Finding Butterflies in Texas

Finding Butterflies in Texas

A Guide to the Best Sites

Roland H. Wauer

Johnson Books
BOULDER
Spring Creek Press
ESTES PARK

Published by Johnson Books, a division of Big Earth Publishing, 3005 Center Green Drive, Suite 220, Boulder, Colorado 80301. E-mail: books@bigearthpublishing.com www.johnsonbooks.com

9 8 7 6 5 4 3 2 1

Cover design: Polly Christensen
Text design and composition: Eric Christensen

Library of Congress Cataloging-in-Publication Data
Wauer, Roland H.
    Finding butterflies in Texas: a guide to the best sites / Roland H. Wauer.
        p. cm.
    Includes bibliographical references and index.
    ISBN 1-55566-366-4
    1. Butterfly watching—Texas—Guidebooks. 2. Texas—Guidebooks.
I. Title
    QL551.T4W39 2005
    595.78'907234764—dc22   2005035299

Printed in the United States of America

Contents

Acknowledgments

I am indebted to numerous individuals who provided assistance during the preparation of this book. I especially want to thank a few people who, in a significant way, have either enhanced the understanding of Texas butterflies, provided valuable time and energy in protecting key habitats, or provided me with constant support. These individuals include: Ben Basham for his enthusiastic support of this project throughout its development; Mike Quinn for much advice and information; Joel Ruiz for his efforts to enhance butterfly populations and protect the Rio Grande floodplain habitat at San Ygnacio; Ellie Thompson for her extensive work in developing the butterfly gardens at Laguna Atascosa National Wildlife Refuge; Bob Stelzer, of Harlingen's Wild Bird Center, for his help regarding binoculars for butterflies; and David Riskind for providing reports of collections from certain state parks.

I also am extremely grateful for the several individuals who reviewed chapters of the book. They include: Phil Schappert; Mike Quinn (Introduction, Lower Rio Grande Valley); Mark Adams and Mike Overton (Trans-Pecos); Richard Howard (Panhandle and Western Plains); Dan Hardy and Barbara Ribble (Edwards Plateau); Dale Clark and Joann Karges (Northern Plains); David Henderson (Pineywoods); Derek Muschalek (Central Plains, South Texas Brushland); P.D. Hulce (Upper Gulf Coast); Glenn Perrigo (Central Gulf Coast); and Dave Hanson (Lower Rio Grande Valley). I also thank Shannon Davies, who provided much time and energy in initial reviews of the manuscript. Her support and interest was greatly appreciated.

Far more people actually accompanied me in the field, suggested places to visit, and/or reviewed site descriptions. For the Trans-Pecos, they included Mark Adams, Kelly Bryan, David and Jan Dauphin, Carl Leib, Bill Reid, Martin Reid, Marc Thompson, and Richard Worthington. Those who helped with the Panhandle and Western Plains included Susan Bryant, Jim and Jason Crites, Anthony Floyd, Richard Howard, Freda Hughes, Rich Kostecke, Rob Lee, John Lombardini, Joann Merritt, Bob and Sylvia Rasa, Brad Simpson, Cliff Stogner, Allen Wemple, Judith Wilington, Burr Williams, and Fred Woerndell. Those who helped with the Edwards Plateau included Mary Cantrell, Shannon Davies, Chris Durden, Tony Gallucci, Gay Gilbert, Patsy Greaves, Carl Green, Erik Holmback, Paul Kisel, Jody Lee, Harold Lemons, Bill Lindemann, Derek Muschalek, Joan Nitschke, Randy Rosales, and Chuck Sexton.

For the Northern Plains, they included Dale Clark, Claire Curry, Fred Gehlbach, Nick Grishin, Peter Heles, Karen Howard, Joann Karges, Jody Lee, David Maple, Mary Lee Middleton, Karen O'Bric, Tom Palmer, Martin Reid, Laurie Simon, and Ken Steigman. Those who helped in the Pineywoods included Bob Behrstock, Charles

Bordelon, Mike Bransford, Keith Hawkins, David Henderson, P.D. Hulce, Ed Knudson, Terry Lamon, Richard Payne, Royce Pendergast, David Powell, Jerald Rashall, Craig Rudolph, Charlie Sassine, and John Tveten.

Those who helped with the Central Plains included Brush Freeman, Martha Gostomski, Dan Hardy, David Henderson, Paul Julian, Brent Leisure, Derek Muschalek, Marvin Schwarzer, and Jim and Lynne Weber. For the Upper Gulf Coast, they included Debbie Alongis, Bob Behrstock, Gary and Kathy Clark, David Dauphin, Jo Evans, David Heinicke, David and Ednelza Henderson, P.D. Hulce, Martha Maglitto, Lynn McBride, Dwight Peake, Mitch Philpot, Janet Rathjen, Cecilia Riley, David Sarkozi, Sallie Sherman, Ken Sztraky, Rob Thacker, Ron Ummel, Mary Ann Welford, and Matt Whitbeck.

For the Central Gulf Coast, they included Sybil Deacon, David and Jan Dauphin, Ray Little, Mary Kathryn Mauel, Glenn Perrigo, Jack Prentiss, Curtis Reemsnyder, Charlie Sassine, Paul Thorton, and Anse Windham. Those who helped with the South Texas Brushland included Eric Finkelstein, Matt Hiendel, Jimmy Jackson, Patty Leslie-Pasztor, Greg Lisciandro, Mary Livingston, Connie Lujan, Craig Marks, Suzanne Melchor, Paul Miliotis, Derek Muschalek, Martin Reid, Helen Rejzek, Georgina Schwartz, Willie Sekula, Fred and Gwen Wallace, Anse Windham, and Jan Wrede.

Those who helped with the Lower Rio Grande Valley included Ben and Jeff Basham, Ray Bieber, Martha and Taylor Blanton, Jim Booker, Terri Bortness, Mark Callanan, Mark Conway, Carrie Cate, Sheridan Coffey, David and Jan Dauphin, Randy Emmitt, Belinda Franco, Susan Fuller, Kim Garwood, Nick Grishin, Martin Hagne, Mike Hannissan, Dave Hanson, Joe Harren, Chris Hathcock, Tina Hernandez, P.D. Hulce, Selena King, Richard Lehman, Jennifer Liston, Derek Muschalek, Mike Overton, Jimmy Paz, Mike Quinn, Gil Quintanilla, Janet Rathjen, Martin Reid, Eugene Rouse, Joel Ruiz, Charles Sassine, Willie Sekula, Ellie Thompson, and Amy Winters.

Many other people provided day-trip reports, either directly or through Tex-Butterflies. They are named in Appendix 3: Regional Checklist Resources.

All the photos in the book are my own, with these exceptions: Cedric Selby provided the scenic photo of Rita Blanca National Grasslands (Site 5). Bob Rogers helped out with a scenic photo of Black Kettle National Grasslands (Site 7). Sue Sill provided the photo of the North American Butterfly Association Garden (Site 69).

I must also thank a few additional folks who helped identify images taken in the field. Charles Bordelon, Jim Brock, John Calhoun, Chris Durden, Nick Grishin, Ed Knudson, Mike Overton, Charlie Sassine, and Andy Warren provided me with vital assistance over the last several years.

I thank them all!

In addition, a very special thanks to my editor, Scott Roederer, for his support and special interest in Texas butterflies. Scott's recommendations significantly improved my initial manuscript. And finally, I thank my wife, Betty Wauer, for putting up with my constant absence from home during the months that I was investigating sites throughout the state. Her continued support is much appreciated!

Introduction

Texas is a huge state, covering approximately 267,000 square miles, and it has a wide diversity of landscapes. These range from the Gulf Coast lowlands to the West Texas highlands, with rolling prairies and plateaus in between. All of these landscapes are distinct. Based on the biogeographic areas they represent, I have split the state into ten regions: Trans-Pecos, Panhandle and Western Plains, Edwards Plateau, Northern Plains, Pineywoods, Central Plains, Upper Gulf Coast, Central Gulf Coast, South Texas Brushlands, and Lower Rio Grande Valley.

I have selected seventy-six butterfly-watching sites in these ten regions. They include city parks, state parks, national forests, and other public lands, as well as private reserves and recreational areas. My main criteria for selecting the sites was their potential to produce regional specialties, i.e., butterfly species not typically found elsewhere in Texas and, sometimes, not in the United States. I have also included sites near major metropolitan areas and other tourist destinations that a visitor with a few spare hours could readily visit.

Planning Your Trip

Within these sites, I describe specific locations, *starting with the one that has the potential to produce the most species and/or the most specialties.* Other locations follow in the order of their potential, with secondary and unproven locations described last. This ranking, along with the species listed for most locations, will help you plan your trip.

Since geography was not considered in the order of the locations, the map of some sites may seem disorganized, with letter "A" next to a letter "G," for example. However, the written directions to the locations are organized with geography in mind. Depending on the site, an efficient route for visiting all the locations is given. In other sites, the directions are given from one or more nearby towns or other landmarks. In most cases, the directions start with the best location first, but they will include nearby locations regardless of their potential for butterflying.

There are too many factors involved—the direction from which you enter an area, the time you have to spend, and the species you want to find—for me to try to plan your route. Using the ranking of locations in the text, you can decide which ones you'd like to visit. Using the directions, you can reach those locations efficiently. Hopefully, this system will allow you to make the best use of your time.

Additional information about many of the sites can be found on the Internet by using a search engine such as Google. The site-specific maps, current access and fees, and even butterfly lists you may find on these web pages can greatly enhance your trip!

Butterfly Specialties

Species that are of special interest to butterfly enthusiasts are considered "specialties." They include species not typically found in other parts of Texas or, sometimes, not found in other parts of the United States. The names of specialties for each region are in **boldface** in the site descriptions.

Specialties usually occur in only one or two regions, but a few may be found in three or, very rarely, four regions. Some of these species are more common in other states. All of the specialty butterflies are resident species and are known to occur at the site at the proper time of year and in appropriate habitat. Stray or accidental species are not included in the lists of specialties but are included in the regional checklists.

Regional Checklists

The butterfly checklist at the end of each region represents a compilation of the species that I know have occurred there. The lists were derived from various sources, including: 1. published checklists for specific sites, such as those for Big Bend National Park and Santa Ana National Wildlife Refuge; 2. site reports by collectors and other serious lepidopterists; 3. U.S. Geological Survey county checklists, when the site is large enough to encompass a majority of a county; 4. annual "Seasonal Summary" lists from the Lepidopterists' Society for the 1994 to 2002 seasons; 5. July 4th Butterfly Counts; and 6. site visits by the author and other knowledgeable individuals.

Many of the checklists should be considered preliminary. They will be enlarged upon as observers gather more data. If you find a new species for a park or refuge, submit a report to officials there. You can report rare or out-of-range species to the Texas butterfly listserv, a mailing list for everyone interested in the state's butterflies. Instructions on how to subscribe and how to access the archives (a good thing to check if you're planning a trip) are found at www.texasento.net/TXBL.htm.

Day lists of unquestionable species can be sent to the North American Butterfly Association at www.naba.org, where they will be archived. Additional trip-planning help can be found by following their "Local Chapters" link and checking out the Texas web sites.

Details about the derivation of the checklists are included in Appendix 3: Regional Checklist Resources. They include the observer, date, and the number of species seen (during a visit of two or more hours). The dates and numbers provide an added perspective on how many species you might expect at various times of the year. An additional perspective on when a species has been recorded (months listed in brackets) can be obtained from Appendix 4: Checklist of Texas Butterflies.

Abundance Status

The abundance status of each species is also included in the regional lists. Assigning abundance status is a judgment call, but it is based on reliable information, such as the numbers recorded on site visits and the habitat available at the site. Abundance status generally represents the highest number recorded at the optimum time of year. However, populations can vary considerably from year to year and from site to site.

In addition, there are a few species that are temporary or periodic colonists (indicated by "TC") in areas beyond their normal range. These populations may last only a few years, or they may survive long enough to expand the species' range.

Abundance status codes are based on visits to appropriate locations and habitats during the flight times of the species. They include:

A = abundant: many can be expected on most visits.
C = common: several can be expected on most visits.
U = uncommon: a few can often be found on most visits.
O = occasional: one or a very few can sometimes be found on visits.
R = rare: one to several occur every few years only.
X = accidental: a non-breeding stray; it may never be found again.
M = migrant: usually occurs only in spring and/or fall. (An example is the Monarch in most of south Texas.)
TC = temporary colonist: out-of-range breeding population likely to persist for a few to several years.
? = unknown: abundance status is not available, usually due to a lack of records.

In a few cases, a double code (such as "A-R") is used to indicate a great fluctuation in populations for a given species.

Butterfly Names

Finally, all common and scientific names used in the checklists are from the *Checklist & English Names of North American Butterflies*, by the North American Butterfly Association (NABA 2001).

In the few cases when a species is so similar to another closely related species that they cannot be readily separated in the field, the two names are given together. Examples include Common/White Checkered-Skipper and Common/Scarce Streaky-Skipper.

In addition, the species status of the Spring Azure complex is unclear at this writing. Although many authors identify the butterflies found in west Texas as "Spring Azure" and those found in east Texas as "Summer Azure," the split into separate species is not yet official. In fact, there is some speculation that the complex may be split into three or more species. Since nothing is definite at this time, I have used "Spring/Summer Azure" in the book to alert you to the possible split and to encourage you to keep records that identify butterflies in this complex by subspecies.

The Checklist of Texas Butterflies includes both common and scientific names, as used by NABA. When another scientific name is used by Paul S. Opler and Andrew D. Warren in *Butterflies of North America 2: Scientific Names List for Butterfly Species of North America, North of Mexico* (2002), that name is included in parentheses. Strays from Mexico that are not yet on the NABA list are indicated by an asterisk.

Map Legend

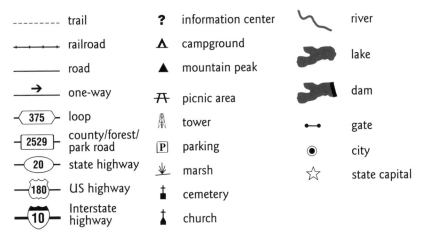

trail	**?** information center	river
railroad	**Λ** campground	lake
road	**▲** mountain peak	dam
→ one-way	**⊼** picnic area	
375 loop	tower	gate
2529 county/forest/park road	**P** parking	city
20 state highway	marsh	state capital
180 US highway	cemetery	
10 Interstate highway	church	

Site Guide

Physiographical Regions of Texas

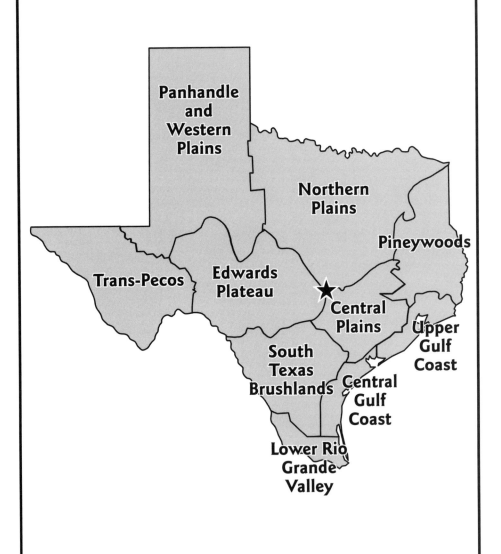

Panhandle and Western Plains

Northern Plains

Pineywoods

Trans-Pecos

Edwards Plateau

Central Plains

Upper Gulf Coast

South Texas Brushlands

Central Gulf Coast

Lower Rio Grande Valley

Trans-Pecos

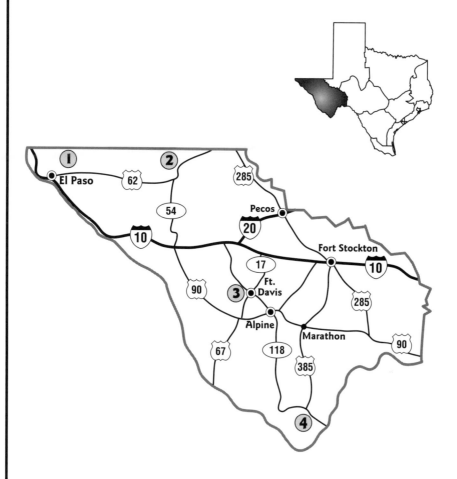

1. El Paso/Franklin Mountains State Park
2. Guadalupe Mountains National Park
3. Davis Mountains
4. Big Bend National Park

Trans-Pecos Region

The Trans-Pecos includes all of Texas west of the Pecos River. With New Mexico to the north, the Rio Grande River forms the western and southern boundaries. Landscapes include arid lowlands, mid-elevation woodlands, and forested highlands. The lowlands are dominated by Chihuahuan Desert, an environment of succulents, such as cacti, agaves, and yuccas. Above the desert, junipers are predominant on the lower slopes, and oak-hackberry woodlands are found in drainages and at slightly higher elevations. The upper slopes and ridges feature pinyon-juniper woodlands. In the highest and coolest canyons, species such as Douglas-fir, yellow pine, and even aspen are found.

Elevations range from about 1,100 feet, where the Pecos River flows into the Rio Grande in western Val Verde County, to 8,749 feet at the summit of Guadalupe Peak in Guadalupe Mountains National Park.

This diverse region is represented by four sites: **1. El Paso/Franklin Mountains State Park**, **2. Guadalupe Mountains National Park**, **3. Davis Mountains**, and **4. Big Bend National Park**. The best time to visit these sites is March through October.

Trans-Pecos Specialties

The region supports a huge number of butterfly species, second only to the Lower Rio Grande Valley Region. Seventy-five of the Trans-Pecos species are area specialties, listed here and in the site descriptions in **boldface**.

Swallowtails, Whites, Sulphurs: **Ornythion Swallowtail** has been recorded irregularly at all elevations in Big Bend NP. Larval foodplants include citrus species. **Mexican Dartwhite** was a temporary colonist in Big Bend's Green Gulch from 1977 to 1982; it may occur again. Larvae feed on mistletoe. **Spring White** occurs during March and April in the El Paso area and Guadalupe Mountains NP. Larval foodplants include mustards, such as rockcress, tansymustard, and twistflower. **Pearly Marble** flies during March and April at mid- to upper elevations in the El Paso area. Larvae feed on mustards, such as rockcress and tansymustard. **Desert** and **Sara orangetips** occur in Texas only in the El Paso area in early spring. Desert Orangetip flies from February to April in lowland areas. Larval foodplants include tansymustard and twistflower. Sara Orangetip flies in March and April at slightly higher elevations. Larvae feed on rockcress and sisymbrium. **Boisduval's Yellow** flies from May to October in brushy areas along the Rio Grande and adjacent arroyos in Big Bend NP. Larval foodplants include sennas.

Hairstreaks: **Poling's Hairstreak** flies in oak woodlands from May to August in all four sites. Larvae utilize gray and Emory oaks. **Xami Hairstreak** frequents patches of stonecrop (its foodplant) from April to September in the pine-oak woodlands of the Davis Mountains and Big Bend NP. **Sandia Hairstreak** is most likely to occur from April to June at mid- to upper elevations in Guadalupe Mountains NP, the Davis Mountains, and Big Bend NP. Larvae feed on beargrass. **Thicket Hairstreak** occurs from May to July in the highlands of Guadalupe Mountains NP and the Davis Mountains. Adults are most often seen in moist canyons but spend considerable time in conifers. Larvae feed on mistletoe. **Red-lined Scrub-Hairstreak** has been recorded very sporadically in April, May, and September at scattered locations in Big Bend NP. Larvae feed on balloonvine and Havard plum. **Bromeliad Scrub-Hairstreak** is possible during July and August in the lowlands of Big Bend NP, where it uses hechtia (its foodplant), a ground bromeliad found on arid limestone slopes along the Rio Grande. **Leda Ministreak** occurs from June to November at low to mid-elevations in the El Paso area, the Davis Mountains, and Big Bend NP. Larvae feed on mesquite foliage. **Arizona Hairstreak** has been recorded only rarely from March to September in the mountain woodlands of Big Bend NP. Larvae feed on Emory oak.

Blues: **Cyna Blue** occurs in desert scrub from March to November in the Davis Mountains and Big Bend NP. Larvae feed on anisacanth. **Rita Blue** has been recorded only in September in desert scrub at mid-elevations of Big Bend NP. Larvae feed on buckwheats. **Melissa Blue** frequents grassy areas from May to August in the El Paso area and Guadalupe Mountains NP. Larvae feed on clover and lupines. **Acmon Blue** is widespread but uncommon from March to October at all four sites. Larvae feed on buckwheats and lupines.

Metalmarks: **Rawson's Metalmark** occurs from April to October at low to mid-elevations in the Davis Mountains and Big Bend NP. Larvae feed on boneset. **Mormon Metalmark** flies at mid-elevations from April to October in all four sites. Larvae feed on buckwheats. **Hepburn's Metalmark** has been recorded only in July in desert scrub and mid-elevation woodlands of Big Bend NP. Very little is known about this small, dark metalmark. **Palmer's Metalmark** occurs from April to October in the lowlands of all four sites. Larvae feed on mesquite. **"Chisos" Nais Metalmark** flies from March to August at mid-elevations only in Big Bend NP. Larvae feed on Havard plum.

Heliconians and Fritillaries: **Mexican Silverspot** has been recorded sporadically from April to September in pinyon-juniper woodlands in Big Bend NP. It is probably a temporary colonist. Larvae feed on passion vine. **Zebra Heliconian** may occur as a stray throughout the region, but it is a temporary colonist from July to September in Big Bend NP. Larvae feed on passion vine.

Checkerspots, Patches, and Crescents: **Chinati Checkerspot** flies from May to September in the mountain woodlands where its larval foodplant, Big Bend silverleaf, occurs. Named for the Chinati Mountains in the southwestern portion of the Trans-Pecos, it occurs in Guadalupe Mountains NP, the Davis Mountains, and Big Bend NP. **Fulvia Checkerspot** flies at mid-elevations from April to September in all four sites. Larvae feed on Indian paintbrush. **Definite Patch** occurs in desert scrub from March to October in the El Paso area and Guadalupe Mountains NP, where its larval foodplant, shaggy stenandrium, grows. **Mylitta Crescent** is a northern species that has been recorded in the Trans-Pecos only in the highlands of Guadalupe Mountains NP. It flies in meadows in midsummer. Larvae feed on thistles.

Ladies, Buckeyes, Leafwings: **West Coast Lady** barely reaches Texas, occurring in the El Paso area and Guadalupe Mountains NP from April to November. Larvae feed on mallow. **Tropical Buckeye**, the dark form only, has been found sporadically from March to October in the Davis Mountains and Big Bend NP. Larvae feed on the Verbenaceae family, including lippia. **Tropical Leafwing** occurs from March to October in wooded areas at all elevations in all four sites. Adults feed primarily on overripe fruit and sap; larvae use crotons.

Satyrs: **Canyonland Satyr** is a mountain species that occurs from May to August in Guadalupe Mountains NP, the Davis Mountains, and Big Bend NP. Adults patrol canyon bottoms and wooded hillsides. Larvae utilize grasses, including grama. **Mead's Wood-Nymph** occurs in mountain woodlands from May to September in Guadalupe Mountains NP, the Davis Mountains, and Big Bend NP. Larvae feed on grasses.

Spread-wing Skippers: **Short-tailed Skipper** has been recorded only rarely in oak woodlands in April and May and again from July to September in the Davis Mountains. Adults frequent areas with mud and/or sap. Larvae feed on oak foliage. **Arizona Skipper** is most likely to be seen on or near its larval foodplant, kidneywood, at mid-elevations from March to October in the El Paso area, the Davis Mountains, and Big Bend NP. Males are known to perch on open branches near cliffs. **Golden Banded-Skipper** occurs from March to September in the highlands, especially in shaded canyons of the Davis Mountains and Big Bend NP. Adults often perch on rock faces. Larvae feed on peas, such as beans and vetch. **Chisos Banded-Skipper** has been recorded sporadically from March to September only in the highlands of Big Bend NP. Larvae feed on clover and beggar's tick. **Desert Cloudywing** occurs from March to October at mid-elevations in the Davis Mountains and Big Bend NP. Larvae feed on tickclover. **Drusius Cloudywing** is most likely to be seen from April to July at flowering plants at mid-elevations in Guadalupe Mountains NP, the Davis Mountains, and Big Bend NP. Larvae feed on cologania. **Acacia Skipper** can usually be found at all elevations from April to September in the El Paso area, the Davis Mountains, and Big Bend NP. Larvae feed on fern acacia. **Golden-headed Scallopwing** occurs at mid-elevations or higher in all four sites from April to October. Adults often rest at moist spots on the ground; larvae feed on pigweed. **Arizona Powdered-Skipper** is a western species that occurs in all four sites, usually below the mountain woodlands, from February to November. Most sightings are at brushy edges, often on the ground. Larvae feed on mallows. **Rocky Mountain Duskywing** is most likely to be found in canyon bottoms of mountain woodlands from April to July in all four sites. Larval foodplants include oak, especially Gambel's oak. **Meridian Duskywing** occurs from March to September in oak woodlands at mid-elevations or higher in all four sites. Adults often rest on the ground at moist locations; larvae feed on oak leaves. **Scudder's Duskywing** occurs in isolated populations in the Davis Mountains and Big Bend NP. It typically frequents oak woodlands from May to August but has been recorded in the Trans-Pecos only in September. Adults commonly hilltop; larvae probably feed on oak leaves. **Small Checkered-Skipper** is most likely to be found in the lowlands but is occasionally at slightly higher elevations in all four sites from March to November. Larvae feed on mallows. **Erichson's White-Skipper** has been recorded from April to October in shady canyons and along woodland edges, usually at mid-elevations, in the El Paso area, the Davis Mountains, and Big Bend NP. Larvae feed on mallows. **Scarce Streaky-Skipper** cannot be separated from Common Streaky-Skipper without examination of the genitalia. Both occur at mid-elevations from March to November in all four sites. Larvae feed on mallows. **Mexican Sootywing** is found at mid-elevation flower patches from May to September in Guadalupe Mountains NP, the Davis Mountains, and Big Bend NP. Larvae feed on amaranth.

Skipperlings, Grass-Skippers: There is a lone spring record for **Four-spotted Skipperling** in Texas from the Texas Nature Conservancy Preserve in the highland forest of the Davis Mountains. **Chisos Skipperling** occurs in grassy areas of the oak-pine woodlands from March to August only in Big Bend NP. **Edwards' Skipperling** is a mountain grassland species that can be common from June to August at mid-elevations in Guadalupe Mountains NP and the Davis Mountains. It is less common in Big Bend NP. Isolated populations of **Sunrise Skipper** occur in mid-elevation grasslands in the Davis Mountains and Big Bend NP. Larvae feed on knotgrass. **Morrison's Skipper** flies only from March to May at mid-elevations in Guadalupe Mountains NP and the Davis Mountains. Adults frequent roadsides and other open areas. **Uncas Skipper** occurs in lowland shortgrass habitat from April to September in Guadalupe Mountains NP and the Davis Mountains. **Apache Skipper** has been recorded only in September and October in grassy areas of pine forests in Guadalupe Mountains NP and the Davis Mountains. Larvae feed on grasses and sedges. **Pahaska Skipper** resides in mid-elevation open grasslands from June to August in all four sites. **Carus Skipper** frequents lowland shortgrass areas in the Davis Mountains and Big Bend NP from April to September. **Taxiles Skipper** has been recorded from June to August in grassy areas in the highlands of the Davis Mountains and Big Bend NP. **Umber Skipper** is most likely to be found at grassy areas in mountain canyons from May to September in the Davis Mountains and Big Bend NP. Males can be very territorial, perching atop a shrub or tree branch and chasing other males away. **Viereck's Skipper** occurs at mid-elevations from March to May in all four sites. Adults often feed on cactus flowers. **White-barred Skipper** has been recorded at mid-elevations in April and May in the Davis Mountains and Big Bend NP. Adults feed on cactus flowers. **Python Skipper** occurs at mid-elevations in all four sites from March to August. **Sheep Skipper** has been recorded at mid-elevations from April to November in Guadalupe Mountains NP, the Davis Mountains, and Big Bend NP. Larvae use sideoats grama. **Simius Roadside-Skipper** occurs in shortgrass areas near mountain woodlands from April to August in Guadalupe Mountains NP, the Davis Mountains, and Big Bend NP. Larvae feed on hairy grama. **Cassus Roadside-Skipper** can be common in the Davis Mountains but is rare in Big Bend NP. It frequents grassy openings in pine-oak woodlands in June and July. Larvae feed on bulb panicum. **Oslar's Roadside-Skipper** occurs in mid-elevation grasslands from April to July in Guadalupe Mountains NP, the Davis Mountains, and Big Bend NP. Larvae feed on sideoats grama. **Texas Roadside-Skipper** frequents mid-elevation open areas from April to September in all four sites. Larvae feed on bulb panicum. **Slaty Roadside-Skipper** occurs from March to September in grassy areas in oak woodlands of Guadalupe Mountains NP, the Davis Mountains, and Big Bend NP. Larvae feed on common beardgrass. **Orange-headed Roadside-Skipper** is most likely to be found in moist forests from June to August in all four sites. Larvae feed on little bluestem.

Giant-Skippers: **Orange Giant-Skipper** occurs in mountains with agaves, its larval foodplant, in all four sites. Adults fly only in September and October. **Mary's Giant-Skipper** flies in desert-scrub from September to November in all four sites. Larvae feed on lechuguilla. **Ursine Giant-Skipper** frequents yucca grasslands in all four sites from April to June. It is known to hilltop. Larvae feed on yucca.

Sites within the Trans-Pecos Region

1. El Paso/Franklin Mountains State Park

This far-western portion of Texas features a number of butterfly species found in the western U.S. but not reported elsewhere in Texas. The entire area is dominated by Chihuahuan Desert, but oaks and junipers occur in the higher canyons of the Franklin Mountains at elevations to 7,192 feet.

More than 700,000 people reside in the city of El Paso. Combined with Mexico's Cuidad Juarez, 2.2 million people live in the region. The El Paso area is the only portion of Texas in the Mountain Time Zone. Butterfly-watching sites include Franklin Mountains State Park (**A-C**), McKelligon Canyon City Park (**D**), the Wilderness Park Museum (**E**), Fred Hervey Water Reclamation Plant (**F**), Memorial Park (**G**), and Arroyo Park (**H**).

Habitats: Desert scrub, sotol grassland, juniper woodland, oak-hackberry woodland, and gardens.

Strategy for finding the most butterflies: In the 24,248-acre Franklin Mountains SP (fee area), three sites should be checked: West Cottonwood Spring Trail; the nature trail; and the park roadsides, which can be especially productive when wildflowers are present. West Cottonwood Spring Trail (**A**), which enters a narrow, brushy canyon leading to a woodland and the spring, is likely to be the most productive site. Specialties possible in this area include **Tropical Leafwing**; **Acacia, Arizona, Viereck's,** and **Python skippers**; and **Ursine Giant-Skipper**. **Rocky Mountain Duskywing** is possible in spring and **Meredian Duskywing** somewhat later.

The half-mile nature trail (**B**) along a desert arroyo and the roadsides (**C**) are likely to produce **Pearly Marble, Spring White,** and **Desert** and **Sara orangetips** in March

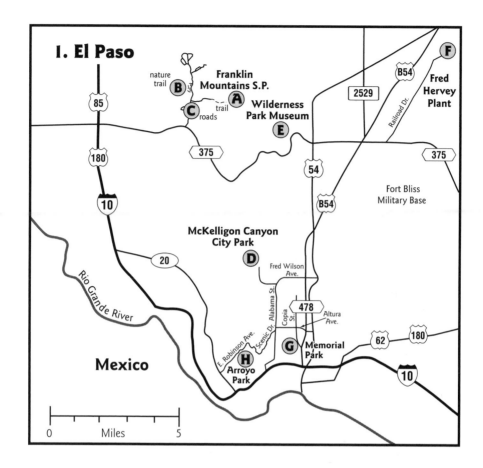

I. El Paso

nature trail

Franklin Mountains S.P.

(B)

(A) trail roads

(C)

Wilderness Park Museum

(E)

85

180

10

375

B54

2529

Railroad Dr.

375

(F)

Fred Hervey Plant

54

B54

Fort Bliss Military Base

375

McKelligon Canyon City Park

(D)

20

Fred Wilson Ave.

Alabama St.

Copia St.

478

Altura Ave.

62

180

Rio Grande River

Scenic Dr.

E. Robinson Ave.

(H)

(G) **Memorial Park**

10

Mexico

Arroyo Park

0 Miles 5

and April. **Leda Ministreak**, **West Coast Lady**, **Golden-headed Scallopwing**, and **Erichson's White-Skipper** occur later. Some of the more numerous butterflies include Pipevine Swallowtail; Cloudless, Large Orange, and Lyside sulphurs; Southern Dogface; Mexican and Little yellows; Sleepy Orange; Western Pygmy-Blue; Gulf Fritillary; Tiny and Elada checkerspots; Empress Leilia; Queen; and Common/White and Desert checkered-skippers.

Another worthwhile site—McKelligon Canyon City Park (**D**)—is on the south side of the mountains closer to downtown El Paso. Many of the species mentioned above can be found there. In addition, **Acmon Blue**, Theona Checkerspot, **Definite Patch**, and **Arizona Powdered-Skipper** are more likely.

There are two good sites east of the state park. At Wilderness Park Museum (**E**), near US 54, check the flowering plants around the parking area and walk the loop trail where **Fulvia Checkerspot**, **Small Checkered-Skipper**, Common Streaky-Skipper, **Pahaska Skipper**, and Bronze and **Texas roadside-skippers** are possible. Farther east, off SH 375, is the Fred Hervey Water Reclamation Plant (**F**). Walk the

Franklin Mountains State Park, El Paso Area

roadsides and the area around the pond where Giant Swallowtail, Great Purple Hair-streak, Marine and Ceraunus blues, **Mormon** and **Palmer's metalmarks**, Bordered Patch, Painted Crescent, and Tropical Least Skipper are possible.

In addition, there are two worthwhile parks near downtown El Paso—Memorial Park (**G**) and Arroyo Park (**H**), where many of those species may be found. There are also a few records of **Melissa Blue** and **Mary's Giant-Skipper** in the El Paso area at unknown locations.

Directions: All the areas are in El Paso County, north and east of I-10. **Franklin Mountains SP (A-C)** is off the Trans-Mountain Road (Loop 375), accessed from I-10 north of downtown El Paso. Take Loop 375 east to the state park entrance road on the west slope of the mountains. **Wilderness Park Museum (E)** is located on the east slope. Continue east on Loop 375, watching on the left for the museum entrance as you near US 54. To find **Fred Hervey Water Reclamation Plant (F)** continue east on SH 375 past US 54 and Bus. 54. Turn north on Railroad Dr. The entrance is three miles ahead, across the tracks, on the right. To continue to McKelligon Canyon Park, return to US 54 and go south.

McKelligon Canyon Park (D) is located off Alabama St. Take Fred Wilson Ave. west from US 54 to its merging with Alabama St. southbound. The turn to the park will be on the right. To find Memorial and Arroyo parks, continue south on Alabama St.

For **Memorial Park (G)**, take Altura Ave. east from Alabama St. Continue to N. Copia St. and turn south. Turn west on N. Copper Ave. to access the main part of the park. Altura Ave. is also accessible from Loop 478 and US 54, north of I-10. To reach

Arroyo Park (H) from Alabama St., go one block south of Altura and turn west on Richmond Ave./Scenic Dr. Scenic Dr. leads to E. Robinson Ave. and the park. Alternately take SH 20 (N. Mesa St.) northwest from I-10 to a right turn on E. Robinson Ave.

Nearest food, gas, and lodging: Throughout the El Paso area.

Nearest camping: Commercial sites in El Paso; primitive, walk-in tent camping and a limited number of RV sites without hook-ups in Franklin Mountains SP.

2. Guadalupe Mountains National Park

Guadalupe Mountains NP (fee area) encompasses 76,293 acres of rugged terrain and includes Guadalupe Peak (8,749 feet), the highest point in Texas. It is also the southern terminus of a limestone ridge that is an extension of the forested New Mexico plateau. For that reason, some of the park's flora and fauna have an affinity to more northern locales, suggesting the possibility of butterfly species not found elsewhere in Texas.

The park has more than eighty miles of trails that provide access to remote areas. Be sure to carry adequate water with you, since it is not available in the high country. The best places to find butterflies include Pine Springs (**A**), Frijole Ranch (**B**), McKittrick Canyon (**C**), Rattlesnake Springs (**D**) in New Mexico, The Bowl (**E**), Dog Canyon (**F**), and the Williams Ranch Road (**G**).

Habitats: Ponderosa pine forest, pinyon-juniper-oak woodland, oak-maple woodland, sotol grassland, desert scrub, and riparian.

Strategy for finding the most butterflies: Start at Pine Springs (**A**) by checking the vegetation around the visitor center parking lot and nearby campground. Some of the more numerous butterflies include Large Orange and Dainty sulphurs; Sleepy Orange; Marine and Ceraunus blues; Gulf Fritillary; Queen; and Common and Desert checkered-skippers. Also watch for Mexican Yellow; Great Purple and Oak hairstreaks; **Leda Ministreak**; **Acmon Blue**; Red Satyr; and **Simius, Oslar's, Texas**, and **Slaty roadside-skippers. Poling's** and **Sandia hairstreaks, Tropical Leafwing**, **Canyonland Satyr**, and **Mead's Wood-Nymph** are also possible in the woodland around the campground.

Then drive to Frijole Ranch (**B**) and walk the 2.3-mile loop trail through sotol grasslands to Manzanita and Smith springs, where you'll find an overstory of oaks and other broadleaf trees. **Python Skipper** is likely along the entrance road, and Pipevine Swallowtail, Cloudless Sulphur, Vesta Crescent, Empress Leilia, and Bronze Roadside-Skipper are often found along the trail. **Definite Patch** is less dependable. At the springs, watch for Two-tailed Swallowtail, Spring/Summer Azure, Red-spotted Purple, Arizona Sister, and **Rocky Mountain Duskywing**.

Next, drive to McKittrick Canyon (**C**) and follow the trail up-canyon. The canyon bottom and slopes, especially when rains have produced wildflowers, can be very productive. Specialty butterflies, such as **Fulvia Checkerspot**, **West Coast Lady**, **Golden-**

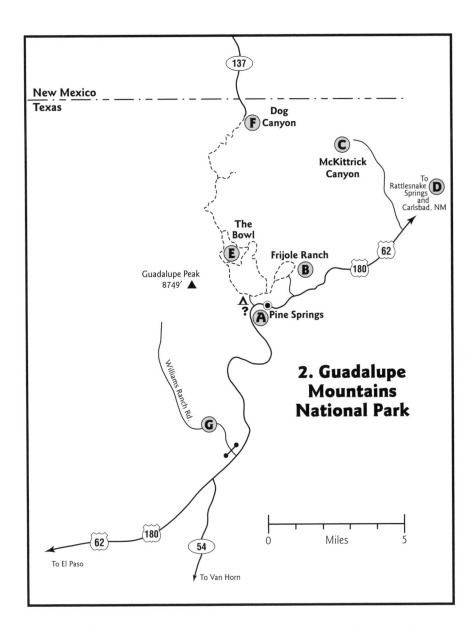

137

F Dog
Canyon

C
McKittrick
Canyon

To
Rattlesnake **D**
Springs
and
Carlsbad, NM

The
Bowl

Frijole Ranch

E

B

62

180

Guadalupe Peak
8749' ▲

Δ
? **A** Pine Springs

2. Guadalupe Mountains National Park

Williams Ranch Rd.

G

0   Miles   5

62   180

54

To El Paso

To Van Horn

headed Scallopwing, and **Orange Giant-Skipper**, are possible. Two-tailed Swallowtail, Lyside Sulphur, Spring/Summer Azure, Fatal Metalmark, Bordered Patch, Elada Checkerspot, Northern Cloudywing, Sleepy and Mournful duskywings, and Common Streaky-Skipper are likely.

In the upper oak woodlands, watch for **Melissa Blue**; **Drusius Cloudywing**; **Meridian Duskywing**; **Carus**, **Viereck's**, and **Sheep skippers**; and **Orange-headed**

McKittrick Canyon, Guadalupe Mountains National Park

Roadside-Skipper. In spring, watch for **Spring White**, Henry's Elfin, **Morrison's Skipper**, and Yucca Giant-Skipper.

While you're this far north, you may want to cross the New Mexico state line to Rattlesnake Springs (**D**). It's also a convenient stop on your way to Dog Canyon (see below). With its stately cottonwoods and thickets of riparian shrubs, this site may produce the area's greatest butterfly diversity. Specialties not mentioned above but possible here include **Arizona Powdered-Skipper**, **Small Checkered-Skipper**, and **Uncas Skipper** at shortgrass edges, as well as **Mexican Sootywing** and **Pahaska Skipper**. Phaon and Painted crescents and Tropical Least Skipper can be numerous. Check the saltbush edges for Saltbush Sootywing.

Two high-country areas are also worth visiting, if time and energy permit. The Bowl (**E**) requires a 9.1-mile round-trip hike from Pine Springs to reach the highland meadows and coniferous forest where **Thicket Hairstreak** and **Mylitta Crescent** are possible. Watch along the trail for **Ursine Giant-Skipper**.

Dog Canyon (**F**) requires a long drive to the northern side of the park. **Edwards' Skipperling** and **Sunrise Skipper** frequent grassy areas just above the camping area, and Nysa and Dotted roadside-skippers are also probable.

Finally, when lowland wildflowers are present, walk a portion of the gated Williams Ranch Road (**G**) at the south end of the park. **Mormon** and **Palmer's metalmarks**, **Chinati Checkerspot**, and **Mary's Giant-Skipper** (September and October) are possible.

Directions: In Culberson County, park headquarters and the trail to **The Bowl (E)** are located at **Pine Springs (A)**, along US 62/180, 110 miles northeast of El Paso and 65 miles southwest of Carlsbad, New Mexico. **Frijole Ranch (B)** and the trail to Mazanita and Smith springs are north of US 62/180 one mile northeast of Pine Springs. The **McKittrick Canyon (C)** entrance road is off US 62/180, five miles northeast of Pine Springs. **Rattlesnake Springs (D)** is west of US 62/180, about 10 miles into New Mexico. Watch for NPS signs. **Dog Canyon (F)** is accessible from US 62/180 south of Carlsbad, N.M., by taking NM 408 (Dark Canyon Rd.) west to NM 137 and turning south. It can also be reached north of Carlsbad on US 285 by turning south on NM 137. Follow NM 137 to the end of the road, just inside the Texas border. The **Williams Ranch Road** is southwest of Pine Springs and north of US 62/180 at a gated National Park Service road with a small parking area.

Nearest food, gas, and lodging: White's City, New Mexico, 35 miles northeast of Pine Springs; food and gas at Nickel Creek, three miles northeast of Pine Springs.

Nearest camping: Pine Springs and Dog Canyon.

3. Davis Mountains

The Davis Mountains have a marvelous diversity of habitats, including extensive lowlands of Chihuahuan Desert and grasslands, large areas of pinyon-juniper woodlands and ponderosa pine forests, and a higher upland forest of pines and firs, aspen groves, and open rocky summits that rise to 8,382 feet in elevation. However, much of the Davis Mountains is privately owned and access is zealously protected.

The highest-elevation lands (432,000 acres above 5,500 feet) are part of the Texas Nature Conservancy's Davis Mountains Preserve, which is not accessible to the public without special arrangements. Participation in "Open Weekends" offers the occasional opportunity to visit the preserve.

Public-use areas included as butterflying sites are limited to highway right-of-ways and some public lands. Recommended roads include SH 118 **(A)**, the side road to McDonald Observatory **(C)**, SH 166 **(G)**, and FM 1832 **(H)**. Other sites include the Lawrence E. Wood Picnic Area **(B)**, Davis Mountains State Park **(D)**, Limpia Creek **(E)**, the Chihuahuan Desert Research Institute **(F)**, and the Hotel Limpia grounds **(I)** in Fort Davis.

Habitats: Pinyon-juniper-oak woodland, ponderosa pine forest, oak savannah, sotol grassland, desert scrub, riparian, and open field.

Strategy for finding the most butterflies: Drive SH 118 **(A)** northwest from Fort Davis, stopping at pull-offs within the open grasslands and pinyon-juniper woodlands to check flowering plants along the roadway. Some of the more numerous butterflies include Dainty Sulphur, Sleepy Orange, Reakirt's Blue, Queen, and Common/White Checkered-Skipper.

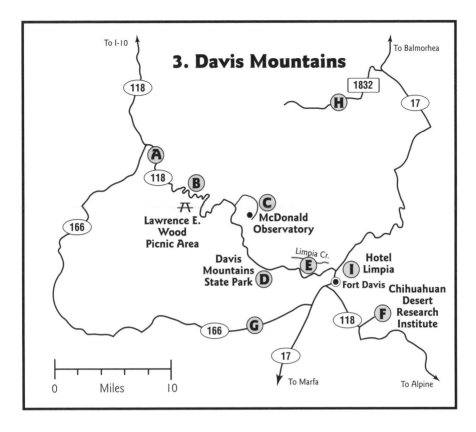

3. Davis Mountains

To I-10

To Balmorhea

118

1832

H

17

A

118

B

⛺

Lawrence E.
Wood
Picnic Area

166

C
● McDonald
Observatory

Davis
Mountains
State Park **D**

Limpia Cr.
E

I Hotel
Limpia
● Fort Davis

118

Chihuahuan
Desert
F Research
Institute

166 **G**

17

To Marfa

To Alpine

0   Miles   10

Stop at the Lawrence E. Wood Picnic Area (**B**) and wander through this grassy area, amid the ponderosa pines. When wildflowers are in bloom, it can have a wide variety of butterfly species. They include the following specialties: **Canyonland Satyr**; **Mead's Wood-Nymph**; **Sunrise** and **White-barred skippers**; and **Simius**, **Cassus**, **Oslar's**, **Texas**, **Slaty**, and **Orange-headed roadside-skippers**. Look for **Morrison's Skipper** in March and April.

Additional butterflies possible in and adjacent to the picnic area include Mexican Yellow, Juniper Hairstreak, Marine and Ceraunus blues, Spring/Summer Azure, Phaon Crescent, Arizona Sister, Red Satyr, Northern Cloudywing, and Mournful Duskywing.

Drive the side road to McDonald Observatory (**C**), checking the roadside wildflowers, and walk around the visitor parking area. This site can produce many of the same butterflies mentioned above, and an **Orange Giant-Skipper** was recorded here in October 2002.

Davis Mountains SP (**D**), a fee area, can also be worthwhile in spring and after summer rains. Check the overlook area on Skyline Drive for hilltopping Pipevine and Black swallowtails and look for **Poling's** and **Sandia hairstreaks** and **Tropical**

Lawrence E. Wood Picnic Area, Davis Mountains

Leafwing in the tree-lined canyon in the camping area. Other likely butterflies here include Two-tailed Swallowtail, Red-spotted Purple, Empress Leilia, Tawny Emperor, and Goatweed Leafwing.

Then, walk along Limpia Creek (**E**), accessible only during bird-banding operations in spring; the site is located across the highway from the park entrance. This creek has the right habitat for **Scarce Streaky-Skipper**, although it cannot be separated from the very similar Common Streaky-Skipper (also present) without examination of the genitalia.

Next, drive south of Fort Davis toward Alpine and stop at the Chihuahuan Desert Research Institute (**F**), another fee area. Check the plantings around the visitor center and walk some of the trails; Modesto Canyon Trail has the greatest potential for variety. Although this area may produce many of the same butterfly species mentioned above, a few additions are possible. **Sheep Skipper** frequents the rocky walls in the canyon, and **Acmon Blue**, **Desert Cloudywing**, **Arizona Powdered-Skipper**, and **Pahaska Skipper** are possible in the open grasslands. Additional expected species include Southern Dogface, Cloudless Sulphur, and Desert Checkered-Skipper.

Next, drive SH 166 (**G**), southwest of Fort Davis. When wildflowers are present, **Leda Ministreak**, **Cyna Blue**, **Mormon Metalmark**, **Chinati** and **Fulvia checkerspots**, and **Acacia Skipper** are possible. In addition, you may want to drive 25 miles north of Fort Davis on SH 17 to FM 1832 (**H**), the Buffalo Trail Boy Scout Ranch Road. This 12-mile-long road passes through desert scrub and a rocky canyon in its upper portion. Many of the specialties mentioned above can be found here, but also watch for **Golden-headed Scallopwing**, **Mexican Sootywing**, and **Small Checkered-Skipper**. This road is also a good place to find several species not already mentioned: Theona, Tiny, and Elada checkerspots; Bordered Patch; Hackberry Emperor; **Python Skipper**; and Bronze, Nysa, and Dotted roadside-skippers.

At the flower garden around the Hotel Limpia (**I**) in downtown Fort Davis, you're likely to find Giant Swallowtail, Gulf Fritillary, Vesta Crescent, Funereal Duskywing, Sachem, and Dun Skipper.

Many of the higher mountain specialties are probably available only in TNC's Davis Mountain Preserve. Examples include: **Golden Banded-Skipper**; **Drusius Cloudywing**; **Rocky Mountain**, **Meridian**, and **Scudder's duskywings**; **Four-spotted** and **Edwards' skipperlings**; **Taxiles** and **Umber skippers**; and **Ursine Giant-Skipper**.

Directions: In Jeff Davis and Reeves counties, Fort Davis and its **Hotel Limpia (I)** are 39 miles south of I-10 via SH 17 or 23 miles north of US 90 via SH 118. Most sites are along **SH 118 (A)**, northwest of Fort Davis, and that road provides the best pull-offs for butterflying. It also leads to **Limpia Creek (E)**, **Davis Mountains SP (D)**, **the side road to McDonald Observatory (C)**, and the **Lawrence E. Wood Picnic Area (B)**. The **Chihuahan Desert Research Institute (F)** is southeast of Fort Davis about four miles on SH 118. **SH 166 (G)** goes west from SH 17, south of Fort Davis. **FM 1832 (H)** goes west from SH 17, 25 miles north of Fort Davis.

Nearest food, gas, and lodging: Fort Davis, Alpine, and Balmorhea, near I-10.

Nearest camping: Davis Mountains SP and Balmorhea SP.

4. Big Bend National Park

One of the nation's finest birding sites, Big Bend NP (fee area) has the largest butter-fly list (180+ species) of any of America's national parks. Few other locations in Texas offer as many specialty butterflies. July 4th Butterfly Counts are held here most years.

The reasons for this high diversity include the park's southern location and its variety of habitats, extending from 1,800 feet in elevation along the Rio Grande River in Boquillas Canyon to 7,825 feet at the summit of Emory Peak in the Chisos Mountains.

The majority of the park's landscape is Chihuahuan Desert, but desert grasslands form a mid-elevation belt between the desert scrub and pinyon-juniper woodlands that extend to the top of the mountains. Moist canyons with forest-type habitat also occur in the highlands.

Numerous roads and trails provide good access to a wide variety of habitats at all elevations. Among the best locations for butterflies are the Green Gulch roadway (**A**), Chisos Basin (**B**), Laguna Meadow Trail (**C**), the Rio Grande Village-Boquillas Canyon area (**D**), Blue Creek Canyon (**E**), and Cottonwood Campground (**F**).

Habitats: Desert scrub, sotol grassland, pinyon-juniper woodland, pine-maple-oak woodland, and riparian.

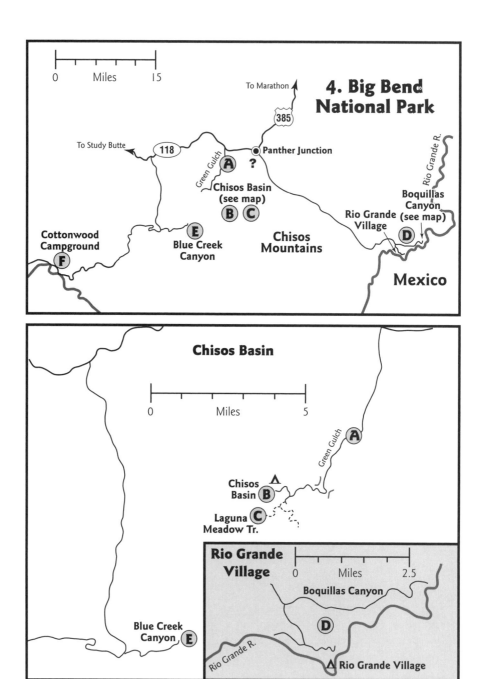

Upper Green Gulch, Big Bend National Park

Strategy for finding the most butterflies: The Green Gulch roadway **(A)** offers the greatest potential for butterfly diversity. This route is a transect between the desert lowlands and mountain highlands. Park only at pull-offs and walk along the road and into the adjacent vegetation. In the lower desert scrub and grassland areas, some of the more common butterflies include Pipevine Swallowtail; Lyside and Dainty sulphurs; Sleepy Orange; Reakirt's Blue; Tiny and Elada checkerspots; Queen; Common/White and Desert checkered-skippers; and Orange Skipperling. Also watch for **Mormon** and **"Chisos" Nais metalmarks**, **Desert Cloudywing**, and **Acacia Skipper**. **Leda Ministreak** and **Rita Blue** are possible in summer, and in September and October, **Orange Giant-Skipper** is possible near century plants.

In the pinyon-juniper woodlands of the upper reaches of Green Gulch, likely species include Two-tailed Swallowtail, Mexican Yellow, Juniper Hairstreak, Vesta and Texan crescents, Red-spotted Purple, Arizona Sister, **Tropical Leafwing**, **Mead's Wood-Nymph**, Red Satyr, **Golden Banded-Skipper**, Northern Cloudywing, Mournful Duskywing, and Dun and Eufala skippers. Less numerous are **Acmon Blue**; **Rawson's Metalmark**; Empress Leilia; **Canyonland Satyr**; **Arizona Powdered-Skipper**; Sleepy, **Rocky Mountain** (spring), and **Meridian duskywings**; and **Arizona** and **Umber skippers**. **Chisos Banded-Skipper** occurs sporadically. **Mexican Silverspot** and **Zebra Heliconian** are temporary colonists.

Next, walk around Chisos Basin **(B)** and the adjacent short trails. Check the shrubbery around and behind the store. **Poling's** and **Sandia hairstreaks** are possible in spring. "Dark" **Tropical Buckeye**, Common/**Scarce Streaky-Skipper**, **Erichson's White-Skipper**, and **Simius Roadside-Skipper** have been recorded in openings and on flowering plants in the brushy areas beyond.

For higher-elevation species, walk the Laguna Meadow Trail (**C**) from its trailhead in Chisos Basin. If time permits, make a loop into Boot Canyon and return via the Pinnacles Trail. The species you'll encounter will be mostly the same as those mentioned for upper Green Gulch, but also watch for **Xami Hairstreak**, **Hepburn's Metalmark**, **Chisos** and **Edwards' skipperlings**, **Sunrise** and **Taxiles skippers**, and **Orange-headed Roadside-Skipper**.

For lowland species, drive to the Rio Grande Village-Boquillas Canyon area (**D**). Watch for **Boisduval's Yellow** in moist, grassy areas, such as ditches. Fatal Metalmark can be abundant along edges, especially in the Daniel's Ranch area. Mourning Cloak is sometimes found along the nature trail. Look for **Small Checkered-Skipper** on low wildflowers, Southern Skipperling in grassy areas, and **Bromeliad Scrub-Hairstreak** and **Palmer's Metalmark** on flowering shrubs along the Boquillas Canyon roadway.

On the west side of the park, walk the trail up Blue Creek Canyon (**E**) for a mile or two in the early morning and look for butterflies on the return trip. This canyon, dominated by desert-scrub vegetation, can be extremely warm by mid-morning. The trail is likely to offer many of the same butterflies mentioned for lower Green Gulch, but **Chinati Checkerspot**; **Golden-headed Scallopwing**; **Viereck's**, **White-barred**, **Python**, and **Sheep skippers**; and Bronze, **Oslar's**, **Texas**, and **Slaty roadside-skippers** are more likely here. Theona and **Fulvia checkerspots** are also possible.

On the far west side of the park, Cottonwood Campground (**F**) can also be worthwhile. Check the saltbush flat at the rear of the group-camping area for Saltbush Sootywings. There are also a few lowland records of **Red-lined Scrub-Hairstreak** and **Cyna Blue**. **Mary's Giant-Skipper** occurs during September and October near lechuguilla. In addition, **Ornythion Swallowtail** and **Drusius Cloudywing** can be encountered almost anywhere in this area but are rare.

Directions: In Brewster County, take either US 385 south from Marathon (69 mi.) or SH 118 south from Alpine (102 mi.) to Panther Junction and Big Bend NP headquarters. The **Green Gulch roadway (A)** to **Chisos Basin (B)** and the **Laguna Meadow Trail (C)** is three miles west of Panther Junction. For the **Rio Grande Village-Boquillas Canyon area (D)**, return to Panther Junction and take the road southeast for 20 miles. For western sites, return to Panther Junction and proceed west past the Green Gulch turn-off for 10 miles to a left turn on Ross Maxwell Scenic Dr. to **Blue Creek Canyon (E)**. Continue to Castolon (22 miles) and nearby **Cottonwood Campground (F)**. Scenic Santa Elena Canyon is 13 miles beyond.

Nearest food, gas, and lodging: In the park, with lodging only in the Chisos Basin; other nearby lodging at the town of Study Butte on SH 118.

Nearest camping: Chisos Basin, Rio Grande Village, and Cottonwood campgrounds; primitive sites by permit.

Additional Worthwhile Sites in the Trans-Pecos Region

Hueco Tanks State Park. Located 32 miles northeast of El Paso, off US 62/180, this 860-acre state park (fee area) offers good butterflying opportunities during wet years when wildflowers are abundant. However, because of the abundance of valuable Indian pictographs on the cliffs, the park is open only on a guided basis. Arrangements must be made in advance.

Balmorhea State Park. This small park (fee area) is located along SH 17, four miles southwest of the town of Balmorhea. A butterfly garden has been developed at the park entrance. The park is best known for the large springs that surface here, providing water for a 1.75-acre swimming pool and the restored San Solomon Cienega. The nearby 600-acre Balmorhea Lake is an excellent wintertime birding location.

Post Park. Located five miles south of Marathon on Post Rd., this county park is known locally as "The Post" because of its historic importance. Fort Pena Colorado was established here in 1879. The park has a picnic area and year-round running water with resultant riparian growth. Check the edges for butterflies, especially along the north side. The entrance road also can be worthwhile.

Big Bend Ranch State Natural Area. Located along the Rio Grande just west of Big Bend NP, this protected land (fee area) offers the same lowland butterflies found in Big Bend but does not have the highland species. Access to the heart of this 300,000-acre park must be arranged at Barton Warnock Environmental Education Center at Lajitas or at Fort Leaton State Historic Park near Presidio.

Butterfly Checklist for the Trans-Pecos Region

The following checklist includes the species seen in four sites: **1. El Paso/Franklin Mountains SP, 2. Guadalupe Mountains NP, 3. Davis Mountains**, and **4. Big Bend NP.**

Status symbols include: A = abundant; C = common; U = uncommon; O = occasional; R = rare; X = accidental; M = migrant; TC = temporary colonist; ? = status unknown. (For a full definition of these terms, see p. 3.)

For trip notes, including dates and numbers of species seen, refer to the entry for this checklist in Appendix 3: Regional Checklist Resources.

Butterfly Species	1	2	3	4
Pipevine Swallowtail	C	C	C	C
Black Swallowtail	U	O	U	U
Thoas Swallowtail			X	
Giant Swallowtail	O	U	U	U

Butterfly Species	1	2	3	4
Ornythion Swallowtail		X	X	R
Broad-banded Swallowtail				X
Eastern Tiger Swallowtail			X	X
Western Tiger Swallowtail		X		
Two-tailed Swallowtail	U	C	C	C
Mexican Dartwhite				?
Florida White				X
Spring White	R	R		
Checkered White	C	A	A	C
Cabbage White	U	R	R	R
Great Southern White				X
Pearly Marble	U			
Desert Orangetip	R			
Sara Orangetip	R			
Clouded Sulphur	R	U	R	R
Orange Sulphur	C	C	C	C
Southern Dogface	C	A	U	A
White Angled-Sulphur		X	X	X
Yellow Angled-Sulphur			X	
Cloudless Sulphur	C	C	U	C
Orange-barred Sulphur				O
Large Orange Sulphur	C	A	O	C
Lyside Sulphur	U	C	C	C
Boisduval's Yellow		X		R
Mexican Yellow	C	U	U	C
Tailed Orange	X		X	X
Little Yellow	C		O	O
Mimosa Yellow				X
Sleepy Orange	C	A	A	A
Dainty Sulphur	C	A	A	A
Colorado Hairstreak		X		
Great Purple Hairstreak	O	U	O	C
Soapberry Hairstreak	R	R	R	
Coral Hairstreak				X
Striped Hairstreak				R
Oak Hairstreak			U	
Poling's Hairstreak		U	O	O
Xami Hairstreak			R	R
Sandia Hairstreak		O	R	O
Henry's Elfin		U	U	R
Thicket Hairstreak		O	R	
Juniper Hairstreak		U	C	U

Butterfly Species	1	2	3	4
Gray Hairstreak	U	A	C	C
Red-lined Scrub-Hairstreak				R
Mallow Scrub-Hairstreak			X	X
Bromeliad Scrub-Hairstreak				R
Dusky-blue Groundstreak		X	R	R
Mountain Groundstreak				U
Leda Ministreak	O	R	O	R
Gray Ministreak			X	X
Arizona Hairstreak			X	R
Western Pygmy-Blue	C	U	C	C
Cassius Blue		R		R
Marine Blue	O	C	O	A
Cyna Blue	X	X	R	R
Ceraunus Blue	U	C	O	U
Reakirt's Blue	A	A	A	C
Eastern Tailed-Blue			X	X
Western Tailed-Blue		X		
Spring/Summer Azure		C	U	U
Rita Blue			X	R
Melissa Blue	R	U	X	
Acmon Blue	R	U	O	U
Lupine Blue		X		
Fatal Metalmark		U	R	A
Rounded Metalmark				X
Rawson's Metalmark			R	U
Arizona Metalmark				X
Zela Metalmark				X
Mormon Metalmark	C	U	R	O
Hepburn's Metalmark				R
Palmer's Metalmark	C	U	R	O
"Chisos" Nais Metalmark				C
American Snout	A-R	A-R	A-R	A-R
Gulf Fritillary	C	C	U	U
Mexican Silverspot				TC
Isabella's Heliconian				X
Zebra Heliconian	X	X		TC
Variegated Fritillary	A	A	A	A
Mexican Fritillary				X
Dotted Checkerspot			X	
Theona Checkerspot	U	U	R	U
Chinati Checkerspot		R	R	U
Fulvia Checkerspot	R	O	R	O

Butterfly Species	1	2	3	4
Bordered Patch	U	U	U	C
Definite Patch	O	R	X	
Crimson Patch				X
Tiny Checkerspot	U	U	O	U
Elada Checkerspot	C	C	R	A
Texan Crescent	U	U	U	C
Vesta Crescent		U	U	U
Phaon Crescent	U	A	O	U
Pearl Crescent	U	A	R	U
Painted Crescent	C	C	O	R
Mylitta Crescent		O		
Question Mark	U	U	U	U
Satyr Comma		X		
Mourning Cloak	U	U	U	U
American Lady	C	C	A	C
Painted Lady	C	C	C	C
West Coast Lady	U	R	X	X
Red Admiral	C	C	C	A
Common Buckeye	U	U	U	U
Tropical Buckeye		X	R	O
Malachite		X	X	
Red-spotted Purple		U	C	C
Viceroy	R	U	R	U
Weidemeyer's Admiral	X			
Arizona Sister	U	C	A	A
Common Mestra		R	R	U
Red Rim			X	X
Many-banded Daggerwing				X
Ruddy Daggerwing				X
Tropical Leafwing	U	U	R	C
Goatweed Leafwing		U	U	U
Hackberry Emperor	U	C	U	U
Empress Leilia	C	U	U	A
Tawny Emperor	U	U	C	U
Nabokov's Satyr		X		
Canyonland Satyr		U	C	U
Red Satyr	U	A	A	A
Mead's Wood-Nymph		C	C	U
Monarch	M	M	M	M
Queen	C	A	C	C
Soldier				X
Dull Firetip			X	

Butterfly Species	1	2	3	4
Silver-spotted Skipper		X	X	X
Hammock Skipper			X	
White-striped Longtail		X	R	
Zilpa Longtail			X	X
Short-tailed Skipper		X	R	
Arizona Skipper	R		R	O
Long-tailed Skipper			R	
Two-barred Flasher			X	
Golden Banded-Skipper			U	C
Chisos Banded-Skipper				R
Desert Cloudywing			C	C
Northern Cloudywing		C	A	A
Mexican Cloudywing			X	
Drusius Cloudywing		U	U	R
Acacia Skipper	U		R	C
Golden-headed Scallopwing	O	R	U	U
Texas Powdered-Skipper		R	R	O
Arizona Powdered-Skipper	U	O	R	U
Sickle-winged Skipper			X	X
Hermit Skipper			X	X
Sleepy Duskywing	U	U	X	U
Juvenal's Duskywing			R	O
Rocky Mountain Duskywing	R	U	R	U
Meridian Duskywing	R	C	U	U
Scudder's Duskywing			R	X
Mournful Duskywing	U	U	U	C
Funereal Duskywing	U	U	U	C
Small Checkered-Skipper	U	O	R	O
Com./White Checkered-Skipper	C	C	C	C
Desert Checkered-Skipper	C	U	U	U
Erichson's White-Skipper	R	X	R	O
Common Streaky-Skipper	U	U	U	C
Scarce Streaky-Skipper			C	U
Common Sootywing	O	U	U	U
Mexican Sootywing		R	U	R
Saltbush Sootywing		U		O
Russet Skipperling			X	
Four-spotted Skipperling			R	
Chisos Skipperling				R
Julia's Skipper			X	U
Clouded Skipper		X	O	C
Tropical Least Skipper	U	C	R	R

Butterfly Species	1	2	3	4
Edwards' Skipperling		C	C	R
Orange Skipperling	C	C	A	C
Southern Skipperling			R	C
Sunrise Skipper		U	O	R
Fiery Skipper	U	U	R	C
Morrison's Skipper		C	C	
Uncas Skipper		R	R	
Apache Skipper		R	R	
Pahaska Skipper	R	U	O	R
Green Skipper		U	R	
Carus Skipper		R	R	
Whirlabout			X	
Sachem	U	U	C	C
Delaware Skipper		O	U	R
Taxiles Skipper		R	R	
Umber Skipper		R	O	
Dun Skipper		C	U	U
Viereck's Skipper	U	U	R	C
White-barred Skipper		O	U	
Python Skipper	U	U	O	U
Sheep Skipper		R	O	C
Simius Roadside-Skipper		U	O	R
Cassus Roadside-Skipper		O	R	
Bronze Roadside-Skipper	U	C	U	C
Oslar's Roadside-Skipper		U	U	U
Texas Roadside-Skipper	U	U	U	O
Slaty Roadside-Skipper		U	O	O
Nysa Roadside-Skipper		U	U	U
Dotted Roadside-Skipper		U	O	O
Celia's Roadside-Skipper		R	R	
Orange-headed Roadside-Skipper		U	U	U
Eufala Skipper		X	U	U
Brazilian Skipper		X	X	
Ocola Skipper		X	X	
Orange Giant-Skipper		R	R	R
Mary's Giant-Skipper	R	R	R	R
Yucca Giant-Skipper		R	R	
Ursine Giant-Skipper	R	R	U	R

Panhandle and Western Plains

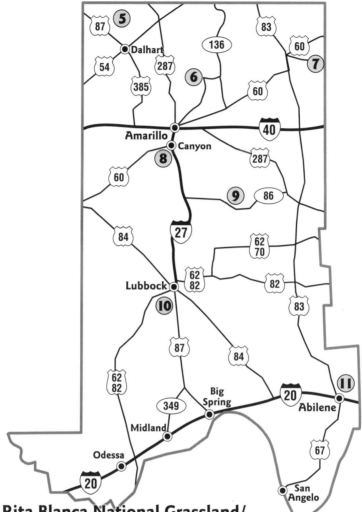

5. Rita Blanca National Grassland/
   Lake Rita Blanca
6. Lake Meredith National
   Recreation Area
7. Black Kettle National Grassland/
   Gene Howe Wildlife Management Area
8. Palo Duro Canyon State Park/
   Buffalo Lake National Wildlife Refuge
9. Caprock Canyon State Park

10. Lubbock
11. Abilene

Panhandle and Western Plains Region

The Texas Panhandle and Western Plains Region is located north of the Trans-Pecos and Edwards Plateau regions. It is bordered by New Mexico to the west and Oklahoma to the north and east.

Landscapes are rugged in places, but the region generally consists of open flatlands with scattered valleys and playa lakes. Major topographic features include the Caprock Escarpment and the Canadian River Breaks. Vegetation is dominated by mixed prairie habitats with scattered scrub oak, mesquite, and yucca. Croplands, especially cotton fields, are widespread. Elevations range from about 1,000 to 4,500 feet.

The region is represented by seven sites: **5. Rita Blanca National Grassland/Lake Rita Blanca, 6. Lake Meredith National Recreation Area, 7. Black Kettle National Grassland/Gene Howe Wildlife Management Area, 8. Palo Duro Canyon State Park/Buffalo Lake National Wildlife Refuge, 9. Caprock Canyon State Park, 10. Lubbock**, and **11. Abilene**. The best time to visit these sites is April through October.

Panhandle and Western Plains Specialties

The Panhandle and Western Plains Region has a good diversity of butterflies, partly due to its position in the Great Plains. Several species enter the state from the north and rarely occur farther south in Texas. Sixteen are considered area specialties.

Whites, Coppers, Hairstreaks: **Olympia Marble** flies in open prairies from March to May at Lake Meredith NRA, Black Kettle NG/Gene Howe WMA, and Palo Duro Canyon SP/Buffalo Lake NWR. Larvae feed on rockcress. **Gray Copper** has been recorded in moist prairies in Texas only in Black Kettle NG/Gene Howe WMA and Palo Duro Canyon SP/Buffalo Lake NWR. Larvae feed on docks. **Coral Hairstreak** occurs at brushy areas in Black Kettle NG/Gene Howe WMA and Palo Duro Canyon SP/Buffalo Lake NWR. Larvae feed on wild cherry and plum. **Behr's Hairstreak** has been recorded in Texas only during July in Palo Duro Canyon SP. Larvae feed on mountain mahogany.

Blues, Checkerspots: **Melissa Blue** can be widespread at patches of wildflowers and in alfalfa fields in Rita Blanca NG/Lake Rita Blanca, Lake Meredith NRA, Palo Duro Canyon SP/Buffalo Lake NWR, and the Lubbock area. Larvae feed on legumes, including alfalfa, lupines, and rattleweed. **Acmon Blue** is most likely to occur at patches of wildflowers in Black Kettle NG/Gene Howe WMA and Palo Duro Canyon SP/Buffalo Lake NWR. Larvae feed on legumes and buckwheats. **Dotted Checkerspot** has been recorded at wildflowers in Palo Duro Canyon SP/Buffalo Lake NWR, Caprock Canyon SP, and the Lubbock area. Larvae feed on beard-tongue. **Fulvia Checkerspot** frequents grassy areas with Indian paintbrush, its larval foodplant, in Palo Duro Canyon SP/Buffalo Lake NWR, Caprock Canyon SP, and the Lubbock area.

Spread-wing Skippers: **Outis Skipper** has been recorded in grasslands with acacia, its larval foodplant, from April and May and again from July to August in Caprock Canyon SP. **Meridian Duskywing** is possible at patches of wildflowers near oak, its larval foodplant, in Lake Meredith NRA.

Grass-Skippers: **Uncas Skipper** is most likely to occur in the sparse prairies of Rita Blanca NG/Lake Rita Blanca, Lake Meredith NRA, Palo Duro Canyon SP/Buffalo Lake NWR, and Caprock Canyon SP. Larvae feed on blue grama. **Ottoe Skipper** has been recorded at undisturbed grasslands in Black Kettle NG/Gene Howe WMA. Larvae use grasses, including bluestem. **Arogos Skipper** flies near bluestem grass, its larval foodplant, in Black Kettle NG/Gene Howe WMA and Palo Duro Canyon SP/Buffalo Lake NWR. **Dusted Skipper** occurs in patches of bluestem grass, its larval foodplant, in May and June in Black Kettle NG/Gene Howe WMA, Palo Duro Canyon SP/Buffalo Lake NWR, and Caprock Canyon SP. **Oslar's Roadside-Skipper** is most likely to occur in sparse prairies in Rita Blanca NG/Lake Rita Blanca, Lake Meredith NRA, Palo Duro Canyon SP/Buffalo Lake NWR, and Caprock Canyon SP. Larvae feed on sideoats grama.

Giant-Skippers: **Strecker's Giant-Skipper** occurs in grasslands with yucca, its larval foodplant, from April to July, in Lake Meredith NRA, Palo Duro Canyon SP, Caprock Canyon SP, and the Lubbock area.

Sites within the Panhandle and Western Plains Region

5. Rita Blanca National Grassland/Lake Rita Blanca

Rita Blanca National Grassland is in the northwest corner of the Panhandle, so butterflies not typically found in Texas are possible. Managed by the U.S. Forest Service, it includes 77,463 acres in Texas, divided into separate tracts with private ranchlands interspersed. The 1,668-acre Lake Rita Blanca Park (fee area) is located just south of Dalhart. Operated as a city park, it features a 150-acre lake and nine miles of trails. Rita Blanca is Spanish for "Little White River."

Specific locations within the Rita Blanca NG include roads north of US 87 (**A-C**). Sites within Lake Rita Blanca Park include a lakeside trail (**D**), the picnic area (**E**), and the area near the dam (**F**).

Habitats: Prairie, marsh, riparian, field, and cropland.

Strategy for finding the most butterflies: In Rita Blanca NG, drive the highways north of US 87, including FM 1879 (**A**), FM 296 (**B**), and FM 2586 (**C**). Walk the roadsides and side roads and survey the Thompson Grove Recreation Area along FM 296. Some of the more numerous butterflies include Pipevine and Black swallowtails, Orange and Dainty sulphurs, American Snout, Painted Crescent, Queen, Green Skipper, and

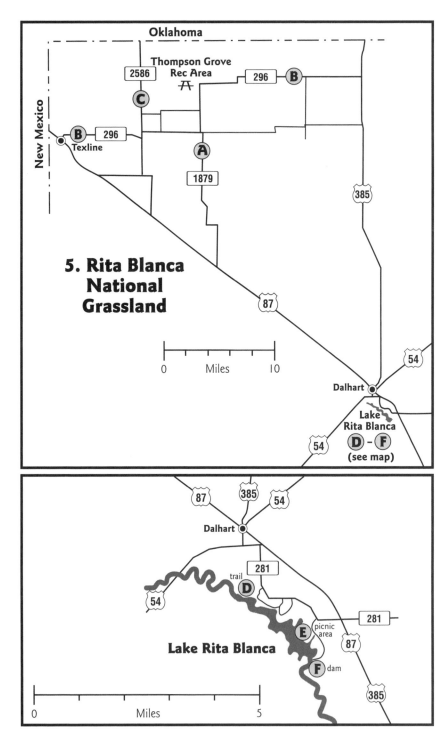

5. Rita Blanca National Grassland

Oklahoma

New Mexico

Thompson Grove
Rec Area

2586

296

B

C

B 296

Texline

A

1879

385

87

54

Dalhart

Lake
Rita Blanca

54

D – F

(see map)

0   Miles   10

Lake Rita Blanca

87

385

54

Dalhart

281

trail

D

54

281

E

picnic
area

87

F

dam

385

0   Miles   5

Rita Blanca National Grassland

Sachem. Look for **Uncas Skipper** on low-growing wildflowers. **Oslar's Roadside-Skipper** is also possible.

At Lake Rita Blanca Park, drive to the boat ramp area and walk the lakeside trail **(D)** along the northern portion of the lake. Likely butterflies along the trail not already mentioned above include Marine and Reakirt's blues, Gorgone Checkerspot, Pearl Crescent, Goatweed Leafwing, and Hackberry Emperor. **Melissa Blue** is also possible. Then check the edges of the picnic area **(E)**, and walk the track to and beyond the dam **(F)** at the southern end of the park. Sleepy Orange and Western Pygmy-Blue are likely.

Directions: In Dallam and Hartley counties, access to Rita Blanca NG is north of Dalhart via US 87. **FM 1879 (A)**, north from US 87, and **FM 296 (B)**, east from US 87 in Texline, traverse the heart of the area. **FM 2586 (C)** goes north from FM 296. To reach **Lake Rita Blanca (D-F)**, take US 87/385 south of Dalhart to FM 281 and turn west.

Nearest food, gas, and lodging: Dalhart; food and gas in Texline.

Nearest camping: Lake Rita Blanca Park; primitive sites in Rita Blanca NG, particularly at Thompson Grove Recreation Area.

6. Lake Meredith National Recreation Area

Lake Meredith is in the geographic center of the Texas Panhandle. The 45,000-acre recreation area, managed by the National Park Service, is dominated by the lake, created by construction of Sanford Dam on the Canadian River. The extensive

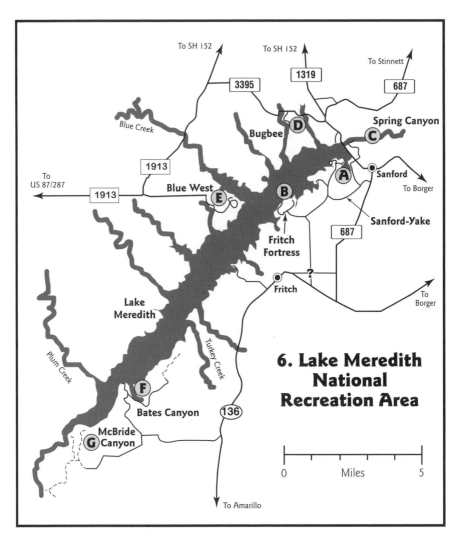

To SH 152

To SH 152

To Stinnett

1319

3395

687

Blue Creek

Spring Canyon

Bugbee

D

C

1913

To
US 87/287

A

Sanford

1913

Blue West

To Borger

E

B

Sanford-Yake

687

**Fritch
Fortress**

?

Fritch

To
Borger

**Lake
Meredith**

Turkey Creek

6. Lake Meredith
National
Recreation Area

Plum Creek

F

Bates Canyon

136

McBride
G **Canyon**

0   Miles   5

To Amarillo

shoreline offers numerous side roads to camping and/or boat-launching sites, a few of which offer short trails.

Specific locations for butterfly watching include the Sanford-Yake area (**A**), the Fritch Fortress area (**B**), Spring Canyon (**C**), the Bugbee entrance road (**D**), Blue West (**E**), Bates Canyon (**F**), and McBride Canyon (**G**).

Habitats: Prairie, mesquite grassland, juniper woodland, marsh, riparian, and field.

Strategy for finding the most butterflies: The most productive butterfly-finding locations are along the eastern and southern shores of the lake. Near the east end of the lake, the Sanford-Yake area (**A**) can be very good, especially the brushy canyon below

View from Fritch Fortress, Lake Meredith National Recreation Area

the Canadian River Municipal Water Authority office. Some of the more numerous butterflies include Pipevine and Black swallowtails; Checkered White; Large Orange Sulphur; Southern Dogface; Sleepy Orange; Marine and Reakirt's blues; Gulf Fritillary; Gorgone Checkerspot, Pearl Crescent; Queen; Common Checkered-Skipper; Orange Skipperling; and Sachem.

The nearby Fritch Fortress area (**B**) should also be checked; watch there for Dainty Sulphur, Green Skipper, and Bronze and Nysa roadside-skippers. **Uncas Skipper** is also possible on low-growing wildflowers. Spring Canyon (**C**), the wetland below the dam, including the north-side roadway, also has considerable potential.

On the north shore, the Bugbee entrance road (**D**) can also be productive, especially the little wetland at the base of the hill, where **Melissa Blue** and **Oslar's Roadside-Skipper** have been recorded. Also drive farther west to Blue West (**E**) and walk through this juniper- and yucca-dotted land. Juniper Hairstreak, Western Pygmy-Blue, and Monarch are likely, and **Strecker's Giant-Skipper** is possible from April to July.

On the southeast shore, Bates Canyon and McBride Canyon should be visited. Bates Canyon (**F**), with its overgrown riparian area, offers many of the same butterflies mentioned above, plus Funereal Duskywing and Dotted Roadside-Skipper. McBride Canyon (**G**), with wooded, juniper-clad hillsides and a cottonwood floodplain, can also be productive. Giant Swallowtail, Soapberry Hairstreak (April to July), Question Mark, Goatweed Leafwing, Hackberry Emperor, and Silver-spotted Skipper are likely. **Meridian Duskywing** is also possible.

Watch throughout the entire area for **Olympia Marble** during March and April.

Directions: In Moore, Potter, and Hutchinson counties. From Borger, take SH 136 west and FM 1319 north to Sanford (10 miles). To reach **Sanford-Yake (A)** and **Fritch Fortress (B)** take FM 687 south from Sanford to the Sanford-Yake Rd. and turn right. Sanford Dam and **Spring Canyon (C)** are just west of Sanford on FM 1319. To reach **Bugbee (D)** on the north shore, continue northwest on FM 1319 and turn west on FM 3395 to Bugbee Dr., the entrance road. For **Blue West (E)**, continue on FM 3395 to FM 1913. Turn south to Blue West Rd., the entrance road. The southeast-shore sites, including **Bates Canyon (F)** and **McBride Canyon (G)**, are accessible off SH 136, eight miles south of Fritch.

Nearest food, gas, and lodging: Borger and Fritch; food and gas in Sanford.

Nearest camping: Lake Meredith NRA.

7. Black Kettle National Grassland/ Gene Howe Wildlife Management Area

Only 576 acres of the 31,399-acre Black Kettle NG are in Texas. The rest are in a separate tract in Oklahoma. The Texas section is at Lake Marvin **(A)**. The lake and its adjacent prairie lands **(B)**, east of Canadian on FM 2266, offer two productive butterfly-watching sites.

The 5,824-acre Gene Howe WMA, managed by the Texas Parks and Wildlife Department, is on both sides of FM 2266 on the way to Lake Marvin. The side road to West Bull Slough and West Bull Slough Trail **(C)**, are good butterfly-watching areas. The vicinity of the headquarters **(D)** is also a good spot to find butterflies. FM 2266 **(E)** and the floodplain below the nearby Canadian River Bridge **(F)** provide additional opportunities.

Habitats: Prairie, pasture, cottonwood grove, riparian, field, and cropland.

Strategy for finding the most butterflies: Start at Lake Marvin **(A)** by checking the road-sides and walking the network of trails that circle most of the lake, passing through riparian vegetation. Some of the more numerous butterflies include Dainty Sulphur; Sleepy Orange; Gorgone Checkerspot; Pearl Crescent; Viceroy; Goatweed Leafwing; Hackberry and Tawny emperors; Common Checkered-Skipper; Least, Dun, and Eufala skippers; Sachem; and Nysa, Dotted, and Common roadside-skippers.

In addition, **Dusted Skipper** occurs along the trail on the north side of the lake in open bluestem grasslands. (Look behind the "Sand Sagebrush" interpretive sign, for example.) Less common species include Black and Giant swallowtails, Cloudless Sulphur, and Common Sootywing. Also check the outflow area along the south side of the lake.

Across FM 2266 to the north, the pond and adjacent prairie **(B)** has potential. **Gray Copper** is possible in brushy areas, and **Arogos Skipper** may be present in the prairie.

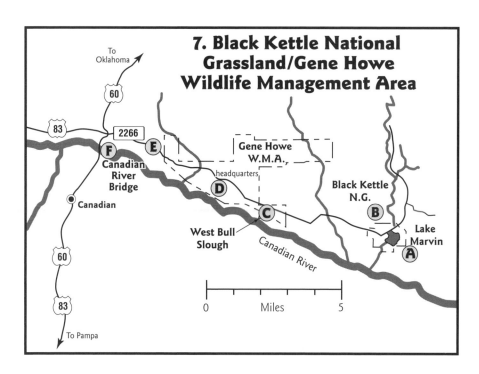

7. Black Kettle National Grassland/Gene Howe Wildlife Management Area

To Oklahoma

60

83

2266

F Canadian River Bridge

E

Canadian

60

83

To Pampa

Gene Howe W.M.A.

headquarters

D

C

West Bull Slough

Canadian River

Black Kettle N.G.

B

A

Lake Marvin

0   Miles   5

Black Kettle National Grassland

Sites of interest in Gene Howe WMA include the roadsides along West Bull Slough, the West Bull Slough Trail **(C),** and the vicinity of the headquarters **(D)**. In these locations, watch for Southern Dogface; Soapberry Hairstreak (spring); **Coral Hairstreak** in brushy areas; Eastern Tailed-Blue; Marine, **Acmon**, and **Melissa blues**; and Queen.

Check wildflower patches along FM 2266 **(E)**, a good place for Painted Crescent. If time permits, visit the floodplain on both sides of the Canadian River Bridge **(F)** on US 60, north of Canadian.

In addition, **Olympia Marble** flies in open areas from March to May, and **Behr's Hairstreak** and **Ottoe Skipper** have been recorded in the area at unknown locations.

Directions: In Hemphill County, **FM 2266 (E)** is located north of Canadian off US 60, just beyond the **Canadian River Bridge (F)**. Follow it east to **Gene Howe WMA (C, D)** and to **Lake Marvin (A, B)**, 13 miles from the turn.

Nearest food, gas, and lodging: Canadian.

Nearest camping: Lake Marvin and Canadian.

8. Palo Duro Canyon State Park/ Buffalo Lake National Wildlife Refuge

Palo Duro Canyon State Park and Buffalo Lake National Wildlife Refuge, east and west of Canyon, respectively, offer a diversity of habitats for butterflies. The 16,402-acre Palo Duro Canyon SP (fee area), situated at the eastern edge of the Llano Estacado (Texas High Plains), was carved by the Prairie Dog Fork of the Red River. The canyon—120 miles long, 20 miles wide, and 800 feet deep—has been called "The Grand Canyon of Texas." Sites to visit include the entrance **(A)**, pull-offs along the entrance road **(B)**, Hackberry Campground **(C)**, Chinaberry Day Use Area **(D)**, Juniper Trail-Riverside **(E)**, Cottonwood Campground **(F)**, and Sunflower Campground **(G)**.

The 7,664-acre Buffalo Lake NWR is situated on rolling hills and features 300-acre Stewart Marsh, fed by rainfall, and little Tierra Blanca Creek. Good butterfly watching can be found at the entrance and along the roadsides **(H)**, in the picnic and camping areas **(I)**, and along the Cottonwood Canyon Birding Trail **(J)**.

Habitats: Juniper woodland, mesquite grassland, prairie, riparian, field, and cropland.

Strategy for finding the most butterflies: Start near the Palo Duro Canyon SP entrance **(A)** by walking the open, juniper-dotted grassland and picnic area in search of **Olympia Marble**, Yucca Giant-Skipper (March to May), and **Strecker's Giant-Skipper** (April to July). Some of the more numerous butterflies include Dainty Sulphur, Southern Dogface, Sleepy Orange, Juniper Hairstreak, Reakirt's Blue, Variegated Fritillary, Common Checkered-Skipper, and Sachem. Black Swallowtail, Green and **Dusted skippers**, and **Oslar's Roadside-Skipper** are also possible.

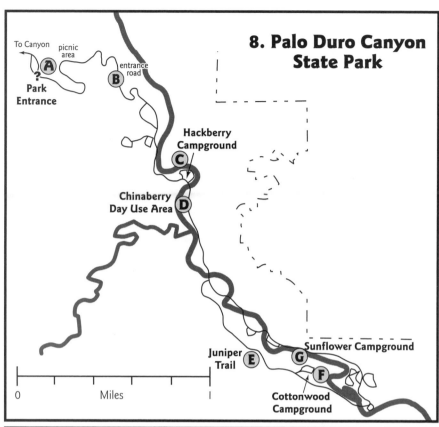

8. Palo Duro Canyon State Park

To Canyon

picnic area

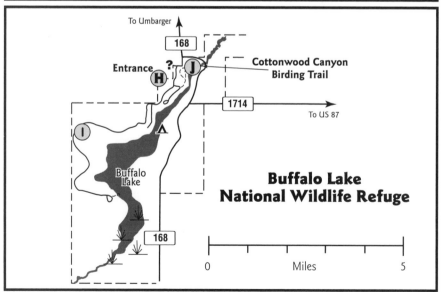

A

?

Park Entrance

entrance road

B

Hackberry Campground

C

Chinaberry Day Use Area

D

Juniper Trail

E

Sunflower Campground

G

F

Cottonwood Campground

0   Miles

To Umbarger

168

Entrance **?**

H

J

Cottonwood Canyon Birding Trail

1714

To US 87

Δ

I

Buffalo Lake

Buffalo Lake National Wildlife Refuge

168

0   Miles   5

Palo Duro Canyon State Park

Then drive into the canyon, checking the roadsides **(B)** at each pull-off for Marine Blue, Eastern Tailed-Blue, Gulf Fritillary, Gorgone Checkerspot, Phaon Crescent, Fiery and Eufala skippers, and Dotted and Common roadside-skippers.

Within the canyon, visit sites along the loop road. Hackberry Campground **(C)** is a good place to find Hackberry and Tawny emperors. Nysa Roadside-Skipper has been recorded at Chinaberry Day Use Area **(D)**. Walk a portion of Juniper Trail-Riverside **(E)**, a likely place for Pearl Crescent; Red-spotted Purple; Goatweed Leafwing; Red Satyr; and Silver-spotted, Least, and Delaware skippers. If time permits, walk around Cottonwood Campground **(F)** and Sunflower Campground **(G)**.

Gray Copper, **Coral Hairstreak**, **Melissa** and **Acmon blues**, Bordered Patch, **Dotted Checkerspot**, Juvenal's (April to June) and Funereal duskywings, and Orange Skipperling are possible at flowering plants throughout the canyon.

At Buffalo Lake NWR, check the entrance and roadsides **(H)**, likely places for Pipevine Swallowtail, Western Pygmy-Blue, **Fulvia Checkerspot**, and Queen. Then walk the edges of the picnic and camping areas **(I)** and the .5-mile Cottonwood Canyon Birding Trail **(J)**, excellent places to find Painted Crescent and Bronze Roadside-Skipper. Also watch for **Uncas** and **Arogos skippers** in short-grass prairie.

Directions: In Randall and Armstrong Counties, **Palo Duro Canyon SP (A-G)** is located 12 miles east of US 87 from Canyon via SH 217. **Buffalo Lake NWR (H-J)** is 13 miles west of Canyon. Take US 60 to Umbarger and turn south on FM 168 for 1.5 miles.

Nearest food, gas, and lodging: Palo Duro Canyon SP, Canyon, and Umbarger.

Nearest camping: Both areas.

9. Caprock Canyon State Park

The 13,906-acre Caprock Canyon SP (fee area) is noted for its marvelous scenic diversity. The exposed red sandstones and siltstones are some of the most colorful found anywhere. The park also features the 100-acre Lake Theo, the South Prong and Little Red rivers, and sixteen miles of hiking trails.

The best butterfly-watching spots include Lake Theo (**A**), Little Red Camping Area (**B**), South Prong Camping Area (**C**), Upper Canyon Trail (**D**), North Prong Primitive Camping Area (**E**), and the park roadsides (**F**).

Habitats: Mesquite grassland, juniper woodland, prairie, wetland, and riparian.

Strategy for finding the most butterflies: Start at Lake Theo (**A**) by walking the brushy and willow-lined edges. Some of the more numerous butterflies include Black and Giant swallowtails; Dainty Sulphur; Sleepy Orange; Western Pygmy-Blue; Marine and

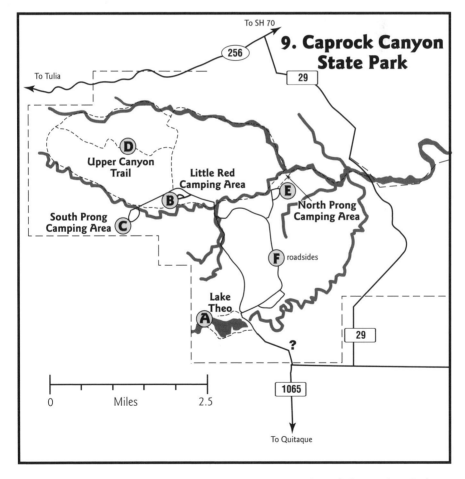

Caprock Canyon State Park

Reakirt's blues; Variegated Fritillary; Painted, Phaon, and Pearl crescents; Goatweed Leafwing; and Queen. Less common but possible are Ceraunus Blue, Gulf Fritillary, and **Dotted** and **Fulvia checkerspots**.

Then drive to Little Red Camping Area (**B**); walk around the campground and along the floodplain of the South Prong River. Little Yellow, Common Buckeye, Common Streaky-Skipper, and Eufala Skipper are likely. South Prong Camping Area (**C**) should also be checked. Especially when wildflowers are in bloom, this sparse juniper woodland is likely to harbor Juniper Hairstreak, American Snout, Red Satyr, and Green Skipper. Two-tailed Swallowtail is also possible.

Also walk a portion of the Upper Canyon Trail (**D**), which begins in the campground. Watch for **Oslar's Roadside-Skipper** on low-growing wildflowers. **Uncas Skipper** is also possible.

At the North Prong Primitive Camping Area (**E**), check the edges and walk adjacent trails. **Dusted Skipper** is possible in patches of bluestem grasses. Finally, all the roadsides (**F**) should be perused for flowering plants. Several butterflies mentioned above are possible, but also watch for Orange Skipperling; Sachem; Delaware Skipper; and Bronze, Nysa, and Dotted roadside-skippers.

In addition, **Outis Skipper** has been recorded in the area in the past, and **Strecker's Giant-Skipper** has been recorded from April to July.

Note: If you're traveling east, you may want to visit Copper Breaks State Park. See Additional Worthwhile Sites in the Northern Plains Region.

Directions: In Briscoe County, go east from Tulia and Silverton to SH 86 at Quitaque (pronounced *kitty-quay*); take FM 1065 north for three miles to the **Caprock Canyon SP (A-F)** entrance.

Nearest food, gas, and lodging: Quitaque.

Nearest camping: In the park.

10. Lubbock

Located at an elevation of about 3,200 feet in the "South Plains," Lubbock is a city of approximately 200,000 people that was established in the 1880s with the Texas cattle industry. It is better known today for the surrounding abundance of cotton fields, a wine industry, and Texas Tech University.

The city has a number of lakes and parks that provide good opportunities to watch butterflies, including Lake Six (**A, B**), Buffalo Springs Lake (**C, D**), Lubbock Lake Landmark (**E**), the Texas Tech Horticultural Garden (**F**), and the Lubbock Memorial Arboretum at Clapp Park (**G**).

Habitats: Prairie, mesquite grassland, riparian, park, garden, and cropland.

Strategy for finding the most butterflies: The Lake Six area within Yellow House Canyon Lakes Park is most likely to have the greatest butterfly diversity. Walk the network of trails (**A**) through the open mesquite grassland above the road to the north on the eastern side of Lake Six. Some of the more numerous butterflies include Clouded and Dainty sulphurs; Southern Dogface; Sleepy Orange; Marine and Reakirt's blues; Common Checkered-Skipper; and Orange Skipperling. Also watch for the less common Black Swallowtail, Great Purple and Juniper hairstreaks, Gorgone Checkerspot, and Nysa Roadside-Skipper.

Then walk the loop trail (**B**) along a small stream and through riparian vegetation between the spillway and the railroad trestle. This is a good place for Cloudless Sulphur, Pearl Crescent, Question Mark, Red Admiral, Goatweed Leafwing, Hackberry and Tawny emperors, and Funereal Duskywing. Also watch for **Melissa Blue**.

Next, drive to Buffalo Springs Lake (fee area), checking the roadsides (**C**), especially when wildflowers are plentiful. Many of the butterflies mentioned above are possible, but also watch for Western Pygmy-Blue, **Dotted** and **Fulvia checkerspots**, Common Buckeye, and Fiery Skipper. Park at the Llano Estacado Audubon Society hut at the top of the hill and search the upper slope from April to July for **Strecker's Giant-Skipper**. Additional butterflies possible here include Pipevine and Giant swallowtails, Large Orange and Lyside sulphurs, Gulf Fritillary, Theona Checkerspot, Green Skipper, and Common Roadside-Skipper.

Then walk the network of trails (**D**) from the upper hillside to the riparian habitat below the spillway. Watch there for Two-tailed Swallowtail; Mexican Yellow; Soapberry Hairstreak (April to July); American Snout; Bordered Patch; Texan, Vesta, Phaon, and Pearl crescents; Common Mestra; Red Satyr; and Silver-spotted and Delaware skippers.

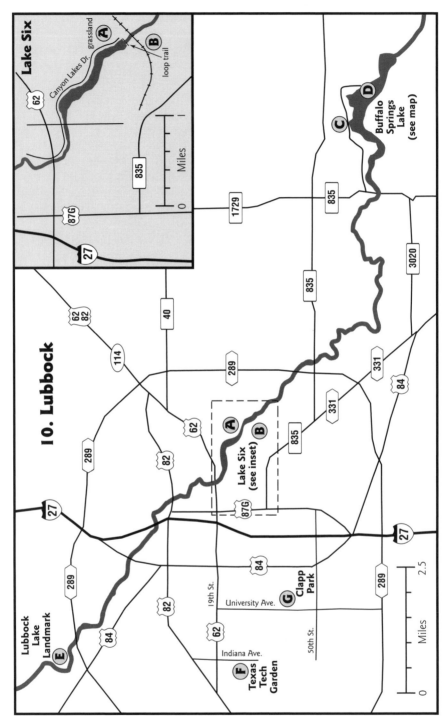

10. Lubbock

Lake Six

Canyon Lakes Dr.

grassland

Ⓐ

Ⓑ

loop trail

62

835

Miles

0

87G

27

62
82

114

40

289

289

27

82

62

Ⓐ

Ⓑ

Lake Six
(see inset)

87G

289

84

82

62

Indiana Ave.

Ⓕ
Texas
Tech
Garden

University Ave.

Ⓖ
Clapp
Park

19th St.

50th St.

84

289

27

Miles

0   2.5

Lubbock
Lake
Landmark

Ⓔ

289

1729

835

835

835

331

331

84

Ⓒ

Ⓓ

Buffalo
Springs
Lake
(see map)

3020

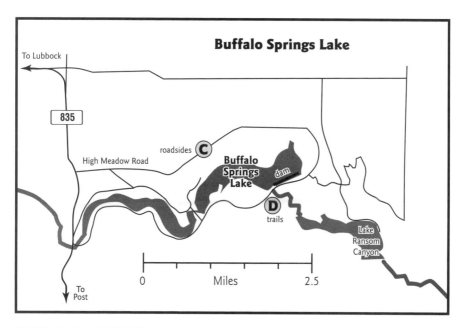

Buffalo Springs Lake

To Lubbock

835

High Meadow Road

roadsides **C**

Buffalo Springs Lake

dam

D

trails

Lake Ransom Canyon

0   Miles   2.5

To Post

Buffalo Springs dam, Lubbock area

In spring, visit Lubbock Lake Landmark (**E**) on the northwest side of the city. Check the plantings around the parking area and below the Interpretive Center, and if wildflowers are blooming, walk a portion of the 2.5-mile hiking trail.

Two additional in-town sites are worthwhile: the Texas Tech Horticultural Garden (**F**) and the Lubbock Memorial Arboretum at Clapp Park (**G**). At the latter, walk through the arboretum and across the dike that divides the two playa ponds below the arboretum proper, a good place to find Viceroy.

Directions: In Lubbock County, **Lake Six (A, B)** is accessible via 19th Street (US 62); turn south on Canyon Lakes Dr. and continue past Martin Luther King Blvd. to the east side of the lake. **Buffalo Springs Lake (C, D)** is east of town. Take FM 835 east of Loop 289 and follow it south to High Meadow Rd., which goes to the spillway. **Lubbock Lake Landmark (E)** is accessed via Landmark Ln. north of the intersection of Loop 289 and US 84. The **Texas Tech Horticultural Garden (F)** is at the corner of 19th St. (US 62) and Indiana Ave., immediately north of United Spirit Arena. The **Lubbock Memorial Arboretum at Clapp Park (G)** is located south of 19th St. (US 62) on University Ave. between 40th and 46th streets.

Nearest food, gas, and lodging: Throughout the Lubbock area.

Nearest camping: Buffalo Springs Lake and in Lubbock.

11. Abilene

The city of Abilene, established in 1821 as a shipping point for cattle, is today an oil town and home to Dyess Air Force Base and three universities—Abilene Christian, Hardin-Simmons, and McMurray. Among the best sites to find butterflies in the Abilene area are Kirby Lake Park (**A**), Abilene State Park (**B**), Lake Abilene (**C**), and Seabee Park (**D**).

Habitats: Oak-hackberry woodland, juniper-oak woodland, riparian, and field.

Strategy for finding the most butterflies: The greatest butterfly diversity in the Abilene area occurs at Kirby Lake Park (**A**), south of the city. Walk the paved and unimproved roads between the lake and recreation area. Some of the more numerous butterflies in this brushy area include Pipevine Swallowtail; Orange and Dainty sulphurs; Sleepy Orange; Reakirt's Blue; Vesta, Phaon, and Pearl crescents; Common Buckeye; Tawny Emperor; Horace's and Funereal duskywings; Common Streaky-Skipper; and Sachem.

Then drive to the 621-acre Abilene SP (**B**), southwest of the city. This state park (fee area) is located at the northern edge of the Edwards Plateau and the southern edge of the Rolling Plains. Walk the roadsides and nature trail through a dense, brushy, juniper woodland and riparian area. Black and Giant swallowtails, Cloudless Sulphur, Great Purple and Juniper hairstreaks, Marine Blue, American Snout, Texan Crescent, Red Satyr, Goatweed Leafwing, and Orange Skipperling are likely. Less common butterflies include Two-tailed Swallowtail, Lyside Sulphur, Desert Checkered-Skipper, and Delaware Skipper.

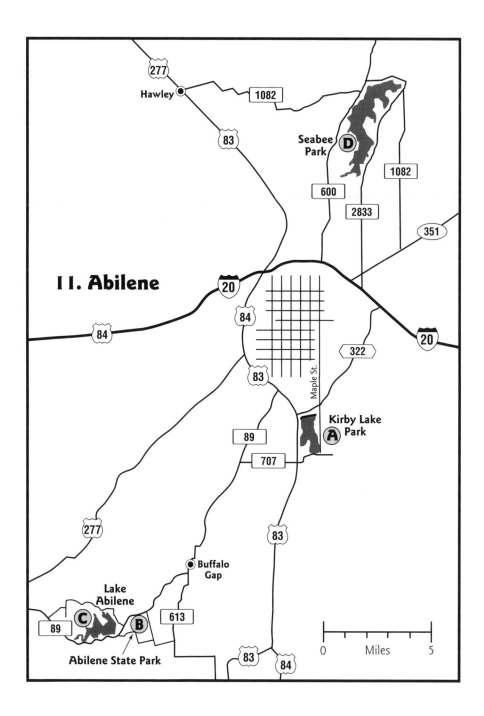

11. Abilene

Hawley

Seabee Park (D)

Kirby Lake Park (A)

Maple St.

Buffalo Gap

Lake Abilene

Abilene State Park

0   Miles   5

277
1082
83
1082
600
2833
351
20
84
84
20
322
83
89
707
277
83
613
89
B
83
84

Kirby Lake Park, Abilene

Next, drive across FM 89 to Lake Abilene **(C)**. Check the roadsides and shoreline, especially when wildflowers are prevalent. If time allows, visit Seabee Park **(D)**, north of Abilene. Walk the edges of the park, where Green Skipper is possible.

Directions: In Taylor County, Kirby Lake is located southeast of the junction of US 83 and Loop 322; **Kirby Lake Park (A)** provides access to the east side of the lake from Maple St. (CR 125) between Loop 322 and Beltway South (FM 707). **Abilene SP (B)** and **Lake Abilene (C)** are located 16 miles southwest of Abilene via FM 89 from US 83. Continue past Buffalo Gap to PR 32, the park entrance road. **Seabee Park (D)** is northeast of Abilene. Take FM 600 (West Lake Rd.) north from I-20 six miles to the park.

Nearest food, gas, and lodging: Abilene; food and gas in Buffalo Gap, near Abilene SP.

Nearest camping: Abilene SP and Seabee Park (primitive sites).

Additional Worthwhile Sites in the Panhandle Region

Muleshoe National Wildlife Refuge. The oldest NWR in Texas, this 5,809-acre refuge northwest of Lubbock was established as wintering grounds for migratory waterfowl and sandhill cranes. It has prairie, locust-hackberry woodland, and mesquite grassland. It is located in Bailey County, 20 miles south of Muleshoe on SH 214 and 30 miles west of Littlefield via FM 54 and SH 214.

Dickens County Spring Park. Located on the eastern outskirts of Dickens, this park has a beautiful riparian area, with a carpet of ferns and an overstory of cottonwoods, set in a canyon along a caprock escarpment. The rimrock is heavily "forested" with juniper. The varied habitats offer a good diversity of plants and butterflies. The park is located 60 miles east of Lubbock near the junction of US 82 and SH 70.

Midland. Known as the "Tall City" of West Texas because of the numerous sky-scrapers constructed primarily by oil companies working the Permian Basin, Midland has only a few butterfly sites. However, the butterfly list is extensive, largely due to the long-term surveys by Francis Williams and Joann Merritt. **Melissa Blue**, the area's only specialty, is common. Key Midland sites include the Sibley Nature Center, Jal Draw on the south side of Midland College campus, and Burr Williams' "Gone Native" home site.

Butterfly Checklist for the Panhandle and Western Plains Region

The following list includes seven sites: **5. Rita Blanca NG/Lake Rita Blanca, 6. Lake Meredith NRA, 7. Black Kettle NG/Gene Howe WMA, 8. Palo Duro Canyon SP/Buffalo Lake NWR, 9. Caprock Canyon SP, 10. Lubbock**, and **11. Abilene.**

Status symbols include: A = abundant; C = common; U = uncommon; O = occasional; R = rare; X = accidental; M = migrant; TC = temporary colonist; ? = status unknown. (For a full definition of these terms, see p. 3.)

For trip notes, including dates and numbers of species seen, refer to the entry for this checklist in Appendix 3: Regional Checklist Resources.

Butterfly Species	5	6	7	8	9	10	11
Pipevine Swallowtail	C	U		U		U	C
Black Swallowtail	C	U	U	C	C	C	A
Thoas Swallowtail				X			
Giant Swallowtail		U	U	U	U	U	U
Two-tailed Swallowtail		R		O	O	C	O
Ruby-spotted Swallowtail						X	
Checkered White	C	A	A	O	C	A	C
Cabbage White	U	R		C	O	C	
Olympia Marble		U	R	U		X	
Clouded Sulphur	C	U	U	U		A	
Orange Sulphur	A	C	C	C	A	A	A
Southern Dogface		U	U	U		A	C
White Angled-Sulphur				X			
Cloudless Sulphur		U	U	C		U	C
Orange-barred Sulphur				X			

Butterfly Species	5	6	7	8	9	10	11
Large Orange Sulphur		U	R	X		U	
Lyside Sulphur		O		X	X	C	U
Mexican Yellow				X	X	U	
Little Yellow					U	C	U
Sleepy Orange	U	U	U	C	C	C	A
Dainty Sulphur	A	C	A	A	C	C	A
Gray Copper			O	O			
Great Purple Hairstreak					U	O	U
Soapberry Hairstreak		C	C	C		U	C
Coral Hairstreak			O	O	X		
Behr's Hairstreak			R				
Oak Hairstreak					U		
Juniper Hairstreak		C		U	C	U	U
Gray Hairstreak	U	U	U	C	U	C	C
Mallow Scrub-Hairstreak						X	
Red-banded Hairstreak				X			
Dusky-blue Groundstreak						O	
Western Pygmy-Blue	U	C		C	C	C	
Marine Blue	O	C	U	C	C	A	U
Ceraunus Blue					U		
Reakirt's Blue	U	U	U	C	C	A	C
Eastern Tailed-Blue			O	O		X	
Spring/Summer Azure						X	
Silvery Blue						X	
Melissa Blue	O	O		O	X	U	
Acmon Blue			O	O			
Lupine Blue					X	X	
American Snout	A-R	A-R	A-R	A-R	A-R	A-R	A-R
Gulf Fritillary		U		U	U	U	
Julia Heliconian						X	
Zebra Heliconian						X	
Variegated Fritillary	U	C	C	A	C	A	C
Dotted Checkerspot					O	U	C
Theona Checkerspot						O	
Fulvia Checkerspot			X	O	U	O	
Bordered Patch		X		U		C	
Crimson Patch				X		X	
Rosita Patch						X	
Gorgone Checkerspot	U	C	C	U	U	C	
Tiny Checkerspot							X
Elada Checkerspot						X	
Texan Crescent				X		U	U

Butterfly Species	5	6	7	8	9	10	11
Vesta Crescent						U	U
Phaon Crescent				C	C	U	C
Pearl Crescent	C	C	C	A	U	A	C
Painted Crescent	C		U	C	C	X	
Question Mark		U		U		C	U
Mourning Cloak		U	U	U		C	O
American Lady	C	C	U	C		C	C
Painted Lady	A	U	C	A	U	C	U
West Coast Lady	X	X		X		X	
Red Admiral	U	C	C	U	C	A	C
Common Buckeye			C	U	U	C	C
Tropical Buckeye						X	
Red-spotted Purple				C			
Viceroy	U	C	C	U	U	U	U
Arizona Sister				O		X	X
Common Mestra				U	X	U	U
Ruddy Daggerwing				X			
Tropical Leafwing						X	
Goatweed Leafwing	C	A	U	C	U	C	U
Hackberry Emperor	U	U	U	U	U	C	C
Tawny Emperor			U	U		C	A
Red Satyr				U	U	C	C
Common Wood-Nymph		U	A	C	C	C	U
Monarch	M	M	M	M	M	C	M
Queen	C	U	U	A	U	C	U
Silver-spotted Skipper		U		U		C	
Arizona Skipper				X			
Hoary Edge				X			
Acacia Skipper						X	
Outis Skipper					?		
Hayhurst's Scallopwing				X			
Sleepy Duskywing						R	
Juvenal's Duskywing				O	U		
Meridian Duskywing		O					
Horace's Duskywing							U
Mournful Duskywing					X	X	
Mottled Duskywing				X			
Funereal Duskywing		O		U	U	U	U
Com. Checkered-Skipper	C	C	C	A	U	A	C
Desert Checkered-Skipper							R
Common Streaky-Skipper					O	X	O
Common Sootywing	O	U	U	C	U	C	O

Butterfly Species	5	6	7	8	9	10	11
Saltbush Sootywing				X			
Clouded Skipper							C
Least Skipper			C	C		X	
Orange Skipperling		U		C	C	C	C
Southern Skipperling		R					
Fiery Skipper				C		U	
Uncas Skipper	O	O		O	O	X	
Ottoe Skipper			R	X	X		
Green Skipper	O	O		U	U	U	U
Rhesus Skipper				X			
Crossline Skipper				X			
Whirlabout				X			
Southern Broken-Dash						R	
Northern Broken-Dash				X			
Sachem	C	C	C	C	U	A	C
Arogos Skipper			U	U			
Delaware Skipper			U	C	C	U	U
Hobomok Skipper				X			
Zabulon Skipper				X			
Dun Skipper				C			C
Dusted Skipper				C	C	U	
Viereck's Skipper		X					
Simius Roadside-Skipper				X			
Bronze Roadside-Skipper			O	U	U	O	
Oslar's Roadside-Skipper	O	U		R	O	X	
Texas Roadside-Skipper						X	
Lace-winged Roadside-Skipper				X			
Nysa Roadside-Skipper			R	C	U	U	U
Dotted Roadside-Skipper			U	U	U	U	U
Common Roadside-Skipper				C	C	R	
Celia's Roadside-Skipper						R	
Eufala Skipper		U	C	C	U	U	U
Brazilian Skipper				U			
Ocola Skipper						X	
Yucca Giant-Skipper				R			
Strecker's Giant-Skipper			R		O	R	O

Edwards Plateau

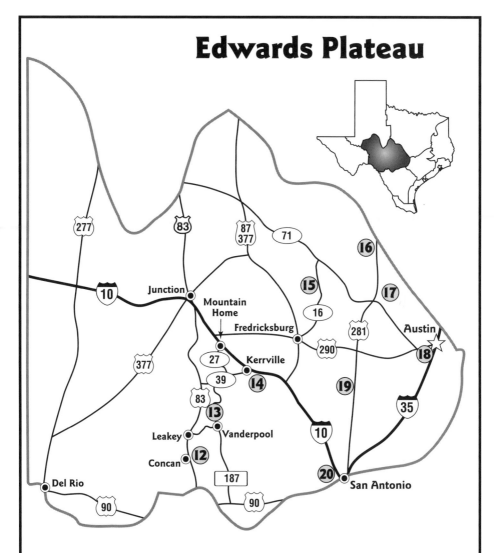

12. Concan/Garner State Park
13. Lost Maples State Natural Area
14. Kerrville
15. Enchanted Rock State Natural Area
16. Inks Lake/Longhorn Cavern State Parks
17. Balcones Canyonlands National Wildlife Refuge
18. Austin
19. Guadalupe River State Park
20. Government Canyon State Natural Area

Edwards Plateau Region

The Edwards Plateau covers about 37,500 square miles (13,500,000 acres) or seventeen percent of Texas, in about the center of the state. The topography of the Plateau includes numerous ravines and rugged slopes, drained by several major rivers, including the Colorado, Guadalupe, Lavaca, Nueces, and San Antonio. All flow southeast from the "Hill Country" to the Gulf of Mexico. Elevations range from 1,500 to 3,000 feet.

Vegetation on the Plateau includes climax grasses on the open slopes and valley bottoms, broadleaf trees in the wetter drainages, and a juniper-oak woodland on the higher slopes. Ashe juniper, required by nesting golden-cheeked warblers, is the most renowned of the Plateau's plants.

The Edwards Plateau Region is represented by nine sites: **12. Concan/Garner State Park**, **13. Lost Maples State Natural Area**, **14. Kerrville**, **15. Enchanted Rock State Natural Area**, **16. Inks Lake State Park/Longhorn Cavern State Park**, **17. Balcones Canyonlands National Wildlife Refuge**, **18. Austin**, **19. Guadalupe River State Park**, and **20. Government Canyon State Natural Area**. The best time to visit these sites is March through October.

Edwards Plateau Specialties

Although the region features a good diversity of butterflies, principally due to its central location within the state, only sixteen species are considered area specialties.

Hairstreaks, Metalmarks: **Coral Hairstreak** has been recorded only in the Kerrville area, where there is an isolated population. It flies from late May to July. Larvae feed on cherry and serviceberry. **Lacey's Scrub-Hairstreak** occurs at scattered growths of myrtlecroton, its foodplant, in the Concan area, Government Canyon SNA, and the Austin area. **Rounded Metalmark** is most likely to be found at flowering plants in the Concan area, Lost Maples SNA, the Kerrville area, and Government Canyon SNA. Larvae feed on eupatoriums. **Rawson's Metalmark** occurs in the Concan area, Kerrville area, Guadalupe River SP, Government Canyon SNA, and the Austin area. Look for it at flowering plants near its larval foodplant, boneset.

Heliconians, Patches, Buckeyes, Leafwings: **Zebra Heliconian** may only be a temporary colonist in Government Canyon SNA and the Austin area. Larvae feed on passion vine. **Crimson Patch** has been recorded in the Concan and Kerrville areas, apparent northward extensions of its range. Larvae use anisacanth, which typically grows on rocky soils along arroyos. **Tropical Buckeye** (the dark form, *nigrosuffusa*) is known from the Concan area, Balcones Canyonlands NWR, and the Austin area. Larvae feed on stemodia. **Tropical Leafwing** frequents woodlands in the Kerrville area, Government Canyon SNA, and the Austin area. It is similar to the more common Goatweed Leafwing, which uses the same habitat. Adults feed on sap and fruit; larvae feed on crotons.

Spread-wing Skippers: **Golden Banded-Skipper** is known only from the Kerrville area, in an isolated population near Mountain Home; it has not been seen in recent years. Larvae feed on legumes, such as butterfly pea and beans. **Coyote Cloudywing** is known only from the Austin area, apparently the northwestern edge of its range. It is most likely to be found at flowering shrubs. Larvae feed on blackbrush acacia. **Outis Skipper** has been recorded in the Austin area, the southern edge of its range, but it has not been seen for many years. Larvae feed on fern acacia in semi-open areas. **Meridian Duskywing** reaches the eastern edge of its range in the Concan, Kerrville, and Austin areas. It prefers oak woodlands on hillsides; males often perch on hilltops. Larvae feed on oaks. **Laviana White-Skipper** is a resident only in Government Canyon SNA, apparently the northern edge of its range. Larvae feed on mallows.

Grass-Skippers, Giant-Skippers: **Apache Skipper** has been recorded in upland grassy areas in the Concan, Kerrville, and Austin areas during September and October. Larvae feed on grasses. **Arogos Skipper** is known only from the Austin area, the southern edge of its range. It flies in spring and late summer in mixed prairies where larvae feed on native grasses, including big bluestem. Males perch near foodplants during midday on cloudy days. **Strecker's Giant-Skipper** has been recorded only in the Kerrville area, apparently an isolated population. It flies from April to July in yucca grasslands; larvae feed on yucca. Females make "clicking" sounds in flight.

Sites within the Edwards Plateau Region

12. Concan/Garner State Park

A number of butterfly hot spots, as well as a network of roads, are located within about twenty miles of Concan. Widespread wildflowers usually provide for a colorful landscape in spring. The Frio River, lined with stately bald cypress trees, flows through the area. Sites include the popular 1,419-acre Garner State Park (**A, B**), the River Road (**C**), House Pasture Resort (**D**), River Oaks Resort (**E**), and the Reagan Wells Road (**F**).

Habitats: Mesquite grassland, oak savannah, juniper-hackberry woodland, prairie, field, and riparian.

Strategy for finding the most butterflies: At Garner SP (fee area), walk at least a portion of the Old Entrance Road (**A**), where Pipevine and Two-tailed swallowtails, Texan Crescent, Common Buckeye, Goatweed Leafwing, Little Wood-Satyr, and Red Satyr are likely. **Meridian Duskywing** is possible in summer. Then drive on to the Pavilion and Pecan Grove Area (**B**). Walk along the roadsides and check the edges of the parking areas. Some of the additional butterflies possible here include Black and Giant swallowtails, Cloudless and Dainty sulphurs, Reakirt's Blue, Spring/Summer Azure, Gulf Fritillary, Pearl Crescent, and Southern Broken-Dash.

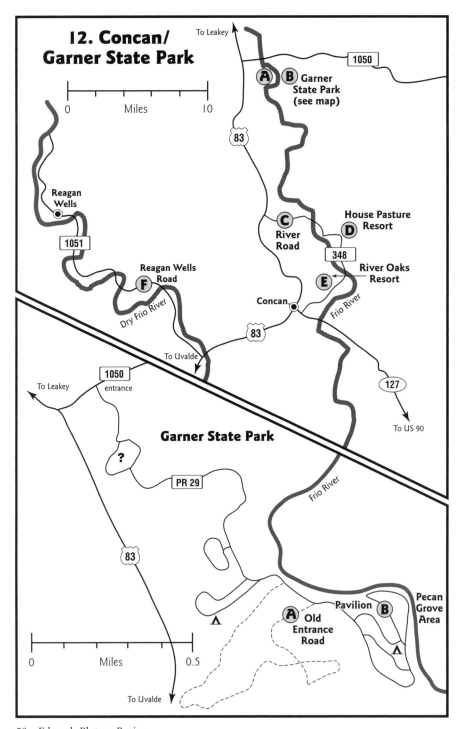

12. Concan/ Garner State Park

0 Miles 10

To Leakey

1050

A **B** Garner State Park (see map)

83

Reagan Wells

1051

C River Road

D House Pasture Resort

348

Reagan Wells Road

F

E River Oaks Resort

Dry Frio River

Concan

Frio River

83

To Uvalde

1050 entrance

To Leakey

Garner State Park

?

PR 29

Frio River

127

To US 90

83

0 Miles 0.5

A Old Entrance Road

Pavilion

B Pecan Grove Area

To Uvalde

Field of wildflowers near Concan

Next, take US 83 south to CR 348, the River Road **(C)** and drive it, stopping at pull-offs. Also stop at House Pasture Resort **(D)**, where you should check the plants in front and the fields behind the restaurant (open for special occasions only). Several butterflies mentioned above are possible but also watch for Southern Dogface, Lyside Sulphur, Sleepy Orange, Silvery Checkerspot, Vesta and Phaon crescents, Queen, Northern Cloudywing, and Fiery and Green skippers. **Apache Skipper** is possible in fall.

At River Oaks Resort **(E)**, park at the office and walk the nature trail, including the Hill Top Trail. The resort has juniper-hackberry woodland, riparian, and field habitats and is likely to have the greatest butterfly diversity. Some of the possible butterflies not already mentioned include Large Orange Sulphur; Juniper Hairstreak; Marine Blue; Red-spotted Purple; Arizona Sister; Common Mestra; Hackberry and Tawny emperors; Empress Leilia; Carolina Satyr; Hayhurst's Scallopwing; Texas Powdered-Skipper; Horace's and Funereal duskywings; Common Streaky-Skipper; and Bronze, Nysa, and Dotted roadside-skippers. **Lacey's Scrub-Hairstreak**, **Crimson Patch**, and "Dark" **Tropical Buckeye** have also been recorded. In spring, Falcate Orangetip, Soapberry and Banded hairstreaks, Henry's Elfin, and Juvenal's Duskywing can be expected.

Finally, drive FR 1051, the Reagan Wells Road **(F)**, stopping at pull-offs to check roadside wildflowers. Watch for **Rounded** and **Rawson's metalmarks**.

Directions: This area encompasses Real, Bandera, and Uvalde counties. **Concan** is situated at the junction of US 83 and SH 127. **Garner SP (A, B)** is located north of

Concan on US 83. Turn right on FR 1050 to the entrance. CR 348, the **River Road** (**C-E**), runs between US 83 and SH 127. FR 1051, the **Reagan Wells Road** (**F**), goes west from US 83, eight miles south of Concan.

Nearest food, gas, and lodging: Concan, Leakey, Utopia, and Vanderpool.

Nearest camping: Garner SP and several sites along the River Road.

13. Lost Maples State Natural Area

Best known as a good place to find black-capped vireos, golden-cheeked warblers, and green kingfishers, the 2,174-acre Lost Maples State Natural Area (fee area) is a hiker's park with lots of good trails. Its name comes from the numerous bigtooth maples that occur within the area's moist canyons. Sites include the East Trail (**A**, **B**, **F**), West Trail (**C**), picnic area (**D**), Maple Trail (**E**), and the campground (**G**).

Habitats: Juniper woodland, oak-juniper woodland, riparian, and field.

Strategy for finding the most butterflies: Start at the East Trail parking area (**A**), a good place for spotting Pipevine and Black swallowtails, Sleepy Orange, Dainty Sulphur, White M Hairstreak, Dusky-blue Groundstreak, Reakirt's Blue, Silvery Checkerspot, Empress Leilia, Queen, Northern Cloudywing, and Horace's and Funereal dusky-wings. Henry's Elfin is possible in spring.

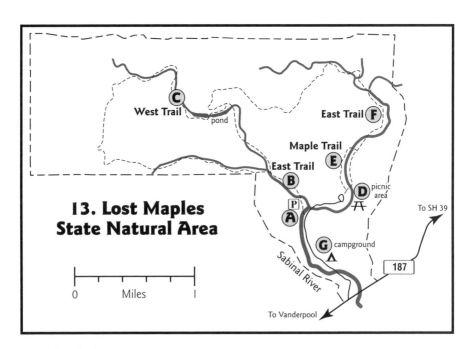

Maple Trail, Lost Maples State Natural Area

Then walk East Trail to the ponds (**B**) through an oak-juniper woodland. Butterflies likely along this trail include Eastern Tiger and Two-tailed swallowtails, Juniper Hairstreak, Texan and Phaon crescents, Red-spotted Purple, Arizona Sister, Little Wood-Satyr, Red Satyr, and Orange Skipperling.

From the ponds continue another mile or so on West Trail (**C**). The entire loop is worthwhile but rather extensive. Additional butterflies possible along this trail include Pearl Crescent, Common Checkered-Skipper, and Green Skipper.

Later, check the picnic area (**D**). If it hasn't been recently mowed, it can also be productive. Then walk the Maple Trail (**E**) starting at the picnic area and a mile or so of the nearby East Trail (**F**). Another area to check is the weedy edges of the campground (**G**), a good place to find Little Yellow, Ceraunus Blue, Gulf Fritillary, Common and Tropical checkered-skippers, and Fiery and Dun skippers.

Directions: In Bandera County, **Lost Maples SNA (A-G)** is located along RM 187, five miles north of Vanderpool.

Nearest food, gas, and lodging: Vanderpool.

Nearest camping: Lost Maples SNA.

14. Kerrville

Kerrville is located along the Guadalupe River, in the heart of the Edwards Plateau. The town has become a popular tourist destination due to the healthy environment and the internationally known Kerrville Folk Music Festival. July 4th Butterfly Counts are held here most years.

Several good butterfly-watching sites are found here, including the Riverside Nature Center (**A**), Louise Hays City Park (**B**), Kerrville-Schreiner Park (**C, D**), Flat Rock Lake Park (**E**), the Kerrville Municipal Airport (**F**), Third Creek Canyon (**G**), and additional sites northwest of Kerrville near Mountain Home (**H-K**).

Habitats: Garden, park, riparian, mesquite grassland, juniper-oak woodland, field, and cropland.

Strategy for finding the most butterflies: Start at Kerrville's Riverside Nature Center (**A**), which has an excellent garden. Walk the trails behind the visitor center and take the streamside loop. Some of the more numerous butterflies include Pipevine Swallowtail, Dainty Sulphur, Reakirt's Blue, American Snout, Gulf Fritillary, Texan Crescent, Red-spotted Purple, Tawny Emperor, Horace's and Funereal duskywings, Desert Checkered-skipper, and Clouded and Fiery skippers. Falcate Orangetip, Soapberry Hairstreak, and Henry's Elfin are likely in spring. Banded Hairstreak is also possible.

Next, drive to nearby Louise Hays City Park (**B**). Check the brushy places around the parking areas, especially at the west end. Many of the same butterflies mentioned above are also here, but Black and Giant swallowtails, Southern Dogface, Large Orange Sulphur, Sleepy Orange, Ceraunus Blue, Bordered Patch, Vesta and Pearl crescents, Queen, and Sachem are also likely.

Southeast of town is the 500-acre Kerrville-Schreiner Park (fee area). Visit the Butterfly Garden beyond the entrance to the left and check the small garden at the entrance station (**C**), where **Rounded** and **Rawson's metalmarks** are possible. West of SH 173, check the roadsides and walk a portion of the trails below and above the campground (**D**). The juniper woodland trail above the campground is likely to have Juniper Hairstreak, Arizona Sister, Little Wood-Satyr, and Red Satyr.

Southeast of the state park, Flat Rock Lake Park (**E**) has brushy draws and edges worth checking; watch for **Meridian Duskywing**. Farther southeast at Kerrville Municipal Airport (**F**), check the entrance road and fields along the wooded edge beyond the terminal; **Apache Skipper** is possible in fall. Third Creek Canyon (**G**), off SH 1341 to the northeast of Kerrville, offers another good woodland site with many side roads and picnic areas.

Additional worthwhile sites are located northwest of Kerrville, near Mountain Home: Heart of the Hills Fisheries Research Center (**H**), Mountain Home Bridge (**I**), Kerr Wildlife Management Area (**J**), and Boneyard Draw (**K**) at Stowers Ranch Overlook. **Lacey's Scrub-Hairstreak** is possible at the last two sites.

Coral Hairstreak, **Crimson Patch**, **Tropical Leafwing,** and **Strecker's Giant-Skipper** have also been recorded in the Kerrville area at unknown locations.

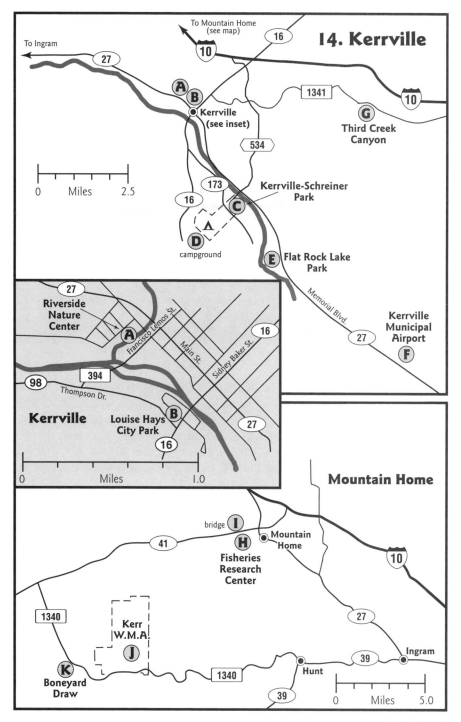

14. Kerrville

To Mountain Home (see map)

To Ingram

27

16

10

10

1341

A
B

Kerrville
(see inset)

534

G

Third Creek
Canyon

173

16

C

Kerrville-Schreiner
Park

D

campground

E

Flat Rock Lake
Park

Memorial Blvd.

27

Kerrville
Municipal
Airport

F

0   Miles   2.5

Kerrville

27

Riverside
Nature
Center

Francisco Lemos St.

A

Main St.

Sidney Baker St.

16

98

394

Thompson Dr.

Kerrville

Louise Hays
City Park

B

16

27

0   Miles   1.0

Mountain Home

bridge **I**

41

H

Fisheries
Research
Center

Mountain
Home

10

1340

Kerr
W.M.A.

J

27

39

Ingram

K

Boneyard
Draw

1340

Hunt

39

0   Miles   5.0

Riverside Nature Center, Kerrville

Directions: In Kerr County, the **Riverside Nature Center (A)** is located in downtown Kerrville. From I-10, take SH 16 into town, turn right on Main Street and left after five blocks onto Francisco Lemos St.; the nature center is just ahead on the right. **Louise Hays City Park (B)** is nearby; continue south on Lemos St. to Thompson Dr. Turn left to SH 16. The park is situated on both sides of SH 16, just north of Thompson Dr. **Kerrville-Schreiner Park (C, D)** can be reached by exiting I-10 south on SH 16 and going a half mile to Loop 534. Turn left and go four miles to SH 173. Turn left to the entrance just ahead on the left. **Flat Rock Lake Park (E)** is located south and on the other side of the river from Kerrville-Schreiner; return to Loop 534, turn right, and take SH 27 (Memorial Blvd.) southeast. Turn right on Cherry Way to the park entrance. Continue southeast on SH 27 for **Kerrville Municipal Airport (F)** on the left.

Third Creek Canyon (G) is northeast of Kerrville along SH 1341 (Cypress Creek Rd.), accessed from Loop 534. The turn is well marked. Mountain Home is located 15 miles west of Kerrville off I-10. Exit on SH 27 and turn right on SH 41 for the **Mountain Home Bridge (I)** and the **Fisheries Research Center (H)**. Continue west on SH 41 to FM 1340 and turn left for **Boneyard Draw (K)** and **Kerr WMA (J)**.

Nearest food, gas, and lodging: Kerrville.

Nearest camping: Kerrville-Schreiner Park.

15. Enchanted Rock State Natural Area

One of the state's best nature parks, the 1,643-acre Enchanted Rock State Natural Area (fee area) has five miles of hiking trails. The domed Enchanted Rock, which rises 425 feet above the surrounding terrain and covers 640 acres, consists of pink granite that is some of the oldest exposed rock in North America. It is the second largest batholith (underground rock formation uncovered by erosion) in the U.S. Weekends and holidays can be extremely busy.

The best sites for butterfly-watching include the entrance station (**A**), Sandy Creek (**B**), the base of Enchanted Rock (**C**), Moss Lake (**D**), the Loop Trail (**E**), and the top of Enchanted Rock (**F**).

Habitats: Mesquite grassland, oak savannah, riparian, and hilltop.

Strategy for finding the most butterflies: First, check the wildflowers around the parking area at the entrance station (**A**). Some of the more numerous butterflies include Pipevine Swallowtail; Cloudless and Dainty sulphurs; Southern Dogface; Gulf Fritillary; Queen; Fiery, Dun, and Eufala skippers; and Sachem.

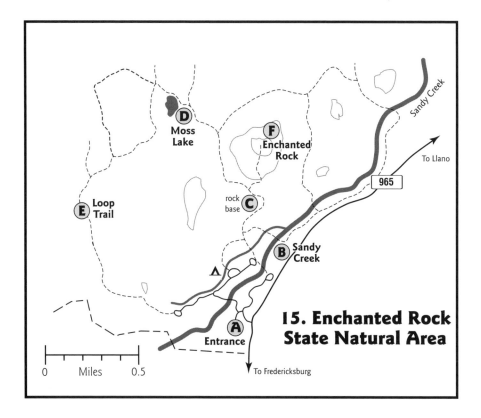

Enchanted Rock, Enchanted Rock State Natural Area

Then walk along Sandy Creek (**B**), which flows along the southeastern corner of the park. Although many of the butterflies mentioned above are likely, other probable species include Giant Swallowtail, Little Yellow, Ceraunus and Reakirt's blues, Bordered Patch, Vesta and Pearl crescents, Arizona Sister, Goatweed Leafwing, Horace's and Funereal duskywings, and Orange Skipperling. Falcate Orangetip is likely to be seen in spring.

Next, walk through the oak woodlands along the base of Enchanted Rock (**C**), watching for butterflies on the flowering shrubs and wildflowers. Great Purple Hairstreak, American Snout, Tawny Emperor, Red Satyr, and Nysa Roadside-Skipper are possible.

If time allows, hike to Moss Lake (**D**) through woodland habitat where Checkered White, Variegated Fritillary, Common Wood-Nymph, and Common Checkered-Skipper are present much of the year. Oak Hairstreak can be seen in April and May. When wildflowers are plentiful, also hike the western portion of the Loop Trail (**E**), where Lyside Sulphur, Juniper Hairstreak, Desert Checkered-Skipper, and Green Skipper are likely.

Finally, if you are up to it, a hike to the top of Enchanted Rock (**F**) might possibly produce hill-topping species, including Black Swallowtail and Yucca Giant-Skipper.

Directions: In Gillespie County, take SH 965 north of Fredericksburg for 18 miles to the **Enchanted Rock SNA (A-F)** entrance on the left.

Nearest food, gas, and lodging: Fredericksburg.

Nearest camping: Tent sites within the SNA; full hook-ups at Crabapple Crossing, four miles south of the entrance on SH 965.

16. Inks Lake State Park/Longhorn Cavern State Park

These two state parks and a nearby national fish hatchery provide a diversity of environments and a variety of visitor activities, including camping, boating, fishing, and hiking, especially within the 1,201-acre Inks Lake State Park (**A-D**). Inks Lake is the second of numerous reservoirs and marshes on the Colorado River between Lake Buchanan and where it flows into the Gulf of Mexico below Matagorda. Inks Dam National Fish Hatchery (**E, F**) offers minimally disturbed surroundings. The 646-acre Longhorn Cavern State Park (**G, H**) supports a small population of golden-cheeked warblers.

Habitats: Mesquite grassland, oak-juniper woodland, field, and riparian.

Strategy for finding the most butterflies: Start at Inks Lake SP (fee area) by walking the Pecan Flats Trail (**A**), which circles a rocky promontory with scattered oaks and shrubs. Some of the more numerous butterflies include Pipevine and Giant swallowtails, Cloudless and Dainty sulphurs, Sleepy Orange, Reakirt's Blue, Common Buckeye, Queen, and Common Checkered-Skipper. Then drive to the boat ramp (**B**), checking roadside wildflowers where Little Yellow, Fiery Skipper, Whirlabout, Southern Broken-Dash, and Sachem are likely. Ocola Skipper can be common in fall.

Next walk along the lake shore (**C**) to the edge of the trailer sites. Pearl Crescent, Viceroy, and Goatweed Leafwing can be expected. Also walk the loop trail (**D**) between PR 4 and the south arm, through an oak-juniper woodland where Juniper Hairstreak and Horace's Duskywing are likely. In spring, Falcate Orangetip is also likely to be seen.

Drive to Inks Dam Fish Hatchery and walk the dirt road (**E**) north of the visitor parking lot. Also walk around the ponds (**F**). Many of the same butterflies mentioned above are possible, but Vesta and Phaon crescents, Red Admiral, and Tawny Emperor are also likely.

At Longhorn Cavern SP, south on PR 4, check the plantings in front of the visitor center and the fields around the parking and picnic areas (**G**). Orange Sulphur, Gulf and Variegated fritillaries, and Question Mark are likely. Great Purple Hairstreak and Funereal Duskywing are also possible. Then walk the nature trail (**H**) through an oak-juniper woodland, where Red Satyr and Common Wood-Nymph are likely to occur and Little Wood-Satyr has been recorded in June and July.

Directions: In Burnet County, all three sites are located along PR 4, which runs for 12 miles between SH 29 west of Burnet and US 281 south of Burnet. To reach **Inks Lake SP (A-D)**, take SH 29 west from Burnet for nine miles. Turn south on PR 4 for three miles to the park entrance. Continue on PR 4 south to CR 117 on the right. Follow it to Fish Hatchery Rd. and the **Inks Dam National Fish Hatchery (E, F)**. Return to PR 4 and turn south to **Longhorn Cavern SP (G, H)**.

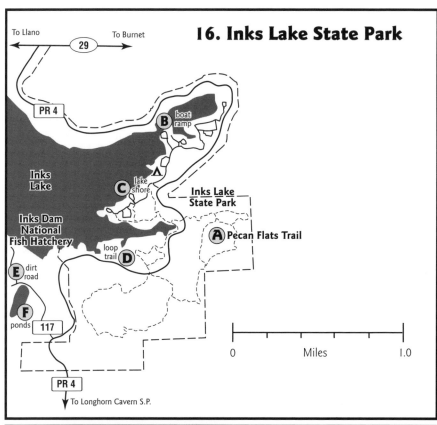

16. Inks Lake State Park

To Llano

To Burnet

29

PR 4

boat ramp

B

Inks
Lake

C lake shore

Inks Lake
State Park

Inks Dam
National
Fish Hatchery

A Pecan Flats Trail

loop trail

D

E dirt road

F

ponds

117

0   Miles   1.0

PR 4

To Longhorn Cavern S.P.

Lake
Buchanan

29

To Burnet

29

National
Fish
Hatchery

Inks Lake
State Park

To Llano

**Longhorn Cavern
State Park**

Colorado River

PR 4

0   Miles   5

nature trail

H

G

To US 281

picnic area

Longhorn Cavern
State Park

View from Pecan Flat Trail, Inks Lake State Park

Nearest food, gas and lodging: Food at Inks Lake SP; gas and lodging at Hoovers Valley, between Inks Lake SP and Longhorn Cavern SP.

Nearest camping: Inks Lake SP.

17. Balcones Canyonlands National Wildlife Refuge

Balcones Canyonlands National Wildlife Refuge was established in 1992. It encompasses 46,000 acres of rugged terrain along the southeastern edge of the Edwards Plateau. Created principally to protect the nesting habitat of black-capped vireos and golden-cheeked warblers, the refuge also has a good diversity of butterflies. The greatest diversity is most likely at Doeskin Ranch (**A-C**). Other sites include Cow Creek Road (**D**) and the Shin Oak Observation Station (**E**).

Habitats: Oak-juniper woodland, oak savannah, prairie, field, and riparian.

Strategy for finding the most butterflies: At Doeskin Ranch, start by walking the short Pond and Prairie Trail (**A**) that loops through a prairie habitat and past a sparse oak-juniper woodland. Some of the more numerous butterflies include Pipevine and Giant swallowtails; Cloudless Sulphur; Little Yellow; Reakirt's Blue; Gulf Fritillary; Queen; Northern Cloudywing; Funereal Duskywing; and Julia's, Fiery, and Eufala skippers. Falcate Orangetip is possible in spring.

Then walk the Rimrock Trail (**B**), all 2.2 miles if time allows, passing through an open prairie edged with oak-juniper woodlands. Although many of the same species

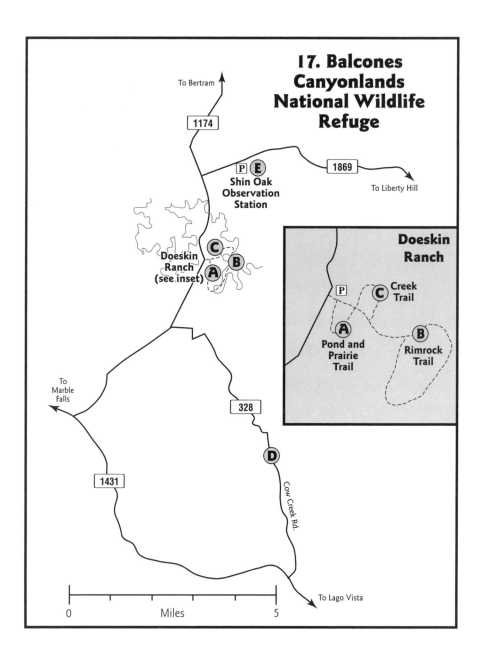

17. Balcones Canyonlands National Wildlife Refuge

To Bertram

1174

P E
Shin Oak Observation Station

1869

To Liberty Hill

C
B
Doeskin Ranch (see inset)
A

Doeskin Ranch

P
C Creek Trail

A
Pond and Prairie Trail

B Rimrock Trail

To Marble Falls

328

D

1431

Cow Creek Rd.

0   Miles   5

To Lago Vista

are likely, additional possibilities include Black Swallowtail, Southern Dogface, Dainty Sulphur, Sleepy Orange, and Oak (April and May) and Juniper hairstreaks. Also watch for Mexican Yellow, "Dark" **Tropical Buckeye**, Bronze Roadside-Skipper, and Yucca Giant-Skipper (March and April).

Shin Oak Observation Station, Balcones Canyonlands National Wildlife Refuge

Finally, walk the .6-mile Creek Trail (**C**) through an oak savannah and along a narrow riparian zone. This is a good spot for Two-tailed Swallowtail, Texan and Pearl crescents, Arizona Sister, Goatweed Leafwing, Hackberry and Tawny emperors, and Red Satyr. Also watch for Silvery Checkerspot, Red-spotted Purple, Juvenal's Dusky-wing (spring), and Least Skipper.

Next, drive Cow Creek Road (**D**), stopping at pull-offs to check flowering plants; drive at least 5.4 miles to where water usually flows across the roadway. This road may offer several additional butterfly species, such as Eastern Tiger Swallowtail, Large Orange Sulphur, Great Purple and Soapberry (April through June) hairstreaks, Bordered Patch, Phaon Crescent, Viceroy, Common Mestra, Empress Leilia, and Desert Checkered-Skipper.

Finally, visit the Shin Oak Observation Station (**E**), checking flowering plants at the parking area and along the short trail. This black-capped vireo site may have some of the same brushy-area butterflies mentioned above.

Directions: In Travis and Burnett Counties, from Austin, take US 183 north to SH 29 and turn west to Liberty Hill, where you will take FM 1869 west for 8.9 miles to the **Shin Oak Observation Station** (**E**), where you may wish to start butterflying. For **Doeskin Ranch** (**A-C**), continue west on FM 1869 for 1.4 miles to the intersection with FM 1174. Turn south for 2.5 miles. **Cow Creek Road** (**D**), CR 328, turns off FM 1174, 1.3 miles south of Doeskin Ranch.

Nearest food, gas, and lodging: Liberty Hill, Lago Vista (east on FM 1431), Austin, and surrounding communities.

Nearest camping: Commercial campgrounds along US 183 and around Lake Travis near Lago Vista.

18. Austin

The capital of Texas, Austin has several good butterfly-watching sites within and near the city. In spite of the city's population of nearly a half-million people, there are several productive greenbelts and parks with easy access. These include St. Edward's Park (**A**), the Barton Creek Greenbelt (**B**), the Zilker Botanical Garden (**C**), Mount Bonnell Park (**H**), Mayfield Park (**I**), and Emma Long Metropolitan Park (**K**). The largest and most varied site is the 1,200-acre Hornsby Bend Biosolids Management Facility (**D-F**) southeast of town.

There is also an excellent butterfly garden at Lady Bird Johnson Wildflower Center (**G**), and the Natural Gardener Nursery (**J**) is worth visiting. Both are in southwest Austin. Austin Butterfly Forum members hold annual butterfly counts in the area.

Habitats: Garden, park, juniper-oak woodland, juniper-hackberry woodland, mesquite grassland, field, and riparian.

Strategy for finding the most butterflies: The three most productive Austin sites include St. Edward's Park, Barton Creek Greenbelt, and Hornsby Bend. At St. Edward's Park (**A**), walk the extended trail system along the creek's riparian and juniper-hackberry woodland habitats. Some of the more numerous butterflies include Cloudless and Dainty sulphurs; Sleepy Orange; Juniper Hairstreak; Texan, Phaon, and Pearl crescents; Common Buckeye; Goatweed Leafwing; Carolina and Red satyrs; Clouded and Fiery skippers; and Sachem. **Meridian Duskywing** is also possible.

Closer to downtown, the Barton Creek Greenbelt (**B**) features a seven-mile trail that runs between Zilker Park on Barton Springs Road and Gus Fruh Park on Capital of Texas Highway/Loop 360. Although many of the butterflies mentioned above are possible here, this trail also offers Pipevine, Giant, and Two-tailed swallowtails; Southern Dogface; Large Orange Sulphur; Little Yellow; Great Purple Hairstreak; Mallow Scrub-Hairstreak; Dusky-blue Groundstreak; **Rawson's Metalmark**; **Zebra Heliconian**; Bordered Patch; Silvery Checkerspot; Red-spotted Purple; Hackberry and Tawny emperors; Queen; Horace's and Funereal duskywings; and Orange Skipperling. Arizona Sister, **Coyote Cloudywing**, Texas Powdered-Skipper, and Juvenal's Duskywing (spring) are less dependable. Spicebush Swallowtail is also possible. In spring, Falcate Orangetip; Soapberry, Banded, and Oak hairstreaks; and Henry's Elfin are likely.

While you're at Zilker Park, visit the Zilker Botanical Garden (**C**), which has a section in the northeast portion of the garden that has been planted to attract butterflies. Expected butterflies not already mentioned include Gulf Fritillary, Question

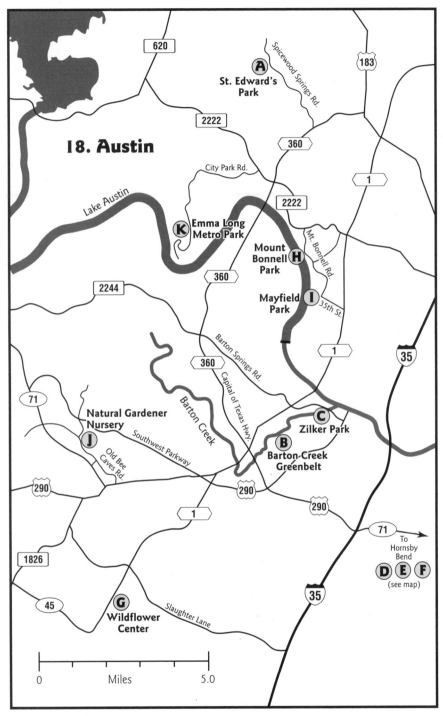

18. Austin

620

Spicewood Springs Rd.

A
St. Edward's
Park

183

2222

360

City Park Rd.

1

Lake Austin

2222

K Emma Long
Metro Park

Mount
Bonnell
Park

H

Mt. Bonnell Rd.

360

Mayfield
Park

I

35th St.

2244

360

1

71

Barton Springs Rd.

Capital of Texas Hwy.

35

Barton Creek

Natural Gardener
Nursery

J

Southwest Parkway

C

Zilker Park

B

Barton Creek
Greenbelt

Old Bee
Caves Rd.

290

1

290

290

71
To
Hornsby
Bend

D E F
(see map)

1826

45

G
Wildflower
Center

Slaughter Lane

35

0   Miles   5.0

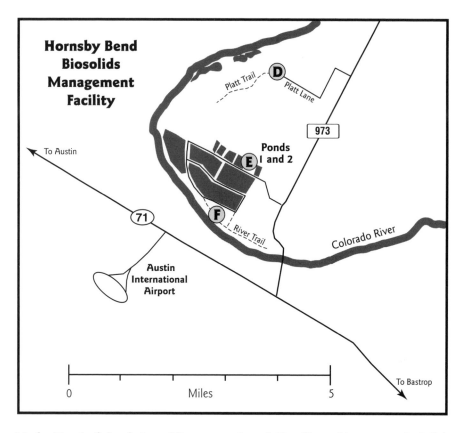

Mark, **Tropical Leafwing**, Silver-spotted and Brazilian skippers, and Celia's Roadside-Skipper.

Hornsby Bend Biosolids Management Facility, southeast of the city, has open fields, mesquite grasslands, juniper-hackberry woodlands, and riparian habitats. Start by walking Platt Lane and the Platt Trail (**D**) to the river, where many of the same species mentioned above are likely. Also watch for Eastern Tiger Swallowtail, Lyside Sulphur, Fatal Metalmark, Hayhurst's Scallopwing, and Tropical Checkered-Skipper. Then walk the roadsides around Ponds 1 and 2 (**E**) and the River Trail (**F**). "Dark" **Tropical Buckeye** is possible in open areas.

Southwest of town, the Lady Bird Johnson Wildflower Center (**G**), with its butterfly garden and scattered plantings, should also be visited. It is a fee area and is closed on Mondays. Many of the species mentioned above are likely to be found there.

In addition, Mount Bonnell Park (**H**) is the most likely place for **Lacey's Scrub-Hairstreak**; walk the brushy trails between the parking area and the overlook. Nearby Mayfield Park (**I**) is yet another good spot, offering many of the same species. Finally, if time allows, visit Natural Gardener Nursery (**J**) and Emma Long Metropolitan Park (**K**), other worthwhile sites.

Zilker Botanical Garden, Austin

There are historic records of **Outis, Apache,** and **Arogos skippers** in the Austin area, but these species have not been recorded in many years.

Directions: In Travis County, **St. Edward's Park (A)** is located in north Austin. Take Loop 360 southwest from US 183 to Spicewood Springs Rd. and go two miles north to the park. To reach nearby **Emma Long Metropolitan Park (K)** continue southwest on Loop 360 and turn northwest on FM 2222. Shortly after the turn, find City Park Rd. on the left and follow it to the park. You can also use FM 2222 southeast of Loop 360 to reach **Mount Bonnell Park (H)**. Turn right from FM 2222 on Mount Bonnell Rd. to the park. Continue on Mount Bonnell Rd. to **Mayfield Park (I)** at the intersection with Old Bull Creek Rd.

To continue, follow Old Bull Creek Rd. to the north end of the park and turn right on 35th St.; take it to Loop 1 (Mo-Pac Expressway). Turn south and drive across the river to Barton Springs Rd. (exit 2244). Zilker Park, including access to **Barton Creek Greenbelt (B)** and the **Zilker Botanical Garden (C)** at 2220 Barton Springs Rd., is just east of Loop 1. (The south access to the Barton Creek Greenbelt is located off Capitol of Texas Hwy./Loop 360 at Gus Fruh Park.)

To continue from Zilker Park to **Hornsby Bend Biosolids Management Facility (D-F)**, located southeast of town and north of the airport, return to Loop 1 and take it south to Capitol of Texas Hwy./Loop 360 where you will turn southeast. SH 71 joins this highway in a few miles. Stay on SH 71 past its intersections with I-35 and Loop 111 (alternate access points). Just past the airport, turn north on FM 973 to Hornsby Bend.

Lady Bird Johnson Wildflower Center (G) is located southwest of the city at 4801 La Crosse Ave. From Hornsby Bend, retrace your route back to Loop 1 and turn southwest. Continue past the stoplight at Slaughter Lane to the stoplight at La Crosse Ave. and turn left to the Center. The final stop is the **Natural Gardener Nursery (J)**, located at 8648 Old Bee Caves Rd. From the Wildflower Center, return to Loop 1 and go north to Slaughter Ln. Take it west to FM 1826 and turn north. At US 290, turn right to the intersection with SH 71 and turn left (west). In about a mile, turn right on Fletcher at a stoplight. Follow it to Old Bee Caves Rd. and turn left to the nursery.

Nearest food, gas, and lodging: Austin.

Nearest camping: Emma Long Metropolitan Park to the north, McKinney Falls State Park (see Additional Worthwhile Sites below), south of town off US 183, and the Austin Lone Star RV Resort on I-35 (exit 227 southbound/228 northbound), with easy access to Loop 1 via Ben White Blvd.

19. Guadalupe River State Park

The 1,900-acre Guadalupe River State Park is dominated by the river and its bald cypress trees. A network of upland trails provides good access into adjacent woodlands. The Guadalupe River originates from aquifer springs near Kerrville and runs for 250 miles to the Gulf of Mexico. The park, primarily used for water recreation, can be extremely busy on weekends and holidays.

Sites for butterflies within the park include the picnic area (**A**), the amphitheater (**B**), an open field (**C**), the Wagon Ford Camping Area (**D**), the trail along the river (**E**), a loop trail (**F**), roadways (**G**), and the park entrance (**H**).

Habitats: Oak-juniper woodland, field, and riparian.

Strategy for finding the most butterflies: In Guadalupe River SP (fee area), start at the picnic area (**A**) at the end of PR 31. Walk the edges and the short trails at the west end, along the river. Some of the more numerous butterflies include Pipevine and Black swallowtails, Dusky-blue Groundstreak, Gulf Fritillary, and Vesta and Phaon crescents. Also watch for Giant and Eastern Tiger swallowtails and Question Mark. Then walk through the woodland around the adjacent amphitheater (**B**), a good place for Juniper Hairstreak, Little Wood-Satyr, and Red Satyr. Continue on the trail into the open field (**C**), where Dainty Sulphur, Reakirt's Blue, Variegated Fritillary, Common Buckeye, and Green Skipper are possible.

Then drive to the Wagon Ford Camping Area parking lot (**D**) and walk the woodland edges and adjacent field. Falcate Orangetip is likely in March and April; Soapberry Hairstreak occurs from April to July; Banded Hairstreak is occasional in May and June; and Oak Hairstreak is possible during July and August. Ceraunus Blue; Silvery Checkerspot; Goatweed Leafwing; Queen; Horace's Duskywing; and Fiery, Dun, and Eufala skippers are likely most of the year. Also walk the trail along the river

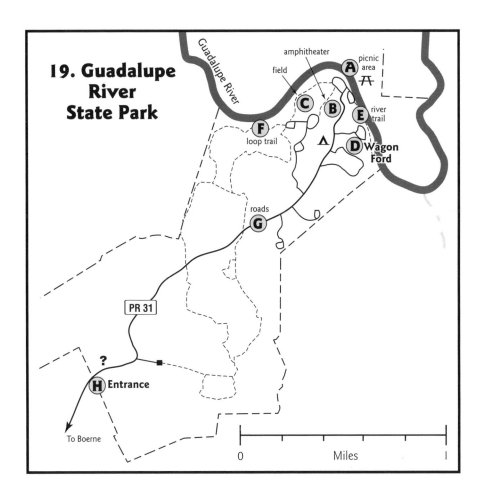

19. Guadalupe River State Park

Guadalupe River

amphitheater

field

picnic area

river trail

loop trail

Wagon Ford

roads

PR 31

? **H** Entrance

To Boerne

0   Miles

(**E**) between the parking lot and the picnic area at the end of PR 31. This riparian habitat is likely to produce Tawny Emperor. Watch also for Red-spotted Purple, Common Mestra, and Hackberry Emperor.

In addition, drive to the Cedar Sage Camping Area and walk a portion of the loop trail (**F**), starting at campsite 34 and passing through open oak-juniper woodlands. Sleepy Orange is likely to be seen, and Northern Cloudywing and Tropical and Desert checkered-skippers are possible. Finally, if wildflowers are plentiful, check the flowering plants along all the roadways (**G**) and near the park entrance (**H**). These locations usually offer most of the same species mentioned above, but also watch for **Rawson's Metalmark**.

Directions: In Kendall County, from Boerne, northwest of San Antonio on I-10, take SH 46 east for 13 miles to PR 31 and go north for three miles to the **Guadalupe River SP (A-H)** entrance.

Entrance to Guadalupe River State Park

Nearest food, gas, and lodging: Boerne; food at Bergheim three miles west of SP on SH 46; gas eight miles east on SH 46 at the junction of US 281.

Nearest camping: Guadalupe River SP.

20. Government Canyon State Natural Area

Opened to the public in mid-2005, this 8,201-acre preserve near San Antonio has an amazing variety of wildflowers in spring and a great diversity of butterflies. Because it is new and without a long-term database, the butterfly list provided here is only preliminary. The area is situated directly on the fault line of the Balcones Escarpment, and Government Canyon Creek carries water much of the year. July 4th Butterfly Counts are held here most years.

Sites include the visitor center garden (**A**), the Joseph E. Johnston Historic Road Trail (**B**), the Far Reaches Trail (**C**), and the entrance road (**D**).

Habitats: Juniper-oak woodland, mesquite grassland, field, and riparian.

Strategy for finding the most butterflies: Start at the visitor center garden (**A**) where Dusky-blue Groundstreak, Vesta and Phaon crescents, Queen, Horace's and Funereal duskywings, Common/White Checkered-Skipper, Southern Broken-Dash, Dun and Eufala skippers, and Celia's Roadside-Skipper can be expected. Then walk the Joseph E. Johnston Historic Road (**B**), now a trail, checking flowering plants along the edges and especially in open canyon bottoms. I like to walk the 3.5 miles to the spring in the early morning and survey butterflies on the way back.

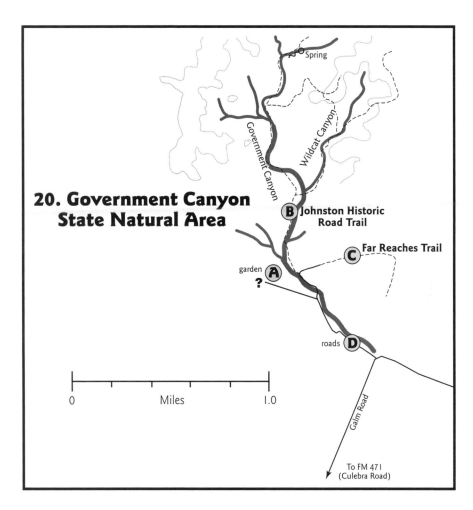

20. Government Canyon State Natural Area

Spring

Government Canyon

Wildcat Canyon

B Johnston Historic Road Trail

C Far Reaches Trail

garden **A**
?

roads **D**

0   Miles   1.0

Galm Road

To FM 471
(Culebra Road)

Specialty butterflies possible along this route include **Lacey's Scrub-Hairstreak**, **Rounded** and **Rawson's metalmarks**, **Zebra Heliconian**, and **Tropical Leafwing**. Some of the additional species to be expected include Cloudless and Dainty sulphurs, Southern Dogface, Juniper Hairstreak, Bordered Patch, Texan Crescent, White-striped Longtail, Northern Cloudywing, Texas Powdered-Skipper, Desert Checkered-Skipper, and Orange Skipperling. Also watch along the trail and in the canyon bottom for Two-tailed Swallowtail, Great Purple Hairstreak, Mallow Scrub-Hairstreak, Eastern Tailed-Blue, Fatal Metalmark, Red-spotted Purple, Common Mestra, Hackberry and Tawny emperors, Common Streaky-Skipper, and Nysa and Dotted roadside-skippers.

If time allows, walk a portion of the Far Reaches Trail **(C)**, starting at the Volunteer/Research Station. This route is likely to produce most of the same species mentioned above. Also check the sides of the entrance road **(D)**, which can be rich

Government Canyon Creek, Government Canyon State Natural Area

with wildflowers. Likely butterflies include Pipevine and Giant swallowtails, Lyside Sulphur, Gulf Fritillary, and Tropical Checkered-Skipper. Also watch for **Laviana White-Skipper**; Falcate Orangetip can be expected in spring.

Note: While you're in the area, you may want to visit nearby locations in San Antonio (site 64 in the South Texas Brushlands Region).

Directions: In Bexar County, the area is west of San Antonio. Take Culebra Road (FM 471) west from Loop 1604 for 3.5 miles to Galm Rd. Turn north and drive 1.6 miles to the **Government Canyon SNA (A-D)** entrance on the left.

Nearest food, gas, and lodging: San Antonio and surrounding areas.

Nearest camping: Government Canyon SNA (primitive only) and at commercial campgrounds along Loop 1604.

Additional Worthwhile Sites in the Edwards Plateau Region

Fredericksburg. The 20-acre Lady Bird Johnson Municipal Park, located three miles southwest of town off SH 16, features the .25-mile Live Oak Wilderness Trail. This site offers a variety of habitats and a good diversity of butterflies for such a small area.

South Llano River State Park. This 507-acre state park (fee area), located off SH 77 five miles south of I-10 at Junction, is dominated by a grove of huge pecan trees on the floodplain of the South Llano ("yawn-oh") River. A two-mile trail loops through the area. The Walter Buck WMA (2,123 acres), at the southern edge of the park, is dominated by juniper-oak woodlands.

Pedernales Falls State Park. Located 12 miles east of Johnson City on FM 2766, this 4,860-acre state park (fee area) offers about the same butterflies as Guadalupe River SP, but it has more trails (20 miles) for access into the backcountry. The park can be very busy on weekends.

Cibolo Nature Center. Located in Boerne, approximately 30 miles northwest of San Antonio on I-10, this is a 75-acre private preserve. It has trails through a diversity of habitats, including restored prairie, marsh, and a riparian corridor lined with majestic bald cypress trees. The Center promotes conservation and offers a number of environmental education programs. Take SH 46 east to a right turn on City Park Rd.

McKinney Falls State Park. This 726-acre state park (fee area) is located at the southern edge of Austin. Take US 183 south to the McKinney Falls Parkway and drive two miles west to the park, where you'll find a visitor center and several trails, including a loop trail that follows a portion of Onion Creek.

Butterfly Checklist for the Edwards Plateau Region

The following list includes nine sites: **12. Concan/Garner State Park, 13. Lost Maples State Natural Area, 14. Kerrville, 15. Enchanted Rock State Natural Area, 16. Inks Lake State Park /Longhorn Cavern State Park, 17. Balcones Canyonlands National Wildlife Refuge, 18. Austin, 19. Guadalupe River State Park,** and **20. Government Canyon State Natural Area**.

Status symbols include: A = abundant; C = common; U = uncommon; O = occasional; R = rare; X = accidental; M = migrant; TC = temporary colonist; ? = status unknown. (For a full definition of these terms, see p. 3.)

For trip notes, including dates and numbers of species seen, refer to the entry for this checklist in Appendix 3: Regional Checklist Resources.

Butterfly Species	12	13	14	15	16	17	18	19	20
Pipevine Swallowtail	A	A	C	C	A	A	A	A	A
Polydamas Swallowtail	X		X				X		
Zebra Swallowtail			X						
Black Swallowtail	C	U	U	U	U	C	C	C	U
Thoas Swallowtail			X				X		
Giant Swallowtail	C	U	C	U	C	C	C	U	C

Butterfly Species	12	13	14	15	16	17	18	19	20
Ornythion Swallowtail	X		X						
Eastern Tiger Swallowtail	U	U	U			C	C	U	
Two-tailed Swallowtail	U	U	O			U	U		U
Spicebush Swallowtail	O	X	O				U		
Palamedes Swallowtail			X			X	X		
Ruby-spotted Swallowtail			X				X		
Florida White	X						X		
Checkered White	A	C	C	A	A	C	A	A	A
Cabbage White			R				O		
Great Southern White	X		X	X			X		
Giant White	X								
Olympia Marble							X		
Falcate Orangetip	U		O	U	U	U	U	U	C
Clouded Sulphur	R					R			
Orange Sulphur	A	C	A	A	A	C	C	A	C
Southern Dogface	A	U	C	U	U	A	C		C
White Angled-Sulphur	X		X						
Yellow Angled-Sulphur	X		X				X		
Cloudless Sulphur	C		O	U	U	C	C	U	A
Orange-barred Sulphur	U						R		
Large Orange Sulphur	A	O	C			U	U	U	O
Statira Sulphur	X						X		
Lyside Sulphur	A	U	C	U		U	U		C
Barred Yellow							X		
Mexican Yellow	O	O	O			O	U		
Tailed Orange	X						X		
Little Yellow	C	U	C		C	C	C	U	A
Mimosa Yellow	X						X		R
Sleepy Orange	A	A	C	A	C	C	A	C	A
Dainty Sulphur	A	A	A	A	A	A	C	C	C
Harvester			X				X		
Great Purple Hairstreak	U		O	U	U	U	C		U
Silver-banded Hairstreak	X						X		
Soapberry Hairstreak	U		U			R	O	C	
Coral Hairstreak			R						
Banded Hairstreak	C		O				R	O	
Oak Hairstreak	C		O	U		C	C	O	
Xami Hairstreak	X								
Henry's Elfin	U	U	U			U	C		
Juniper Hairstreak	C	C	C	U	C	A	C	C	A
White M Hairstreak	X	O	X				U		
Gray Hairstreak	A	A	C	A	C	C	C	C	C

Butterfly Species	12	13	14	15	16	17	18	19	20
Red-crescent Scrub-Hairstreak							X		
Lacey's Scrub-Hairstreak	R		R				U		U
Mallow Scrub-Hairstreak	O	O	O	O			C		U
Dusky-blue Groundstreak	C	U	O			U	C	U	C
Red-spotted Hairstreak			X						
Clytie Ministreak	X								
Gray Ministreak	X		X						
Western Pygmy-Blue	U		O			R	R		
Cassius Blue	R		R				X		
Marine Blue	U	O	O				R		U
Cyna Blue	X						X		
Ceraunus Blue	U	U	U	U			U	U	U
Reakirt's Blue	C	C	C	U	U	C	C	C	C
Eastern Tailed-Blue	O		R			U	U		U
Spring/Summer Azure	R		O				O		
Fatal Metalmark	U		O				C		O
Rounded Metalmark	R	X	R				X		O
Rawson's Metalmark	U		O				U	O	U
Red-bordered Metalmark	X								
Mormon Metalmark							X		
American Snout	A-R	A-R	A-R	A-R	A-R	A-R	A-R	A-R	A-R
Gulf Fritillary	C	C	C	C	U	C	C	C	A
Mexican Silverspot	X						X		
Julia Heliconian	X		X			X	X		
Isabella's Heliconian							X		
Zebra Heliconian	X		X				TC		C
Variegated Fritillary	A	C	A	A	A	A	C	C	C
Mexican Fritillary	X		X				X		
Theona Checkerspot	U		O				U		
Bordered Patch	C		C	C		C	C	R	A
Crimson Patch	U		O				X		
Gorgone Checkerspot			X			R	R		
Silvery Checkerspot	C	U	O		O	U	C	U	O
Tiny Checkerspot	O								
Elada Checkerspot	C					R	R		
Texan Crescent	A	U	U			U	C	A	A
Pale-banded Crescent	X								
Vesta Crescent	C	R	C	U	U	U	C	C	A
Phaon Crescent	C	C	A	U	C	A	A	C	C
Pearl Crescent	U	U	U	U	U	U	A	U	U
Question Mark	U	U	C	U	U	U	C	U	U
Eastern Comma	X		X				X		

Butterfly Species	12	13	14	15	16	17	18	19	20
Mourning Cloak	U		U	U		U	O		
American Lady	C	C	C	C	C	C	C	C	C
Painted Lady	U	U	U	U	C	C	C	U	
Red Admiral	A	A	C	A	C	A	A	A	C
Common Buckeye	C	U	C	C	C	A	C	C	A
Tropical Buckeye	O					O	O		
White Peacock	X		X			X			
Malachite	X		X						
Red-spotted Purple	U	C	U			U	U	U	U
Viceroy	O		O	U	C	U	U		
Arizona Sister	U	U	U	U		U	O		O
Dingy Purplewing	X								
Blue-eyed Sailor	X					X			
Common Mestra	C		O	U		U	C	O	C
Red Rim	X					X			
Many-banded Daggerwing			X			X			
Ruddy Daggerwing			X			X			
Tropical Leafwing	X		O				U		U
Goatweed Leafwing	U		O	C	C	C	C	C	C
Hackberry Emperor	C		U		U	A	C	U	U
Empress Leilia	U	U	O			R	R		
Tawny Emperor	U		C	U	C	C	C	A	U
Gemmed Satyr						R			
Carolina Satyr	U		O			U	C		
Little Wood-Satyr	U	A	U	O	C	C	C	C	U
Red Satyr	C	C	U	U	U	A	C	A	U
Common Wood-Nymph	C		O	C	C	C	C	A	
Monarch	M	M	M	M	M	M	M	M	M
Queen	C	U	C	U	A	C	C	C	A
Soldier	X		X			X	X		
Mercurial Skipper			X						
Silver-spotted Skipper	U		U				C		
Hammock Skipper			X						
White-striped Longtail	X		O				X		A
Zilpa Longtail	X		X			X	X		
Gold-spotted Aguna	X								
Long-tailed Skipper	U		O				X		
Dorantes Longtail	R		R				X		
Brown Longtail			X						
Two-barred Flasher	X						X		
Golden Banded-Skipper			?						
Hoary Edge	X								

Butterfly Species	12	13	14	15	16	17	18	19	20
Desert Cloudywing			X						
Coyote Cloudywing	X		X				O		
Jalapus Cloudywing	X								
Southern Cloudywing	X								
Northern Cloudywing	C	U	O		U	C	C	U	C
Confused Cloudywing			X				R		
Acacia Skipper	X								
Outis Skipper			X				R		
Mazans Scallopwing	X								O
Hayhurst's Scallopwing	O		R				O		
Variegated Skipper	X								
Glassy-winged Skipper	X								
Texas Powdered-Skipper	U						U		C
Sickle-winged Skipper	X		X				X		
Hermit Skipper	X		X						
Brown-banded Skipper			X						
White-patched Skipper	X						X		
False Duskywing	X		R				R		
Sleepy Duskywing			R						
Juvenal's Duskywing	O		O	O		O	U		
Meridian Duskywing	R		R				R		
Scudder's Duskywing			X						
Horace's Duskywing	C	C	C	U	C		C	C	A
Mournful Duskywing	X		O						
Mottled Duskywing			R						
Zarucco Duskywing	X						X		
Funereal Duskywing	C	U	C	U	U	C	C	C	C
Wild Indigo Duskywing							O	O	
Com./White Checkered-Skipper	C	C	C	A	C	A	A	C	C
Tropical Checkered-Skipper	U	U					U	U	C
Desert Checkered-Skipper	U	O	O	U		O	U	O	A
Erichson's White-Skipper			X						
Laviana White-Skipper	X		X				X		R
Turk's-cap White-Skipper	X								
Common Streaky-Skipper	U		O				O		U
Common Sootywing	O		R				U		U
Swarthy Skipper			X						
Julia's Skipper	O	U	O	O	U	C	C		U
Neamathla Skipper			X				X		
Fawn-spotted Skipper	X								
Clouded Skipper	U		C	U		U	A	U	U
Least Skipper	X		R			U	R		

Butterfly Species	12	13	14	15	16	17	18	19	20
Tropical Least Skipper	X							X	
Orange Skipperling	C	U	O	A	U	U	C	C	C
Southern Skipperling	C		U			U	C	O	C
Fiery Skipper	C	U	C	A	U	C	A	C	U
Apache Skipper	R		R				R		
Green Skipper	U	C	O	C		U	O	C	
Dotted Skipper							X		
Crossline Skipper			X						
Whirlabout	X		O		U		U	U	U
Southern Broken-Dash	C	U	U	U	U		C	U	C
Sachem	A	C	A	A	A	A	A	C	C
Arogos Skipper							R		
Delaware Skipper	X		R				R		
Glowing Skipper	X						X		
Zabulon Skipper							X		
Broad-winged Skipper							X		
Dun Skipper	A	C	U	C	U	A	A	A	C
Bronze Roadside-Skipper	O	O	O			O	O	O	
Oslar's Roadside-Skipper	X		X						
Nysa Roadside-Skipper	U		U	U			O		U
Dotted Roadside-Skipper	O		O				O		O
Celia's Roadside-Skipper	O	U	O		U	U	C		U
Eufala Skipper	C	U	O	C	U	C	A	C	C
Olive-clouded Skipper							X		
Brazilian Skipper	U						U		
Ocola Skipper	C	U	U		C	C		C	U
Hecebolus Skipper							X		
Purple-washed Skipper							X		
Yucca Giant-Skipper	O		O	O		U	O		
Strecker's Giant-Skipper			R						

Northern Plains

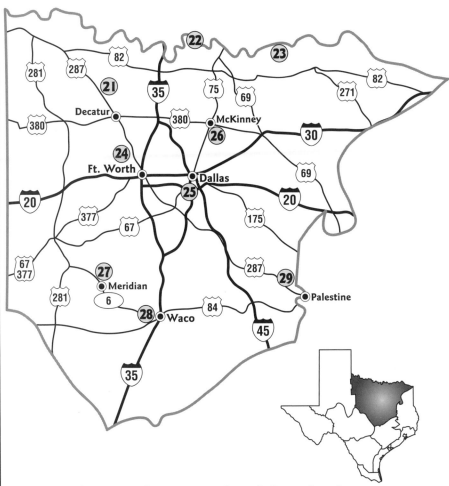

21. Lyndon B. Johnson National Grassland
22. Lake Texoma/Hagerman N.W.R.
23. Caddo National Grassland/Bonham State Park
24. Fort Worth
25. Dallas
26. Heard Natural Science Museum and
    Wildlife Sanctuary
27. Meridian State Park
28. Waco
29. Gus Engeling Wildlife Management Area

Northern Plains Region

The Northern Plains Region is a huge area that runs from the Oklahoma border southward to the Edwards Plateau and Central Plains regions and from the Panhandle and Western Plains Region east to the Pineywoods Region. Landscapes vary from rolling hills to deep stream valleys, all between approximately 300 and 1,000 feet in elevation. Vegetation is often classified into three zones: cross timbers and prairies in the west, blackland prairie in the center, and post-oak savannah in the east.

The Northern Plains Region is represented by nine sites: **21. Lyndon B. Johnson National Grassland**, **22. Lake Texoma/Hagerman National Wildlife Refuge**, **23. Caddo National Grassland/Bonham State Park**, **24. Fort Worth**, **25. Dallas**, **26. Heard Natural Science Museum and Wildlife Sanctuary**, **27. Meridian State Park**, **28. Waco**, and **29. Gus Engeling Wildlife Management Area**. The best time to visit these sites is April through October.

Northern Plains Specialties

Because of the region's location at the northern edge of the state and the influence from adjacent regions, butterfly diversity is moderate to high. Twenty-one species are considered area specialties.

Swallowtails, Whites, Hairstreaks: **Zebra Swallowtail** has been recorded at Gus Engeling WMA in spring and again in summer. Larvae feed on pawpaw. **Olympia Marble** flies only in spring in the open areas of Lyndon B. Johnson NG, the Fort Worth area, the Dallas area, and Gus Engeling WMA. Larvae feed on rockcress. **Coral Hairstreak** has been recorded at woodland edges where larval foodplants (cherry and plum) occur in Lyndon B. Johnson NG and the Fort Worth and Dallas areas. **Frosted Elfin** occurs during April and May in grassy woodlands in the Dallas area and Gus Engeling WMA. It is most likely to occur in recent burns where lupines and wild indigo (larval foodplants) are present. **Eastern Pine Elfin** frequents pine woodlands, often perching on pines, in Gus Engeling WMA. Larvae feed on pine foliage.

Spread-wing Skippers: **Outis Skipper** is most likely to be seen in open acacia (larval foodplant) grasslands in Lyndon B. Johnson NG, the Fort Worth and Dallas areas, and Gus Engeling WMA. Two broods have been reported, one in April/May and another in July/August.

Grass-Skippers: **Cobweb Skipper** can be found in spring at bluestem (larval foodplant) grassy areas in Lyndon B. Johnson NG and the Fort Worth and Dallas areas. **Dotted Skipper** frequents short-grass areas in pine woodlands in Lyndon B. Johnson NG and the Dallas and Waco areas. **Meske's Skipper** frequents grassy areas in sandy pine woodlands during May and June and again during September and October in Lyndon B. Johnson NG, the Fort Worth and Dallas areas, and Gus Engeling WMA. **Tawny-edged Skipper** occurs in disturbed grassy areas, including lawns, in Caddo NG and the Dallas area.

Crossline Skipper prefers open grassy areas in Caddo NG, the Dallas area, and Gus Engeling WMA. Males are known to perch in "grassy swales and valley bottoms" to await passing females. **Northern Broken-Dash** prefers grassy areas in moist woodlands in Caddo NG, the Dallas area, the Heard Museum site, and Gus Engeling WMA. Adults are slow fliers, and males often perch on vegetation from three to six feet above the ground. **Little Glassywing** frequents woodlands at the Heard Museum site and Gus Engeling WMA. Males often perch in small, sunny clearings. Larvae feed on purple top grass. **Arogos Skipper** prefers undisturbed prairies in spring and again in late summer in Lyndon B. Johnson NG, Lake Texoma, and the Fort Worth and Dallas areas. Males are known to be active during midday under cloudy skies. Larvae feed on big bluestem grass.

Zabulon Skipper occurs in grassy, often-shady openings in moist woodlands in Lyndon B. Johnson NG, Lake Texoma, the Fort Worth and Dallas areas, and the Heard Museum site. **Yehl Skipper** has been found in swampy woodlands only in the Gus Engeling WMA. Two flights have been recorded—from May to June and from August to October. **Broad-winged Skipper** is most likely to occur in and adjacent to wetlands in the Fort Worth and Dallas areas and Gus Engeling WMA. Males fly among vegetation with a slow and somewhat bobbing flight. Larvae feed on sedges. **Dion Skipper** occurs at wetlands where sedges (larval foodplant) grow during spring and again in late summer in Lyndon B. Johnson NG, the Fort Worth and Dallas areas, the Heard Museum site, and the Waco area.

Dusted Skipper is most likely to occur in open grassy areas in spring in Lyndon B. Johnson NG and the Fort Worth and Dallas areas. Males often perch in clearings to await passing females. Larvae feed on bluestem grasses. **Bell's Roadside-Skipper** occurs in a variety of locations, from gardens to roadsides, usually near moist woodlands in Lyndon B. Johnson NG, Lake Texoma, Caddo NG, the Fort Worth and Dallas areas, the Heard Museum site, and Meridian SP. **Dusky Roadside-Skipper** frequents grassy areas in open pine stands in Lyndon B. Johnson NG, Caddo NG, the Dallas area, and Gus Engeling WMA.

Sites within the Northern Plains Region

21. Lyndon B. Johnson National Grassland

The 20,313-acre Lyndon B. Johnson National Grassland has four lakes fifteen to forty acres in size, a network of roads, and nearly fifty miles of trails. The area's location along the state's northern border, its environmental diversity, and its close proximity to the Fort Worth-Dallas region (resulting in an extensive species database) make it one of the state's favorite butterfly-watching destinations.

Places to visit in the grassland include Cottonwood Lake (**A**), Cottonwood Lake Dam (**B**), the area near an oil/gas well (**C**), road F 900 (**D**), Black Creek Lake (**E**), and the Black Creek-Cottonwood Hiking Trail (**F**).

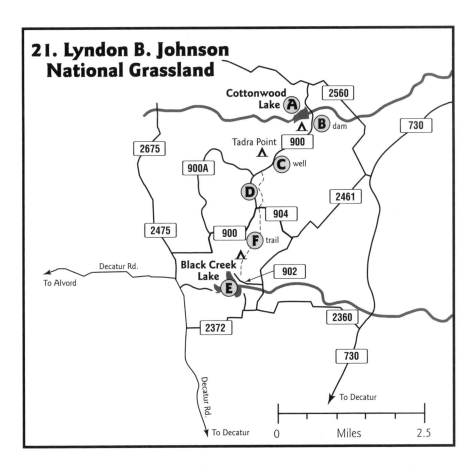

21. Lyndon B. Johnson National Grassland

Cottonwood Lake (A)

2560

dam (B)

730

Tadra Point 900

2675

900A

(C) well

(D)

2461

904

2475

900

(F) trail

902

Decatur Rd.

Black Creek Lake

To Alvord

(E)

2360

2372

730

Decatur Rd.

To Decatur

To Decatur

0   Miles   2.5

Habitats: Prairie, oak-juniper woodland, pine stand, riparian, wetland, and field.

Strategy for finding the most butterflies: Start at Cottonwood Lake (**A**). Park near the "Black Creek-Cottonwood Hiking Trail 901" sign and walk north half a mile to the gate along the north side of the lake. Some of the more numerous butterflies include Giant and Eastern Tiger swallowtails; Cloudless Sulphur; Red-banded Hairstreak; Dusky-blue Groundstreak; Reakirt's Blue; Eastern Tailed-Blue; Bordered Patch; Gorgone and Silvery checkerspots; Phaon Crescent; Question Mark; Red-spotted Purple; Hackberry Emperor; Common Wood-Nymph; Monarch; Northern Cloudywing; Horace's Duskywing; Clouded, Fiery, and Dun skippers; Sachem; and Common Roadside-Skipper.

Less common butterflies include Juniper Hairstreak; Texan Crescent; Tawny Emperor; Gemmed, Carolina, and Red satyrs; Little Wood-Satyr; Silver-spotted, Green, and Eufala skippers; Hoary Edge; Southern and Confused cloudywings; Hayhurst's Scallopwing; Funereal Duskywing; and Dotted Roadside-skipper. Check the adjacent lakeshore sedges for **Dion Skipper**.

Early spring at Lyndon B. Johnson National Grassland

In spring, also watch for **Olympia Marble**; Falcate Orangetip; Soapberry, Striped, Banded, and Oak hairstreaks; Henry's Elfin; Juvenal's Duskywing; **Cobweb** and **Zabulon skippers**; **Bell's Roadside-Skipper**; and Yucca Giant-Skipper.

Then walk between Cottonwood and Little Cottonwood lakes and below the Cottonwood Lake Dam **(B)**. This open area is likely to produce Little Yellow, Sleepy Orange, Dainty Sulphur, Variegated Fritillary, Common Buckeye, Monarch, and Queen.

Next, drive south on F 900 to an oil/gas well **(C)**. Park there and walk the track to the east that circles the adjacent hill; watch for **Cobweb** and **Dusted skippers** in spring. Climb the hill for hill-topping species, including Black Swallowtail and Sleepy Duskywing. Then continue south (except after heavy rains when the road can be next to impassable) on F 900 **(D)**, stopping at fields and other places with flowering plants. Many of the same butterflies mentioned above are possible. F 900 eventually turns into CR 2474 and terminates at CR 2475 (Old Decatur Road).

Afterwards, backtrack to CR 2461 and drive south to the east side of Black Creek Lake **(E)**. Walk around this area and, when wildflowers are plentiful, walk a portion of the Black Creek-Cottonwood Hiking Trail **(F)**. **Dusky Roadside-Skipper** is possible where pines grow.

There are also reports of **Coral Hairstreak**, a species that frequents brushy woodland edges, and **Outis**, **Meske's**, and **Arogos skippers**, three grassland species. Specific locations are not known.

Directions: From Decatur in Wise County, take FM 730 nine miles north of US 380 to CR 2560/CR 2461 (at the cemetery sign) and turn left. Follow CR 2560 to **F 900 (D)** and turn left to **Cottonwood Lake (A, B)**. Continue on F 900 to the **oil/gas well (C)**. After exploring the lake and F 900, take F 904 to CR 2461 and turn right (southwest) to **Black Creek Lake (E)** and the **hiking trail (F)**. Note: Some roads may be impassable after heavy rains.

Nearest food, gas, and lodging: Decatur.

Nearest camping: Cottonwood Lake, Tadra Point, and Black Creek Lake. *Note: Drinking water is not available.*

22. Lake Texoma/Hagerman National Wildlife Refuge

There are three key sites in the Lake Texoma area: Hagerman National Wildlife Refuge, the 423-acre Eisenhower State Park, and Spillway Park. The 11,320-acre NWR is situated on the Big Mineral Arm of Lake Texoma, an 89,000-acre impoundment of the Red River, which forms the border between Texas and Oklahoma. Productive butterfly-watching sites include the Meadow Pond Road (**A**), Crow Hill Trail (**B**), Muleshoe Marsh loop road (**C**), and Goode Picnic Area (**D**).

In Eisenhower SP, check out the garden (**E**), pull-offs along the roads (**F**), and woodland trails (**G**). The roads and fields near Spillway Park (**H**) are also good.

Habitats: Mesquite grassland, oak-hackberry woodland, bottomland-hardwood forest, prairie, riparian, field, and cropland.

Strategy for finding the most butterflies: Start at Hagerman NWR by walking the shaded Meadow Pond Road (**A**) past the gate for a mile or so. Some of the more numerous butterflies include Pipevine and Black swallowtails, Cloudless and Dainty sulphurs, Southern Dogface, Little Yellow, Marine and Reakirt's blues, Gulf Fritillary, Phaon Crescent, Goatweed Leafwing, Hackberry Emperor, Monarch, Queen, Horace's Duskywing, Fiery and **Tawny-edged skippers**, Sachem, and **Bell's Roadside-Skipper**.

Less numerous butterflies include Giant and Eastern Tiger swallowtails, Large Orange Sulphur, Sleepy Orange, Red-banded Hairstreak, Gorgone Checkerspot, Texan Crescent, Tawny Emperor, Northern Cloudywing, Funereal and Wild Indigo duskywings, Southern Broken-Dash, and Delaware and Dun skippers. In spring, Falcate Orangetip and Soapberry Hairstreak are also likely.

Next, walk the wooded Crow Hill Trail (**B**), a suitable place for Juniper Hairstreak, Little Wood-Satyr, Common Wood-Nymph, and **Dotted Skipper**. Also, drive the Muleshoe Marsh loop road (**C**), checking flowering plants; watch for Eastern Tailed-Blue and Least Skipper.

Walk around the wooded Goode Picnic Area (**D**), including the gated road at the entrance. Many of the same butterflies mentioned above are possible, but also watch for **Zabulon Skipper** in moist woodland clearings and **Arogos Skipper** in the adjacent prairie habitat.

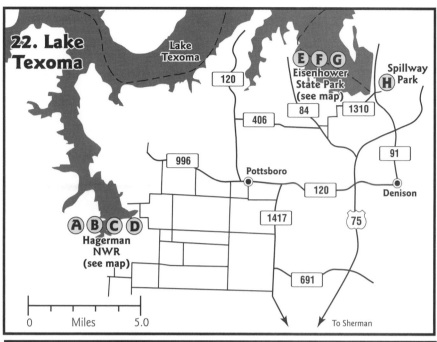

22. Lake Texoma

Lake Texoma

120

E **F** **G**
Eisenhower
State Park
(see map)

Spillway
H Park

84   1310

406

91

996

Pottsboro

120

Denison

1417

75

A **B** **C** **D**
Hagerman
NWR
(see map)

691

0   Miles   5.0

To Sherman

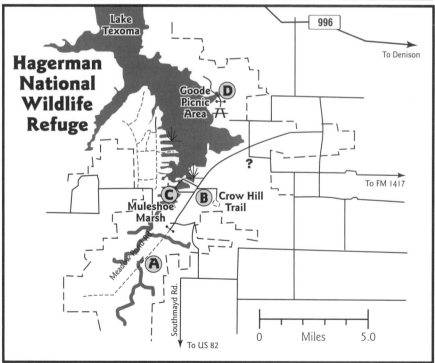

Lake
Texoma

996

To Denison

Hagerman
National
Wildlife
Refuge

Goode
Picnic
Area   **D**

?

To FM 1417

C   **B** Crow Hill
Muleshoe   Trail
Marsh

Meadow Pond Rd.

A

Southmayd Rd.

0   Miles   5.0

To US 82

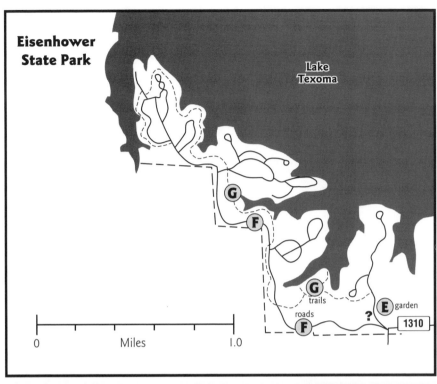

Eisenhower State Park

Lake Texoma

G

F

G
trails
roads
F

E garden

?

1310

0   Miles   1.0

Crow Hill Trail, Hagerman National Wildlife Refuge

Next, drive to Eisenhower SP, where many of the same butterflies mentioned above are possible. First check the garden (**E**) at the park entrance; then drive the roads, stopping at pull-offs (**F**) near patches of wildflowers. It can also be productive to walk some of the 4.5 miles of woodland trails (**G**).

In Spillway Park (**H**), drive the road to the Project Office below the dam, checking the roadsides and fields beyond, good places to find Variegated Fritillary.

Directions: In Grayson County near the Oklahoma border, **Hagerman NWR (A-D)** is northwest of Sherman. From US 75 in Sherman, take FM 1417 north for 13 miles to the refuge sign. Turn west and go six miles to the entrance. To reach **Spillway Park (H)**, take SH 91 from Denison or from US 75 north of Denison to the park entrance. **Eisenhower SP (E-G)** is west on FM 1310 W (Eisenhower Rd.) 1.8 miles from Spillway Park.

Nearest food, gas, and lodging: Denison and Sherman.

Nearest camping: Eisenhower SP and at several parks along Lake Texoma.

23. Caddo National Grassland/Bonham State Park

Established in 1935, the 17,785-acre Caddo National Grassland was the first national grassland dedicated in Texas. It is divided into two main units and provides a rather diverse environment, including three small lakes; the largest, Coffee Mill Lake, is 651 acres. Neither unit has very much accessible native prairie. Caddo NG is administered by the U.S. Forest Service and is managed under an agreement with the Texas Parks and Wildlife Department.

Sites in the north unit include campgrounds (**A, C**) and roadsides (**B**). In the south unit, visit roadsides (**E**) and a cemetery (**F**) for the best butterfly watching.

The 251-acre Bonham SP (fee area) has a 65-acre lake and 11 miles of trails. Sites here include roadsides and trails (**D**).

Habitats: Prairie, mixed hardwood forest, pine woodland, riparian, field, and cropland.

Strategy for finding the most butterflies: Three sites in the north unit of Caddo NG should be visited first. East Coffee Mill Lake Camping Area (**A**), including the trail that runs west through the woodland, offers the most diversity. Some of the more numerous butterflies include Black Swallowtail, Red-banded Hairstreak, Eastern Tailed-Blue, Hackberry Emperor, Common Wood-Nymph, Fiery and Eufala skippers, Southern Broken-Dash, and Sachem. Several less common butterflies are also possible: Harvester, Spring/Summer Azure, Texan Crescent, Red-spotted Purple, Tawny Emperor, Carolina and Gemmed satyrs, Little Wood-Satyr, Southern Cloudywing, Hayhurst's Scallopwing, Horace's Duskywing, and **Bell's Roadside-Skipper**.

Next, check the CR 2710 roadsides (**B**). Pipevine, Giant, Eastern Tiger, and Spicebush swallowtails; Cloudless and Dainty sulphurs; Little Yellow; Gulf Fritillary; Gorgone Checkerspot; Question Mark; Common Buckeye; Monarch; Queen; and Common Roadside-Skipper can be expected.

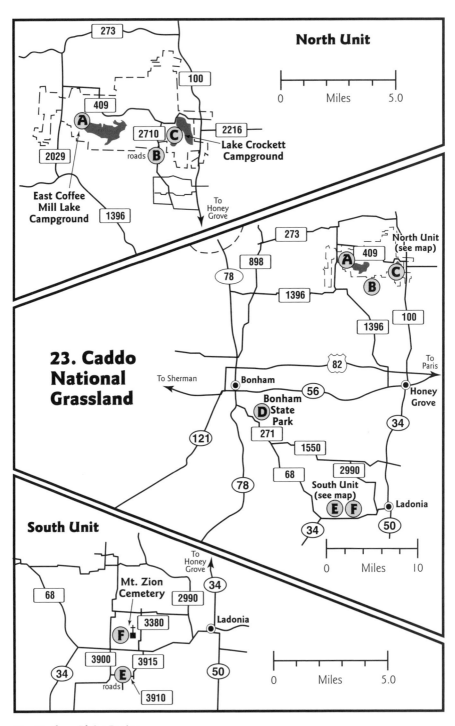

North Unit

273

100

409

A

2710 C

2216

Lake Crockett
Campground

2029

roads B

East Coffee
Mill Lake
Campground

1396

To
Honey
Grove

0   Miles   5.0

273

North Unit
(see map)

898

409

A

78

C

B

1396

1396

100

To
Paris

82

To Sherman

Bonham

Honey
Grove

**23. Caddo
National
Grassland**

56

Bonham
State
Park

D

34

121

271

1550

68

2990

78

South Unit
(see map)

E   F

Ladonia

34

50

0   Miles   10

South Unit

To
Honey
Grove

Mt. Zion
Cemetery

34

68

2990

3380

Ladonia

F

3900

3915

34

E

50

roads

3910

0   Miles   5.0

Coffee Mill Lake, Caddo National Grassland

Then walk around West and East Lake Crockett camping areas (**C**), including the roadsides and lakeshore. Likely species include Phaon Crescent, Viceroy, and Silver-spotted and Least skippers. **Crossline Skipper, Northern Broken-Dash**, and **Dusky Roadside-Skipper** are also possible. In spring, Falcate Orangetip and Juvenal's Duskywing are likely.

Next, drive to Bonham SP (**D**); check the pine-shaded roadsides and walk some of the woodland trails. Several of the butterflies mentioned above are possible, including **Dusky Roadside-Skipper**.

Finally, the south unit of Caddo NG can be productive in spring: check the roadsides (**E**) along CR 3915, 3910, and 3900, and also walk through Mt. Zion Cemetery (**F**), a good place for Cabbage White.

Directions: In Fannin County, **the north unit of Caddo NG (A-C)** is northeast of Bonham and northwest of Paris. Take US 82 from either town to Honey Grove. Turn north on SH 100 for 12 miles to FM 409. Turn west into the heart of the north unit. To reach the **south unit of Caddo NG (E, F)**, take SH 34 south from Honey Grove to Ladonia and follow SH 34 west to the entrance. **Bonham SP (D)** is southeast of Bonham. Take SH 78 south for 1.5 miles and turn left on FM 271 for two miles to the entrance.

Nearest food, gas, and lodging: Bonham; food and gas at numerous sites along US 82.

Nearest camping: Caddo NG and Bonham SP.

24. Fort Worth

There are five very good but widely spaced sites for watching butterflies in the area around Fort Worth, which was named for a military post established on the Trinity River in 1849. These include the 3,500-acre Fort Worth Nature Center (**A-D**), the Fort Worth Botanical Garden (**E**), several parks along the north and west side of Benbrook Lake (**F, G, H**), and River Legacy Park (**I**) and the adjacent Village Creek Wastewater Treatment Plant (**J**). Fort Worth Nature Center has the greatest habitat diversity and is likely to produce the greatest number of butterflies, but the botanical garden offers easy access with a variety of habitats.

Habitats: Oak savannah, oak-hackberry woodland, bottomland-hardwood forest, prairie, marsh, garden, riparian, and field.

Strategy for finding the most butterflies: Start at the Fort Worth Nature Center. Check the small garden and trail at the Hardwicke Interpretive Center (**A**) and walk a portion of the adjacent Prairie Trail (**B**). Some of the more numerous butterflies include Pipevine, Black, Giant, and Eastern Tiger swallowtails; Cloudless and Dainty sulphurs; Little Yellow; Gulf Fritillary; Gorgone and Silvery checkerspots; Phaon Crescent; Monarch; Queen; Northern Cloudywing; Horace's and Funereal dusky-wings; Clouded, Fiery, Delaware, Dun, and Eufala skippers; Southern Skipperling; Sachem; and Common Roadside-Skipper.

Spicebush Swallowtail, Checkered White, and Southern Dogface are less common. In spring, watch for Falcate Orangetip; Soapberry, Banded, and Striped hairstreaks; Henry's Elfin; Juvenal's Duskywing; and **Cobweb Skipper**.

Next, drive to the Marsh Boardwalk (**C**), a good place for **Dion Skipper**. Also walk the adjacent Equestrian Trail that runs north from the parking area through a woodland. Red-banded Hairstreak, Dusky-blue Groundstreak, Marine Blue, Eastern Tailed-Blue, Pearl Crescent, Little Wood-Satyr, and **Bell's Roadside-Skipper** are likely. Then drive to Greer Island (**D**). Check the roadsides and walk the loop trail. Watch for **Northern Broken-Dash** in moist, grassy areas; **Broad-winged Skipper** is also possible.

In Fort Worth proper, the Fort Worth Botanical Garden (**E**) can be superb. Check the plantings in front of the Garden Center and along the entrance road. Walk the trails through the courtyard and Fuller Garden, the Fragrance Garden, Four Seasons Garden, and Trial Garden. Also walk the trail through the lower woodlands. Many of the same butterflies mentioned above can be found here, but this area also offers a good opportunity to find Great Purple, Juniper, and White M hairstreaks; Texan Crescent; Question Mark; Green and **Zabulon skippers** (in shady, open areas); and Nysa Roadside-Skipper.

At Benbrook Lake, southwest of the city, drive into Mustang Park (**F**), Holiday Park (**G**), and Dutch Branch Park (**H**). Sleepy Orange, Ceraunus Blue, Common Buckeye, and Gemmed Satyr are likely; Tropical Checkered-Skipper (probably a temporary colonist) has been found along the track behind the first restroom on the right in the

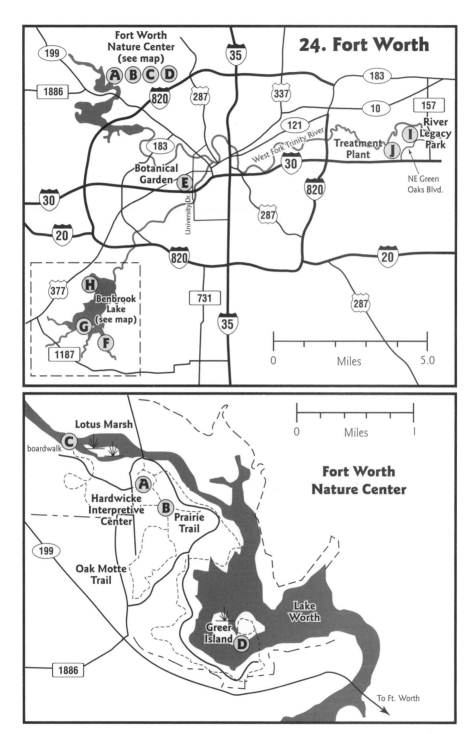

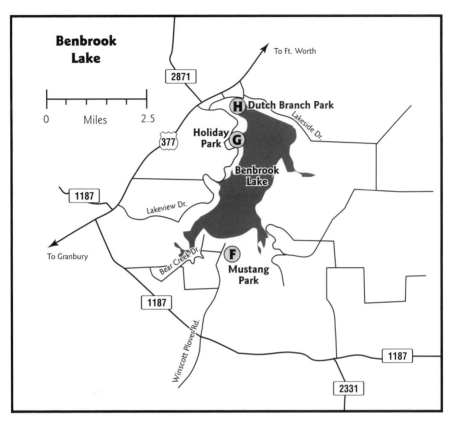

Benbrook
Lake

To Ft. Worth

2871

0   Miles   2.5

H Dutch Branch Park

Lakeside Dr.

Holiday
Park

377

G

Benbrook
Lake

1187

Lakeview Dr.

To Granbury

Bear Creek Dr.

F

Mustang
Park

1187

Winscott Plover Rd.

1187

2331

Holiday Park Campground. Look for **Dusted Skipper** in spring and **Arogos Skipper** in undisturbed prairie along the western edge.

Finally, in east Fort Worth, drive to River Legacy Park (**I**), explore the roads and walk a portion of the trail through the riparian vegetation along the West Fork of the Trinity River. Also visit the nearby Village Creek Wastewater Treatment Plant (**J**); walk the outer levee and some of the connecting levees.

Olympia Marble flies in open areas throughout the sites in early spring, and a few rare species are possible: **Coral Hairstreak** has been recorded in open woodlands in May and June; **Outis Skipper** has been found on sunny, open hillsides; **Dotted Skipper** has been recorded in short-grass prairies; and **Meske's Skipper** frequents open pinelands.

Directions: In Tarrant County, the **Fort Worth Nature Center (A-D)** is 10 miles northwest of downtown. It is located north off SH 199, four miles west of Loop 820. Return to SH 199 and drive southwest on Loop 820 to I-30. Go east on I-30 to University Dr. Go north a short distance to the **Fort Worth Botanical Garden (E)**.

To reach Benbrook Lake from the Botanical Garden, take I-30 west. Exit on US 377 and continue southwest past Loop 820 and through Benbrook to the park on the left.

Entrance to the Marsh Boardwalk, Ft.Worth Nature Center

Just past the intersection with FM 2871, take Stevens Dr. left into the park. Take the first left on Park Dr. for **Dutch Branch Park (H)**. Return to Stevens Dr. and continue southeast to a left turn on Lakeview Dr. **Holiday Park (G)** is along both sides of the road as it winds its way along the lakeshore and returns to US 377. Turn left on US 377 and drive a short distance to FM 1187. Turn left and continue to Winscott Plover Rd. Turn left (north) to **Mustang Park (F)**.

River Legacy Park (I) and **Village Creek Wastewater Treatment Plant (J)** are east of downtown. Take I-30 east past Loop 820 to FM 157 and turn north for 2.3 miles. Turn west on NE Green Oaks Blvd. to the park entrance 1.8 miles ahead. The treatment plant is a short distance beyond.

Nearest food, gas, and lodging: Fort Worth.

Nearest camping: Benbrook Lake and commercial sites in the area.

25. Dallas

There are several good butterfly-watching sites in and around the city of Dallas, the third largest city in Texas (after Houston and San Antonio) and locally known as "Big D." The principal sites include the sixty-six-acre Dallas Arboretum and Botanical Garden **(A)** and White Rock Lake Park **(B-E)** in east Dallas; the 633-acre Dallas Nature Center **(F, G)**, with its ten miles of hiking trails, and the 1,826-acre Cedar Hill State Park **(H-J)** on the south side.

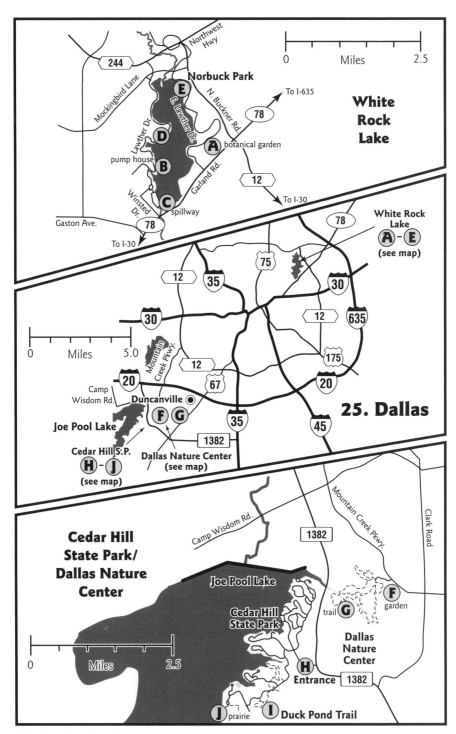

244

Northwest Hwy

Mockingbird Lane

Norbuck Park

E. Lawther Dr.

Lawther Dr.

E

N. Buckner Rd.

78

To I-635

D

A botanical garden

pump house

B

Garland Rd.

White Rock Lake

12

Winsted Dr.

C

spillway

Gaston Ave.

78

To I-30

To I-30

78

White Rock Lake

A - **E**

(see map)

75

12

35

30

30

12

635

Mountain Creek Pkwy.

12

175

0 Miles 5.0

20

Camp Wisdom Rd.

Duncanville

F **G**

67

35

20

45

25. Dallas

Joe Pool Lake

Cedar Hill S.P.

H - **J**

(see map)

1382

Dallas Nature Center (see map)

Cedar Hill State Park/ Dallas Nature Center

Camp Wisdom Rd.

1382

Mountain Creek Pkwy.

Clark Road

Joe Pool Lake

Cedar Hill State Park

trail **G**

F garden

Dallas Nature Center

0 Miles 2.5

H

Entrance 1382

J prairie

I Duck Pond Trail

Entrance to Dallas Nature Center

Habitats: Juniper-hackberry woodland, scrub-oak woodland, mesquite grassland, bottomland hardwood forest, prairie, garden, riparian, and field.

Strategy for finding the most butterflies: The Dallas Arboretum and Botanical Garden and White Rock Lake Park are located closest to downtown Dallas. Start at the botanical garden (**A**) and wander around the abundant plantings. Some of the more numerous butterflies include Pipevine, Black, Giant, and Eastern Tiger swallowtails; Cloudless and Dainty sulphurs; Southern Dogface; Little Yellow; Sleepy Orange; Red-banded Hairstreak; Dusky-blue Groundstreak; Eastern Tailed-Blue; Gulf Fritillary; Gorgone and Silvery checkerspots; Monarch; Silver-spotted, Clouded, Fiery, Dun, and Eufala skippers; Horace's and Funereal duskywings; Sachem; Southern Broken-Dash; and **Bell's Roadside-Skipper**. In spring, watch for Falcate Orangetip, Soapberry and Banded hairstreaks, Henry's Elfin, and Juvenal's Duskywing.

Then visit the White Rock Lake area. Enter on Winsted Drive and walk the roads near the old pump house (**B**) and through the forested area north of the spillway (**C**). **Zabulon Skipper** is possible near the old pump house and **Dion Skipper** is likely along the lakeshore. In spring, **Frosted Elfin** may be seen in the pine woodland. Check for flowering plants along Lawther Drive (**D**) and walk around Norbuck Park (**E**) in the northwest corner. Additional butterflies possible here include Harvester, Least Skipper, and Southern Skipperling.

Next, drive to the Dallas Nature Center. Start at the butterfly garden (**F**) near the entrance, a good place to find Great Purple Hairstreak; Phaon Crescent; Long-tailed, Delaware, and Brazilian skippers; and Celia's Roadside-Skipper. Then walk one or more of the trails, such as the Cattail Pond Trail (G). Watch for Juniper and White M hairstreaks, Northern and Confused cloudywings, Hayhurst's Scallopwing, Mottled and Wild Indigo duskywings, **Cobweb Skipper** (in spring), and Common and Nysa roadside-skippers. **Broad-winged Skipper** is possible at or near the pond.

Nearby Cedar Hill SP is likely to have the highest butterfly diversity, especially when wildflowers are present. Check the plantings at the park entrance (H), walk the Duck Pond Trail (I), and survey the "Native Tall Grass Prairie" (J), where several prairie species are possible. Many of the same butterflies mentioned above are likely, but also expect Tawny Emperor, Queen, and Orange Skipperling. Watch for Hoary Edge; Sleepy Duskywing; Southern Cloudywing; **Dotted**, **Crossline**, **Arogos**, and **Dusted skippers**; and Dotted Roadside-Skipper.

Olympia Marble is possible in open areas during early spring throughout the site. Other rare species include **Coral Hairstreak** at brushy areas and **Outis Skipper** in acacia grasslands. **Northern Broken-Dash** has also been recorded.

Directions: In Dallas County, the **Dallas Arboretum and Botanical Garden (A)** is located at 8525 Garland Rd. (SH 78). Take SH 78 southwest from I-635 or northeast from I-30. To explore **White Rock Lake Park (B, C)**, turn right on Garland Rd. from the botanical garden and go just past the lake to a right turn on Winsted Dr. To reach **Lawther Dr. (D)**, continue on Winsted to White Rock Rd. and turn right to Lawther, which goes along the lakeshore to Mockingbird Ln. Turn right on Mockingbird and cross the bridge to **Norbuck Park (E)**.

To reach **Dallas Nature Center (F, G)** and **Cedar Hill SP (H-J)**, take I-30 west to I-35E. Go south on I-35E until US 67 splits off. Follow US 67 toward Duncanville. Then take I-20 west, go to Mountain Creek Parkway, and take it south to the Nature Center. Return north to Camp Wisdom Rd. and turn west for a short distance to FM 1382. Turn south and proceed to Cedar Hill SP on the right. FM 1382 is also accessible from I-20.

Nearest food, gas, and lodging: Dallas.

Nearest camping: Cedar Hill SP and commercial sites in Dallas.

26. Heard Natural Science Museum and Wildlife Sanctuary

This fairly small site (fee area) of 289 acres offers excellent butterfly-watching opportunities. Located in the blackland prairie bioregion of the state, the Heard Natural Science Museum and Wildlife Sanctuary has a marvelous garden, a restored prairie, and 3.5 miles of trails. The preserve was established by Bessie Heard in 1967 to "bring nature and people together to discover, enjoy, experience, preserve and restore our precious environment." Sites to visit include a garden (A), prairie areas (B, C), and Bullfrog Pond (D).

Habitats: Garden, prairie, bottomland-deciduous forest, oak savannah, field, and riparian.

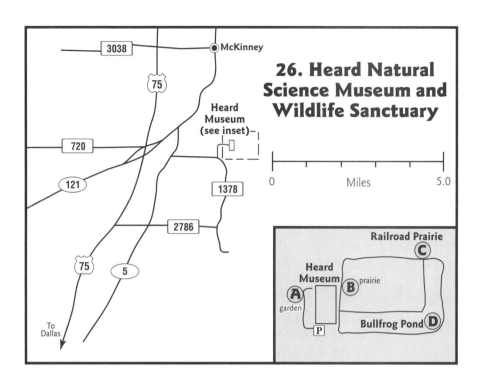

26. Heard Natural Science Museum and Wildlife Sanctuary

3038

75

McKinney

720

121

Heard Museum (see inset)

1378

2786

75

5

To Dallas

0   Miles   5.0

Railroad Prairie

C

Heard Museum

B prairie

A

garden

P

Bullfrog Pond D

Visitor Center, Heard Natural Science Museum and Wildlife Sanctuary

Strategy for finding the most butterflies: Start at the visitor center garden (**A**) and be sure to return to check it again before you depart. Some of the more numerous butterflies include Red-banded Hairstreak; Dusky-blue Groundstreak; Phaon Crescent; Horace's Duskywing; Clouded, Least, Fiery, Delaware, Dun, and Eufala skippers; Sachem; Southern Broken-Dash; and Common and Celia's roadside-skippers.

Next, walk into the open prairie area (**B**) below the visitor center and continue to the woods. Pipevine, Black, Giant, and Eastern Tiger swallowtails; Sleepy Orange; Marine Blue; Spring/Summer Azure; Gulf Fritillary; Gorgone and Silvery checkerspots; Vesta Crescent; Monarch; and Northern Cloudywing are likely here. Juniper Hairstreak, Goatweed Leafwing, Hackberry and Tawny emperors, and **Bell's Roadside-Skipper** are possible along the woodland edge. In spring, watch for Falcate Orangetip, Soapberry and Banded hairstreaks, Henry's Elfin, and Juvenal's Duskywing.

Then follow the trail north through the woods to the wetlands and Railroad Prairie (**C**). Watch for Carolina Satyr, Little Wood-Satyr, and Common Wood-Nymph in the woods, Viceroy near willows, **Northern Broken-Dash** and **Little Glassywing** in moist, shady areas, and **Zabulon Skipper** in shady clearings. Return to the garden via Bullfrog Pond (**D**), where **Dion Skipper** is probable.

Directions: In Collin County, southwest of McKinney, take SH 5 south and turn east on FM 1378. The **Heard Natural Science Museum (A-D)** is one mile ahead on the left, just past the country club.

Nearest food, gas, and lodging: McKinney.

Nearest camping: Commercial campgrounds along US 75.

27. Meridian State Park

The 503-acre Meridian State Park (fee area) is best known to the naturalist as a good site to find golden-cheeked warblers, but its varied habitats also offer a diverse environment for other wildlife. The park has five miles of hiking trails, including one that circles the 70-acre Lake Meridian. The name of the park is derived from its location on the one-hundredth meridian. Visit the area of the dam (**A**), the bridge (**B**), Shinnery Ridge Trail (**C**), the one-way drive (**D**), and Bosque Hiking Trail (**E**).

Habitat: Juniper-oak woodland, wetland, riparian, and field.

Strategy for finding the most butterflies: Start at the Lake Meridian dam (**A**). Walk across the dam (part of the Bosque Hiking Trail) and check the moist area below the dam. Some of the more numerous butterflies include Pipevine, Giant, and Eastern Tiger swallowtails; Little Yellow; Sleepy Orange; Phaon Crescent; Horace's Duskywing; Fiery and Dun skippers; and Sachem. Less common butterflies include Great Purple Hairstreak, Dusky-blue Groundstreak, Silvery Checkerspot, Question Mark, Monarch, Queen, Funereal Duskywing, Orange and Southern skipperlings, and Southern Broken-Dash.

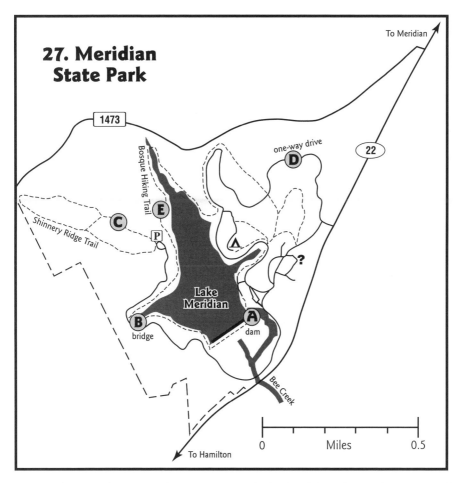

27. Meridian State Park

1473

Bosque Hiking Trail

one-way drive

22

To Meridian

Shinnery Ridge Trail

C

E

P

D

A

?

Lake Meridian

B

bridge

A

dam

Bee Creek

To Hamilton

0   Miles   0.5

Next, drive to Shinnery Ridge, stopping at the bridge (**B**) at the southwest arm of the lake to check there and to walk the trail to the open beach on the left side of the stream. Watch for Marine Blue, Texan Crescent, Red-spotted Purple, and **Bell's Roadside-Skipper** along the trail. Then continue on to Shinnery Ridge Trail (**C**) parking area and walk a good portion of the trail. Juniper Hairstreak, Reakirt's Blue, Hackberry and Tawny emperors, and Red Satyr are usually common.

Next, return to near the park entrance and drive the one-way drive (**D**), stopping at pull-offs to check patches of wildflowers. In spring, Soapberry Hairstreak can be common at soapberry trees. If time allows, walk a section of the Bosque Hiking Trail (**E**).

Directions: In Bosque County, from Meridian, southwest of Dallas, take SH 22 southwest for three miles to **Meridian SP (A-E)**.

Nearest food, gas, and lodging: Meridian.

Nearest camping: Meridian SP.

Bosque Hiking Trail on dam, Meridian State Park

28. Waco

The greater Waco area, situated along the Brazos and Bosque rivers, offers a number of butterfly-watching locations. These include the 416-acre Cameron Park (**A**, **B**), the 16-acre Carleen Bright Arboretum (**C**), and several locations surrounding Waco Lake (**D-J**), a 7,270-acre impoundment on the northwestern edge of the city. Waco is the home of Baylor University.

Habitats: Garden, oak savannah, juniper-oak woodland, mesquite grassland, bottomland-hardwood forest, field, and riparian.

Strategy for finding the most butterflies: Start in Cameron Park at "Miss Nellie's Pretty Place" (**A**), where you're likely to find the highest butterfly diversity, at least in spring. Some of the more numerous butterflies include Pipevine, Giant, and Eastern Tiger swallowtails; Cloudless and Dainty sulphurs; Little Yellow; Ceraunus Blue; Eastern Tailed-Blue; Gulf Fritillary; Tawny Emperor; Monarch; Queen; Horace's Duskywing; Clouded and Fiery skippers; Whirlabout; Sachem; and Ocola Skipper (in fall).

Less common butterflies include Black Swallowtail; Large Orange Sulphur; Southern Dogface; Mallow Scrub-Hairstreak; Red-banded Hairstreak; Gorgone Checkerspot; Texan, Vesta, and Phaon crescents; Silver-spotted and Long-tailed skippers; Northern Cloudywing; Funereal Duskywing; Celia's Roadside-Skipper; and Eufala and Brazilian skippers. In spring, look for Soapberry and Banded hairstreaks in the soapberry trees along the northern edge of Miss Nellie's.

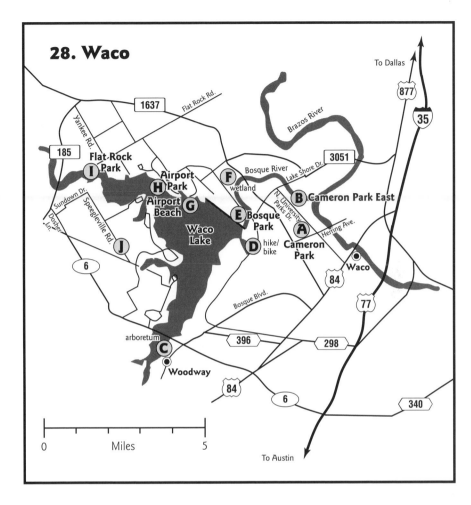

28. Waco

1637

Flat Rock Rd.

Brazos River

To Dallas

877

35

185

Flat-Rock Park

I

Yankee Rd.

3051

Airport Park

H **F**

Bosque River

Lake Shore Dr.

wetland

B Cameron Park East

Airport Beach **G**

N. University Parks Dr.

Sundown Dr.

Speegleville Rd.

Dosher Ln.

Waco Lake

E Bosque Park

A

Herring Ave.

J

D hike/ bike

Cameron Park

6

Waco

84

77

Bosque Blvd.

arboretum

C

396

298

Woodway

84

6

340

0   Miles   5

To Austin

Also in Cameron Park, visit the wetland at Cameron Park East (**B**), across the river. Watch there for Pearl Crescent and Least Skipper; this is the westernmost site for **Dion Skipper**.

Southwest of town is the Carleen Bright Arboretum (**C**) in Woodway. Check the plantings and walk the network of trails. Great Purple and Juniper hairstreaks, Dusky-blue Groundstreak, American Snout, Question Mark, Little Wood-Satyr, Red Satyr, Hayhurst's Scallopwing, and Whirlabout are likely.

Additional worthwhile sites surround Waco Lake. Start from near Cameron Park East. A small butterfly garden at the entrance to the Hike and Bike Trail (**D**) along Lake Shore Drive is worth a stop. Other sites include Bosque Park (**E**), below the dam, the Research Wetlands (**F**) farther north, nearby Airport Beach (**G**), Airport Park (**H**), a fee area, and Flat Rock Park (**I**), another fee area. Speegleville Road (**J**) on the west side of the lake is good for roadside butterflying. The open prairies offer many of the

Miss Nellie's Pretty Place, Waco

same butterflies mentioned above, but also watch for Sleepy Orange, Oak Hairstreak (in spring), Western Pygmy-Blue, Viceroy (in willows), and **Dotted Skipper** (possible in prairie-like habitat at locations G-J).

Directions: In McLennan County, Cameron Park is located north of US 84. Turn on N. University Parks Dr. and continue across Herring Ave. to a right turn into the park. Take the left fork ahead on Sturgis Rd. **Miss Nellie's Pretty Place (A)** is at the corner of Sturgis and Mt. Lookout Rd. To visit **Cameron Park East (B)**, return to Herring Dr. and go east to Martin Luther King, Jr. Blvd. (Lake Brazos Dr.). Turn north to the park on the left.

To find Waco Lake and related sites, continue on Martin Luther King to Lake Shore Dr. (FM 3051) where you will turn west. Continue past 19th St. and Airport Rd. to the **Hike and Bike Trail (D)** at the south end of the dam. Then return to Airport Rd. and turn north to **Bosque Park (E)** below the dam. The **Research Wetlands (F)** are also along Airport Rd. farther north. Continue across Steinbeck Bend Dr. into the airport area and turn left on Skeet Eason Rd. to find access to **Airport Beach (G)** along the lake. Part of **Airport Park (H)** is accessible by turning left from Skeet Eason Rd. as it follows the airport boundary northwest. Then continue to Flat Rock Rd. and turn left. Go past a subdivision and turn left on an access road to the rest of the park. Return to Flat Rock Rd. and turn left. Follow it to the end to find **Flat Rock Park (I)**.

Return on Flat Rock Rd. to the first left on Yankee Rd. At North River Crossing (FM 185), turn left and take it to a left turn on Dosher Ln. just before the intersection with

SH 6. Make a left on Sundown Dr. and follow it to **Speegleville Rd. (J)** where side roads will take you to the lake.

When you're through there, return by convenient side roads to SH 6 to the west and turn south. Cross Waco Lake on SH 6 and take a right turn on Bosque Blvd. in Woodway. Follow a well-marked route two miles to **Carleen Bright Arboretum (C)**. You can also access Bosque Blvd. from US 84 by taking N. Valley Mills Dr. (Loop 396) or SH 6 west and turning left.

Nearest food, gas, and lodging: Waco.

Nearest camping: Parks around Waco Lake and in the Waco area.

29. Gus Engeling Wildlife Management Area

Managed by the Texas Parks and Wildlife Service, the 10,960-acre Gus Engeling Wildlife Management Area offers easy access to typical post-oak savannah habitat, but many of the butterfly species are representative of the Pineywoods. The WMA is drained by Catfish Creek, a tributary to the Trinity River. The WMA was named for its first wildlife biologist, who was killed by a poacher in December 1951.

Among the sites to visit are the road to Day Camps 3 and 4 (**A**), the Dogwood Nature Trail (**B**), the Beaver Pond Nature Trail (**C**), and Catfish Creek (**D**).

Habitats: Deciduous forest, post-oak savannah, swamp, riparian, and field.

Strategy for finding the most butterflies: Roadsides offer the greatest butterfly diversity, particularly after rain has produced wildflowers. The roadway to Day Camps 3 and 4 (**A**), which passes through oaks and wetlands, may be most productive. Some of the more numerous butterflies include Black and Eastern Tiger swallowtails; Cloudless and Dainty sulphurs; Juniper and Red-banded hairstreaks; Eastern Tailed-Blue; Reakirt's Blue; Viceroy; Hackberry and Tawny emperors; Horace's Duskywing; Clouded, Fiery, Dun, and Delaware skippers; and Southern Broken-Dash.

Less common butterflies include Pipevine, Giant, and Spicebush swallowtails; Sleepy Orange; Dusky-blue Groundstreak; Eastern Comma; Red-spotted Purple; **Meske's Skipper**; and **Dusky Roadside-Skipper**. **Yehl** and **Broad-winged skippers** can be expected at the edges of wetlands and in adjacent fields. In spring, **Olympia Marble**, Falcate Orangetip, Oak Hairstreak, Henry's Elfin, and Juvenal's Duskywing are possible.

Next, visit the Dogwood Nature Trail (**B**) where **Crossline Skipper** is possible in the sandy grassland near the entrance. The Beaver Pond Nature Trail (**C**) beyond is likely to produce Pearl Crescent and Least Skipper.

Continue north to Eubanks Road (CO 473) and go east to where it crosses Catfish Creek (**D**). Check the moist roadsides and the picnic area for **Northern Broken-Dash** and **Little Glassywing**. Yucca Giant-Skipper flies in spring in yucca grasslands along the western portion of the road.

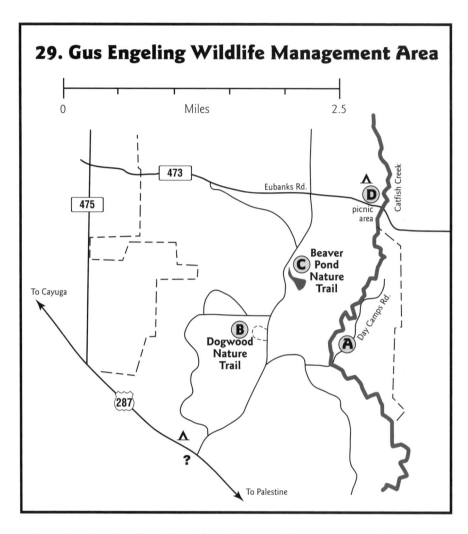

29. Gus Engeling Wildlife Management Area

In spring, Gus Engeling WMA also offers specialties more typical of the Piney-woods. **Zebra Swallowtail** can be widespread, and **Frosted Elfin** and **Eastern Pine Elfin** may be found in pine woodlands and along their edges. In addition, **Outis Skipper** has been recorded in open acacia grasslands.

Directions: In Anderson County, **Gus Engeling WMA (A-D)** is along US 287, 20 miles northwest of Palestine.

Nearest food, gas, and lodging: Palestine.

Nearest camping: Palestine; primitive sites in the WMA.

Along Day Camps Road, Gus Engeling Wildlife Management Area

Additional Worthwhile Sites in the Northern Plains Region

Lake Arrowhead Area. Southeast of Wichita Falls, the site includes Lake Arrowhead SP (fee area), located along the northwestern edge of 13,500-acre Lake Arrowhead, a reservoir on the Little Wichita River. Roads and trails within the park offer easy access to mesquite grassland, prairie, and riparian habitats. Take US 281 south from Wichita Falls to FM 1954. Turn east and follow it to the park.

Possum Kingdom Lake Area. This extensive area west of Fort Worth provides easy access to Possum Kingdom Lake and the riparian habitat along the Brazos River. The 1,615-acre Possum Kingdom SP (fee area) lies along the southwestern edge of the 19,800-acre lake. It offers a diversity of habitats, including juniper woodland, oak savannah, mesquite grassland, field, and riparian. From Mineral Wells, take US 180 west 37 miles to Caddo and go north 17 miles on PR 33 to the park.

Lake Mineral Wells State Park. This 2,809-acre park (fee area) features 646-acre Lake Mineral and 16 miles of trails that provide access to mesquite grassland, oak savannah, field, wetland, and riparian habitats. The park is only four miles east of Mineral Wells on US 180.

Dinosaur Valley State Park. Established to protect the numerous dinosaur tracks in the riverbed of the Paluxy River, this 1,523-acre park (fee area) also harbors many butterflies. David Powell coordinates July 4th Butterfly Counts here annually. The area is dominated by juniper-oak woodland with some bottomland-hardwood forest and riparian habitats. The park is located in Somervell County, four miles west of Glen Rose, southwest of Fort Worth. Take US 67 west to FM 205 and turn right to the park.

Parkhill Prairie/Clymer Meadow. These two sites are located east of McKinney off US 380. Beyond Farmersville, turn north on FM 36. Parkhill Prairie Preserve, county-owned, is located north of Merit. Turn west on CR 1130/CR 668. For Clymer Meadow, continue north on FM 36; turn east on FM 1562 and north on CR 1140. Clymer Meadow Preserve, including an undisturbed portion, is owned and managed by the Texas Nature Conservancy. Access to Clymer Meadow Preserve is by appointment only.

Fairfield Lake State Park. This 1,460-acre state park (fee area), located six miles northeast of Fairfield off FM 2570 or about 60 miles east of Waco, lies on the east and south sides of 2,400-acre Fairfield Lake, with constant warm water produced by the Big Brown Steam Electric Power Plant. The site has a diversity of habitats, including juniper-oak woodland, oak savannah, bottomland-hardwood forest, riparian, and marsh. Camping is available.

Copper Breaks State Park. This 1,933-acre state park features the 60-acre Lake Copper Breaks, an impoundment on Devil's Creek that flows south into the Pease River. The landscape is dominated by prairie and mesquite grassland; trails provide good access. It is located in Hardeman County west of Vernon along SH 6 between Quanah and Crowell.

Butterfly Checklist for the Northern Plains Region

The following list includes nine sites: **21. Lyndon B. Johnson National Grassland, 22. Lake Texoma/Hagerman National Wildlife Refuge, 23. Caddo National Grassland/Bonham State Park, 24. Fort Worth, 25. Dallas, 26. Heard Natural Science Museum and Wildlife Sanctuary, 27. Meridian State Park, 28. Waco,** and **29. Gus Engeling Wildlife Management Area**.

Status symbols include: A = abundant; C = common; U = uncommon; O = occasional; R = rare; X = accidental; M = migrant; TC = temporary colonist; ? = status unknown. (For a full definition of these terms, see p. 3.)

For trip notes, including dates and numbers of species seen, refer to the entry for this checklist in Appendix 3: Regional Checklist Resources.

Butterfly Species	21	22	23	24	25	26	27	28	29
Pipevine Swallowtail	U	C	U	A	C	C	C	C	U
Polydamas Swallowtail				X					
Zebra Swallowtail									O
Black Swallowtail	U	C	C	C	C	C	C	U	C
Thoas Swallowtail				X					
Giant Swallowtail	C	U	U	C	C	C	C	C	U
Eastern Tiger Swallowtail	C	U	U	C	C	C		C	C
Spicebush Swallowtail			U	O	X				U
Florida White		X			X				
Checkered White	U	A	C	U	U	C	C	C	C
Cabbage White	U		U	C	C	C	O	U	
Great Southern White	X			X	X			X	
Olympia Marble	U			O	O				R
Falcate Orangetip	C	U	U	C	U	U		U	U
Clouded Sulphur	U	U	U		O	U		U	
Orange Sulphur	A	A	A	A	C	C	C	A	C
Southern Dogface	C	C		U	C	U	C	U	C
White Angled-Sulphur					X				
Yellow Angled-Sulphur					X				
Cloudless Sulphur	C	A	C	C	C	C	C	C	C
Orange-barred Sulphur				X	X				
Large Orange Sulphur	U	U		X	X	U		R	
Lyside Sulphur	X		X	X	X				
Barred Yellow					X			X	
Mexican Yellow	U	X	X	U	R	U	U		X
Tailed Orange				X	X				
Little Yellow	A	A	C	C	C	C	A	C	C
Sleepy Orange	C	U		C	C	C	C	C	U
Dainty Sulphur	A	A	A	A	C	C	A	C	A
Harvester			U	O	O	U			
Great Purple Hairstreak	U			C	C	U	U	U	
Soapberry Hairstreak	A	C		C	C	C	U	C	
Coral Hairstreak	R			R	R				
Edwards' Hairstreak					X				
Banded Hairstreak	C			U	C	U		C	
Striped Hairstreak	U			R	U				
Oak Hairstreak	C			U	U			O	O
Frosted Elfin	X			X	R				U
Henry's Elfin	C			C	C	U		U	U
Eastern Pine Elfin									O
Juniper Hairstreak	U	U	U	C	C	C	A	C	C
White M Hairstreak	TC		U	U	O			R	U

Butterfly Species	21	22	23	24	25	26	27	28	29
Gray Hairstreak	C	A	C	A	C	A	A	C	C
Mallow Scrub-Hairstreak	R			X	X			U	
Red-banded Hairstreak	C	U	C	U	C	C		U	C
Dusky-blue Groundstreak	C			U	C	U	U	U	U
Gray Ministreak					X				
Western Pygmy-Blue		U		O	U			U	
Cassius Blue			X		X				
Marine Blue	TC	C		U	U	O	U		
Ceraunus Blue	U			U	U		O	C	
Reakirt's Blue	C	C	U	A	C	C	C	U	C
Eastern Tailed-Blue	A	A	A	C	C		C	C	C
Spring/Summer Azure				U	O	O	O		C
American Snout	A-R	A-R	A-R	A-R	A-R	A-R	A-R	A-R	A-R
Gulf Fritillary	U	C	U	A	C	C	C	A	C
Mexican Silverspot	X								
Julia Heliconian				X	X			X	
Zebra Heliconian				X	X	X		X	
Variegated Fritillary	C	U	A	C	C	C	C	C	C
Mexican Fritillary				X	X				
Theona Checkerspot					X				
Bordered Patch	C			U	U	U		U	
Crimson Patch					X				
Gorgone Checkerspot	A	U	U	C	C	U		U	
Silvery Checkerspot	C			C	C	U	U	C	C
Texan Crescent	U	U	U	C	U	U	R	R	
Vesta Crescent	TC		X	R	R	U		U	
Phaon Crescent	C	A	A	A	C	C	A	U	U
Pearl Crescent	C	A	C	A	C	C	C	A	C
Question Mark	C	U	U	C	C	U	U	C	C
Eastern Comma				X	R			X	U
Mourning Cloak	C		O	C	C			U	C
American Lady	A	U	U	C	C	C	C	C	C
Painted Lady	C	C	C	C	C	C	C	C	U
Red Admiral	A	U	U	A	C	C	C	A	C
Common Buckeye	C	C	C	C	C	C	C	C	C
White Peacock					X				
Malachite								X	
Red-spotted Purple	C		R	C	C	U	C	C	U
Viceroy	C	U	U	C	C	C		C	C
Arizona Sister	TC			R	X	X	X	R	
Common Mestra	R			R	R			R	
Many-banded Daggerwing					X				

Butterfly Species	21	22	23	24	25	26	27	28	29
Ruddy Daggerwing					X				
Tropical Leafwing					X				
Goatweed Leafwing	A	C	C	C	C	C	C	C	C
Angled Leafwing					X				
Hackberry Emperor	A	C	C	A	C	C	A	C	C
Empress Leilia					X				
Tawny Emperor	U	U	U	C	C	C	C	C	C
Northern Pearly-Eye	X								
Creole Pearly-Eye					X				
Gemmed Satyr	U		U	U	C	U			C
Carolina Satyr	U		U		U	O		O	C
Little Wood-Satyr	U	C	U	U	C	C	U	C	C
Red Satyr	R			R	R		C	C	
Common Wood-Nymph	C	A	A	U	U	U	A	C	U
Monarch	C	C	U	C	C	C	U	C	U
Queen	U	C	C	A	C	C	U	C	
Soldier					X				
Silver-spotted Skipper	U		U	C	C	O		U	U
Long-tailed Skipper	TC			O	U			U	
Dorantes Longtail					R	X			X
Hoary Edge	U			U	U				
Southern Cloudywing	U		R	O	U			R	
Northern Cloudywing	C	U		C	C	U	U	U	C
Confused Cloudywing	R			R	U				U
Outis Skipper	R			O	R				U
Mazans Scallopwing					X				
Hayhurst's Scallopwing	U	U	U	C	C	U		U	
Sickle-winged Skipper			X	C	X			X	
Hermit Skipper					X				
White-patched Skipper				X	X				
Sleepy Duskywing	U		R	R	U	U			R
Juvenal's Duskywing	C		U	U	C	U		U	U
Horace's Duskywing	C	C	U	C	C	C	C	C	C
Mottled Duskywing				X	U				U
Zarucco Duskywing				X	X				
Funereal Duskywing	U	U		C	C	U	U	U	
Wild Indigo Duskywing		U		U	U				U
Com. Checkered-Skipper	C	A	A	C	C	U	C	C	U
Tropical Checkered-Skipper				TC	TC				
Erichson's White-Skipper					X				
Laviana White-Skipper					X				
Common Streaky-Skipper				R	R				

Butterfly Species	21	22	23	24	25	26	27	28	29
Common Sootywing		U	C	U	U		U	U	
Swarthy Skipper				R	R				
Julia's Skipper	R			C	U		R		
Clouded Skipper	A			C	C	A		C	C
Least Skipper		U	C	U	C	C		U	C
Orange Skipperling		O	U	U	U		U	U	
Southern Skipperling				C	U		U	O	U
Fiery Skipper	C	C	A	A	C	C	C	C	C
Cobweb Skipper	C			R	U			X	
Green Skipper	U			U	U				
Dotted Skipper		U		R	R			R	
Meske's Skipper	R			R	R				C
Tawny-edged Skipper		C		U					
Crossline Skipper	X		C		U				C
Whirlabout				U		O		C	
Southern Broken-Dash	U	U	C	U	C	C	U	U	C
Northern Broken-Dash			C	R	R	R	X		U
Little Glassywing	X			X	X	U			O
Sachem	C	A	C	A	A	C	C	A	A
Arogos Skipper	R	U		R	R				
Delaware Skipper	R	U		C	C	U		O	
Zabulon Skipper	U	O		C	U	U			
Yehl Skipper									O
Broad-winged Skipper				R	O				A
Dion Skipper	U			U	C	C		U	
Two-spotted Skipper	X								
Dun Skipper	C	U	U	C	C	C	C	U	C
Dusted Skipper	O			O	R				
Bronze Roadside-Skipper				R					
Texas Roadside-Skipper			X						
Nysa Roadside-Skipper				U	U				
Dotted Roadside-Skipper	O			O	X				
Common Roadside-Skipper	C			C	U	U			U
Celia's Roadside-Skipper				C	C	O		R	
Bell's Roadside-Skipper	C	C	U	C	C	U	U		
Dusky Roadside-Skipper	O		O		R				O
Eufala Skipper	C	C	C	C	C	C	U	C	
Brazilian Skipper				U	U			U	U
Ocola Skipper	X	U		U	C	U		C	R
Yucca Giant-Skipper	O			U					U

Pineywoods

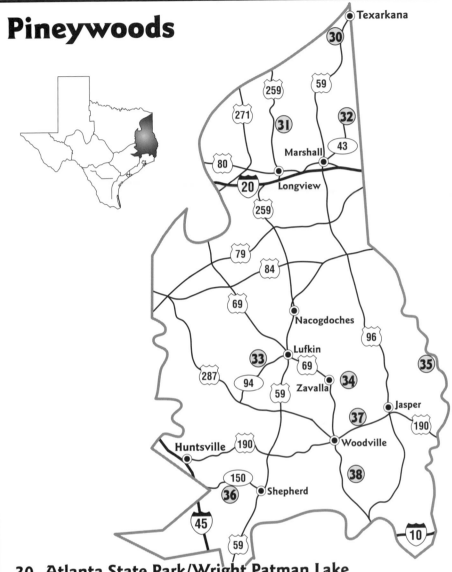

30. Atlanta State Park/Wright Patman Lake
31. Lake O' The Pines/Daingerfield State Park
32. Caddo Lake State Park and W.M.A.
33. Davy Crockett National Forest
34. Angelina National Forest/Sam Rayburn Reservoir
35. Sabine National Forest
36. Sam Houston National Forest
37. Martin Dies, Jr. State Park/B.A. Steinhagen Lake
38. Big Thicket Area

Pineywoods Region

The Texas Pineywoods are located in the eastern Texas "timber belt" along the border with Arkansas and Louisiana. The region covers about 15 million acres and extends westward to the Northern Plains and Central Plains regions. The landscape features gently rolling hills, open valleys, and the drainages of four major rivers: Angelina, Sabine, Neches, and Trinity. Hardwood trees dominate the floodplains, while conifers occur on the higher, drier slopes and ridges. Elevations range from 200 to 500 feet.

The Pineywoods Region is represented by nine sites: **30. Atlanta State Park/Wright Patman Lake**, **31. Lake O' The Pines/Daingerfield State Park**, **32. Caddo Lake State Park and Wildlife Management Area**, **33. Davy Crockett National Forest**, **34. Angelina National Forest/Sam Rayburn Reservoir**, **35. Sabine National Forest**, **36. Sam Houston National Forest**, **37. Martin Dies, Jr. State Park/B.A. Steinhagen Lake**, and **38. Big Thicket Area**. The best time to visit these sites is March through October.

Pineywoods Specialties

Butterfly diversity in this region, with 28 area specialties, ranks third behind the Lower Rio Grande Valley and Trans-Pecos regions.

Swallowtails, Hairstreaks: **Zebra Swallowtail** is usually widespread and abundant in early spring, often absent or rare in April, with a second, less numerous but longer-tailed summer population that can appear as early as mid-May. Larvae feed on pawpaw. An isolated population of **Edwards' Hairstreak** has been recorded in scrub-oak woodlands of Hardin County in the Big Thicket Area. Adults fly June to August; larvae feed on scrub-oak foliage. **King's Hairstreak** has been recorded in May and June in "brushy hardwood forests" where common sweetleaf (larval foodplant) grows in Sabine NF, Martin Dies, Jr. SP/B. A. Steinhagen L., and the Big Thicket Area. **Frosted Elfin** occurs throughout the region during March and April, most often along roadsides, in fields, and in open woods where lupines and false indigo (larval foodplants) grow. **Eastern Pine Elfin** prefers pine woodlands and their edges throughout the region, often perching on pine foliage (larval foodplants) in spring. Jarring pines may flush perched females.

Blues, Metalmarks: **Silvery Blue**, one of the earliest spring butterflies, has been recorded from March to June only in Cass County at Atlanta SP/Wright Patman L. Larval foodplants include species of legumes, such as lupines, locoweeds, and vetch. **Little Metalmark** occurs in grassy fields in or near pine woodlands in Martin Dies, Jr. SP/B. A. Steinhagen L. and the Big Thicket Area. Males usually perch on or near the ground; larvae feed on yellow thistle.

Pearly-eyes, Satyrs: **Southern Pearly-eye** frequents stands of giant cane (larval food-plant) in moist, shady woodlands throughout most of the Pineywoods. Males are very territorial, returning constantly to a favorite perch. **Creole Pearly-eye** prefers dense, moist woodlands in Angelina NF, Sabine NF, Sam Houston NF, Martin Dies, Jr. SP/ B. A. Steinhagen L., and the Big Thicket Area. Males are very territorial and often fly at dusk. Larvae feed on giant cane. **Georgia Satyr** is most likely to be found in grassy wetlands, such as pitcherplant bogs, in open woodlands, in Sabine NF, Sam Houston NF, and the Big Thicket Area. Larvae feed on Indiangrass.

Spread-wing Skippers: **Zarucco Duskywing** occurs in open areas such as roadsides and right-of-ways. Although its range extends throughout the region, it has been recorded only in Atlanta SP/Wright Patman L., Sam Houston NF, and the Big Thicket Area. Larval foodplants include legumes, such as black locust, bushclover, and sesbania.

Grass-Skippers: **Neamathla Skipper** occurs in open, grassy areas near moist woodlands in Martin Dies, Jr. SP/B. A. Steinhagen L. and the Big Thicket Area. **Cobweb Skipper** flies near bluestem grass in March and April. It has been recorded only in the northern Pineywoods in Atlanta SP/Wright Patman L., Lake O' The Pines/ Daingerfield SP, and Martin Dies, Jr. SP/B. A. Steinhagen L. **Meske's Skipper** occurs along roadsides and in clearings in open woods in Angelina NF, Sabine NF, Martin Dies, Jr. SP/B. A. Steinhagen L., and the Big Thicket Area. **Tawny-edged Skipper** prefers short-grass areas, even lawns, in Davy Crockett NF, Sabine NF, Martin Dies, Jr. SP/B. A. Steinhagen L., and the Big Thicket Area. **Crossline Skipper** frequents sandy grasslands from June to August in Atlanta SP/Wright Patman L., Angelina NF, Sabine NF, Martin Dies, Jr. SP/B. A. Steinhagen L., and the Big Thicket Area. **Northern Broken-Dash** is occasional to rare throughout the Pineywoods in moist, grassy areas near woodlands. **Little Glassywing** frequents moist, shady areas near woodlands throughout the region. It has two broods, in April-May and July-August. **Zabulon Skipper** is most likely to be found in grassy clearings in moist woods in Atlanta SP/Wright Patman L., Caddo Lake SP, and Angelina NF. **Yehl Skipper** occurs throughout the region in swampy woods and wetland thickets with giant cane, its larval foodplant. It has two broods, in May-June and August-September. **Broad-winged Skipper** frequents wetlands with sedges, but it often perches on taller grasses, such as cattails. It has been recorded only in Davy Crockett NF and Sam Houston NF. **Dion Skipper** utilizes wetland edges with sedges (its larval foodplant) in Atlanta SP/Wright Patman L., Lake O' The Pines/Daingerfield SP, and Caddo Lake SP. **Dukes' Skipper** frequents wetlands where sedges grow in Caddo Lake SP, Martin Dies, Jr. SP/B. A. Steinhagen L., and the Big Thicket Area, but it is seldom encountered. An earlier name for this species was "Scarce Swamp Skipper." **Pepper and Salt Skipper** is most likely to be seen at brushy areas near streams or in moist woods in Atlanta SP/Wright Patman L., Caddo Lake SP, Angelina NF, Sabine NF, and the Big Thicket Area. **Lace-winged Roadside-Skipper** occurs at patches of cane (larval foodplant) in pine woodlands in Caddo Lake SP, Angelina NF, Sabine NF, Sam Houston NF, Martin Dies, Jr. SP/B. A. Steinhagen L., and the Big Thicket Area. **Bell's Roadside-Skipper** is found along the edges of dense woodlands and moist clearings and fields in Atlanta SP/Wright Patman L., Lake O' The Pines/Daingerfield SP, Caddo Lake SP, Sabine NF, and the Big Thicket Area. **Dusky Roadside-Skipper** has been recorded at the edges of moist pine forests in Atlanta SP/Wright Patman L., Angelina NF, Martin Dies, Jr. SP/B. A. Steinhagen L., and the Big Thicket Area. **Twin-spot Skipper** frequents patches of wildflowers near swampy areas and moist woodlands in Sam Houston NF, Martin Dies, Jr. SP/B. A. Steinhagen L., and the Big Thicket Area. Two broods have been recorded, in April-May and August-September.

Sites within the Pineywoods Region

30. Atlanta State Park/Wright Patman Lake

The 1,474-acre Atlanta State Park (fee area) is located on the southern edge of Wright Patman Lake in the extreme northeastern corner of Texas, near the Arkansas border. Butterfly-watching spots in the park include roadsides (**A**), Hickory Hollow Nature Trail (**B**), and the trail along the shoreline (**C**).

Wright Patman's 18,500-foot-long dam formed a 20,300-acre impoundment on the Sulphur River, which flows east to the Red River in southwestern Arkansas. Several parks (fee areas) along the lakeshore provide good butterflying. These include Clear Springs (**D**), Paradise Cove (**E**), Piney Point (**F**), and Rocky Point (**G**).

Habitats: Bottomland-hardwood forest, pine forest, field, pasture, and riparian.

Strategy for finding the most butterflies: Start at Atlanta SP by walking the roads, checking the roadsides and woodland edges (**A**). Some of the more numerous butterflies include **Zebra** and Spicebush swallowtails, Cloudless and Dainty sulphurs, Little Yellow, Juniper Hairstreak, Eastern Tailed-Blue, Gulf Fritillary, Phaon Crescent, Red-spotted Purple, Carolina Satyr, Horace's Duskywing, Southern Broken-Dash, and Sachem. Less numerous butterflies include Black, Giant, and Eastern Tiger swallowtails; Sleepy Orange; Great Purple and Red-banded hairstreaks; Silvery Checkerspot; Hackberry Emperor; Silver-spotted Skipper; Hoary Edge; Southern and Confused cloudywings; Sleepy and Funereal duskywings; and Common, **Bell's**, and **Dusky roadside-skippers**.

In spring, Falcate Orangetip, Banded Hairstreak, Henry's Elfin, and Juvenal's Duskywing can be expected throughout the area; **Frosted** and **Eastern Pine elfins** are possible in pine woodlands; **Cobweb Skipper** frequents big-bluestem areas, and **Zabulon Skipper** is possible in shaded openings in woodlands. **Silvery Blue** has been reported in early spring, and Ocola Skipper is likely to be found in fall.

Next, walk the Hickory Hollow Nature Trail (**B**) and the shoreline trail (**C**) that begins at the boat ramp. Most of the butterflies mentioned above are possible here, but additional species of interest include Viceroy, Gemmed Satyr, Little Wood-Satyr, Hayhurst's Scallopwing, and Least Skipper. Look for **Southern Pearly-eye** where cane grows, **Northern Broken-Dash** and **Little Glassywing** in moist, grassy areas, **Yehl Skipper** in swampy areas, **Dion Skipper** in sedges, and **Pepper and Salt Skipper** in brushy areas.

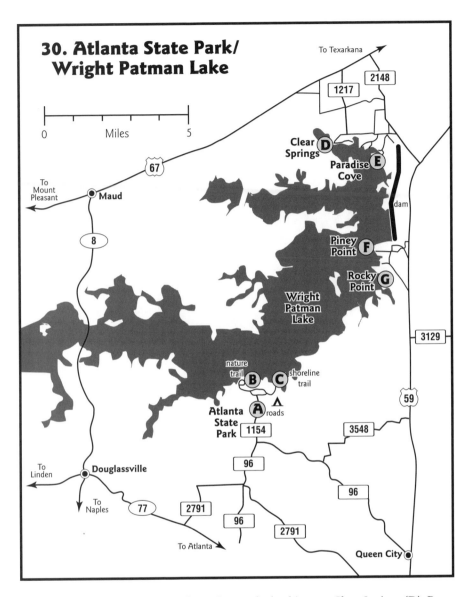

30. Atlanta State Park/ Wright Patman Lake

To Texarkana

2148

1217

0 Miles 5

67

To Mount Pleasant

Maud

8

Clear Springs **D**

Paradise Cove **E**

dam

Piney Point **F**

Rocky Point **G**

Wright Patman Lake

3129

nature trail

B **C**

shoreline trail

Atlanta State Park **A** roads

1154

59

3548

96

To Linden

Douglassville

To Naples

77

2791

96

96

2791

To Atlanta

Queen City

Among the Wright Patman Lake parks worth checking are Clear Springs (**D**), Paradise Cove (**E**), Piney Point (**F**), and Rocky Point (**G**). Walk the open and gated roadways, where **Zarucco Duskywing** and **Crossline Skipper** are possible, as well as many of the species mentioned above.

Directions: In Bowie and Cass Counties, the lake is located west of US 59 between Atlanta and Texarkana. To reach **Atlanta SP (A-C)**, take FM 96 northwest from Queen City to FM 1154. Turn north and go two miles to the park. **Piney Point (F)**

Paradise Cove, Wright Patman Lake

and **Rocky Point (G)** are south of the Wright Patman Lake dam off US 59, 2.5 miles north of FM 3129. Turn left and follow the signs. **Clear Springs (D)** and **Paradise Cove (E)** are north of the dam. Proceed to FM 2148 and turn left on Clear Springs Rd. for both parks.

Nearest food, gas and lodging: Queen City and Texarkana; food and gas three miles south of Atlanta SP.

Nearest camping: Atlanta SP and lakeside parks.

31. Lake O' The Pines/Daingerfield State Park

The 18,700-acre Lake O' The Pines was created in the 1950s when Cypress Creek was dammed for flood control. It is primarily a recreational lake and has numerous hidden bays and side streams. Key butterfly sites include parks (fee areas) around the 18-mile-long lake: Cypress Creek **(A)**, Lakeside and Shady Grove Parks **(B)**, Cedar Springs Park **(C)**, and Lone Star Ramp **(D)**.

The 551-acre Daingerfield State Park (fee area) features 88-acre Lake Daingerfield. A 2.5-mile hiking trail that circles the lake **(E)** and park roadsides **(F)** are the best places for finding butterflies. Roadsides **(G, H, I)** between the park and the lake provide additional opportunities.

Habitats: Bottomland-hardwood forest, pine forest, riparian, field, and cropland.

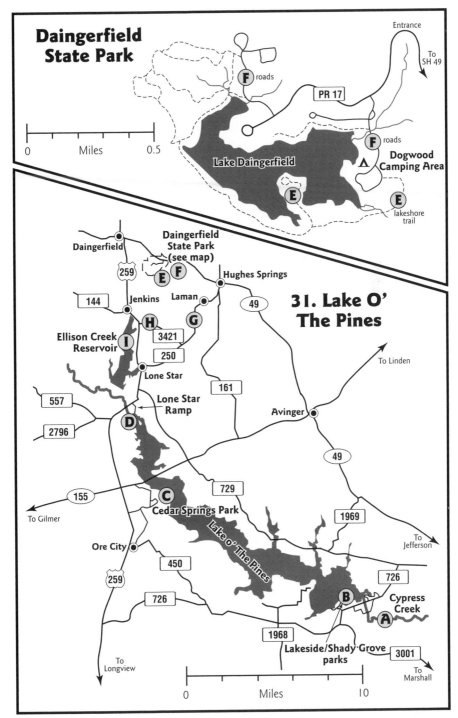

Daingerfield
State Park

Entrance

To
SH 49

F roads

PR 17

F roads

0 Miles 0.5

Lake Daingerfield

Dogwood
Camping Area

E

E

lakeshore
trail

Daingerfield
State Park
(see map)

E **F**

Daingerfield

259

Hughes Springs

144 Jenkins Laman

H **G**

3421

250

I

Ellison Creek
Reservoir

Lone Star

31. Lake O'
The Pines

49

To Linden

Lone Star
Ramp

161

Avinger

557

D

2796

49

155

729

To Gilmer

1969

C

Cedar Springs Park

To
Jefferson

Ore City

726

259

450

726

3001

1968

Lakeside/Shady Grove
parks

B

Cypress
Creek

A

To Longview

0 Miles 10

To
Marshall

Lake Daingerfield, Daingerfield State Park

Strategy for finding the most butterflies: The highest butterfly diversity is most likely to be found at the park lands adjacent to Lake O' The Pines. They include Cypress Creek (**A**) and Lakeside and Shady Grove parks (**B**) at the south end and Cedar Springs Park (**C**) and Lone Star Ramp (**D**) to the north. Some of the more numerous butterflies include Pipevine, **Zebra**, Eastern Tiger, and Spicebush swallowtails; Cloudless Sulphur; Red-banded Hairstreak; Eastern Tailed-Blue; Gulf Fritillary; Gorgone Checkerspot; Red-spotted Purple; and Least Skipper.

Less numerous species include Black and Giant swallowtails, Harvester, Silvery Checkerspot, Eastern Comma, Gemmed and Carolina satyrs, Little Wood-Satyr, Silver-spotted Skipper, Hoary Edge, Northern and Confused cloudywings, Sleepy and Funereal duskywings, and **Bell's Roadside-Skipper**. In spring, Falcate Orangetip, Banded and Striped hairstreaks, Henry's Elfin, and Juvenal's Duskywing can be expected throughout the area. **Frosted** and **Eastern Pine elfins** frequent pine woodlands, and **Cobweb Skipper** occurs in big-bluestem areas. Ocola Skipper can be expected in fall.

Next, drive to Daingerfield SP and walk the hiking trail around the lake (**E**) or at least the section that starts at the Dogwood Camping Area. Also check the roadsides (**F**). Several of the butterflies mentioned above are likely, but watch for **Southern Pearly-eye** where cane grows, **Northern Broken-Dash** and **Little Glassywing** in moist, grassy areas, and **Dion Skipper** at sedges.

In addition, the roadsides between Lake O' The Pines and the state park are worth checking when wildflowers are present. Principal roads to explore include FM 250 (**G**) and FM 3421 (**H**) southwest of Laman and roads near Ellison Creek Reservoir (**I**).

Directions: In Marion and Morris counties, Lake O' The Pines is between I-20 and I-30, 26 miles northwest of Marshall. Take FM 1997 to FM 3001; turn left and follow it to FM 726. Turn right. **Lakeside and Shady Grove parks (B)** are about a mile ahead on the left. Access to **Cypress Creek (A)** is on the right in the same vicinity. You can also reach this area from Jefferson by taking SH 49 to a left on FM 729. Then turn left on FM 726 to the parks.

Return to FM 726 and go west. Where it joins FM 450, continue north on FM 450 to Ore City. Turn right on US 259 and go to SH 155. Turn right and go a half-mile to a right turn on Old Highway 155 to **Cedar Springs Park (C)**. Return to US 259 and drive north to where the highway curves right before entering Lone Star. Find the road to the **Lone Star Ramp (D)** on the right, just past the bridge over Big Cypress Creek.

West of US 259 in Lone Star, explore roads along **Ellison Creek Reservoir (I)**. Then take **FM 250 (G)** east from Lone Star. Check its roadsides and those of **FM 3421 (H)** to the northwest, off FM 250. When you're finished, take FM 250 to Hughes Springs or take FM 3421 and US 259 to Daingerfield. **Daingerfield SP (E, F)** is located off SH 49 between those two towns.

Nearest food, gas, and lodging: Jefferson and Daingerfield; food and gas in Hughes Springs and at sites around Lake O' The Pines.

Nearest camping: Daingerfield SP and at lakeside parks.

32. Caddo Lake State Park and Wildlife Management Area

Caddo Lake (32,000 acres) predates any other large lake in Texas. The state park is dominated by one of the finest cypress swamps in the state, with numerous stands of bald cypress trees from 250 to 400 years old. The significance of the area is recognized by the Ramsar Convention on Wetlands of International Importance. The best example of this fascinating environment occurs in 478-acre Caddo Lake State Park (fee area). Surrounding areas have been designated a wildlife management area.

Specific sites to visit in the WMA include roadsides along CR 314 **(A)**, FM 134 **(B)**, and FM 2198 **(C)**. At the state park, check the roads **(D)** and the hiking trails **(E)**.

Habitats: Cypress swamp, marsh, bottomland-hardwood forest, mixed conifer-deciduous forest, pine forest, riparian, field, and pasture.

Strategy for finding the most butterflies: Start along the CR 314 loop **(A)** north of the lake within Caddo Lake WMA. Its weedy roadsides and forested habitats can produce a variety of common butterflies, including **Zebra**, Eastern Tiger, and Spicebush swallowtails; Cloudless Sulphur; Red-banded Hairstreak; Phaon Crescent; Red-spotted Purple; Gemmed and Carolina satyrs; Northern Cloudywing; Funereal Duskywing; and Common Roadside-Skipper.

A few of the less numerous butterflies include Pipevine, Black, and Giant swallow-tails; Harvester; Great Purple Hairstreak; Eastern Tailed-Blue; Gulf Fritillary; Gorgone Checkerspot; Eastern Comma; Little Wood-Satyr; Silver-spotted Skipper; Southern

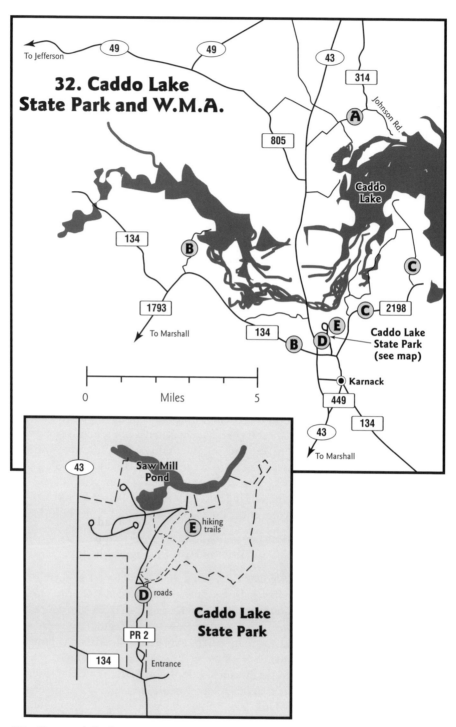

32. Caddo Lake State Park and W.M.A.

To Jefferson

49

49

43

314

805

Johnson Rd.

A

Caddo Lake

134

B

C

1793

C

2198

To Marshall

134

E

B

D

Caddo Lake State Park (see map)

Karnack

449

43

134

To Marshall

0   Miles   5

43

Saw Mill Pond

E hiking trails

D roads

Caddo Lake State Park

PR 2

134 Entrance

Caddo Lake, Caddo Lake State Park

and Confused cloudywings; Horace's Duskywing; **Northern Broken-Dash**; and **Bell's Roadside-Skipper**. Also drive south on SH 43 to FM 134 **(B)**, FM 2198 **(C)**, and nearby side roads, where you should check the roadsides and pull-offs.

In spring, Falcate Orangetip, Banded and Striped hairstreaks, Henry's Elfin, and Juvenal's Duskywing occur throughout the area. **Frosted** and **Eastern Pine elfins** frequent open pine stands, and **Cobweb Skipper** is possible in places where big bluestem grass grows.

At Caddo Lake SP, check the roadsides and parking lot edges **(D)** and walk the network of hiking trails **(E)**. The lower trail near the boat ramp provides access to stands of cane, where **Southern Pearly-eye** and **Lace-winged Roadside-Skipper** are likely to be found, and sedge areas, where **Dion** and **Dukes' skippers** are possible. Other possibilities include **Pepper and Salt Skipper** along brushy shorelines and **Zabulon Skipper** in clearings along the upper woodland trail.

Directions: In Marion and Harrison Counties, Caddo Lake SP and WMA is along SH 43. **Caddo Lake SP (D, E)** is 15 miles northeast of Marshall. Take SH 43 to the intersection with **FM 134 (B)** and FM 2198; turn right to the entrance on the left. **FM 2198 (C)** continues east beyond that point. **CR 314 loop (A)** is 5.5 miles north of FM 134, east off SH 43 just past the intersection with FM 805.

Nearest gas, food, and lodging: Marshall; gas and food at Karnack, near the state park.

Nearest camping: Caddo Lake SP.

33. Davy Crockett National Forest

The 161,497-acre Davy Crockett National Forest, named for the legendary pioneer, has several areas managed for red-cockaded woodpeckers, which also provide habitat for a number of woodland butterflies. The NF has a network of roadways, and a portion of the twenty-mile-long Four C Hiking Trail runs between the first two butterfly stops, Ratcliff Lake Recreation Area (**A**) and Neches Overlook (**B**). The Neches River forms the eastern boundary of the NF. Other sites include Holly Bluff Swamp (**C**), Alabama Creek WMA (**D**), and roadsides along FR 509 (**E**) and FR 541 (**F**).

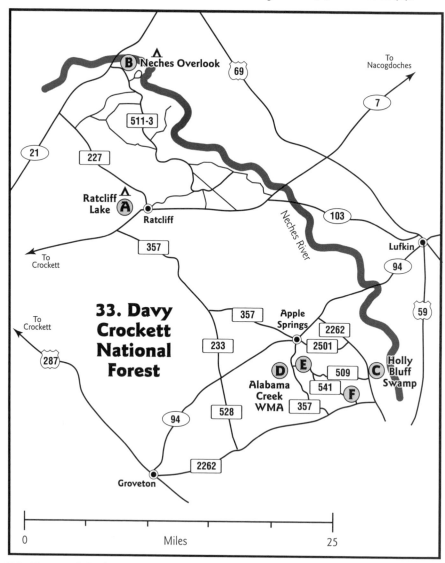

Ratcliff Lake, Davy Crockett National Forest

Habitats: Bottomland-hardwood forest, mixed pine-hardwood forest, pine forest, swamp, field, pasture, and riparian.

Strategy for finding the most butterflies: There are four principal butterfly-watching locations, two north of SH 7 and two south. Start on the north side at Ratcliff Lake Recreation Area (**A**) by checking the roadsides, walking the edges of the campground, and walking a portion of the Four C Trail (in spring). Some of the more numerous butterflies include **Zebra**, Giant, Eastern Tiger, Spicebush, and Palamedes swallowtails; Cloudless Sulphur; Red-banded Hairstreak; Eastern Tailed-Blue; Carolina Satyr; Little Wood-Satyr; Horace's and Wild Indigo duskywings; and Southern Broken-Dash.

Less numerous butterflies include Pipevine and Black swallowtails; Great Purple Hairstreak; Gulf Fritillary; Silvery Checkerspot; Eastern Comma; Red-spotted Purple; Gemmed Satyr; and Silver-spotted, **Tawny-edged**, and **Twin-spot skippers**. **Little Glassywing** may be seen in moist, grassy areas. In spring, Falcate Orangetip, Henry's Elfin, and Juvenal's Duskywing are widespread, while **Frosted** and **Eastern Pine elfins** occur in pine woodlands.

Farther north, Neches Overlook (**B**) can be productive in spring when wildflowers are present. To the south are Holly Bluff Swamp (**C**) and nearby Alabama Creek WMA (**D**). Both are especially productive in spring and fall. Phaon Crescent and Least Skipper are likely. **Yehl Skipper** is possible in swampy areas with cane growth, and **Broad-winged Skipper** is most likely to be found at wetlands with sedge. Also check the roadsides along FR 509 (**E**) and FR 541 (**F**) and walk into the adjacent forest.

Directions: In Houston and Trinity Counties, **Ratcliff Lake (A)** is along SH 7, 20 miles east of Crockett and 25 miles west of Lufkin (via SH 103). **Neches Overlook (B)** is located northeast of Crockett along SH 21. Take FR 511-3 south a short distance to the overlook on the left. To reach the overlook from Ratcliff Lake, go east on SH 7 to a left turn on FM 227. Follow it to SH 21 and turn right to FR 511-3.

To continue to the areas south of SH 7 from Ratcliff Lake, go west on SH 7 and turn south on FM 357. To find **Holly Bluff Swamp (C)**, follow FM 357 to SH 94; turn east and go about two miles to FM 2262. Turn south and continue past the intersection with FM 2501 to FR 510A (Holly Bluff Rd.); turn east to the swamp. Return to FM 2262 and turn south a short distance to **FR 509 (E)**. Turn west to check the roadsides. The intersection with **FR 541 (F)** is a few miles ahead. Turn south and explore it to FM 2262. Turn west on FM 2262 and north on FM 357 to reach **Alabama Creek WMA (D)**.

Nearest food, gas, and lodging: Groveton, Crockett, and Lufkin; food and gas at Apple Springs.

Nearest camping: Ratcliff Lake and Holly Bluff.

34. Angelina National Forest/Sam Rayburn Reservoir

Sam Rayburn Reservoir, one of the largest lakes in Texas at 114,500 acres, is surrounded by Angelina National Forest, the smallest in Texas, with 154,307 acres. The site has several parks along the reservoir's shoreline and a variety of recreation areas administered by the U.S. Forest Service. The most productive is Boykin Springs Recreation Area **(A)**, with its extensive campground, pond and stream, trails, and adjacent utility right-of-way. Other good places to find butterflies include Sandy Creek Recreation Area **(B)**, Caney Creek Recreation Area **(C)**, Pouland Road **(D)**, a wetland **(E)**, Jackson Hill Park **(F)**, Monterey Park **(G)**, and Hanks Creek Park **(H)**.

Habitats: Bottomland-hardwood forest, mixed pine-hardwood forest, longleaf-pine savannah, riparian, field, and pasture.

Strategy for finding the most butterflies: Start at the Boykin Springs RA **(A)** by exploring the edges of the campground and walking the adjacent trails. Some of the more numerous butterflies include Pipevine, **Zebra**, Eastern Tiger, Spicebush, and Palamedes swallowtails; Cloudless Sulphur; Red-banded Hairstreak; Eastern Tailed-Blue; Silvery Checkerspot; Red-spotted Purple; Gemmed and Carolina satyrs; Little Wood-Satyr; Northern Cloudywing; Horace's Duskywing; Least Skipper; Southern Broken-Dash; and Common Roadside-Skipper.

Less numerous are Black and Giant swallowtails, Large Orange and Dainty sulphurs, Sleepy Orange, Great Purple and White M hairstreaks, Gulf Fritillary, Gorgone Checkerspot, Silver-spotted Skipper, Hoary Edge, Southern and Confused cloudywings, Sleepy Duskywing, and Tropical Checkered-Skipper. Also possible are **Dusky Roadside-Skipper** along the entrance road, **Meske's** and **Crossline skippers** in open, grassy areas along the utility right-of-way, **Northern Broken-Dash** at moist,

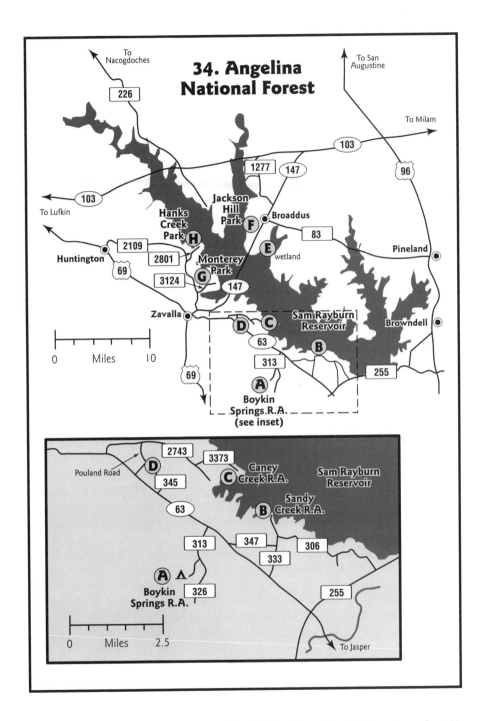

34. Angelina National Forest

To Nacogdoches

226

To San Augustine

To Milam

103

1277 147

96

To Lufkin

103

Jackson Hill Park **F**

Broaddus

Hanks Creek Park **H**

83

Pineland

2109

Huntington

2801

Monterey Park

E wetland

69

3124

G

147

Zavalla

D **C**

Sam Rayburn Reservoir

Browndell

0 Miles 10

63

B

313

255

69

A

Boykin Springs R.A.
(see inset)

Pouland Road

D 2743 3373

345

C Caney Creek R.A.

Sam Rayburn Reservoir

63

B Sandy Creek R.A.

313 347

306

333

A △

Boykin Springs R.A. 326

255

0 Miles 2.5

To Jasper

Angelina National Forest

brushy areas, and **Pepper and Salt Skipper** along the stream. Look for **Southern Pearly-eye** and **Lace-winged Roadside-Skipper** behind the campground where cane grows; **Creole Pearly-eye** prefers deep, moist forests.

In spring, Falcate Orangetip, Banded and Oak hairstreaks, Henry's Elfin, and Juvenal's Duskywing usually are widespread. **Frosted** and **Eastern Pine elfins** frequent pine woodlands. Yucca Giant-Skipper may be seen in the utility right-of-way.

Nearby Sandy Creek RA (**B**) can also be worthwhile. Many of the butterflies mentioned above are possible but also watch for **Little Glassywing** at moist, grassy areas. Just north is Caney Creek RA (**C**) with its lakeshore environment, where **Yehl Skipper** is possible in brushy areas.

Also visit Pouland Road (**D**), between Caney Creek and SH 63, a good area for elfins in spring. **Zabulon Skipper** is possible in shaded clearings. Watch for **Twin-spot Skipper** at roadside wildflowers.

Two potentially good locations northeast of Zavalla off SH 147 include a small wetland (**E**) just north of the bridge on the east side and Jackson Hill Park (**F**) west of the road. North of Zavalla are Monterey Park (**G**) and Hanks Creek Park (**H**), also worth checking.

Directions: In Angelina, Jasper, and San Augustine counties, take US 69 from Lufkin 22 miles southeast to Zavalla. Continue 10.5 miles on SH 63 to a turn south on FM 313 and go 2.5 miles to **Boykin Springs RA (A)**. For **Sandy Creek RA (B)**, return to SH 63 and turn right. Watch for a sign at FM 333 and go north to the park. To reach **Caney Creek RA (C)**, return to SH 63 and turn northwest toward Zavalla. Turn right on CR 345, **Pouland Rd. (D)**. Check the roadsides as you continue to FM 2743. Turn east and go to FM 3373. Turn left and follow it to the park. Return to SH 63 on FM 2743 and turn west to Zavalla.

From Zavalla, go northeast on SH 147. Just across the bridge, check out the small **wetland (E)** on the right. Continue on SH 147 to FM 3185 and turn left to **Jackson Hill Park (F)**. Return to Zavalla and take FM 2109 north to CR 3124. Turn east to **Monterey Park (G)**. For **Hanks Creek Park (H)**, return to FM 2109 and turn north. Find a turn east on FM 2801 to the park.

Nearest food, gas, and lodging: Lufkin and Nacogdoches; food and gas at Zavalla and Broaddus.

Nearest camping: Townsend, Jackson Hill, Hanks Creek, Monterey, Caney Creek, Sandy Creek, and Boykin Springs.

35. Sabine National Forest

Sabine National Forest is situated along the western shore of Toledo Bend Reservoir, the eastern shore of which is in Louisiana. The lake, formed by damming the Sabine River, and the various parks are administered by the Texas Sabine River Authority. The recreation areas within the 157,951-acre national forest are managed by the U.S. Forest Service.

Specific sites for butterflying include the following recreation areas: Lakeview Recreation Area **(A)**, Indian Mounds Recreation Area **(B)**, Red Hills Lake Recreation Area **(E)**, and Ragtown Recreation Area **(F)**. Roadsides along FR 113 **(C)** and CR 3315 **(D)** provide other viewing opportunities.

Habitats: Mixed pine-hardwood forest, pine forest, field, pasture, and riparian.

Strategy for finding the most butterflies: Start at Lakeview RA **(A)** by walking along the lake beyond the primitive camping area. Some of the more numerous butterflies in this riparian habitat include Pipevine, **Zebra**, Giant, Eastern Tiger, and Spicebush swallowtails; Cloudless Sulphur; Little Yellow; Red-banded Hairstreak; Eastern Tailed-Blue; Gorgone Checkerspot; Carolina Satyr; and Northern Cloudywing. A few of the less numerous but widespread butterflies include Black and Palamedes swallowtails, Southern Dogface, Sleepy Orange, Reakirt's Blue, Gulf Fritillary, Phaon Crescent, and Silver-spotted Skipper.

In spring, Falcate Orangetip, Henry's Elfin, and Juvenal's Duskywing are widespread. **Frosted** and **Eastern Pine elfins** are likely to be found in pine woodlands, and **Crossline** and **Pepper and Salt skippers** are possible in moist, grassy areas. **King's Hairstreak** has been reported in brushy, hardwood forests in May and June.

Next, drive to nearby Indian Mounds RA **(B)** and check the brushy slopes below the campground; watch for **Southern Pearly-eye** and **Lace-winged Roadside-**

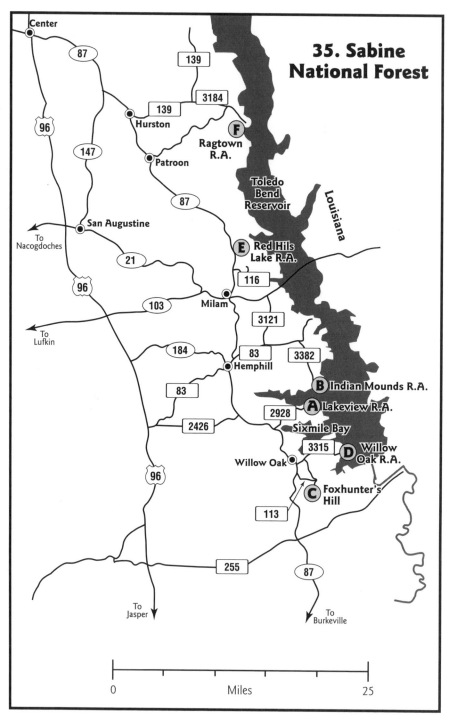

35. Sabine National Forest

Center

87

139

139   3184

Hurston   F   Ragtown R.A.

96

147   Patroon

87   Toledo Bend Reservoir   Louisiana

San Augustine

To Nacogdoches

21   E   Red Hils Lake R.A.

96   116

103   Milam

To Lufkin   3121

184   83   3382

Hemphill   B   Indian Mounds R.A.

83   A   Lakeview R.A.

2928

2426   Sixmile Bay

3315   D   Willow Oak R.A.

Willow Oak

C   Foxhunter's Hill

96   113

255   87

To Jasper   To Burkeville

0   Miles   25

Polydamas Swallowtail

Southern Dogface

Zebra Swallowtail

Great Purple Hairstreak

Spicebush Swallowtail

Great Southern White, mating pair

Soapberry Hairstreak

Oak Hairstreak

Poling's Hairstreak

Henry's Elfin

Juniper Hairstreak

Mallow Scrub-Hairstreak

Dusky-blue Groundstreak

Rounded Metalmark

"Chisos" Nais Metalmark

Mormon Metalmark

Red-bordered Pixie

Gulf Fritillary

Zebra Heliconian

Theona Checkerspot

Crimson Patch

Pale-banded Crescent

Texan Crescent

Question Mark

Mangrove Buckeye

White Peacock

Red-spotted Purple

Tropical Leafwing

Mexican Bluewing

Arizona Sister

Southern Pearly-Eye

Common Wood-Nymph

Queen

White-striped Longtail

Two-barred Flasher

Golden Banded-Skipper

Coyote Cloudywing

Texas Powdered-Skipper

Sickle-winged Skipper

Turks-cap White-Skipper, mating pair

Common Streaky-Skipper

Fawn-spotted Skipper

Double-dotted Skipper

Green Skipper

Zabulon Skipper

Aaron's Skipper

Lace-winged Roadside-Skipper

Obscure Skipper

Sabine National Forest

Skipper among the patches of cane growth. **Creole Pearly-eye** prefers dense, moist forests, and **Georgia Satyr** frequents marshy habitats.

Farther south, drive FR 113 (**C**), a forested road good for Red-spotted Purple, Little Wood-Satyr, Hoary Edge, Southern and Confused cloudywings, Sleepy and Horace's duskywings, and **Bell's Roadside-Skipper**. Also watch for **Meske's Skipper** and **Northern Broken-Dash**.

Nearby CR 3315 (**D**) to Willow Oak RA is also worthwhile. To the north of Milam are Red Hills Lake RA (**E**) and Ragtown RA (**F**). Check the roadsides, edges, and trails at each of them. Swarthy Skipper frequents grassy areas, including lawns; **Little Glassywing** prefers moist, grassy places, even ditches; and **Twin-spot Skipper** is most likely to be seen at low-growing wildflowers.

Directions: In Sabine and Newton Counties, all the recreation areas are accessed from SH 87. Begin in Hemphill, east of US 96. Take SH 87 south to FM 2928 just before the highway crosses the lake. Turn east to **Lakeview RA (A)**. Return to SH 87. Before continuing to the next key site, you may want to explore **CR 3315 (D)** and **FR 113 (C)** a short distance south. Both are east of SH 87. Return to Hemphill and continue on US 87 to a turn east on FM 83. Follow it to a right turn on CR 3382, which leads to **Indian Mounds RA (B)**. Return to SH 87 and turn north. Continue past SH 103 to FR 116 and turn east to **Red Hills Lake RA (E)**. To reach **Ragtown RA (F)**, continue north on SH 87 to Hurston and turn east on CR 139. Follow it to FM 3184, which leads to the park.

Nearest food, gas, and lodging: Center, San Augustine, and Hemphill; food and gas in Milam.

Nearest camping: Ragtown, Red Hills Lake, Indian Mounds, Lakeview, and Willow Oak recreation areas.

36. Sam Houston National Forest

The 158,411-acre Sam Houston National Forest, only fifty miles north of downtown Houston along the east and west sides of I-45, is home to numerous enclaves of the endangered red-cockaded woodpecker. It has some of the best remaining stands of native pinewood forest in Texas and offers many easily accessible butterfly-watching spots. There are approximately 150 miles of hiking trails, including the Lone Star NR Hiking Trail, and several open and gated forest roadways.

Sites east of I-45 include Big Creek Scenic Area (**A**) and several roadsides (**B-E**). West-side sites include a loop trail (**F**), Cagle Recreation Area (**G**), and Stubblefield Recreation Area (**H**).

Habitats: Pine forest, hardwood forest, lakeshore, riparian, field, and cropland.

Strategy for finding the most butterflies: Sam Houston NF is divided into two sections, east and west of I-45. Start on the east side at Big Creek Scenic Area (**A**), which provides the best butterfly-watching; walk the roadsides and trails. Some of the more numerous butterflies include Pipevine, **Zebra**, Eastern Tiger, and Palamedes swallowtails; Southern Dogface; Red-banded Hairstreak; and Common Roadside-Skipper. Less numerous are White M Hairstreak and Eastern Tailed-Blue. **Southern** and **Creole pearly-eyes** are possible along streamsides where giant cane grows, and **Lacewinged Roadside-Skipper** is possible at cane growth in somewhat drier sites.

Next, walk the nearby side roads, including FR 217 (**B**) and FR 221 (**C**). Some of the likely butterflies here include Spicebush Swallowtail, Dusky-blue Groundstreak, Gulf Fritillary, Phaon Crescent, Hoary Edge, Southern and Northern cloudywings, Horace's and Wild Indigo duskywings, Tropical Checkered-Skipper, and Swarthy Skipper. These roads may also offer other less numerous but generally widespread butterflies, including Black and Giant swallowtails, Cloudless and Large Orange sulphurs, Gorgone Checkerspot, Eastern Comma, Queen, Least Skipper, and Southern Broken-Dash. In spring, Falcate Orangetip, Striped Hairstreak, Henry's Elfin, and Juvenal's Duskywing are widespread. **Frosted** and **Eastern Pine elfins** frequent pine woodlands.

South of Liberty Hill, walk sections of FR 261 and FR 262 (**D**) and the gated roadway at FR 203 (**E**) farther south. The roadsides offer Red-spotted Purple, Tawny Emperor, Hayhurst's Scallopwing, and **Tawny-edged Skipper**. Also watch for **Little Glassywing** and **Yehl Skipper** in clearings in moist forests.

West of I-45, walk the loop trail (**F**) at the national forest headquarters parking lot, where Gemmed and Carolina satyrs and Little Wood-Satyr can be expected. Visit the campground at Cagle RA (**G**) along FR 205, including the gated side road at the

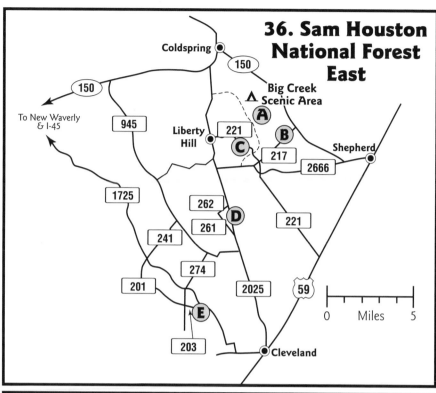

36. Sam Houston National Forest East

Coldspring

150

150

To New Waverly & I-45

Big Creek Scenic Area

945

Liberty Hill

221

A

B

C

217

Shepherd

2666

1725

262

261

D

221

241

274

201

2025

59

E

203

Cleveland

0   Miles   5

Sam Houston National Forest West

To Huntsville

0   Miles   5

To Huntsville

45

Stubblefield R.A.

H

216

Stubblefield Lake Rd.

F

loop trail

New Waverly

216

215

233

?

1375

To SH 90

205

149

G Cagle R.A.

Lake Conroe

To Conroe

Sam Houston National Forest

wetland across the road. Check there for **Broad-winged Skipper**. Finally, Stubble-field RA (**H**), north of FM 1375, is also worth a visit: check the roadsides and walk the Little Lake Creek Loop.

Directions: In Montgomery, San Jacinto, and Walker counties, the national forest is along I-45 north of Conroe. From New Waverly off I-45, take SH 150 east toward Coldspring and turn south on FM 2025 (also accessible more directly from Houston via US 59 to Cleveland and then north on FM 2025). Turn east on FM 2666 and then north on **FR 221** (**C**). Turn east on **FR 217** (**B**) to **Big Creek Scenic Area** (**A**) Return to FM 2025, turn south, and go to **FR 262/FR 261** (**D**) where you'll walk these roads. Farther south, take FM 945 west to FR 274 and turn south. It crosses FM 1725 and becomes paved. Watch for **FR 203** (**E**) on the left and walk this gated roadway.

For sites west of I-45, take FM 1375 west from New Waverly to FR 233 and the headquarters **loop trail** (**F**). Then continue west on FM 1375 to FR 205 on the left before the bridge over the lake. Take it south to **Cagle RA** (**G**). Return to FM 1375 and turn west. Drive over the lake to a right turn on FR 215 (Stubblefield Lake Rd.). Turn right on FR 216 and continue to **Stubblefield RA** (**H**), located where the road crosses the west fork of the San Jacinto River.

Nearest food, gas, and lodging: Conroe, Cleveland, and Huntsville; food and gas in New Waverly and Coldspring.

Nearest camping: Cagle RA, Double Lake RA, Stubblefield RA, in Cleveland, and at Huntsville State Park.

37. Martin Dies, Jr. State Park/B. A. Steinhagen Lake

The area surrounding B. A. Steinhagen Lake includes Martin Dies, Jr. State Park (fee area) and several other recreation units (fee areas). The 705-acre state park is located on the eastern shore of the lake and features several lakeshore and forest trails. The park can be extremely busy on weekends and holidays.

Sites for the best butterfly-watching include East End Park (**A**), the Walnut Ridge Unit (**B**), Hen House Ridge Unit (**C**), Cherokee Unit (**D**), Magnolia Ridge Park (**E**), and Campers Cove Park (**F**).

Habitats: Mixed pine-hardwood forest, hardwood forest, riparian, wetland, field, and pasture.

Strategy for finding the most butterflies: Start at East End Park (**A**) by walking a short way on the dam, the adjacent gated roadway, and along the edge of the wetland

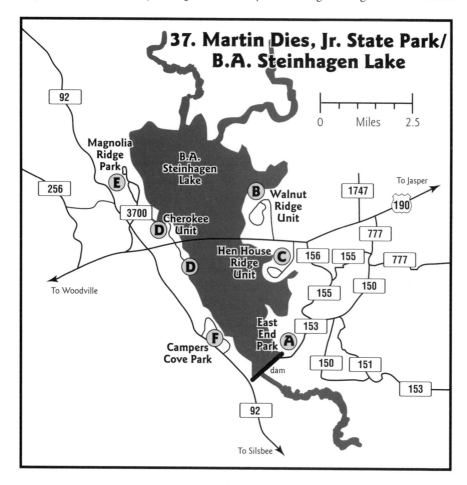

Gated roadways and dam, East End Park.

behind the picnic area. Some of the more numerous butterflies include **Zebra**, Giant, Spicebush, and Palamedes swallowtails; Cloudless and Large Orange sulphurs; Red-banded Hairstreak; Eastern Tailed-Blue; Northern Cloudywing; Southern Skipper-ling; and Southern Broken-Dash. Less numerous are Pipevine, Black, and Eastern Tiger swallowtails; Dainty Sulphur; Marine Blue; Gulf Fritillary; Silver-spotted Skipper; Confused Cloudywing; and Wild Indigo Duskywing. Watch for **Neamathla Skipper** and **Little Glassywing** along the gated roadway and **Little Metalmark** and **Tawny-edged** and **Crossline skippers** in the grassy field at the picnic area. **Lace-winged Roadside-Skipper** is possible at cane growth along the edge of the wetland.

Next, drive to the Walnut Ridge Unit (**B**) and walk the woodland trails. **Southern Pearly-eye** frequents patches of cane, and **Creole Pearly-eye** has been recorded in the dense woodlands. At the Hen House Ridge Unit (**C**), drive the roads and walk the nature trail. Watch for **King's Hairstreak** in brushy hardwood forests along the trail and for **Dusky Roadside-Skipper** along the entrance road. Additional butterflies likely to be found along the roadsides include Red-spotted Purple, Gemmed and Carolina satyrs, Little Wood-Satyr, Hoary Edge, and Tropical Checkered-Skipper.

Springtime butterflies include Falcate Orangetip; Banded, Striped, and Oak hair-streaks; Henry's Elfin; and Juvenal's Duskywing throughout the area. **Frosted** and **Eastern Pine elfins** are more likely to be seen in pine woodlands.

Next, drive west on US 190 across the lake to the Cherokee Unit (**D**); walk the road-sides on both sides of US 190. Then drive north to Magnolia Ridge Park (**E**) and walk the roadsides and the swampy lakeshore. Phaon Crescent, Question Mark, Long-tailed Skipper, and Common Roadside-Skipper are likely to be found. Watch for **Yehl Skipper** in swampy woodlands with cane growth.

Last, drive south to Campers Cove Park (**F**), which has a long lakeside border that can be excellent for butterflying. Many of the butterflies mentioned above are likely to be seen, and several additional specialties are possible: **Dukes' Skipper** at sedges along the lake, **Meske's Skipper** in open areas, **Northern Broken-Dash** in grassy locations, and **Twin-spot Skipper** at patches of wildflowers.

Directions: In Tyler County, Martin Dies, Jr. State Park is along US 190, eight miles west of Jasper and 10 miles east of Woodville. From Jasper, take US 190 west to FM 777 and turn south. When FM 777 turns sharply left, go south on CR 150. Follow it to CR 153 and turn west to **East End Park (A)** near the dam. Return to US 190 and turn left. The **Hen House Ridge Unit (C)** of the state park is ahead on the left. The **Walnut Ridge Unit (B)** is on the right before the bridge over the lake.

Continue west on SH 190. The **Cherokee Unit (D)** is on both sides of the highway just over the lake. Farther west on SH 190, turn north on FM 92. At FM 3700, turn east to **Magnolia Ridge Park (E)**. **Campers Cove Park (F)** is located south of SH 190 on FM 92. Watch for FM 4130 (Campers Cove Rd.) on the left.

Nearest food, gas, and lodging: Jasper and Woodville; food and gas along US 190.

Nearest camping: In the state park and at Sandy Creek Park.

38. Big Thicket Area

The Big Thicket Area extends from Woodville south to Lumberton and west to the Menard Creek Corridor Unit of Big Thicket National Preserve. It includes four major and several additional sites, all within national preserve, state park and forest, and Texas Nature Conservancy lands, as well as one private site, Watson Pineland Preserve (fee area).

Sites include John H. Kirby State Forest (**A**), Watson Pineland Preserve (**B**), Sundew Trail (**C**), Pitcher Plant Trail (**D**), Kirby Nature Trail (**E**), Roy E. Larsen Sandyland Sanctuary (**F**), Village Creek State Park (**G**), and several roadsides (**H-M**).

Habitats: Bottomland-hardwood forest, mixed pine-hardwood forest, pine forest, pine-oak savannah, prairie, field, riparian, and wetland.

Strategy for finding the most butterflies: Start at John H. Kirby State Forest (**A**) by walking the network of roadways. Some of the more numerous butterflies include Pipevine, **Zebra**, and Spicebush swallowtails; Cloudless, Large Orange, and Dainty sulphurs; Southern Dogface; Red-banded Hairstreak; Eastern Tailed-Blue; Carolina Satyr; Little Wood-Satyr; Horace's and Wild Indigo duskywings; Southern Broken-Dash; and Common Roadside-Skipper. Some of the less numerous but expected butterflies include Black, Giant, and Palamedes swallowtails; Sleepy Orange; Juniper Hairstreak; Gulf Fritillary; Gorgone Checkerspot; Phaon Crescent; Eastern Comma; Swarthy Skipper; and Southern Skipperling. **Neamathla** and **Tawny-edged skippers**, **Northern Broken-Dash**, and **Bell's** and **Dusky roadside-skippers** are also possible.

In spring, Falcate Orangetip; Banded, Striped, and Oak hairstreaks; Henry's Elfin; and Juvenal's Duskywing are widespread. **Frosted** and **Eastern Pine elfins** frequent pine woodlands, and Yucca Giant-Skipper is possible along the roadway.

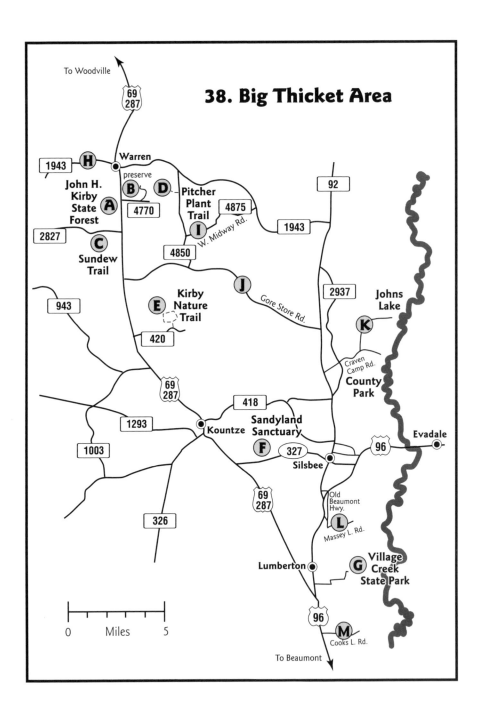

38. Big Thicket Area

To Woodville

69
287

1943

H

Warren

preserve

John H.
Kirby
State
Forest

A

B

D

Pitcher
Plant
Trail

4770

4875

92

I

W. Midway Rd.

1943

2827

C

4850

Sundew
Trail

943

Kirby
Nature
Trail

E

J

Gore Store Rd.

2937

Johns
Lake

K

420

Craven
Camp Rd.

County
Park

69
287

418

1293

Kountze

Sandyland
Sanctuary

F

327

Evadale

96

1003

Silsbee

69
287

Old
Beaumont
Hwy.

L

Massey L. Rd.

326

Lumberton

G

Village
Creek
State Park

96

M

Cooks L. Rd.

To Beaumont

0   Miles   5

John H. Kirby State Forest, Big Thicket

Nearby worthwhile sites include Watson Pineland Preserve (**B**), where **Yehl Skipper** is possible along the edges, the Sundew Trail (**C**) in the Hickory Creek Savannah Unit, and the Pitcher Plant Trail (**D**) in the Turkey Creek Unit, a good place for **Georgia Satyr**. Also check beyond the boardwalk there for **King's Hairstreak**. Other possibilities in these areas include Harvester, Hoary Edge, Southern and Confused cloudywings, and **Crossline Skipper**.

To the south are Kirby Nature Trail (**E**), behind the Turkey Creek Visitor Information Center in the Turkey Creek Unit of the Big Thicket Preserve, and Roy E. Larsen Sandyland Sanctuary (**F**), which includes the Floodplain Loop Trail where **Pepper and Salt Skipper** and **Lace-winged Roadside-Skipper** are likely to be seen. **Dukes' Skipper** is also possible.

Village Creek SP (**G**), a fee area, offers many of the same butterflies mentioned above; in addition, **Edwards' Hairstreak** has been recorded in scrub-oak growth. Watch the roadsides for **Zarucco Duskywing**, **Meske's Skipper**, and **Little Glassywing**.

Several less-traveled roadways can be worthwhile: FM 1943 (**H**), west of Warren; W. Midway Road (**I**), east of the Turkey Creek Unit; Gore Store Road (**J**); the roads to County Park and Johns Lake (**K**), west of Neches Bottom and Jack Gore Baygall Unit; Massey Lake Road (**L**), just above Lumberton; and Cooks Lake Road (**M**) on the west side of the Beaumont Unit.

Little Metalmark can occur throughout the area in open fields with yellow thistle, and **Twin-spot Skipper** is possible at patches of wildflowers.

Directions: In Hardin, Polk, and Tyler counties, sites are scattered along US 69 and FM 92, and US 96 north of Beaumont. Five sites are near Warren on US 69. **John H.**

Kirby State Forest (A) is on the west side of US 69 south of town. On the east side of the highway, take CR 4770 for 1.2 miles to CR 4777 and go north .2 mile to **Watson Pineland Preserve (B)**. **Sundew Trail (C)** is south on US 69; take FM 2827 west to the Hickory Creek Savannah Unit. One of the recommended roads is **FM 1943 (H)**. Take it west from Warren.

To find **Pitcher Plant Trail (D)**, take FM 1943 east from Warren to CR 4850 and go south to the Turkey Creek Unit. You can continue south to **W. Midway Rd. (I)**, CR 4875, which heads east. Farther south on CR 4850 is the **Gore Store Rd. (J)**, which can be used to access sites near Kountze and Silsbee.

From where Gore Store Rd. meets US 69, turn south and drive about five miles to FM 420. Turn east and proceed to the visitor center and the **Kirby Nature Trail (E)**. Return to US 69 and go south past Kountze to SH 327. Turn east and go 2.6 miles to **Roy E. Larsen Sandyland Sanctuary (F)**. After exploring that area, you can drive 6.4 miles east on SH 327 to Silsbee. The **roads to County Park and Johns Lake (K)** are north of Silsbee off FM 92. Take Craven Camp Rd. east.

To reach **Massey Lake Rd. (L)** from Silsbee, take Bus 96 south and take the Old Beaumont Hwy. across the tracks just before the merger with US 96. Continue south to Massey Lake Rd. on the left. **Village Creek SP (G)** is in Lumberton. From US 96 (Main St.), go east on Matthews Rd. to Village Creek Parkway. Turn left a short distance to Alma Dr. Cross the railroad tracks and veer left .5 mile to the entrance. For the final site, take US 96 south from Lumberton and exit east on **Cooks Lake Rd. (M)**.

Nearest food, gas, and lodging: Beaumont, Kountze, and Silsbee.

Nearest camping: Village Creek SP and commercial sites along US 69 and SH 92.

Additional Worthwhile Sites in the Pineywoods Region

Tyler State Park. This 994-acre state park (fee area) is just north of Tyler on SH 14. It features a 64-acre spring-fed lake that is popular for fishing and boating. There is a network of trails around the lake. Vegetation is dominated by oak-pine woodland and bottomland-hardwood forest.

Huntsville State Park. Located south of Huntsville along the west side of I-45, this 2,083-acre park (fee area) is dominated by Lake Raven, a 210-acre impoundment. There is a pine woodland on the drier uplands. Eight miles of hiking and biking trails circle the lake. The park can be extremely busy on weekends.

W. G. Jones State Forest. This 1,725-acre forest is dominated by native loblolly pines. Prescribed burns are utilized as a management tool to enhance the habitat for red-cockaded woodpeckers, and they also benefit woodland butterflies. This area is along I-45, five miles south of Conroe and 30 miles north of Houston.

Jesse H. Jones Nature Center. Only 225-acres in size, this private area (donation expected) offers a diversity of habitats, including wetlands and mixed hardwood-pine forest. Easy access is provided by five miles of paved, all-weather trails. The nature center is located west of US 59 northeast of Houston. Take the Humble exit (FM 1960) and go north on Kenswick Drive for 1.3 miles.

Tyrrell Park. This park is at the southern edge of Beaumont. Exit I-10 at Walden Road and turn east. Cross the railroad tracks to the entrance and drive the park loop road. Cattail Marsh (900 acres) is located at the far side. Other habitats include pine woodland, riparian, field, and garden. Eight miles of hiking trails are available.

Butterfly Checklist for the Pineywoods Region

The following list includes nine sites: **30. Atlanta State Park/Wright Patman Lake, 31. Lake O' The Pines/Daingerfield State Park, 32. Caddo Lake State Park and Wildlife Management Area, 33. Davy Crockett National Forest, 34. Angelina National Forest/Sam Rayburn Reservoir, 35. Sabine National Forest, 36. Sam Houston National Forest, 37. Martin Dies, Jr. State Park/B.A. Steinhagen Lake,** and **38. Big Thicket Area**.

Status symbols include: A = abundant; C = common; U = uncommon; O = occasional; R = rare; X = accidental; M = migrant; TC = temporary colonist; ? = status unknown. (For a full definition of these terms, see p. 3.)

For trip notes, including dates and numbers of species seen, refer to the entry for this checklist in Appendix 3: Regional Checklist Resources.

Butterfly Species	30	31	32	33	34	35	36	37	38
Pipevine Swallowtail	R	C	U	U	C	C	C	U	C
Zebra Swallowtail	C-U	A-U	C-U	C-U	A-U	C-U	A-U	C-U	A-U
Black Swallowtail	U	U	U	U	U	U	U	U	U
Giant Swallowtail	U	U	U	C	U	C	U	C	U
Eastern Tiger Swallowtail	U	C	C	C	C	C	C	U	C
Spicebush Swallowtail	C	C	C	C	C	A	A	C	A
Palamedes Swallowtail					C	C	U	C	C	A
Florida White								X		X
Checkered White	U	U	U				R	U	U
Cabbage White	R								X
Great Southern White		X				X	R		U
Falcate Orangetip	C	C	C	C	C	C	C	C	C
Clouded Sulphur		U						O		R
Orange Sulphur	U	U	C	U	U	U	U	C	C
Southern Dogface	C		U			U	U	U	C

Butterfly Species	30	31	32	33	34	35	36	37	38
White Angled-Sulphur									X
Cloudless Sulphur	C	C	A	C	A	C	U	C	C
Orange-barred Sulphur									X
Large Orange Sulphur	R		O	U			U	C	A
Lyside Sulphur	X								
Barred Yellow		X	X						
Mexican Yellow		X						X	X
Little Yellow	C	A	U	C	A	A	A	C	C
Sleepy Orange	U	U	U		U	U	U	U	U
Dainty Sulphur	C	U			U	U	U	U	C
Harvester		U	U						U
Great Purple Hairstreak	U	O	U	U	U		U	U	C
Edwards' Hairstreak									O
Banded Hairstreak	C	C	C		U			C	C
King's Hairstreak						O		O	O
Striped Hairstreak		U	U				U	U	R
Oak Hairstreak					U			U	U
Frosted Elfin	U	U	U	U	U	U	U	U	U
Henry's Elfin	C	C	C	U	U	C	C	C	U
Eastern Pine Elfin	U	U	U	U	U	C	U	U	U
Juniper Hairstreak	C						C	C	U
White M Hairstreak					O		O		R
Gray Hairstreak	C	U	U	C	U	U	C	C	C
Red-banded Hairstreak	U	A	C	C	C	C	A	C	A
Dusky-blue Groundstreak			R				U	C	U
Western Pygmy-Blue									U
Eastern Pygmy-Blue									X
Marine Blue								U	
Reakirt's Blue	U				X	U	O	O	O
Eastern Tailed-Blue	C	C	U	C	C	C	U	A	A
Spring/Summer Azure	C	U				C	U	U	U
Silvery Blue	R								
Little Metalmark								U	U
American Snout	A-R	C-R	A-R	A-R	A-R		A-R	A-U	A-R
Gulf Fritillary	C	C	U	U	U	U	C	U	U
Julia Heliconian									X
Variegated Fritillary	A	C	C	U	C	C	C	U	U
Gorgone Checkerspot		C	U		U	C	U		U
Silvery Checkerspot	U	U		U	C		O		C
Phaon Crescent	C	U	C	C	U	U	U	C	U
Pearl Crescent	C	C	C	C	C	C	C	C	A
Question Mark	U	U	U		U	U	C	C	U

Butterfly Species	30	31	32	33	34	35	36	37	38
Eastern Comma		O	U	U			U		U
Mourning Cloak		R	U	U	U				C
American Lady	C	U	C	U	C	U	U	C	C
Painted Lady	U	U	U				U	U	U
Red Admiral	C	C	A	C		C	C	A	A
Common Buckeye	U	C	U	U	U	C	C	U	C
Red-spotted Purple	C	C	C	U	C	C	C	C	C
Viceroy	C	C	U	C	U	U	U	U	U
Common Mestra					X				O
Goatweed Leafwing	C	U	C	U	C	C	C	A	C
Hackberry Emperor	U	C	C	C	C		U	C	C
Tawny Emperor		C	U	C			U	C	C
Southern Pearly-eye	U	U	C		U	C	U	C	C
Creole Pearly-eye					C	O	U	O	U
Gemmed Satyr	C	U	C	U	C	U	U	C	U
Carolina Satyr	C	U	C	A	A	A	A	A	C
Georgia Satyr						O		R	U
Little Wood-Satyr	C	U	U	C	C	U	C	C	C
Red Satyr						X			
Common Wood-Nymph	C			R	C	O		C	C
Monarch	C	C	U		U	M	M	M	M
Queen							U		U
Silver-spotted Skipper	U	U	U	U	U	U	U	C	C
White-striped Longtail				X					
Long-tailed Skipper		R	R	O	O			O	O
Dorantes Longtail									U
Golden Banded-Skipper	X								
Hoary Edge	U	U			U	U	O	U	U
Southern Cloudywing	U	R	U		U	U	O	U	U
Northern Cloudywing	U	U	C	C	C	C	U	C	C
Confused Cloudywing	U	U	U		C	U	R	U	U
Drusius Cloudywing							X		
Outis Skipper							X		
Mazans Scallopwing							X		
Hayhurst's Scallopwing	C						U		
Sickle-winged Skipper							X	X	X
False Duskywing									X
Sleepy Duskywing	U	U			U	U			R
Juvenal's Duskywing	U	O	C	U	C	C	C	U	U
Horace's Duskywing	C	U	U	C	C	U	C	C	C
Zarucco Duskywing	U								U
Funereal Duskywing	U	U	C	U	U	C	U	C	C

Butterfly Species	30	31	32	33	34	35	36	37	38
Wild Indigo Duskywing				C	O		U	U	C
Com./White Checkered-Skipper	C	C	C	C	U	C	C	U	C
Tropical Checkered-Skipper				U	U	R	U	U	R
Swarthy Skipper					U	U	U	U	U
Julia's Skipper		U					U		
Neamathla Skipper								U	U
Clouded Skipper	C	U	A	C	C	A	C	C	C
Least Skipper	U	C	C	C	C	C	C	C	C
Orange Skipperling		C							
Southern Skipperling	U	O	U	U	C	U	U	C	U
Fiery Skipper	C	C	C	C	U	C	C	A	C
Cobweb Skipper	U	U	U						
Meske's Skipper					U	R		R	U
Tawny-edged Skipper				U			O	U	C
Crossline Skipper	U				U	C		U	U
Whirlabout		U		C	A	U	R	U	C
Southern Broken-Dash	C	U		C	C	C	U	C	C
Northern Broken-Dash	O	O	O		O	R	R	R	R
Little Glassywing	C	U		C	C	C	C	C	C
Sachem	A	C		C	C	A	U	C	U
Delaware Skipper	U	U			U	C		U	U
Zabulon Skipper	U		U		U				
Aaron's Skipper						X			X
Yehl Skipper	R			U	O		U	U	O
Broad-winged Skipper				U			O		
Dion Skipper	U	C	C						
Bay Skipper									X
Dukes' Skipper				R				U	U
Dun Skipper	C	C	C		C	U	C	U	C
Dusted Skipper						X			X
Pepper and Salt Skipper	U		U		U	U			U
Lace-winged Roadside-Skipper		U			U	U	U	U	U
Dotted Roadside-Skipper									X
Common Roadside-Skipper	U		C		C		C	C	C
Celia's Roadside-Skipper		R	R				U		
Bell's Roadside-Skipper	U	U	U			U			R
Dusky Roadside-Skipper	U				U			U	R
Eufala Skipper	C	U					C	C	C
Twin-spot Skipper				U	R	U		O	U
Brazilian Skipper	R				U		O	U	U
Ocola Skipper	C	C	C		U	C	U	U	C
Yucca Giant-Skipper					O			O	U

Central Plains

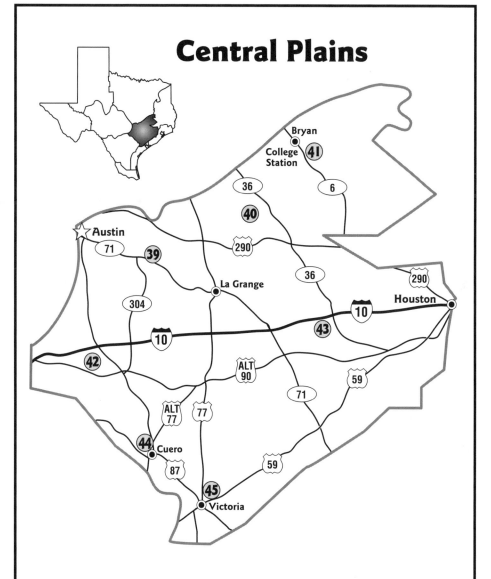

39. **Buescher State Park/Bastrop State Park**
40. **Somerville Lake**
41. **Bryan–College Station**
42. **Palmetto State Park**
43. **Attwater Prairie-Chicken National Wildlife Refuge**
44. **DeWitt County**
45. **Victoria**

Central Plains Region

The Central Plains Region is bordered on the north by the Northern Plains, on the east by the Pineywoods and Upper Gulf Coast, on the south by the Central Gulf Coast and South Texas Brushlands, and on the west by the Edwards Plateau. The landscape consists of gently rolling hills with numerous river valleys, including those of the Brazos, Lavaca, San Jacinto, Colorado, and Guadalupe rivers. Vegetation in open areas is dominated by southern extensions of the post-oak savannah and blackland prairie, and some of the river floodplains contain extensive bottomland hardwoods. The prairie that once was prevalent on the drier hills has largely been replaced by mesquite and yucca grasslands. Elevations range between 300 and 800 feet.

The Central Plains Region is represented by seven sites: **39. Buescher State Park/ Bastrop State Park**, **40. Somerville Lake**, **41. Bryan–College Station**, **42. Palmetto State Park**, **43. Attwater Prairie-Chicken National Wildlife Refuge**, **44. DeWitt County**, and **45. Victoria**. The best time to visit these sites is from March to November.

Central Plains Specialties

Because this region is closely associated with so many surrounding regions, the butterfly diversity is moderate to high, but only twelve species are considered specialties.

Metalmarks, Heliconians, Peacocks: **Rounded Metalmark** frequents patches of flowers in Palmetto SP, DeWitt County, and the Victoria area. Adults usually remain low to the ground; larvae feed on eupatoriums. **Julia Heliconian** occurs as a temporary colonist at Somerville Lake and Palmetto SP. Adults are most likely to be seen in late summer and fall; larvae feed on passion vines. **Zebra Heliconian** is a temporary colonist in Palmetto SP and the Victoria area. Larvae feed on passion vines. **White Peacock** is most likely to be seen along rivers and at wetlands in DeWitt County and the Victoria area. Adults are likely to be temporary colonists, not appearing until midsummer; larvae feed on frog-fruit and water hyssop.

Spread-wing Skippers: **Coyote Cloudywing** frequents flowering plants in DeWitt County and the Victoria area. Adults are fast-flying, "jumping" from one flower to the next when feeding. Larvae feed on blackbrush acacia. In the past, **Outis Skipper** has been recorded in open grasslands with acacia (larval foodplants) in the "Bastrop area." There are no specifics on location and no recent records. **Mazans Scallopwing** occurs in Palmetto SP, DeWitt County, and the Victoria area. Adults nectar on low-growing wildflowers and often perch on the ground. Larvae feed on lamb's-quarters and pigweed. **Laviana White-Skipper**, most often seen in flight along the edges of vegetation, occurs in Buescher/Bastrop SP, DeWitt County, and the Victoria area. Larvae feed on mallows. **Turk's-cap White-Skipper** is a fast, active species, usually found flying along the edge of vegetation in DeWitt County and the Victoria area. Larvae feed on mallows, including Turk's cap.

Grass-Skippers: **Neamathla Skipper** has been recorded only in Attwater Prairie-Chicken NWR. **Little Glassywing** is also known only from Attwater Prairie-Chicken NWR; two broods occur, in April-May and July-August. **Dusky Roadside-Skipper** has been recorded only in Buescher/Bastrop SP; it is most likely to be found near the ground at the edge of moist pine stands.

Sites within the Central Plains Region

39. Buescher State Park/Bastrop State Park

These two state parks—3,550-acre Bastrop and 1,017-acre Buescher—and Lake Bastrop South Shore are located in a scenic remnant of an extensive pine forest that once covered much of central Texas. This land of isolated loblolly pines, sometimes called "lost pines," is located approximately 100 miles west of the more extensive loblolly pine stands of the Pineywoods Region. In addition, the two state parks protect the majority of the remaining population of the endangered Houston toad. Hiking trails—7.7 miles at Buescher, 8.5 miles at Bastrop, and three miles at Lake Bastrop—provide access into the environment.

Butterfly-watching sites at Buescher SP (fee area) include the dam (**A**), day use area (**B**), campground (**C**), and a hiking trail (**D**). Park Road 1C (**E**) provides butterflying opportunities on the way to Bastrop SP (fee area), where you should investigate the campground road (**F**) and a garden (**G**) at the entrance station. Hike some of the trails, including Lost Pines Hiking Trail (**H**). Also visit the Lake Bastrop South Shore Park (**I**) with its different habitats.

Habitats: Pine forest, juniper woodland, post-oak savannah, oak-yaupon woodland, riparian, wetland, and field.

Strategy for finding the most butterflies: Start at Buescher SP by walking across Park Lake Dam (**A**) and checking the flowering vegetation along the edges. Then drive to the Picnic/Day Use Area (**B**) and explore the oak-juniper woodland there. At the north end of the lake, walk around the Lakeview Camping Area (**C**), a park-like area with large cottonwoods. If time permits, walk a portion of the trail along the east side of the lake between the campground and the picnic area. Some of the more numerous butterflies include Pipevine and Giant swallowtails, Cloudless Sulphur, Ceraunus Blue, Gulf Fritillary, Phaon and Pearl crescents, Tawny Emperor, Horace's Duskywing, Common/White and Tropical checkered-skippers, Clouded and Eufala skippers, Southern Broken-Dash, and Sachem. In spring, Falcate Orangetip and Soapberry Hairstreak can be expected; Banded and Striped hairstreaks, Henry's Elfin, and Juvenal's Duskywing are also possible.

When wildflowers are present, walk a portion of the nearby Buescher Hiking Trail (**D**). This juniper-oak woodland is likely to produce Juniper Hairstreak, Carolina

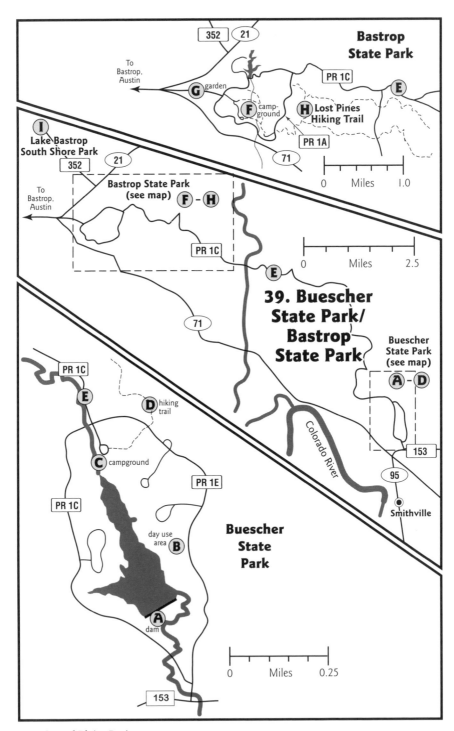

352 21

**Bastrop
State Park**

To
Bastrop.
Austin

G garden

PR 1C

E

F camp-
ground

H Lost Pines
Hiking Trail

I

PR 1A

**Lake Bastrop
South Shore Park**

352 21

71

0   Miles   1.0

To
Bastrop.
Austin

**Bastrop State Park
(see map)**

F - H

PR 1C

E

0   Miles   2.5

**39. Buescher
State Park/
Bastrop
State Park**

**Buescher
State Park
(see map)**

A - D

71

PR 1C

E

Colorado River

153

95

D hiking
trail

C campground

PR 1E

Smithville

PR 1C

day use
area B

**Buescher
State Park**

A
dam

0   Miles   0.25

153

Powerline right-of-way, Bastrop State Park

Satyr, Little Wood-Satyr, and Common Wood-Nymph. Oak Hairstreak and Red-spotted Purple are also possible.

Next, drive Park Road 1C (**E**) toward Bastrop SP, stopping at open areas with wild-flowers, especially at powerline right-of-ways, which can be very productive. Although many of the butterflies mentioned above are possible, watch for Western Pygmy-Blue, Silvery Checkerspot, Queen, Northern and Confused cloudywings, Wild Indigo Duskywing, **Laviana White-Skipper**, and Common and **Dusky roadside-skippers** in these open areas.

At Bastrop SP, key sites include the road into Piney Hill Camping Area (**F**) and the small garden around the park entrance station (**G**). Watch for Great Purple Hair-streak, Dusky-blue Groundstreak, and Long-tailed Skipper. If time allows, hike some of the trails, such as the Lost Pines Hiking Trail (**H**) near the Scout Camping Area. Finally, visit Lake Bastrop South Shore Park (**I**), a fee area, north of Bastrop SP, which has a slightly different environment and a network of trails.

There are historical records of **Outis Skipper** for this general area but no recent sightings.

Directions: In Bastrop County, the state parks are along SH 71, east of Austin. **Buescher SP (A–D)** is two miles north of Smithville. From SH 71, take FM 153 east to the entrance on the left. **PR 1C (E)**, a 13-mile scenic drive, leaves the north side of park and goes to **Bastrop SP (F–H)**, located along SH 21, one mile east of Bastrop. To reach **Lake Bastrop South Shore Park (I)**, continue two miles on SH 21 to South Shore Rd. (CR 352) and go north to the entrance.

Nearest food, gas, and lodging: Bastrop and Smithville; cabins and screened shelters at the state parks.

Nearest camping: All three areas.

40. Somerville Lake

The 11,460-acre Somerville Lake has eighty-five miles of shoreline. The principal watershed, Yegua (pronounced *yah-wha*) Creek, drains approximately 850,500 acres and is dammed by a 20,210-foot earthfill embankment near Somerville, twenty miles above its confluence with the Brazos River. Lake Somerville State Park (fee area) and lakeside parks provide recreational opportunities.

Key butterfly-watching sites include Big Creek Park (**A**), the state park's Birch Creek Unit (**B**), Yegua Creek Park (**C**), Rocky Creek Park (**D**), and Nails Creek Unit (**E**), also part of the state park.

Habitats: Juniper woodland, oak savannah, oak-hickory woodland, lakeshore, riparian, field, and cropland.

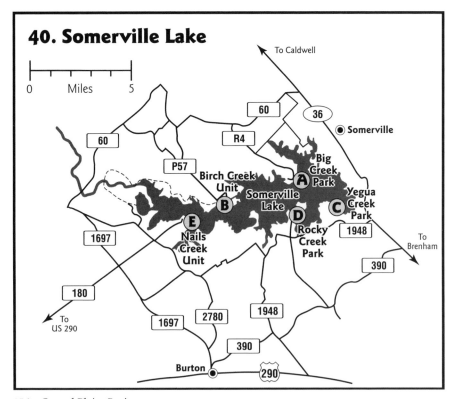

Late summer wildflowers, Somerville Lake

Strategy for finding the most butterflies: There are five worthwhile butterfly-watching sites around the lake; the two best are located on the north side. Start at Big Creek Park (**A**), a privately managed area; walk along a section of the roadway and the nature trail. Some of the more numerous butterflies include Pipevine Swallowtail, Cloudless Sulphur, Little Yellow, Gulf Fritillary, Silvery Checkerspot, Texan and Phaon crescents, Tawny Emperor, Clouded and Fiery skippers, and Sachem. Less numerous species include Eastern Tiger Swallowtail, Ceraunus Blue, Queen, and Horace's Duskywing. In spring, Falcate Orangtip and Soapberry Hairstreak are likely to be seen; Ocola Skipper is usually present in fall.

Next, drive to the Birch Creek Unit (**B**) of the state park and walk along the open roadsides when wildflowers are present. Also walk the woodland trail, as well as the lakeside trail that starts at the Yaupon Camping Area. Most of the same butterflies mentioned above are likely, but several other species are possible: Dusky-blue Groundstreak, Bordered Patch, Carolina Satyr, Common Wood-Nymph, Southern Skipperling, Southern Broken-Dash, and Celia's Roadside-Skipper.

Afterwards, drive to the south side of the lake to Yegua Creek Park (**C**). Check the areas along the north Boat Ramp Road and walk the nature trail. Watch for **Julia** and **Zebra heliconians**, probably temporary colonists, although they may only be strays. Other possibilities here include Large Orange Sulphur, Juniper and White M hairstreaks, Red Satyr, and Julia's and Dun skippers.

Then drive to Rocky Creek Park (**D**) and walk a section of the rather extensive trail system. If time allows, also drive to the Nails Creek Unit (**E**) and walk along the edge of the picnic area.

Directions: In Burleson and Washington Counties, Somerville Lake is situated about 30 miles southwest of Bryan-College Station, west of SH 36 between Brenham and Caldwell. North of Somerville on SH 36, turn west on FM 60. Find R 4 and turn south to **Big Creek Park (A)**. Return to FM 60 and go west to P 57. Turn south to the **Birch Creek Unit (B)**. South of Somerville on SH 36, take FM 1948 west for **Yegua Creek Park (C)** and **Rocky Creek Park (D)**, on the south shore. To reach the **Nails Creek Unit (E)**, turn northwest on FM 1697 from US 290 in Burton. Continue to FM 180 and turn northeast to the park.

Nearest food, gas, and lodging: Somerville and Caldwell; food at Birch Creek Unit and Overlook Park (off SH 36 at the turn to Yegua Creek Park); gasoline at Birch Creek Unit; lodging at Big Creek and Overlook parks.

Nearest camping: Yegua Creek and Rocky Creek parks and Birch Creek and Nails Creek units.

41. Bryan–College Station

Best known as the home of Texas A&M University, these two cities are advertised as "Smack in the Heart of Texas." They are ninety miles east of Austin, 165 miles south of Dallas, and ninety miles northwest of Houston. They have numerous parks and areas dedicated to recreational activities. A few of them, such as the 515-acre Lick Creek Park **(A)**, Bee Creek Park **(B)**, Texas A&M University Horticultural Garden **(C)**, and Lake Bryan Park **(D)**, also offer good butterfly-watching opportunities.

Habitats: Mesquite grassland, juniper-hackberry woodland, oak-hickory woodland, riparian, and field.

Strategy for finding the most butterflies: Start at Lick Creek Park **(A)** by walking the extensive trail system beyond the parking area through woodland and riparian habitats. Some of the more numerous butterflies include Pipevine and Giant swallowtails, Little Yellow, Juniper Hairstreak, Dusky-blue Groundstreak, Gulf Fritillary, Bordered Patch, Silvery Checkerspot, Phaon Crescent, Queen, Northern Cloudywing, Horace's and Wild Indigo duskywings, and Clouded and Dun skippers. In spring, Falcate Orangetip is likely to occur, and Sickle-winged and Ocola skippers are possible in fall.

Then drive into town to Bee Creek Park **(B)** and its D. A. Anderson Arboretum; walk the network of short trails and the edges. Some of the same butterflies mentioned above are likely, but Spicebush Swallowtail, Question Mark, Tawny Emperor, Common Wood-Nymph, Southern Skipperling, and Whirlabout can usually be expected.

Next, drive to the Texas A&M University Horticultural Garden **(C)**. Check the plantings around the parking area and walk through the gardens where Eastern Tiger Swallowtail, Red-banded Hairstreak, Least and Eufala skippers, and Celia's Roadside-Skipper are possible.

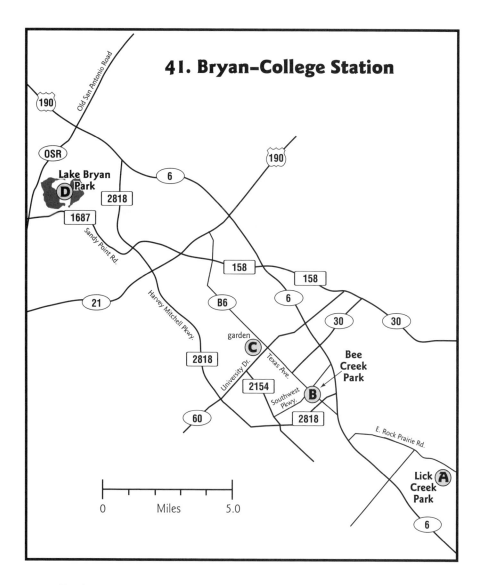

41. Bryan–College Station

Finally, drive west of Bryan to Lake Bryan Park (**D**). Check the flowering plants along the roadways and walk the trail across the dam. Black Swallowtail, Orange Sulphur, Southern Dogface, Sleepy Orange, Queen, and Tropical Checkered-Skipper may be added to your list.

Directions: In Brazos County, **Lick Creek Park (A)** is located on E. Rock Prairie Rd., 4.4 miles east of SH 6. Return to SH 6 and turn north. Exit northwest on Texas Ave. (Bus. 6). Turn south on Southwest Parkway and left on Anderson St. to **Bee Creek Park (B)**. Return to Texas Ave. and continue northwest past University Dr. (SH 60) to

Lick Creek Park, Bryan–College Station

Hensel Dr. and turn left to the **Texas A&M Horticultural Garden (C)**. To reach **Lake Bryan Park (D)** from that point, return to Texas Ave. and turn southeast. Turn southwest on University Dr. and proceed to Harvey Mitchell Parkway (FM 2818) and turn north. At Sandy Point Road, (FM 1687), turn west for 3.4 miles to the park.

Nearest food, gas, and lodging: Bryan and College Station.

Nearest camping: Lake Bryan Park and commercial sites.

42. Palmetto State Park

Palmetto State Park is one of the oldest Texas state parks, evident by the large number of CCC structures. This 263-acre park (fee area) was named for the dwarf palmettos that are prominent in Ottine Swamp along the San Marcos River. Several trails offer good access into the unique swampland and adjacent woodlands. July 4th Butterfly Counts are held here annually.

The best sites for butterflies include the Oxbow Lake Trail (**A**), Palmetto Trail (**B**), River Trail (**C**), the road to the Palmetto Trail (**D**), Ottine Cemetery (**E**), and other roadsides (**F-H**).

Habitats: Post-oak woodland, bottomland-hardwood forest, riparian, wetland, field, and cropland.

Strategy for finding the most butterflies: Start in Palmetto SP by walking the Oxbow Lake Trail (**A**) around the lake, where the greatest butterfly diversity is likely. Some of the more numerous butterflies include Pipevine Swallowtail; Little Yellow; Dusky-

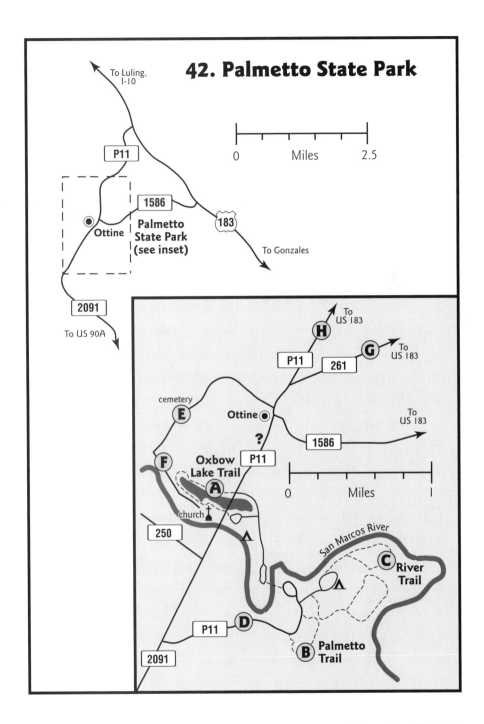

42. Palmetto State Park

To Luling, I-10

P11

0   Miles   2.5

1586

183

Ottine

Palmetto
State Park
(see inset)

To Gonzales

2091

To US 90A

To
US 183

H

P11

261

G To
US 183

cemetery

E

Ottine

To
US 183

?

1586

F

Oxbow
Lake Trail

P11

A

0   Miles

church

250

San Marcos River

C River
Trail

P11

D

B Palmetto
Trail

2091

Palmetto State Park

blue Groundstreak; Reakirt's Blue; Texan and Phaon crescents; Tawny Emperor; Carolina Satyr; Silver-spotted, Clouded, and Fiery skippers; Southern Broken-Dash; and Celia's Roadside-Skipper. In spring, Falcate Orangetip and Soapberry and Oak hairstreaks are also likely to be seen.

Then walk the Palmetto Trail (**B**), a good place for Eastern Tiger Swallowtail, and a portion of the River Trail (**C**), both through woodlands. Several of the butterflies mentioned above are likely, but watch for Cloudless and Large Orange sulphurs, Hackberry Emperor, and Gemmed Satyr. Little Wood-Satyr, **Mazans Scallopwing**, and Nysa Roadside-Skipper have also been found along these trails. Afterwards, walk along road P 11 (**D**), which leads to the Palmetto Trail.

Next, visit Ottine Cemetery (**E**), which is worthwhile unless recently mowed, and the roadside beyond to the church (**F**). North of Ottine, drive CR 261 (**G**) and P 11 (**H**), checking flowering plants along the roadsides. These more open areas are likely to produce Black and Giant swallowtails, Dainty Sulphur, Southern Dogface, Ceraunus Blue, Fatal and **Rounded metalmarks**, Gulf Fritillary, Silvery Checkerspot, Tropical Checkered-Skipper, and Eufala and Brazilian skippers. **Julia** and **Zebra heliconians** can sometimes be found along P 11 in summer, and Ocola Skipper is likely to be seen in fall.

Directions: In Gonzales County east of San Antonio, **Palmetto State Park (A-H)** is south of I-10. The park is southwest of US 183, eight miles south of Luling and 13 miles north of Gonzales, adjacent to the town of Ottine.

Nearest food, gas, and lodging: Luling and Gonzales.

Nearest camping: Palmetto SP.

43. Attwater Prairie-Chicken National Wildlife Refuge

The 8,000-acre Attwater Prairie-Chicken National Wildlife Refuge (fee area) features one of the largest remnants of coastal prairie in southeast Texas. The refuge was established in 1972 to protect habitat for the endangered Attwater's prairie-chicken. The population has continued to decline, but restoration efforts are underway. The NWR also offers an undeveloped environment for prairie butterflies. July 4th Butterfly Counts are held here some years.

Key butterfly sites include the Auto Tour Route (**A**), Sycamore Trail (**B**), Pipit Trail (**C**), a butterfly garden (**D**), and the entrance road (**E**).

Habitats: Prairie, field, oak motte, marsh, and riparian.

Strategy for finding the most butterflies: First, drive the five-mile Auto Tour Route (**A**), stopping at the few pull-offs to check roadside wildflowers. Some of the more numerous butterflies include Pipevine and Giant swallowtails, Little Yellow, Reakirt's Blue, Gulf Fritillary, Queen, Tropical Checkered-Skipper, and Clouded and Fiery skippers. Falcate Orangetip and Soapberry Hairstreak are possible in spring.

Next, walk the Sycamore Trail (**B**) and Pipit Trail (**C**). Butterflies likely among the prairie flowers and shrubs include many of those mentioned above, but Dusky-blue Groundstreak, Phaon Crescent, Carolina Satyr, Horace's and Wild Indigo duskywings, Southern Skipperling, and Dun Skipper are also likely to be found. **Neamathla**

Pairie lands, Attwater Prairie-Chicken National Wildlife Refuge

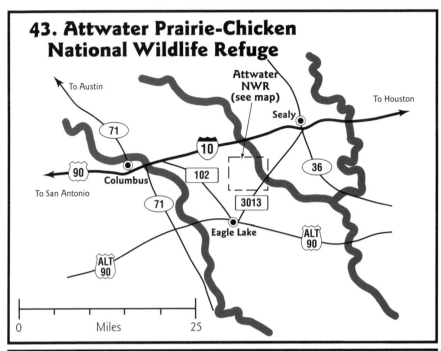

43. Attwater Prairie-Chicken National Wildlife Refuge

To Austin

Attwater
NWR
(see map)

To Houston

71

Sealy

10

90

Columbus

102

36

To San Antonio

3013

71

Eagle Lake

ALT
90

ALT
90

0   Miles   25

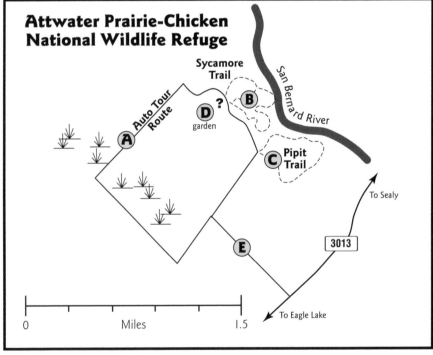

Attwater Prairie-Chicken National Wildlife Refuge

Sycamore
Trail

San Bernard River

Auto Tour Route

D ?

B

garden

A

Pipit
Trail

C

To Sealy

E

3013

0   Miles   1.5

To Eagle Lake

Skipper has also been recorded. Check the small butterfly garden (**D**) at the head-quarters and wildflowers along the entrance road (**E**); watch for **Little Glassywing** in moist ditches.

Directions: In Colorado County, **Attwater Prairie-Chicken NWR (A-E)** is located west of Houston and 10 miles south of Sealy (on I-10). Take SH 36 south to FM 3013 and turn southwest. Follow it to the entrance, seven miles northeast of Eagle Lake.

Nearest food, gas, and lodging: Eagle Lake and Sealy.

Nearest camping: Commercial sites in Eagle Lake.

44. DeWitt County

This county has the state's greatest diversity of wildflowers; an annual Wildflower Festival is held each April. The festival is headquartered in Cuero, in the center of the county. Cuero (Spanish for cowhide) is primarily an agricultural and ranching center, but it's also known for its turkey races. Area roadsides are left unmowed through spring, providing easy access to the plentiful wildflowers. Butterflies can also be abundant.

Sites for butterfly watching are primarily roads (**A-E**). The better butterfly-watching sites lie to the west of the Guadalupe River. In Cuero, visit Cuero City Park (**F**) and the DeWitt County Museum (**G**).

Habitats: Hackberry-oak woodland, riparian, field, cropland, and garden.

Strategy for finding the most butterflies: Although the best roadsides for wildflowers vary from year to year, the more popular routes include Dreyer and Steen roads (**A**), Concrete-Edgar Road (**B**), Bellevue Cemetery Road and roads near Westhoff (**C**), Arneckville-Meyersville Road (**D**), and Stratton Road (**E**). Some of the more numerous butterflies include Pipevine and Giant swallowtails; Large Orange Sulphur; Little Yellow; Dusky-blue Groundstreak; Ceraunus and Reakirt's blues; Gulf Fritillary; Bordered Patch; Vesta, Phaon, and Pearl crescents; Queen; Horace's Duskywing; Clouded and Fiery skippers; and Tropical Checkered-Skipper. At roadsides edged with trees, Goatweed Leafwing and Hackberry and Tawny emperors are likely to occur.

The less common Eastern Tailed-Blue, **Rounded Metalmark**, **Coyote Cloudy-wing**, False Duskywing, and **Laviana** and **Turk's-cap white-skippers** are also possible along roadsides. In spring, Falcate Orangetip and Soapberry Hairstreak can be common; Oak Hairstreak and Henry's Elfin are likely.

In Cuero, check the flowers and shrubs at Cuero City Park (**F**) and the DeWitt County Museum (**G**), headquarters for the Wildflower Festival. These plantings may also attract Eastern Tiger Swallowtail; Lyside Sulphur; Mallow Scrub-Hairstreak; Marine Blue; Long-tailed Skipper; Dorantes Longtail; Northern Cloudywing; and Least, Dun, and Eufala skippers. Sickle-winged and Ocola skippers are usually common in fall.

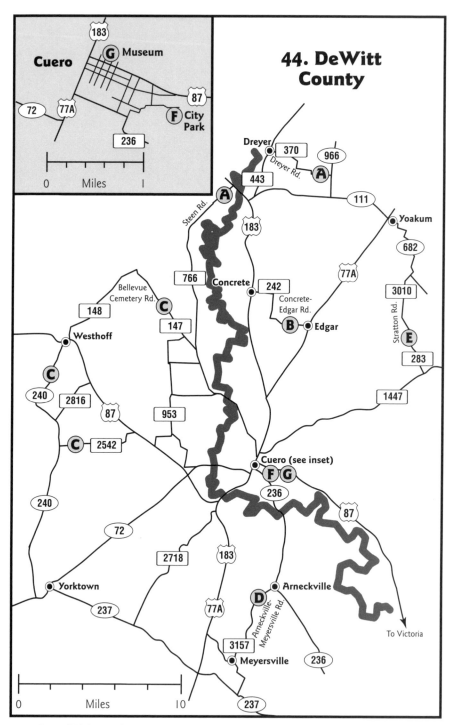

Cuero

183

G Museum

72   77A

87

F City Park

236

0   Miles   1

44. DeWitt County

Dreyer

370

966

A

Dreyer Rd.

443

A

Steen Rd.

111

183

Yoakum

682

766

Concrete

242

77A

3010

Bellevue Cemetery Rd.

C

Concrete-Edgar Rd.

148

147

B

Edgar

Stratton Rd.

E

283

Westhoff

C

240   2816

87

953

1447

C   2542

240

Cuero (see inset)

F G

236

87

72

2718

183

Yorktown

Arneckville

D

To Victoria

237

77A

Arneckville-Meyersville Rd.

3157

Meyersville

236

0   Miles   10

237

Bluebonnets and Indian paintbrush, DeWitt County

Directions: In Dewitt County, Cuero is located at the junction of SH 183 and US 87, 28 miles northwest of Victoria. See the map for the locations of **recommended roads (A-E)**. **Cuero City Park (F)** is located south of US 87 (E. Broadway), across the highway from the high school. **DeWitt County Museum (G)** is located at 312 E. Broadway.

Nearest food, gas, and lodging: Cuero and Yorktown.

Nearest camping: Commercial RV parks in Cuero and Yorktown.

45. Victoria

One of the oldest cities in the state, Victoria was founded in 1824. The area is often called the "Crossroads" for numerous reasons. Biologically, it encompasses several rather distinct ecosystems, all within close proximity of the city: the northeastern edge of the South Texas plains, the southern edges of the post-oak savannah and blackland prairie, the western edge of the Gulf Coast and marshes, and the free-flowing Guadalupe River.

Key sites include a garden **(A)**, Saxet Lake Recreation Area **(C)**, roadsides **(B, D, E)**, and Riverside Park **(F-H)**.

Habitats: Oak-hackberry woodland, coastal prairie, coastal scrub, riparian, field, park, and garden.

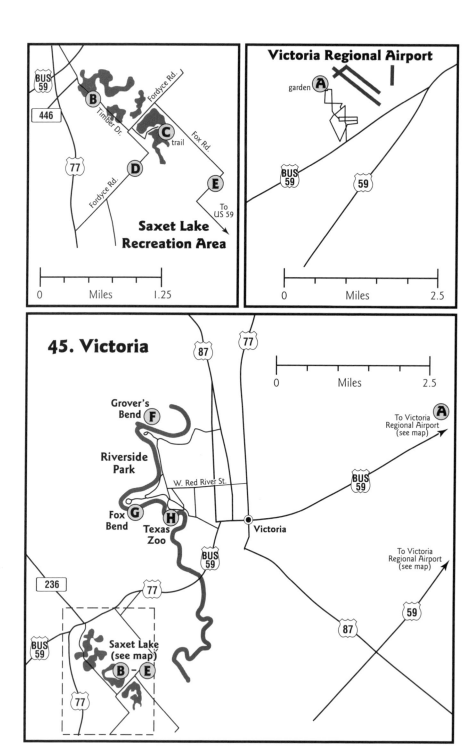

Victoria Regional Airport

garden **A**

BUS 59

59

Saxet Lake Recreation Area

BUS 59

446

77

Fordyce Rd.

Timber Dr.

B

Fordyce Rd.

C

trail

Fox Rd.

D

E

To US 59

0   Miles   1.25

0   Miles   2.5

45. Victoria

87

77

0   Miles   2.5

Grover's Bend **F**

To Victoria Regional Airport (see map) **A**

Riverside Park

W. Red River St.

BUS 59

Fox Bend **G**

H

Texas Zoo

Victoria

236

77

BUS 59

To Victoria Regional Airport (see map)

BUS 59

Saxet Lake (see map)

B – **E**

59

87

77

Riverside Park, Victoria

Strategy for finding the most butterflies: Start at the Master Gardeners Demonstration Garden (**A**) near the airport. Some of the more numerous butterflies include Pipevine and Giant swallowtails; Cloudless and Large Orange sulphurs; Ceraunus Blue; Gulf Fritillary; Queen; Horace's Duskywing; Clouded, Fiery, and Eufala skippers; and Whirlabout. **Coyote Cloudywing** and **Mazans Scallopwing** are also possible, and Ocola Skipper is usually common in fall.

Next, take US 77 southwest to Saxet Lake RA (**C**). Enter by way of Timber Drive (**B**), and check the roadsides along the way to the park. In the park, walk the edges along the entrance road, take the short loop trail at the far end of the road, and check the nearby lake edges. The end of the loop trail is a good place to find **White Peacock** in summer, and the area can have many butterflies. Besides those already mentioned, Mallow Scrub-Hairstreak; Dusky-blue Groundstreak; Reakirt's Blue; **Rounded Metalmark**; Silvery Checkerspot; Hackberry and Tawny emperors; Gemmed and Carolina satyrs; Little Wood-Satyr; White-striped Longtail; Long-tailed, Sickle-winged, and Julia's skippers; and **Laviana** and **Turk's-cap white-skippers** can be expected. In spring, Falcate Orangetip and Henry's Elfin can be common, and Soap-berry, Banded, Striped, and Oak hairstreaks are possible.

Next, drive Fordyce Road (**D**) to US 77, and Fox Road (**E**) to US 59, stopping at pull-offs to check wildflower patches. These routes are good locations to find Little Yellow; Sleepy Orange; and Common/White, Tropical, and Desert checkered-skippers.

Then, drive into town to Riverside Park. Walk along the river, especially within the Grover's Bend (**F**) and Fox Bend (**G**) areas, and also walk the roadside across from the Texas Zoo (**H**), a good place for Texan and Phaon crescents and Southern Skipperling. Many of the same butterflies mentioned above are possible, but these riparian habitats may offer a few additional butterflies, including **Julia** and **Zebra heliconians**.

Directions: In Victoria County, the **Master Gardeners Demonstration Garden (A)** is situated off Bus. 59 on the north side of the airport-parking complex, at the end of Waco Circle. **Saxet Lake RA (C)** is south of Bus. 59, at its intersection with FM 236. Turn south on **Timber Dr. (B)**. Turn left on **Fordyce Rd. (D)** to the park entrance. Return to Fordyce and turn right to **Fox Rd. (E)**. **Riverside Park (F-H)** is accessible from W. Red River St., west from US 87 in Victoria.

Nearest food, gas, and lodging: Victoria.

Nearest camping: Commercial sites, including an RV park adjacent to Riverside Park.

Additional Worthwhile Sites in the Central Plains Region

Granger Lake Area. There are several sites worth checking around 4,400-acre Granger Lake. They include Willis Creek Wildlife Area, Friendship Park, Pecan Grove Wildlife Area below the dam, Wilson H. Fox Park, and Taylor Park. Located in Williamson County, the site is east of Austin via I-35, US 79, SH 95, and FM 1331.

McKinney Roughs Nature Park. This 1,100-acre site (fee area), owned by the Lower Colorado River Authority, has a small butterfly garden at the headquarters, two miles of river frontage, and 18 miles of trails. Habitats include oak-hackberry-juniper woodlands, fields, and riparian. The main entrance is located along SH 71 between Austin and Bastrop; the north entrance and river are accessible from Pope Bend Road (just west of the main entrance).

Fayette Lake Area. Located off SH 159, west of Houston and east of La Grange in Fayette County, the 5,400-acre Fayette Lake is a cooling basin for the coal-fired Fayette Power Plant. Two private shoreline parks (fee areas) with trails, including the Lake Fayette-Rice Osborne Nature Trail, offer habitats that include oak-hackberry-juniper woodland, wetland, and field.

Peters-San Felipe, Grubbs, Steck Bottom Roads. This Austin County site, northeast of Sealy from I-10, consists almost entirely of gravel and chuckholed farm roads (high-clearance vehicles suggested) that meander for nine miles between Stephen F. Austin State Historical Park and FM 331. The route offers a diversity of habitats, including acacia thickets, roadsides filled with swamp milkweed, sugarberry hedgerows, and a riparian woodland. The route is part of the annual Brazos Valley July 4th Butterfly Count.

To reach the site from I-10, exit north on FM 1458 east of Sealy and drive toward the state park. Turn west .1 mile before the park entrance onto Peters-San Felipe Road. In four miles, turn north onto Grubbs Road, which turns into Steck Bottom Road and then meanders for 3.5 miles to FM 331.

Butterfly Checklist for the Central Plains Region

The following list includes seven sites: **39. Buescher State Park/Bastrop State Park, 40. Somerville Lake, 41. Bryan–College Station, 42. Palmetto State Park, 43. Attwater Prairie-Chicken National Wildlife Refuge, 44. DeWitt County,** and **45. Victoria.**

Status symbols include: A = abundant; C = common; U = uncommon; O = occasional; R = rare; X = accidental; M = migrant; TC = temporary colonist; ? = status unknown. (For a full definition of these terms, see p. 3.)

For trip notes, including dates and numbers of species seen, refer to the entry for this checklist in Appendix 3: Regional Checklist Resources.

Butterfly Species	39	40	41	42	43	44	45
Pipevine Swallowtail	C	A	C	A	A	A	A
Polydamas Swallowtail							X
Zebra Swallowtail	X						
Black Swallowtail	U	C	U	U	U	U	U
Giant Swallowtail	C	U	C	C	C	C	C
Ornythion Swallowtail	X						
Eastern Tiger Swallowtail	U	U	U	C		U	O
Spicebush Swallowtail				U		R	
Palamedes Swallowtail	X	X				X	X
Florida White	X						X
Checkered White	U	U	C	C	U	C	C
Cabbage White	R						
Great Southern White	X				U	O	O
Falcate Orangetip	C	C	U	C	U	C	C
Clouded Sulphur		X					
Orange Sulphur	C	A	A	A		C	C
Southern Dogface	C	U	C	C		A	C
White Angled-Sulphur						X	X
Yellow Angled-Sulphur						X	X
Cloudless Sulphur	C	A	U	C	A	C	A
Orange-barred Sulphur		O					O
Large Orange Sulphur	U	U	U	C		A	A
Lyside Sulphur				U		U	U
Mexican Yellow	X			X		O	R
Tailed Orange	X					X	X
Little Yellow	A	A	C	A	A	A	A
Sleepy Orange		C	C	C	C	C	C
Dainty Sulphur	A	C	C	C	C	A	C
Great Purple Hairstreak	C		U	U		U	U
Silver-banded Hairstreak						X	

Butterfly Species	39	40	41	42	43	44	45
Soapberry Hairstreak	C	C		U	O	C	O
Banded Hairstreak	U					R	O
Striped Hairstreak	R		X				R
Oak Hairstreak	O	U		U		U	O
Henry's Elfin	U					R	U
Juniper Hairstreak	C		U				
White M Hairstreak				O			
Gray Hairstreak	C	C	C	C	C	C	C
Mallow Scrub-Hairstreak			U			U	U
Lantana Scrub-Hairstreak	X					X	
Red-banded Hairstreak	O	R	R				X
Dusky-blue Groundstreak	C	U	U	C	U	C	A
Clytie Ministreak						X	
Western Pygmy-Blue	U			U		U	U
Cassius Blue						X	X
Marine Blue						O	O
Cyna Blue	X					X	
Ceraunus Blue	C	U		U	O	C	C
Reakirt's Blue	O			U	O	C	U
Eastern Tailed-Blue	R		O			O	O
Spring/Summer Azure	O		O	O			X
Fatal Metalmark				U		U	U
Rounded Metalmark				O		U	U
Red-bordered Metalmark					X	X	
Mormon Metalmark	X						
American Snout	A-R	A-R	A-R	A-R		A-R	A-R
Gulf Fritillary	C	A	C	U	A	A	A
Julia Heliconian	X	X	X	TC		X	X
Zebra Heliconian	X	X	X	TC	X	X	TC
Variegated Fritillary	C	A	C	A	C	A	C
Theona Checkerspot						U	
Bordered Patch	O	U	U	U		C	C
Gorgone Checkerspot	R		R				
Silvery Checkerspot	C	C	U	C	R	U	U
Texan Crescent	U	C		A		U	C
Vesta Crescent	U			U		C	C
Phaon Crescent	A	C	C	A	C	A	A
Pearl Crescent	C	C	C	A	U	C	A
Question Mark	U	U	U	U		C	C
Mourning Cloak	O						
American Lady	C	U	C	C		A	C
Painted Lady	C	C	U	U		C	U

Butterfly Species	39	40	41	42	43	44	45
Red Admiral	C	C	C	C	U	C	C
Common Buckeye	C	C	C	U	C	C	C
Tropical Buckeye	X						
White Peacock						TC	TC
Red-spotted Purple	O			R			
Viceroy	U	U	O	O	C	U	C
Dingy Purplewing						X	
Blue-eyed Sailor				X			
Common Mestra	O	O	O	U		U	U
Red Rim	X						
Blomfild's Beauty						X	
Many-banded Daggerwing	X						
Ruddy Daggerwing				X		X	
Goatweed Leafwing	A	C	U	U	C	U	C
Hackberry Emperor	C	C	U	C	U	A	U
Empress Leilia				X		R	X
Tawny Emperor	C	C	C	A	C	A	A
Gemmed Satyr	U		O	U		C	C
Carolina Satyr	U	U	U	C	O	C	A
Little Wood-Satyr	C			O		C	C
Red Satyr		U					
Common Wood-Nymph	C	U	U	U		X	
Monarch	M	M	M	M	M	M	M
Queen	U	U	U	C	C	C	C
Soldier						X	X
Silver-spotted Skipper	U			O		X	X
White-striped Longtail		O	X	O		U	C
Zilpa Longtail						X	X
Long-tailed Skipper	O	O	O	U		O	U
Dorantes Longtail	X		O	O		U	O
Hoary Edge	R						
Desert Cloudywing	X						
Coyote Cloudywing		X				C	C
Southern Cloudywing	R	R	?				X
Northern Cloudywing	U	U	U	U		U	U
Confused Cloudywing	O		O				
Outis Skipper	?			?			
Mazans Scallopwing	X	X		R	X	R	R
Hayhurst's Scallopwing	R			U			X
Texas Powdered-Skipper						U	R
Sickle-winged Skipper	X	U	R			U	C
Hermit Skipper		X					

Butterfly Species	39	40	41	42	43	44	45
White-patched Skipper							X
False Duskywing	U			U		U	U
Sleepy Duskywing	O						
Juvenal's Duskywing	U						
Horace's Duskywing	C	U	U	U	C	A	C
Mournful Duskywing							O
Mottled Duskywing	O						
Funereal Duskywing	C	U	O	U	U	C	U
Wild Indigo Duskywing	C	O	O		C	U	O
Com./White Checkered-Skipper	C	C	C	A	C	A	A
Tropical Checkered-Skipper	U	C	U	C	U	C	A
Desert Checkered-Skipper				O	O	U	U
Laviana White-Skipper	O					R	O
Turk's-cap White-Skipper	X					U	O
Common Streaky-Skipper	R			O		R	
Common Sootywing		U		U			R
Julia's Skipper	U	U		O		U	U
Neamathla Skipper	X		X		R		
Clouded Skipper	C	A	C	A	C	C	C
Least Skipper	R		O	U	C	C	U
Orange Skipperling	U	U		O		O	O
Southern Skipperling	U	U	O	C	U	C	C
Fiery Skipper	A	A	C	C	U	A	C
Cobweb Skipper	X						
Meske's Skipper	X						
Tawny-edged Skipper	X						
Whirlabout		C	U	C	O	U	C
Southern Broken-Dash	C	U	U	C	O	U	C
Little Glassywing					R		X
Sachem	C	A	U	C	C	A	A
Dun Skipper	C	U	C	U	U	C	A
Bronze Roadside-Skipper				X			
Nysa Roadside-Skipper					O		U	O
Dotted Roadside-Skipper			R				X
Common Roadside-Skipper	C						
Celia's Roadside-Skipper	U	U	U	C		A	A
Bell's Roadside-Skipper	X						
Dusky Roadside-Skipper	R						
Eufala Skipper	C	C	U	C	U	C	C
Brazilian Skipper			O	O	O	U	U
Ocola Skipper	C	C	C	U	U	C	A
Yucca Giant-Skipper	R						

Upper Gulf Coast

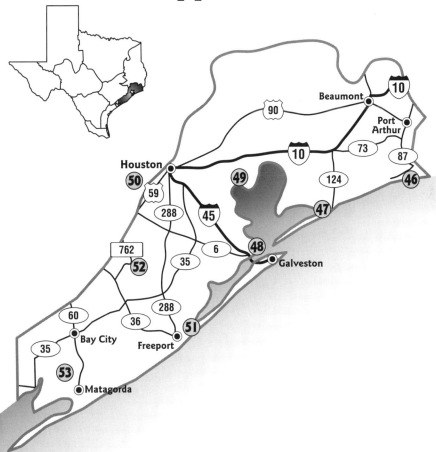

46. **Texas Point/Sabine Woods**
47. **Anahuac National Wildlife Refuge/High Island**
48. **Galveston–Texas City**
49. **Baytown**
50. **Houston**
51. **Freeport**
52. **Brazos Bend State Park**
53. **Matagorda County**

Upper Gulf Coast Region

The Upper Gulf Coast Region lies between the Gulf of Mexico and the Pineywoods and Central Plains regions, stretching from the Sabine River in the northeast to Matagorda Bay in the southwest. The landscape is generally flat with numerous drainages, including three major rivers—the Brazos, Lavaca, and Colorado. Vegetation consists primarily of coastal prairie and coastal scrub with oak mottes situated on slightly higher, drier sites. Elevations range from sea level to about 300 feet.

The Upper Gulf Coast Region is represented by eight sites: **46. Texas Point/Sabine Woods**, **47. Anahuac National Wildlife Refuge/High Island**, **48. Galveston–Texas City**, **49. Baytown**, **50. Houston**, **51. Freeport**, **52. Brazos Bend State Park**, and **53. Matagorda County**. The best time to visit these sites is March through November.

Upper Gulf Coast Specialties

The region's butterfly fauna is moderate in diversity and includes several species that owe their presence to the region's proximity to the Southeast U.S. and the Pineywoods. Fourteen are considered specialties.

Blues, Buckeyes, Pearly-eyes: **Eastern Pygmy-Blue** has been recorded in stands of glasswort (larval foodplant) on coastal flats only at Texas Point/Sabine Woods. **Tropical Buckeye**, at least the dark form, has been recorded in the areas of Galveston–Texas City, Baytown, Freeport, and Matagorda County. Larvae feed on woolly stemodia. **Southern Pearly-eye**, apparently at the southern edge of its range, has been recorded in patches of giant cane (larval foodplant) in the Freeport area.

Grass-Skippers: **Neamathla Skipper** frequents open, grassy areas near moist woodlands at Texas Point/Sabine Woods, Anahuac NWR/High Island, the Galveston–Texas City area, Baytown area, Freeport area, and Brazos Bend SP. **Tawny-edged Skipper** has been recorded only at Texas Point/Sabine Woods; it is most likely to be found in open, short-grass areas, including lawns. **Little Glassywing** occurs in moist, shady habitats, including ditches, near woodlands at Anahuac NWR/High Island, the Baytown area, Freeport area, and Brazos Bend SP. It has two broods, in April–May and July–August. **Aaron's Skipper** has been recorded in and near brackish marshes only at Texas Point/Sabine Woods and the Baytown area. These skippers apparently represent an isolated population in Texas. **Broad-winged Skipper** occurs in and adjacent to sedge wetlands, often roosting on cattails, throughout the region. Larvae feed on common reeds, sedges, and wild rice. **Bay Skipper** has been recorded only rarely at the edge of saltwater marshes at Texas Point/Sabine Woods, Anahuac NWR/High Island (in September), and the Baytown area (in July). Very little is known about this coastal species. **Lace-winged Roadside-Skipper**, apparently at the southern edge of its range, has been recorded in cane patches in the Big Bog Tract of San Bernard NWR in the Freeport area. **Twin-spot Skipper** frequents wildflowers near moist woodlands in the Galveston–Texas City area, Baytown area, and Houston area. **Salt Marsh Skipper** is most likely to be seen on shrubs near saltgrass in sites throughout the region. **Obscure Skipper** occurs in brushy areas near marine wetlands in sites throughout the region.

Sites within the Upper Gulf Coast Region

46. Texas Point/Sabine Woods

Texas Point is at the extreme southeastern tip of the state, across the Sabine River from Louisiana. The principal site, Sabine Woods (**A**), featuring thirty-two acres of woodlands and fields, is owned and maintained by the Texas Ornithological Society. An entry contribution is expected. Sabine Pass Battleground State Park (**B**), with its riverside vegetation, and Sea Rim State Park (**C-E**) offer additional sites. Because of the site's location on the border with Louisiana, butterfly strays from the southeastern U.S. are always possible. July 4th Butterfly Counts are held here annually.

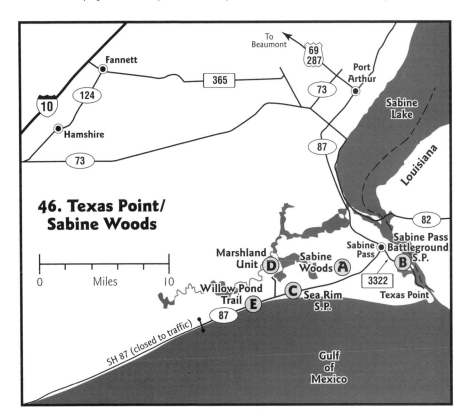

Sabine Woods, near Texas Point

Habitats: Coastal prairie, coastal scrub, oak motte, riparian, and saltwater marsh.

Strategy for finding the most butterflies: Start at Sabine Woods (**A**) by walking the woodland and perimeter trails, including those that radiate out into the adjacent prairie. Some of the more numerous butterflies include Giant Swallowtail, Great Southern White, Cloudless Sulphur, Little Yellow, Gulf Fritillary, Phaon Crescent, Tawny Emperor, Carolina Satyr, Horace's Duskywing, Tropical Checkered-Skipper, and Clouded and Fiery skippers. Some of the less numerous butterflies include Eastern Tiger, Spicebush, and Palamedes swallowtails; Red-banded Hairstreak; Dusky-blue Groundstreak; White-striped Longtail; Long-tailed, Least, Dun, and Eufala skippers; and Funereal Duskywing. Also watch along the edges for **Aaron's Skipper**. In fall, expect Ocola Skipper. Next, drive to Sabine Pass Battleground SP (**B**), a fee area. Walk the edges and also check the vegetation on the historic bunkers and along the entrance roads. Pipevine and Black swallowtails, Monarch, and Queen can be expected, and **Neamathla, Tawny-edged,** and **Twin-spot skippers** are possible.

Then drive to Sea Rim SP (fee area) and check the entrance roadsides (**C**), especially those with wildflowers, and the road into the Marshland Unit (**D**). Walk the Willow Pond Trail (**E**), watching for **Broad-winged Skipper** around sedges or cattails. **Salt Marsh** and **Obscure skippers** are likely to be seen in brushy areas along the salt-marsh edges. **Eastern Pygmy-Blue** and **Bay Skipper** are also possible.

Note: Watch, also, for Palatka Skipper at all these sites. It has been recorded in sawgrass areas in nearby Louisiana.

Directions: In Jefferson County, take SH 87 south from Port Arthur to Sabine Pass. **Sabine Pass Battleground SP (B)** is located just beyond the town on FM 3322. **Sabine Woods (A)** is four miles west of Sabine Pass on the north side of SH 87. **Sea Rim SP (C, D)** is 10 miles west of Sabine Pass. The **Willow Pond Trail (E)** is located past park headquarters on SH 87, which is closed beyond McFadden NWR.

Nearest food, gas, and lodging: Sabine Pass.

Nearest camping: At the two state parks.

47. Anahuac National Wildlife Refuge/High Island

Anahuac National Wildlife Refuge and High Island, approximately fifteen miles apart, are located on the coastal prairie north of Galveston Bay. The 34,000-acre Anahuac NWR (fee area) was established in 1963 to provide habitat for wintering waterfowl along the Central Flyway; a butterfly garden **(A)** was opened in 2004. The Shoveler Pond loop road **(B)** and Frozen Point Road **(C)** are also good spots for butterflies.

High Island features two well-known birding sites (fee areas) that are also good for butterflies: Smith Oaks Sanctuary **(D)** and the Boy Scout Woods **(E)**. Both are owned

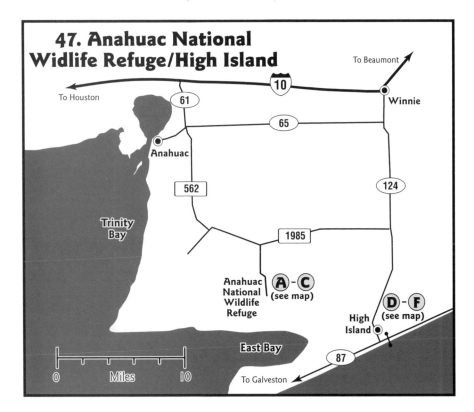

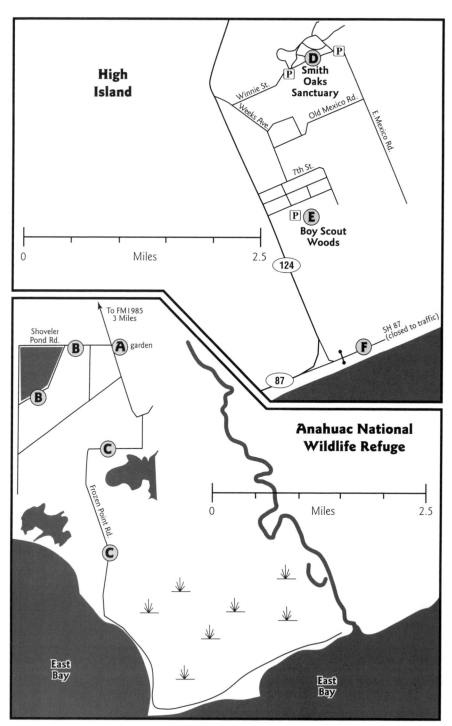

High
Island

Smith
Oaks
Sanctuary

Winnie St.
Weeks Ave.
Old Mexico Rd.
E. Mexico Rd.

7th St.

Boy Scout
Woods

0   Miles   2.5

124

To FM1985
3 Miles

Shoveler
Pond Rd.

garden

SH 87
(closed to traffic)

87

Anahuac National
Wildlife Refuge

Frozen Point Rd.

0   Miles   2.5

East
Bay

East
Bay

Entrance garden, Anahuac National Wildlife Refuge

and operated by the Houston Audubon Society. Walking a portion of SH 87 (**F**) that is closed to vehicular traffic is also recommended. July 4th Butterfly Counts are held annually in the area.

Habitats: Coastal prairie, coastal scrub, oak motte, fresh and saltwater wetlands, garden, field, and cropland.

Strategy for finding the most butterflies: At Anahuac NWR, start at the butterfly garden (**A**) near the refuge entrance and visit it again during your stay. Some of the more numerous butterflies include Pipevine, Black, and Giant swallowtails; Little Yellow; Western Pygmy-Blue; Ceraunus Blue; Gulf Fritillary; Phaon Crescent; Monarch; Horace's Duskywing; Clouded, Fiery, and Eufala skippers; and Southern Skipperling. Less numerous species include Eastern Tiger, Spicebush, and Palamedes swallowtails; Red-banded Hairstreak; Dusky-blue Groundstreak; White-striped Longtail; and Funereal Duskywing. Also walk to The Willows, where Viceroy is probable. In spring, Falcate Orangetip is also likely, and Ocola Skipper can be expected in fall.

Then drive the Shoveler Pond Road (**B**) and at least a portion of the Frozen Point Road (**C**), checking flowering plants along the edges. Great Southern White, Dainty Sulphur, Sleepy Orange, and Tropical Checkered-Skipper can be expected. Wild Indigo Duskywing, **Neamathla** and **Bay skippers**, and **Little Glassywing** are also possible.

Then drive to High Island and visit both Smith Oaks Sanctuary (**D**) and the Boy Scout Woods (**E**). At both sites, check the hummingbird gardens near the parking areas and walk the extended network of woodland trails. Many of the same butterflies mentioned above are possible, but Texan Crescent; American Lady; Red-spotted Purple; Carolina Satyr; and Silver-spotted, Long-tailed, Least, and Brazilian skippers are also likely. Watch, too, for **Broad-winged Skipper** at swampy areas with sedges.

In addition, when wildflowers are present, walk a section of SH 87 (**F**) that is closed to traffic and runs east along the Gulf; **Salt Marsh** and **Obscure skippers** are likely to occur.

Directions: In Chambers and Galveston counties, all sites are south of I-10 from Winnie. Take SH 124 south for 13 miles to FM 1985 and drive west for eight miles to the **Anahuac NWR (A-C)** entrance. High Island is 12 miles south of FM 1985 on SH 124. **Smith Oaks Sanctuary (D)** and the **Boy Scout Woods (E)** are east of SH 124. From Galveston, High Island is 27 miles northeast of the ferry landing on SH 87. *Note: SH 87 is closed to vehicular traffic east of its junction with SH 124.*

Nearest food, gas, and lodging: High Island, Winnie, and Galveston; food and gas at Gilchrist and Crystal Beach along SH 87.

Nearest camping: High Island and along SH 87 at Gilchrist.

48. Galveston–Texas City

Galveston is the oldest active seaport in Texas. It is located on Galveston Island, and Texas City is across the bay on the mainland. Several butterflying sites are located within a ten-mile circle. On Galveston Island, visit the 2,013-acre Galveston Island State Park (**A**) and nearby Stewart Road (**B**). Also stop at Galveston's Moody Gardens (**C**) and Corps Woods (**D**), before heading north to Texas City's Sundance Garden (**E**) and the nearby 2,303-acre Texas City Preserve (**F**). July 4th Butterfly Counts are held in the area some years.

Habitats: Coastal prairie, coastal scrub, marsh, beach, garden, and field.

Strategy for finding the most butterflies: Start on Galveston Island at Galveston Island SP (**A**), a fee area. Drive the park roads north of FM 3005 and walk the trails. Some of the more numerous butterflies include Giant Swallowtail, Great Southern White, Western Pygmy-Blue, Ceraunus Blue, Gulf Fritillary, Phaon Crescent, Queen, Tropical Checkered-Skipper, and Clouded and Fiery skippers. "Dark" **Tropical Buckeye** is possible, and also watch for **Salt Marsh** and **Obscure skippers**.

Then drive northeast on Stewart Road (**B**), paralleling FM 3005. Stop at flowering plants along the roadside. Along with many of the butterflies mentioned above, Sleepy Orange, Reakirt's Blue, American Lady, Southern Skipperling, and Whirlabout can be expected. **Neamathla Skipper** is possible at open, grassy areas. In spring, Falcate Orangetip and Soapberry Hairstreak are likely. In fall, Ocola Skipper can be expected.

At 81st Street, go north to the 145-acre Moody Gardens (**C**), a fee area with a rainforest pyramid housing tropical vegetation and butterflies. Check the plantings on

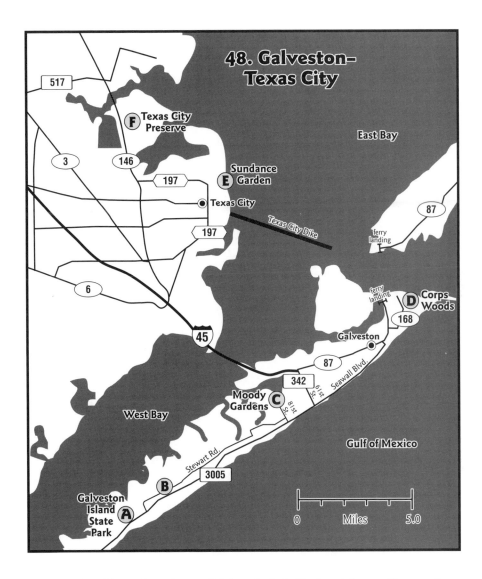

48. Galveston–
Texas City

the grounds. Additional species possible here include Black and Eastern Tiger swallow-tails; Red-banded Hairstreak; Dusky-blue Groundstreak; Long-tailed, Dun, Eufala, and Brazilian skippers; Southern Broken-Dash; and Celia's Roadside-Skipper.

Next, drive east on FM 3005 toward the ferry landing to Corps Woods (**D**). Short trails pass through a wooded area where Goatweed Leafwing, Hackberry and Tawny emperors, Gemmed and Carolina satyrs, and Little Wood-Satyr are possible; also watch for **Broad-winged Skipper** at sedges.

Drive across Galveston Bay to Texas City and visit Sundance Garden (**E**). Walk the adjacent trails. In addition to many of the butterflies mentioned above, also watch

Sundance Garden, Texas City

for **Twin-spot Skipper**. Then drive to the nearby Texas City Preserve **(F)**, a Texas Nature Conservancy property that protects a small population of Attwater's prairie-chickens. Report in at the office first and then check the garden in front and walk the nearby trails.

Directions: In Galveston County and situated between San Luis Pass to the south and the Bolivar Peninsula across the bay to the north, Galveston is 50 miles from Houston via I-45. Exit I-45 on 61st St. in Galveston and go south to Seawall Blvd. (FM 3005). Drive 10 miles southwest to **Galveston Island SP (A)**. After exploring the park, turn north at the park boundary on 13 Mile Rd. It curves right and becomes **Stewart Rd. (B)**. In Galveston, turn north on 81st St. from Stewart Rd. Where it curves east, take Hope Blvd. to **Moody Gardens (C)**. Then return to Seawall Blvd. and go east. **Corps Woods (D)** is located at the edge of the Coast Guard Base, .7 mile east of Ferry Rd. via SH 168.

Return to I-45 and go north to Texas City. Exit on Loop 197 northeast, follow it to 9th Ave., and turn right. Then turn left onto Bay St. **Sundance Garden (E)** is in Bay Street Park on the right side of Bay St. Return to Loop 197 and follow it to a right turn on SH 146. **Texas City Preserve (F)** is located east of SH 146 on the northern edge of Texas City.

Nearest food, gas, and lodging: Galveston and Texas City.

Nearest camping: Galveston Island SP.

49. Baytown

Near Baytown, east of Houston, the 450-acre Baytown Nature Center (fee area) and the 1,900-acre Armand Bayou Nature Center (fee area) feature two of only a few semi-wild tracts left in the Houston area. Both offer a variety of environmental education programs. San Jacinto Battleground State Historical Park (fee area) is directly across the bay to the west and offers another opportunity for butterflying.

The Baytown Nature Center is located on lands that once held the community of Brownwood, which sank as much as fifteen feet, allowing the sea to invade the land. Sites for butterfly watching include a butterfly garden (**A**), MacArthur Trail (**B**), and Bayshore Trail (**C**). At San Jacinto Battleground SHP, the main site is the loop road (**D**). Armand Bayou Nature Center is restoring a native prairie. Sites to visit include the facilities area (**E**), Karankawa Trail (**F**), Marsh Trail (**G**), and Martyn Trail (**H**). July 4th Butterfly Counts are held here annually.

Habitats: Coastal prairie, oak-hackberry woodland, riparian, marsh, and garden.

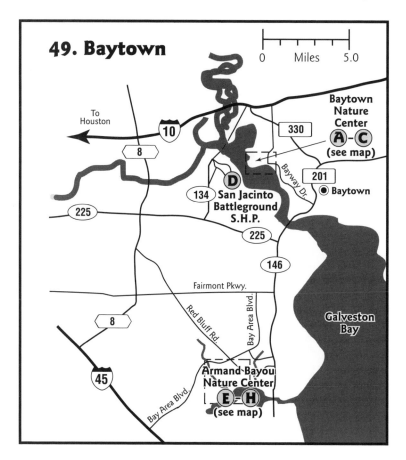

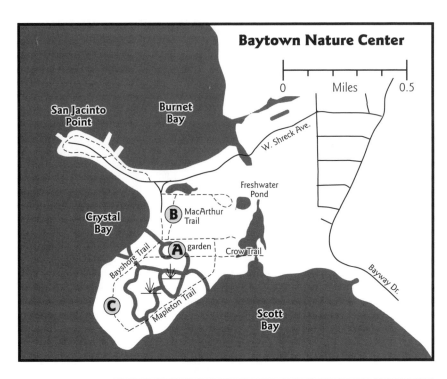

Baytown Nature Center

0 — Miles — 0.5

San Jacinto Point

Burnet Bay

W. Shreck Ave.

Crystal Bay

Freshwater Pond

B MacArthur Trail

Bayshore Trail

A garden

Crow Trail

Bayway Dr.

C

Mapleton Trail

Scott Bay

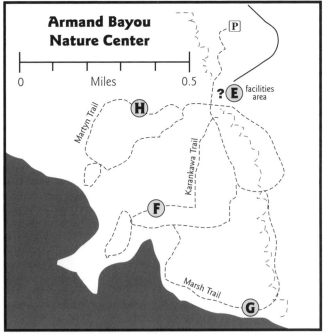

Armand Bayou Nature Center

0 — Miles — 0.5

P

? E facilities area

H

Martyn Trail

Karankawa Trail

F

Marsh Trail

G

Crystal Bay Butterfly Garden, Baytown Nature Center

Strategy for finding the most butterflies: The Baytown Nature Center is likely to offer the greatest butterfly diversity. Start at the Crystal Bay Butterfly Garden **(A)** and return there later in the day to check for additional species. Some of the more numerous butterflies include Black, Giant, and Palamedes swallowtails; Cloudless Sulphur; Red-banded Hairstreak; Ceraunus Blue; Queen; Horace's Duskywing; and Clouded, Dun, and Eufala skippers. Eastern Tiger and Spicebush swallowtails, Dusky-blue Groundstreak, White-striped Longtail, and Brazilian Skipper are less numerous. In spring, Soapberry Hairstreak is likely; Monarch and Ocola Skipper are usually abundant in fall.

Next walk MacArthur Trail **(B)** to Freshwater Pond, and Bayshore Trail **(C)** to Wooster Pavilion. These trails pass through a lush coastal prairie where Pipevine Swallowtail, Great Southern White, Little Yellow, Western Pygmy-Blue, Marine and Reakirt's blues, Phaon Crescent, Northern Cloudywing, and Tropical Checkered-Skipper are likely to be seen. Cassius Blue; "Dark" **Tropical Buckeye**; and **Broad-winged, Salt Marsh**, and **Obscure skippers** are also possible.

Next, drive to San Jacinto Battleground SHP **(D)** and take the loop road, stopping at pull-offs to check flowering plants. Walk the Marsh and Boardwalk Trail. Many of the butterflies mentioned above can be expected, and Least Skipper is also likely.

Then drive to Armand Bayou Nature Center and start by checking the flowering shrubs around the facilities **(E)**, a good place to find **Twin-spot Skipper**. Walk the Karankawa Trail **(F)** to Armand Bayou overlook and return via the Marsh Trail **(G)**.

Watch for **Neamathla** and **Aaron's skippers** and **Little Glassywing**. Finally, walk the Martyn Trail (**H**) for woodland butterflies. Texan Crescent, Gemmed and Carolina satyrs, and Little Wood-Satyr are likely to be found here.

Directions: In east Harris County, take I-10 east from Houston. Exit at Spur 330 (Decker Dr.) to Bayway Dr., where you'll turn south and go to W. Shreck Ave. Turn west to Westwood Park and the **Baytown Nature Center (A-C)**. **San Jacinto Battleground SHP (D)** is also accessible from I-10; take SH 134 south to PR 1836. From the south, take SH 225 west from SH 146 to SH 134 and turn north to PR 1836. **Armand Bayou Nature Center (E-H)** is located to the south, off SH 146. Take Fairmont Pkwy. west to Bay Area Blvd. and turn south. The entrance is on the left past Red Bluff Rd. From I-45 southeast of Houston, take Bay Area Blvd. (exit 28) northeast for 6.5 miles to the entrance.

Nearest food, gas, and lodging: Along I-45 and SH 146.

Nearest camping: Commercial sites in Baytown, League City, Dickinson, La Marque, and Texas City.

50. Houston

Butterfly-watching sites in the Houston area include six principal locations, all within the western portion of Loop 610: Houston Arboretum and Nature Center (**A**), a 155-acre wildlife sanctuary; nearby 1,468-acre Memorial Park (**B**), including the utility right-of-way; 20-acre 11th Street Park (**C**), owned by the Houston Independent School District but maintained by Harris County; the parkway along T.C. Jester Boulevard (**D**); Allen Park (**E**) along the Allen Parkway; and 398-acre Hermann Park (**F**). The Cockrell Butterfly Center and Houston Museum of Natural Science are located at Hermann Park. July 4th Butterfly Counts are held in Houston annually.

Habitats: Mixed-hardwood forest, pine forest, garden, riparian, and field.

Strategy for finding the most butterflies: The greatest butterfly diversity is most likely to be found at the Houston Arboretum and Nature Center (**A**). Check the flowering plants in front of the visitor center and around the parking area and walk at least the Inner Loop Trail through the woodlands. Some of the more numerous butterflies include Great Purple and Red-banded hairstreaks; Dusky-blue Groundstreak; Cassius Blue; Texan Crescent; American and Painted ladies; Tawny Emperor; Horace's Duskywing; Silver-spotted, Clouded, Fiery, and Eufala skippers; and Celia's Roadside-Skipper. Ocola Skipper can be common in fall.

Then, drive to nearby Memorial Park (**B**) and walk the utility right-of-way on both sides of Memorial Drive. This open, grassy area is likely to produce Pipevine, Black, and Eastern Tiger swallowtails; Sleepy Orange; Reakirt's Blue; Gulf Fritillary; Queen; Northern Cloudywing; Tropical Checkered-Skipper; Southern Skipperling; and Swarthy and Dun skippers. Also, watch for Confused Cloudywing and **Twin-spot Skipper** at patches of wildflowers and **Broad-winged Skipper** at wetlands with sedges.

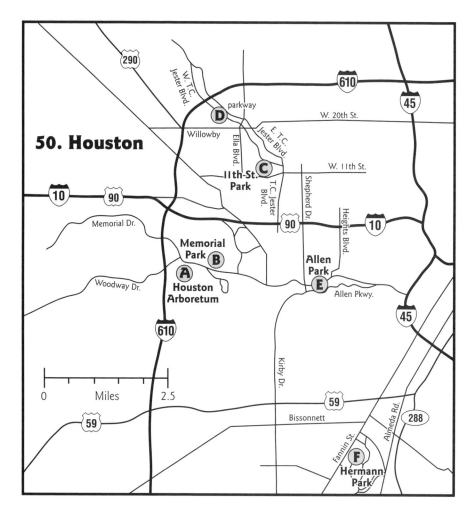

50. Houston

The next spot is 11th Street Park (**C**). Walk the mowed trails through this wooded area. Giant and Spicebush swallowtails and Long-tailed Skipper can be expected. Three additional areas are worth visiting. At the parkway along T.C. Jester Blvd. (**D**), walk a section of the paved trail along the cement bayou. At Allen Park (**E**), walk a section of the hiking/biking trail, and at Hermann Park (**F**), check the wildflowers growing near the marsh, as well as the plantings in front of and on the north side of the Cockrell Butterfly Center.

Directions: In Harris County, the **Houston Arboretum and Nature Center** (**A**) is west of downtown Houston at 4501 Woodway Dr. From Loop 610 south of I-10, exit on Woodway Dr. east and go a quarter mile. **Memorial Park** (**B**) is immediately beyond the Nature Center. Woodway Dr. turns into Memorial Dr., and parking is available at the first entry road. **Allen Park** (**E**) is situated along Allen Parkway

Houston Arboretum and Nature Center

between Shepherd Dr. and Heights Blvd. From Memorial Park, continue east on Memorial Dr. to Shepherd Dr. and turn south. Then turn east on Allen Parkway.

11th Street Park (C) and **T.C. Jester Blvd. (D)** are north of I-10: from Allen Park, return to Shepherd Dr. and travel north to 11th St. Turn west to reach 11th Street Park, located between Shelterwood Dr. and Shirkmere Rd. From 11th Street Park, go east on 11th St. to T.C. Jester Blvd. Turn north and continue to a right turn on E. T.C. Jester Blvd., which provides access to the parkway. The recommended area is between Ella Blvd. and Loop 610. **Hermann Park (F)**, the southernmost site, is located south of US 59 on Fannin St.

Nearest food, gas, and lodging: Throughout Houston.

Nearest camping: Commercial sites along I-10 and Loop 610.

51. Freeport

Although the Freeport area has long been known to naturalists as a marvelous winter birding destination, it also supports a great variety of butterflies. It incorporates much of eastern Brazoria County and has at least seven sites worth visiting, including gardens, parks, and two national wildlife refuges. The Gulf Coast Bird Observatory (**A**) features a butterfly garden, hiking trails, and a nature store. Other sites include Sea Center (**B**), Peach Point Wildlife Management Area (**C**), the Quintana area (**D**), Brazosport Nature Center (**E**), and the Brazoria (**F**) and San Bernard (**G**) national wildlife refuges. Two July 4th Butterfly Counts, Freeport and Dancinger, are held annually.

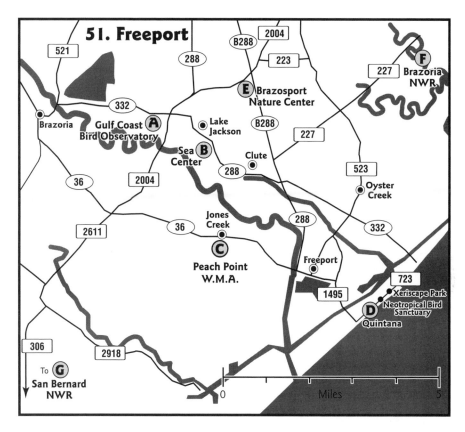

Habitats: Coastal prairie, coastal scrub, mesquite grassland, marsh, riparian, field, and cropland.

Strategy for finding the most butterflies: Start at the Gulf Coast Bird Observatory (**A**) by checking the butterfly garden and walking the trails into the adjacent woodlands. Some of the butterflies most likely to be seen in the garden and open areas include Giant and Eastern Tiger swallowtails; Little Yellow; Red-banded Hairstreak; Dusky-blue Groundstreak; Reakirt's Blue; Gulf Fritillary; Phaon Crescent; Queen; Horace's Duskywing; Tropical Checkered-Skipper; Clouded, Fiery, and Dun skippers; Whirlabout; and Southern Broken-Dash. In the woodlands, expect Goatweed Leafwing and Hackberry and Tawny emperors. In fall, Ocola Skipper is likely.

Next, drive to nearby Sea Center (**B**), which also has a small garden, as well as a boardwalk over a marsh. Many of the same butterflies mentioned above are likely to occur, but Marine and Ceraunus blues, Viceroy, and Least and **Broad-winged skippers** are also possible.

Peach Point WMA (**C**) offers a loop trail through a wooded wetland as well as a mile of roadsides, a good place to find **Little Glassywing**. Pearl Crescent and Gemmed and Carolina satyrs can also be expected.

Neotropical Bird Sanctuary, Quintana

The area around Quintana (**D**), including the Neotropical Bird Sanctuary, Xeriscape Park, and roadsides, may be the best of the sites. Many of the butterflies mentioned above can be expected, but several additional species are likely: Pipevine and Black swallowtails, Great Southern White, Western Pygmy-Blue, Monarch, White-striped Longtail, and **Salt Marsh** and **Obscure skippers**. Also watch for "Dark" **Tropical Buckeye**, Confused Cloudywing, and **Neamathla Skipper**.

Also worthwhile are Brazosport Nature Center (**E**), Brazoria NWR (**F**), with its butterfly garden and Big Slough Auto Tour, and San Bernard NWR (**G**), with its Moccasin Auto Tour, Bobcat Woods Trail, and Big Pond Tract (open only by prior arrangement), where **Southern Pearly-eye** and **Lace-winged Roadside-Skipper** have been recorded in stands of giant cane.

Directions: In Brazoria County, the **Gulf Coast Bird Observatory (A)** is located south of SH 332, just west of the junction with SH 288. **Sea Center (B)** is five miles southeast of the junction on SH 288; follow the signs. The entrance to **Peach Point WMA (C)** is along SH 36, on the south side of Jones Creek. You can reach one of the more remote sites, **San Bernard NWR (G)**, from this point by going west on SH 36 to FM 2611. Take that road southwest until it curves sharply right. Continue straight on FM 2918 and follow it to a turn southwest on CR 306 to the refuge entrance road.

To reach Quintana, return to SH 36 and go east through Freeport to a right turn on FM 1495. Continue over the Intracoastal Waterway to FM 723. Turn left and go 2.1 miles to **Quintana (D)** and the Neotropical Bird Sanctuary and Xeriscape Park. After exploring that area, return to SH 36 and turn west. Turn north on SH 288 and continue on Bus. 288 to **Brazosport Nature Center** (**E**) near the intersection of Bus. 288 and FM 2004. To reach **Brazoria NWR** (**F**) from there, go east on FM 2004 a half-mile past Bus. 288 and turn right on CR 223. Turn south on FM 523 to CR 227, where you will turn northeast to the refuge. From Quintana, you can take FM 1495 and FM 523 north past Oyster Creek to CR 227. Turn right to the refuge.

Nearest food, gas, and lodging: Communities in the area.

Nearest camping: Quintana Beach County Park, the two NWRs, and commercial sites in the area.

52. Brazos Bend State Park

The 4,897-acre Brazos Bend State Park, named for a bend in the Brazos River, has a variety of natural environments, in spite of being only twenty-eight miles from downtown Houston. The park (fee area) has two lakes and 21.6 miles of trails that provide good access. Key butterfly sites include the Hale Lake Trail (**A**), 40-Acre Lake Trail (**B**), Prairie Trail (**C**), Elm Lake Trail (**D**), wildflower gardens at the visitor center (**E**) and entrance station (**F**), and the park entrance road (**G**). July 4th Butterfly Counts are held here annually.

Habitats: Bottomland-hardwood forest, oak motte, oak savannah, coastal prairie, riparian, freshwater marsh, field, and cropland.

Strategy for finding the most butterflies: Start at the Hale Lake Trail (**A**), probably the location with the greatest variety of butterflies. Some of the more numerous species include Black, Giant, and Eastern Tiger swallowtails; Little Yellow; Dusky-blue Groundstreak; Gulf Fritillary; Phaon Crescent; Gemmed and Carolina satyrs; Little Wood-Satyr; White-striped Longtail; Southern and Northern cloudywings; Horace's Duskywing; Tropical Checkered-Skipper; Clouded, Fiery, and Dun skippers; and Southern Broken-Dash.

A few of the less reliable species include Dainty Sulphur, Great Purple and White M hairstreaks, Ceraunus and Reakirt's blues, Silvery Checkerspot, and Wild Indigo Duskywing. In spring, Falcate Orangetip; Soapberry, Striped, and Oak hairstreaks; and Juvenal's Duskywing are possible.

Next, walk the 40-Acre Lake Trail (**B**), checking the wildflowers and shrubbery and also the open grassland at the parking area. Many of the butterflies mentioned above are possible here, but likely additional species include Spicebush Swallowtail, Large Orange Sulphur, Texan Crescent, Red-spotted Purple, Least Skipper, and Southern Skipperling.

In spring, walk the Prairie Trail (**C**) and at least a portion of the Elm Lake Trail (**D**). Expect **Broad-winged Skipper** among the cattails and adjacent sedges. Afterwards, check the wildflower gardens at the visitor center (**E**) and entrance station (**F**). These gardens are likely to offer a few different butterflies: Red-banded Hairstreak; Dusky-blue Groundstreak; and Long-tailed, Julia's, and Brazilian skippers. Ocola Skipper can be added in the fall.

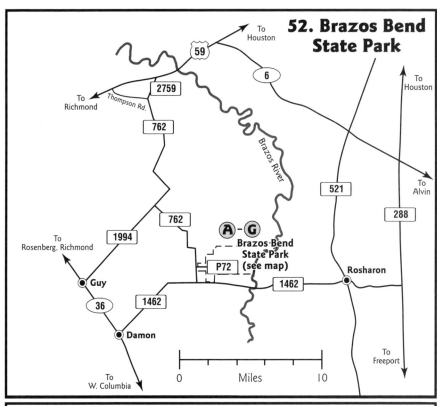

52. Brazos Bend State Park

To Houston

To Houston

59

6

2759

To Richmond

Thompson Rd.

762

Brazos River

To Alvin

521

288

762

A - G
Brazos Bend
State Park
(see map)

1994

To Rosenberg, Richmond

P72

Rosharon

Guy

1462

1462

36

Damon

To Freeport

To W. Columbia

0   Miles   10

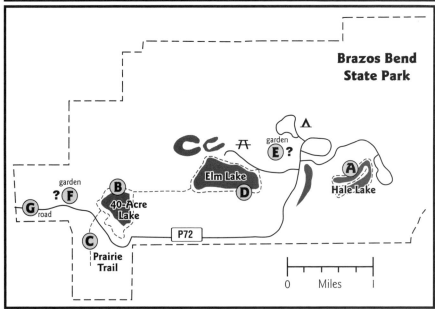

Brazos Bend State Park

garden
E ?

Elm Lake
D

A

Hale Lake

garden
? F

B

G road

40-Acre Lake

P72

C

Prairie Trail

0   Miles   1

40-Acre Lake Trail, Brazos Bend State Park

Finally, walk the roadsides along the entrance road **(G)**, where Swarthy and **Neamathla skippers** and **Little Glassywing** are possible.

Directions: In Fort Bend County, take US 59 west from Houston to FM 2759 south and continue south on FM 762 to P 72 and the **Brazos Bend SP (A-G)** entrance. From Freeport, take SH 288 north to a turn west on FM 1462. Continue to a turn north on FM 762 and go two miles to P 72.

Nearest food, gas, and lodging: Food and gas at the junction of FM 762 and FM 1462; lodging in Rosenberg, West Columbia (southeast via FM 1462 and US 36), and Alvin (each about 15 miles).

Nearest camping: Brazos Bend SP.

53. Matagorda County

This is a large area, extending from Bay City south to Matagorda and including Mad Island Marsh, best known for its high number of wintering birds. Principal sites within the county include Bay City's Matagorda County Birding Nature Center **(A)**, South Gulf Road **(B)**, Selkirk Island residential area **(C)**, North Gulf Road **(D)**, a county park **(E)**, a power plant visitor center **(F)**, and the Mad Island Marsh Preserve and nearby wildlife management area **(G)**.

Habitats: Coastal prairie, coastal scrub, saltwater and freshwater marshes, riparian, field, and cropland.

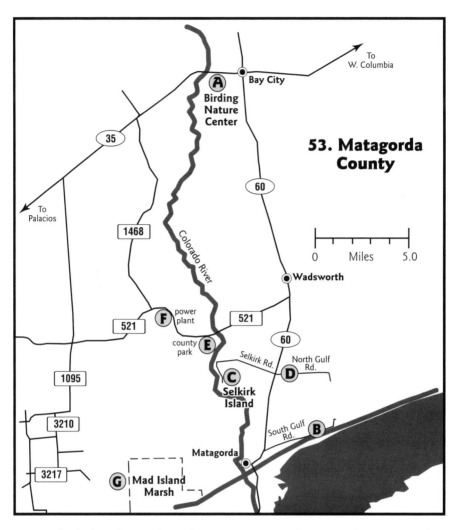

To
W. Columbia

Bay City

A

Birding
Nature
Center

35

**53. Matagorda
County**

60

To
Palacios

1468

Colorado River

0   Miles   5.0

Wadsworth

power
plant **F**

521

521

county
park **E**

60

Selkirk Rd.

North Gulf
Rd.

1095

C

D

Selkirk
Island

3210

South Gulf
Rd.

B

Matagorda

3217

G | Mad Island
Marsh

Strategy for finding the most butterflies: Start at Bay City's Matagorda County Birding Nature Center (**A**). Check the butterfly, hummingbird, and herb garden plots and walk the extended network of trails. Some of the more numerous butterflies include Pipevine and Giant swallowtails; Cloudless Sulphur; Little Yellow; Gulf Fritillary; Texan Crescent; Tawny Emperor; Monarch; Queen; Clouded, Fiery, Dun, and Eufala skippers; Southern Skipperling; and Southern Broken-Dash. Less common butterflies include Black, Eastern Tiger, and Palamedes swallowtails; Large Orange Sulphur; White-striped and Dorantes longtails; and False and Horace's duskywings. In fall, Sickle-winged and Ocola skippers can also be expected.

Next, drive south to Matagorda and take the South Gulf Road (**B**) that runs east from the city cemetery. Stop at pull-offs and check the roadsides. In addition to the

Matagorda County Birding Nature Center, Bay City

species mentioned above, expect Great Southern White, Dainty Sulphur, Southern Dogface, Reakirt's Blue, Phaon Crescent, Tropical Checkered-Skipper, and **Obscure Skipper**. "Dark" **Tropical Buckeye** and **Salt Marsh Skipper** are also possible.

En route back toward Bay City, drive into the Selkirk Island residential area **(C)** and check flowering plants along the entrance road and at the front office. Then cross SH 60 and take North Gulf Road **(D)**, checking roadside wildflowers. Continue north on SH 60 and take FM 521 west toward the South Texas Nuclear Power Plant, stopping at FM 521 County Park **(E)** along the way. Then visit the power plant visitor center **(F)** to check the small garden plot there.

If time allows, drive to the 7,063-acre Clive Runnells Family Mad Island Marsh Preserve **(G)**, managed by the Texas Nature Conservancy, and nearby Mad Island WMA, stopping along the roadsides at flowering plants.

Directions: The **Matagorda County Birding Nature Center (A)** is south of SH 35 1.7 miles west of Bay City. **South Gulf Road (B)** runs east from SH 60 at the Matagorda Cemetery. **Selkirk Island (C)** and **North Gulf Road (D)** are north of Matagorda off SH 60. Take Selkirk Rd. west to Selkirk Island. The N. Gulf Rd. goes east from the same intersection. **FM 521 County Park (E)** and the **South Texas Nuclear Power Plant (F)** are west along FM 521, which leaves SH 60 a few miles north of Selkirk Rd. **Mad Island Marsh (G)** is located farther west; take FM 1095 south from SH 35 or FM 521 toward Collegeport. Then take Brazos Tower Rd. (CR 3210) to AP Ranch Rd. (CR 3217) and the visitor center.

Nearest food, gas, and lodging: Bay City and Matagorda; food and gas in Wadsworth.

Nearest camping: Le Tulle Park, next to the Birding Nature Center, and at locations around Bay City and Matagorda.

Additional Worthwhile Site in the Upper Gulf Coast Region

Palacios. Situated along SH 35, across Tres Palacios Bay from Collegeport and Mad Island Marsh, this area offers easy access to coastal prairie, coastal scrub habitat, saltwater marshes, and mesquite grasslands. East Bayshore Drive and the Palacios Marine Education Center, at the end of Camp Hulen Road, are the two principal sites for finding butterflies.

Butterfly Checklist for the Upper Gulf Coast Region

The following list includes eight sites: **46. Texas Point/Sabine Woods, 47. Anahuac National Wildlife Refuge/High Island, 48. Galveston–Texas City, 49. Baytown, 50. Houston, 51. Freeport, 52. Brazos Bend State Park**, and **53. Matagorda County**.

Status symbols include: A = abundant; C = common; U = uncommon; O = occasional; R = rare; X = accidental; M = migrant; TC = temporary colonist; ? = unknown. (For a full definition of these terms, see p. 3.)

For trip notes, including dates and numbers of species seen, refer to the entry for this checklist in Appendix 3: Regional Checklist Resources.

Butterfly Species	46	47	48	49	50	51	52	53
Pipevine Swallowtail	U	C	U	U	U	U	U	C
Polydamas Swallowtail		X	X		X		X	
Zebra Swallowtail								X
Black Swallowtail	U	A	U	C	U	C	C	O
Giant Swallowtail	C	C	C	C	C	C	C	C
Eastern Tiger Swallowtail	U	U	U	U	O	U	C	O
Two-tailed Swallowtail			X					
Spicebush Swallowtail	U	R	O	U	C	O	U	X
Palamedes Swallowtail	R	U		C	R	C		O
Checkered White	C	U	U	U		C	C	U
Cabbage White			X				X	
Great Southern White	C	A	A	C		A	U	C
Giant White			X					
Falcate Orangetip		U	O					O

Butterfly Species	46	47	48	49	50	51	52	53
Clouded Sulphur			X				X	
Orange Sulphur	C	C	C	U	O	C	C	U
Southern Dogface	C	U	U	U		U		U
Yellow Angled-Sulphur			X					
Cloudless Sulphur	C	C	C	A	A	A	C	C
Orange-barred Sulphur					X			
Large Orange Sulphur		O		U	U	U	O	U
Lyside Sulphur							X	
Little Yellow	A	A	A	A	A	A	A	C
Sleepy Orange	U	U	C	U	O	C	C	U
Dainty Sulphur		C	U			C	U	U
Great Purple Hairstreak					U		O	
Soapberry Hairstreak			O	U			C	
Striped Hairstreak							R	
Oak Hairstreak	R		R	O			O	R
White M Hairstreak					O		U	
Gray Hairstreak	C	U	C	C	C	C	C	C
Red-banded Hairstreak	U	U	O	C	C	C	U	
Dusky-blue Groundstreak	U	O	U	U	U	U	U	U
Western Pygmy-Blue	O	A	A	A		A	U	
Eastern Pygmy-Blue	O			?				
Cassius Blue				R	C			
Marine Blue		R	R	U	O	R		
Ceraunus Blue		C	C	C	O	C	O	
Reakirt's Blue			U	U	O	C	O	U
Eastern Tailed-Blue			?					R
Spring/Summer Azure				O				
American Snout	U	A-R	A-R	A-R	A-R	A-R	A-R	A-R
Gulf Fritillary	C	A	C	A	A	A	A	A
Julia Heliconian				X	X	X	X	
Zebra Heliconian						X	X	
Variegated Fritillary	C	C	U	C	C	A	C	C
Bordered Patch						R		
Silvery Checkerspot				U		O	O	
Texan Crescent		U	C	U	C		U	C
Phaon Crescent	A	A	A	U	U	A	A	C
Pearl Crescent	U	A	C	A	U	A	A	A
Question Mark	U	C	O	U	C	C	C	U
Mourning Cloak							X	
American Lady	U	C	U	U	U	U	U	C
Painted Lady		C	U	U	C	A		U
Red Admiral	C	C	U	C	C	U	U	C

Butterfly Species	46	47	48	49	50	51	52	53
Common Buckeye	C	C	C	C	C	C	C	U
Tropical Buckeye			R	R		O		O
Red-spotted Purple		U	X		O		O	
Viceroy	C	A		U		C	A	C
Common Mestra						O	O	
Ruddy Daggerwing			X					
Goatweed Leafwing			U	U	U	C	U	C
Hackberry Emperor		U	U	U	U	C	A	U
Tawny Emperor	C	C	A	C	C	A	A	C
Southern Pearly-eye						R		
Gemmed Satyr			O	C		C	A	
Carolina Satyr	C	U	U	U		A	A	U
Little Wood-Satyr		U	C				C	U
Monarch	U	C	C	M	M	U	U	C
Queen	U	U	U	U	U	A	U	C
Mercurial Skipper			X					
Silver-spotted Skipper		U	O		U	R		
White-striped Longtail	O	U		U	U	C	C	U
Tailed Aguna			X					
Long-tailed Skipper	U	U	U	U	O	U	U	U
Dorantes Longtail		O	O			O	U	U
Southern Cloudywing			R			U	C	
Northern Cloudywing				U	U	C	U	
Confused Cloudywing						R	U	R
Mazans Scallopwing						X	X	X
Hayhurst's Scallopwing							?	
Sickle-winged Skipper						X		X
False Duskywing			X					R
Juvenal's Duskywing							U	
Horace's Duskywing	C	C	C	C	A	C	C	U
Funereal Duskywing	U	U	O	U	C	C	C	U
Wild Indigo Duskywing		O		U		U	R	O
Com./White Checkered-Skipper	C	A	A	A	A	A	C	C
Tropical Checkered-Skipper	C	C	C	A	C	A	C	C
Turk's-cap White-Skipper						X	X	
Swarthy Skipper			R		U	U	R	
Julia's Skipper		U	O	U		O	O	U
Neamathla Skipper	U	O	O	U		U	R	
Clouded Skipper	C	C	C	C	C	A	C	C
Least Skipper	U	C			U	A	A	U
Orange Skipperling			U			U	R	
Southern Skipperling	A	A	A	C	A	A	A	C

Butterfly Species	46	47	48	49	50	51	52	53
Fiery Skipper	C	A	A	C	A	A	A	C
Tawny-edged Skipper	U		X					
Whirlabout	U	O	C	U	O	C	U	U
Southern Broken-Dash			U	U	U	C	C	C
Little Glassywing		U		U		U	O	
Sachem			O	C	C	U	U	C
Delaware Skipper				X				
Aaron's Skipper	O			R				
Broad-winged Skipper	U	C	U	C	U	C	A	
Dion Skipper				X				
Bay Skipper	O	R		R				
Dun Skipper	U	U	U	C	U	A	A	C
Lace-winged Roadside-Skipper						R		
Dotted Roadside-Skipper		X						
Celia's Roadside-Skipper			R		U	U		
Eufala Skipper	U	C	C	C	C	U	U	C
Twin-spot Skipper	U		O	C	R			
Brazilian Skipper	U	U	U	O	U	U	U	
Salt Marsh Skipper	U	C	C	R		U		U
Obscure Skipper	C	C	C	U		A	R	C
Ocola Skipper	U	C	U	A	C	C	U	C
Purple-washed Skipper	X							

Central Gulf Coast

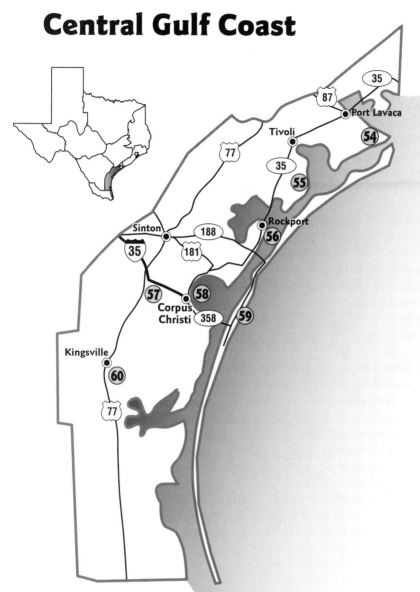

54. Indianola/Magic Ridge
55. Aransas National Wildlife Refuge
56. Rockport/Goose Island State Park
57. Hazel Bazemore County Park/Pollywog Pond
58. Corpus Christi
59. Padre Island/Mustang Island
60. Kingsville

Central Gulf Coast Region

The Central Gulf Coast Region begins at Matagorda Bay in the north and runs south to the Lower Rio Grande Valley Region. It is bordered on the west by the South Texas Brushlands Region. Like the Upper Gulf Coast Region, the landscape is dominated by the coastal plain and is bisected by several streams and rivers. The largest of these are the Guadalupe, San Antonio, and Nueces rivers. Coastal prairie and coastal scrub, with scattered oak mottes, are prevalent.

The Central Gulf Coast Region is represented by seven sites: **54. Indianola/Magic Ridge**, **55. Aransas National Wildlife Refuge**, **56. Rockport/Goose Island State Park**, **57. Hazel Bazemore County Park/Pollywog Pond**, **58. Corpus Christi**, **59. Padre Island/Mustang Island**, and **60. Kingsville**. The best time to visit these sites is March through November.

Central Gulf Coast Specialties

There is about the same number of butterfly species in this region as in the Upper Gulf Coast, with fewer southeastern U.S. species but more tropical species. There are fourteen area specialties.

Hairstreaks, Blues, Metalmarks: **Lacey's Scrub-Hairstreak** occurs in brushy areas near its larval foodplant, myrtlecroton, only at Hazel Bazemore CP/Pollywog Pond. **Eastern Pygmy-Blue** has been recorded in an isolated population only at Indianola/Magic Ridge. Larvae feed on glasswort. **Rounded Metalmark** is most likely to be seen at patches of wildflowers at Indianola/Magic Ridge, Aransas NWR, Rockport/Goose Island SP, Hazel Bazemore CP/Pollywog Pond, the Corpus Christi area, and the Kingsville area. Larvae feed on eupatoriums. **Red-bordered Metalmark** has been recorded at flowering plants at Hazel Bazemore CP/Pollywog Pond, the Corpus Christi area, and the Kingsville area. Larvae feed on spiny hackberry.

Patches, Buckeyes, Peacocks: **Definite Patch** occurs only in Dick Kleberg Park in the Kingsville area. Adults roost overnight in tall grasses; larvae feed on stenandrium. **Crimson Patch** has been recorded in fall at Hazel Bazemore CP/Pollywog Pond. Although the species may only be a stray, adequate anisacanth, its larval foodplant, is available. **Tropical Buckeye** occurs at Indianola/Magic Ridge, Aransas NWR, Hazel Bazemore CP/Pollywog Pond, Padre Island/Mustang Island, and the Kingsville area, usually along roads and in other open locations. Larvae feed on woolly stemodia. **White Peacock** appears in late summer and fall along wetland edges at Indianola/Magic Ridge, Aransas NWR, Hazel Bazemore CP/Pollywog Pond, the Corpus Christi area, and the Kingsville area. Adults may be temporary colonists; larvae feed on frog-fruit and water hyssop.

Spread-wing Skippers: **Coyote Cloudywing** frequents flowering shrubs at Rockport/Goose Island SP, Hazel Bazemore CP/Pollywog Pond, and the Corpus Christi area. Larvae feed on blackbrush acacia. **Mazans Scallopwing** has been recorded at the edge of brushy areas at Hazel Bazemore CP/Pollywog Pond. Adults often rest on the ground; larvae feed on lamb's-quarters and pigweed. **Laviana White-Skipper** occurs throughout the region, flying swiftly about and only occasionally perching on wildflowers or on the ground. Larvae feed on mallows. **Turk's-cap White-Skipper** is a fast, active species, usually found flying along the edge of vegetation at Indianola/Magic Ridge, Rockport/Goose Island SP, and Hazel Bazemore CP/Pollywog Pond. Turk's-cap and other mallow species are utilized by the larvae.

Grass-Skippers: **Salt Marsh Skipper** is most likely to be found on shrubs near salt-grass (larval foodplant) at Indianola/Magic Ridge, and Aransas NWR. **Obscure Skipper** can be common on flowering plants near marine wetlands throughout the coastal areas. Larvae feed on saltgrass.

Sites within the Central Gulf Coast Region

54. Indianola/Magic Ridge

Once the most popular seaport in Texas, Indianola was wiped out twice by major hurricanes in the late 19th century. Now a small port for shrimpers and fishermen, Indianola offers easy access to the Central Gulf Coast. The site features Zimmerman Road (**A**), which runs down "Magic Ridge," a shell ridge between a broad tidal slough and Lavaca Bay. It is owned and maintained by the Texas Ornithological Society.

Other sites include a picnic area (**B**), Indianola Cemetery (**C**), a beach road (**D**), and other roads (**E, F**). July 4th Butterfly Counts are held here annually.

Habitats: Coastal prairie, coastal scrub, saltwater marsh, beach, and salt flat.

Strategy for finding the most butterflies: Start at Zimmerman Road (**A**) on Magic Ridge by driving its full length, stopping often to check flowering plants and roadside shrubbery. Some of the more numerous butterflies include Pipevine and Giant swallowtails; Great Southern White; Cloudless and Large Orange sulphurs; Little Yellow; Sleepy Orange; Reakirt's Blue; Gulf Fritillary; Phaon Crescent; Queen; Tropical Checkered-Skipper; and Clouded, Fiery, and **Obscure skippers**.

Some of the less numerous species include Lyside Sulphur; Mallow Scrub-Hairstreak; Fatal and **Rounded metalmarks**; Silvery Checkerspot; Tawny Emperor; White-striped Longtail; Long-tailed, Dun, and **Salt Marsh skippers**; False Duskywing; and Celia's Roadside-Skipper.

At the cemetery on Magic Ridge, walk a circle outside the fence. A stray Dingy Purplewing was found here on July 11, 2002, and three **Eastern Pygmy-Blues** were found along the roadside beyond on April 14, 2004. In fall, Sickle-winged and Ocola skippers can also be expected.

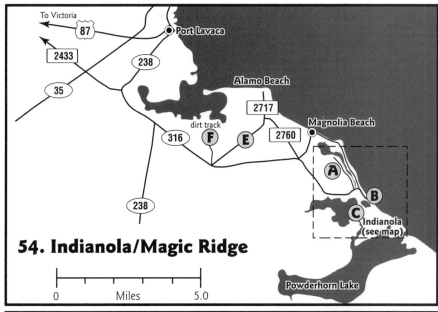

54. Indianola/Magic Ridge

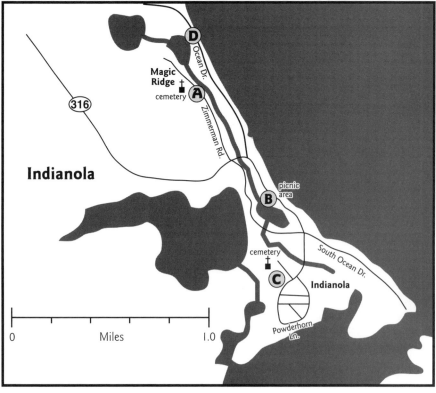

Zimmerman Road on Magic Ridge

Next, stop at the open field near the picnic area (**B**) and drive to Indianola, stopping to check roadside wildflowers. Although most of the butterflies mentioned above are likely, these open areas usually offer a few additional species, such as Black Swallowtail, Ceraunus Blue, Monarch, Horace's Duskywing, Desert Checkered-Skipper, **Laviana** and **Turk's-cap white-skippers**, Southern Skipperling, and Brazilian Skipper.

Then, drive Powderhorn Lane and the side road to Indianola Cemetery (**C**); "Dark" **Tropical Buckeye** is likely to be found along the roadway. Afterwards, take Ocean Dr., the beach road (**D**), north to Magnolia Beach. Next, drive FM 2717 (**E**) to Alamo Beach, stopping at pull-offs with flowering plants. Also walk north on the dirt track (**F**) at the junction of FM 2717 and SH 316.

Directions: In Calhoun County, from SH 35 southwest of Port Lavaca, turn southeast on FM 2433 (also accessible from US 87 southeast of Victoria) to SH 238 and turn right. At the intersection with SH 316, continue southeast on SH 316, past the turns to Alamo Beach and Magnolia Beach. Turn left on **Zimmerman Road (A)** to butterfly along Magic Ridge. Then, return to SH 316 and take S. Ocean Dr. to Indianola, where you'll find the **picnic area (B)**, Powderhorn Lane, and the side road to the **cemetery (C)**. From the Indianoloa area, take Ocean Dr., the **beach road (D)**, to Magnolia Beach. **FM 2717 (E)** and the **dirt track (F)** are accessible via FM 2760 or SH 316.

Nearest food, gas, and lodging: Port Lavaca; food at Indianola.

Nearest camping: Magnolia Beach County Park, Indianola, and Port Lavaca.

55. Aransas National Wildlife Refuge

Best known as the winter home of endangered whooping cranes, the 115,670-acre Aransas National Wildlife Refuge (fee area) also offers a good variety of butterflies. Located on the Blackjack Peninsula, the refuge has several productive trails, such as Heron Flats (**A**), Rail (**B**), Jones Lake (**G**), and Big Tree (**I**). Other good butterflying sites include a garden (**C**), a utility right-of-way (**E**), a boardwalk to the bay (**H**), and roads (**D, F, J**) with productive pull-offs. July 4th Butterfly Counts are held here annually.

Habitats: Coastal prairie, oak motte, oak savannah, freshwater and saltwater marshes, and field.

Strategy for finding the most butterflies: Start by walking the Heron Flats Trail (**A**) and Rail Trail (**B**) near the Aransas NWR entrance. Some of the more numerous butterflies include Pipevine, Giant, and Palamedes swallowtails; Great Southern White; Cloudless, Large Orange, and Dainty sulphurs; Little Yellow; Dusky-blue Groundstreak; Western Pygmy-Blue; Ceraunus and Reakirt's blues; Gulf Fritillary; Phaon Crescent; Tawny Emperor; Carolina Satyr; Queen; Tropical Checkered-Skipper; **Turk's-cap White-Skipper**; and Clouded, Fiery, Dun, Eufala, and **Obscure skippers**. **Laviana White-Skipper**, Nysa Roadside-Skipper, and **Salt Marsh Skipper** are also possible.

Next, check the small garden (**C**) around the refuge headquarters, and walk a portion of the entrance roadway (**D**). Many of the same butterflies mentioned above are likely, but Black Swallowtail, Mallow Scrub-Hairstreak, **Rounded Metalmark**, Southern Skipperling, and Celia's Roadside-Skipper are also possible. In spring, Falcate Orangetip and Soapberry Hairstreak are likely. **White Peacock** and Sickle-winged and Ocola skippers can be expected in fall.

Then, drive south to the picnic area and walk behind the restroom into the utility right-of-way (**E**); walk a section of this open area. This is a good place to find Bordered Patch; Goatweed Leafwing; Hackberry Emperor; White-striped and Dorantes longtails; False, Horace's, Mournful, Funereal, and Wild Indigo duskywings; and Orange Skipperling.

Afterwards, drive the entrance road (**F**) to the observation tower, checking flowering plants at pull-offs. "Dark" **Tropical Buckeye** can be expected on the roadway beyond the Dagger Point side road and on the loop drive. Near the observation tower, walk the Jones Lake Trail (**G**), the boardwalk to the bay (**H**), and the Big Tree Trail (**I**). Then drive the sixteen-mile Wildlife Drive (**J**), a one-way loop road, stopping at pull-offs with flowering plants.

Directions: In Aransas County, from Rockport, take SH 35 north to FM 774, turn right and follow it to FM 2040. Turn right for seven miles to **Aransas NWR (A-J)**. From Tivoli, take SH 35 south to a turn southeast on SH 239 and go to Austwell and FM 2040.

Nearest food, gas, and lodging: Food and gas at Tivoli (north 15 miles); lodging at Rockport (south 36 miles) and Port Lavaca (north 35 miles).

Nearest camping: Austwell RV Park (seven miles) and Goose Island SP (south 33 miles).

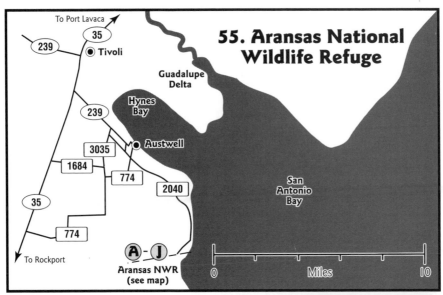

55. Aransas National Wildlife Refuge

To Port Lavaca
239
35
Tivoli
Guadalupe Delta
Hynes Bay
239
3035
1684
774
Austwell
2040
35
774
(A)-(J)
Aransas NWR (see map)
San Antonio Bay

0   Miles   10

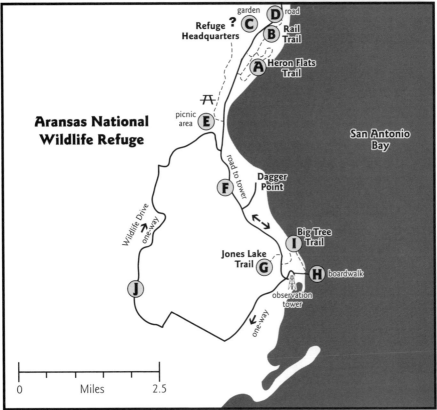

Aransas National Wildlife Refuge

Refuge Headquarters
garden (C) (D) road
(B) Rail Trail
(A) Heron Flats Trail
picnic area (E)
road to tower
(F)
Dagger Point
San Antonio Bay
Wildlife Drive one-way
Big Tree Trail (I)
Jones Lake Trail (G)
(H) boardwalk
(J)
observation tower
one-way

0   Miles   2.5

Heron Flats Trail, Aransas National Wildlife Refuge

56. Rockport/Goose Island State Park

Located on the south side of the Copano Bay Bridge on SH 35, the Rockport-Fulton area is one of North America's best-known birding spots. Less is known about the butterfly fauna. The city is home to the annual "Hummer/Bird Festival" in September and is the port for whooping crane boat tours in winter. Butterfly sites include demonstration gardens (**A**, **C**), a sanctuary (**B**), Rockport Cemetery (**D**), Memorial Park (**E**), Cape Valero Drive (**F**), and Port Bay Road (**G**).

On the north side of the Copano Bay Bridge, in the 307-acre Goose Island State Park (fee area) and surrounding urban environment, roads (**H**, **J**) and a nature trail (**I**) offer good opportunities. Goose Island SP is at the southern end of the Lamar Peninsula. July 4th Butterfly Counts are held in Rockport annually.

Habitats: Coastal prairie, oak woodland, mesquite grassland, saltwater and freshwater wetlands, cemetery, and garden.

Strategy for finding the most butterflies: In Rockport, start at the Green Acres Demonstration Garden (**A**), and check back later in the day. Some of the more numerous butterflies include Pipevine and Giant swallowtails, Cloudless Sulphur, Gulf Fritillary, Phaon Crescent, Monarch, Queen, Clouded and Fiery skippers, and Sachem. Less numerous butterflies may include Palamedes Swallowtail, Large Orange Sulphur, Mallow Scrub-Hairstreak, Dusky-blue Groundstreak, **Rounded Metalmark**, Long-tailed and Brazilian skippers, **Coyote Cloudywing**, and Horace's Duskywing.

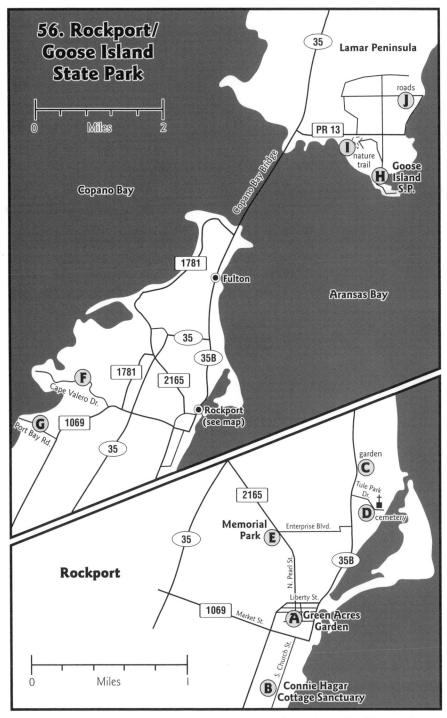

56. Rockport/ Goose Island State Park

0 Miles 2

Copano Bay

Lamar Peninsula

35

roads

J

PR 13

I

nature trail

Goose Island S.P.

H

1781

Fulton

Aransas Bay

35

35B

1781

2165

F

Cape Valero Dr.

Rockport (see map)

G

Port Bay Rd.

1069

35

garden

C

Tule Park Dr.

D cemetery

2165

Memorial Park

E

Enterprise Blvd.

35

N. Pearl St.

35B

Rockport

Liberty St.

1069

Market St.

A Green Acres Garden

0 Miles 1

S. Church St.

B Connie Hagar Cottage Sanctuary

Green Acres Demonstration Garden, Rockport

Next, drive to the nearby Connie Hagar Cottage Sanctuary (**B**) and walk the network of short trails. This is a good place to find Reakirt's Blue, "Dark" **Tropical Buckeye**, White-striped Longtail, False Duskywing, Tropical Checkered-Skipper, and **Turk's-cap White-Skipper**. **Laviana White-Skipper** is also possible. In spring, Falcate Orangetip is likely, and Sickle-winged and Ocola skippers can be expected in fall.

Then drive to the Hummingbird Demonstration Garden (**C**) and walk the edges and the short boardwalk. Watch here for Goatweed Leafwing and Tawny Emperor. Afterwards, visit the nearby Rockport Cemetery (**D**), which can be productive unless recently mowed. This open, short-grass habitat is a good place to find Checkered White, Dainty Sulphur, and Gulf and Variegated fritillaries.

Next, drive to Memorial Park (**E**) and walk the loop around the pond. Return to your car and continue on to Cape Valero Drive (**F**), where there is a good place near its end to find **Obscure Skipper**, and Port Bay Road (**G**), where you should walk a portion of the roadsides and the adjacent side roads. A few additional butterflies likely along these salt flats and edges include Great Southern White, Little Yellow, Sleepy Orange, Western Pygmy-Blue, Ceraunus Blue, and **White Peacock** (in fall).

Finally, drive north across Copano Bay to the vicinity of Goose Island SP. Check the roadsides (**H**), walk the nature trail (**I**) inside the park, and drive the network of roads (**J**) outside the park.

Directions: In Aransas County, the **Green Acres Demonstration Garden** (**A**) is located in Rockport at 611 E. Mimosa St. in the center of town. From there, go east to N. Church St. and turn right. Continue south on Church St. to the **Connie Hagar Cottage Sanctuary** (**B**), located at 1st and Church. Then go north on Bus. 35 to the

Rockport Cemetery (**D**), located east on Tule Park Dr. The **Hummingbird Demonstration Garden (C)** is a short distance beyond on Bus. 35.

To reach **Memorial Park (E)**, return south on Bus. 35 and turn right on Pirate Dr. Turn left on Omohondro St. Take a right on Enterprise Blvd. and follow it to its end. The park is across FM 2165. To find **Cape Valero Drive (F)** and **Port Bay Road (G)**, turn right on FM 2165 from the park and go to a right turn on Liberty St. (Bus. 35). Take it to Market St. (FM 1069) and turn right. Follow it past SH 35 to the two roads on the right.

To reach **Goose Island SP (H, I)** take SH 35 north to a right turn on PR 13 just over the Copano Bay Bridge. Continue 1.4 miles to the entrance. The **network of roads (J)** in the nearby residential area offers one more butterflying opportunity.

Nearest food, gas, and lodging: The Rockport-Fulton area.

Nearest camping: Goose Island SP and at RV parks in Rockport and Fulton.

57. Hazel Bazemore County Park/Pollywog Pond

Hazel Bazemore County Park, northwest of Corpus Christi, is best known as America's most productive hawk-watch site (with peak flights from Sept. 22–25), but it also has excellent butterfly habitat. The general topography of the region just west of Nueces Bay is flatlands, but adjacent hillsides offer additional butterfly-watching

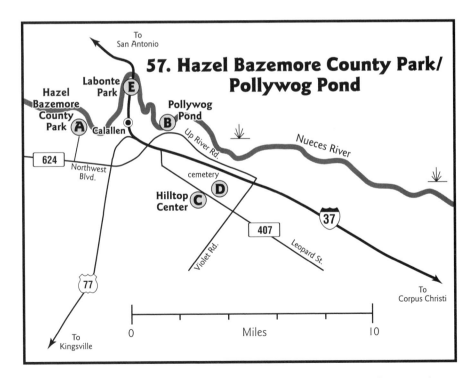

Hazel Bazemore County Park

opportunities. All of the sites are located within a ten-mile circle. In addition to Hazel Bazemore County Park (**A**), other sites include Pollywog Pond (**B**), Hilltop Community Center (**C**), Nueces County Cemetery (**D**), and Labonte Park (**E**).

Habitats: Coastal prairie, coastal scrub, oak-hackberry woodland, saltwater marsh, field, and riparian.

Strategy for finding the most butterflies: Hazel Bazemore County Park (**A**) has a loop road and numerous trails. Drive the roads, stopping at patches of flowering plants, and walk the Lucas Kimmel Nature Trail. Some of the more numerous butterflies include Pipevine and Giant swallowtails; Large Orange Sulphur; Little Yellow; Western Pygmy-Blue; Reakirt's Blue; Gulf and Variegated fritillaries; Bordered Patch; Phaon Crescent; Tawny Emperor; Tropical Checkered-Skipper; and Clouded, Fiery, and Eufala skippers.

Less common butterflies may include Black Swallowtail, Great Southern White, **Lacey's** and Mallow scrub-hairstreaks, Queen, **Mazans Scallopwing**, Horace's Duskywing, Southern Broken-Dash, and Celia's Roadside-Skipper. In fall, Sickle-winged and Ocola skippers are likely, and stray White-patched and Brown-banded skippers were recorded here on October 30, 2002.

Next, drive to Pollywog Pond (**B**) and walk the loop trail, which is best in summer, particularly after rains. This trail through a riparian habitat is likely to offer Ceraunus Blue, Texan and Vesta crescents, Common Mestra, White-striped Longtail, Southern Skipperling, and Whirlabout.

Then drive to Hilltop Community Center (**C**) and walk the network of trails that can be especially productive when plants are flowering. Many of the butterflies mentioned above are likely, but additional species may include Lyside Sulphur, **Rounded** and **Red-bordered metalmarks**, Theona Checkerspot, **Crimson Patch**, Gemmed and Carolina satyrs, **Coyote Cloudywing**, and **Laviana** and **Turk's-cap white-skippers**. Across the highway is the Nueces County Cemetery (**D**), which can also be worth a visit unless it has been recently mowed.

One more site, Labonte Park (**E**), can be productive, especially its southern corner and along the edges; **White Peacock** can be common, and **Obscure Skipper** is possible.

Directions: In Nueces and San Patricio Counties northwest of Corpus Christi, take US 77 south from I-37 at Calallen and turn right on Northwest Blvd. (FM 624). Go about a mile to Hazel Bazemore Pkwy. and turn right to **Hazel Bazemore County Park (A)**. Nearby **Labonte Park (E)** is along US 77 and I-37, two miles north of Calallen. Use the US 77 frontage roads to access this park (formerly called Nueces River Park) on the west side of I-37. To reach **Pollywog Pond (B)**, return to the US 77 and Northwest Blvd. intersection and turn east on Up River Rd. Follow it to the other side of I-37 and watch for the parking area on the left. For **Hilltop Community Center (C)**, continue east on Up River Rd. to Violet Rd. and turn right (south). Go beyond I-37 to Leopard St. and turn right for .3 mile to 11426 Leopard St. on the left. **Nueces County Cemetery (D)** is directly across the street from the center.

Nearest food, gas, and lodging: Calallen and along I-37 northwest of Corpus Christi.

Nearest camping: Labonte Park.

58. Corpus Christi

Located between Nueces Bay and Corpus Christi Bay, the city of Corpus Christi was built on two levels: one at sea level and the second on a forty-foot bluff. Corpus Christi is Spanish for "Body of Christ." Over the years the city has acquired three additional names: "Texas Riviera," "Sparkling City by the Sea," and "Naples of the Gulf." Today, the city has a thriving seaport, the Texas State Aquarium, the Corpus Christi Museum of Science and History (where replicas of Columbus' ships, the Pinta and Santa Maria, are docked), the 180-acre Botanical Garden, several parks, and Texas A&M University at Corpus Christi. This area features five widely spaced butterfly-watching locations: Blucher Park (**A**) and nearby gardens (**B**), Hans Suter Wildlife Park (**C**), Corpus Christi Botanical Gardens (**D**), and the Xeriscape Learning Garden (**E**).

Habitats: Park, garden, coastal prairie, coastal scrub, and riparian.

Strategy for finding the most butterflies: Start in downtown Corpus Christi behind the public library at Blucher Park (**A**) and across the street at the gardens (**B**) in front and behind the South Texas Audubon Society Headquarters and adjacent Blucher House. Some of the more numerous butterflies include Giant Swallowtail; Cloudless Sulphur;

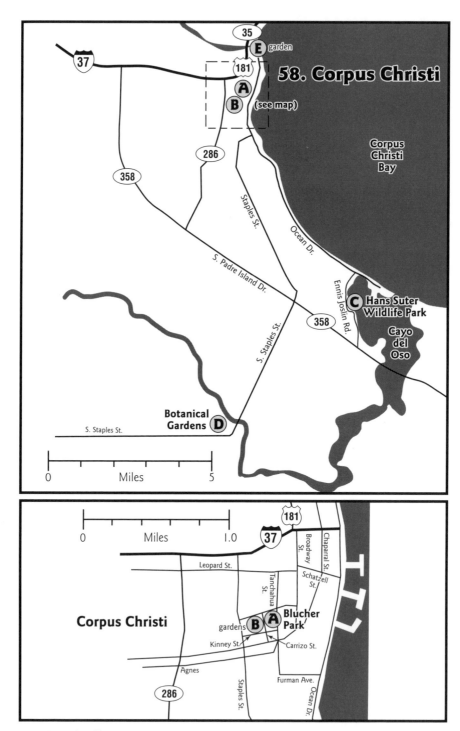

58. Corpus Christi

(see map)

garden

Corpus
Christi
Bay

Staples St.

Ocean Dr.

S. Padre Island Dr.

Ennis Joslin Rd.

Hans Suter
Wildlife Park

Cayo
del
Oso

S. Staples St.

Botanical
Gardens

S. Staples St.

0   Miles   5

0   Miles   1.0

Broadway St.

Chaparral St.

Leopard St.

Tancahua St.

Schatzell St.

Corpus Christi

gardens

Blucher
Park

Kinney St.

Carrizo St.

Agnes

Furman Ave.

Staples St.

Ocean Dr.

Corpus Christi Botanical Gardens

Little Yellow; Mallow Scrub-Hairstreak; Dusky-blue Groundstreak; Gulf Fritillary; Bordered Patch; Phaon Crescent; Red Admiral; Clouded, Fiery, and Eufala skippers; and Sachem. **Coyote Cloudywing** and **Laviana** and **Turk's-cap white-skippers** have also been recorded along the edges.

Then drive south to Hans Suter Wildlife Park **(C)**; visit the small garden next to the north parking area. Black Swallowtail, Great Southern White, Reakirt's Blue, and Southern Skipperling can be expected.

Continue south to the Corpus Christi Botanical Gardens **(D)** and check the flowering plants in front and around the office and walk the trails. Pipevine Swallowtail, Lyside and Large Orange sulphurs, Great Purple Hairstreak, Western Pygmy-Blue, **Rounded** and **Red-bordered metalmarks**, Texan Crescent, Common Mestra, Monarch, Celia's Roadside-Skipper, and **Obscure Skipper** can be expected. Nysa Roadside-Skipper is also possible on the trail. In spring, Falcate Orangetip can be expected, and **White Peacock** and Sickle-winged and Ocola skippers are usually common in fall.

Finally, drive across town to the Xeriscape Learning Garden **(E)** at the Corpus Christi Museum of Science and History; there is also a small garden inside (fee area), at the plaza for the Columbus ships.

Directions: In Nueces County, all sites are in Corpus Christi. Starting at the most northern site, from the end of I-37 east of the US 181 intersection continue to Chaparral St. and turn north. The **Xeriscape Learning Garden (E)** and the Museum of

Science and History are ahead along Corpus Christi Bay, near the ship channel. Return on Chaparral south to Schatzell St. and turn west, following it until it becomes Leopard St. Continue west to Tancahua St. Turn south and go past the library to Kinney St. Turn west to Carrizo St., where you'll turn north to **Blucher Park (A)**. The **South Texas Audubon Society gardens (B)** are across Carrizo St.

To reach **Hans Suter Wildlife Park (C)**, return to Tancahua St. and go south to Furman Ave. Turn east to Ocean Dr. and take it south to a southwest turn on Ennis Joslin Rd. The park is just ahead on the left along Cayo del Oso Bay. Then continue on Ennis Joslin to S. Padre Island Dr. (SH 385). Turn northwest to Staples St. (FM 2444) and take it southwest. The **Corpus Christi Botanical Gardens (D)** are located at 8545 S. Staples St.

Nearest food, gas, and lodging: Corpus Christi.

Nearest camping: Commercial sites along the southeastern end of S. Padre Island Dr. and at Padre Island National Seashore (see next site).

59. Padre Island/Mustang Island

These two barrier islands run from South Padre Island, east of Brownsville, north to Port Aransas. The Port Mansfield Channel divides South Padre Island from the Padre Island National Seashore (fee area), which covers 130,454 acres, including sixty miles of undeveloped seashore. In Padre Island NS, butterfly sites include the entrance road **(B)**, the Grassland Nature Trail **(C)**, a gated roadway **(D)**, and a campground **(E)**. Additional sites include Packery Channel County Park **(A)**, Mustang Island State Park (fee area) campground **(F)**, Mollie Beattie Preserve **(G)**, the Port Aransas Birding Center **(H)**, and a park **(I)**.

Habitats: Coastal scrub, coastal prairie, dune, beach, salt marsh, oak motte, and garden.

Strategy for finding the most butterflies: When approaching the islands from Corpus Christi on SH 358, stop first at Packery Channel County Park **(A)**. Drive the roadways and walk the edges when flowering plants are present. Some of the likely butterflies include Giant Swallowtail, Great Southern White, Cloudless and Dainty sulphurs, Little Yellow, Dusky-blue Groundstreak, Western Pygmy-Blue, Ceraunus and Reakirt's blues, Gulf Fritillary, Phaon Crescent, Queen, and Monarch. Also watch for Cassius and Marine blues and "Dark" **Tropical Buckeye**. Ocola Skipper can be common in fall.

Then drive south on P 22 to Padre Island NS. Stop at roadside pull-offs along the entrance road **(B)** and walk the Grassland Nature Trail **(C)**. The gated roadway **(D)** across from the Bird Island Basin Road is a good place to find **Obscure Skipper**. Also check the edges of the visitor center parking area and campground **(E)**. Additional butterflies expected here include Pipevine and Black swallowtails, Large Orange Sulphur, Mallow Scrub-Hairstreak, Horace's and Mournful duskywings, Tropical Checkered-Skipper, and Southern Skipperling.

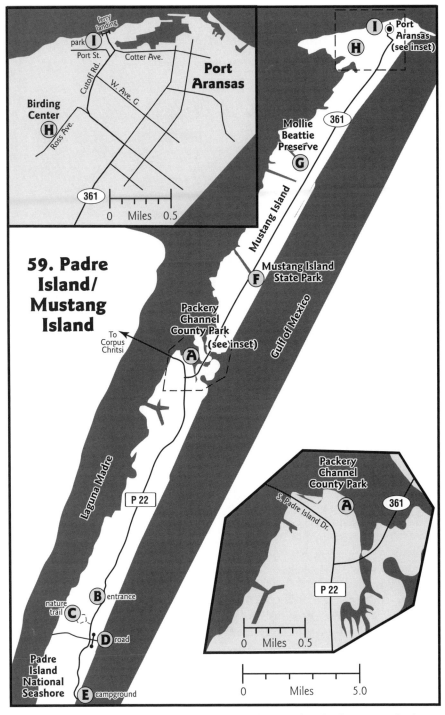

Port Aransas

ferry landing

park **I**

Port St.

Cotter Ave.

Cutoff Rd.

W. Ave. G

Birding Center H

Ross Ave.

361

0 Miles 0.5

I Port Aransas (see inset)

H

361

Mollie Beattie Preserve G

Mustang Island

Mustang Island State Park F

Gulf of Mexico

59. Padre Island/ Mustang Island

Packery Channel County Park (see inset) A

To Corpus Chritsi

Laguna Madre

P 22

B entrance

nature trail **C**

D road

Padre Island National Seashore

E campground

Packery Channel County Park

A 361

S. Padre Island Dr.

P 22

0 Miles 0.5

0 Miles 5.0

Grassland Nature Trail, Padre Island National Seashore

Then drive north on SH 361 onto Mustang Island. Check the edges of the Mustang Island SP parking area and campground **(F)**. Next, walk the trail into the Mollie Beattie Preserve **(G)**. At Port Aransas, visit the garden at the entrance to the Port Aransas Birding Center **(H)**, where Fiery and Eufala skippers, Whirlabout, and Sachem can be expected.

Lastly, walk throughout the little park **(I)** in Port Aransas near the ferry landing along the Intracoastal Waterway.

Directions: In Nueces County, from Corpus Christi, take S. Padre Island Dr. (SH 358) southeast across Laguna Madre on the John F. Kennedy Causeway. **Packery Channel County Park (A)** is on the north side of the road at the end of the causeway. To explore **Padre Island NS (B-E)**, take P 22. Return on P 22 and take SH 361 north to **Mustang Island SP (F)**. **Mollie Beattie Preserve (G)** is between the state park and Port Aransas. The **Port Aransas Birding Center** is located on Ross Ave., west of SH 361 via W. Avenue G. The **ferry-landing park** is on Port St. Port Aransas is also accessible from Aransas Pass, south of Rockport, via the ferry.

Nearest food, gas, and lodging: Corpus Christi and Port Aransas.

Nearest camping: Padre Island NS, Mustang Island SP, and Port Aransas.

60. Kingsville

Named for the King Ranch founder, Richard King, Kingsville is home to the Naval Air Station of Kingsville and Texas A&M University at Kingsville, as well as Dick Kleberg Park. Located along the western portion of the coastal prairie, with considerable influence from the south Texas brush country, the area offers several good butterfly-watching locations. In addition to Kleberg Park (**A**), they include a demonstration garden (**B**), the King Ranch Visitor Center (**C**), the Texas A&M campus (**D**),

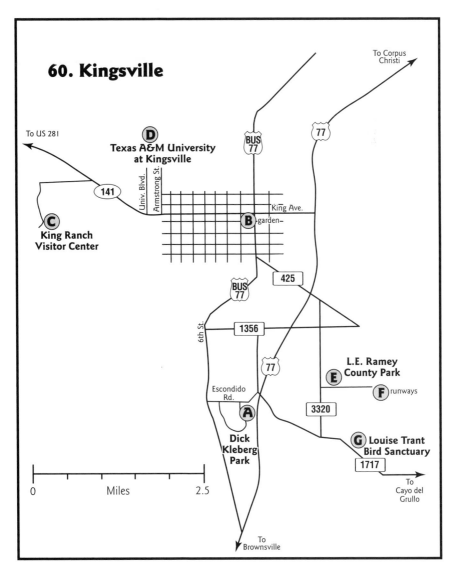

Dick Kleberg Park, Kingsville

L.E. Ramey County Park (**E**, **F**), and the Louise Trant Bird Sanctuary (**G**). July 4th Butterfly Counts are conducted annually in the area.

Habitats: Garden, Tamaulipan scrub, mesquite savannah, pasture, and field.

Strategy for finding the most butterflies: Start at Dick Kleberg Park (**A**), concentrating along the southwestern corner where **Definite Patch** can be common and **Red-bordered Metalmark** and **Crimson Patch** are possible. Some of the more numerous butterflies include Pipevine Swallowtail; Cloudless, Lyside, and Dainty sulphurs; Mallow Scrub-Hairstreak; Dusky-blue Groundstreak; Ceraunus Blue; Gulf Fritillary; Vesta and Phaon crescents; Queen; Desert Checkered-Skipper; Southern Skipperling; and Fiery Skipper. Texan Crescent and Horace's Duskywing are less numerous.

Also watch for "Dark" **Tropical Buckeye** in open areas, **Laviana White-Skipper** along brushy edges, and Western Pygmy-Blue and **Obscure Skipper** along Escondido Creek. **White Peacock** and Sickle-winged and Ocola skippers can be expected in late summer and fall. Also visit the garden on the park office patio.

Then drive into town to the Master Gardener's Demonstration Garden (**B**) and explore it. Large Orange Sulphur and Bordered Patch can be common, and watch, too, for **Rounded Metalmark**.

Next, drive west on King Ave. (SH 141) to the King Ranch Visitor Center (**C**). Check the plantings in front and on the sides, walk into the field to the north, and stop along the roadsides when wildflowers are present. Although many of the butter-flies mentioned above are possible, Black and Giant swallowtails; Great Southern White; Reakirt's Blue; Fatal Metalmark; Hackberry and Tawny emperors; Tropical Checkered-Skipper; and Clouded, Dun, Eufala, and Brazilian skippers are also likely.

Additional sites include the Texas A&M University at Kingsville campus (**D**), where you should visit four planted gardens: in front of the biology building, in front of Conner Museum, in front of the library, and at the Howe Agricultural Lab.

Finally, if time allows, drive to L.E. Ramey County Park and golf course (**E**); check out the brushy edges there and the edges of the old runways (**F**) beyond the tennis courts. Also visit nearby Louise Trant Bird Sanctuary (**G**).

In addition, consider visiting Bishop City Park, discussed in the "Additional Worth-while Sites" section at the end of this site description.

Directions: In Kleberg County, Kingsville is along US 77; the butterfly-watching sites are located in town and south of town. In town, take King Ave. west from US 77 to 14th St. and turn south one block. The **Master Gardener's Demonstration Garden (B)** is located on the northwest corner of 14th St. and Kenedy Ave. **Texas A&M University (D)** is north of King Ave. via either N. Armstrong St. or University Blvd. The **King Ranch Visitor Center (C)** is located west of town west off SH 141.

On the south side of town **Dick Kleberg Park (A)** is south of Escondido Rd., between US 77 and Bus. 77 (6th St.). From there go east on Escondido to FM 1717 and turn southwest. Follow it to FM 3320 and turn north to **L.E. Ramey County Park (E, F)**. **Louise Trant Bird Sanctuary** is located along FM 1717 east of FM 3320.

Nearest food, gas, and lodging: Kingsville.

Nearest camping: Commercial locations, including Country Estates, adjacent to Louise Trant Bird Sanctuary.

Additional Worthwhile Sites in the Central Gulf Coast Region

Bishop City Park. This site is located along Bus. 77 just north of Kingsville in Bishop. The park, situated along Carreta Creek, offers an extensive trail that circles a nine-acre lake and passes through a brushy riparian habitat. Take E. Joyce St. into the park and also take S. Birch St. on the east end of the park to the "Wildlife Viewing Area."

Riviera Beach/Cayo del Grullo Area. Located along the Gulf Coast southeast of Kingsville, the area extends from Drum Point on the north, including Kaufer-Hubert Memorial Park, to Riviera Beach on the south. From US 77 south of Kingsville, take FM 628 east to the coast. Drum Point is north from that point. The park and Riviera Beach are south. FM 771 returns to US 77 from Riviera Beach. Side roads offer access to good coastal prairie, coastal scrub habitats, salt marshes, and fields.

Sarita. This little town, actually the county seat of Kenedy County, is along US 77, 20 miles south of Kingsville. The immediate area has considerable potential for a good diversity of butterflies, especially after spring and summer rains. Drive past the courthouse to Garcia Road and check the side roads and fields.

Butterfly Checkist for the Central Gulf Coast Region

The following list includes seven sites: **54. Indianola/Magic Ridge**, **55. Aransas National Wildlife Refuge**, **56. Rockport/Goose Island State Park**, **57. Hazel Bazemore County Park/Pollywog Pond**, **58. Corpus Christi**, **59. Padre Island/Mustang Island**, and **60. Kingsville**.

Status symbols include: A = abundant; C = common; U = uncommon; O = occasional; R = rare; X = accidental; M = migrant; TC = temporary colonist; ? = status unknown. (For a full definition of these terms, see p. 3.)

For trip notes, including dates and numbers of species seen, refer to the entry for this checklist in Appendix 3: Regional Checklist Resources.

Butterfly Species	54	55	56	57	58	59	60
Pipevine Swallowtail	C	A	A	C	C	U	A
Polydamas Swallowtail		X			X		
Black Swallowtail	U	U	O	U	U	U	U
Giant Swallowtail	C	C	C	C	C	C	C
Eastern Tiger Swallowtail		X					
Spicebush Swallowtail		X					
Palamedes Swallowtail		A	U		O		
Checkered White	C	C	U	O	U	U	C
Great Southern White	A	A	A	U	A	C	C
Giant White	X	X					
Falcate Orangetip		U	O		O		U
Clouded Sulphur		X					
Orange Sulphur	C	C	U	U	C	U	C
Southern Dogface	U	C			C	C	C
White Angled-Sulphur		X			X		
Cloudless Sulphur	C	A	C	U	C	C	C
Orange-barred Sulphur	R					R	R
Large Orange Sulphur	C	A	U	C	U	U	A
Statira Sulphur		X			X		
Lyside Sulphur	U	U	U	A	U		C
Mexican Yellow							O
Little Yellow	A	A	C	A	A	A	A

Butterfly Species	54	55	56	57	58	59	60
Mimosa Yellow		X					
Sleepy Orange	C	C	U	U	C		A
Dainty Sulphur	A	C	C	C	A	C	A
Great Purple Hairstreak				U	U		
Silver-banded Hairstreak							X
Soapberry Hairstreak		U					
Gray Hairstreak	A	C	C	C	C	U	U
Red-crescent Scrub-Hairstreak						X	
Lacey's Scrub-Hairstreak				U			
Mallow Scrub-Hairstreak	U	U	U	U	C	U	C
Red-banded Hairstreak		X					
Dusky-blue Groundstreak		A	U	U	C	C	U
Clytie Ministreak						X	
Western Pygmy-Blue	A	A	C	A	A	C	C
Eastern Pygmy-Blue	R						
Cassius Blue						O	
Marine Blue		R			U		
Ceraunus Blue	A	A	A	A	C	A	C
Reakirt's Blue	C	C	C	C	C	C	U
Eastern Tailed-Blue				R	U		
Fatal Metalmark	U			U			C
Rounded Metalmark	U	U	C	C	U		U
Red-bordered Metalmark				U	U		O
American Snout	A-R	A-R	A-R	A-R	A-R	A-R	A-R
Gulf Fritillary	A	C	A	C	C	U	A
Julia Heliconian		X	X				
Zebra Heliconian				X	X		
Variegated Fritillary	A	C	C	A	U	C	A
Mexican Fritillary				X			
Theona Checkerspot				U			O
Bordered Patch		C	C	C	C		A
Definite Patch							A
Crimson Patch				O			O
Silvery Checkerspot	U						
Tiny Checkerspot							R
Elada Checkerspot		R			U		
Texan Crescent				U	U		U
Vesta Crescent			U	A	C		C
Phaon Crescent	A	A	C	A	A	C	A
Pearl Crescent	U	C		C	U	C	C
Question Mark				U	U		
American Lady	U	A	U	U	C	U	U

Butterfly Species	54	55	56	57	58	59	60
Painted Lady	U	U	U	C	U	U	R
Red Admiral	C	C	C	C	C	C	U
Common Buckeye	A	C	C	U	C	C	C
Tropical Buckeye	U	C	U			C	O
White Peacock	U	U	U	C	U		C
Malachite							X
Viceroy		C		U			
Dingy Purplewing	X						
Common Mestra		C		C	C		U
Gray Cracker					X		
Ruddy Daggerwing					X		
Goatweed Leafwing		U	U	U	U		U
Hackberry Emperor		C		R	U		U
Tawny Emperor	R	C	U	C	C		C
Gemmed Satyr		U		U	U		U
Carolina Satyr		C		O	U		
Monarch	C	U	C	M	U	U	M
Queen	C	C	C	U	C	C	A
Soldier				X			X
Silver-spotted Skipper						X	
White-striped Longtail	U	C	C	U	C		X
Long-tailed Skipper	O	U	C		U		R
Dorantes Longtail		U		R	R	U	X
Coyote Cloudywing			O	O	U		
Mimosa Skipper					X		
Mazans Scallopwing					U		
Texas Powdered-Skipper				R	U		O
Sickle-winged Skipper	C	C	U	A	C		U
Brown-banded Skipper					X		
White-patched Skipper					X		
False Duskywing	U	C	U				
Horace's Duskywing	U	C	U	U		U	U
Mournful Duskywing		U				U	
Funereal Duskywing	U	C	U	C	U		U
Wild Indigo Duskywing		O					
Com./White Checkered-Skipper	A	C	C	C	A	C	A
Tropical Checkered-Skipper	C	C	C	C	A		C
Desert Checkered-Skipper	U	O	O	R			C
Laviana White-Skipper	U	U	O	U	U		C
Turk's-cap White-Skipper	U	C	U	U	U		O
Common Streaky-Skipper							R
Common Sootywing		R	U	U	R		U

Butterfly Species	54	55	56	57	58	59	60
Julia's Skipper		U		R	U		U
Clouded Skipper	U	A	C	A	A		A
Least Skipper		U					
Orange Skipperling	O	U		U	U		U
Southern Skipperling	U	C	C	U	C	U	A
Fiery Skipper	C	C	A	A	C	C	A
Green Skipper					X		
Whirlabout	U	C	U	U	U		C
Southern Broken-Dash		U	U	U	A	U	
Sachem	U	C	A	C	C	U	A
Dun Skipper	U	C	U	U			
Nysa Roadside-Skipper		U			U		R
Celia's Roadside-Skipper	U	C		U	U	U	U
Eufala Skipper	U	C	U	C	C	C	C
Brazilian Skipper	U	R	U	O	O		
Salt Marsh Skipper	U	U					
Obscure Skipper	A	A	U	O	C	U	U
Ocola Skipper	C	U	A	C	C	C	U

South Texas Brushlands

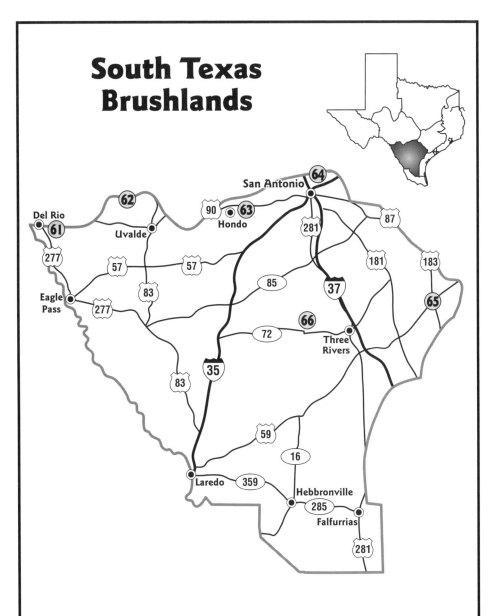

61. **Del Rio/Amistad National Recreation Area**
62. **Park Chalk Bluff**
63. **Hondo–Castroville**
64. **San Antonio**
65. **Goliad**
66. **Choke Canyon State Park**

South Texas Brushland Region

The South Texas Brushlands, also known as the South Texas Plains, is an extensive region of about ten million acres that runs from the Edwards Plateau south to the Rio Grande Valley and from the Trans-Pecos east to the Central Gulf Coast. The landscape is dominated by flatlands and rolling hills that are dissected by numerous drainages. Rivers include the Atascosa, Frio, Medina, Nueces, and San Antonio. Dense Tamaulipan scrub covers the majority of the land, although scattered oak mottes are fairly common, and oak-hackberry woodlands grow in arroyos and other moist places. Elevations range from sea level to about 1,200 feet.

The region is represented by six sites: **61. Del Rio/Amistad National Recreation Area**, **62. Park Chalk Bluff**, **63. Hondo–Castroville**, **64. San Antonio**, **65. Goliad**, and **66. Choke Canyon State Park**. The best time to visit these sites is from March through November.

South Texas Brushland Specialties

The South Texas Brushland Region owes its relatively high butterfly diversity primarily to its close proximity to the tropics. Nineteen area specialties have been recorded in the region.

Sulphurs, Hairstreaks: **Mimosa Yellow** has been found at weedy places along the Rio Grande River and in adjacent arroyos at Del Rio/Amistad NRA and in the Hondo–Castroville area. Unlike the similar Little Yellow, which usually remains in the open when disturbed, Mimosa Yellow will immediately seek protected, shady areas. Larvae feed on mimosa shrubs. **Lacey's Scrub-Hairstreak** has been recorded at brushy areas where its larval foodplant (myrtlecroton) occurs in Del Rio/Amistad NRA and in the San Antonio area.

Metalmarks: **Rounded Metalmark** frequents patches of wildflowers in the Hondo–Castroville area, San Antonio area, Goliad area, and Choke Canyon SP. Its flight is usually short in duration; larvae feed on eupatoriums. **Rawson's Metalmark** is most likely to be found at patches of wildflowers, usually in shady areas, at Del Rio/Amistad NRA, Park Chalk Bluff, the Hondo–Castroville area, San Antonio area, and Choke Canyon SP. Larvae feed on eupatorium. **Red-bordered Metalmark** occurs at Choke Canyon SP, usually near its larval foodplant, spiny hackberry. **Mormon Metalmark** has been recorded only along the western edge of Del Rio/Amistad NRA, representing the eastern edge of its range. Larvae feed on buckwheats.

Patches, Buckeyes, Peacocks, and Leafwings: **Crimson Patch** occurs in a huge colony along Hondo Creek and is also seen in the San Antonio area. Adults fly slowly near their foodplants, anisacanth. **Tropical Buckeye** is known only from Choke Canyon SP, where adults frequent open areas; larvae feed on woolly stemodia. **White Peacock** occurs in late summer and fall in the San Antonio area, Goliad area, and Choke Canyon SP. Larval foodplants include frog-fruit and water hyssop. **Tropical Leafwing** frequents woodlands at Del Rio/Amistad NRA, Park Chalk Bluff, and the San Antonio area. It is a swift flier, often flying out into open areas and returning to perch on a tree trunk or limb. Larvae feed on crotons.

Spread-wing Skippers: **Coyote Cloudywing** is most likely to be found at flowering plants near brushy areas with blackbrush acacia (larval foodplant) at Park Chalk Bluff and in the Hondo–Castroville, San Antonio, and Goliad areas. Adults typically "skip" about from one flower to the next when feeding. **Outis Skipper** is represented by very old records from the Del Rio/Amistad NRA and San Antonio area; there are no recent reports. It is known to utilize acacia grasslands in spring and summer; larvae feed on acacia. **Mazans Scallopwing** is known from the Hondo–Castroville, San Antonio, and Goliad areas. It is most likely to be seen at the edges of shaded wildflowers. **Golden-headed Scallopwing** has been recorded only in the Del Rio/Amistad NRA; it is most likely to be seen along the edge of brushy areas or perched on the ground. Larvae feed on pigweed. **Arizona Powdered-Skipper** is known only in the Del Rio/Amistad NRA; larvae feed on mallows. **Meridian Duskywing** is possible at wooded areas, such as Lowry Spring, in the Del Rio/Amistad NRA. Adults often rest on the ground at moist locations; larvae feed on oak leaves. **Laviana White-Skipper** flies swiftly along the edge of brushy areas with mallows (larval foodplants) in the San Antonio and Goliad areas. It only occasionally stops to feed or rest, often on the ground. **Turk's-cap White-Skipper** is most likely to be found along the edge of brushy areas with Turk's cap, a larval foodplant, along with other mallows, in the San Antonio area, Goliad area, and Choke Canyon SP.

Grass-Skippers and Giant-Skippers: **Viereck's Skipper** has been recorded only in the Del Rio/Amistad NRA, the eastern edge of its range. Adults often feed on cactus flowers in spring. **Mary's Giant-Skipper** occurs where lechuguilla (larval foodplant) grows extensively from September to November in Del Rio/Amistad NRA.

Sites within the South Texas Brushland Region

61. Del Rio/Amistad National Recreation Area

Del Rio and the Amistad National Recreation Area are located within the northwestern edge of the Tamaulipan-scrub vegetation zone at the eastern edge of the Chihuahuan Desert. The city of Del Rio is a major entry point into Mexico. The best butterflying sites in the city include a church garden (**A**), Moore Park (**E**), and Loma de la Cruz (**F**), a wetlands area.

The nearby 67,000-acre Amistad Reservoir has 850 miles of shoreline and a number of side streams. San Pedro Campground (**B**), Lowry Springs (**C**), and the Rio Grande floodplain (**D**) are good places to find butterflies.

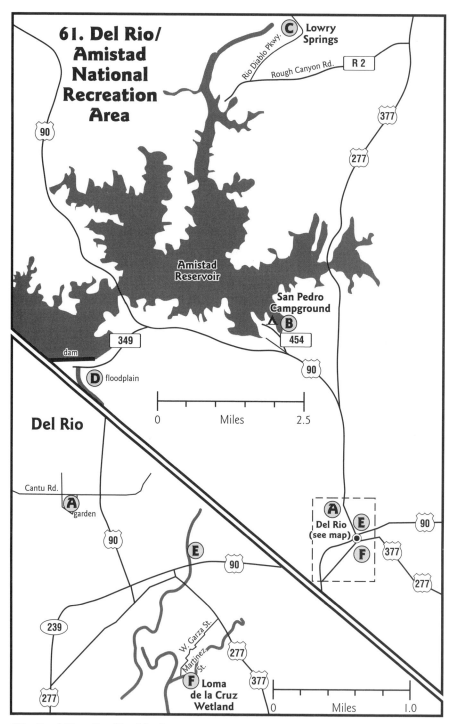

61. Del Rio/ Amistad National Recreation Area

C Lowry Springs

Rio Diablo Pkwy.

Rough Canyon Rd.   R 2

90

377

277

Amistad Reservoir

San Pedro Campground
B

349   454

dam

90

D floodplain

Del Rio

0   Miles   2.5

Cantu Rd.

A garden

90

E

90

239

A Del Rio (see map)

E

90

377

277

F

377

W. Garza St.

Martinez St.

277

F Loma de la Cruz Wetland   377

0   Miles   1.0

Tamaulipan scrub habitat, Amistad Reservoir

Habitats: Tamaulipan scrub, desert scrub, garden, floodplain, riparian, and lakeshore.

Strategy for finding the most butterflies: Start in downtown Del Rio at the rather extensive garden at the Central Church of Christ **(A)**. The garden is worth checking again during your visit. Some of the more numerous butterflies include Pipevine Swallowtail, Large Orange and Lyside sulphurs, Ceraunus and Reakirt's blues, Gulf Fritillary, Theona and Elada checkerspots, Bordered Patch, Queen, Clouded and Fiery skippers, and Celia's Roadside-Skipper. Other common butterflies include Henry's Elfin in spring and Ocola Skipper in fall. Less common butterflies include Giant Swallowtail, Great Purple Hairstreak, and Goatweed Leafwing; also watch for **Rawson's Metalmark** and **Golden-headed Scallopwing**.

Next, drive to San Pedro Campground **(B)** in the Amistad NRA, with its extensive shoreline and low-growing wildflowers. Orange Sulphur, Little Yellow, Western Pygmy-Blue, Variegated Fritillary, Phaon and Pearl crescents, Common/White and Desert checkered-skippers, and Southern Skipperling can be expected, and Monarchs roost here in great numbers in the fall.

Then, drive north to Lowry Springs **(C)**, an isolated drainage within an arid environment. Several of the butterflies mentioned above can be expected, but also possible are Two-tailed Swallowtail; **Lacey's Scrub-Hairstreak**; Fatal Metalmark; Texan and Vesta crescents; Red-spotted Purple; **Tropical Leafwing**; Tawny Emperor; **Arizona Powdered-Skipper**; False, **Meridian**, and Funereal duskywings; Orange

Skipperling; and Green Skipper. Also search the lechuguilla flats along the entrance roadway from September into November for **Mary's Giant-Skipper**.

Below Amistad Dam (open by permission only; see "Directions" below), the Rio Grande floodplain (**D**) has considerable potential as well. Expect Black Swallowtail, Marine Blue, Empress Leilia, and Eufala Skipper. **Mimosa Yellow**, **Coyote Cloudywing**, Common Streaky-Skipper, and Nysa Roadside-Skipper are also possible.

A secondary site in Del Rio, Moore Park (**E**), is located along San Felipe Creek. Enter through the golf course (permission necessary) or drive to the adjacent Elks Lodge parking lot and walk along the creek beyond. At Loma de la Cruz (**F**), a wetlands area, walk the edges and along the creeks.

In addition, **Mormon Metalmark** and **Outis** and **Viereck's skippers** have been recorded at unknown locations in the Del Rio/Amistad NRA.

Directions: In Val Verde County, most sites are located off US 90. The **Central Church of Christ garden (A)** is located at 402 Cantu Rd. west of US 90. Return to US 90 and go south and then east to the US 277 intersection. Continue east on US 90 a short distance to San Felipe Springs Rd. Turn north to **Moore Park (E)**. To reach **Loma de la Cruz (F)**, return to US 277 and go southeast. Take W. Garza St. southwest from US 277 to Broadbent Ave. and turn left. At Martinez St., turn right to the wetlands area.

North of Del Rio, **San Pedro Campground (B)**, one of the Amistad NRA sites, is off SH 454 Spur north of US 90. **Lowry Springs (C)** is north off US 277. Take the Rough Canyon Rd. (R 2) west and turn northeast on Rio Diablo Parkway. Watch on the left for a gate with a park service sign for the springs; the gate is just before the road crosses a major drainage. The **Rio Grande floodplain (D)**, off SH 349 Spur below Amistad Dam, is accessible only with permission from the National Park Service. Inquire at headquarters, located near the Blackbrush boat ramp entry road along US 90, a few miles west of the turn to San Pedro Campground.

Nearest food, gas, and lodging: Del Rio.

Nearest camping: Amistad NRA and sites along US 90.

62. Park Chalk Bluff

The 500-acre Park Chalk Bluff is a privately owned park (fee area), located along the Nueces River as it flows along the base of a 300-foot bluff. Butterfly-watching sites include a butterfly garden (**A**), an adjacent field (**B**), a woodland (**D**), a riparian habitat (**E**), and a network of trails and old roads (**C, F, G**). The level of recreational use can be extensive on weekends and holidays, but weekdays are usually quiet.

Habitats: Tamaulipan scrub, pecan grove, garden, riparian, field, and cropland.

Strategy for finding the most butterflies: Start at the butterfly garden (**A**) at the park entrance and also walk the edges of the adjacent field (**B**). Some of the more numerous butterflies include Pipevine and Giant swallowtails, Lyside Sulphur, Southern Dogface, Little Yellow, Sleepy Orange, Ceraunus and Reakirt's blues, Gulf

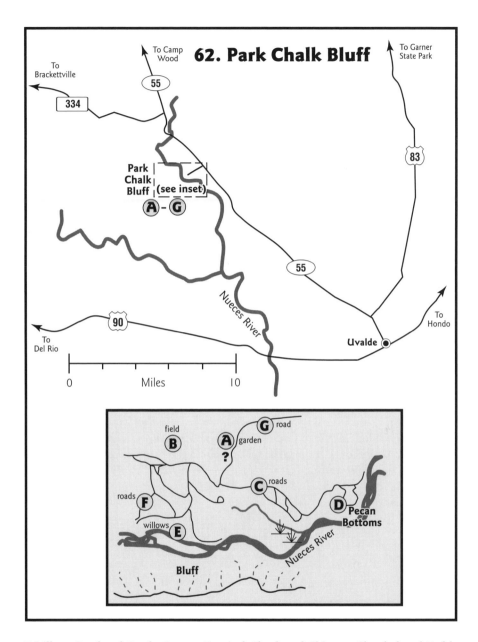

62. Park Chalk Bluff

To Camp Wood

To Brackettville

To Garner State Park

55

334

83

Park Chalk Bluff (see inset)

Ⓐ-Ⓖ

55

Nueces River

90

To Hondo

To Del Rio

Uvalde

0   Miles   10

field

Ⓖ road

Ⓑ

Ⓐ garden

?

Ⓒ roads

roads Ⓕ

Ⓓ **Pecan Bottoms**

willows Ⓔ

Nueces River

Bluff

Fritillary, Bordered Patch, Queen, Tropical Checkered-Skipper, Clouded and Eufala skippers, Sachem, and Celia's Roadside-Skipper.

Also watch for the less common Great Purple Hairstreak, Mallow Scrub-Hairstreak, Dusky-blue Groundstreak, **Rounded** and **Rawson's metalmarks**, Elada Checkerspot, **Coyote Cloudywing**, Funereal Duskywing, and Fiery Skipper. In spring,

Park Chalk Bluff

Falcate Orangetip can be expected, and Sickle-winged and Ocola skippers can be common in fall. Migrating Monarchs can be abundant in fall.

Then, drive eastward toward Pecan Bottoms. Check the roadsides (**C**) where Black Swallowtail, Marine Blue, Fatal Metalmark, Theona Checkerspot, Vesta and Phaon crescents, Question Mark, Empress Leilia, Desert Checkered-Skipper, Common Streaky-Skipper, and Dun Skipper are likely. At Pecan Bottoms (**D**) and other wooded locations, watch for Goatweed Leafwing; **Tropical Leafwing** has also been recorded.

Next, look for Viceroys among the willows along the river (**E**) and then walk the network of roads (**F**) on the west end of the park. Texan and Pearl crescents, Red Admiral, Common Mestra, Red Satyr, and False Duskywing are possible. Also, the open and shaded roadsides along the entrance road (**G**) can be productive, especially when wildflowers are present.

Directions: In Uvalde County, from Uvalde take US 83 north to SH 55 and go 15 miles to the signed Park Chalk Bluff entrance on the left.

Nearest food, gas, and lodging: Uvalde; food and lodging at Park Chalk Bluff.

Nearest camping: Park Chalk Bluff.

63. Hondo–Castroville

Located along US 90, these two nearby towns are at the northern edge of the South Texas brushlands and at the southern edge of the Edwards Plateau. The topography, therefore, is rough, with numerous perennial streams that flow southward. Butterfly

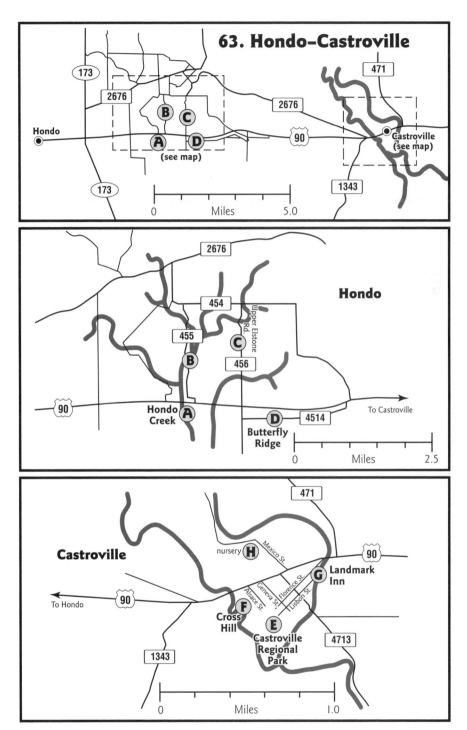

63. Hondo–Castroville

173

2676

Hondo

(A) (B) (C) (D)

(see map)

173

2676

90

471

Castroville
(see map)

1343

0   Miles   5.0

2676

454

455

Upper Elstone Rd.

(C)

(B)

456

90

Hondo
Creek (A)

(D)   4514

Butterfly
Ridge

To Castroville

Hondo

0   Miles   2.5

471

Castroville

nursery (H)

Mexico St.

90

Landmark
Inn (G)

Geneva St.

Florence St.

Alsace St.

Lisbon St.

90

To Hondo

(F)

Cross
Hill

(E)

Castroville
Regional
Park

4713

1343

0   Miles   1.0

Crimson Patch habitat along Hondo Creek

sites near Hondo include Hondo Creek (**A**) and several roadsides (**B**-**D**). Castroville, settled by Alsatians in 1846, is located in the valley formed by the Medina River. It features the Castroville Regional Park (**E**), a hilltop walk (**F**), the restored Landmark Inn (**G**), and a nursery (**H**).

Habitats: Tamaulipan scrub, park, garden, riparian, field, and cropland.

Strategy for finding the most butterflies: Start at Hondo Creek (**A**) on the south side of US 90; enter the area from the west on a weedy track. This is the best location for observing the huge colony of **Crimson Patch** that extends along the creek above and below US 90. Some of the other butterflies you should expect to find here include Pipevine and Giant swallowtails, Little Yellow, Sleepy Orange, Vesta Crescent, Common Mestra, Hackberry and Tawny emperors, and Clouded and Eufala skippers.

Then, cross US 90 and drive CR 455 (**B**) north along Hondo Creek, stopping near the railroad bridge to walk the roadsides and the trail along the south side of the tracks. This location usually provides the site's greatest butterfly diversity. Cloudless, Large Orange, and Lyside sulphurs; Mallow Scrub-Hairstreak; Dusky-blue Ground-streak; Marine, Ceraunus, and Reakirt's blues; Fatal Metalmark; Gulf Fritillary; Bordered Patch; Northern Cloudywing; False Duskywing; Common Streaky-Skipper; Southern Skipperling; and Celia's Roadside-Skipper can usually be found. In addition, **Mimosa Yellow**, **Rounded** and **Rawson's metalmarks**, Tiny Checkerspot, **Coyote Cloudywing**, **Mazans Scallopwing**, and Nysa Roadside-Skipper also frequent the area. In spring, Falcate Orangetip can be expected; Sickle-winged and Ocola skippers occur in fall.

Next, continue to CR 454 and turn right to Upper Elstone Rd., CR 456 (**C**), which loops back to US 90. Although many of the butterflies mentioned above are likely, additional species may include Eastern Tiger Swallowtail; Great Purple and Juniper hairstreaks; Western Pygmy-Blue; Theona, Silvery, and Elada checkerspots; Empress Leilia; Texas Powdered-Skipper; **Laviana** and **Turk's-cap white-skippers**; and Least Skipper. In spring, watch for Soapberry, Banded, and Oak hairstreaks.

Then cross US 90 and drive the CR 4514 loop (**D**)—"Butterfly Ridge"—located along the south side of US 90, checking the roadsides; this area may be best in the morning. The road may be closed to vehicular traffic.

In Castroville, visit Castroville Regional Park (**E**), stopping at the butterfly garden at the entrance and walking the far edges, where Texan Crescent can be common. Then, just beyond the cemetery, walk the dirt track that goes to the top of Cross Hill (**F**), where hilltopping species, such as Black Swallowtails, can be expected. Finally, visit the Landmark Inn (**G**), a private fee area. Check the flowering plants around the buildings and walk the nature trail. If time allows, visit the Medina Valley Nursery (**H**) at the end of Mexico Street.

Directions: In Medina County, along US 90 between Hondo and Castroville, **Hondo Creek (A)** is located along US 90 east of Hondo. Start on the south side of US 90. Across US 90 to the north, take **CR 455 (B)** to the railroad bridge. Continue north to CR 454 and turn east for about a mile to **Upper Elstone Rd., CR 456 (C)**. Take it south to US 90 and cross the highway. Butterfly Ridge is located along **CR 4514 (D)**, a two-mile loop south of US 90.

Continue east on US 90 to Castroville. The dirt track to the top of **Cross Hill (F)** is beyond the cemetery, located at US 90 and Alsace St. To reach **Castroville Regional Park (E)**, turn south from US 90 on Geneva St. and drive to Florence St. or Lisbon St. and turn right. The **Landmark Inn (G)**, with a bed and breakfast, is located at 402 E. Florence St., northeast from the park. East of Geneva St. on US 90, take Mexico St. north to reach the **Medina Valley Nursery (H)**.

Nearest food, gas, and lodging: Hondo and Castroville.

Nearest camping: Hondo and Castroville and at Hondo RV Park at Hondo Creek.

64. San Antonio

The San Antonio area includes scattered sites in and around the city. The eleven-acre San Antonio Botanical Garden (**A**), a fee area, features representative plants from all regions of Texas and can be superb. It is owned and operated by the City of San Antonio. Other worthwhile sites include Calaveras Lake Park (**B**) and Braunig Lake Park (**C**), both fee areas, and Mitchell Lake Audubon Center (**D**), open Saturdays or by special arrangement.

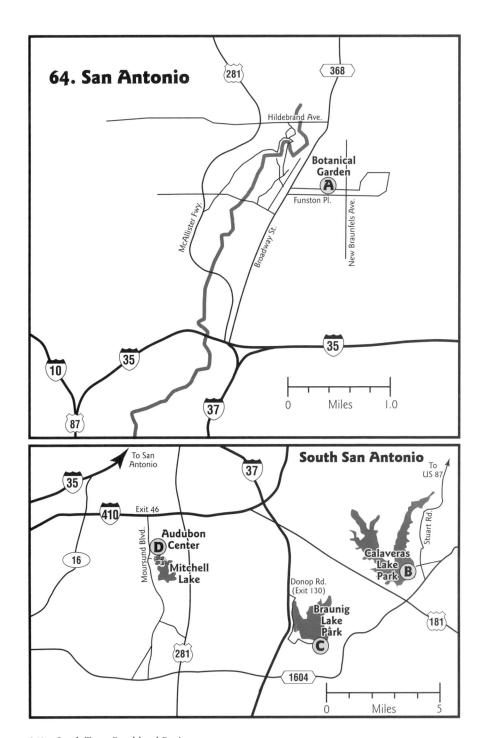

64. San Antonio

281

368

Hildebrand Ave.

**Botanical
Garden**
Ⓐ

Funston Pl.

McAllister Fwy.

Broadway St.

New Braunfels Ave.

35

10

35

37

87

0   Miles   1.0

To San
Antonio

35

37

South San Antonio

To
US 87

410   Exit 46

Moursund Blvd.

**Audubon
Center**
Ⓓ

**Mitchell
Lake**

16

Stuart Rd.

**Calaveras
Lake
Park**
Ⓑ

Donop Rd.
(Exit 130)

**Braunig
Lake
Park**
Ⓒ

181

281

1604

0   Miles   5

San Antonio Botanical Garden

Habitats: Juniper-oak woodland, broadleaf woodland, Tamaulipan scrub, garden, and riparian.

Strategy for finding the most butterflies: The San Antonio Botanical Garden (**A**) offers the most accessible and productive butterflying in this area. Walk the trails, returning to the best spots later, since butterflies come and go throughout the day. Some of the more numerous species include Pipevine and Giant swallowtails, Large Orange Sulphur, Little Yellow, Sleepy Orange, Gulf Fritillary, Bordered Patch, Texan Crescent, Horace's Duskywing, and Fiery and Eufala skippers.

Some of the less numerous species include Black and Eastern Tiger swallowtails, Great Purple Hairstreak, Dusky-blue Groundstreak, Reakirt's Blue, Fatal Metalmark, Vesta Crescent, Queen, Common Streaky-Skipper, and Brazilian Skipper. Also watch for Two-tailed Swallowtail, **Rounded** and **Rawson's metalmarks** at flowering plants, and **Tropical Leafwing** in wooded locations. In spring, Falcate Orangetip can be expected, and Soapberry and Oak hairstreaks, Henry's Elfin, and Juvenal's Duskywing are also possible. In fall, Sickle-winged and Ocola skippers can be common.

Next, drive to the south side of town where there are three worthwhile sites: Calaveras Lake Park, Braunig Lake Park, and Mitchell Lake. Calaveras Lake Park (**B**) is best; drive the roadsides, stopping at pull-offs with flowering plants, and walk the nature trail. Although many of the butterflies mentioned above are likely, also expect Cloudless and Lyside sulphurs; Phaon Crescent; Elada Checkerspot; Funereal Duskywing; Common/White, Tropical, and Desert checkered-skippers; and Southern Broken-Dash. Also possible are Mexican Yellow, Cassius Blue, Theona Checkerspot,

Coyote Cloudywing, and **Mazans Scallopwing** at patches of flowering plants; the fast-flying **Laviana White-Skipper** along the lakeshore in the northern portion of the park; and **White Peacock** in summer and fall.

At Braunig Lake Park (**C**), walk the roadsides, the nature trail, and the edges along the lakeshore in the northern portion of the park. Butterflies possible are very similar to those at Calaveras Lake Park. Mitchell Lake Audubon Center (**D**) butterflies are also similar to those at Calaveras Lake Park, but it is only open Saturdays, 8 a.m. to 4 p.m. or for scheduled tours.

Note: While you're in the area, consider a visit to nearby Government Canyon State Natural Area, just northwest of San Antonio (site 20 in the Edwards Plateau Region).

Directions: In Bexar County, the **San Antonio Botanical Garden** (**A**) is located in the middle of the city; take Broadway St. north from I-35 near its intersection with US 281 and turn right on Funston Pl. The address is 555 Funston Place. Calaveras, Braunig, and Mitchell lakes are south of the city between Loop 410 and Loop 1604. To reach **Calaveras Lake Park** (**B**) take US 181 south from Loop 410 to Loop 1604. Go east on Loop 1604 for two miles and turn north on Stuart Rd. **Braunig Lake Park** (**C**) is along I-37. Take Donop Rd. (Exit 130) and follow the signs to the park. **Mitchell Lake Audubon Center** (**D**) is located off Moursund Blvd. (Exit 46), .7-mile south of Loop 410. Currently the Center is only open on Saturdays and for scheduled events. For more information, call 210-628-1639 or visit their web site.

Nearest food, gas, and lodging: San Antonio.

Nearest camping: Commercial sites in San Antonio and the nearby Government Canyon SNA (site 20, Edwards Plateau Region).

65. Goliad

The Goliad area is located in the northeastern corner of the Tamaulipan-scrub zone of Texas. Butterflying sites include Goliad State Park (**A-D**), the two-mile, paved Angel of Goliad Nature Trail (**E**) between downtown and the state park, the Presidio la Bahía (**F**), and a nearby road (**G**). The trail passes through a rich riparian habitat along the San Antonio River. Goliad is best known for its significance in Texas history.

Habitats: Tamaulipan scrub, coastal prairie, oak motte, riparian, field, and cropland.

Strategy for finding the most butterflies: Start at Goliad SP (fee area) by walking the perimeter of the Group Trailer Area (**A**), including the track to the swimming pool. Some of the more numerous butterflies include Pipevine and Giant swallowtails; Cloudless, Large Orange, and Lyside sulphurs; Little Yellow; Reakirt's Blue; Gulf Fritillary; Bordered Patch; Phaon Crescent; Queen; Clouded, Fiery, and Eufala skippers; and Sachem.

Next, drive the park roads (**B**), stopping at patches of wildflowers. The roadsides and adjacent fields usually have many of the butterflies mentioned above, but a

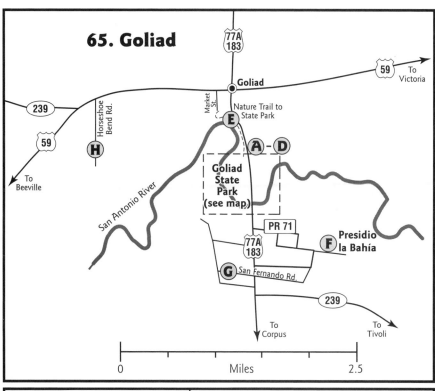

65. Goliad

77A
183

Goliad

59 To
Victoria

239

Horseshoe Bend Rd.

Market St.

Nature Trail to
State Park

E

59

To
Beeville

H

A D

San Antonio River

Goliad
State
Park
(see map)

PR 71

77A
183

Presidio
la Bahía

F

G San Fernando Rd.

239

To
Corpus

To
Tivoli

0   Miles   2.5

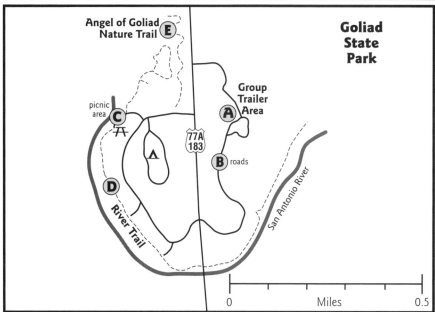

Angel of Goliad
Nature Trail E

Goliad
State
Park

picnic
area C

Group
Trailer
Area

A

77A
183

B roads

D

River Trail

San Antonio River

0   Miles   0.5

Roadside in spring, Goliad State Park

number of other species also occur. They may include Great Purple Hairstreak, Mallow Scrub-Hairstreak, Dusky-blue Groundstreak, Fatal Metalmark, Silvery Checkerspot, Vesta Crescent, Common Mestra, White-striped and Dorantes longtails, Long-tailed Skipper, Texas Powdered-Skipper, Horace's Duskywing, and **Laviana** and **Turk's-cap white-skippers**. **Rounded Metalmark** and **Coyote Cloudywing** are also possible. In spring, Falcate Orangetip can be expected; Sickle-winged and Ocola skippers are usually common in fall.

Walk the edges of the picnic area (**C**) and at least the portion of the River Trail (**D**) between the picnic area and Tent Camping Pad 1. Texan Crescent, Gemmed and Carolina satyrs, and Little Wood-Satyr are likely to be seen. Next, walk the Angel of Goliad Nature Trail (**E**) between the state park and the end of Market Street in town; watch for False Duskywing at the midway point and **Mazans Scallopwing** anywhere along the edges at shaded locations. **White Peacock** is likely to be found in late summer and fall.

Also, check the fields (**F**) surrounding Presidio la Bahía, birthplace of General Ignacio Zaragoza, and nearby Fannin Memorial Monument. Across the highway, drive San Fernando Road (**G**) to the cemetery. Finally, west of town, drive Horseshoe Bend Road (**H**), checking the roadsides and adjacent fields. Goatweed Leafwing and Tawny Emperor can be abundant.

Directions: In Goliad County, from US 59, take US 183 south for .3 mile to **Goliad SP** (**A-D**) on the right. The **Angel of Goliad Nature Trail** (**E**) runs from the end of Market Street in downtown Goliad through the state park to Presidio la Bahía.

Presidio la Bahía (**F**) and the Fannin Memorial Monument are farther south on US 183. Take PR 71 east. **San Fernando Road (G)** to the cemetery is west of the highway just south of the junction with PR 71. West of downtown, **Horseshoe Bend Road (H)** goes south from US 59 near its junction with SH 239.

Nearest food, gas, and lodging: Goliad.

Nearest camping: Goliad SP.

66. Choke Canyon State Park

The name for Choke Canyon State Park (fee area) was derived from the steep banks near the dam site that "chokes" the Frio River during floods. The 26,000-acre reservoir serves as a water supply for the city of Corpus Christi. The site offers several widely spaced butterfly-watching locations, including the FM 99 Boat Ramp (**A**), P 7 road (**B**), the Calliham Unit (**C**), South Shore Unit (**D**), nearby roadsides (**E, F**), and Tips Park (**G**) in Three Rivers. The Calliham and South Shore units offer the greatest biological diversity. The nearby town of Three Rivers was named for its location at the confluence of the Frio, Atascosa, and Nueces rivers.

Habitats: Tamaulipan scrub, mesquite grassland, riparian, wetland, and field.

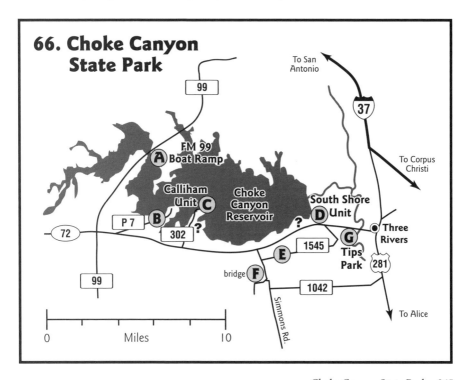

Tamaulipan scrub habitat, Choke Canyon State Park

Strategy for finding the most butterflies: Start at the far western edge of the site at the FM 99 Boat Ramp (**A**), along the Frio River floodplain, and walk the trails above the parking area and along the reservoir. Some of the more numerous butterflies include Pipevine and Giant swallowtails; Large Orange, Lyside, and Dainty sulphurs; Little Yellow; Sleepy Orange; Ceraunus and Reakirt's blues; Gulf Fritillary; Theona Checkerspot; Phaon Crescent; Empress Leilia; Queen; and Fiery, Dun, and Eufala skippers.

A few of the less common butterflies include Cloudless Sulphur, Western Pygmy-Blue, Silvery Checkerspot, Mallow Scrub-Hairstreak, and Desert Checkered-Skipper. Also watch for **Rawson's Metalmark**, "Dark" **Tropical Buckeye**, and Nysa Roadside-Skipper. In spring, Falcate Orangetip and Henry's Elfin can be expected; Yucca Giant-Skipper is also possible. In fall, **White Peacock**, Monarch, and Sickle-winged and Ocola skippers are likely to occur.

Next, drive south on FM 99 to SH 72 and turn east toward the Calliham Unit, but first take P 7 road (**B**) northeast through rather dense Tamaulipan scrub to a boat ramp. Check for nectaring butterflies at flowers along the main and side roads. Fatal Metalmark, Elada Checkerspot, Common Buckeye, and Red Admiral are usually present.

Then return to SH 72 and continue east to FM 302. Turn north to the Calliham Unit (**C**), checking the roadsides along the way. Walk the nature trail and side trails. Although many of the butterflies mentioned above are possible, additional species may include Texas Powdered-Skipper, **Laviana** and **Turk's-cap white-skippers**, and Southern Skipperling.

Next, visit the South Shore Unit (**D**), also north of SH 72 nearer Three Rivers. Drive the roadways, walk through the picnic area along the river below the dam, and take the short nature trail. Expect American Snout, Vesta Crescent, Question Mark, Hackberry and Tawny emperors, and Tropical Checkered-Skipper. Also stop and walk the short, gated side road just before the cabins, where **Red-bordered** and **Rounded metalmarks** are possible.

Afterwards, turn east on SH 72 and go a short distance to a turn south on FM 1545 (**E**). Follow it as it goes south and then west to Simmons Road. Turn south to the Nueces River bridge (**F**); check the roadsides along the way and the floodplain below the bridge. Then return to SH 72 and drive toward Three Rivers. Stop at Tips Park (**G**) south of the highway just west of the bridge; park near the river and walk along the edges, including the area below the bridge. Black and Eastern Tiger swallowtails, Viceroy, and Common Mestra can usually be added to your list. Brazilian Skipper larvae can often be found at the cannas near the park entrance.

Directions: In McMullen and Live Oak Counties, all the sites are located west of US 281 from Three Rivers. The Frio River floodplain site at the **FM 99 Boat Ramp** (**A**)—locally known as "Possum Creek Crossing"—is located off FM 99, six miles north of its junction with SH 72. Return to SH 72 and go east to **P 7 (B)** and the boat ramp. Return to SH 72 and go east to FM 302. Turn north to the end of the road and the **Calliham Unit (C)**, 14.4 miles west of Three Rivers. The **South Shore Unit (D)** is north of SH 72, 10.2 miles east of FM 302 and 4.2 miles west of Three Rivers. For **FM 1545 (E)** and the route to the **Nueces River bridge (F)** go south from SH 72 a short distance east of the South Shore Unit entrance road. **Tips Park (G)** is located west of Three Rivers along the Frio River on the south side of SH 72.

Nearest food, gas, and lodging: Three Rivers and Calliham (at the entrance to the Calliham Unit).

Nearest camping: Choke Canyon SP and Tips Park.

Additional Worthwhile Sites in the South Texas Brushland Region

Fort Clark Springs. One of the most appealing sites in the region because of the abundance of fresh water, this private community is well worth a visit. The 2,700-acre development, within the town of Bracketville, west of Uvalde on US 90, has the remains of the 1852 U.S. Army Fort Clark, as well as roads and trails for easy access into the varied habitats. Camping, a golf course, swimming pool, and restaurant are available.

Lake Corpus Christi State Park. This 365-acre park is located at the southeastern corner of Lake Corpus Christi, the principal water source for Corpus Christi. It is located off I-37, northwest of the city. The park can be very busy on holidays and weekends. Its butterfly fauna is similar to that found in the Choke Canyon area.

Rio Bravo Nature Center. This is a new site, within Shelby Park in Eagle Pass, which has considerable promise. Located along the Rio Grande River, it includes access to a three-mile-long Border Patrol road. Proceed west on Main Street (Bus. 277), crossing Commercial St., to Shelby Park. Park at the extreme right in the parking lot; an unmarked dirt road hugs the river bank and runs about one mile, passing the city water catchment pond and proceeding to a timber bridge over a deep arroyo.

Butterfly Checkist for the South Texas Brushland Region

The following list includes six sites: **61. Del Rio/Amistad National Recreation Area**, **62. Park Chalk Bluff**, **63. Hondo–Castroville**, **64. San Antonio**, **65. Goliad**, and **66. Choke Canyon State Park**.

Status symbols include: A = abundant; C = common; U = uncommon; O = occasional; R = rare; X = accidental; M = migrant; TC = temporary colonist; ? = unknown status. (For a full definition of these terms, see p. 3.)

For trip notes, including dates and numbers of species seen, refer to the entry for this checklist in Appendix 3: Regional Checklist Resources.

Butterfly Species	61	62	63	64	65	66
Pipevine Swallowtail	C	C	A	A	A	A
Polydamas Swallowtail	X			X		
Black Swallowtail	U	O	O	U	O	U
Thoas Swallowtail	X					
Giant Swallowtail	U	C	C	C	A	A
Ornythion Swallowtail				X		
Eastern Tiger Swallowtail			U	O		U
Two-tailed Swallowtail	R			U		
Ruby-spotted Swallowtail			X	X		
Florida White				X		X
Checkered White	C	A	A	A	C	U
Cabbage White				X		
Great Southern White	X			X	X	
Giant White				X		
Falcate Orangetip		U	C	U	C	U
Clouded Sulphur				X		
Orange Sulphur	C	A	A	A	A	C
Southern Dogface	C	C	C	U	C	C
White Angled-Sulphur	X		X	X		X
Yellow Angled-Sulphur			X	X		
Cloudless Sulphur	C	A	U	C	C	U
Orange-barred Sulphur			O	O		R

Butterfly Species	61	62	63	64	65	66
Large Orange Sulphur	C	U	A	C	C	C
Tailed Sulphur				X		
Lyside Sulphur	C	A	A	C	C	A
Boisduval's Yellow				X		
Mexican Yellow	O		O	O		O
Tailed Orange			X	X		
Little Yellow	C	C	A	C	A	A
Mimosa Yellow	R	X	U	X		X
Sleepy Orange	A	A	A	A	C	A
Dainty Sulphur	A	A	A	A	A	A
Harvester				X		
Great Purple Hairstreak	U	U	U	U	O	O
Silver-banded Hairstreak				X		
Soapberry Hairstreak	O		U	U		
Banded Hairstreak			O	R		
Oak Hairstreak	X		R	R		
Xami Hairstreak				X		
Henry's Elfin	U			O		U
Juniper Hairstreak			U	U		
White M Hairstreak				X		
Gray Hairstreak	C	C	C	C	C	C
Lacey's Scrub-Hairstreak	U			O		
Mallow Scrub-Hairstreak	U	O	U	O	U	U
Lantana Scrub-Hairstreak			X	X		X
Red-banded Hairstreak				X		
Dusky-blue Groundstreak	O	O	U	O	U	U
Clytie Ministreak			X	X		
Western Pygmy-Blue	A		U	U		U
Cassius Blue			R	R		
Marine Blue	C	O	U	U		
Cyna Blue				R		
Ceraunus Blue	C	C	A	U	A	A
Reakirt's Blue	C	C	A	U	C	C
Eastern Tailed-Blue				R		
Spring/Summer Azure				X		
Fatal Metalmark	A	A	A	U	U	O
Rounded Metalmark		R	U	U	U	U
Rawson's Metalmark	O	O	O	O		O
Red-bordered Metalmark						O
Mormon Metalmark	O					
American Snout	A-R	A-R	A-R	A-R	A-R	A-R
Gulf Fritillary	C	C	C	C	A	C

Butterfly Species	61	62	63	64	65	66
Mexican Silverspot				X		
Julia Heliconian				X	X	
Isabella's Heliconian				X		
Zebra Heliconian	X	X	X	X	X	X
Variegated Fritillary	A	A	C	C	C	C
Mexican Fritillary				X		
Theona Checkerspot	C	A	C	U	U	A
Bordered Patch	U	A	C	C	A	A
Crimson Patch			A	O		
Silvery Checkerspot			U	U	U	O
Tiny Checkerspot		O	O	O		
Elada Checkerspot	A	U	U	U		U
Texan Crescent	U	U	C	C	C	
Pale-banded Crescent				X		
Vesta Crescent	C	A	A	C	U	C
Phaon Crescent	A	A	A	C	A	A
Pearl Crescent	U	O	C	U	C	C
Painted Crescent	O					
Question Mark		O	U	U	U	U
Mourning Cloak	O		O	O		
American Lady	U	U	U	C	U	
Painted Lady	U	U	U	C	U	U
Red Admiral	U	U	C	C	C	C
Common Buckeye	U	U	C	C	C	U
Tropical Buckeye						O
White Peacock	X		X	TC	O	U
Malachite				X		
Red-spotted Purple	U			R		
Viceroy	U	U	C	U	U	C
Band-celled Sister						X
California Sister				O		
Dingy Purplewing	X					
Blue-eyed Sailor				X		
Common Mestra	O	C	C	U	U	C
Red Rim			X	X		X
Many-banded Daggerwing	X		X			
Ruddy Daggerwing				X		
Tropical Leafwing	U	O		O		
Goatweed Leafwing	O	U	C	U	C	C
Hackberry Emperor	U		C	U	C	U
Empress Leilia	C	C	A	C	U	C
Tawny Emperor	C		A	C	A	C

Butterfly Species	61	62	63	64	65	66
Gemmed Satyr				C		
Carolina Satyr				U	U	
Little Wood-Satyr				R	U	
Red Satyr		R		U		
Common Wood-Nymph				O		
Monarch	M	M	M	M	M	M
Queen	C	C	C	C	C	A
Soldier				X	X	
Mercurial Skipper				X		
Silver-spotted Skipper				U		
Hammock Skipper				X		
White-striped Longtail	X		X	O	U	
Zilpa Longtail				X		
Long-tailed Skipper			U	U	O	
Dorantes Longtail			R	U	U	
Brown Longtail				X		X
Two-barred Flasher				X		
Sonoran Banded-Skipper			X			
Hoary Edge				X		
Desert Cloudywing				X		
Coyote Cloudywing	R	R	U	O	U	
Southern Cloudywing				X		
Northern Cloudywing	U	U	U	U		
Confused Cloudywing			X	X		
Potrillo Skipper				X		
Fritzgaertner's Flat				X		
Outis Skipper	?			?		
Golden-headed Scallopwing	R			R		
Mazans Scallopwing			R	O	U	
Hayhurst's Scallopwing			R	R		
Texas Powdered-Skipper	O		O	O	U	U
Arizona Powdered-Skipper	R					
Sickle-winged Skipper		U	U	O	C	C
Hermit Skipper				X		
White-patched Skipper				X		
False Duskywing	O	U	U	O	U	
Juvenal's Duskywing	O			O		
Meridian Duskywing	R			R		
Horace's Duskywing				C	U	U
Funereal Duskywing	U	U	U	U	C	U
Com./White Checkered-Skipper	A	A	A	C	A	A
Tropical Checkered-Skipper	R	C	U	U	A	U

Butterfly Species	61	62	63	64	65	66
Desert Checkered-Skipper	C	U	U	U	U	U
Laviana White-Skipper			R	O	U	U
Turk's-cap White-Skipper			R		U	U
Common Streaky-Skipper	U	U	U	O		O
Common Sootywing	U	O	O	U		
Swarthy Skipper				X		
Julia's Skipper	O		U	O	U	
Clouded Skipper	U	A	A	C	A	C
Least Skipper	R		U	O	U	
Tropical Least Skipper	U			R		
Orange Skipperling	C		U	C	U	
Southern Skipperling	U	U	C	C	A	C
Fiery Skipper	C	U	U	A	C	C
Green Skipper	R		R	R		
Whirlabout	R		U	U	U	O
Southern Broken-Dash		R	U	U	U	O
Little Glassywing				X		
Sachem	U	C	U	A	C	C
Arogos Skipper				X		
Delaware Skipper				X		
Broad-winged Skipper				X		
Dun Skipper		U	U	C	U	U
Viereck's Skipper	R					
Bronze Roadside-Skipper				X		
Oslar's Roadside-Skipper			X	X		
Nysa Roadside-Skipper	U		O	O		U
Dotted Roadside-Skipper	R		R	R		
Celia's Roadside-Skipper	C	C	U	U	C	O
Eufala Skipper	C	C	C	U	C	C
Brazilian Skipper	U			U		
Ocola Skipper	U	U	U	U	C	U
Purple-washed Skipper				X		
Violet-banded Skipper				X		
Chestnut-marked Skipper				X		
Mary's Giant-Skipper	U					
Yucca Giant-Skipper			R	R		
Strecker's Giant-Skipper				X		
Manfreda Giant-Skipper				?		

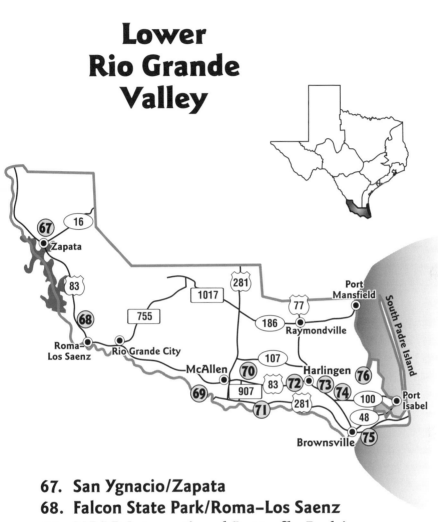

Lower Rio Grande Valley

67. **San Ygnacio/Zapata**
68. **Falcon State Park/Roma–Los Saenz**
69. **NABA International Butterfly Park/
    Bentsen-Rio Grande Valley State Park**
70. **Edinburg World Birding Center**
71. **Santa Ana National Wildlife Refuge**
72. **Weslaco**
73. **Hugh Ramsey Nature Park**
74. **Los Ebanos Preserve**
75. **Sabal Palm Audubon Center and Sanctuary**
76. **Laguna Atascosa National Wildlife Refuge**

Lower Rio Grande Valley Region

The Lower Rio Grande Valley Region encompasses the Rio Grande Valley from San Ygnacio east to the Gulf of Mexico (about 165 miles). It includes Zapata, Starr, Hidalgo, Cameron, and Willacy counties. Most of the recommended sites are within twenty miles of the border with Mexico. The landscape is dominated by the Rio Grande floodplain, with scattered subtropical woodlands, and the adjacent uplands, with numerous arroyos. The riparian habitat along drainages in the region is typically oak-hackberry woodland, which supports a fascinating and often unique butterfly fauna. Tamaulipan scrub occurs on the higher flats and slopes. Elevations range from sea level to about 500 feet.

The region is represented by nine sites: **67. San Ygnacio/Zapata, 68. Falcon State Park/Roma–Los Saenz, 69. NABA International Butterfly Park/Bentsen-Rio Grande Valley State Park, 70. Edinburg World Birding Center, 71. Santa Ana National Wildlife Refuge, 72. Weslaco, 73. Hugh Ramsey Nature Park, 74. Los Ebanos Preserve, 75. Sabal Palm Audubon Center and Sanctuary**, and **76. Laguna Atascosa National Wildlife Refuge**. Visits to these sites are worthwhile year-round, but the peak of butterfly activity is from October to mid-December.

Lower Rio Grande Valley Specialties

The Lower Rio Grande Valley Region supports the largest and most diverse butterfly fauna in the entire United States, including a total of eighty specialties. The high number of specialties, plus the numerous Mexican strays (not considered specialties) and the possibility of discovering a new U.S. species, add to the excitement of the Valley for butterfly enthusiasts.

Swallowtails: **Polydamas Swallowtail** can occur anywhere in the Valley but is most likely to be found at Falcon SP/Roma and at the Golden Raintree Garden in Weslaco. Adults fly quickly from one flowering plant to the next; larvae feed on pipevines. **Ornythion Swallowtail** is sporadic in occurrence but is most likely to be seen in Falcon SP/Roma, NABA Park/Bentsen SP, and Santa Ana NWR. Adults are difficult to separate from Giant Swallowtails without careful observation; larvae are known to feed on citrus foliage. **Ruby-spotted Swallowtail** has been recorded in Falcon SP/Roma, NABA Park/Bentsen SP, Santa Ana NWR, and Weslaco. Adults fly slowly about when feeding, usually in and adjacent to wooded areas where larval foodplants, jopoy, grow; larvae also feed on citrus foliage.

Whites, Sulphurs: **Florida White** is possible at gardens and wildflowers at Falcon SP/Roma, NABA Park/Bentsen SP, Edinburg WBC, Santa Ana NWR, Weslaco, Sabal Palm Sanctuary, and Laguna Atascosa NWR. Larvae feed on capers. **Giant White** has been recorded throughout the Valley. Adults wander widely, occasionally stopping to feed in gardens and patches of crucitas. Larval foodplants include capers. **White Angled-Sulphur** is possible throughout the Valley but is most likely to be found at

NABA Park/Bentsen SP, Santa Ana NWR, and Weslaco. It is most often seen in flight, usually above the canopy. Adults generally feed on flowers high above the ground; larvae feed on cassias. **Yellow Angled-Sulphur** is possible anywhere in the Valley but is most likely to be found at NABA Park/Bentsen SP, Edinburg WBC, Santa Ana NWR, Weslaco, and Hugh Ramsey Nature Park. It usually is seen in flight, often high above the ground, and occasionally stopping to feed on flowers. Larvae utilize cassias. **Barred Yellow** has been recorded at Falcon SP/Roma, NABA Park/Bentsen SP, Santa Ana NWR, and Sabal Palm Sanctuary. Adults usually fly near the ground. Larvae feed on various members of the pea family, including bur-clover, mimosa, senna, and tick-clover. **Boisduval's Yellow** frequents weedy areas throughout the Valley but is most likely to be found at Sabal Palm Sanctuary. Adults remain low to the ground; larvae feed on cassias. **Tailed Orange** is widespread but sporadic in occurrence. It uses a wide variety of habitats, from brushy fields to woodland edges. Larvae feed on members of the pea family, such as mesquite and senna. **Mimosa Yellow** occurs throughout the valley in weedy and grassy areas; it is rarely found in the open. Unlike the very similar Little Yellow, it retreats immediately to shaded areas when disturbed. Larval foodplants are limited to mimosas.

Hairstreaks: **Silver-banded Hairstreak** has been recorded at most Valley sites, usually near its larval foodplant, balloonvine, which grows on shrubs and fences. **Clench's Greenstreak** was once resident in the Valley but has recently been recorded only at the NABA Butterfly Garden. Larvae feed on ratama. **Xami Hairstreak** has been found at NABA Park/Bentsen SP, Santa Ana NWR, Weslaco, and Sabal Palm Sanctuary. It is most dependable at two of the "Additional Worthwhile Sites:" Palo Alto Battlefield National Historic Site and Old Port Isabel Road. Larvae feed on echeveria and stonecrop. **Red-crescent Scrub-Hairstreak** is widespread but unexpected. Look for it at NABA Park/Bentsen SP, Santa Ana NWR, and Weslaco. Adults frequent low-growing wildflowers; larvae feed on mallows. **Red-lined Scrub-Hairstreak** is known only from NABA Park/Bentsen SP, Santa Ana NWR, and Sabal Palm Sanctuary. Adults feed on a variety of flowers, including the larval foodplant, balloonvine. **Yojoa Scrub-Hairstreak** has been recorded only at NABA Park/Bentsen SP, Santa Ana NWR, and Weslaco. Adults feed at flowering plants; larvae use tickclover and hibiscus. **White Scrub-Hairstreak**, although possible at several sites, may only breed in NABA Park/Bentsen SP. Larval foodplants may be limited to Indianmallow. **Lacey's Scrub-Hairstreak** frequents flowering plants in San Ygnacio/Zapata, Falcon SP/Roma, NABA Park/Bentsen SP, and Santa Ana NWR, never far from myrtlecrotons, its larval foodplant. **Lantana Scrub-Hairstreak** is widespread but only occasional at shaded areas, usually feeding on flowering plants in gardens. Larvae feed on lantana, lippia, and frog-fruit. **Clytie Ministreak** is possible throughout the Valley and can be abundant near its larval foodplants, including mesquite, following an emergence. **Gray Ministreak** is seldom seen due to its small size and solitary habits. It has been recorded at Falcon SP/Roma, NABA Park/Bentsen SP, Santa Ana NWR, Weslaco, Hugh Ramsey Nature Park, Sabal Palm Sanctuary, and Laguna Atascosa NWR. Larvae feed on soft-leaf mimosa.

Blues, Metalmarks: **Cyna Blue** is at best occasional at patches of wildflowers in NABA Park/Bentsen SP, Santa Ana NWR, Weslaco, Hugh Ramsey Nature Park, and Laguna Atascosa NWR. Larval foodplants are unknown. **Rounded Metalmark** occurs throughout the Valley, and adults can be expected at a wide variety of flowering plants. Larvae feed on eupatorium. **Rawson's Metalmark** is most likely to be seen in the western portion of the Valley in San Ygnacio/Zapata and Falcon SP/Roma. Adults frequent flowering plants along the edges of brushy areas; larvae feed on eupatorium and frog-fruit. **Red-bordered Metalmark** occurs throughout the Valley. Adults are usually found on shrubs; larvae feed on spiny hackberry foliage. **Blue Metalmark** is one the Valley's most charismatic species, found primarily in the eastern half of the Valley, especially in gardens at Los Ebanos Preserve, Sabal Palm Sanctuary, and Laguna Atascosa NWR. Larval foodplants are unknown. **Red-bordered Pixie** is most likely to be found in the vicinity of guamachil trees, its larval foodplant, which have been planted in much of the eastern half of the Valley. Loners can occasionally be found feeding in gardens.

Heliconians, Fritillaries: **Mexican Silverspot** has been recorded at Falcon SP/Roma, NABA Park/Bentsen SP, Santa Ana NWR, Weslaco, and Los Ebanos Preserve, usually in shaded areas near passion vine, its larval foodplant. **Julia Heliconian** is possible throughout the Valley but is most often seen in shaded areas, especially at Santa Ana NWR. Adults only occasionally frequent gardens. Larvae feed on passion vine. **Zebra Heliconian** is widespread in the Valley but prefers shaded areas such as those at Santa Ana NWR. Larvae feed on passion vine. **Mexican Fritillary** is possible throughout the Valley, usually as loners in shaded areas, rarely in gardens. Larvae use a number of plants, including passion vine and morningglory.

Patches, Buckeyes, Other Brushfoots: **Definite Patch** has been recorded at San Ygnacio/Zapata, Falcon SP/Roma, NABA Park/Bentsen SP, Santa Ana NWR, Hugh Ramsey Nature Park, and Laguna Atascosa NWR. It is most likely to be found at Palo Alto Battlefield National Historic Site (see Additional Sites). Larvae feed on shaggy stenandrium. **Crimson Patch** is most likely to be found in the western half of the Valley at Falcon SP/Roma, NABA Park/Bentsen SP, Santa Ana NWR, and Weslaco. Larval foodplants include species of anisacanth. **Pale-banded Crescent** is sporadic in occurrence but is most likely to be found at NABA Park/Bentsen SP, Santa Ana NWR, Weslaco, Hugh Ramsey Nature Park, and Sabal Palm Sanctuary. Adults frequent trails and woodland openings. Larvae feed on dicliptera and ruellia. **Tropical Buckeye** has been recorded in San Ygnacio/Zapata, Falcon SP/Roma, NABA Park/Bentsen SP, Santa Ana NWR, Weslaco, and Sabal Palm Sanctuary, usually in gardens. The "Dark" form frequents open areas. Larval foodplants include black mangroves in littoral areas and woolly stemodia elsewhere. **Mangrove Buckeye** is mainly a coastal species that has been recorded only at Edinburg WBC, Santa Ana NWR, and Sabal Palm Sanctuary. It should be expected at Laguna Atascosa NWR. Larvae feed on black mangroves. **White Peacock** can be expected in numbers throughout the Valley in a variety of habitats; it is common in gardens. Larval foodplants include lippia, ruellia, and frog-fruit. **Banded Peacock** has been recorded with some regularity only at Santa Ana NWR and Hugh Ramsey Nature Park, although it is a possible stray elsewhere. Larvae are known to feed on justicia and ruellia. **Malachite** is a large, charismatic species that occasionally occurs at Falcon SP/Roma, NABA Park/Bentsen SP, Santa Ana NWR, and Weslaco. Larval foodplants include justicia and ruellia.

Bluewings, Crackers, Daggerwings: **Mexican Bluewing** frequents woodlands, including those at Falcon SP/Roma, NABA Park/Bentsen SP, Santa Ana NWR, Weslaco, and Hugh Ramsey Nature Park; it can be especially numerous in Los Ebanos Preserve and Sabal Palm Sanctuary. Larvae feed on Vasey adelia. **Blue-eyed Sailor** had not been recorded for many years before it was found to be breeding at Santa Ana NWR during the fall of 2003; it has also been recorded at NABA Park/Bentsen SP. Records elsewhere in the Valley are probably only strays. Larvae feed on noseburn. **Red Rim** does not occur every year, but it has recently been recorded at Falcon SP/Roma, NABA Park/Bentsen SP, Santa Ana NWR, and Weslaco. It probably breeds some years; larvae feed on noseburn. **Gray Cracker** is probably the only cracker that actually breeds in the Valley. It is recorded most years at Falcon SP/Roma, NABA Park/Bentsen SP, Santa Ana NWR, Weslaco, and Sabal Palm Sanctuary. Larvae feed on noseburn. **Many-banded Daggerwing** is found almost every year in Weslaco, where it probably breeds; it is likely to be a stray at other sites. It is most often found in shady locations. **Ruddy Daggerwing** probably breeds only at Santa Ana NWR and Weslaco. The larvae of both daggerwings feed on fig foliage.

Leafwings, Emperors, Monarchs: **Tropical Leafwing** is widespread but local in the Valley, residing only in woodlands. Most sightings are of fast-flying individuals that can be followed to a perch on a tree trunk or branch. Larvae feed on crotons. **Pavon Emperor** is probably a breeding species only in Santa Ana NWR, where several females were recorded during October and November 2003. Larvae utilize hackberry. **Soldier** can be expected at flowering plants almost anywhere in the Valley, but never in large numbers. It is most likely to be found in gardens. Larval foodplants include milkweeds.

Spread-wing Skippers: **Guava Skipper** is most likely at flowering olive trees but can occur at other flowering trees and vines throughout the Valley. It is most active early and late in the day. Larvae feed on guavas. **Zilpa Longtail** has been recorded throughout the Valley but is most likely to be found at NABA Park/Bentsen SP, Santa Ana NWR, Weslaco, Hugh Ramsey Nature Park, Los Ebanos Preserve, and Sabal Palm Sanctuary. Larvae feed on legume vines, including nissolia. **Gold-spotted Aguna** is known only from Falcon SP/Roma, NABA Park/Bentsen SP, Santa Ana NWR, and Weslaco. Most sightings are of lone individuals feeding on flowering shrubs. Larvae feed on Mexican orchid tree foliage. **Teleus Longtail** is rare in the Valley but has been recorded at flowering shrubs. It can easily be confused with female Brown Longtails. **Brown Longtail** can be expected throughout the Valley, usually at flowering shrubs.

It is the most abundant of the Valley longtails. Larvae of Brown and Teleus longtails feed on grasses. **Two-barred Flasher** is widespread but occasional at best, most often found on flowering shrubs in shaded locations. Larvae feed on coyotillo, a small shrub or tree. **Coyote Cloudywing** is most likely to be seen at flowering plants, especially in gardens and along roadsides, at San Ygnacio/Zapata, Falcon SP/Roma, NABA Park/Bentsen SP, Edinburg WBC, and Weslaco. Larvae feed on Texas ebony and blackbrush acacia. **Potrillo Skipper** occurs on flowering shrubs in shady areas at Falcon SP/Roma, NABA Park/Bentsen SP, Edinburg WBC, Santa Ana NWR, Weslaco, Sabal Palm Sanctuary, and Laguna Atascosa NWR. Larvae feed on Barbados-cherry. **Stallings' Flat** probably breeds at Santa Ana NWR, although it is rare and sporadic in occurrence. Larvae feed on members of the Acanthaceae family. **Falcate Skipper** has only been recorded at Falcon SP/Roma, NABA Park/Bentsen SP, and Santa Ana NWR. Adults feed on flowering shrubs; larvae use legumes, including beans and peas.

Mimosa Skipper frequents a variety of habitats, from wetlands to dry scrub habitat and gardens, at Falcon SP/Roma, NABA Park/Bentsen SP, Santa Ana NWR, Weslaco, Sabal Palm Sanctuary, and Laguna Atascosa NWR. Larvae feed on black mimosa. **Glazed Pellicia** has been recorded on flowering plants in fields and gardens at NABA Park/Bentsen SP, Santa Ana NWR, Weslaco, and Hugh Ramsey Nature Park. Larval foodplants are unknown. **Golden-headed Scallopwing** is found only rarely at San Ygnacio/Zapata, Falcon SP/Roma, NABA Park/Bentsen SP, Santa Ana NWR, and Weslaco. It frequents open areas and frequently perches on the ground. Larvae feed on goosefoot. **Mazans Scallopwing** is widespread in the Valley, preferring shady edges and often resting on the ground. Larval foodplants include lamb's-quarters and pigweed. **Hermit Skipper** has been recorded at Falcon SP/Roma, NABA Park/Bentsen SP, Santa Ana NWR, and Sabal Palm Sanctuary. Larvae utilize Runyon esenbeckia. **Brown-banded Skipper** is most likely to be found at flowering plants at Falcon SP/Roma, NABA Park/Bentsen SP, Edinburg WBC, Santa Ana NWR, Hugh Ramsey Nature Park, Sabal Palm Sanctuary, and Laguna Atascosa NWR. Its principal larval foodplant is Barbados-cherry. **White-patched Skipper** is widespread and often found in numbers, usually feeding on flowering plants along woodland edges and in gardens. Larvae feed on Barbados-cherry. **Erichson's White-Skipper** can occur anywhere in the Valley but is occasional at best. Larval foodplants include mallows. **Laviana White-Skipper** is a common, widespread species that often is first encountered flying swiftly from one location to another. Larvae feed on mallows. **Turk's-cap White-Skipper** is another common, widespread species that is usually encountered in flight along the edge of woodlands and on trails. Larval foodplants include mallows, especially Turk's cap.

Grass-Skippers: **Malicious Skipper** is known to breed only at Falcon SP/Roma, where most sightings are on low-growing wildflowers or on the ground. **Pale-rayed Skipper** is known only from Sabal Palm Sanctuary and Laguna Atascosa NWR, usually feeding on flowering shrubs in the gardens. **Violet-patched Skipper** has been recorded only at Falcon SP/Roma, NABA Park/Bentsen SP, and Santa Ana NWR. It is most likely to be seen at flowering plants in gardens and along roadsides and trails. **Fawn-spotted Skipper** is widespread, feeding on low-growing wildflowers or perched on the ground, especially in shaded locations. **Double-dotted Skipper** has been recorded at several Valley sites, but it is most likely to be found at Hugh Ramsey Nature Park, Sabal Palm Sanctuary, and Laguna Atascosa NWR, feeding on flowering plants in shaded areas. **Common Mellana** occurs at flowering plants at Falcon SP/Roma, NABA Park/Bentsen SP, Santa Ana NWR, Sabal Palm Sanctuary, and Laguna Atascosa NWR. **Olive-clouded Skipper** is widespread but only rare to occasional, usually at flowering plants in gardens at Falcon SP/Roma, NABA Park/Bentsen SP, Santa Ana NWR, Weslaco, Hugh Ramsey Nature Park, Sabal Palm Sanctuary, and Laguna Atascosa NWR. **Obscure Skipper** is a coastal species most likely to be found at Laguna Atascosa NWR. Larval foodplants are limited to saltgrass. **Hecebolus Skipper** is rare or occasional at Falcon SP/Roma, NABA Park/Bentsen SP, and Santa Ana NWR. Most are found feeding on crucitas in shaded spots or asters in fields. Larvae likely feed on sugarcane. **Purple-washed Skipper** is widespread but occasional at best. It is most likely to be seen in gardens. Larval foodplants are limited to grasses, including sugarcane. **Violet-banded Skipper** has been recorded at NABA Park/Bentsen SP, Santa Ana NWR, Weslaco, and Sabal Palm Sanctuary. Most sightings have been on crucitas in fall. Larval foodplants are limited to grasses, including sugarcane and corn.

Sites within the Lower Rio Grande Valley Region

67. San Ygnacio/Zapata

This site extends for fourteen miles along the Rio Grande River from San Ygnacio to Zapata, a village first settled as "Carrizo" in 1770. For birders, San Ygnacio offers the best bet for finding white-collared seedeaters in the U.S. There are several access points to the Rio Grande floodplain and a few roadside pull-offs and side roads that can offer a rich diversity of flowering plants, especially after rains. Because of its westernmost position in the Valley, western and arid-land butterflies are possible.

The best butterflying can be found at three sites in San Ygnacio (**A**-**C**), a rest stop north of town (**D**), and a side road (**E**) on the way to the final spot, Zapata's library grounds (**F**).

Habitats: Floodplain, riparian, garden, and Tamaulipan scrub.

Strategy for finding the most butterflies: Start at San Ygnacio by walking the old roadway at the end of Washington Street (**A**) onto the floodplain; follow the network of trails downriver into this private land (fee area) that has been enhanced to attract birds and butterflies by owner Joel Ruiz. Some of the more numerous butterflies

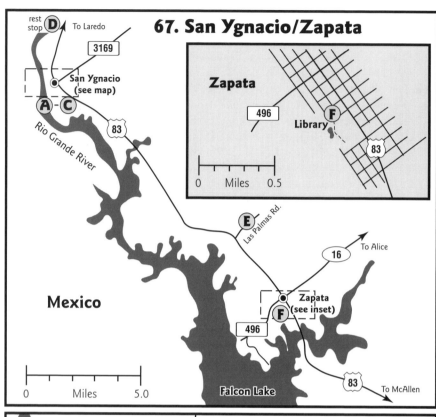

67. San Ygnacio/Zapata

rest stop To Laredo

3169

San Ygnacio
(see map)

Ⓐ-Ⓒ

Rio Grande River

83

Zapata

496

Library

Ⓕ

83

0 Miles 0.5

Ⓔ

Las Palmas Rd.

16 To Alice

Mexico

Zapata
(see inset)

Ⓕ

496

83 To McAllen

0 Miles 5.0

Falcon Lake

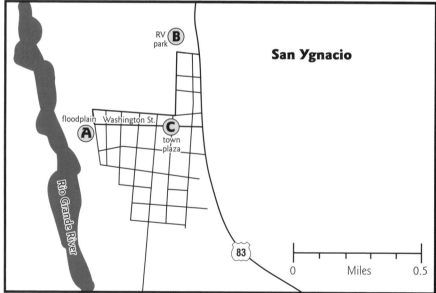

RV park Ⓑ

San Ygnacio

floodplain Washington St. Ⓒ

Ⓐ

town plaza

Rio Grande River

83

0 Miles 0.5

Flood plain, San Ygnacio

within this riparian environment, especially at patches of flowering plants, include Large Orange Sulphur; Little Yellow; Sleepy Orange; Western Pygmy-Blue; Ceraunus Blue; Fatal Metalmark; Bordered Patch; Phaon Crescent; **White Peacock**; Common Mestra; Queen; Sickle-winged, Clouded, Fiery, and Eufala skippers; Common/White and Tropical checkered-skippers; and Southern Skipperling.

Other less numerous but likely species include Giant Swallowtail, Cloudless and Orange-barred sulphurs, Mexican Yellow, Mallow Scrub-Hairstreak, Marine and Reakirt's blues, Texan Crescent, Empress Leilia, Tawny Emperor, Texas Powdered-Skipper, Desert Checkered-Skipper, Common Streaky-Skipper, Celia's Roadside-Skipper, and Ocola Skipper.

Also watch for some of the uncommon specialties: **Giant White**; **Boisduval's** and **Mimosa yellows**; **Tailed Orange**; **Lacey's Scrub-Hairstreak**; **Rounded** and **Red-bordered metalmarks**; **Mexican Fritillary**; **Soldier**; **Brown Longtail**; **Mazans Scallopwing**; **White-patched** and **Fawn-spotted skippers**; and **Erichson's, Laviana**, and **Turk's-cap white-skippers**. Rare specialties possible at flower patches include **Red-crescent, White** and **Lantana scrub-hairstreaks, Definite Patch, Malachite, Two-barred Flasher**, and **Golden-headed Scallopwing**.

Also in San Ygnacio, drive into the San Ygnacio RV Park (**B**), on the north side of town, and walk the half-mile nature trail (check in first at the manager's trailer). **Julia** and **Zebra heliconians, Tropical Leafwing**, and Gemmed and Carolina satyrs are likely to be seen along the wooded trail, and "Dark" **Tropical Buckeye** is possible in open areas. Before leaving San Ygnacio, check the concrete flower boxes that border the town plaza (**C**).

Afterwards, drive north of San Ygnacio 3.3 miles to the Zapata County Rest Stop (**D**) overlooking the Rio Grande River; walk the short trails through the Tamaulipan scrub below and to the right. This shrubby area is likely to contain Pipevine, Black, and Giant swallowtails; Great Southern White; Lyside Sulphur; Gulf Fritillary; Theona and Elada checkerspots; and Desert Checkered-Skipper. Also watch for Tiny Checkerspot, Saltbush Sootywing, and Nysa Roadside-Skipper.

Next, return to San Ygnacio on US 83 and continue twelve miles toward Zapata to the Las Palmas Road (**E**). Turn northeast from US 83 and drive the two miles to Las Palmas; flowering roadside plants can be especially productive after rains. Although many of the same butterflies mentioned above are likely, **Rawson's Metalmark** and **Coyote Cloudywing** are also possible. At Zapata, park at the library (**F**) and walk the edge of the wetland behind it and the weedy field to the west.

Directions: In Zapata County, San Ygnacio and Zapata are along US 83, south of Laredo. The **San Ygnacio Rest Stop (D)**, the westernmost site in this region, is about 30 miles from Laredo and 3.3 miles north of **San Ygnacio (A-C)**. Twelve miles south of San Ygnacio and two miles north of Zapata, **Las Palmas Road (E)** goes two miles northeast from US 83. The **Zapata County Library (F)** is on the south side of US 83, just east of FM 496.

Nearest food, gas, and lodging: Zapata; food and gas in San Ygnacio.

Nearest camping: San Ygnacio RV Park and Falcon State Park, 26 miles southeast of Zapata.

68. Falcon State Park/Roma–Los Saenz

This area, twenty-six miles southeast of Zapata along US 83, extends approximately fifteen miles along the Rio Grande River, from the 573-acre Falcon State Park (**C**) and adjacent Falcon County Park (**D**) downriver to Chapeño (**B**), Salineño (**A**), Santa Margarita Ranch (**E**), and Roma–Los Saenz (**F, G**). Most of these areas, which contain significant tracts of native vegetation, are part of the Rio Grande Wildlife Corridor, a multi-agency project to protect tracts of natural landscape between Falcon Dam and the mouth of the Rio Grande. July 4th Butterfly Counts are held in the area most years. *(Note: "Falcon Woodlands," a worthwhile area below Falcon Dam spillway, has not been accessible to the public since 9/11.)*

Habitats: Thorn forest, Tamaulipan scrub, riparian, field, and cropland.

Strategy for finding the most butterflies: Start at Salineño (**A**); drive through the small town to the river and walk the woodland trails upstream and downstream from the parking area. Some of the more numerous butterflies include Cloudless, Large Orange, and Lyside sulphurs; Sleepy Orange; Mallow Scrub-Hairstreak; Reakirt's Blue; Fatal and **Rounded metalmarks**; Bordered Patch; Texan and Phaon crescents; Common

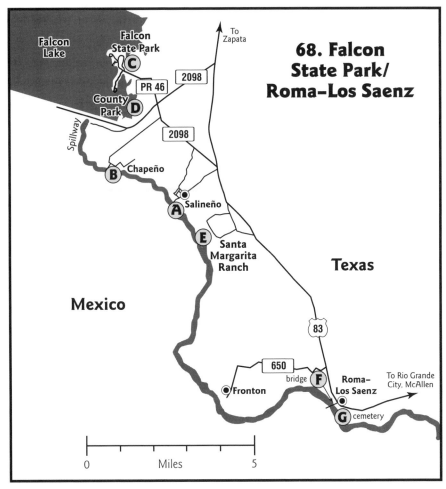

68. Falcon
State Park/
Roma–Los Saenz

Mestra; **Tropical Leafwing**; Empress Leilia; Tawny Emperor; Carolina Satyr; Sickle-winged, Clouded, Fiery, and Eufala skippers; and **Laviana White-Skipper**.

Some of the less numerous but likely species include Orange-barred Sulphur, Mexican and **Mimosa yellows, Tailed Orange, Lantana Scrub-Hairstreak, Red-bordered Metalmark, Julia** and **Zebra heliconians, Mexican Fritillary, White Peacock, Mexican Bluewing,** Gemmed Satyr, **Soldier,** White-striped and **Brown longtails, Mimosa** and **White-patched skippers**, and **Turk's-cap White-Skipper**. Additional rare to occasional specialties include **Giant White; Barred** and **Bois-duval's yellows; Lacey's Scrub-Hairstreak; Clytie** and **Gray ministreaks; Crimson Patch; Malachite; Coyote Cloudywing; Potrillo, Malicious,** and **Violet-patched skippers;** and **Erichson's White-Skipper**.

Next, drive to nearby Chapeño (**B**), a fee area; walk eastward along the river, making a loop onto the upper roadway and back to the start. Chapeño's butterflies are

Picnic site, Falcon State Park

likely to be the same as those at Salineño, but also watch for some of the rarities that have been recorded in the area: **Florida White**; **Red-crescent**, **Yojoa**, and **Lantana scrub-hairstreaks**; **Definite Patch**; **Zilpa Longtail**; **Golden-headed Scallopwing**; **Hermit**, **Brown-banded**, **Olive-clouded**, **Hecebolus**, and **Purple-washed skippers**; and **Common Mellana**.

Then travel to Falcon SP (**C**), a fee area, and drive the side roads and walk the right-of-ways, including the edges of the boat ramp parking area, a good spot for Western Pygmy-Blue, Marine and Ceraunus blues, and Common Buckeye. "Dark" **Tropical Buckeye** is also possible. At the adjacent Falcon County Park (**D**) along FM 2098, drive to the restroom and walk the tracts beyond. When wildflowers are present, watch for **Pale-banded Crescent**, **Mazans Scallopwing**, and **Fawn-spotted Skipper**. **Guava Skipper** can sometimes be found at the wild olive trees.

Afterwards, drive southeast on US 83 to the Santa Margarita Ranch (**E**), a fee area, and walk the available trails. In spring, Yucca Giant-Skipper is possible around yuccas. Farther southeast at Roma–Los Saenz, drive or walk to the river below the international bridge (**F**) and walk along the short roadway. **Polydamas Swallowtail**, **Julia** and **Zebra heliconians**, **Mexican Bluewing**, and **Tropical Leafwing** occur in the dense woodlands. **Ornythion Swallowtail**, **Red Rim**, **Gray Cracker**, **Gold-spotted Aguna**, and **Two-barred Flasher** have also been found here. In addition, east of town along US 83, walk through the little roadside cemetery (**G**), where some of the common species mentioned above are likely to occur.

Directions: In Starr County, these sites are along US 83. Start at the north end of the area by taking FM 2098 west from US 83. Continue to PR 46 and turn north to

Falcon SP (**C**). **Falcon County Park** (**D**) is just west of the PR 46 intersection on Spur FM 2098. Return to the intersection and continue southeast on FM 2098 to a right turn on the road to **Chapeño** (**B**). Then continue on FM 2098 to US 83 and the turn west to **Salineño** (**A**). Return to US 83 and go 1.2 miles to the old highway on the right (if you get to the US 83 rest area, you've gone too far). A dirt road leads to the river and **Santa Margarita Ranch** (**E**). Return to US 83 and continue south to Roma–Los Saenz, at the southern edge of the area, 65 miles west of Mission. The **international bridge** (**F**) is on Bravo Ave. The **cemetery** (**G**) is on the south side of US 83.

Nearest food, gas, and lodging: Roma–Los Saenz, Falcon Heights, and Rio Grande City.

Nearest camping: Falcon SP, with rough camping at the county park.

69. NABA International Butterfly Park/ Bentsen-Rio Grande Valley State Park

Situated in the center of the Lower Rio Grande Valley Region, this site features the eighty-three-acre North American Butterfly Association International Butterfly Park (**A**). The World Birding Center (WBC), established in 2004, maintains butterfly gardens (**B**) near the entrance to the 587-acre Bentsen-Rio Grande Valley State Park (**C-F**), which has the highest diversity of both birds and butterflies of any of the Texas state parks. Mission West RV Park (**G**) has a long hedge of sky-flower plants that can be superb when they're flowering in summer and fall. Anzalduas County Park (**H, I**) features a more open area along the Rio Grande River. Finally, try the nearby La Lomita Mission Picnic Area (**J**).

These state and county parks are important links in the Rio Grande Valley Wildlife Corridor and offer great butterfly-watching opportunities. July 4th Butterfly Counts are held in the area annually.

Habitats: Garden, thorn forest, Tamaulipan scrub, mesquite grassland, riparian, field, and cropland.

Strategy for finding the most butterflies: Start at the NABA International Butterfly Park (**A**). Walk the extensive network of trails on both sides of the canal and revisit key sites again during your stay. Some of the more numerous butterflies include Pipevine and Giant swallowtails; Large Orange Sulphur; Little Yellow; Mallow Scrub-Hairstreak; Ceraunus Blue; **Red-bordered Metalmark**; Gulf Fritillary; Bordered Patch; Phaon Crescent; **White Peacock**; Tawny Emperor; Queen; Long-tailed, Sickle-winged, Clouded, and Fiery skippers; **Brown Longtail**; Tropical Checkered-Skipper; and **Laviana** and **Turk's-cap white-skippers**.

Some of the less common butterflies include Black Swallowtail; Great Southern White; **Boisduval's** and **Mimosa yellows**; **Tailed Orange**; **Silver-banded Hairstreak**; **Red-crescent** and **Lantana scrub-hairstreaks**; **Clytie Ministreak**; Reakirt's Blue; **Rounded Metalmark**; **Soldier**; White-striped, **Zilpa**, and Dorantes longtails;

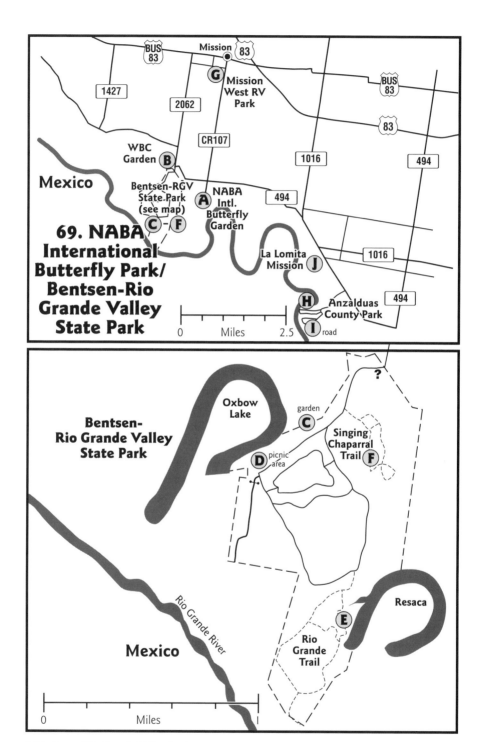

69. NABA International Butterfly Park/ Bentsen-Rio Grande Valley State Park

Mexico

Bentsen-Rio Grande Valley State Park

Mexico

Rio Grande River

Oxbow Lake

Resaca

Rio Grande Trail

Singing Chaparral Trail

picnic area

garden

NABA International Butterfly Park

Mimosa, **White-patched**, and Julia's skippers; **Glazed Pellicia**; **Mazans Scallop-wing**; and Common Streaky-Skipper.

Several additional rare and occasional specialties are also possible in and about the gardens: **Polydamus, Ornythion**, and **Ruby-spotted swallowtails**; **Florida** and **Giant whites**; **White** and **Yellow angled-sulphurs**; **Barred Yellow**; **Xami Hairstreak**; **Red-lined, Yojoa**, and **Lacey's scrub-hairstreaks**; **Gray Ministreak**; **Cyna Blue**; **Blue Metalmark**; **Red-bordered Pixie**; **Mexican Silverspot**; **Definite** and **Crimson patches**; **Pale-banded Crescent**; **Tropical Buckeye**; **Malachite**; **Blue-eyed Sailor**; **Red Rim**; **Gold-spotted Aguna**; **Two-barred Flasher**; **Coyote Cloudywing**; **Potrillo, Falcate, Hermit, Brown-banded, Violet-patched, Fawn-spotted, Olive-clouded, Hecebolus**, and **Violet-banded skippers**; **Golden-headed Scallopwing**; **Erichson's White-Skipper**; and **Common Mellana**.

Also walk the woodland trail where **Julia** and **Zebra heliconians**, **Mexican Bluewing**, **Gray Cracker**, **Tropical Leafwing**, and Gemmed and Carolina satyrs are possible.

Next, drive to Bentsen-Rio Grande Valley SP and visit the World Birding Center butterfly gardens (**B**) located just outside the park entrance. Butterflies here can be similar to those at the NABA butterfly park, but "Dark" **Tropical Buckeye** has been reported on the outer edges. Then take the tram into the state park to a second garden (**C**), located near the Oxbow Lake boat ramp. Walk along the edge of the lake and through the picnic area (**D**), a good place to find **Mexican Bluewing.** If there has been adequate rain to produce wildflowers, walk the Rio Grande Trail (**E**) off the outer loop road and the Singing Chaparral Trail (**F**). Be sure to check the wild olive blossoms near the entrance, a good place to look for **Guava Skipper**. **Polydamas Swallowtail** has also been found here.

Drive to Mission West RV Park (**G**). After reporting in at the office, walk along the long hedge of sky-flower shrubs at the eastern edge of the park. This hedge, in full sun during the afternoon, has hosted many of the butterflies mentioned above, but **Red-bordered Pixie**, **Zilpa Longtail**, and **Common Mellana** may be more common here.

Then drive to Anzalduas County Park (**H**), which charges a fee on weekends. Drive the loop road to the right, stopping to check out flowering plants along the way, and walk through the picnic grounds, another good place for **Mexican Bluewing**. Also drive across the dike to the south and take that loop road (**I**). Walk along the outer edges and through the woodland; Guatemalan Cracker was found here in the fall of 2003. If time allows, drive into the nearby La Lomita Mission Picnic Area (**J**) and explore the surroundings.

Directions: In Hidalgo County, all the sites are located south of US 83. In Mission, take FM 2062 (Bentsen Palm Dr.) south of Bus. 83 to the end of the road. The **WBC butterfly garden (B)** is on the right, just before the entrance to **Bentsen-Rio Grande Valley SP (C-F)**. The **NABA International Butterfly Park (A)** is one mile east of the park entrance on the Old Military Highway (FM 494). Continue east on FM 494 to the junction with FM 1016 (Conway Rd.). Turn right on the merged roads for a short distance and take FM 494 south to **La Lomita Mission Picnic Area (J)** and **Anzalduas County Park (H, I)**. **Mission West RV Park (G)** is located at 3805 W. Hwy. 83, east of FM 2062 on Bus. 83.

Nearest food, gas, and lodging: Mission.

Nearest camping: Mission West RV Park and near the entrance to Bentsen-Rio Grande Valley SP; tent camping only within the park.

70. Edinburg World Birding Center

Opened in 2003, the forty-acre Edinburg World Birding Center is located north of US 83 and east of US 281 at the edge of Edinburg's 155-acre Municipal Park. It features a six-acre butterfly garden (**A**) and a series of trails (**B-D**) along a wetland and ditch. The site also has an impressive interpretive center and a dragonfly pond. Edinburg WBC was the first to be built of the nine WBC sites planned in the Valley between Starr County and the Gulf. The butterfly list is only preliminary; the large garden is sure to attract many additional species.

Habitats: Garden, mesquite brush, and wetland.

Strategy for finding the most butterflies: First, walk through the extensive garden at the Edinburg WBC (**A**), where some of the more numerous butterflies include Pipevine

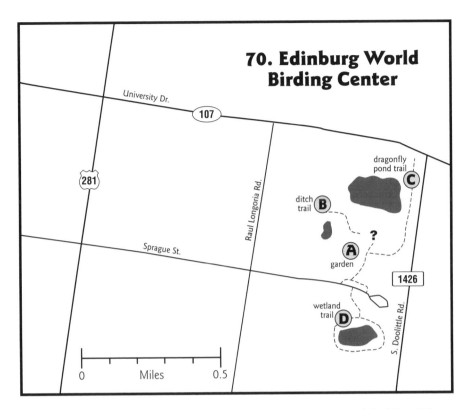

70. Edinburg World Birding Center

University Dr.

107

281

Raul Longoria Rd.

dragonfly pond trail

C

ditch trail **B**

?

A

garden

1426

Sprague St.

wetland trail **D**

S. Doolittle Rd.

0   Miles   0.5

and Giant swallowtails; Great Southern White; Large Orange and Lyside sulphurs; Little Yellow; Western Pygmy-Blue; Ceraunus and Reakirt's blues; Fatal and **Red-bordered metalmarks**; Gulf Fritillary; Bordered Patch; Texan and Phaon crescents; **White Peacock**; Common Mestra; Tawny Emperor; Queen; Long-tailed, Sickle-winged, Clouded, Fiery, and Ocola skippers; **Brown Longtail**; Tropical Checkered-Skipper; **Laviana White-Skipper**; Southern Skipperling; Southern Broken-Dash; and Whirlabout.

Some of the less numerous butterflies to be expected include Black Swallowtail; Orange-barred Sulphur; Mallow Scrub-Hairstreak; Dusky-blue Groundstreak; **Rounded Metalmark**; **Red-bordered Pixie**; Elada Checkerspot; Empress Leilia; **Soldier**; White-striped and Dorantes longtails; **White-patched**, Eufala, and Brazilian skippers; Desert Checkered-Skipper; **Turk's-cap White-Skipper**; and Celia's Roadside-Skipper. Also watch for **Guava Skipper** at flowering wild olive trees.

Additional rare or occasional specialties possible in the garden include **Florida** and **Giant Whites**; **Yellow Angled-Sulphur**; **Tailed Orange**; **Mimosa Yellow**; **Lantana Scrub-Hairstreak**; **Clytie Ministreak**; **Mexican Fritillary**; **Coyote Cloudywing**; and **Potrillo**, **Brown-banded**, **Fawn-spotted**, and **Purple-washed skippers**.

Next, walk the trail along the ditch (**B**) to the west of the interpretive center, as well as the trail to the east of the center that circles the small dragonfly pond (**C**). **Mexican**

Garden and interpretive center, Edinburg World Birding Center

Bluewing and **Julia** and **Zebra heliconians** are possible in the shaded areas. Then walk the Scenic Wetland Trail (**D**) south of the entrance road; **Silver-banded Hairstreak** is possible at balloonvines. In addition, **Red-bordered Pixie** can be abundant at the large guamachil tree directly behind a nearby Burger King on Raul Longoria Road, just south of the junction with Sprague Street.

Directions: In Hidalgo County, from US 281 in Edinburg, exit at University Drive (SH 107) and go east to Raul Longoria Rd. Turn south and proceed to E. Sprague St. and the **Edinburg WBC (A-D)**.

Nearest food, gas, and lodging: Edinburg.

Nearest camping: At commercial sites in Edinburg.

71. Santa Ana National Wildlife Refuge

One of the true jewels of the national wildlife refuge system, the 2,088-acre Santa Ana National Wildlife Refuge (fee area) is one of the premier butterfly-finding sites in all of North America, with more than 300 species recorded. The reasons for the high number include an abundance of long-term records, superb butterfly gardens, and seven miles of trails that provide access into undeveloped parts of the refuge. Among the best butterflying spots are the gardens along the entrance road and near the visitor center (**A**), the old manager's residence (**B**), the old cemetery (**C**), three trails (**D-F**), and the loop road, Wildlife Drive (**G**). July 4th Butterfly Counts are held here annually.

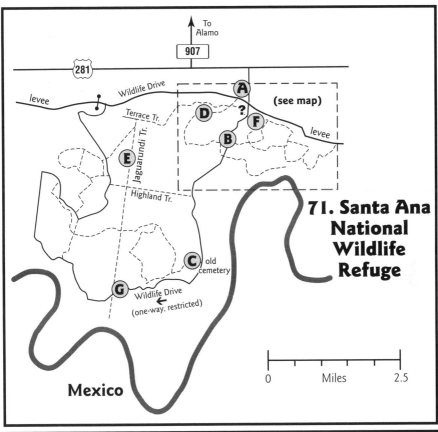

To
Alamo

907

281

levee

Wildlife Drive

(see map)

A

D

?

F

B

levee

Terrace Tr.

Jaguarundi Tr.

E

Highland Tr.

C old
cemetery

G

Wildlife Drive
(one-way, restricted)

71. Santa Ana National Wildlife Refuge

Mexico

0   Miles   2.5

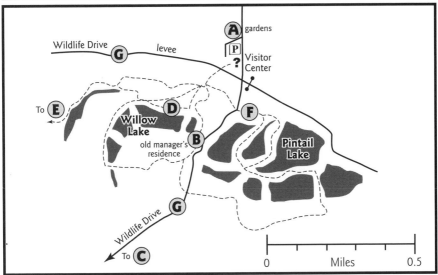

Wildlife Drive

G

levee

A gardens

P

? Visitor
Center

To E

D

Willow
Lake

F

old manager's
residence

B

Pintail
Lake

Wildlife Drive

G

To C

0   Miles   0.5

Thorn forest habitat along Trail A, Santa Ana National Wildlife Refuge

Habitats: Garden, thorn forest, Tamaulipan scrub, wetland, riparian, and field.

Strategy for finding the most butterflies: Start at the butterfly gardens along the entrance road, in front of the visitor center, and on the west side of the parking lot (**A**); return to these gardens again during your stay. Some of the more numerous butterflies include Pipevine and Giant swallowtails; Cloudless, Large Orange, and Lyside sulphurs; Little Yellow; Mallow Scrub-Hairstreak; Dusky-blue Groundstreak; Fatal, **Rounded**, and **Red-bordered metalmarks**; Gulf Fritillary; Phaon Crescent; **White Peacock**; Common Mestra; Queen; **Brown Longtail**; **Mimosa**, Sickle-winged, and Clouded skippers; **Mazans Scallopwing**; Tropical Checkered-Skipper; and **Laviana** and **Turk's-cap white-skippers**.

Some of the less common butterflies in the gardens include Great Southern White; Orange-barred Sulphur; **Boisduval's**, Mexican, and **Mimosa yellows**; **Tailed Orange**; **Lantana Scrub-Hairstreak**; **Clytie Ministreak**; **Red-bordered Pixie**; **Soldier**; White-striped and Dorantes longtails; **Potrillo, White-patched, Fawn-spotted**, and **Olive-clouded skippers**; and **Glazed Pellicia. White** and **Yellow angled-sulphurs** occasionally are seen overhead in flight, and **Guava Skipper** is most likely to be seen at the flowering wild olive trees, especially during the morning and evening hours.

Several additional rare or occasional specialties are also possible in and about the gardens: **Polydamas** and **Ornythion swallowtails**; **Florida** and **Giant whites**; **Barred Yellow**; **Xami Hairstreak**; **Red-crescent, Red-lined**, and **Yojoa scrub-hairstreaks**; **Gray Ministreak, Cyna Blue**; **Blue Metalmark**; **Definite** and **Crimson patches**;

Tropical Buckeye; Banded Peacock; **Malachite**; **Many-banded** and **Ruddy dagger-wings**; **Zilpa Longtail**; **Coyote Cloudywing**; **Falcate, Hermit, Brown-banded, Violet-patched, Hecebolus, Purple-washed**, and **Violet-banded skippers**; **Golden-headed Scallopwing**; and **Common Mellana**.

Next (or earlier, if something really unusual has been reported) walk the Wildlife Drive, at least to the old manager's residence site (**B**) and check the garden there. You may want to continue an additional mile or so to another garden, just beyond the "old cemetery" (**C**). Recent sightings of special interest along the roadway and in these two gardens, not regularly seen in the gardens near the visitor center, include **Ruby-spotted Swallowtail, Lacey's Scrub-Hairstreak, Mexican Silverspot, Mexican Fritillary, Banded Peacock, Blue-eyed Sailor, Red Rim, Gray** and Guatemalan **crackers, Pavon Emperor, Gold-spotted Aguna, Two-barred Flasher, Stallings' Flat**, and **Erichson's White-Skipper**.

Also walk Trail A (**D**) to Willow Lake from the visitor center and, if time allows, circle the lake on Trail B. Jaguarundi Trail (**E**), between Highland and Terrace trails, can be especially good in fall. Take Trail C (**F**) to Pintail Lake and circle the lake; watch for **Silver-banded Hairstreak** at patches of balloonvines.

Finally, when Wildlife Drive (**G**) is open to vehicle traffic, drive this seven-mile loop road, stopping at pull-offs to check flowering plants along the roadway or to walk side roads and trails. A few expected species on the interior woodland trails and along Wildlife Drive include **Julia** and **Zebra heliconians, Mexican Bluewing, Tropical Leafwing**, and Gemmed and Carolina satyrs. **Mexican Silverspot** and **Pale-banded Crescent** are also possible.

Directions: In Hidalgo County, from US 83 take FM 907 south through Alamo for 7.5 miles and jog east on US 281 for .5-mile to the refuge entrance; open daily. The Wildlife Drive is open to vehicles only on weekends, from May to November, 9 a.m. to 4 p.m. From Thanksgiving to the end of April, access to Wildlife Drive is available by tram.

Nearest food, gas, and lodging: Cities along US 83.

Nearest camping: Commercial sites in Alamo and along Bus. 83, including Mission West RV Park.

72. Weslaco

The town of Weslaco, named by combining the initials of the W.E. Steward Land Company, which promoted the townsite in 1919, features three principal sites. The six-acre Valley Nature Center (**A**) is a fee area operated by a non-profit organization, whose mission is "to provide environmental education about the unique South Texas ecosystem to the Valley Community." It has a half-mile of trails through a native plant garden. The second site, Frontera Audubon Society Center (**B**), is also a fee area. It has a one-mile-long network of trails. The third site is the Golden Raintree Garden (**C**), a citrus nursery that welcomes visitors. A secondary site at a church (**D**) offers the chance to see another specialty butterfly.

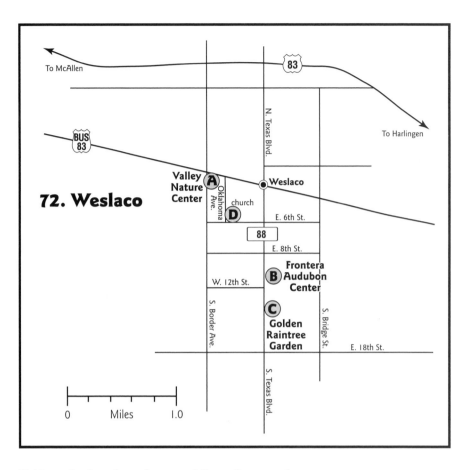

Habitats: Garden, thorn forest, and Tamaulipan scrub.

Strategy for finding the most butterflies: Start at the Valley Nature Center (**A**); walk the trails directly behind the headquarters building and beyond, especially in the northern corner. Then drive to the Frontera Audubon Society Center (**B**). Check the edge of the parking area and the front garden and walk the network of trails. These two properties have similar habitats and butterflies, although one may be better than the other at any given time. Some of the more numerous species include Giant Swallowtail; Cloudless and Large Orange sulphurs; Little Yellow; Mallow Scrub-Hairstreak; Ceraunus Blue; Fatal Metalmark; Gulf Fritillary; Bordered and **Crimson patches**; Texan, Vesta, and Phaon crescents; **White Peacock**; Common Mestra; **Tropical Leafwing**; Tawny Emperor; Queen; Long-tailed, Sickle-winged, Clouded, Fiery, and Eufala skippers; **Brown Longtail**; and **Laviana White-Skipper**.

Other less common butterflies along the woodland trails include Orange-barred Sulphur; **Tailed Orange**; **Boisduval's**, Mexican, and **Mimosa yellows**; **Silver-banded Hairstreak**; **Gray Ministreak**; Cassius and Marine blues; **Rounded** and **Red-**

Garden, Frontera Audubon Society Center

bordered metalmarks; **Julia** and **Zebra heliconians**; **Pale-banded Crescent**; **Tropical Buckeye**; **Banded Peacock**; **Mexican Bluewing**; Hackberry Emperor; Carolina Satyr; **Soldier**; White-striped and Dorantes longtails; **Mimosa, White-patched**, and **Fawn-spotted skippers**; **Glazed Pellicia**; **Mazans Scallopwing**; **Turk's-cap White-Skipper**; and Celia's Roadside-Skipper. Watch at wild olive blossoms, especially in the morning and evening hours, for **Guava Skipper**.

The more open spaces, such as the plantings at the Frontera entrance, often have a somewhat different variety of butterflies. They may include Pipevine and Black swallowtails; Great Southern White; Dainty Sulphur; Western Pygmy-Blue; Horace's and Mournful duskywings; and Tropical Checkered-Skipper.

These two sites also offer an opportunity to find some of the rare and occasional species: **Ruby-spotted Swallowtail**; **Florida** and **Giant whites**; **White** and **Yellow angled-sulphurs**; **Red-crescent, Yojoa**, and **Lantana scrub-hairstreaks**; **Clytie Ministreak**; **Cyna Blue**; **Blue Metalmark**; **Mexican Silverspot**; **Mexican Fritillary**; **Malachite**; **Red Rim**; **Gray Cracker**; **Ruddy Daggerwing**; **Zilpa Longtail**; **Gold-spotted Aguna**; **Two-barred Flasher**; **Coyote Cloudywing**; **Potrillo, Hermit, Olive-clouded, Purple-washed**, and **Violet-banded skippers**; **Golden-headed Scallop-wing**; and **Erichson's White-Skipper**.

Nearby is the Golden Raintree Garden (**C**), a commercial citrus nursery. The owners, who have planted areas specifically to attract butterflies, welcome visitors. Park near the office and walk the trails and edges. Many of the same butterflies mentioned above are possible. This is the single best location in the Valley for **Polydamas Swallowtail**.

In addition, **Red-bordered Pixies** are likely in the guamachil trees across the street from the Catholic church parking lot (**D**), located at 6th St. and Oklahoma Ave.

Note: It may be worthwhile to adjust your itinerary if some out-of-the-ordinary species has been reported.

Directions: In Hidalgo County, the **Valley Nature Center** (**A**) is located in Gibson Park, one block south of Bus. 83, at 301 S. Border Ave. Currently, hours are 9 a.m. to 5 p.m. Tuesday through Friday, 8 a.m. to 5 p.m. on Saturday, and 1 p.m. to 5 p.m. on Sunday. The center is closed on Monday. Also south of Bus. 83 is **Frontera Audubon Society Center** (**B**), located at 1101 S. Texas Blvd. It is open daily. **Golden Raintree Garden** (**C**) is located nearby at 1303 S. Texas Blvd. The **Catholic church** (**D**) is on 6th St. between S. Border Ave. and S. Texas Blvd.

Nearest food, gas, and lodging: Weslaco.

Nearest camping: Commercial sites in Weslaco and nearby communities.

73. Hugh Ramsey Nature Park

Located in Harlingen, the fifty-five-acre Hugh Ramsey Nature Park along the north bank of the Arroyo Colorado was part of a landfill closed in 1983. A visitor center is planned southwest of the Ed Carey Drive bridge. The site is operated by the Arroyo Colorado Audubon Society and is a satellite of the World Birding Center. The park has a good network of trails—four of which are recommended here (**A-D**)—offering easy access into the habitat. The site's butterfly list is only preliminary, and numerous additions can be expected.

Habitats: Garden, thorn scrub, and riparian.

Strategy for finding the most butterflies: Start by walking the short Ebony Loop Trail (**A**) from the southeast corner of the parking lot; then walk the Indigo Trail (**B**) to the Upper Arroyo Trail, which loops back to the parking lot. These trails offer most of the more numerous butterflies, including Pipevine and Giant swallowtails; Large Orange, Lyside, and Dainty sulphurs; Little Yellow; Mallow Scrub-Hairstreak; Ceraunus Blue; Gulf Fritillary; Bordered Patch; Texan, Vesta, and Phaon crescents; **White Peacock**; Common Mestra; Carolina Satyr; Queen; Sickle-winged, Clouded, Fiery, and Eufala skippers; Tropical Checkered-Skipper; **Laviana White-Skipper**; Southern Broken-Dash; and Sachem.
 Some of the less numerous butterflies that can be expected along the trails include Mexican and **Mimosa yellows**; **Tailed Orange**; Western Pygmy-Blue; Reakirt's Blue; Fatal, **Rounded**, and **Red-bordered metalmarks**; **Soldier**; White-striped Longtail; Long-tailed, **White-patched**, **Fawn-spotted**, and Dun **skippers**; **Brown Longtail**; Texas Powdered-Skipper; **Turk's-cap White-Skipper**; and Celia's Roadside-Skipper. **Guava Skipper** often feeds at wild olive flowers. **Definite Patch, Pale-banded**

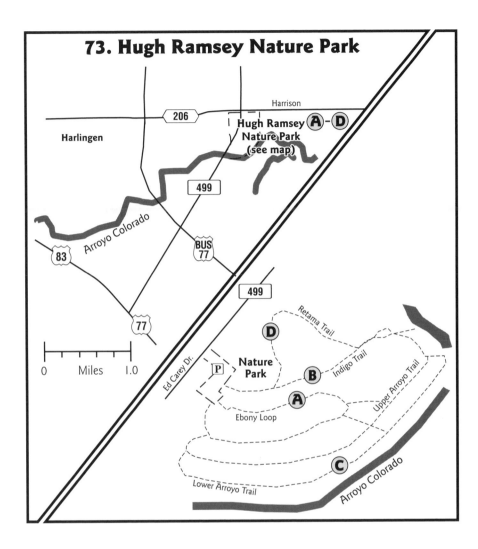

73. Hugh Ramsey Nature Park

Crescent, Two-barred Flasher, Mazans Scallopwing, and **Fawn-spotted Skipper** are more likely along the edges, and **Julia** and **Zebra heliconians, Mexican Bluewing**, and **Tropical Leafwing** prefer woodlands.

A few additional rare and occasional specialties are also possible: **Giant White**; **Yellow Angled-Sulphur**; **Boisduval's Yellow**; **Silver-banded Hairstreak**; **Clytie** and **Gray ministreaks**; **Mexican Fritillary**; **Banded Peacock**; **Zilpa Longtail**; **Glazed Pellicia**; **Brown-banded, Double-dotted, Olive-clouded,** and **Purple-washed skippers**; and **Erichson's White-Skipper**.

If time allows, also walk the Lower Arroyo Trail (**C**), which is especially good for **Blue Metalmarks**, and the Retama Trail (**D**).

Indigo Trail, Hugh Ramsey Nature Park

Directions: From US 77/83 or Bus. 77 in southeast Harlingen, exit on Loop 499 (Ed Carey Dr.) and drive northeast just past the Arroyo Colorado bridge to **Hugh Ramsey Nature Park (A-D)**. Park on the right side of the road.

Nearest food, gas, and lodging: Harlingen.

Nearest camping: Commercial sites in Harlingen.

74. Los Ebanos Preserve

This private eighty-two-acre nature park (fee area), located between Harlingen and Brownsville, offers a significant butterfly garden as well as trails through a thorn-scrub woodland and along a portion of a resaca. Sites include a garden **(A)**, trails **(B, C)**, and the entrance road **(D)**.

Opened in 2002, there is still much to learn about the preserve's butterfly fauna; the list will undoubtedly increase. From October through April, the preserve is currently open daily except Thursdays and major holidays; from May through September, it is open only by special arrangement.

Habitats: Garden, thorn scrub, riparian, and field.

Strategy for finding the most butterflies: Start in the garden **(A)** beyond the pavilion and return here again during your stay. Some of the more numerous butterflies include Pipevine and Black swallowtails; Southern Dogface; Large Orange and Lyside

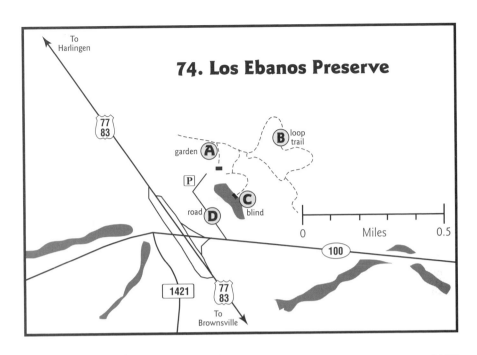

74. Los Ebanos Preserve

To Harlingen

77
83

garden (A)

(B) loop trail

P

(C)

road (D) blind

100

0   Miles   0.5

1421   77
83

To Brownsville

Garden, Los Ebanos Preserve

sulphurs; Little Yellow; Dusky-blue Groundstreak; **Red-bordered** and **Blue metal-marks**; Gulf Fritillary; Bordered Patch; Elada Checkerspot; Phaon Crescent; **White Peacock**; Queen; Sickle-winged, Julia's, **Fawn-spotted**, Clouded, Fiery, Eufala, and Ocola skippers; **Laviana White-Skipper**; and Sachem.

Several less numerous butterflies are also possible in the garden: Giant Swallowtail; Great Southern and **Giant whites**; **Boisduval's**, Mexican, and **Mimosa yellows**; **Tailed Orange**; Mallow Scrub-Hairstreak; **Clytie Ministreak**; Ceraunus and Reakirt's blues; **Rounded Metalmark**; **Red-bordered Pixie**; **Mexican Silverspot**; Theona Checkerspot; Vesta Crescent; Common Mestra; **Soldier**; **Zilpa**, Dorantes, and **Brown long-tails**; **Two-barred Flasher**; **White-patched** and **Purple-washed skippers**; Tropical Checkered-Skipper; and **Turk's-cap White-Skipper**. Also, check the edges for **Mazans Scallopwing** and **Fawn-spotted Skipper**. Watch for **Guava Skipper** feeding on wild olive flowers. **Yellow Angled-Sulphur** has also been recorded in flight.

Next, walk the loop trail (**B**) east of the garden. Texan Crescent and **Mexican Bluewing** can be common, and **Julia** and **Zebra heliconians**, **Tropical Leafwing**, and Gemmed and Carolina satyrs are also likely to be seen.

Afterwards, walk the trail (**C**) to the blind along the east side of the resaca and check the flowering shrubs along the entrance road (**D**).

Directions: From US 77/83, south of Harlingen, take SH 100 east toward South Padre Island. The entrance to **Los Ebanos Preserve (A-D)** is on the left only 100 yards east of the turn.

Nearest food, gas, and lodging: Sites along US 77/83 between Harlingen and Brownsville.

Nearest camping: Commercial sites in Harlingen.

75. Sabal Palm Audubon Center and Sanctuary

Protecting one of two remaining sabal palm groves in the U.S. (along with the Texas Nature Conservancy's Southmost Preserve), this 527-acre National Audubon Society preserve (fee area) offers easy trails (**B-D**) through the palm grove and adjacent woodlands. The butterfly garden (**A**) near the parking area can be one of the most productive in the Valley. The sanctuary is open daily year-round, except for Thanksgiving, Christmas, and New Years Day. This site is the centerpiece of the Brownsville July 4th Butterfly Count.

Habitats: Garden, palm grove, second-growth thorn scrub, coastal scrub, freshwater wetland, riparian, and field.

Strategy for finding the most butterflies: Start at the butterfly garden (**A**) behind the headquarters. Some of the more numerous butterflies include Giant Swallowtail; Great Southern White; Large Orange and Lyside sulphurs; **Boisduval's Yellow**; Dusky-blue Groundstreak; **Clytie Ministreak**; Ceraunus and Reakirt's blues; **Red-bordered** and **Blue metalmarks**; Gulf Fritillary; Bordered Patch; Phaon Crescent;

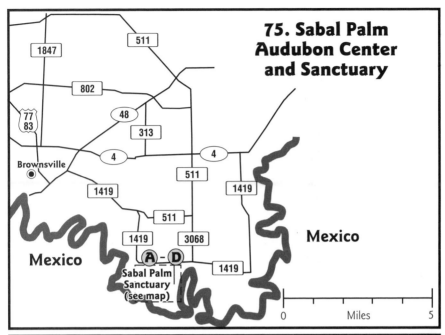

75. Sabal Palm Audubon Center and Sanctuary

1847
511
802
77
83
48
313
4
4
Brownsville
511
1419
1419
511
Mexico
1419   3068
A-**D**
Sabal Palm
Sanctuary
(see map)
1419
Mexico

0   Miles   5

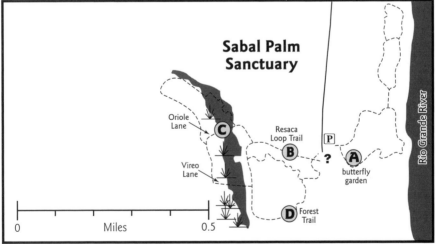

Sabal Palm Sanctuary

Oriole
Lane   **C**

Resaca
Loop Trail
P
B
?   **A**
Vireo
Lane   butterfly
garden

Rio Grande River

D Forest
Trail

0   Miles   0.5

White Peacock; Common Mestra; Queen; **Brown Longtail**; **Mazans Scallopwing**; Sickle-winged, **White-patched**, Clouded, Fiery, Eufala, and Ocola skippers; Tropical Checkered-Skipper; **Laviana White-Skipper**; and Celia's Roadside-Skipper.

Less numerous butterflies possible in the garden include Black Swallowtail, **Mimosa Yellow**, **Silver-banded Hairstreak**, Mallow Scrub-Hairstreak, Cassius Blue, Fatal and **Rounded metalmarks**, **Red-bordered Pixie**, Elada Checkerspot, Vesta

Garden, Sabal Palm Audubon Center and Sanctuary

Crescent, **Soldier**, **Guava** and Long-tailed **skippers**, White-striped Longtail, Mournful Duskywing, and **Turk's-cap White-Skipper**.

Additional rare and occasional species possible in the garden include **Florida** and **Giant whites**; **Barred Yellow**; **Xami Hairstreak**; **Red-lined** and **Lantana scrub-hairstreaks**; **Gray Ministreak**; **Definite Patch**; **Tropical** and **Mangrove buckeyes**; **Malachite**; **Zilpa Longtail**; **Two-barred Flasher**; **Potrillo, Mimosa, Hermit, Brown-banded, Pale-rayed, Double-dotted, Olive-clouded, Purple-washed**, and **Violet-banded skippers**; **Erichson's White-Skipper**, and **Common Mellana**.

Next, walk the 1.1-mile Resaca Loop Trail (**B**) and detour onto Oriole Lane (**C**), returning via Vireo Lane and Forest Trail (**D**). These well-shaded trails are likely to produce several additional butterflies, including Orange-barred Sulphur, **Tailed Orange, Julia** and **Zebra heliconians, Mexican Fritillary, Pale-banded Crescent, Tropical Leafwing**, Empress Leilia, Tawny Emperor, Gemmed and Carolina satyrs, and **Fawn-spotted Skipper**. **Mexican Bluewing** and **Gray Cracker** are also possible along the trails.

Directions: In Cameron County, from US 77/83 in Brownsville take Boca Chica Blvd. (SH 48 and SH 4) east to FM 511; turn south and continue on FM 511 and FM 3068 to FM 1419. Turn west and drive one mile. From Rancho Viejo (north of Brownsville on US 77/83), take FM 511 south and follow the same directions.

Nearest food, gas, and lodging: Brownsville.

Nearest camping: Commercial sites in Brownsville, including nearby Rio R.V. Park at 8801 Boca Chica Blvd.

76. Laguna Atascosa National Wildlife Refuge

The 45,000-acre Laguna Atascosa National Wildlife Refuge (fee area) is situated on a former delta of the Rio Grande River. The refuge, named for the large lake located along the west side of the refuge, was established to provide winter habitat for waterfowl; the refuge's bird list includes more than 400 species.

Although the butterfly list is less impressive, recently developed butterfly gardens (**A**) will undoubtedly greatly increase it. Other worthwhile sites to visit include the Kiskadee Trail (**B**), Mesquite Trail (**C**), Osprey Overlook (**D**), Alligator Pond Road (**E**), Lakeside Trail (**F**), and Bayside Drive (**G**). July 4th Butterfly Counts are held here annually.

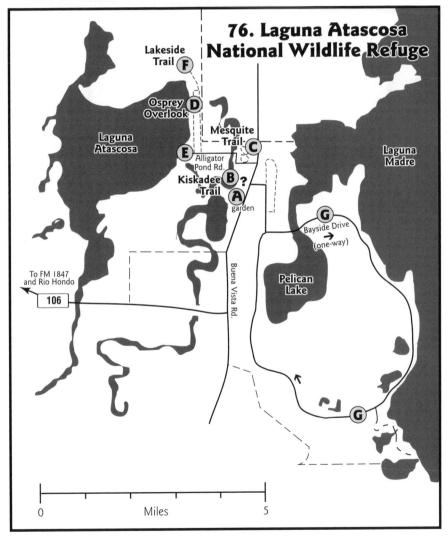

Butterfly garden, Laguna Atascosa National Wildlife Refuge

Habitats: Garden, coastal prairie, coastal scrub, mesquite grassland, field, and salt-water marsh.

Strategy for finding the most butterflies: Start at the rather extensive gardens (**A**) in front and behind the visitor center and check them again during your visit. Some of the more numerous butterflies include Giant Swallowtail; Great Southern White; Large Orange, Lyside, and Dainty sulphurs; Little Yellow; Mallow Scrub-Hairstreak; Dusky-blue Groundstreak; **Clytie Ministreak**; Western Pygmy-Blue; Ceraunus Blue; **Red-bordered** and **Blue metalmarks**; Gulf Fritillary; Theona Checkerspot; Bordered Patch; Vesta and Phaon crescents; **White Peacock**; Monarch; Queen; Sickle-winged, **White-patched**, Clouded, Fiery, Eufala, and Ocola skippers; Tropical Checkered-Skipper; **Laviana White-Skipper**; Whirlabout; Sachem; and Celia's Roadside-Skipper.

Less common but expected butterflies include Pipevine and Black swallowtails; Orange-barred Sulphur; Mexican and **Mimosa yellows**; **Silver-banded Hairstreak**; Cassius, Marine, and Reakirt's blues; Fatal and **Rounded metalmarks**; Elada Checkerspot; Common Mestra; **Soldier**; **Guava**, Long-tailed, **Mimosa**, **Brown-banded**, **Fawn-spotted**, and Tropical Least **skippers**; White-striped, Dorantes, and **Brown longtails**; Mournful and Funereal duskywings; **Mazans Scallopwing**; and **Turk's-cap White-Skipper**.

Several rare and occasional specialty butterflies have also been recorded in the gardens. These include **Florida** and **Giant whites**; **Tailed Orange**; **Red-crescent** and

Lantana scrub-hairstreaks; **Gray Ministreak**; **Cyna Blue**; **Mexican Fritillary**; Definite Patch; **Zilpa Longtail**; **Two-barred Flasher**; **Potrillo, Pale-rayed, Double-dotted, Olive-clouded**, and **Purple-washed skippers**; and **Erichson's White-Skipper**.

Next, walk the adjacent, very short Kiskadee Trail (**B**), a good place for Texan Crescent, **Julia** and **Zebra heliconians**, **Tropical Leafwing**, Tawny Emperor, and Carolina Satyr. Also walk the nearby 1.5-mile Mesquite Trail (**C**). Then drive to Osprey Overlook (**D**); check around the parking area (a good place to find **Silver-banded Hairstreak**) and walk the Alligator Pond Road (**E**), where Desert Checkered-Skipper is likely to occur. Also walk a portion of the Lakeside Trail (**F**).

Finally, drive the fifteen-mile Bayside Drive (**G**), a one-way loop road, stopping at pull-offs to check flowering plants; watch for **Obscure Skipper**. In spring, also watch for Yucca Giant-Skipper where yucca grows. In addition, watch for **Xami Hairstreak**, which occurs nearby; see the Old Port Isabel Road site in "Additional Worthwhile Sites" below.

Directions: In Cameron County, from US 77 in Harlingen, take FM 106 east to Rio Hondo and continue 15 miles to Buena Vista Rd.; turn north and go three miles to the refuge headquarters. From Brownsville, go north on FM 1847 (Paredes Line Rd.) through Los Fresnos to FM 106, then east to Buena Vista Rd.

Nearest food, gas, and lodging: Food and gas in Laguna Vista (12 miles southeast); lodging in Port Isabel (17 miles southeast) and Harlingen (25 miles southwest).

Nearest camping: Adolph Thomae, Jr. County Park, north of the refuge at the end of FM 1847, 20 miles from the NWR headquarters.

Additional Worthwhile Sites in the Lower Rio Grande Valley Region

La Grulla. From Alto Bonito on US 83 west of Sullivan City, take FM 2360 south through the village of La Grulla and continue on a dirt track that leads past open fields to a section of the USFWS wildlife corridor (closed to public access). In fall when crucita is blooming, this area can produce a variety of butterflies.

Chihuahua Woods Preserve. This 243-acre Texas Nature Conservancy property west of Mission has a one-mile trail through dense woodland and cactus habitats. It is located off Bus. 83, .8 mile west of FM 492. Where Bus. 83 curves to the northwest, go straight on a blacktop road for .1 mile to the entrance on the left.

Mission. The city hosts the annual Texas Butterfly Festival each October. There are two small gardens that have produced an amazing number of butterflies. "Lucy's Garden" and the Parks and Recreation Building garden are located along 8th Street, west of Bryan Road and just south of Bus. 83.

Longoria Wildlife Management Area. From US 83 west of Harlingen, take FM 506 north for 11 miles; the site is north of Santa Rosa. It has a series of trails that provide access into the thick Tamaulipan-scrub vegetation. Two water drippers attract butterflies.

Resaca de la Palma State Park. This is a new park (not yet open at this writing) with numerous trails; it is Brownsville's World Birding Center satellite site. It and adjacent USFWS sites, including the Olmito Fish Hatchery, comprise almost 2,000 acres. The park is located approximately four miles west of Brownsville off Military Highway (SH 281), with the park entrance north on New Carmen Rd.

Inn at Chachalaca Bend. There is an excellent butterfly garden near the parking lot at the entrance to this 40-acre private resort, located two miles northeast of Los Fresnos off FM 2480. From the stoplight in Los Fresnos, go north .25 mile and take a right turn on FM 2480. Go two miles to Track 43 Rd. Turn left and proceed over the resaca to Chachalaca Bend Dr. Turn right and proceed through the gate to the Inn. From SH 100, take Track 43 Rd. north to the entrance. The garden and additional plantings inside the gate have produced several rare butterflies.

Palo Alto Battlefield National Historic Site. Located at the junction of FM 511 and FM 1847, north of Brownsville and south of Los Fresnos, this 3,400-acre unit (fee area) of the National Park Service commemorates the U.S-Mexican War. It is also one of the best places to find **Definite Patch**. Check around the parking area and along the short nature trail.

Old Port Isabel Road. This is the only known site in Texas where **Xami Hairstreak** can be found consistently. It is situated off a dirt road (don't drive when wet) that runs between FM 511 and SH 100. Drive approximately two miles southeast of FM 1847 (Paredes Line Rd.) on FM 511 and turn northeast on Old Port Isabel Rd. Continue 1.8 miles from FM 511 (5.6 miles southwest of SH 100) and walk through the coastal scrub near the "Loma Alta Skeet & Trap, Inc." gate.

Port Isabel. At two intersections in town, **Red-bordered Pixie** can sometimes be found at guamachil trees (larval foodplant). Check at Adams and Tarnava and at Manautou and Monroe, both south of SH 100.

South Padre Island Convention Center Garden. The convention center is four miles north of the SH 100 causeway exit onto the island, on the west side of Padre Blvd. The garden is located in front and on the side of the convention center. It is the best bet for finding **Mangrove Buckeye**.

Boca Chica Tract. Located at the eastern end of Boca Chica Blvd. (SH 4), the property is part of the Lower Rio Grande NWR. Although the land appears somewhat sterile, **Xami Hairstreak** can sometimes be found at sedum plants on the "lomas" (low, sandy hills), and Yucca Giant-Skipper, which flies in March and April, occurs on the lomas where Spanish daggers (yuccas) grow.

Butterfly Checklist for the Lower Rio Grande Valley Region

The following list includes nine sites: **67. San Ygnacio/Zapata, 68. Falcon State Park/Roma–Los Saenz, 69. NABA International Butterfly Park/Bentsen-Rio Grande Valley State Park, 70. Edinburg World Birding Center, 71. Santa Ana National Wildlife Refuge, 72. Weslaco, 73. Hugh Ramsey Nature Park, 74. Los Ebanos Preserve, 75. Sabal Palm Audubon Center and Sanctuary,** and **76. Laguna Atascosa National Wildlife Refuge**.

Status symbols include: A = abundant; C = common; U = uncommon; O = occasional; R = rare; X = accidental; M = migrant; TC = temporary colonist; ? = unknown status. (For a full definition of these terms, see p. 3.)

For trip notes, including dates and numbers of species seen, refer to the entry for this checklist in Appendix 3: Regional Checklist Resources.

Note: Strays from Mexico that are not yet on the NABA list are indicated by an asterisk.

Butterfly Species	67	68	69	70	71	72	73	74	75	76
Pipevine Swallowtail	C	C	C	C	C	U	C	C	O	U
Polydamas Swallowtail		U	O		O	O				
Dark Kite-Swallowtail			X		X					
Black Swallowtail	U	U	U	U	U	O	U	C	U	O
Thoas Swallowtail	X	X			X					
Giant Swallowtail	U	C	C	C	C	C	C	U	C	C
Ornythion Swallowtail		R	R		R					X
Broad-banded Swallowtail			X		X	X				
Three-tailed Swallowtail	X	X								
Ruby-spotted Swallowtail		X	O		O	O				
Florida White		R	O	R	O	O			O	O
Green-eyed White*					X					
Cross-barred White*		X								
Checkered White	A	A	U	C	C	U	U	U	U	U
Cabbage White		X			X					
Great Southern White	U	U	U	C	C	U	U	U	C	A
Giant White	R	O	O	O	O	O	O	O	O	O
Falcate Orangetip			R		O					
Orange Sulphur	A	C	U	U	U	U				U
Southern Dogface	C	C	C	C	C	C	C	C	C	C
Common Melwhite*			X							
White Angled-Sulphur	X	X	R		O	O			X	
Yellow Angled-Sulphur		X	R	R	O	O	X	X	X	X
Cloudless Sulphur	U	C	C	C	A	C	C	C	C	C
Orange-barred Sulphur	U	U	U	U	U	U	U	U	U	O
Large Orange Sulphur	C	A	C	C	C	C	C	C	C	C

Butterfly Species	67	68	69	70	71	72	73	74	75	76
Statira Sulphur		X	X							
Lyside Sulphur	C	A	A	A	A	C	C	C	C	C
Barred Yellow		R	R		R				R	
Ghost Yellow		X								
Boisduval's Yellow	U	O	U		U	U	O	O	C	
Mexican Yellow	U	U	U		U	U	U	U		O
Salome Yellow			X		X					
Tailed Orange	O	U	U	R	U	U	U	U	U	O
Little Yellow	C	A	C	C	C	C	C	C	A	A
Mimosa Yellow	U	O	U	O	U	O	U	U	U	U
Dina Yellow					X					
Sleepy Orange	C	A	C	C	C	U	U	C	C	C
Dainty Sulphur	A	A	A	A	C	U	U	U	C	A
Costa-spotted Mimic-White			X		X					
Strophius Hairstreak					X					
Great Purple Hairstreak		U	U	U	U	O	U	U	O	O
Gold-bordered Hairstreak			X		X					
Marius Hairstreak			X		X					
Black Hairstreak					X					
Stag Hairstreak*				X						
Silver-banded Hairstreak		R	U	O	U	U	O		U	U
Clench's Greenstreak			X		?					
Goodson's Greenstreak			X		X					
Tropical Greenstreak			X	X	X					
Xami Hairstreak			O		R	R			O	
Aquamarine Hairstreak				X		X				
Gray Hairstreak	U	C	C	C	C	C	C	C	C	C
Red-crescent Scrub-Hairstreak	R	R	U			O	O			R
Red-lined Scrub-Hairstreak			R		O			R		
Yojoa Scrub-Hairstreak			R		O	R				
White Scrub-Hairstreak			R		X			X		
Lacey's Scrub-Hairstreak	O	O	O		O					
Mallow Scrub-Hairstreak	U	C	C	O	C	C	C	U	U	C
Tailless Scrub-Hairstreak					X					
Lantana Scrub-Hairstreak	R	U	U	O	U	O			O	O
Ruddy Hairstreak			X		X					
Muted Hairstreak					X					
Dusky-blue Groundstreak	U	U	C	C	A	U	C	C	C	C
Mountain Groundstreak*	X		X							
Red-spotted Hairstreak		X			X					
Pearly-gray Hairstreak			X		X					
Clytie Ministreak		R	O	O	U	O	O	U	A-R	A-R

Butterfly Species	67	68	69	70	71	72	73	74	75	76
Gray Ministreak		R	R		R	R	R		O	R
Western Pygmy-Blue	C	A	C	A	C	U	U	U	U	C
Cassius Blue			O		O	O			U	O
Marine Blue	U	U	O		U	O	O			O
Cyna Blue	X	X	R		O	R				R
Ceraunus Blue	C	A	C	C	C	C	C	U	C	A
Reakirt's Blue	U	C	U	C	C	U	U	U	C	U
Eastern Tailed-Blue		X			X					
Fatal Metalmark	C	C	C	C	C	C	U		U	U
Rounded Metalmark	U	C	U	U	C	U	U	O	U	U
Rawson's Metalmark		O	R	X						
Red-bordered Metalmark	U	U	C	C	C	U	U	C	C	C
Blue Metalmark		X	O		O	O	U	C	C	A
Red-bordered Pixie			O	U	U	U		U	U	
Curve-winged Metalmark			X		X	X				
Falcate Metalmark					X					
Narrow-winged Metalmark		X			X					
Walker's Metalmark		X	X		X			X	X	
American Snout	A-R	A-R	A-R	A-R	A-R	A-R	A-R	A-R	A-R	A-R
Gulf Fritillary	C	C	C	C	C	C	C	C	C	C
Mexican Silverspot		X	O		O	O		O		
Banded Orange Heliconian			X			X				
Julia Heliconian	U	U	U	U	C	U	U	U	U	O
Isabella's Heliconian		X	X		X	X				
Zebra Heliconian	U	U	U	U	C	U	U	U	U	O
Erato Heliconian			X		X	X			X	
Variegated Fritillary	C	C	C	C	C	C	U	U	U	U
Mexican Fritillary	U	U	U	O	U	O	O		U	O
Theona Checkerspot	C	A	U		U	O		U		C
Bordered Patch	C	C	A	C	C	A	C	C	C	C
Definite Patch	R	R	R		O		U			O
Banded Patch					X					
Crimson Patch	X	O	O		O	U				
Rosita Patch			X		X					
Elf					X					
Tiny Checkerspot	O									
Elada Checkerspot	C	U	U	O	C	U	U	C	U	O
Texan Crescent	U	C	C	C	U	C	C	C	C	U
Pale-banded Crescent		R	O		O	U	O		O	
Black Crescent			X		X					
Chestnut Crescent					X					
Vesta Crescent	C	C	C	U	C	C	C	U	U	C

Butterfly Species	67	68	69	70	71	72	73	74	75	76
Phaon Crescent	A	A	C	A	A	C	C	C	C	C
Pearl Crescent	C	C	C	U	C	C	C	U	U	C
Question Mark	U	C	U		U	U	U		U	O
American Lady	C	U	U	U	C	U	U		U	U
Painted Lady	U	U	U	C	C	U	U		U	U
Red Admiral	C	U	C	C	C	A	C	C	C	C
Mimic									X	
Common Buckeye	C	U	U	U	C	U	U	U	U	U
Tropical Buckeye	O	O	O		R	R			O	
Mangrove Buckeye				X	X				R	
White Peacock	C	U	C	C	C	C	C	C	C	C
Banded Peacock	X	X	X		R	R	O			
Malachite	R	R	R		O	O			R	
Red-spotted Purple	X	X			X					
Viceroy	O				R					
Band-celled Sister		X	X		X	X				
Common Banner		X	X		X					
Orange Banner*		X								
Mexican Bluewing		U	U	U	C	U	U	C	R	
Dingy Purplewing		X	X		X					X
Florida Purplewing		X			X					
Blue-eyed Sailor	X	X	X	R	R				X	
Common Mestra	C	C	C	C	C	C	C	U	C	U
Red Rim	X	O	O		O	O		X		
Red Cracker		X			X					
Gray Cracker	R	O			O	R			R	X
Variable Cracker		X			X					
Guatemalan Cracker	X	X			X					
Brownish Cracker*					X					
Blomfild's Beauty		X			X	X				
Many-banded Daggerwing		X	X	X	O					
Ruddy Daggerwing		X	X		O	O				X
Waiter Daggerwing*		X			X					
Tropical Leafwing	U	C	C		C	C	C	C	U	O
Goatweed Leafwing	U	U	U		U	U		U		O
Angled Leafwing		X			X					
Pale-spotted Leafwing		X	X		X	X				
Hackberry Emperor	C	U	U	O	C	U			U	U
Empress Leilia	C	C	C	O	C	R			U	
Tawny Emperor	C	A	A	C	A	C			C	C
Pavon Emperor		X	X		R					
Silver Emperor		X	X		X					

Butterfly Species	67	68	69	70	71	72	73	74	75	76
Gemmed Satyr	U	U	U		C	R		U	U	
Carolina Satyr	U	A	A		A	U	A	A	C	U
Frosty-tipped Clearwing*			X							
Monarch	M	M	M	M	M	M	M		M	C
Queen	C	C	A	A	C	A	A	C	A	C
Soldier	U	U	U	U	U	U	U	U	U	U
Beautiful Beamer*			X							
Guava Skipper		U	U	U	U	U	U	U	U	U
Mercurial Skipper			X		X					
Silver-spotted Skipper			X							
Broken Silverdrop					X					
Hammock Skipper			X		X					
White-striped Longtail		U	U	U	U	U	U		U	U
Zilpa Longtail	R	U			O	O	O	O	O	R
Gold-spotted Aguna	R	O			O	R				X
Emerald Aguna			X		X	X				
Tailed Aguna		X	X		X	X				
Mexican Longtail			X		X					
Eight-spotted Longtail			X		X					
White-crescent Longtail			X		X					
Long-tailed Skipper		U	C	C	C	C	U		U	U
Pronus Longtail					X					
Esmeralda Longtail					X					
Double-striped Longtail								X		
Turquoise Longtail*			X		X					
Dorantes Longtail			U	U	U	U	U	U	U	U
Teleus Longtail		R	R	R	R	R	R		R	X
Tanna Longtail					X					
Plain Longtail			X		X					
Brown Longtail	U	U	C	C	C	C	U	U	C	U
White-tailed Longtail			X		X		X			
Two-barred Flasher	R	R	O		O	O	O	O	O	O
Small-spotted Flasher			X		X					
Frosted Flasher			X		X					
Gilbert's Flasher			X		X					
Yellow-tipped Flasher			X		X	X				
Coyote Cloudywing	O	O	O	O	O	O				
Jalapus Cloudywing		X	X							
Potrillo Skipper	O	O	O	U	O				O	O
Fritzgaertner's Flat			X		X					X
Stallings' Flat			X		R					
Falcate Skipper		X	O		R					

Lower Rio Grande Valley Region   291

Butterfly Species	67	68	69	70	71	72	73	74	75	76
Mimosa Skipper		U	U		C	U			U	U
Acacia Skipper			X		X	X				
Starred Skipper			X		X	X				
Purplish-black Skipper		X	X		X					
Glazed Pellicia			U		U		O			
Mottled Bolla					X					
Golden-headed Scallopwing	R	R	R		R	R				
Mazans Scallopwing	U	U	U		C	U	U	U	C	U
Variegated Skipper		X	X		X					
Blue-studded Skipper			X		X					
Shining Blue-Skipper*			X							
Tropical Duskywing*			X							
Hoary Skipper	X		X		X	X				
Glassy-winged Skipper					X	X				
Red-studded Skipper					X					
Texas Powdered-Skipper	U	O	O		U	O	O		O	R
Sickle-winged Skipper	C	C	C	C	A	C	A	C	A	C
Hermit Skipper		R	R		O	R			O	
Brown-banded Skipper		R	R	O	O		O		O	O
Everlasting Skipper*		X	X							
White-patched Skipper	U	U	U	U	U	U	U	U	C	C
Horace's Duskywing			X		O	O				
Mournful Duskywing			O		O	O			U	O
Funereal Duskywing	U	U	U	U	U	U	U	U	O	U
Com./White Checkered-Skipper	C	C	C	C	C	C	C	U	C	A
Tropical Checkered-Skipper	C	U	C	C	C	U	C	C	C	C
Desert Checkered-Skipper	U	U	U	O	U	U			O	U
Erichson's White-Skipper	O	O	O		O	O	O		O	R
Laviana White-Skipper	U	C	C	C	C	C	C	C	C	C
Turk's-cap White-Skipper	U	U	C	U	C	U	U	U	U	U
East-Mexican White-Skipper*					X	X				
Veined White-Skipper	X	X	X							
Common Streaky-Skipper	O		O		O					
Common Sootywing	U	U	U		U	U	U	U	U	U
Saltbush Sootywing	O									
Malicious Skipper		R	X		X					
Salenus Skipper					X					
Redundant Skipper			X		X					
Pale-rayed Skipper									R	O
Violet-patched Skipper		R	R		R					
Julia's Skipper	U	U	O	U	U	U			U	U
Fawn-spotted Skipper	U	U	O	O	U	U	U	U	U	U

Butterfly Species	67	68	69	70	71	72	73	74	75	76
Clouded Skipper	C	C	A	C	A	A	A	C	C	C
Liris Skipper		X	X		X					
Fantastic Skipper					X	X				
Green-backed Ruby-eye		X	X		X		X			
Osca Skipper					?				?	
Double-dotted Skipper		X	X		X		O		U	O
Hidden-ray Skipper			X		X					
Least Skipper		U	U		O					
Tropical Least Skipper										O
Orange Skipperling	U	U	U		U	O	O		U	
Southern Skipperling	C	C	C	C	C	U	U	U	C	U
Fiery Skipper	C	C	C	C	A	A	C	C	C	C
Whirlabout	U	U	C	C	C	U	U	U	C	A
Southern Broken-Dash	U	U	C	C	C	C	C	U	C	C
Sachem	U	C	A	O	A	C	C	C	C	A
Common Mellana		R	O		O				O	X
Dun Skipper		U			U	U	U		O	
Nysa Roadside-Skipper	O	U	U		U	O				U
Celia's Roadside-Skipper	U	U	U	O	C	U	U		C	C
Eufala Skipper	C	C	C	U	C	C	C	C	C	A
Olive-clouded Skipper		R	O		U	O	O		U	O
Brazilian Skipper		U	O	O	O					R
Obscure Skipper		X			X	X				U
Ocola Skipper	U	U	C	A	C	C	C	C	C	C
Hecebolus Skipper	X	R	R		O					
Purple-washed Skipper	X	R	O	R	O	R	O	R	O	O
Evans' Skipper		X			X	X				
Violet-banded Skipper		O			O	O			O	
Chestnut-marked Skipper					X					
Yucca Giant-Skipper		R								O

Appendix 1
Plant Names

The following plant species are included in the "Specialty" sections of the ten regions, as well as in the "Habitat" discussions for each site. The common and scientific names were derived from "Checklist of the Vascular Plants of Texas" by Stephen L. Hatch, Kencheepuram N. Gandhi, and Larry E. Brown (1990).

Acacia *Acacia* sp.
Acacia, blackbrush *Acacia rigidula*
Acacia, fern *Acacia angustissima*
Adelia, Vasey *Adelia vaseyi*
Agave *Agave* sp.
Alfalfa *Medicago sativa*
Amaranth *Amaranthus* sp.
Anisacanth *Anisacanthus* sp.
Aspen *Populus tremuloides*
Aster *Aster* sp.

Balloonvine *Cardiospermum* sp.
Barbados-cherry *Malpighia glabra*
Bean *Phasealus* sp.
Beardgrass, common *Andropogon scoparius*
Beargrass *Nolina* sp.
Beard-tongue *Penstemon* sp.
Beggar's tick *Bidens* sp.
Bluestem *Schizachyrium* sp.
Bluestem, big *Andropogon gerardii*
Bluestem, little *Schizachyrium scoparim*
Boneset *Eupatorium* sp.
Buckwheat *Eriogonum* sp.
Bur-Clover *Medicago* sp.
Bushclover *Lespedeza* sp.
Butterfly pea *Centrosema virginianum*

Cane *Arundinaria* sp.
Cane, giant *Arundinaria gigantea*
Caper *Capparis* sp.
Cassia *Cassia* sp.
Cattail *Typha* sp.
Cherry *Prunus* sp.
Clover *Trifolium* sp.
Cologania *Cologania* sp.
Corn *Zea mays*
Cottonwood *Populus* sp.
Coyotillo *Karwinskia humboldtiana*
Croton *Croton* sp
Crucita *Eupatorium odoratum*

Dicliptera *Dicliptera* sp.
Dock *Rumex* sp.
Douglasfir *Pseudotsuga menziesii*

Ebony, Texas *Pithecellobium flexicaule*
Echeveria *Echeveria strictiflora*
Esenbeckia, Runyon *Esenbeckia berlandieri*
Eupatorium *Eupatorium* sp.
False indigo *Baptisia alba*

Fig *Ficus* sp.
Frog-fruit *Phyla* sp.

Glasswort *Salicornia virginica*
Goatweed *Croton* sp.
Goosefoot *Chenopodium* sp.
Grama *Bouteloua* sp.
Grama, blue *Bouteloua gracilis*
Grama, hairy *Bouteloua hirsuta*
Grama, sideoats *Bouteloua curtipendula*
Guava *Psidium* sp.
Guamachil *Pithecellobium dulce*
Guayacan *Guaiacum angustifolium*
Gumbo Limbo *Bursera simaruba*

Hackberry *Celtis* sp.
Hackberry, spiny *Celtis pallida*
Hechtia *Hechtia texensis*
Hickory *Carya* sp.
Hibiscus *Hibiscus* sp.

Indian paintbrush *Castilleja* sp.
Indiangrass *Sorghastrum* sp.
Indianmallow *Abutilon* sp.
Indigo *Indigofera* sp.

Jopoy *Esenbeckia berlandieri*
Juniper *Juniperus* sp.
Juniper, Ashe *Juniperus ashei*
Justicia *Justicia* sp.

Kidneywood *Eysenhardtia texana*
Knotgrass *Setaria firmula*

Lamb's-quarters *Chenopodium album*
Lantana *Lantana* sp.
Lechuguilla *Agave lechuguilla*
Legume Leguminosae family
Lippia *Lippia alba*
Locoweed *Astragalus* sp.
Locust, black *Robinia pseudo-acacia*
Lupine *Lupinus* sp.

Mallow Malvaceae family
Manfreda *Manfreda maculosa*
Mangrove, black *Avicennia germinans*
Mesquite *Prosopis* sp.
Milkweed *Asclepias* sp.
Mimosa *Mimosa* sp.
Mimosa, black *Mimosa pigra*
Mimosa, soft-leaf *Mimosa malacophylla*
Mistflower *Eupatorium* sp.
Mistletoe *Phoradendron sp.*
Morningglory *Ipomoea* sp.
Myrtlecroton *Bernardia myricifolia*

Nettle *Urtica* sp.
Nissolia *Nissolia platycalyx*
Noseburn *Tragia* sp.

Oak *Quercus* sp.
Oak, Emory *Quercus emoryi*
Oak, Gambel's *Quercus gambelii*
Oak, gray *Quercus grisea*
Oak, post *Quercus stellta*
Oak, scrub *Quercus ilicifolia*
Orchid tree *Bauhinia purpurea*

Palm, Sabal *Sabal mexicana*
Palmetto, dwarf *Sabal minor*
Panicum, bulb *Panicum bulbosum*
Passion vine *Passiflora* sp.
Pawpaw *Asimina* sp.
Pea *Lathyrus* sp.
Pecan *Carya illinioensis*
Pigweed *Chenopodium* sp.
Pine *Pinus* sp.
Pine, longleaf *Pinus palustris*
Pine, ponderosa *Pinus ponderosa*
Pine, yellow *Pinus* sp.
Pipevine *Aristolochia* sp.
Pitcherplant *Sarraceaia alata*
Plum *Prunus* sp.

Plum, Havard *Prunus havardii*
Pricklyash *Zanthoxylum* sp.
Purpletop *Tridens flavus*

Ratama *Parkinsonia aculeata*
Rattleweed *Astragalus* sp.
Reed, common *Phragmites australis*
Rockcress *Arabis* sp.
Ruellia *Ruellia* sp.

Saltbush *Atriplex* sp.
Saltgrass *Distichlis* sp.
Sawgrass *Cladium jamaicense*
Sedge *Carex* sp.
Senna *Chamaecrista* sp.
Serviceberry *Amelanchier* sp.
Sesbania *Sesbania* sp.
Silverleaf, Big Bend *Leucophyllum minus*
Sisymbrium *Sisymbrium* sp.
Soapberry *Sapindus drummondii*
Sotol *Dasylirion* sp.
Spanish dagger *Yucca treculeana*
Stemodia, woolly *Stemodia tomentosa*
Stenandrium, shaggy *Stenadrium dulce*
Stonecrop *Sedum* sp.
Sugarcane *Saccharum officinarum*
Sweetleaf, common *Symplocos tinctoria*

Tansymustard *Descurainia* sp.
Thistle *Cirsium* sp.
Thistle, yellow *Cirsium horridulum*
Tickclover *Desmodium* sp.
Tubetongue *Siphonoglossa* sp.
Tubetongue, hairy *Siphonoglossa pilosella*
Turk's cap *Malvaviscus drummondii*
Twistflower *Streptanthus* sp.

Vetch *Vicia* sp.

Water hyssop *Bacopa* sp.
Whitebrush *Aloysia* sp.
Wildrice *Zizania texana*
Willow *Salix* sp.

Yucca *Yucca* sp.
Yaupon *Ilex vomitoria*

Appendix 2
References

Field Guides

Brock, Jim P., and Kenn Kaufman. 2003. *Butterflies of North America*. Boston: Houghton Mifflin Company.

Glassberg, Jeffrey. 1999. *Butterflies through Binoculars: The East*. NY: Oxford University Press.

Glassberg, Jeffrey. 2001. *Butterflies through Binoculars: The West*. NY: Oxford University Press.

Howe, William H. 1975. *The Butterflies of North America*. NY: Doubleday & Company, Inc.

Neck, Raymond W. 1996. *A Field Guide to Butterflies of Texas*. Houston: Gulf Publishing Co.

Opler, Paul A., and Vichai Malikul. 1998. *Peterson Field Guides Eastern Butterflies*. Boston: Houghton Mifflin Company.

Opler, Paul A., and Amy Bartlett Wright. 1999. *Peterson Field Guides Western Butterflies*. Boston: Houghton Mifflin Company.

Pyle, Robert Michael. 1981. *National Audubon Society Field Guide to North American Butterflies*. NY: Alfred A. Knopf.

Scott, James A. 1986. *The Butterflies of North America: A Natural History and Field Guide*. Stanford, CA: Stanford University Press.

Tveten, John L. & Gloria. 1996. *Butterflies of Houston & Southeast Texas*. Austin: University of Texas Press.

Wauer, Roland H. 2004. *Butterflies of the Lower Rio Grande Valley*. Boulder, CO: Johnson Books.

Wauer, Roland H. 2002. *Butterflies of West Texas Parks and Preserves*. Lubbock, TX: Texas Tech University Press.

Other Useful References

Ajilvsgi, Geyata. 1991. *Butterfly Gardening for the South*. Dallas: Taylor Trade Publishing Company.

Durden, Chris. 1998. *Checklist of Texas Butterflies*. Austin: Memorial Museum, University of Texas.

North American Butterfly Association. 2001. *Checklist & English Names of North American Butterflies, Second Edition*. Morristown, NJ: North American Butterfly Association.

Opler, Paul A., and Andrew D. Warren. 2002. *Butterflies of North America 2. Scientific Names List for Butterfly Species of North America, North of Mexico*. Colorado Springs: C.P. Gillette Museum of Arthropod Biodiversity.

Pyle, Robert Michael. 1992. *Handbook for Butterfly Watchers*. Boston: Houghton Mifflin Company.

Ross, Gary Noel. 1995. *Everything You Ever Wanted to Know About Butterflies*. Baton Rouge, LA: Gary Noel Ross.

Schappert, Phil. 2000. *A World for Butterflies: Their Lives, Behavior and Future*. Buffalo, NY: Firefly Books, Ltd.

Sutton, Patricia Taylor & Clay. 1999. *How to Spot Butterflies*. Boston: Houghton Mifflin Company.

Additional Worthwhile Reading

Halpern, Sue. 2002. *Four Wings and a Prayer*. NY: Vintage.

Johnson, Kurt, and Steve Coates. 1999. *Nabokov's Blues The Scientific Odyssey of a Literary Genius*. Cambridge, MA: Zoland Books.

Pyle, Robert Michael. 1999. *Chasing Monarchs: Migrating with the Butterflies of Passage*. Boston: Houghton Mifflin Company.

Russell, Sharman Apt. 2003. *An Obsession with Butterflies*. NY: Basic Books.

Appendix 3
Regional Checklist Resources

The resources used to create the checklists at the end of each region are given here. By doing so, the author acknowledges the time and effort put in by the many people who contributed their butterfly sightings to this book and the work of the authors of the site checklists and articles used here.

The number of species seen on site visits is given in parentheses, if known. This information can aid in planning a trip to the sites at a time of year when the most species can be seen.

Information on the regional checklists was derived from the sources listed below.

Trans-Pecos Region
1. El Paso/Franklin Mountains SP—"Distribution of Butterflies in New Mexico (Lepidoptera: Hesperioidea and Papilionoidea), 2nd ed." by Michael E. Toliver, Richard Holland, and Steven J. Cary (privately published by Holland, Albuquerque, NM, 1994); "Lepidoptera of El Paso County, Texas" by Ed Knudson, Charles Bordelon, Jr., and Richard Worthington (photocopy, 1997); reports to TPWD on collections by Floyd and June Preston: 2/27-28/96, 4/16-17/97, 2/24-25/98, 2/28/99, 3/1/99; and site visits by Bob Behrstock: 6/30/02; Mike Overton: 8/6/01 (28 sp), 8/2/02 (10 sp); Wauer: 3/30/01 (16 sp), 6/7/04 (26 sp). **2. Guadalupe Mountains NP**—*Butterflies of West Texas Parks and Preserves* by Wauer (Texas Tech Univ. Press, 2000); "Checklist of the Lepidoptera of the Guadalupe Mountains National Park, Texas" by Ed Knudson and Charles Bordelon (Texas Lep. Survey Publ. 4, 1999); and site visits by Mark Adams, Rex Barrick: 4/8/01 (15 sp); Bob Behrstock: 6/27-28/02; Nick Block: 8/13/03 (20 sp); Jeff Glassberg: 5/28/02 (25 sp); Lee Hoy: 6/15/02 (10 sp), 6/14/03 (17 sp); Rich Kostecke, Brandon Best: 7/23-24/04 (31 sp); Craig Marks: 7/4-6/02 (19 sp); Mike Overton: 8/4/01 (24 sp), 8/2-6/02 (63 sp), 9/16-17/02 (56 sp); Herschel Raney: 9/14/02 (38 sp); Wauer, Bill Reid: 6/16-17/02 (43 sp). **3. Davis Mountains**—"Lepidoptera Checklist of the Davis Mountains, Texas" by Ed Knudson (1955); "Comprehensive List of Spring Butterflies (1998 & 1999) Recorded on the Davis Mountains Preserve" by Wauer (1998); report on a 7/17-18/99 trip by Chuck Sexton; July 4th Counts (Wauer, coord.) on 7/17/99 (33 sp), 6/23/00 (52 sp), 7/15/01 (57 sp); and (Mark Adams, coord.) on 7/20/03 (46 sp); and site visits by Adams: 11/2/03 (13 sp); Adams, Laura Long: 3/15/03 (16 sp); Nick Block: 8/14/03 (25 sp); Jeff Glassberg: 6/2/99 (16 sp); Joann Karges: 9/20/97 (16 sp), 8/26&28/99 (41 sp), 8/18-19/00 (36 sp), 7/13-15/01 (39 sp); Rich Kostecke: 6/25-26/04 (23 sp); Derek Muschalek, Rob Thacker: 6/7-8/01 (40 sp); Mike Overton: 8/3/01 (12 sp); Wauer: 6/18-24/00 (56 sp), 8/17-20/04 (58 sp). **4. Big Bend NP**—"Butterfly Checklist Big Bend National Park, Texas" (Wauer 2003); "Checklist of Lepidoptera of Big Bend National Park, Texas" by Ed Knudson and Charles Bordelon (1999); reports to the NPS by Wauer for 1/10-15/99 (19 sp), 3/3-5/99 (27 sp), 4/24/99-5/12/99 (76 sp), 8/28/99-9/12/99 (99 sp), late April to mid-May 2000 (71 sp), 8/31/00-9/11/00 (67 sp), 4/24/01-5/22/01 (82 sp); July 4th Count (Mark Adams, coord.) on 7/8/01 (58 sp), 6/28/03 (47 sp); and site visits by Adams, Mark and Maryann Eastman, Laura Long: 12/28-29/02 (10 sp); Adams, Long: 4/5/03 (19 sp); Adams, Eastmans: 10/7/01 (25 sp); Adams, Rex Barrick: 3/6/00 (11 sp), 9/10/00 (19 sp); Nick Block: 7/17-19/03 (60 sp); Jim Brock: 5/29-30/99 (51 sp); Cathy Clark: 6/23/01-7/4/01 (63 sp); Jeff Glassberg: 5/29/99-6/1/99 (53 sp); Nick Grishin: 5/28-29/04 (76 sp); Dan Hardy, Jeff Detweiler: 5/4-8/02 (44 sp); Lee Hoy: 6/21-23/03 (34 sp); Rich Kostecke: 6/7-10/01 (31 sp); Craig Marks: 6/14-16/01 (25 sp); Derek Muschalek, Rob Thacker: 6/20-25/00 (54 sp), 6/2-5/01 (62 sp); Mike Overton: 6/30/00 (62 sp); Dan Peak: 6/24/02 (16 sp); Wauer: 6/2-6/04 (73 sp), 8/11-16/04 (65 sp).

Panhandle and Western Plains Region
5. Rita Blanca NG/Lake Rita Blanca—the USGS checklist, "Butterflies of Dallam and Hutchinson Counties, Texas," and site visits by Mike Overton: 8/16/01 (16 sp); Wauer: 8/14/02 (12 sp). **6. Lake Meredith NRA**—the USGS checklist, "Butterflies of Carson and Hutchinson Counties, Texas," and site visits by Wauer: 8/15/02 (23 sp), 5/6/03 (27 sp). **7. Black Kettle NG/Gene Howe WMA**—the USGS Checklist, "Butterflies of Hemphill County, Texas," and site visits by Wauer: 8/16/02 (25 sp), 5/7/03 (21 sp). **8. Palo Duro Canyon SP/Buffalo Lake NWR**—a draft list of Lepidoptera by Richard Howard (2001) and site visits by Charles Jones: 9/26-27/03 (15 sp); Mike Overton: 8/15/01 (10 sp); Wauer: 8/17/02 (11 sp), 5/5/03 (27 sp). **9. Caprock Canyon SP**—the USGS checklist, "Butterflies of Briscoe County, Texas," and site visits by Barry Lombardini: 9/3-5/99 (19 sp);

Wauer: 8/17/02 (16 sp). **10. Lubbock**—two papers by John B. Lombardini: "The Butterflies of Lubbock County, Texas" (*So. Lep. News, 9*, 1989) and "Butterflies of Lubbock County, Texas, and the Llano Estacado: A Continuing Saga" (*So. Lep. News, 6*, 1996); and site visits by Wauer, Anthony Floyd: 5/4/03 (28 sp); Wauer, Jim and Jason Crites, Rob Lee, Bob and Sylvia Rasa, Cliff Stogner: 6/4/03 (24 sp). **11. Abilene**—the USGS checklist, "Butterflies of Taylor County, Texas," and site visits by Wauer: 5/12/02 (34 sp), 8/19/02 (23 sp), 6/5/03 (36 sp).

Edwards Plateau Region

12. Concan/Garner SP—"Butterflies of the Upper Frio-Sabinal Region, Central Texas, and Distribution of Faunal Elements Across the Edwards Plateau" by David Gaskin (*Jour. Lep. Soc.* 52(3): 229-61, 1998); "Checklist of Lepidoptera of the Texas Hill Country," by Ed Knudson and Charles Bordelon (*Tex. Lep. Survey Pub. 8*, 2001); a comprehensive "List of Butterflies from Nature Quest Festivals 1999-2002" by John Tveten; and site visits by Derek Muschalek: 4/20/01 (34 sp); Wauer: 4/23/01 (28 sp), 9/22/03 (37 sp); Wauer, Mike Overton: 4/16-17/02 (50 sp); Wauer, John and Gloria Tveten: 4/23-24/03 (45 sp). **13. Lost Maples SNA**—site visits by Mitch Heindel: 4/15/01 (20 sp), 4/5/03 (17 sp), 4/26/04; Derek Muschalek: 5/21/01 (34 sp), 5/15/04 (44 sp); Wauer: 4/23/01 (7 sp), 4/24/02 (39 sp). **14. Kerrville**—"Checklist of the Butterflies of Kerr County" by Tony Gallucci and colleagues (photocopy, 2001); July 4th Count (Wauer, coord.) on 6/20/02 (29 sp) and (Bill Lindemann, coord.) on 7/2/03 (26 sp); and site visits by Gallucci: 4/8&10/03 (23 sp), 4/13/03 (25 sp), 5/4-5/03 (28 sp), 9/26/03 (26 sp); Wauer: 3/27/01 (27 sp), 5/16/01 (22 sp), 6/6/01 (17 sp), 12/3/01 (6 sp). **15. Enchanted Rock SNA**—site visits by Dan Hardy: 5/22/01 (29 sp), 11/6/01 (26 sp), 4/15/03 (10 sp), 4/22/03 (31 sp); Joann Karges: 4/25/95 (29 sp); Mike Overton: 4/14/02 (20 sp); Wauer: 6/6/01 (8 sp), 5/13/02 (23 sp). **16. Inks Lake SP/Longhorn Cavern SP**—a July 4th Count (Bill Lindemann, coord.) on 8/10/02 (15 sp); and site visits by Joann Karges: 4/14-15/02 (17 sp); Mike Overton: 4/14/02 (12 sp); Wauer: 6/7/01 (36 sp), 4/11/02 (32 sp). **17. Balcones Canyonlands NWR**—"Butterflies of Balcones Canyonlands NWR," by Chuck Sexton (2002); and site visits by Wauer: 5/3/03 (19 sp), 6/1/03 (36 sp). **18. Austin**—"Guide to Butterflies of Austin" by Chris Durden (Texas Memorial Museum, 1990); Austin Butterfly Forum counts (Durden, coord.) on 7/13/03 (42 sp), 7/10/04 (43 sp); and site visits by Robert Brewer: 9/2/02 (18 sp), 9/2/03 (17 sp); Sibyl Deacon: 4/7/03 (21 sp); Durden: 10/25/01 (24 sp), 2/9/02 (15 sp), 2/15/02 (20 sp), 3/21/02 (16 sp), 3/27/02 (29 sp), 5/8/02 (26 sp), 11/12/02 (28 sp); Durden, Dan Hardy, Frank Hedges, Barbara Ribble: 7/12/03 (46 sp); Durden, Janet Rathjen: 2/20/02 (20 sp); Hardy: 7/22/99 (12 sp), 8/9/99 (12 sp), 9/21/99 (33 sp), 2/26/00 (14 sp), 7/7/01 (24 sp), 9/24/01 (24 sp), 10/24/01 (30 sp), 10/28/01 (39 sp), 12/5/01 (29 sp), 9/1-2/02 (33 sp), 4/23/03 (31 sp), 5/27/03 (46 sp), 11/19/03 (34 sp), 2/21/04 (15 sp); Mike Quinn: 5/5/01 (15 sp); Jeff Taylor: 11/16/03 (16 sp); Wauer: 1/23/02 (11 sp), 4/12-13/02 (42 sp), 11/6/02 (32 sp), 5/22/04 (32 sp); Wauer, Shannon Davies: 9/23/02 (36 sp), 5/2/03 (34 sp); Wauer, Hardy, Ribble: 4/12/03 (33 sp). **19. Guadalupe River SP**—site visits by Wauer: 5/22/01 (35 sp), 11/10/01 (28 sp), 4/10/02 (35 sp), 5/14/02 (36 sp), 8/20/02 (25 sp), 6/7/03 (27 sp). **20. Government Canyon SNA**—site visits by Wauer: 4/5/02 (25 sp); Wauer, Carl Green: 11/5/03 (43 sp); Wauer, Derek Muschalek, Green: 4/16/03 (51 sp), 5/23/03 (46 sp); Wauer, Muschalek, Barbara Ribble: 7/20/04 (60 sp).

Northern Plains Region

21. Lyndon B. Johnson NG—the USGS checklist, "Butterflies of Wise County, Texas;" "Species List for the LBJ Grasslands" (5/15/02) from Dale Clark's Dallas Butterflies web page (www.dallasbutterflies.com/Hotspots/html/lbj.html); a July 4th Wise/Montague Count (Claire Curry, coord.) on 7/8/04 (49 sp); a March 2003 Wise County list (82 sp) by Nick Grishin; and site visits by Clark and Dallas County Lep. Society: 4/5/03 (36 sp); Curry: 5/29/03, 6/26/03, 9/19/03; Joann Karges: 8/16/92 (13 sp), 6/13/93 (14 sp), 3/19/95 (7 sp), 5/17/97 (19 sp), 5/9/98 (27 sp), 5/13/00 (25 sp), 4/13/01 (22 sp), 5/12/02 (20 sp); Wauer: 10/4/02, 12/5/02; Wauer, Clark, Karges, Henry Turner: 5/8/03 (44 sp). **22. Lake Texoma/Hagerman NWR**—the USGS checklist, "Butterflies of Grayson County, Texas," and site visits by Joann Karges: 6/8-10/99 (21 sp); Mike Overton: 4/12/02 (9 sp), 9/20/02 (35 sp); Wauer: 10/4/02 (35 sp). **23. Caddo NG/Bonham SP**—the USGS checklist, "Butterflies of Fannin County, Texas," and site visits by Lucie Bruce: 3/23/02 (10 sp); Mike Overton: 9/21/02 (40 sp); Wauer: 10/5/02 (23 sp). **24. Fort Worth**—"Butterflies of Tarrant County, A Checklist" by Joann Karges (2002); July 4th Tarrant County Counts (Karges, coord.) on 6/21/97 (38 sp), 6/20/98 (44 sp), 6/19/99 (56 sp), 6/17/00 (60 sp), 6/16/01 (54 sp), 6/15/02 (52 sp), 6/14/03 (64 sp); and site visits by Karges: 5/8/92 (14 sp), 8/1/92 (14 sp), 10/31/92 (18 sp), 3/18/94 (13 sp), 10/29/94 (21 sp), 9/22/96 (27 sp), 10/29/96 (26 sp), 8/28/97 (17 sp), 9/6/98 (18 sp), 10/21/99 (24 sp), 11/28/99 (21 sp), 7/30/00 (22 sp), 10/1/00 (21 sp),

5/21/01 (28 sp), 6/23/01 (23 sp), 8/19/01 (22 sp), 11/25/01 (25 sp), 12/1/01 (20 sp), 1/25-26/04 (11 sp); Karges, Bill Edwards: 9/4/00 (24 sp), 1/3/03 (13 sp); Karges, Martin Reid: 5/24/01 (24 sp), 7/19/01 (22 sp); David Powell: 9/1/04 (31 sp); Reid: 6/18/01 (36 sp), 6/26/01 (41 sp), 7/13/01 (37 sp), 7/19/01 (31 sp), 3/25-26/03 (21 sp), 11/21/03 (32 sp); Reid, Karges: 11/1/03; Reid, Barbara Ribble: 7/3/03 (39 sp); Wauer, Karges, Reid: 10/2-3/02 (39 sp); Wauer, Ben and Jeff Basham, Karges: 3/29-30/04 (44 sp). **25. Dallas**—the on-line butterfly checklist of the Dallas County Lepidopterist Society at www.dallasbutterflies.com/ (maintained by Dale Clark) and site visits by Joann Karges: 6/9/01 (18 sp); Wauer: 10/6/02 (29 sp). **26. Heard Natural Science Museum and Wildlife Sanctuary**—the "Heard Butterfly Checklist;" July 4th Counts (Kenneth Steigman, coord.) on 6/28/97 (33 sp), 6/20/98 (46 sp); chapter review (add-ons) by Peter Heles; and site visits by Mike Moore: 11/2/03; Wauer: 10/7/02 (23 sp). **27. Meridian SP**—site visits by Joann Karges: 4/16 72 (11 sp), 3/16/94 (10 sp), 4/10/98 (9 sp), 5/8/99 (14 sp), 9/26-27/00 (23 sp); Wauer: 5/10/02 (33 sp), 6/6/03 (35 sp). **28. Waco**—the USGS checklist, "Butterflies of McLennan County, Texas;" a checklist of butterflies by Fred Gehlbach (photocopy, 1979); and site visits by Wauer: 10/1/02 (36 sp), 6/2/03 (30 sp); Wauer, Gehlbach: 5/9/02 (35 sp). **29. Gus Engeling WMA**—the USGS checklist, "Butterflies of Anderson County, Texas;" and site visits by Nick Grishin: 5/24/03 (31 sp); Wauer: 9/1/02 (26 sp), 5/9/03 (31 sp).

Pineywoods Region

30. Atlanta SP/Wright Patman Lake—the USGS checklist, "Butterflies of Cass County, Texas;" and site visits by Joann Karges: 5/24-25/99 (15 sp); Mike Overton: 5/1/01 (8 sp); Wauer: 7/3/02 (22 sp), 8/30/02 (31 sp). **31. Lake O' The Pines/Daingerfield SP**—the USGS checklist, "Butterflies of Harrison County, Texas," July 4th Daingerfield Counts (David Powell, coord.) on 7/20/97 (19 sp), 7/19/98 (15 sp), 7/16/00 (23 sp), 7/15/01 (40 sp), 7/14/02 (34 sp), 7/20/03 (38 sp), 8/2/04 (42 sp); and site visits by Mike Overton: 4/11/02 (17 sp); Wauer: 7/2/02 (24 sp). **32. Caddo Lake SP and Wildlife Management Area**—the USGS checklist, "Butterflies of Harrison County, Texas," and site visits by Mike Overton: 4/11/02 (16 sp); Wauer: 6/30/02 (23 sp). **33. Davy Crockett NF**—the USGS checklist, "Butterflies of Trinity County, Texas;" July 4th Davy Crockett NF Count (Lee Hoy, coord.) on 6/13/03 (22 sp); and site visits by Mike Overton: 4/9/02 (12 sp); Wauer: 6/28/02 (16 sp). **34. Angelina NF/Sam Rayburn Reservoir**—the USGS checklist, "Butterflies of San Augustine County, Texas;" a July 4th Angelina NF Count (David Henderson, coord.) on 7/25/04 (32 sp); and site visits by Derek Muschalek: 4/29/02 (32 sp); Mike Overton: 4/10/02 (20 sp); Wauer: 7/3/02 (21 sp), 8/30/02 (31 sp). **35. Sabine NF**—the USGS checklist, "Butterflies of San Augustine County, Texas;" July 4th Sabine NF Count (David Henderson, coord.) on 7/1/03 (32 sp); and site visits by Mike Overton: 4/10/02 (22 sp); Wauer: 6/29/02 (25 sp). **36. Sam Houston NF**—USGS checklists, "Butterflies of Montgomery, Walker and San Jacinto counties, Texas;" July 4th San Jacinto County Counts (David Henderson, coord.) on 6/25/01 (30 sp), 6/26/02 (17 sp), 6/26/03 (19 sp); July 4th Raven Butterfly Counts (Henderson, coord.) on 6/14/02 (30 sp) and (Diane Cabiness, coord.) on 6/13/03 (14 sp); and site visits by Bob Behrstock: 2/14/01 (9 sp), 4/4/01 (26 sp); David and Jan Dauphin: 2/24/01 (19 sp); Derek Muschalek: 4/28/02 (10 sp); Mike Overton: 7/11/01 (20 sp); Janet Rathjen: 2/16/02 (8 sp), 3/10/02 (13 sp), 4/14/02 (19 sp), 4/12/03 (19 sp); Wauer: 3/21/01 (32 sp), 8/28/01 (27 sp), 10/28/01 (19 sp), 6/29/03 (32 sp). **37. Martin Dies, Jr. SP/B.A. Steinhagen Lake**—the USGS checklist, "Butterflies of Tyler County, Texas;" a July 4th Martin Dies, Jr. SP Count (P.D. Hulce, coord.) on 7/21/02 (15 sp); and site visits by Joann Karges: 4/22-25/01 (14 sp); Wauer: 3/23/02 (17 sp), 6/12/02 (27 sp), 8/29/02 (24 sp), 7/1/03 (19 sp), 5/19/04 (31 sp). **38. Big Thicket Area**—the USGS checklists, "Butterflies of Hardin, Polk and Tyler counties, Texas;" "Checklist of the Lepidoptera of the Big Thicket National Preserve, Texas," by Charles Bordelon and Ed Knudson (*Tex. Lep. Survey Pub. 2*, 1999); July 4th Roy Larsen Sandylands Sanctuary Counts (Ken Sztraky, coord.) on 7/1/01 (31 sp), 6/30/02 (24 sp), 7/13/03 (29 sp); and site visits by P.D. Hulce: 3/22-23/03 (24 sp); Wauer: 3/22/02 (19 sp), 8/31/02 (26 sp), 7/2/03 (14 sp), 5/20/04 (26 sp); Wauer, Bordelon, Knudson: 3/23/02 (25 sp).

Central Plains Region

39. Buescher SP/Bastrop SP—the USGS checklist "Butterflies of Bastrop County, Texas," and site visits by Lee Hoy: 5/23/03 (16 sp); Derek Muschalek: 5/31/03 (23 sp); Wauer: 9/21/01 (26 sp), 3/23/02 (33 sp), 5/19/02 (34 sp), 6/27/02 (27 sp), 5/10/03 (28 sp); Wauer, Dan Hardy, Barbara Ribble: 6/9/03 (30 sp); Wauer: 4/13/03 (26 sp). **40. Somerville Lake**—the USGS checklists, "Butterflies of Burleson and Washington Counties, Texas," and site visits by Wauer: 10/29/01 (41 sp), 11/3/01 (37 sp), 5/17/02 (24 sp), 6/27/03 (28 sp). **41. Bryan**—

College Station—the USGS checklist, "Butterflies of Brazos County, Texas," and site visits by Wauer: 7/5/02 (20 sp), 6/28/03 (30 sp). **42. Palmetto SP**—a 1978 report, "Palmetto State Park Natural Resource Handbook: Appraisal, Synthesis, Management," by Laurence N. Lodwick and David N. Riskind; July 4th Palmetto SP Counts (Wauer, coord.) on 6/12/01 (31 sp), 8/1/02 (22 sp), 7/13/03 (34 sp), 7/22/04 (26 sp); and site visits by Wauer: 10/26/01 (37 sp), 4/1/02 (39 sp), 5/15/02 (24 sp). **43. Attwater Prairie-Chicken NWR**—July 4th Attwater Prairie-Chicken NWR Counts (P.D. Hulce, coord.) on 7/30/99 (23 sp), 6/27/00 (38 sp), 6/26/01 (30 sp), 6/25/02 (18 sp), 6/24/03 (27 sp); and a site visit by Wauer: 5/18/02 (21 sp). **44. DeWitt County**— "Butterfly Checklist for Dewitt County" (June 2002) by Derek Muschalek, and site visits by Muschalek: 11/01 (27 sp), 12/22/01 (24 sp), 1/23/02 (23 sp), 1/27/02 (24 sp), 3/21/02 (31 sp), 3/30/02 (37 sp), 4/1/02 (39 sp), 4/11/02 (35 sp), 4/25/02 (35 sp), 6/9/02 (30 sp), 7/13/02 (25 sp), 8/17/02 (38 sp), 9/17/02 (42 sp), 9/21/02 (46 sp), 9/28/02 (32 sp), 11/19/02 (45 sp), 1/1/03 (12 sp), 3/21/03 (35 sp), 4/7/03 (27 sp), 4/13/03 (44 sp), 5/11/03 (54 sp), 5/27/03 (30 sp), 5/28/03 (34 sp), 6/8/03 (45 sp), 7/3/03 (27 sp), 8/28/03 (38 sp), 10/23/03 (46 sp), 11/19/03 (49 sp), 5/31/04 (36 sp), 7/13/04 (28 sp), 8/1/04 (44 sp), 12/9/04 (48 sp); Wauer: 3/24/03 (24 sp). **45. Victoria**—the USGS checklist, "Butterflies of Victoria County, Texas;" July 4th Victoria Counts (Wauer, coord.) on 6/13/98 (47 sp), 6/26/99 (53 sp), 6/3/00 (52 sp), 7/14/01 (53 sp), 6/25/02 (33 sp), 6/24/03 (51 sp), 6/27/04 (49 sp); and site visits by Wauer: 6/2/99 (19 sp), 6/9/99 (21 sp), 6/29/99 (26 sp), 8/15/99 (12 sp), 8/26/99 (9 sp), 11/10/99 (43 sp), 11/11/99 (27 sp), 11/29/99 (24 sp), 3/13/00 (8 sp), 5/29/00 (25 sp), 8/12/00 (13 sp), 9/18/00 (8 sp), 5/29/03 (34 sp), 9/5/03 (41 sp), 9/16/03 (37 sp).

Upper Gulf Coast Region

46. Texas Point/Sabine Woods—an article "Collecting in Sabine Pass, Texas," by Ed Knudson and Charles Bordelon (*So. Lep. Soc. News*, 2002); July 4th Sea Rim Counts (Ken Sztraky, coord.) on 6/21/98 (12 sp), 7/18/99 (13 sp), 7/16/00 (25 sp), 6/10/01 (26 sp), 6/23/02 (28 sp), 6/22/03 (26 sp); and site visits by David Dauphin: 6/16/01 (21 sp); Mike Overton: 4/7/02 (12 sp); Wauer: 5/1/02 (15 sp). **47. Anahuac NWR/High Island**—"Butterfly list for Anahuac NWR" by David Sarkozi (Sept. 2001); July 4th High Island Counts (P.D. Hulce, coord.) on 7/26/97 (26 sp), 7/11/98 (24 sp), 7/3/99 (36 sp), 7/1/00 (32 sp), 6/30/01 (42 sp), 6/29/02 (33 sp), 6/29/03 (33 sp); and (Sarkozi, coord.) on 7/11/04 (36 sp); and site visits by David Dauphin: 10/28/01 (26 sp); Mike Overton: 4/7/02 (9 sp); Janet Rathjen: 5/17/03 (13 sp), 10/4/03 (17 sp); Wauer: 4/30/02, 4/3/03 (13 sp). **48. Galveston–Texas City**—the USGS Checklist, "Butterflies of Galveston County, Texas," July 4th Galveston Counts (P.D. Hulse, coord.) on 8/5/00 (26 sp), 7/5/01 (38 sp), 7/27/02 (29 sp), 7/5/03 (36 sp); and site visits by Nick Block: 3/13/02 (12 sp); Bob Behrstock: 2/15/01; Wauer: 5/30/02 (12 sp), 11/8/02 (16 sp), 4/5/03 (11 sp). **49. Baytown**—"Butterflies of the Baytown Nature Center" (photocopy); July 4th Baytown Counts (Sallie Sherman, coord.) on 7/2/99 (26 sp), 7/14/00 (30 sp), 7/6/02 (37 sp), 7/5/03 (33 sp), 7/3/04 (43 sp); and site visits by Craig Marks: 5/26/02 (16 sp); Derek Muschalek: 4/28/01 (20 sp); Wauer: 5/2/02 (33 sp), 11/9/02 (20 sp). **50. Houston**—July 4th Houston Counts (P.D. Hulce, coord.) on 8/3/00 (31 sp), 7/4/01 (40 sp), 7/4/02 (39 sp), 7/4/03 (39 sp); and a site visit by Wauer, David and Ednelza Henderson: 11/17/02 (21 sp). **51. Freeport**—July 4th Freeport Counts (David Heinicke, coord.) on 7/8/00 (55 sp), 7/7/01 (55 sp), 6/23/03 (54 sp); and (Gardner Cambell, coord.) on 7/6/02 (44 sp); the nearby July 4th Dancinger Counts (Charles Brower, coord.) on 7/8/01 (63 sp), and (Campbell, coord.) on 7/7/02 (49 sp), and (Heinicke, coord.) on 6/30/03 (44 sp); and site visits by Brower: 10/5/99 (6 sp), 11/2/99 (14 sp), 12/6/99 (9 sp), 3/3/00 (15 sp), 8/21/00 (8 sp), 9/11/00 (22 sp), 6/11/01 (28 sp); Wauer: 3/6/02 (15 sp), 9/12/02 (17 sp). **52. Brazos Bend SP**—"The Butterflies of Brazos Bend State Parks A Checklist," compiled by P.D. Hulce, Sandra West, Mike Quinn, and David Heinicke (TPWD); July 4th Brazos Bend Counts (Hulce, coord.) on 6/21/97 (38 sp), 6/20/98 (47 sp), 6/26/99 (40 sp), 6/24/00 (50 sp), 6/23/01 (57 sp), 6/23/02 (41 sp), 6/21/03 (50 sp); and (Rich and Sandy Jespersen, coord.) on 6/19/04 (40 sp); and site visits by Hulce and others: 5/24/03 (32 sp); Joann Karges: 4/27-30/98 (21 sp), 10/20/01 (21 sp); Wauer, Rob Thacker: 6/23/00 (43 sp). **53. Matagorda County**—the USGS checklist, "Butterflies of Matagorda County, Texas," and site visits by Wauer: 3/12/01 (9 sp), 9/11/02 (36 sp), 12/15/02 (15 sp), 4/2/03 (16 sp), 6/13/03 (26 sp), 8/4/04 (34 sp).

Central Gulf Coast Region

54. Indianola/Magic Ridge—July 4th Indianola Counts (Wauer, coord.) on 6/17/01 (36 sp), 7/11/02 (28 sp), 6/20/03 (30 sp), 7/16/04 (26 sp); and site visits by Wauer: 10/30/00 (14 sp), 3/22/01 (13 sp), 6/2/01 (30 sp), 10/14/01 (40 sp), 12/14/01 (26 sp), 3/7/02 (17 sp), 5/5/02 (26 sp), 9/18/02 (24 sp), 11/11/02 (35 sp),

12/21/02 (16 sp), 4/25/03 (32 sp), 4/14/04 (20 sp), 11/6/04 (37 sp); Wauer, David and Jan Dauphin: 4/25/03 (29 sp). **55. Aransas NWR**—a report, "Butterfly Summary of Aransas National Wildlife Refuge 1997," by Charlie Sassine; July 4th Aransas NWR Counts (Wauer, coord.) on 6/27/98 (47 sp), 6/12/99 (52 sp), 6/10/00 (61 sp), 7/7/01 (62 sp), 6/22/02 (40 sp), 6/22/03 (40 sp), 7/17/04 (35 sp); and site visits by Derek Muschalek: 5/17/03 (46 sp); Wauer: 9/29/03 (30 sp), 4/8/04 (46 sp); Wauer, Muschalek: 5/29/04 (29 sp). **56. Rockport/ Goose Island SP**—July 4th Rockport Counts (Wauer, coord.) on 7/11/03 (40 sp), 7/24/04 (37 sp); and site visits by Wauer: 9/11/01 (22 sp), 11/1/01 (29 sp), 2/22/02 (26 sp), 5/30/02 (31 sp), 7/20/02 (37 sp). **57. Hazel Bazemore County Park/Pollywog Pond**—"List of Butterfly Species Observed from September 2001 through June 3, 2003," by Mary Kathryn Mauel (email); "List of Butterfly Species Nueces County Cemetery," by Mauel (email); and site visits by Mauel: 8/28/03; Derek Muschalek: 10/22/01 (45 sp), 10/21/02 (45 sp); Wauer: 9/18/01 (31 sp), 2/24/02 (40 sp), 5/29/02 (30 sp), 10/20/02 (39 sp). **58. Corpus Christi**—"Checklist of the Butterflies of Hans Suter Wildlife Area" by Charlie Sassine (1995); "List of Butterfly Species Observed on Museum Grounds," by Mary Kathryn Mauel (2003); "Comprehensive List of Butterfly Species, Botanical Gardens," by Mauel (2003); and site visits by Mauel: 2/8/02 (23 sp), 3/16/02 (16 sp), 9/24/02 (11 sp), 11/6/02 (17 sp), 12/22/02 (15 sp), 2/1/03 (11 sp), 4/5/03 (12 sp), 4/8/03 (16 sp), 4/9/03 (20 sp), 4/19/03 (15 sp), 4/26/03 (17 sp), 5/13/03 (22 sp), 6/21/03 (20 sp), 7/2/03 (17 sp), 8/28/03 (11 sp), 9/23/03 (10 sp), 10/25/03 (24 sp), 11/29/03 (27 sp), 1/25-26/04 (21 sp); Mike Overton: 4/1/02 (28 sp); Sassine: 11/19/01, 1/15&17/02 (32 sp), 1/21/02, 3/21/02; Wauer: 9/18/01 (13 sp), 5/29/02 (12 sp), 3/27/03 (27 sp); Wauer, Mauel: 5/15/03 (29 sp). **59. Padre Island/Mustang Island**—"Padre Island Checklist as of 6/21/2003" by Charlie Sassine (2003), and site visits by Sassine: 12/29/01 (11 sp); Willie Sekula: 8/23/03; Wauer: 9/19/01 (19 sp), 2/23/02 (21 sp). **60. Kingsville**—July 4th Kleberg County Counts (Sibyl Deacon, coord.) on 6/26/03 (42 sp), 7/23/04 (51 sp); and site visits by Deacon: 2/25/02 (20 sp), 3/22/02 (26 sp), 1/30/03 (11 sp), 4/14/03 (26 sp), 8/25/03, 11/14/03 (36 sp), 1/25/04 (26 sp), 11/21/04 (32 sp); Derek Muschalek: 10/21/02 (37 sp); Muschalek, Rob Thacker: 1/21/03 (15 sp); Wauer: 5/30/02 (24 sp), 1/31/03 (12 sp), 11/21/03 (43 sp); Wauer, Deacon: 11/27/01 (26 sp), 7/23/02 (37 sp), 10/20/02 (43 sp); Wauer, Deacon, Anse Windham: 3/14/02 (35 sp).

South Texas Brushland Region

61. Del Rio/Amistad NRA—the USGS checklist, "Butterflies of Val Verde County, Texas," and site visits by Mike Overton: 8/1-2/01 (32 sp), 7/30-31/02 (49 sp), 10/30/02 (32 sp); Wauer, Eric Finkelstein: 11/11/01 (14 sp), 6/12-13/02 (38 sp); Wauer, Eric and Sally Finkelstein: 9/30/04 (46 sp). **62. Park Chalk Bluff**—site visits by Wauer: 4/22/02 (35 sp), 11/13/02 (46 sp), 4/21/03 (28 sp), 9/22/03 (49 sp), 5/7/04 (34 sp). **63. Hondo–Castroville**—the USGS checklist, "Butterflies of Medina County, Texas;" "Butterflies of Landmark Inn State Historic Park" by June Secrist (1999); and site visits by Craig Marks: 8/22/01 (19 sp); Derek Muschalek: 4/21/02 (41 sp), 6/2/02 (31 sp), 9/25/02 (40 sp); Muschalek, Rob Thacker: 6/10/01 (26 sp); Wauer: 11/29/01 (7 sp), 4/14/02 (15 sp), 4/16/02 (32 sp), 11/14/02 (44 sp), 4/21/03 (40 sp), 9/23/03 (47 sp), 9/24/04 (48 sp), 11/19/04 (35 sp); Wauer, Paul Miliotis: 6/6/01 (16 sp). **64. San Antonio**—the USGS Checklist, "Butterflies of Bexar County, Texas," and site visits by Sheridan Coffey: 11/16/03 (24 sp); Matt Heindel: 9/3/01 (31 sp), 2/23/02 (20 sp); Heindel, Willie Sekula: 7/27/02 (15 sp); Wauer: 4/5/02 (25 sp), 5/16/02 (23 sp), 11/15/02 (24 sp), 3/21/02 (37 sp), 9/24/03 (40 sp); Wauer, Paul Miliotis: 6/5/01 (37 sp). Note: The extensive list, with numerous strays and accidentals, is due to a long-term database developed by Roy Kendall and included in the USGS checklist. **65. Goliad**—a July 4th Count (Wauer, coord.) on 7/2/04 (47 sp), and site visits by Derek Muschelek: 9/21/02 (46 sp), 1/4/03 (8 sp), 4/5/03 (26 sp), 3/6/04 (30 sp); Muschelek, Rob Thacker: 4/8/01 (38 sp), 4/15/02 (35 sp); Wauer: 5/30/01 (28 sp), 11/7/01 (45 sp), 5/23/02 (32 sp), 3/31/03 (32 sp), 4/18/03 (36 sp), 6/18/03 (47 sp). **66. Choke Canyon SP**—a July 4th Count (Wauer, coord.) on 7/26/04 (43 sp); and site visits by Matt Heindel: 11/9/02 (36 sp); Willie Sekula: 12/5/04 (29 sp); Wauer: 9/6/01 (14 sp), 10/16/01 (45 sp), 10/22/01 (35 sp), 3/13/02 (33 sp), 4/27/02 (36 sp), 6/3/02 (34 sp); Wauer, Jimmy Jackson: 9/28/02 (40 sp); Wauer, Jackson: 6/21/03 (31 sp).

Lower Rio Grande Valley Region

67. San Ygnacio/Zapata—the USGS checklist, "Butterflies of Zapata County, Texas;" and site visits by Martin Reid: 11/2/04; Mike Overton: 7/30/02 (28 sp), 10/24/02 (43 sp); Wauer: 9/5/01 (28 sp), 10/16/01 (42 sp), 2/7/02 (32 sp), 2/2/03 (25 sp); Wauer, Ben Basham: 11/28/00, 10/17/01, 2/27/03 (21 sp). **68. Falcon SP/ Roma–Los Saenz**—a report on collections at Falcon State Park by Floyd and June Preston, 11/5/00; July

4th Falcon Woodlands Counts (Joe Ideker, coord.) on 7/19/97 (26 sp), 8/15/98 (14 sp), 7/6/99 (37 sp); and (P.D. Hulce, coord.) on 7/16/00 (43 sp), 7/12/01 (39 sp), 7/11/02 (34 sp), 7/12/03 (45 sp); and site visits by Buck and Linda Cooper: 10/16/03 (51 sp), 10/28/03 (44 sp); Jerry McWilliams: 11/6/01; Derek Muschalek: 11/2/03 (48 sp); Charlie Sassine: 1/3/02, 3/12/02, 4/7/02, 7/21/02, 9/23/02, 11/3/02, 12/11/02, 5/25/03; Wauer: 12/16/98, 9/3/01, 10/17/01 (40 sp), 2/8/02 (35 sp), 2/2/03 (19 sp), 7/6/03; Wauer, Ben Basham: 11/29/99 (31 sp); Wauer, Mike Overton: 10/21/99 (54 sp). **69. NABA International Butterfly Park/ Bentsen-Rio Grande Valley SP**—"An Annotated Checklist of the Butterflies (Lepidoptera: Rhopalocera) of Bentsen-Rio Grande Valley State Park and Vicinity" by W.W. McGuire and Mike A. Rickard (1974); report of collections by Floyd and June Preston: 3/2/00; July 4th Bentsen-Rio Grande Valley SP Counts (P.D. Hulce, coord.) on 7/14/00 (28 sp), 7/14/01 (46 sp), 7/13/02 (53 sp), 7/11/03 (57 sp); and site visits by Randy Emmitt: 12/6/04 (66 sp); Dave Hanson, Derek Muschalek: 11/7/03; Hanson and others: 12/7/04 (90 sp); Wauer: 10/16/02 (53 sp), 2/7/04 (41 sp); Wauer, Ben Basham: 11/29/99 (37 sp), 11/9/00 (47 sp), 11/27/00 (16 sp), 11/29/00 (36 sp); Wauer, Basham, Hanson: 11/11/02; Wauer, Hanson, Muschalek: 10/14/03 (64 sp). **70. Edinburg World Birding Center**—a preliminary checklist by Richard Lehman (2003); July 4th Edinburg WBC Count (Gil Quintanilla, coord.) on 7/21/04 (52 sp); and site visits by Ben Basham: 12/8/03 (72 sp), 12/14/03 (57 sp); Quintanilla: 10/8/03 (38 sp); Wauer: 2/1/03, 10/15/03 (45 sp). **71. Santa Ana NWR**—"Checklist of Butterflies of Santa Ana National Wildlife Refuge" by Edward Knudson and Mike Quinn (Nov. 2002); July 4th Santa Ana NWR Counts (Joe Ideker, coord.) on 6/1/97 (42 sp), 6/18/98 (28 sp), 6/9/99 (47 sp); and (P.D. Hulce, coord.) on 7/13/00 (52 sp), 7/15/01 (62 sp), 7/14/02 (76 sp), 7/13/03 (65 sp); and site visits by Ben Basham: 12/2/03 (73 sp); Buck and Linda Cooper: 10/14/03 (62 sp), 10/18/03 (74 sp), 10/19/03 (76 sp), 10/25/03 (69 sp), 10/31/03 (72 sp); Dave Hanson: 4/10/03 (27 sp), 3/1/04 (31 sp); Hanson, Mike Overton: 9/27-28/03 (90 sp); Eugene Rouse, Jeff Glassberg, Jane Scott: 6/18/01 (42 sp); Wauer: 12/14/99 (29 sp), 1/7/00 (43 sp), 10/20/01, 2/9/02 (34 sp), 7/28/02 (41 sp), 10/17/02 (57 sp); Wauer, Ben Basham: 10/20/99 (58 sp), 11/27/99 (52 sp), 1/8/00 (41 sp), 11/9/00 (55 sp), 11/27/00 (38 sp), 11/29/00 (34 sp), 12/1/00 (47 sp), 1/5/03 (49 sp); Wauer, Basham, Overton: 10/17/00 (49 sp); Wauer, Ben and Jeff Basham, Hanson: 11/19&23/02 (78 sp); Wauer, Hanson, Derek Muschalek, Janet Rathjen: 10/13/03 (87 sp); Wauer and Overton: 7/16/01 (52 sp); Wauer, David and Jan Dauphin, Rathjen: 10/20/03 (80 sp); Wauer, Richard Lehman, Muschalek: 9/14/04 (46 sp). **72. Weslaco**— the "Seasonal Butterfly Checklist of the Valley Nature Center" by Mike Quinn (2001), and site visits by Carrie Cate: 6/6/01, 8/4/01 (35 sp), 10/7-8/01 (50 sp), 10/13-14/01 (56 sp), 10/27/01 (58 sp), 11/4/01 (60 sp); Elizabeth Cavazos: all of Dec. 2001 (82 sp); Randy Emmitt: 12/5/04 (46 sp); Wauer, Ben Basham: 12/1/00 (26 sp), 12/12/00, 1/4/03 (50 sp); Wauer, Ben and Jeff Basham: 11/19&21/02 (66 sp); Wauer, Muschalek: 9/13/04 (35 sp). **73. Hugh Ramsey Nature Park**—"Hugh Ramsey Nature Park Butterfly List," courtesy of Mark Conway, and site visits by Wauer, Ben Basham: 11/11/00, 11/28/00; Wauer, Basham, Carl and Beverly Swafford: 10/29/03; Wauer, Muschalek: 9/13/04 (29 sp). **74. Los Ebanos Preserve**—a butterfly checklist for Los Ebanos (2003) and site visits by Dave Hanson: 1/25/04 (28 sp); David and Ednelza Henderson: 12/2/02 (20 sp); Wauer: 1/4/03 (38 sp), 1/31/03 (19 sp). **75. Sabal Palm Audubon Center and Sanctuary**— "Checklist of the Audubon Sabal Palm Grove Sanctuary" by Ed Knudson and Charles Bordelon (2001); July 4th Brownsville Counts (P.D. Hulce, coord.) on 7/11/00 (28 sp), 7/10/01 (58 sp), 7/10/02 (44 sp), 7/9/03 (52 sp); and (Gil Quintanilla, coord.) on 7/17/04 (52 sp); and site visits by Ben Basham: 12/15/03 (53 sp); Buck and Linda Cooper: 10/30/03 (32 sp); Knudson, Bordelon, Eugene Rouse: 8/5/01 (57 sp); Jerry McWilliams: 11/19/01 (46 sp); Mike Overton: 11/11/01 (66 sp), 11/19/01 (67 sp), 3/29/02 (51 sp), 7/27/02 (51 sp); Rouse, Jeff Glassberg, Jane Scott: 6/18/01 (42 sp); Wauer: 7/24-25/02 (45 sp); Wauer, Ben Basham: 11/19/00 (29 sp), 11/30/00 (66 sp); Wauer, Overton: 10/17/03 (46 sp). **76. Laguna Atascosa NWR**—the "Laguna Atascosa NWR Butterfly Checklist-09/2001" by Ellie Thompson; July 4th Laguna Atascosa Counts (P.D. Hulse, coord.) on 7/7/03 (46 sp), and (Gil Quintanilla, coord.) on 7/18/04 (56 sp); and site visits by Bob Behrstock: 9/24/01 (30 sp); Buck and Linda Cooper: 10/29/03 (50 sp); Mike Overton: 11/19/01 (69 sp), 3/29/02 (47 sp); Wauer: 12/15/98 (16 sp); Wauer, Mike Hannisian, Susan Fuller, Thompson: 7/27/02 (57 sp); Wauer, Overton: 7/15/01 (33 sp).

Appendix 4
Checklist of Texas Butterflies

The following checklist follows the taxonomic order established by the North American Butterfly Association. It utilizes NABA common and scientific names, but when scientific names used by Opler and Warren (2002) differ, they are included in parentheses. Months when the species have been recorded in Texas are also included; these were derived from several sources, including Glassberg (1999, 2001), Howe (1975), Kendall (1963), Neck (1996), Pyle (1995), Lepidopterist Society Seasonal Summaries (1973 to 2003), and the site-visit reports used for the regional checklists.

Note: Strays from Mexico that are not yet on the NABA list are indicated by an asterisk.

Swallowtails (Family Papilionidae)

Swallowtails (Subfamily Papilioninae)

____ Pipevine Swallowtail *Battus philenor* [Jan-Dec]
____ Polydamas Swallowtail *Battus polydamas* [Mar-Jan]
____ Zebra Swallowtail *Eurytides marcellus* [Mar-May, Jul-Nov]
____ Dark Kite-Swallowtail *Eurytides philolaus* [Jul, Oct]
____ Black Swallowtail *Papilio polyxenes* [Jan-Dec]
____ Thoas Swallowtail *Papilio thoas* [Apr-Jul, Sep, Oct]
____ Giant Swallowtail *Papilio cresphontes* [Jan-Dec]
____ Ornythion Swallowtail *Papilio ornythion* [Mar-Jun, Aug-Nov]
____ Broad-banded Swallowtail *Papilio astyalus* [Apr, Aug-Oct]
____ Eastern Tiger Swallowtail *Papilio glaucus* [Feb-Nov]
____ Western Tiger Swallowtail *Papilio rutulus* [Jun-Jul]
____ Two-tailed Swallowtail *Papilio multicaudata* [Feb-Nov]
____ Three-tailed Swallowtail *Papilio pilumnus* [May]
____ Spicebush Swallowtail *Papilio troilus* [Mar-Nov]
____ Palamedes Swallowtail *Papilio palamedes* [Mar-Dec]
____ Magnificent Swallowtail *Papilio garamas* [Sep, Oct]
____ Victorine Swallowtail *Papilio victorinus* [Aug]
____ Pink-spotted Swallowtail *Papilio pharnaces* (*P. rogeri*) [Apr]
____ Ruby-spotted Swallowtail *Papilio anchisiades* [Apr-Jul, Sep-Dec]

Whites and Sulphurs (Family Pieridae)

Whites (Subfamily Pierinae)

____ Mexican Dartwhite *Catasticta nimbice* [Mar-May]
____ Florida (Tropical) White *Appias drusilla* [Mar-May, Jul-Dec]
____ Mountain White* *Leptophobia aripa* [Oct]
____ Cross-barred White* *Itaballia demophile* [Dec]
____ Spring White *Pontia sisymbrii* [Mar-Apr]
____ Checkered White *Pontia protodice* [Jan-Dec]
____ Mustard White *Pieris napi* (*P. angelika*) [Apr-Aug]
____ Cabbage White *Pieris rapae* [Apr-Jul, Oct-Dec]
____ Great Southern White *Ascia monuste* [Jan-Dec]
____ Giant White *Ganyra josephina* [Mar-Jan]
____ Pearly Marble *Euchloe hyantis* [Mar-May]

_____ Olympia Marble *Euchloe olympia* [Mar-May]
_____ Desert Orangetip *Anthocharis cethura* [Feb-Mar]
_____ Sara Orangetip *Anthocharis sara* [Feb-Apr]
_____ Falcate Orangetip *Anthocharis midea* [Feb-Apr]

Sulphurs (Subfamily Coliadinae)
_____ Clouded Sulphur *Colias philodice* [Mar-Dec]
_____ Orange Sulphur *Colias eurytheme* [Jan-Dec]
_____ Southern Dogface *Colias cesonia* (*Zerene cesonia*) [Jan-Dec]
_____ Common Melwhite* *Melete lycimnia isandra* [Nov]
_____ White Angled-Sulphur *Anteos clorinde* [Mar-May, Jul-Jan]
_____ Yellow Angled-Sulphur *Anteos maerula* [Feb-Dec]
_____ Cloudless Sulphur *Phoebis sennae* [Jan-Dec]
_____ Orange-barred Sulphur *Phoebis philea* [Apr, Jul-Jan]
_____ Large Orange Sulphur *Phoebis agarithe* [Jan-Dec]
_____ Tailed Sulphur *Phoebis neocypris* [Oct, Nov]
_____ Statira Sulphur *Phoebis statira* (*Aphrissa statira*) [Feb, Jun]
_____ Lyside Sulphur *Kricogonia lyside* [Jan-Dec]
_____ Barred Yellow *Eurema daira* [Aug-Dec]
_____ Ghost Yellow *Eurema albula* [Nov]
_____ Boisduval's Yellow *Eurema boisduvaliana* [Apr-Jan]
_____ Mexican Yellow *Eurema mexicana* [Jan-Dec]
_____ Salome Yellow *Eurema salome* [Sep]
_____ Tailed Orange *Eurema proterpia* (*Pyrisitia proterpia*) [Jun-Jan]
_____ Little Yellow *Eurema lisa* (*Pyrisitia lisa*) [Jan-Dec]
_____ Mimosa Yellow *Eurema nise* (*Pyrisitia nise*) [Aug-Jan]
_____ Dina Yellow *Eurema dina* (*Pyrisitia dina*) [Apr, Jul, Sep]
_____ Sleepy Orange *Eurema nicippe* (*Abaeis nicippe*) [Jan-Dec]
_____ Dainty Sulphur *Nathalis iole* [Jan-Dec]

Mimic-Whites (Subfamily Dismorphiinae)
_____ Costa-spotted Mimic-White *Enantia albania* [Sep]

Gossamer-wing Butterflies (Family Lycaenidae)

Harvesters (Subfamily Miletinae)
_____ Harvester *Feniseca tarquinius* [Mar, Jul-Sep]

Coppers (Subfamily Lycaeninae)
_____ Gray Copper *Lycaena dione* [May-Aug]

Hairstreaks (Subfamily Theclinae)
_____ Mexican Cycadian* *Eumaeus toxea* [Mar]
_____ Colorado Hairstreak *Hypaurotis crysalus* [Jun-Aug]
_____ Strophius Hairstreak *Allosmaitia strophius* [Oct, Nov]
_____ Great Purple Hairstreak *Atlides halesus* [Jan-Dec]
_____ Gold-bordered Hairstreak *Rekoa palegon* [Nov]
_____ Zebrina Hairstreak* *Rekoa zebrina* [Sep-Nov]
_____ Marius Hairstreak *Rekoa marius* [Sep-Dec]
_____ Stag (Smudged) Hairstreak* *Rekoa stagira* [Nov]
_____ Black Hairstreak *Ocaria ocrisia* [Jan, Nov]
_____ Telea Hairstreak *Chlorostrymon telea* [Jun]

_____ Silver-banded Hairstreak *Chlorostrymon simaethis* [Jan-Dec]
_____ Soapberry Hairstreak *Phaeostrymon alcestis* [Apr-Aug]
_____ Coral Hairstreak *Satyrium titus* [Jun-Aug]
_____ Behr's Hairstreak *Satyrium behrii* [Jul]
_____ Edwards' Hairstreak *Satyrium edwardsii* [Jan-Jul, Nov-Dec]
_____ Banded Hairstreak *Satyrium calanus* [Mar-Jun]
_____ King's Hairstreak *Satyrium kingi* [May-Jun]
_____ Striped Hairstreak *Satyrium liparops* [May, Jul-Aug]
_____ Oak Hairstreak *Satyrium favonius* [Apr-Jun]
_____ Poling's Hairstreak *Satryrium polingi* [May-Jun, Aug-Sep]
_____ Clench's Greenstreak *Cyanophrys miserabilis* [Apr-Dec]
_____ Goodson's Greenstreak *Cyanophrys goodsoni* [May-Dec]
_____ Tropical Greenstreak *Cyanophrys herodotus* [May, Jun, Oct, Nov]
_____ Xami Hairstreak *Callophrys xami* [Jun-Dec]
_____ Sandia Hairstreak *Callophrys mcfarlandi* [Apr-Aug]
_____ Frosted Elfin *Callophrys irus* [Mar-May]
_____ Henry's Elfin *Callophrys henrici* [Feb-May]
_____ Eastern Pine Elfin *Callophrys niphon* [Feb-Apr]
_____ Thicket Hairstreak *Callophrys spinetorum* [Mar-Oct]
_____ Juniper Hairstreak *Callophrys gryneus* [Mar-Sep]
_____ Aquamarine Hairstreak *Oenomaus ortygnus* [Nov, Dec]
_____ White M Hairstreak *Parrhasius m-album* [Feb-Oct]
_____ Gray Hairstreak *Strymon melinus* [Jan-Dec]
_____ Red-crescent Scrub-Hairstreak *Strymon rufofusca* [Mar-Jan]
_____ Red-lined Scrub-Hairstreak *Strymon bebrycia* [Jan, Oct, Nov]
_____ Yojoa Scrub-Hairstreak *Strymon yojoa* [Apr, Oct-Jan]
_____ White Scrub-Hairstreak *Strymon albata* [Apr, Jun-Dec]
_____ Lacey's Scrub-Hairstreak *Strymon alea* [Apr, Jun-Jul, Sep-Dec]
_____ Mallow Scrub-Hairstreak *Strymon istapa* [Jan-Dec]
_____ Tailless Scrub-Hairstreak *Strymon cestri* [Mar]
_____ Lantana Scrub-Hairstreak *Strymon bazochii* [Jan-Mar, May, Oct-Dec]
_____ Bromeliad Scrub-Hairstreak *Strymon serapio* [Mar-Nov]
_____ Ruddy Hairstreak *Electrostrymon sangala* [Apr, Oct-Dec]
_____ Muted Hairstreak *Electrostrymon canus (E. joya)* [?]
_____ Red-banded Hairstreak *Calycopis cecrops* [Feb-Oct]
_____ Dusky-blue Groundstreak *Calycopis isobeon* [Jan-Dec]
_____ Mountain Groundstreak* *Ziegleria guzanta* [Jan, Mar, Jun, Sep]
_____ Red-spotted Hairstreak *Tmolus echion* [May]
_____ Pearly-gray Hairstreak *Siderus tephraeus (Strephonota tephraceus)* [Sep-Dec]
_____ Leda Ministreak *Ministrymon leda* [Mar-Jul, Sep-Nov]
_____ Clytie Ministreak *Ministrymon clytie* [Jan-Dec]
_____ Gray Ministreak *Ministrymon azia* [Mar-Oct]
_____ Arizona Hairstreak *Erora quaderna* [Mar-May, Jul-Sep]

Blues (Subfamily Polyommatinae)
_____ Western Pygmy-Blue *Brephidium exile* [Jan-Dec]
_____ Eastern Pygmy-Blue *Brephidium isophthalma* [Mar, May, Nov]
_____ Cassius Blue *Leptotes cassius* [Jan-Dec]
_____ Marine Blue *Leptotes marina* [Jan-Dec]
_____ Cyna Blue *Zizula cyna* [Mar-Jan]

____ Ceraunus Blue *Hemiargus ceraunus* [Jan-Dec]
____ Reakirt's Blue *Hemiargus isola* (*Echinargus isola*) [Jan-Dec]
____ Eastern Tailed-Blue *Everes comyntas* (*Cupido comyntas*) [Mar-May, Sep-Dec]
____ Spring Azure *Celastrina ladon* [Jan-Oct]
____ Summer Azure *Celastrina ladon neglecta* (*Celastrina neglecta*) [Jun-Oct]
____ Rita Blue *Euphilotes rita* [Jan-Sep]
____ Silvery Blue *Glaucophsyche lygdamus* [Mar-May]
____ Melissa Blue *Lycaeides melissa* (*Plebejus melissa*) [Apr-Oct]
____ Acmon Blue *Plebejus acmon* [Feb-Dec]

Metalmarks (Family Riodinidae)

____ Little Metalmark *Calephelis virginiensis* [Mar-Oct]
____ Fatal Metalmark *Calephelis nemesis* [Jan-Dec]
____ Rounded Metalmark *Calephelis perditalis* [Jan-Dec]
____ Rawson's Metalmark *Calephelis rawsoni* [Feb-Nov]
____ Arizona Metalmark *Calephelis arizonensis* [May]
____ Red-bordered Metalmark *Caria ino* [Jan-Dec]
____ Blue Metalmark *Lasaia sula* [Jan-Dec]
____ Red-bordered Pixie *Melanis pixe* [Apr, May, Jul-Jan]
____ Zela Metalmark *Emesis zela* [Sep]
____ Curve-winged Metalmark *Emesis emesia* [Feb, May-Dec]
____ Falcate Metalmark *Emesis tenedia* [Oct]
____ Mormon (Mexican) Metalmark *Apodemia mormo mejicanus* (*A. mejicanus*) [Mar-Oct]
____ Mormon (Dury's) Metalmark *Apodemia mormo duryi* (*A. duryi*) [May, Aug-Sep]
____ Narrow-winged Metalmark *Apodemia multiplaga* [Oct, Nov]
____ Hepburn's Metalmark *Apodemia hepburni* [Jul]
____ Palmer's Metalmark *Apodemia palmeri* [Apr-Nov]
____ Walker's Metalmark *Apodemia walkeri* [May-Aug, Oct-Dec]
____ "Chisos" Nais Metalmark *Apodemia nais chisosensis* [Apr-Aug]

Brushfooted Butterflies (Family Nymphalidae)

Snouts (Subfamily Libytheinae)
____ American Snout *Libytheana carinenta* [Jan-Dec]

Heliconians and Fritillaries (Subfamily Heliconiinae)
____ Gulf Fritillary *Agraulis vanillae* [Jan-Dec]
____ Mexican Silverspot *Dione moneta* [Apr-Jan]
____ Banded Orange Heliconian *Dryadula phaetusa* [Mar, Aug, Nov]
____ Julia Heliconian *Dryas iulia* [Jan-Dec]
____ Isabella's Heliconian *Eueides isabella* [Apr-May, Jul, Oct-Dec]
____ Zebra Heliconian *Heliconius charithonia* (*H. charithonias*) [Jan-Dec]
____ Erato Heliconian *Heliconius erato* [Jan, Jun, Aug, Dec]
____ Variegated Fritillary *Euptoieta claudia* [Jan-Dec]
____ Mexican Fritillary *Euptoieta hegesia* [Mar, Jul-Dec]
____ Great Spangled Fritillary *Speyeria cybele* [Sep]

True Brushfoots (Subfamily Nymphalinae)
____ Dotted Checkerspot *Polydryas minuta* [Apr-Oct]
____ Theona Checkerspot *Thessalia theona* (*Chlosyne theona*) [Mar-Jan]
____ Chinati Checkerspot *Thessalia chinatiensis* (*Chlosyne theona chinatiensis*) [May-Oct]

_____ Fulvia Checkerspot *Thessalia fulvia* (*Chlosyne fulvia*) [Apr-Oct]
_____ Bordered Patch *Chlosyne lacinia* [Jan-Dec]
_____ Definite Patch *Chlosyne definita* [Jan-Dec]
_____ Banded Patch *Chlosyne endeis* [Mar, Oct-Dec]
_____ Crimson Patch *Chlosyne janais* [Apr-Dec]
_____ Rosita Patch *Chlosyne rosita* [Oct]
_____ Red-spotted Patch *Chlosyne marina* [Oct]
_____ Gorgone Checkerspot *Chlosyne gorgone* [Mar-Nov]
_____ Silvery Checkerspot *Chlosyne nycteis* [Mar-Oct]
_____ Elf *Microtia elva* [Aug]
_____ Tiny Checkerspot *Dymasia dymas* [Feb-Nov]
_____ Elada Checkerspot *Texola elada* [Feb-Dec]
_____ Texan Crescent *Phyciodes texana* (*Anthanassa texana*) [Jan-Dec]
_____ Pale-banded Crescent *Phyciodes tulcis* (*Anthanassa tulcis*) [Mar, May, Oct-Dec]
_____ Black Crescent *Phyciodes ptolyca* (*Anthanassa ptolyca*) [Mar, Dec]
_____ Chestnut Crescent *Phyciodes argentea* (*Anthanassa argentea*) [Nov, Dec]
_____ Vesta Crescent *Phyciodes vesta* (*P. graphica*) [Jan-Dec]
_____ Phaon Crescent *Phyciodes phaon* [Jan-Dec]
_____ Pearl Crescent *Phyciodes tharos* [Jan-Dec]
_____ Painted Crescent *Phyciodes picta* [Apr-Oct]
_____ Mylitta Crescent *Phyciodes mylitta* [Aug]
_____ Variable Checkerspot *Euphydryas chalcedona* [Aug, Nov]
_____ Baltimore Checkerspot *Euphydryas phaeton* [May-Jun]

Anglewings, Ladies, and Buckeyes (Subfamily Nymphalinae)
_____ Question Mark *Polygonia interrogationis* [Jan-Dec]
_____ Eastern Comma *Polygonia comma* [Mar-Dec]
_____ Mourning Cloak *Nymphalis antiopa* [Jan-May, Aug, Oct-Nov]
_____ American Lady *Vanessa virginiensis* [Jan-Dec]
_____ Painted Lady *Vanessa cardui* [Jan-Dec]
_____ West Coast Lady *Vanessa annabella* (Apr-Nov)
_____ Red Admiral *Vanessa atalanta* [Jan-Dec]
_____ Mimic *Hypolimnas misippus* [Aug]
_____ Common Buckeye *Junonia coenia* [Jan-Dec]
_____ Tropical Buckeye *Junonia evarete* [Jan-Dec]
_____ Mangrove Buckeye *Junonia genoveva* [Mar, Apr, Oct, Nov]
_____ White Peacock *Anartia jatrophae* [Jan-Dec]
_____ Banded Peacock *Anartia fatima* [Mar-Jan]
_____ Malachite *Siproeta stelenes* [Jan-Dec]
_____ Rusty-tipped Page *Siproeta epaphus* [Nov]

Admirals and Relatives (Subfamily Limenitidinae)
_____ Red-spotted Purple *Limenitis arthemis* [Mar-Nov]
_____ Viceroy *Limenitis archippus* [Apr-Nov]
_____ Weidemeyer's Admiral *Limenitis weidemeyerii* [Oct]
_____ Band-celled Sister *Adelpha fessonia* [Jan-Apr, Jul-Dec]
_____ Arizona Sister *Adelpha eulalia* [May-Dec]
_____ Spot-celled Sister *Adelpha basiloides* [Nov]
_____ Common Banner *Epiphile adrasta* [Oct-Jan]
_____ Orange Banner* *Temenis laothoe* [Nov]
_____ Mexican Bluewing *Myscelia ethusa* [Jan-Dec]

____ Blackened Bluewing *Myscelia cyananthe* [Oct]
____ Dingy Purplewing *Eunica monima* [Jun-Nov]
____ Florida Purplewing *Eunica tatila* [Aug-Oct]
____ Blue-eyed Sailor *Dynamine dyonis* [Jun, Sep-Dec]
____ Common Mestra *Mestra amymone* [Jan-Dec]
____ Red Rim *Biblis hyperia* [Mar, May, Jul-Jan]
____ Red Cracker *Hamadryas amphinome* [Jan, Sep]
____ Gray Cracker *Hamadryas februa* [Jul-Dec]
____ Variable Cracker *Hamadryas feronia* [Oct-Dec]
____ Guatemalan Cracker *Hamadryas guatemalena* [Aug, Oct-Feb]
____ Orion Cecropian *Historis odius* [Jul]
____ Blomfild's Beauty *Smyrna blomfildia* [Oct-Jan]
____ Waiter Daggerwing *Marpesia coresia* (*M. zerynthia*) [Jul]
____ Many-banded Daggerwing *Marpesia chiron* [Feb, Apr, Jul-Oct]
____ Ruddy Daggerwing *Marpesia petreus* [Feb, Apr, Jun-Nov]

Leafwings (Subfamily Charaxinae)
____ Tropical Leafwing *Anaea aidea* [Jan-Dec]
____ Goatweed Leafwing *Anaea andria* [Mar-Dec]
____ Angled Leafwing *Anaea glycerium* (*Memphis glycerium*) [Jul, Aug]
____ Pale-spotted Leafwing *Anaea pithyusa* (*Memphis pithyusa*) [Mar, Jul-Jan]

Emperors (Subfamily Apaturinae)
____ Hackberry Emperor *Asterocampa celtis* [Mar-Dec]
____ Empress Leilia *Asterocampa leilia* [Feb-Dec]
____ Tawny Emperor *Asterocampa clyton* [Apr-Feb]
____ Pavon Emperor *Doxocopa pavon* [May, Aug-Dec]
____ Silver Emperor *Doxocopa laure* [Jul-Dec]

Satyrs (Subfamily Satyrinae)
____ Southern Pearly-eye *Enodia portlandia* [Mar-Oct]
____ Northern Pearly-eye *Enodia anthedon* [Apr, Aug]
____ Creole Pearly-eye *Enodia creola* [Apr-Sep]
____ Canyonland Satyr *Cyllopsis pertepida* [May-Oct]
____ Gemmed Satyr *Cyllopsis gemma* [Jan-Dec]
____ Carolina Satyr *Hermeuptychia sosybius* [Jan-Dec]
____ Georgia Satyr *Neonympha areolata* [Apr-Sep]
____ Little Wood-Satyr *Megisto cymela* [Mar-Nov]
____ Red Satyr *Megisto rubricata* [Feb-Dec]
____ Common Wood-Nymph *Cercyonis pegala* [May-Nov]
____ Mead's Wood-Nymph *Cercyonis meadii* [May-Sep]
____ Red-bordered Satyr *Gyrocheilus patrobas* [Aug-Oct]

Clearwings (Subfamily Ithomiinae)
____Klug's Clearwing *Dircenna klugii* [Apr]
____Frosty-tipped Clearwing* *Greto morgane oto* [Dec]

Monarchs (Subfamily Danainae)
____Monarch *Danaus plexippus* [Jan-Dec]
____Queen *Danaus gilippus* [Jan-Dec]
____Soldier *Danaus eresimus* [Apr-Jan]
____Tiger Mimic-Queen *Lycorea cleobaea* [?]

Skippers (Family Hesperiidae)

Firetips (Subfamily Pyrrhopyginae)

____ Dull Firetip *Pyrrhopyge araxes* [Jul]

Spread-wing Skippers (Subfamily Pyrginae)

____ Beautiful Beamer* *Phocides belus* [Apr]
____ Guava Skipper *Phocides polybius* [Jan-Dec]
____ Mercurial Skipper *Proteides mercurius* [Apr, Oct]
____ Silver-spotted Skipper *Epargyreus clarus* [Apr-Nov]
____ Broken Silverdrop *Epargyreus exadeus* [Oct]
____ Hammock Skipper *Polygonus leo* [Mar, Apr, Sep-Nov]
____ Manuel's Skipper *Polygonus manueli* (*P. savigny*) [Aug-Oct]
____ White-striped Longtail *Chioides catillus* (*C. albofasciatus*) [Jan-Dec]
____ Zilpa Longtail *Chioides zilpa* [Mar-Apr, Aug-Nov]
____ Gold-spotted Aguna *Aguna asander* [Apr-Jan]
____ Emerald Aguna *Aguna claxon* [Jan, Oct, Nov]
____ Tailed Aguna *Aguna metophis* [Aug-Jan]
____ Mottled Longtail *Typhedanus undulatus* [Aug-Nov]
____ Mexican Longtail *Polythrix mexicanus* [Jul, Oct]
____ Eight-spotted Longtail *Polythrix octomaculata* [Mar, Sep, Oct]
____ Short-tailed Skipper *Zestusa dorus* [Mar-Oct]
____ White-crescent Longtail *Codatractus alcaeus* [Oct]
____ Arizona Skipper *Codatractus arizonensis* [Apr-Oct]
____ Long-tailed Skipper *Urbanus proteus* [Jan-Dec]
____ Pronus Longtail *Urbanus pronus* [Oct]
____ Esmeralda Longtail *Urbanus esmeraldus* [Aug]
____ Double-striped Longtail *Urbanus belli* [Jun]
____ Turquoise (Scarce) Longtail* *Urbanus evona* [Nov-Dec]
____ Dorantes Longtail *Urbanus dorantes* [Jan-Dec]
____ Teleus Longtail *Urbanus teleus* [May-Jan]
____ Tanna Longtail *Urbanus tanna* [Jun, Dec]
____ Plain Longtail *Urbanus simplicius* [Apr]
____ Brown Longtail *Urbanus procne* [Jan-Dec]
____ White-tailed Longtail *Urbanus doryssus* [Mar-Jul, Oct, Nov]
____ Two-barred Flasher *Astraptes fulgerator* [Mar-Jan]
____ Small-spotted Flasher *Astraptes egregius* [Oct]
____ Frosted Flasher *Astraptes alardus* [Jun, Sep, Oct]
____ Gilbert's Flasher *Astraptes gilberti* (*A. alector*) [Mar, Oct]
____ Yellow-tipped Flasher *Astraptes anaphus* [Apr, Sep-Nov]
____ Golden Banded-Skipper *Autochton cellus* [Feb-Nov]
____ Chisos Banded-Skipper *Autochton cincta* [Mar-Sep]
____ Hoary Edge *Achalarus lyciades* [Mar-Dec]
____ Desert Cloudywing *Achalarus casica* [Apr-Oct]
____ Skinner's Cloudywing *Achalarus albociliatus* [Jul]
____ Coyote Cloudywing *Achalarus toxeus* [Jan-Dec]
____ Jalapus Cloudywing *Achalarus jalapus* (*Thessia jalapus*) [Jul-Nov]
____ Southern Cloudywing *Thorybes bathyllus* [Mar-Dec]
____ Northern Cloudywing *Thorybes pylades* [Feb-Dec]
____ Confused Cloudywing *Thorybes confusis* [Feb-Oct]

_____ Drusius Cloudywing *Thorybes drusius* [Apr-Sep]

_____ Potrillo Skipper *Cabares potrillo* [Apr-Feb]

_____ Fritzgaertner's Flat *Celaenorrhinus fritzgaertneri* [Feb, Jul, Sep-Nov]

_____ Stallings' Flat *Calaenorrhinus stallingsi* [Jun, Aug, Oct-Dec]

_____ Falcate Skipper *Spathilepia clonius* [May-Jul, Oct-Dec]

_____ Mimosa Skipper *Cogia calchas* [Jan-Dec]

_____ Acacia Skipper *Cogia hippalus* [Apr-Sep]

_____ Outis Skipper *Cogia outis* [Mar-Oct]

_____ Starred Skipper *Arteurotia tractipennis* [Sep-Nov]

_____ Purplish-black Skipper *Nisoniades rubescens* [Oct, Nov]

_____ Confused Pellicia *Pellicia angra* [Mar, Oct, Dec]

_____ Glazed Pellicia *Pellicia arina* [Apr, Jun-Jan]

_____ Morning Glory Pellicia *Pellicia dimidiata* [Oct]

_____ Mottled Bolla *Bolla clytius* [Jun-Nov]

_____ Obscure Bolla *Bolla brennus* [Oct]

_____ Golden-headed Scallopwing *Staphylus ceos* [Mar-Dec]

_____ Mazans Scallopwing *Staphylus mazans* [Jan-Dec]

_____ Hayhurst's Scallopwing *Staphylus hayhurstii* [Mar-Nov]

_____ Variegated Skipper *Gorgythion begga* [Mar, Dec]

_____ Dusted Spurwing* *Antigonus erosus* [Oct]

_____ Blue-studded Skipper *Sostrata bifasciata* (*S. nordica*) [Oct]

_____ Shining Blue-Skipper* *Paches polla* [Nov]

_____ Tropical Duskywing* *Anastrus sempiternus* [Oct, Nov]

_____ Hoary Skipper *Carrhenes canescens* [Feb-May, Oct-Dec]

_____ Glassy-winged Skipper *Xenophanes tryxus* [Jul-Nov]

_____ Red-studded Skipper *Noctuana stator* [Oct]

_____ Texas Powdered-Skipper *Systasea pulverulenta* [Jan-Dec]

_____ Arizona Powdered-Skipper *Systasea zampa* [Mar-Oct]

_____ Sickle-winged Skipper *Achlyodes thraso* (*Eantis tamenund*) [Jan-Dec]

_____ Pale Sicklewing* *Achlyodes pallida* [Oct-Dec]

_____ Hermit Skipper *Grais stigmatica* [Apr, May, Jul-Nov]

_____ Brown-banded Skipper *Timochares ruptifasciatus* [Feb-Jun, Aug-Dec]

_____ White-patched Skipper *Chiomara asychis* (*C. georgina*) [Jan-Dec]

_____ False Duskywing *Gesta gesta* (*G. invisus*) [Mar-Nov]

_____ Sleepy Duskywing *Erynnis brizo* [Mar-May]

_____ Juvenal's Duskywing *Erynnis juvenalis* [Mar-Oct]

_____ Rocky Mountain Duskywing *Erynnis telemachus* [Apr-Sep]

_____ Propertius Duskywing *Erynnis propertius* [May-Aug]

_____ Meridian Duskywing *Erynnis meridianus* [Mar-Sep]

_____ Scudder's Duskywing *Erynnis scudderi* [May-Sep]

_____ Horace's Duskywing *Erynnis horatius* [Jan-Nov]

_____ Mournful Duskywing *Erynnis tristis* [Jan-Dec]

_____ Mottled Duskywing *Erynnis martialis* [Apr-Oct]

_____ Zarucco Duskywing *Erynnis zarucco* [Mar-Oct]

_____ Funereal Duskywing *Erynnis funeralis* [Jan-Dec]

_____ Wild Indigo Duskywing *Erynnis baptisiae* [Mar-Oct]

_____ Persius Duskywing *Erynnis persius* [Apr]

_____ Small Checkered-Skipper *Pyrgus scriptura* [Mar-Nov]

_____ Common Checkered-Skipper *Pyrgus communis* [Jan-Dec]

_____ White Checkered-Skipper *Pyrgus albescens* [Jan-Dec]

_____ Tropical Checkered-Skipper *Pyrgus oileus* [Jan-Dec]
_____ Desert Checkered-Skipper *Pyrgus philetas* [Mar-Nov]
_____ Erichson's White-Skipper *Heliopetes domicella* (*Heliopyrgus domicella*) [Jan-Dec]
_____ Laviana White-Skipper *Heliopetes laviana* [Jan-Dec]
_____ Turk's-cap White-Skipper *Heliopetes macaira* [Jan-Dec]
_____ East-Mexican White-Skipper* *Heliopetes sublinea* [Oct]
_____ Veined White-Skipper *Heliopetes arsalte* [Oct]
_____ Common Streaky-Skipper *Celotes nessus* [Jan, Mar-Nov]
_____ Scarce Streaky-Skipper *Celotes limpia* [Mar-Oct]
_____ Common Sootywing *Pholisora catullus* [Mar-Nov]
_____ Mexican Sootywing *Pholisora mejicana* [May-Sep]
_____ Saltbush Sootywing *Hesperopsis alpheus* [Apr-Nov]

Skipperlings (Subfamily Heteropterinae)
_____ Russet Skipperling *Piruna pirus* [May-Aug]
_____ Four-spotted Skipperling *Piruna polingi* (*P. polingii*) [Jul, Aug]
_____ Small-spotted Skipperling *Piruna microstictus* (*P. penaea*) [Oct]
_____ Chisos Skipperling *Piruna haferniki* [Mar-Oct]

Grass-Skippers (Subfamily Hesperiinae)
_____ Malicious Skipper *Synapte malitiosa* [Apr-Dec]
_____ Salenus Skipper *Synapte salenus* [Aug-Oct]
_____ Redundant Skipper *Corticea corticea* [Sep-Dec]
_____ Pale-rayed Skipper *Vidius perigenes* [Mar-Nov]
_____ Violet-patched Skipper *Monca tyrtaeus* (*M. crispinus*) [Mar, Jun-May, Oct-Dec]
_____ Swarthy Skipper *Nastra lherminier* [Apr-Sep]
_____ Julia's Skipper *Nastra julia* [Jan-Dec]
_____ Neamathla Skipper *Nastra neamathla* [Jan-Dec]
_____ Fawn-spotted Skipper *Cymaenes odilia* (*C. trebius*) [Jan-Dec]
_____ Clouded Skipper *Lerema accius* [Jan-Dec]
_____ Liris Skipper *Lerema liris* [Jul-Oct]
_____ Fantastic Skipper *Vettius fantasos* [Oct-Dec]
_____ Green-backed Ruby-eye *Perichares philetes* [Oct-Dec]
_____ Osca Skipper *Rhinthon osca* [Oct]
_____ Double-dotted Skipper *Decinea percosius* [Mar-Dec]
_____ Hidden-ray Skipper *Conga chydaea* [Jul-Oct]
_____ Least Skipper *Ancyloxypha numitor* [Mar-Nov]
_____ Tropical Least Skipper *Ancyloxypha arene* [Apr-Aug]
_____ Edwards' Skipperling *Oarisma edwardsii* [Apr-Jul, Oct]
_____ Orange Skipperling *Copaeodes aurantiacus* [Jan-Dec]
_____ Southern Skipperling *Copaeodes minimus* [Jan-Dec]
_____ Sunrise Skipper *Adopaeoides prittwitzi* [May-Jun, Sep]
_____ Fiery Skipper *Hylephila phyleus* [Jan-Dec]
_____ Morrison's Skipper *Stringa morrisoni* [Mar-May, Sep-Oct]
_____ Uncas Skipper *Hesperia uncas* [May-Nov]
_____ Common Branded Skipper *Hesperia comma* [Jul-Sep]
_____ Apache Skipper *Hesperia woodgatei* [Sep-Oct]
_____ Ottoe Skipper *Hesperia ottoe* [Jun-Aug]
_____ Pahaska Skipper *Hesperia pahaska* [Apr-Oct]
_____ Cobweb Skipper *Hesperia metea* [Mar-Apr]
_____ Green Skipper *Hesperia viridis* [Apr-Jun, Aug-Oct]

_____ Dotted Skipper *Hesperia attalus* [May-Sep]
_____ Meske's Skipper *Hesperia meskei* [May-Oct]
_____ Rhesus Skipper *Polites rhesus* [May-Jun]
_____ Carus Skipper *Polites carus* [Apr-Sep]
_____ Peck's Skipper *Polites peckius* [May-Jun, Aug-Oct]
_____ Tawny-edged Skipper *Polites themistocles* [Jun, Sep]
_____ Crossline Skipper *Polites origenes* [Jun-Aug]
_____ Whirlabout *Polites vibex* [Jan-Dec]
_____ Southern Broken-Dash *Wallengrenia otho* [Jan-Dec]
_____ Northern Broken-Dash *Wallengrenia egeremet* [Apr-Sep]
_____ Little Glassywing *Pompeius verna* [Apr-Sep]
_____ Sachem *Atalopedes campestris* [Jan-Dec]
_____ Arogos Skipper *Atrytone arogos* [May-Aug]
_____ Delaware Skipper *Anatrytone logan* [Apr-Sep]
_____ Glowing Skipper *Anatrytone mazai* [Jun]
_____ Byssus Skipper *Problema byssus* [Apr-Oct]
_____ Hobomok Skipper *Poanes hobomok* [May-Sep]
_____ Zabulon Skipper *Poanes zabulon* [Mar-Sep]
_____ Taxiles Skipper *Poanes taxiles* [May-Aug]
_____ Aaron's Skipper *Poanes aaroni* [May-Jun, Aug-Oct]
_____ Yehl Skipper *Poanes yehl* [Apr-June, Aug-Oct]
_____ Broad-winged Skipper *Poanes viator* [Mar-Nov]
_____ Umber Skipper *Poanes melane* [May-Sep]
_____ Common Mellana *Quasimellana eulogius* [Apr-Feb]
_____ Dion Skipper *Euphyes dion* [May-Oct]
_____ Bay Skipper *Euphyes bayensis* [May, Sep]
_____ Dukes' Skipper *Euphyes dukesi* [May-Oct]
_____ Dun Skipper *Euphyes vestris* [Mar-Dec]
_____ Dusted Skipper *Atrytonopsis hianna* [Apr-Jun]
_____ Viereck's Skipper *Atrytonopsis vierecki* [Mar-Jun]
_____ White-barred Skipper *Atrytonopsis pittacus* [Mar-May]
_____ Python Skipper *Atrytonopsis python* [Mar-Jul, Sep]
_____ Sheep Skipper *Atrytonopsis edwardsii* [Apr-Sep]
_____ Simius Roadside-Skipper *Amblyscirtes sumius* [Apr-Sep]
_____ Cassus Roadside-Skipper *Amblyscirtes cassus* [Jun-Jul]
_____ Bronze Roadside-Skipper *Amblyscirtes aenus* [Mar-Sep]
_____ Oslar's Roadside-Skipper *Amblyscirtes oslari* [Apr-Sep]
_____ Pepper and Salt Skipper *Amblyscirtes hegon* [Mar-Jul]
_____ Texas Roadside-Skipper *Amblyscirtes texanae* [Apr-Sep]
_____ Lace-winged Roadside-Skipper *Amblyscirtes aesculapius* [Feb-Sep]
_____ Slaty Roadside-Skipper *Amblyscirtes nereus* [May-Sep]
_____ Nysa Roadside-Skipper *Amblyscirtes nysa* [Feb-Oct]
_____ Dotted Roadside-Skipper *Amblyscirtes eos* [Apr-Sep]
_____ Common Roadside-Skipper *Amblyscirtes vialis* [Mar-Jul]
_____ Celia's Roadside-Skipper *Amblyscirtes celia* [Jan-Dec]
_____ Bell's Roadside-Skipper *Amblyscirtes belli* [Mar-Oct]
_____ Dusky Roadside-Skipper *Amblyscirtes alternata* [Mar-Nov]
_____ Orange-headed Roadside-Skipper *Amblyscirtes phylace* [Jun-Aug]
_____ Orange-edged Roadside-Skipper *Amblyscirtes fimbriata* [Jun-Jul]
_____ Eufala Skipper *Lerodea eufala* [Jan-Dec]

_____ Olive-clouded Skipper *Lerodea dysaules* (*L. arabus*) [Jan-Dec]
_____ Twin-spot Skipper *Oligoria maculata* [Apr-Sep]
_____ Brazilian Skipper *Calpodes ethlius* [Jan-Dec]
_____ Salt Marsh Skipper *Panoquina panoquin* [Apr-Oct]
_____ Obscure Skipper *Panoquina panoquinoides* [Jan-Dec]
_____ Ocola Skipper *Panoquina ocola* [Jan-Dec]
_____ Hecobolus Skipper *Panoquina hecebola* [Jul-Dec]
_____ Purple-washed Skipper *Panoquina sylvicola* (*P. lucas*) [Aug-Jan]
_____ Evans' Skipper *Panoquina fusina* (*P. evansi*) [Oct, Nov]
_____ Violet-banded Skipper *Nyctelius nyctelius* [May, Sep-Feb]

Giant-Skippers (Subfamily Megathyminae)
_____ Orange Giant-Skipper *Agathymus neumoegeni* [Sep-Oct]
_____ Mary's Giant-Skipper *Agathymus mariae* [Sep-Nov]
_____ Yucca Giant-Skipper *Megathymus yuccae* [Feb-Apr]
_____ Strecker's Giant-Skipper *Megathymus streckeri* [Apr-Jul]
_____ Ursine Giant-Skipper *Megathymus ursus* [May-Sep]
_____ Manfreda Giant-Skipper *Stallingsia maculosa* (*S. maculosus*) [Apr-May, Sep-Nov]

Additional Sightings

The butterflies below have been reported in Texas, but additional documentation is required before they can be added to the state checklist.

Common (Mylotes) Cattleheart *Parides eurimedes*
Apricot Sulphur *Phoebis argante*
Creamy Stripe-Streak *Arawacus jada*
"Cuban" Snout *Libytheans motya*
Green Longwing *Philaethria dido*
Ardys Crescent *Anthanassa ardys*
Huastecan Crescent *Tegosa anieta*
Mexican Eight-eight *Diaethria asteria*
Orange Mapwing *Hypanartia lethe*
Common Morpho *Morpho peleides*
Euribates Skipper *Dyscophellus euribates*
Urania Skipper *Phocides urania*
Foldless Checkered-Skipper *Pyrgus adepta*
Saturn Skipper *Callimormus saturnus*
Glowing Skipper *Antrytone mazai*
Chestnut-marked Skipper *Thespieus macareus*

Index

Roland H. Wauer, a thirty-two year veteran of the National Park Service, is the author of twenty-one books. These include books on birds and bird watching, such as *The American Kestrel, Birding Texas, A Birder's West Indies, Virgin Island's Birdlife, Birder's Mexico,* and several guides to birding national parks. His butterfly titles include *Butterflies of West Texas Parks and Preserves* and *Butterflies of the Lower Rio Grande Valley.* He lives in Texas.

BUILDING CONSTRUCTION INSPECTION
A Guide For Architects

Jay M. Bannister

A WILEY-INTERSCIENCE PUBLICATION

JOHN WILEY & SONS, INC.

New York / Chichester / Brisbane / Toronto / Singapore

Copyright © 1991 by John Wiley & Sons, Inc.

All rights reserved. Published simultaneously in Canada.

Reproduction or translation of any part of this work
beyond that permitted by Section 107 or 108 of the
1976 United States Copyright Act without the permission
of the copyright owner is unlawful. Requests for
permission or further information should be addressed to
the Permissions Department, John Wiley & Sons, Inc.

Library of Congress Cataloging in Publication Data:
Bannister, Jay.
    Building construction inspection : a guide for architects / Jay
Bannister.
        p.   cm.
    "A Wiley-Interscience publication."
    Includes bibliographical references (p.).
    1. Building inspection.   I. Title.
    TH439.B35   1991
    692—dc20   90-13028
    ISBN 0-471-53004-2   CIP

Printed in the United States of America

10   9   8   7   6   5   4   3   2   1

CONTENTS

PART II   SITE AND STRUCTURAL CONSTRUCTION

PART III   GENERAL CONSTRUCTION

PART V   FINAL INSPECTION AND PROJECT CLOSEOUT

PREFACE

Inspection of construction in progress is as vital a function in the construction process as the design itself. After all, if the design is not accomplished correctly in the field, what good is a design? The owner hires a designer to translate his or her requirements into a design that is communicated to the builder through the plans and specifications. The owner also must hire a builder to do the actual construction. The builder must make a profit to stay in business. The profit motive may tempt the constructor to provide less than the design requires in order to minimize costs. The owner has every right to expect that the minimum requirements of the design are produced in the construction. Toward this goal, the owner empowers others (who are not interested in making a profit on the construction) to be his or her informed eyes and ears on the construction site. "Others" may be the firm that produced the design, a third party hired by the owner, or someone on the owner's payroll. Throughout this manual, I will refer to this person or persons as "the inspector."

The construction inspector observes the work and determines whether it conforms to the provisions of the design. The inspector does *not ensure* that the construction is correct. That is the contractor's job. If the work does not conform to the contract, the inspector must tell the constructor. It is up to the constructor to do the work correctly.

Inspection is mostly good common sense. But there are aspects of inspection that call for a special expertise; things that are still good common sense, but which are not part of our early experience. I have assembled a compendium of these kinds of experience in the field to help you gain an understanding of the process and to contribute to better construction. This book is written for those with limited experience in construction—but some experience is assumed.

The general arrangement of this book is the order of construction. Some of the chapters stand on their own, while reference to other chapters is required for some of the segments. This is unfortunate but otherwise the text would be riddled with repeat information. There are some chapters that *must* be used together, such as "Concrete and Concrete Columns." The "Concrete" chapter is general in nature and applies to all the more specific concrete subchapters. "Concrete Applications" is more specific about forming and placing concrete and does not contain repeat general information about concrete.

Some chapters are supplemented with an outline "memory jogger" at the end of the book that may be used in the field or before leaving for the job site. The most benefit will be gained by reading the book cover to cover and then using the memory joggers to refresh your memory for specific tasks.

This manual is not a legal guide to inspection. It does not claim that you will have perfect results from following the memory joggers. It does not cover every provision that might appear in the drawings and specifications. It does not deal with laboratory and field testing as performed by a testing laboratory nor does it cover engineering and design. It is directed to building construction as opposed to engineering structures such as bridges, roads, pipelines, and dams. It is generic in nature and should be used as a guide to good inspection. The thought process and methodology can be applied to all those provisions that are not covered.

This manual must not be substituted for the requirements of the contract documents for a specific project. The provisions of the contract are the provisions of the project, regardless of what is stated in this manual. I have been diligent in stating what is usually required of typical contracts but I also remind readers to check their specific drawings and specifications for different provisions and requirements. These specific requirements may even be diametrically opposed to the advice given in the manual but they are still the basis of the contract and must be respected.

Few students of construction, architecture, or engineering are exposed to this subject extensively in school; yet in most offices, it is the younger architects and engineers who are called upon for on-site observation or inspection of construction projects. One of the goals of this book is to steepen the learning curve for these people. This book can also be used by anyone interested in performing inspection but who has no formal architectural education.

The benefit of years of experience in the construction industry has gone into this book, so that you do not have to learn many of these things the way I did—by trial and error (mostly by error!). We all learn by making errors, but if we can learn from others' errors, and avoid those errors, everyone benefits.

Frequent reference is made to "some contractors" doing this, that, or the other *bad* thing. I do not intend to defame general contractors in general. In a bidding situation, I am referring to those contractors who calculate and submit their bids on the basis that they will be able to circumvent some of the provisions of the contract documents, thereby giving them an unfair advantage in the bidding process. I do not believe that this is the norm, nor that *most* contractors act this way. I also do not think that reputable contractors will even identify with some of the examples because that behavior is not their way of doing business. In fact, I believe that good contractors will appreciate our efforts to eliminate this behavior because it will make competition more fair.

Without the support, encouragement, opportunity, and friendship of a lot of special people, this book would have never been possible. Among these special folks are Fred Buford, Jim Clutts, and Howard Parker—all gentlemen and fine architects. My thanks to them for the opportunity to learn many of the valuable lessons presented in this manual. Thanks also to all the many general contractors who have assisted in my education, with hands-on experience in the construction process.

A sincere "thank you" to my friends at Telpro, Inc. for their help with plotting my illustrations and to the folks at Meisel Commercial Photographic Services for their excellent processing of the photographs. I want to thank the American Institute of Architects and the American Institute of Steel Construction for their permission to use their copyrighted materials in this book.

Finally, my humble thanks to my family for their indulgence and encouragement throughout the writing of this book.

JAY M. BANNISTER

Dallas, Texas
April 1990

BUILDING
CONSTRUCTION
INSPECTION

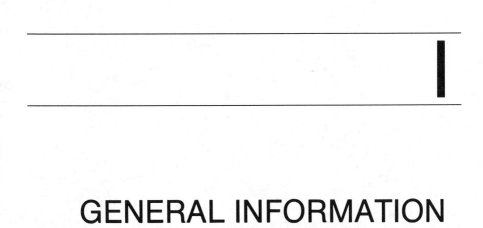

GENERAL INFORMATION

GENERAL CONSIDERATIONS

WHEN TO BE ON SITE

In the ideal situation, the construction inspector should always be on site while construction is going on. If the project is large enough that several critical activities are likely to be occurring simultaneously there should be even more than one inspector on site. As an "on site observer" you may not have the advantage of being on site all the time. It might be that, because of economic or time constraints, it is only possible to be there when important events are taking place. Therefore, you must know what those events are and when they will occur.

Another possibility is for you only to be at the site on a regular, periodic basis, such as once a week. This will decrease your effectiveness because it will largely be a matter of luck to be there at the right times. Regular periodic visits probably will mean that you will be looking at work that is already complete on many of your visits; and will inevitably force compromise on the quality you can effect. After the work is completed you can have very little effect on the quality of the work. Because the main purpose of inspection is to positively effect the quality of the work, you should appeal to those who make this kind of decision to rethink the process, and allow you to be on site when the critical events are taking place. This manual will show you those critical periods.

KNOW YOUR LIMITS

You should quickly learn to recognize when you are in over your head. You cannot know everything about all the disciplines represented in a construction project. The trick is to know what it is that you *don't* know, and what to do about it: ask for help. There is no shame in asking for help. The ''shame on you'' is in not asking for help when you are in a situation that is beyond your area of expertise or competence. Call the electrical engineer, the mechanical engineer, the structural engineer, anyone who might be more knowledgeable about the subject than you are. You also may want some of these same people to help you in your inspection duties from time to time, when you do not have the technical knowledge to do an adequate inspection of some special system. Do not hesitate to ask questions of knowledgeable people. That is the best way to learn.

QUALITY

A word about ''quality.'' In the field of construction, the word has a different meaning than it has in general usage. In general usage, quality has come to mean ''better quality''; and better quality means richer, finer, more costly, materials, better methods or better appearance. The Design & Construction Quality Institute (DCQI) gives four definitions of quality depending on roles. For an owner, quality means fitness for an intended purpose; for a designer, conformance to requirements; for a contractor, reliance and strict adherence to plan documents; and for operational and facilities management people, the ability to have acceptable, predictable performance. For the inspector, I define quality as ''meeting the established requirements.'' These requirements are established by the design.

The design, communicated by the drawings and specifications, establishes the relative quality of the materials and workmanship. The level of quality, however, is established by the requirements of the owner. To the inspector, quality means adherence to the standards established by the design. Better quality means closer adherence to those standards. The quality of the materials and workmanship have already been established, and we, as inspectors, cannot change that standard. We must only interpret the intended quality and judge how closely the work conforms to that standard.

If the drawings call for a 3'0" × 7'0" door and the specifications call for it to be made out of corrugated cardboard of a specified weight and thickness, we need only determine that the door is made of corrugated cardboard the correct weight and thickness and that it is the right size. Of course, this quality standard is low, but, remember, the standard of quality has already been established, and high quality in construction is to provide exactly the quality established by the design.

Quality is not strictly an aesthetic issue. It is also an economic issue. It is widely accepted by experienced members of the DCQI that approximately 30% of the total construction cost can be attributed to quality. About 80% of that can be attributed to *poor* quality—the cost of replacing or repairing substandard work. Therefore, doing the job right the first time saves approximately 24% of the total cost of construction.

Quality cannot be obtained with a checklist, nor come after the fact. In other words, an inspector should not look at a completed product and judge the quality at that point. If the completed work is substandard, the inspector can have little effect on the outcome of the product. The alternatives are to accept substandard work, repair it, or replace it. Each alternative is potentially detrimental to the project in terms of time lost, additional cost and negative effects on morale and good working relationships. Quality assurance must begin at the beginning; at the start of the project, at the first moment of any new task and continue through to the end. It requires being on top of things; preparing for a new activity; being there when the activity first begins; and assuring that it is being done correctly from the start.

Relative quality is determined by the attitudes of those involved in the work. The best quality results when the "culture" of the organization that produces the work is totally committed to the highest standards of quality. You can do your part by inspiring and helping those around you to produce the best product that they can.

THE WORD *INSPECTION*

Inspection has been a word to be avoided by architects and engineers for a long time. It implies legal responsibilities beyond what most architects, engineers, and their insurers are willing to accept. However, you may be in a position where it *is* your right and even your responsibility to inspect the work—for instance, if you are part of a construction manager's quality assurance organization, or if you are employed by the owner or a government agency to inspect the construction. In these cases, you must be actively inspecting, not just observing. You should know where you are in the spectrum between observation and inspection. If your role has not been clearly defined, press your employer for clarification.

The word *inspect* in this manual does not reflect legal responsibilities but describes a process. The process is the same whether you call it "inspection" or "on site observation." It means looking at what the contractor is doing and determining if it meets the standards he or she has contracted to provide. Those standards are enumerated in the contract documents—the agreement, the conditions to the contract, the drawings and specifications. Obviously, then, it is absolutely necessary that an inspector be thoroughly familiar with the contract documents, the subject of the next chapter.

2

THE CONTRACT DOCUMENTS

All of the contract documents are a part of the contract between the owner and the contractor. In most fields, the document on which the signatures appear is called the contract. In construction it is called the agreement. The agreement states that the other contract documents become a part of the contract. The other contract documents are the conditions to the contract (general conditions, supplemental general conditions, special conditions), addenda, drawings, specifications, and change orders. Therefore, drawings and specifications are legal documents (see Figure 2.1).

The Drawings will tell you where the materials, the parts and pieces of construction are located, establish the physical dimensions, and tell you how the various parts fit together. The Specifications tell you what the materials are, establish the quality standards and tell you how they are to be installed.

Before you inspect a project, read the specifications all the way through and study the drawings. This will give you much data to look for in the field. I have not attempted to cover what should be in the specifications, but have gone beyond the specifications to explain additional "watch-outs." By the way, if you write specifications, this book might help you too, because you should write every specification as if you will judge the acceptability of the product or the workmanship of the installation. This approach eliminates vague references to quality such as "in a workmanlike manner" and "workmanship of the first class;" which are impossible to quantify accurately and to enforce.

All projects are different, and, thus, all contracts are different. Just because you have read one contract, do not assume that all contracts will be similar, even if they are based on accepted standard contracts such as the AIA documents. You must read each contract and know its provisions. After you have read and worked with contracts based on standard documents, only

7

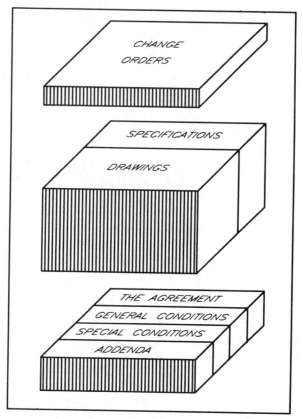

FIGURE 2.1. A schematic diagram of the contract documents.

then you can begin to look for changes and nonstandard provisions. Also, remember that standards change, due to improved technology, better materials, and experience with old standards. One section most likely to change with each project is the general requirements, because this section is highly project-specific. Here is an outline of what you might expect to see in the general requirements:

A. Summary of Work

1. Work by owner,
2. Contractor use of premises,
3. Future work.

B. Contract Considerations

1. Cash allowances,
2. Contingency allowance,

3. Inspection and testing allowances,
4. Schedule of values,
5. Applications for payment,
6. Change procedures,
7. Alternatives.

C. Coordination and Meetings

1. Coordination,
2. Field engineering,
3. Cutting and patching,
4. Conferences,
5. Progress meetings.

D. Submittals

1. Submittal procedures,
2. Construction progress schedules,
3. Proposed products list,
4. Shop drawings,
5. Product data,
6. Samples,
7. Manufacturers' instructions,
8. Manufacturers' certificates,
9. Construction photographs.

E. Quality Control

1. Quality assurance/control of installation,
2. References,
3. Field samples,
4. Inspection and testing laboratory services,
5. Manufacturers' field services and reports.

F. Construction Facilities and Temporary Controls

1. Temporary electricity,
2. Temporary lighting,
3. Temporary heat,
4. Temporary ventilation,
5. Telephone service,
6. Temporary water service,
7. Temporary sanitary facilities,

8. Barriers and fencing,
9. Water control,
10. Exterior enclosures,
11. Interior enclosures,
12. Protection of installed work,
13. Security,
14. Access roads,
15. Parking,
16. Progress cleaning,
17. Project identification,
18. Field offices and sheds,
19. Removal of utilities, facilities, and controls.

G. Material and Equipment

1. Products,
2. Transportation, handling, storage, and protection,
3. Products options,
4. Substitutions.

H. Starting of Systems

1. Starting systems,
2. Demonstration and instructions,
3. Testing, adjusting, and balancing.

I. Contract Closeout

1. Contract closeout procedures,
2. Final cleaning,
3. Adjusting,
4. Project record documents,
5. Operation and maintenance data,
6. Warranties,
7. Spare parts and maintenance materials.

There may be a bound book that contains all the printed portions of the contract documents. Many people call this manual the specifications, but it is more properly called the project manual. There may be more than one project manual for projects that have too many technical specifications to bind in a single manual or on projects in which multiple "bid packages" are issued. In this case, each bid package is likely to have a separate project manual.

TYPES OF CONTRACTS

Contracts may be categorized by (1) method of payment, (2) phasing of contracts, or (3) number and division of prime contracts.

Contracts Determined by Method of Payment

The method of payment may be a lump sum, cost plus, or unit price. A *lump sum* contract has a fixed price. That price is usually based on a competitive bid, and it changes only when the work required changes (by change order). The final sum paid the contractor is the lump sum price plus (or minus) the amount of any change orders.

In a *cost plus* contract, the contractor agrees to charge only what he or she has to pay in the way of materials and labor costs, plus a fee that can be based on a fixed amount (cost plus a fixed fee) or a percentage of the materials and labor costs (cost plus a percentage). Either type of contract can include a guaranteed maximum price. In this case the contractor assumes all costs above the guaranteed maximum. (A time and materials contract is virtually the same.) In a cost plus contract the contractor is usually required to submit actual invoices for materials and time sheets for labor to verify the amount billed to the owner. If there are subcontracts (and there nearly always are), the subcontractor is usually required to give the contractor the same type of documentation required of the contractor. It may be the duty of the inspector to verify that the invoices are correct. If so, the inspector must be thoroughly familiar with the materials that are delivered to the site and know how many workers are on the site each day.

The *unit price* method is not usually encountered in building construction, but it could be. In engineering projects (pipelines, roads, etc.) the quantities of work must be approximations because of the widely varying existing conditions. The route of a pipeline might have to be altered during construction because of unanticipated rock in the path of the excavation, or the cut might have to be deeper than originally planned because of an inherent inaccuracy in the topographical survey. The engineer estimates the quantities, and the bidders quote a lump sum based on this estimate. However, the bidders also bid unit prices for the various categories of work, and the actual basis of payment is the unit price that was bid. In other words, the contractor is paid for the actual linear footage of pipe laid or for the actual cubic footage of excavation done, based the unit prices bid for this work. The inspector is usually responsible for verifying the units of work that the contractor claims on his or her application for payment.

Many building construction contracts call for unit price bids on work that is likely to vary according to site conditions. Some of the required unit prices might be for drilled piers or piles, evacuation of unsuitable soils, and similar tasks. Unit prices also may be requested for common construction items if substantial changes are anticipated.

Contracts Determined by Phasing of Contracts

The phased construction contract is generally used in fast-track construction with a construction manager instead of a general contractor. The work is divided into packages, which usually depend on when the work is needed or on similarity of work. For instance, the rough grading and foundations might be in one package, the structural frame in another, and the outside skin in yet another. The packages are competitively bid, and a contract is executed for each package. The contract is usually with the owner; the construction manager administers and coordinates the work called for in each contract. It is a demanding task to keep all the packages sorted out and to figure out who does what part of the work.

Contracts Determined by Number and Division of Prime Contracts

When contracts are determined by the number and division of prime contracts, there is usually a prime contract for general construction, another for mechanical work, and another for electrical work. The general contractor is usually designated the coordinator of the contracts. This form puts a greater burden on the architect and the inspector, because they must treat each party as a prime contractor, each with its own share of paperwork.

SCHEDULE OF VALUES

In most construction projects, the contract calls for the contractor to submit a *schedule of values* before construction begins. This document (typically AIA document G703) breaks down the total price of the construction into line items, such as general conditions (common nomenclature for the construction trailer, utilities, administrative personnel, Port-A-Cans, etc.), excavation, grading, site drainage, concrete, structural steel, and so forth.

If the contract is using the AIA standard documents, the schedule of values is on the second page of the application for payment (AIA document G702 or G722). See Figures 2.2 and 2.3. The application for payment is prepared by the contractor at the times stipulated in the contract, usually at the end of each month during construction.

In determining the amount of money due the contractor each payment period, the inspector judges what percentage of each line item is complete. Therefore, the inspector must find out from the contractor (or the estimator) what constitutes each line item. For instance, does the line item "concrete" include forming, or is that in "carpentry"? Does "structural steel" include reinforcing for concrete, or is that in the line item "concrete"? I try not to discuss the value of line items with anyone except my employer or the contractor's superintendent. (I have had subcontractors or suppliers accuse me of personally withholding their money.)

APPLICATION AND CERTIFICATE FOR PAYMENT

AIA DOCUMENT G702   (Instructions on reverse side)

TO (OWNER): Newtown Ind. School Dist.
4040 Main Street
Newtown, TX 75099
Mr. I.Q. Testerman, Supt.

PROJECT: Newtown Elementary School
2020 Rough Road
Newtown, TX

APPLICATION NO: Five (5)

PERIOD TO: 7/01/89

Distribution to:
☐ OWNER
☐ ARCHITECT
☐ CONTRACTOR

FROM (CONTRACTOR): John R. Builder and
Company, Inc.

VIA (ARCHITECT): Wright and Richardson,
Architects

ARCHITECT'S PROJECT NO: 8821

CONTRACT FOR: General Construction

CONTRACT DATE: 2/10/89

CONTRACTOR'S APPLICATION FOR PAYMENT

Application is made for Payment, as shown below, in connection with the Contract.
Continuation Sheet, AIA Document G703, is attached.

CHANGE ORDER SUMMARY	ADDITIONS	DEDUCTIONS
Change Orders approved in previous months by Owner		
TOTAL	1,235.00	
Approved this Month		
Number	Date Approved	
TOTALS	1,235.00	
Net change by Change Orders		

1. **ORIGINAL CONTRACT SUM** . . . . $ 5,685,350.00
2. **Net change by Change Orders** . . . . $ 1,235.00
3. **CONTRACT SUM TO DATE** (Line 1 ± 2). . . . . . . $ 5,686,585.00
4. **TOTAL COMPLETED & STORED TO DATE** . . . . . $ 2,353,680.03
   (Column G on G703)
5. **RETAINAGE:**
   a. 10 % of Completed Work $ 235,368.00
      (Column D + E on G703)
   b. 10 % of Stored Material $ 24,918.60
      (Column F on G703)
   Total Retainage (Line 5a + 5b or
   Total in Column I of G703) . . . . $ 235,367.52
6. **TOTAL EARNED LESS RETAINAGE** . . . . $ 2,118,312.51
   (Line 4 less Line 5 Total)
7. **LESS PREVIOUS CERTIFICATES FOR
   PAYMENT** (Line 6 from prior Certificate) . . . . $ 1,639,876.67
8. **CURRENT PAYMENT DUE** . . . . $ 487,435.84
9. **BALANCE TO FINISH, PLUS RETAINAGE** . . . . . $ 4,046,708.33
   (Line 3 less Line 6)

The undersigned Contractor certifies that to the best of the Contractor's knowledge, information and belief the Work covered by this Application for Payment has been completed in accordance with the Contract Documents, that all amounts have been paid by the Contractor for Work for which previous Certificates for Payment were issued and payments received from the Owner, and that current payment shown herein is now due.

CONTRACTOR:

By: _[signature]_   Date: 7/10/89

State of: Texas   County of: Dallas
Subscribed and sworn to before me this tenth day of July , 19 89
Notary Public: Mary Seals
My Commission expires: 9/01/89

ARCHITECT'S CERTIFICATE FOR PAYMENT

In accordance with the Contract Documents, based on on-site observations and the data comprising the above application, the Architect certifies to the Owner that to the best of the Architect's knowledge, information and belief the Work has progressed as indicated, the quality of the Work is in accordance with the Contract Documents, and the Contractor is entitled to payment of the AMOUNT CERTIFIED.

AMOUNT CERTIFIED . . . . $ 487,435.84
(Attach explanation if amount certified differs from the amount applied for.)
ARCHITECT:
By: _[signature]_   Date: 7/15/89
This Certificate is not negotiable. The AMOUNT CERTIFIED is payable only to the Contractor named herein. Issuance, payment and acceptance of payment are without prejudice to any rights of the Owner or Contractor under this Contract.

AIA DOCUMENT G702 • APPLICATION AND CERTIFICATE FOR PAYMENT • MAY 1983 EDITION • AIA • © 1983
THE AMERICAN INSTITUTE OF ARCHITECTS, 1735 NEW YORK AVENUE, N.W., WASHINGTON, D.C. 20006

G702-1983

FIGURE 2.2. G702 form application for payment. Reproduced with the permission of the American Institute of Architects.

CONTINUATION SHEET

AIA Document G702, APPLICATION AND CERTIFICATE FOR PAYMENT, containing Contractor's signed Certification is attached.
In tabulations below, amounts are stated to the nearest dollar.
Use Column I on Contracts where variable retainage for line items may apply.

APPLICATION NUMBER: Five (5)
APPLICATION DATE: 7/10/89
PERIOD TO: 2/10/89
ARCHITECT'S PROJECT NO: 1/01/89
8821

A ITEM NO.	B DESCRIPTION OF WORK	C SCHEDULED VALUE	D WORK COMPLETED FROM PREVIOUS APPLICATION (D + E)	E WORK COMPLETED THIS PERIOD	F MATERIALS PRESENTLY STORED (NOT IN D OR E)	G TOTAL COMPLETED AND STORED TO DATE (D + E + F)	% (G ÷ C)	H BALANCE TO FINISH (C − G)	I RETAINAGE
1	General Conditions	682,242.00	83,915.77	40,934.52		124,850.47	18.3%	557,391.53	12,485.05
2	Earthwork	341,121.00	191,027.78	30,700.89		221,729.30	65.0%	119,391.70	22,172.93
3	Landscaping	125,077.70	0.00			0.00	0.0%	125,077.70	0.00
4	Carpentry	397,974.50	131,331.59	83,574.65		214,906.77	54.0%	183,067.73	21,490.68
5	Concrete	795,949.00	557,164.50	95,513.88		652,679.00	82.0%	143,270.00	65,267.90
6	Structural Steel	682,242.00	409,345.20	15,009.32	75,220.00	499,575.15	73.2%	182,666.85	49,957.51
7	Miscellaneous Metals	227,414.00	79,594.90	25,015.54	35,345.00	139,955.90	61.5%	87,458.10	13,995.59
8	Roofing and Waterproofing	136,448.40	15,009.32	10,915.87	10,500.00	36,425.39	26.7%	100,023.01	3,642.54
9	Masonry	477,569.40	23,878.47	47,756.94	5,600.00	77,235.54	16.2%	400,333.84	7,723.56
10	Drywall	45,482.80	909.66	2,728.97		3,638.70	8.0%	41,844.10	363.87
11	Painting	85,280.25	1,705.61	3,411.21		5,116.88	6.0%	80,163.38	511.69
12	Acoustical	11,370.70	0.00	113.71	2,650.00	2,763.72	24.3%	8,606.98	276.37
13	Resilient Flooring	17,056.05	0.00	0.00		0.00	0.0%	17,056.05	0.00
14	Carpet	39,797.45	0.00	0.00	21,970.00	21,970.00	55.2%	17,827.45	2,197.00
15	Hollow Metal	34,112.10	1,364.48	1,023.26	6,450.00	8,837.92	25.9%	25,274.18	883.79
16	Windows and Glazing	39,797.45	795.95	1,313.32		2,109.22	5.3%	37,688.13	210.93
17	Millwork	68,224.20	0.00	0.00	12,650.00	12,650.00	18.5%	55,574.20	1,265.00
18	Folding Partitions	28,426.75	0.00	0.00		0.00	0.0%	28,426.75	0.00
19	Specialties	73,909.55	2,433.02	0.00	1,500.00	3,939.05	5.3%	69,970.50	393.90
20	Detention Equipment	62,538.85	0.00	0.00		0.00	0.0%	62,538.85	0.00
21	Heating, Ventil'n, Air Cond	460,513.35	41,446.20	50,656.47		92,102.87	20.0%	368,410.48	9,210.29
22	Plumbing	318,379.60	41,339.35	35,021.76	45,321.00	121,732.34	38.2%	196,647.26	12,173.23
23	Fire Protection	113,707.00	37,523.31	12,507.77		50,031.52	44.0%	63,675.48	5,003.15
24	Electrical	420,715.99	21,025.79	8,414.32	31,990.00	61,430.18	14.6%	359,285.72	6,141.02
			0.00						
		5,685,350.00	1,639,876.67	464,612.49	249,186.00	2,353,680.03	41.4%	3,331,669.97	235,368.00

AIA DOCUMENT G703 • APPLICATION AND CERTIFICATE FOR PAYMENT • MAY 1983 EDITION • AIA® • © 1983
THE AMERICAN INSTITUTE OF ARCHITECTS, 1735 NEW YORK AVENUE, N.W., WASHINGTON, D.C. 20006

G703-1983

FIGURE 2.3. G703A form schedule of values. Reproduced with the permission of the American Institute of Architects.

Most contracts allow payment for materials stored on the site or in a bonded warehouse. You must be able to look at these materials and determine if the claimed amount of material is actually there. If not and the contractor defaults, the owner will have to purchase the shortfall even though he or she has already paid for it. The same is true for the percentage complete of each line item of work.

CHANGE ORDERS

A *change order* is an agreement between the owner and the contractor for a change in the work, contract time, or contract sum. It is signed by the owner, the contractor, and the architect. Change orders have always been complicated. If your project is using the 1988 version of the AIA documents, the change orders are even more complicated. In the past, there was no legal alternative to a fully executed change order. If contractors chose to proceed with the work called for in a pending change order, they did so at their own risk. There was no guarantee that the change order would be approved or that the owner would agree to the price quoted for the change. Therefore the project was either stalled or the contractor took a risk. Now there is a provision, called a change directive, for keeping the project moving while change orders are negotiated and executed. A *change directive* is an authorization from the owner for a change in the work, contract time, or contract sum. It is signed only by the owner and the architect. It also may be called a change authorization or a work directive change. You must dig into the contract and understand what provisions are in force pertaining to changes, because they are not all the same and can be complex.

A change may be requested by the owner, by the architect, or, sometimes, by the contractor. If the owner or architect request a change, they should issue a request for a proposal from the contractor, clearly stating the details of the change with supplementary or revised drawings and specifications. When the change order is signed by all parties, it is sent to the field for inclusion in the work and it becomes one of the contract documents.

There are three ways to price a change order: *stipulated sum, unit price,* and *time and materials*. The stipulated sum is based on the contractor's proposal for the change. The unit price change is based on unit prices previously agreed on. The unit price is usually called for in the bids. The price is not determined until the number of units can be established. The time and materials change is based on the contractor's invoices for materials and on the workers' time sheets. The final price cannot be established until the cost of the materials and the time required have been determined.

Check the specifications for actions that may be necessary because of a change order. Some contracts call for the progress schedules, contract time, or the schedule of values to be revised to reflect the change. Others require all changes to be carried separately.

3

PLANNING AND CODES

STAYING AHEAD

One of the inspector's most challenging tasks is to anticipate the contractor's activities and to stay at least one step ahead. Since questions are inevitable, you should be able to anticipate questions based on the scheduled activities and be prepared with answers. (For example, where can the contractor stockpile stripped topsoil?) Therefore, you must have a copy of the contractor's schedule. In the unlikely event that the Contractor lacks a schedule (heaven forbid!) you must know enough about the sequence of construction to anticipate upcoming events and prepare for them.

You need to know when new activities are to begin because one of the most crucial moments in construction is at the beginning of a task. For example, if you aren't watching when the mason begins laying masonry units, a lot of masonry could be in place before it is inspected. If the work is not acceptable to the inspector, there can be a battle over whether to accept it or tear it down and start over.

Of course the masons should know their business, but they may not understand what level of quality is expected. If modular coursing is critical (and it usually is), they should understand the importance of coursing. If the design calls for a clean cavity, they need to know what "clean" means—are they required to have a pull stick in the cavity or just keep it "fairly clean"? If the specifications do not allow acid for cleaning the masonry, the masons would be well-informed to keep mortar off the face of masonry as they go.

The same line of reasoning applies to all the other trades and their tasks as well. It is much easier to have an understanding of what is expected from day one than to haggle over acceptability after some of the work is done. It is also better to do a job right the first time. Redoing, repairing, or replacing cost both time and money that does not have to be expended if it is done right in the first place.

CODES, PERMITS

The common building codes in use are the Standard Building Code, the Uniform Building Code, and the Basic or BOCA (Building Officials and Code Administrators International) codes. Conforming to the codes is the responsibility of the owner and the architect. It is usually the contractor's responsibility to secure building permits. To secure building permits in most places, the contractor must submit the drawings (and sometimes the specifications) to the ruling authority, usually the city, but sometimes the county or even the state, for approval and code checking. There also may be separate checks by the fire marshal, the electrical department, the department of health, the agency responsible for handicapped accommodations, and so forth.

What is important to you as the inspector, is that the set or sets of documents that have been checked by the code officials must be kept, unaltered, on the project site. Sometimes a permit will be issued on the condition that additional requirements, marked on this set of drawings, be met. Meeting these requirements is the contractor's responsibility, but you should know about the requirements. You also should know that a plan check does not relieve any obligation to conform to the codes. A local inspector may see a previously undetected discrepancy on the site, and it will have to be addressed; whether it was noticed during the official plan check or not.

You should know what permits are required and see that the actual permits are properly displayed at the job site. Other than a general building permit, the contractor may need permits for electrical construction, plumbing, excavation, curb cuts, boilers, demolition, and temporary utilities. Most jurisdictions will issue a certificate of occupancy when the construction is complete and they are satisfied that all code provisions have been met. This certificate is usually needed to get the final utility hookups or to have the services turned on.

INSPECTION BY LOCAL AUTHORITIES

Local code authorities usually require multiple inspections. You should know what must be inspected and at what stage of construction it must be expected. Talk to the local code authority and find out exactly what is required. Some common inspections are underground plumbing pressure tests, wiring, concrete reinforcing (usually not as exhaustive as you will make), framing, and boilers. Ensuring that these inspections are made is usually the responsibility of the contractor, but it is in the best interests of the owner if the inspector is informed and does not let these requirements go unmet.

Some jurisdictions also have their building inspectors make unannounced inspections from time to time during the construction. You (and the contractor's superintendent) should accompany these inspectors during the inspection and note all discrepancies pointed out. You also may be able to explain details of the design that may overcome some of the inspector's objections.

I am aware of one state (and there may be others) in which the building code requires the architect to inspect the construction and certify that it was constructed according to the contract documents. This places a legal as well as an ethical responsibility on the construction inspector that cannot be sidestepped.

4

RELATIONS WITH
THE CONTRACTOR

Maintaining good relationships on a construction project is a delicate endeavor. You must walk a thin line between becoming an adversary and becoming too friendly and too lenient. This skill comes with experience, but you can gain a lot of good insight by simply testing your actions with the "Golden Rule" and an unbiased sense of fairness. You should be impartial and neither too harsh nor too lenient.

It is nice to be liked. It is nice to be accepted into the "brotherhood" of construction. But an inspector is on the job not to establish friendships but to provide quality control. You need the respect, not the personal friendship, of others on the site. Be friendly. Just don't get too chummy with them, because they may try to take advantage of your friendly nature. Never accept gifts or favors. They will surely be recalled, subtly or not so subtly, when contractors need a favor, usually when they want you to relax some standard of quality.

Griping is often heard around construction. (This phenomenon is certainly not exclusive to construction.) Architects gripe about contractors. Contractors gripe about architects and subcontractors. Subcontractors gripe about architects, contractors, and suppliers. Everyone gripes about something. It is natural and healthy. On the project site you will be exposed to the gripes of the contractor and the subcontractors almost exclusively. The temptation will be strong to listen to their gripes and become sympathetic. You must not take sides. You must learn to be objective and not judgmental of the personalities involved in the project. Your job is only to be an unbiased, impartial monitor of the provisions of the contract documents, not to satisfy gripes.

The old diplomatic doctrine "speak softly, carry a big stick" applies on the construction site as well. You should let the contractor know that you are not

21

on the job to interfere with the work, but you are going to require that the intent of the drawings and specifications be met. Be very clear that you will call to his or her attention any discrepancy you see and will diligently pursue whatever action is necessary to have the discrepancy corrected. Remind him that you are also there to help him conform to the contract documents.

Never advise a contractor, superintendent, or worker as to the means or methods of construction. That is supervision. If you take the responsibility for supervision, you become responsible for the construction and assume a tremendous liability that rightly belongs to the contractor. If your directions cause a delay or added cost, the contractor may present you with a claim for extra payment. Supervision and methods of construction are solely the constructor's duty and responsibility. For instance, there are many questions you should ask a superintendent before concrete is placed (see Chapter 9). You need to ask these questions in such a way that you avoid becoming responsible for the outcome of the concreting. You're there to help ensure stability of the operation. Concreting is a hectic endeavor. It helps to have already discussed potential problems beforehand, because "in the heat of the battle" people tend to panic when faced with unforeseen problems. You do not want to be placed in the position of needing to stop the work because the superintendent has forgotten to cover some detail, such as making sure that a working vibrator is available.

CLOSE DECISIONS

Quality is also the contractor's responsibility. However, many people involved in construction take the attitude that whatever quality they have provided is good enough and they will leave it to you to prove that it is not. Your judgement must be in strict accordance with the contract documents; no more, no less. But judgment is not quite that black and white. Even if you are going strictly by the book, there will be judgment decisions that can go either way, the close calls. What are some of the other factors that will help you judge?

First, you may be influenced by the type of contract, especially the method of payment. In a lump sum contract, the owner and the contractor have agreed on a price. As long as your decision is in compliance with the contract documents, it will not affect the price. A decision point arrives when the contractor asks you to approve some method or material that does not strictly meet the requirements of the contract, but which he or she believes meets the spirit of the contract. A contractor usually has only one motive for such a request: either it will save money or it will save some time (which will also save money) thus increasing profit. The request may be legitimate, but be cautious about approving these changes without consulting the architect. There may be underlying reasons for the methods or materials specified that may not be apparent in the documents. It also may be that the contractor may not understand the architect's reasoning for specifying certain methods and materials.

In a cost plus contract, close decisions usually immediately affect the price. The saving may go to the contractor or to the owner, or they may split it. Knowing these arrangements may help you make those close calls. Of course, if the call is not close, if it is a clear-cut change in the contract, you are not allowed to make a change without an official change order to the contract.

The second main factor that will influence your judgment is the matter of priority. Every contract has three factors: cost, quality, and schedule. One must have top priority, and one must have the lowest priority. You should know what order they are in to help make decisions. It may be difficult to find out the *real* order of priority. Ideally, priorities should remain the same throughout the project. For example, the owner may have schedule as a top priority during the design. During bidding, price becomes the priority, and then in construction quality will become top priority. This changing of priorities is irrational, and it is unfair to the other parties involved. One can not expect the lowest price and the highest quality, right? You might be surprised to find out how many people *will* expect this to happen.

Discovering the order of priority can be a valuable asset to decision making, though. If schedule, say, is the top priority, you will make decisions that allow the project to be completed sooner. You would not, for instance, reject a tilt-up concrete wall panel with a minor defect after it is in place. That could set a project back two or three weeks. On the other hand, if quality is top priority, you might not hesitate to reject this same panel. If cost were the top priority, you would look at the type of contract to help make a decision.

ANSWERING QUESTIONS

If you don't know the answer to a question, don't fake it. You will lose the respect of the construction people. Admit that you don't know, and ask the project architect or engineer. Don't put it off. Questions usually do not go away. In fact, I find it more common that the question will be asked again, especially if the contractor doesn't like the first answer you've given. If this is the case, the only recourse it to put your answer in writing.

REJECTING WORK

If you have advised the contractor that some portion of the work does not meet the requirements of the drawings or specifications, and he or she seems to be ignoring you, repeat your advice, firmly and without hostility. If the contractor continues to ignore you, take pictures of the defective work and make sure your contractor sees you. Now wait. The builder will probably think about your advice and agree to redo the work. If not, put your position in writing with copies to the contractor and your employer. If this does not have the desired results, you will at least be on record as having given sufficient notice. What follows will probably be out of your hands. It may be a further demand from the architect or the owner. It may also require meetings with all the involved parties to seek a mutually agreeable solution. Ultimately, it could call for arbitration or litigation.

RESOLVING DISAGREEMENTS

Many disputes on the site can be resolved without involving outside parties. Before trying to resolve a dispute, make sure that all the parties to the dispute are present. With the help of those present, try to state the elements of the dispute as carefully and accurately as possible. If there is more than one issue, separate them and handle them separately. Only when everyone agrees to the statement of the problem should you attempt a resolution. You may find that by simply stating the problem there was a misunderstanding that disappears when all the parties understand the nature of the problem.

With the problem clearly stated and understood, the best approach to a resolution is not to press for a ''I win, you lose'', or a ''You win, I lose'' answer. That usually will not solve the dispute. And, if it does, it will usually be a temporary resolution that deteriorates over time. By the same token, compromise is seldom a good solution. Compromise typically is a ''lose–lose'' situation.

The best approach is to look for some new way to solve the problem that will satisfy everyone (the ideal ''win–win'' solution). Brainstorm. Ask a lot of questions. Keep probing until an alternate solution emerges. New ideas or approaches are much easier for the involved parties to accept and to support than giving up something in a compromise.

Such a resolution is not always possible, but it should be your goal in resolving disputes, because when everyone wins the dispute stays resolved. It also promotes better relations on the job and may inspire others to adapt the technique to keep disputes from getting out of hand in the first place.

5

ADMINISTRATIVE
CONSIDERATIONS

PRECONSTRUCTION CONFERENCE(S)

Most construction projects call for at least one preconstruction conference. It is during this meeting that basic understandings (mostly details that are not covered by the contract documents) are brought to the surface, discussed, and resolved. There may be only one preconstruction conference before the construction begins. There also may be preconstruction conferences held before major subcontract portions of work begin. Most typical of these are for blasting, masonry, roofing, and other specialty work that requires special considerations or special coordination.

Preconstruction conferences may be held anywhere, but it is usually most convenient to hold them at the project site. The attendees should be the contractor, superintendent, and any involved subcontractors; the architect and inspector; and, if possible, a representative of the owner.

Because the subjects are vital to the construction process and may or may not be addressed by the contract documents, the following subjects should be discussed.

- Individuals directly involved in the construction should be introduced, their areas of responsibility should be outlined, and their phone numbers distributed. Some of these people will be at the job site, whereas off-site members might be in the contractor's office, major subcontractors' offices, the architect's or engineer's office, and in the owner's office.
- The schedule of construction, sometimes called the progress schedule, should be discussed, particularly with respect to major milestones.
- Regular meetings on the site should be scheduled and attendees should be designated.

- The contractor's safety program should be detailed.
- Quality assurance responsibilities and the responsibility for ensuring that the testing company is notified and present at the proper times should be delegated.
- The appearance, location, and wording of signs should be resolved.
- Site security and the policies concerning admittance to the site must be clarified. For example, an entry gate policy may be needed if there are separate gates for union and nonunion workers.
- Designate materials staging areas.
- Designate construction parking areas and traffic lanes.
- Policy regarding receipt of deliveries.
- Agree on dates for submitting requests for payment; discuss the review and payment schedule.
- The schedule of values.
- Change procedures and cash allowances.
- Quality.

All items on the agenda should be made known in advance to everyone so that they can be prepared to discuss them.

It is advisable to have preconstruction conferences prior to the start of each major construction activity, such as pier drilling, concrete construction, steel erection, masonry, roofing, HVAC, tile, and so on.

TOOLS OF THE TRADE

As with any job, there is a certain minimum number of tools you should have, either on your person or available to you. Those tools you should have with you all the time are:

Pencil or pen,
Writing pad,
Steel tape measure, at least 25 ft long,
Flashlight, and
Pocket knife.

Tools you should have available:

Red pencils,
Hi-liters,
Pocket calculator, preferably one for feet and inches,

Steel measuring tape at least 100 ft long,

Camera, ideally, an SLR 35mm with a 35 to 105mm zoom lens, an automatic flash attachment, and 200 ASA speed print film,

Weather thermometer,

Architect's scale,

Engineer's scale,

Carpenter's level

Small, angled head mirror,

Truck mirror,

Masking tape, and

Duct tape.

Helpful, but not essential are:

Clipboard,

Surveyor's level and rod,

Binoculars,

Drafting equipment,

Pocket recorder or dictation machine, and

Handheld transceiver (Walkie-talkie).

DRESS

Of course, there are no dress codes on a construction project; there are dressing requirements of a practical nature. The first of these is headgear. Any time you are around construction, you should be wearing a hard hat. On most projects, it is not optional but an absolute requirement and just good practice. The contractor will probably furnish one for you but if you are going to be on different projects, you should have your own.

There will be a lot of walking, so wear a *comfortable* pair of shoes or boots but no sneakers or soft soles, and no high-heel shoes. A pair with steel toe reinforcement is a good investment in safety. A construction site always seems to be muddy or dusty, so wear things that you don't mind getting dirty. That doesn't imply that you should look like a tramp. On the contrary, you should look neat and well groomed. You will also find that you never have enough pockets. There are many things in the list above that can be carried in pockets, if you have enough pockets and if they are big enough. Skirts are not recommended.

You should dress for the weather. Do not let the temperature become an excuse for not watching what is going on during construction. When it is cold, especially take care to keep your head warm. Wear a knitted cap that will cover your ears beneath your hard hat.

DAILY LOGS AND RECORDS

Diaries, written memos, logs, and notes on scraps of paper all may carry the force of law. Many courts have relied on such evidence to corroborate testimony in court. Write down and file everything you can and date it. It does not have to be a formal, typewritten document. Handwritten notes, with dates can be just as effective.

Record the basic elements of everyday verbal agreements and telephone conversations. It may surprise you how often "selective amnesia" occurs in the construction business. Whether your company requires it or not, you should keep a daily log of pertinent facts:

Weather,

Work in progress,

Work *not* in progress (if significant),

Estimate of the work force (by major subcontractors),

Major equipment on site, and

Visitors to the site.

Your records should include:

All correspondence,

  Directives to the contractor,

  Answers to questions and interpretations of the drawings and specifications,

  Written communication with your office,

  Log of telephone conversations,

Schedules and schedule changes,

Notes from construction meetings, and

Approved shop drawings and submittals.

If the specifications for some work refer to ambient temperatures, relative humidity, or other environmental measurements, be sure to make measurements and keep careful records. Of course, you should keep your drawings and specifications up-to-date with revisions and change orders. You should also have a place to keep them so that they do not become tattered and unreadable.

HOUSEKEEPING, CLEANUP

Keeping the site clean will probably be a provision of the specifications. Keeping a clean, orderly construction site is not a matter of esthetics. It is a safety issue and one that involves the attitudes of everyone on the site. A site that is littered with construction or demolition debris, disorderly stacks of materials, or trash is potentially dangerous, and tells the workers that no more is expected of them. A poor safety record and poor attention to quality is usually the result. Construction creates a lot of trash. There should be regular cleanups and designated places for depositing rubbish. The rubbish should be removed regularly and not allowed to pile up and become a safety hazard or become a nesting place for pests.

SHOP DRAWINGS AND SUBMITTALS

Shop drawings are not part of the contract documents. To oversimplify, they are merely drawings that show the shop exactly how to make parts that are only generally shown on the drawings. For instance, the structural drawings will not routinely show details of bolted connections. They will be specified as "detailed to develop the imposed stresses." The steel detailer must determine the required bolts and draw the detailed connection so that the shop will know how to make the connecting clips and where to drill holes in the clips and in the beams, columns, or girders. Before any work is done, either in the shop or in the field, the shop drawing should be checked, stamped, and initialed by the structural engineer and the contractor. I am not going to say that the shop drawings should be approved. The wording of these stamps has been a subject of controversy for years, so I will not get into what the stamp should say. Just make sure they have been stamped and initialed before using them.

Submittals are not shop drawings in the strict sense of the word, but they are usually pages from catalogs or manufacturers' literature ("cut sheets") that assure the architect or engineer that the products they are proposing to use conform to the intent of the specifications. Sometimes the submittals are actual samples of the proposed materials. Submittals must also be approved by the architect and the contractor.

No substitutions of materials should be allowed in the field, regardless of the advisability or the reasons for requesting a substitution. Any request for substitutions must be submitted to the architect for a decision.

"AS-BUILT" DRAWINGS

During construction, changes are made for many reasons. Some changes are made to accommodate manufactured items, such as windows, that are not exactly like those shown on the drawings. Others are required when a contractor discovers a conflict (between, e.g., conduit and piping) that does not show up on the drawings, or simply finds a better routing for pipes. Many of these changes are later covered up by construction. It may be important at some time in the future for the owner to locate a pipe that was not routed as was shown on the drawings. That is where "as-built" drawings are helpful. The specifications are affected as well, and they should be included in the same "as-built" procedures as the drawings.

I generally put "as-built" in quotation marks, because some lawyer might take the term literally, and that is beyond the scope of these documents. It is usually the contractor's responsibility to mark up prints to show changes, but sometimes the architect does it. A set of prints and a set of the technical specifications on which changes are marked should be on site. They will be used later to produce the "as-builts." Learn to recognize changes that should be recorded, and see to it that the prints and specifications are properly marked. Maintain this set until the construction is complete, and transmit to the proper party as a part of the closeout procedures.

FIGURE 5.1. A sample panel of exposed aggregate finish at a job site.

SAMPLES, SAMPLE PANELS

In construction, many quality standards are so subjective that they cannot be adequately described in writing. Therefore, the specifications will call for a sample to be made. Specifications commonly call for sample panels of masonry (both face brick and CMU), architectural concrete, and hand-applied finishes such as textured stucco and stained wood. Job site sample panels are illustrated in Figures 5.1 and 5.2.

When the quality of a sample panel has been approved, it will serve as the standard of quality for that material throughout the project. Thus, sample panels must be preserved until there is no chance of a dispute arising over the standard of quality that has been agreed to. If the samples are so large that relocating them will be difficult, if not impossible, they should be placed where they will not interfere with construction and are not likely to be destroyed "accidently."

Panels should also be located where the light will be representative of the light on the finished product. A brick or architectural concrete panel, for instance, should be located where it will be in full sunlight for at least part of the day.

The samples must be made early enough to allow them to be examined and

FIGURE 5.2. A brick sample panel at a job site.

FIGURE 5.3. A curtain wall mock-up in a building under construction.

accepted in ample time before the construction is scheduled to begin. This should include time for remaking the sample should it fail to be approved.

Similar to sample panels are mock-ups. Mock-ups are usually constructed to test procedures and construction techniques. They may also be subjected to testing, and are sometimes destroyed by destructive testing. Figure 5.3 shows a curtain wall mock-up with reflective glazing that has been placed in the corner of a building under construction. It was used to test the assembly procedure and to show the owner what it would look like at full size.

CONSTRUCTION TOLERANCES

No manual on quality assurance would be complete without a discussion of construction tolerances. Tolerances have been the subject of more than one heated discussion about quality assurance in construction. I have participated in projects where the contractor insisted that tolerances can and must be established for all facets of the construction if he was to be held responsible for the quality of his own and his subcontractors' work (which he always is). Specifications can and do establish tolerances for some construction components. Industry standards establish others by reference in the specifications.

But no one can expect all tolerances to be established. That would be an endless task, and it would not put an end to controversy, simply because the contractor might consider any tolerance unattainable. Consider the old concrete slab standard of 1/16 in. in 10 ft. I have never seen a concrete slab built to that tolerance or even close to it. Many contractors say that this tolerance is impossible to achieve and, therefore, is not valid. They probably have good reason to believe it is impossible, but how can you dismiss a tolerance that is stated in the specifications? After all, the contractor agreed to build the project according to the specifications when he or she signed the agreement. In this case, an alternative tolerance would have to be negotiated in order to prevent a breakdown of the quality assurance program.

This is where judgment enters the picture. On the construction site, you will be called on many times during the duration to make a judgment on allowable tolerances, where none have been established or the one's established are unattainable. Part of these situations can be solved by the use of sample panels. Others simply require that you use common sense. If you have taken a position and made a quality call based on your common sense and you can not "sell" your common sense judgment, it is time to call for outside help. Before you do though, ask yourself if your position is a defensible one because you will be asking for someone else to support your position. That outside person must have some reasonable chance of defending and supporting your position, or he or she may have to reverse your decision, leaving you high and dry.

COLOR BOARDS

Color boards are used by most architects to show the client the color scheme designed by the architect. It usually includes all the paint colors and samples of all the other finish materials, such as laminated plastic, stained wood, floor tile, carpet, and so on. It is not one of the contract documents, but it could be a valuable tool to assist you in determining that the correct colors of materials have been used. Whether they are formally presented on mounted boards or not, you should have a complete set of colors and finish materials to compare with those used on the project, and a schedule to denote where each one is to be used.

6

SAFETY AND TESTING

SAFETY

Who is responsible for safety? The simple answer to that question is "The contractor." But the contractor will be the first to tell you that safety is everybody's job, and that is right. You should always be on the lookout for unsafe practices or situations. Even though you do not have the prime responsibility for safety, many courts have seen fit to shift this responsibility to the architect because his or her representative was on site, especially if the attorneys can prove that the architect's representative observed the unsafe act or situation, knew it was unsafe, and did not report it to the contractor. So it behooves you to keep a a sharp eye on safety and report any violations to the contractor *in writing*.

Here are some safety items to look for.

* Rickety ladders, ladders that are not fastened at the top, ladders that are resting on an unsafe surface or have only one foot secured.
* Unprotected openings in upper floor or roof decks, unprotected drop-offs, such as the edge of upper floor decks or retaining walls, stairs without handrails. See Figure 6.1 for a good way to protect small roof openings.
* Workers (or visitors) not wearing safety equipment: lackof hard hats on workers or visitors, lack of safety glasses when required, painters not wearing masks.
* Unsafe equipment or equipment operation (workers riding a headache ball on a crane or the forks of a lift truck), vehicles without backup warnings, frayed or worn cables or ropes.

FIGURE 6.1. Reinforcing bars welded across a roof curb. This is a good way to protect a roof opening.

- Unsafe construction practices such as unshored trenches, boards laid across gaps and used as foot bridges, lack of safety nets or safety harnesses in required situations.

This list is not intended to be a complete listing of all the job site hazards to watch for but a general list of the unsafe practices typically seen on a construction site. It would be a good idea to develop a more extensive list during the preconstruction conference or at the contractor's safety meetings. You should also build yourself a list of things to watch for throughout the construction to be used for future reference.

Hazardous Materials

According to the Occupational Safety and Health Administration (OSHA), a substance is hazardous if "it is a combustible liquid, a compressed gas, an organic peroxide, or if it is pyrophoric, explosive, flammable, unstable, or water-reactive." That covers a lot of ground! You may add to that list materials that might have long-term effects on the health of anyone exposed to them, such as asbestos, silica used in sandblasting, and excessive X-radiation.

Many hazardous materials are used in building construction. Most of them are hazardous because they are solvents or because of the solvents they release with use, such as paints and cleaning solvents. OSHA requires that all such materials must have an accompanying materials safety data sheet (MSDS). These sheets must be available to any worker who is exposed to the materials in question. The MSDS explains all the ingredients and hazards associated with the material, precautions for its use, and antidotes.

Hazardous materials may be present in existing construction that is being rehabilitated, remodeled, or refurbished. The materials may need to be neutralized, encapsulated, or removed. These procedures require special handling methods. Not just anyone should be handling hazardous materials; it requires specialists. This is usually the owner's responsibility but you should be aware that such materials do exist. If you see any suspect materials, or the mishandling of known hazardous materials, do not hesitate to inform your employer.

One of the most common (and prominent) hazardous materials in existing construction is asbestos. Asbestos has been used for fire-proofing, insulation, acoustical ceilings, and resilient floor tile, to name just a few. Asbestos was also used in roofing materials: base flashings, fibrated mastics, ply sheets, and shingles. In fact, there are those who are still using asbestos-containing flashing materials and mastics.

You cannot determine if a material is (or contains) asbestos by looking at it. It must be tested. I have seen materials I would have bet money were asbestos that testing proved were not asbestos. Asbestos removal should only be done by qualified asbestos abatement contractors. Workers must wear protective clothing and the air and workers themselves must be monitored for asbestos concentration (look for the plastic monitoring badge on monitored workers). The removed materials must be bagged and disposed of in a Class 1 landfill expressly for hazardous wastes. Do not monitor the removal of asbestos unless you are trained and certified to do so.

A commonly overlooked health hazard is associated with sandblasting. Anyone sandblasting should wear an approved mask. Many jurisdictions carefully control sandblasting, to prevent others on the project from being exposed to silicosis (derived from breathing the dust from common silica sand). The critical measure in controlling this potential exposure is the size and opacity of the dust plume created by sandblasting. The easiest way to combat an excessive plume is by adding a water spray to the blasting apparatus. There is a downside to water spraying, though. If the sandblasting is being used to clean steel down to bare metal, there is the likelihood of rust forming before the metal can be refinished.

Paint removal can be hazardous. If the paint was applied as late as 1975, it may contain lead or a chromate. Any paint removal residue with greater than 5 parts per million (PPM) lead is classified as a hazardous waste and must be disposed of in a Class 1 landfill, with all the attending administrative measures.

Another common hazard is buried tanks. They are prone to leak and to contaminate the surrounding soil. Contaminated soil can only be discovered through testing, and must be properly disposed of in a Class 1 landfill.

All of these conditions and remedies should be carefully spelled out in the specifications or in the provisions of a separate contract for abatement or monitoring. If they are not, by all means, contact the architect and get specific requirements before allowing work to proceed.

Sanitation

Sanitary facilities must be provided on any construction site. Usually "Port-A-Cans" are used, but if the project is an addition to a building there could be existing toilets. Frequently, though, the owner does not want construction workers using them. Know the rules and abide by them.

If workers are allowed to eat at the site, and they usually are, there should be rules in place regarding the disposal of leftover foods and trash. If left, unattended, on the site, they will attract all manner of pests. A building could be infested with insects or rodents even before it's finished. The situation in Figure 6.2 should never be tolerated on any project site.

INDUSTRY STANDARDS

Industry standards are written to establish (1) minimum quality standards for materials and products, (2) test procedures to verify the integrity of materials and products, and (3) standards for installation of materials and products. Industry standards are written by governmental or quasi-governmental bodies, industry associations, or underwriting associations such as Factory Mutual or Underwriters Laboratories.

Most specification writers will cite industry standards in various sections instead of writing out the entire standard. This makes that part of the standard a part of the contract. The situation is difficult because a virtual library of standards books might be required. If you do not know what a standard requires, ask the person who wrote the specification. Sometimes the standard is not as stringent as the provisions of the specification, but at other times, virtually all the provisions are in the standard. The specification writer should at least know the significance of each standard that he or she has cited.

Some of these standards are published by

ACI	American Concrete Institute
AISC	American Institute of Steel Construction
AISI	American Iron and Steel Institute
ANSI	American National Standards Institute

FIGURE 6.2. This mess should not be allowed. The food leftovers will surely attract rodents and insects.

ASME	American Society of Mechanical Engineers
ASTM	American Society for Testing and Materials
CRSI	Concrete Reinforcing Steel Institute
FM	Factory Mutual
ICBO	International Conference of Building Officials
NFPA	National Fire Protection Association
UL	Underwriters Laboratories

A more complete listing, with addresses and some common reference standards is given in the general references.

TESTING

Some in the construction industry think of quality control *only* in terms of testing. As you can plainly see from the contents of this book, this is a very short-sighted view of quality control. Testing does play a vital role; no one can tell the strength of concrete by looking at it. Nor can anyone tell if soil is compacted to 95 percent Modified Proctor by walking on it. A typical construction project will require many tests to be performed by testing specialists, with specialized equipment.

Some common building construction tests are:

- Concrete cylinder compressive tests at 7, 21, and 28 days
- Concrete air entrainment tests (done on site),
- Concrete slump tests (done on site),
- Mortar cube tests for compressive strength,
- Soil compaction tests,
- Tests on concrete represented by failed compressive strength tests:
    Swiss hammer test,
    Core sample tests,
- Paint film (wet and/or dry) thickness tests, and
- X-ray and Magnaflux testing of shop welding.

Specifications generally call for three concrete test cylinders to be taken for every 75 or 100 cubic yards of each class of concrete placed each day. Some require one additional test cylinder to be taken during cold-weather concreting and for it to be cured on the job site under the same conditions as the concrete it represents. Specifications also usually require one slump test for each set of test cylinders taken. They may also require air entrainment tests for some proportion of concrete used.

It is safe to assume that the testing company people know what they are doing. But some contracts allow the contractor to do some work for the testing company. The most common tasks are the making of concrete cylinders and doing slump tests. You should be familiar with these two at least.

Doing Slump Tests

Why do a slump test? First, it is usually called for in the specifications, which is reason enough to do one. The concrete design nearly always specifies a minimum or maximum slump. The slump test is a final test that can be made before the concrete is placed in the form. It gives a rough indication of the water-cement ratio. The standard test method is based on ASTM C 143.

The test is made with a standard slump cone (see Figure 6.3). The cone is rinsed out and left wet, then placed on a hard level surface. Two samples of concrete are taken from the discharge of the concrete truck in the middle of the batch. The two samples are mixed before they are placed in the cone.

The person making the test should stand on the foot pieces, to hold the cone firmly in place. The first lift should fill one third of the cone. It must be rodded 25 strokes with a 5/8-in. smooth rod, 24 in. long, with a hemispherical end. It must not be rodded with a stick or a piece of re-bar. The second lift should fill two thirds of the cone and be rodded 25 strokes, with the rod just

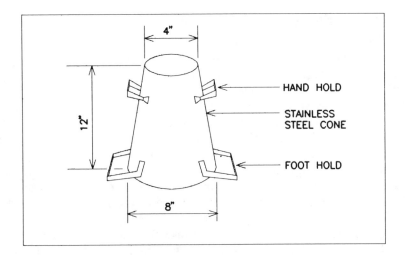

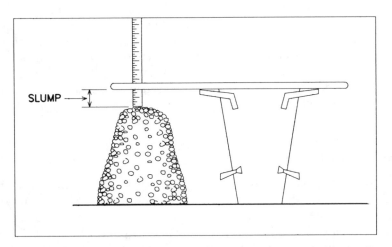

FIGURE 6.3. (top) The cone for making slump tests; (bottom) measuring the slump.

penetrating the first lift. The cone is then filled to overflowing and rodded 25 times, penetrating just into the second lift. The excess concrete is struck off with the rod so that the top of the concrete is just even with the top of the cone.

The cone must be lifted, with no torsional motion, within 3 to 7 seconds after finishing it off. The entire operation must not take longer than 2-1/2 minutes. The tester then places the rod across the inverted cone and measures the amount the concrete has slumped. See Figure 6.3. If the mass has fallen over or a mass has sheared off one side, the test must be redone.

Making Concrete Cylinders for Testing

Concrete test cylinders are made to verify the strength of the concrete delivered to the site. If they are to be useful, two conditions must be met: All cylinders must be made in exactly the same way, and there must be a way of knowing where the tested concrete is located in the construction.

In order to determine where concrete is located, there must be a numbering system for the cylinders. The location can be recorded and keyed to the numbers on the cylinders. This step is essential. If a cylinder fails compressive tests, one must know how to localize and test potentially defective concrete in the construction.

There is a standard method of making concrete cylinders and it must be followed to the letter if results of testing are to be meaningful. The standard method is given in ASTM C 31-75. First, the concrete must be a representative sample. The wheelbarrow used to take the sample should be passed through the stream of flowing concrete at two intervals in the middle of the batch, but neither at the beginning nor at the end of the discharge. The concrete should be hand-mixed before it is placed in the cylinder.

The concrete should be placed in the mold in three lifts. Each lift must be firmly rodded 25 times with a smooth, 5/8-in. rod with a hemispherical tamping end. With each lift, the rod should penetrate the previous lift. The tester must fill the molds uniformly; that is, the first lift is placed in all the molds and rodded, then the second lift is placed in all the molds. After all the molds have been filled and rodded, the tester strikes off and trowels the top evenly with the top of the mold.

Curing the Cylinders

After the cylinders are made, it is mandatory to handle and store them correctly. Nearly every time I have seen concrete cylinders fail compressive tests, the concrete in the building was found to be up to the required strength. Cylinder failures are commonly attributable to either the making of the cylinders or the handling of them after they are made rather than to faulty concrete. For accurate results, cylinders must be handled carefully until the concrete has taken an initial set. If they are set on a board alongside a construction road, for instance, they will surely be affected by the vibration of construction traffic and will fail compressive strength tests. If they are set out in the sun and allowed to dry unevenly and prematurely, they usually fail. If they are thrown in the back of a pick up truck immediately and taken to the lab, I will bet the rent money that they will fail.

Testing Concrete in Place

If concrete cylinders fail testing, then the next step is more testing—testing of the concrete in place. The contractor must be able to locate the concrete that is represented by the sample in the construction. If he or she cannot, the test results may apply to a very large segment of the concrete in place. You have an interest in being able to identify where the tested concrete is also, so you should discuss this with the superintendent and be satisfied that you know how you will locate concrete from a specific set of test cylinders.

The first test is usually the Swiss hammer test (sometimes called the Schmidt hammer test). A Swiss hammer is a spring-loaded device with a rod (the hammer) inside a tube. The device is pressed against the face of the concrete and pushed until the hammer/plunger is released and strikes the concrete. The device measures the rebound of the plunger. It can give a relative indication of the strength of the concrete, but not an absolute value. Many tests must be made before any conclusions may be reached.

If the concrete fails this test or if the results are inconclusive, cores must be cut in the concrete. These cores are then taken to the lab and tested. The location of the cores is determined by the structural engineer, and the holes must be patched. If this fails, the concrete must be removed or reinforced. Removing concrete is seldom justified because it is not structurally "clean," and it is demoralizing to the construction team. Concrete beams can sometimes be reinforced with steel attached to the outside of the beam. This is not always possible, though, and removal becomes a structural engineering decision.

Deciding whether to repair or to remove defective concrete is not to be taken lightly and should be resolved at the highest level of decision making on the project.

7

MISCELLANEOUS CONSIDERATIONS

PHOTOS, FLASHLIGHTS, AND MIRRORS

Photos

These fall into the category "tricks of the trade". Photography should be used throughout the construction. It should be used often and liberally. Photographs are an excellent supplement to your memory or notes. Quite a good project history can be recorded with photos, and they can also document disputed construction that is later covered up. As I said before, you can use your camera to help get the superintendent to be more responsive to your rejection of materials or workmanship.

The camera should be a 35mm SLR, if possible. If a better camera is not available, a Polaroid or a 110 Instamatic will do. In a pinch, go to a drugstore and buy a disposable 110 camera.

You also need a good flash for inside photography. A flash can provide some surprise benefits. Sometimes the finished photographs reveal discrepancies that were not seen when the picture was taken.

Use a color film that is not too fast (ASA speeds of 200 or below). Faster films tend to be grainy when their speed is really needed. Do not bother with black and white. These days, it takes longer to get them developed (if you can even find somewhere to have it done) and they are much more expensive.

Flashlights

A common problem in construction is lack of adequate light, both for the construction and for inspecting the construction. The more powerful a flashlight is, the better. The best available flashlights have halogen bulbs, which put out an extremely bright light. Remember to keep extra batteries on hand.

Mirrors

Mirrors are valuable in several situations. When you inspect drilled pier holes, use a large truck mirror to reflect sunlight into the pier hole. For sheer brightness and the effective distance, sunlight is far better than a flashlight. Obviously, it will work only when the sun is out, so have a flashlight as well, just in case.

You can also use a mirror to inspect the tops and bottoms of doors, especially those made of wood, to ensure that they have received the appropriate finish. Wood doors are usually factory sealed. But the door must be trimmed to fit the frame. The bottom is usually trimmed, and therefore no longer sealed. If it is not refinished, moisture can enter the wood and contribute to warping, swelling, and delaminating of the surface finish. An inexpensive dental mirror (the kind with the mirror on an angled head) is best for looking underneath a door.

INTERIM PUNCH LISTING

The term *punch list* is a construction colloquialism for a list of construction errors, unacceptable workmanship, or damaged construction that must be repaired or replaced. Typically, punch listing means inspecting and writing down the discrepancies. The main inspection associated with punch listing is the final inspection, but no contractor should have to wait until the job is complete to receive a punch list. You should do this as a regular activity. It is especially helpful to the contractor in dealing with the subcontractors.

There is a major pitfall associated with interim punch listing. Some construction people have a tendency to become "legalistic" with punch lists: If it is not on the list, it does not get done or corrected. Interim punch lists also have a tendency to become lists of work to be completed. You should not let interim punchlisting substitute for the contractor's responsibility for quality or responsibility to manage the work. Do not let yourself get led into this position. And if you do, recognize it for what it is and lead yourself out of it.

One general contractor I know that has established a program called "zero punch list". The aim is to eliminate the punch list at the end of the job by doing daily punch listing during the construction. The program was originally established in response to a tight schedule. The only way the scheduler could see to make the deadline was to eliminate the three or four weeks at the end of the job necessary to work off the final punch list. In the follow-up audit of the project, the contractor discovered that he not only saved time but he also made more profit and the overall quality was better.

CHANGES

Changes in construction are as inevitable as changes in the weather. That does not make them any more palatable, but it helps to recognize that there will be changes before they actually happen. Changes in existing work are the worst kind. Who likes to redo or tear out work that they have completed?

It always helps to be candid about changes. Find out for yourself why the changes are required. Then share that information freely. There usually are good, understandable reasons and it will usually help the workers that are involved to accept the necessity for the change.

MISCELLANEOUS

Generic Inspection

What if you are expected to inspect a part of the construction that is not covered specifically in this manual? I am already ahead of you. Turn to Part V, Final Inspection. The first section is a discourse on the *generic inspection;* the inspection of an unknown element that is not specifically addressed. It is a method that may be applied to the inspection of almost anything in construction. It is not intended to be all-inclusive, but it should give a good basis for developing a specific inspection procedure for anything you might need to inspect.

Hand Signals

Construction sites are usually noisy, especially if a piece of equipment is running nearby. In most instances, when one is guiding the operator of a piece of equipment, voice communication is out of the question because of the noise. That is why hand signals are extensively used for communication. There are no "official" hand signals. However, there are signals that are commonly recognized because they clearly communicate what action is intended. The signals shown in Figure 7.1 are some of the most commonly used and understood.

You will see others, depending on what part of the country you are in and what piece of equipment is being guided. For instance, you might see a worker who is guiding a crane operator setting a piece of equipment. The worker will have his face close to the equipment base and hold an outstretched fist for the crane operator to see. He will rub the forefinger with the thumb. This means to move the load v-e-r-y slowly. He will clinch the fist to indicate "stop"—which is a common signal to say "stop." Make an effort to learn the meaning of any project-specific hand signals you do not understand because you may be called on to use them in an emergency.

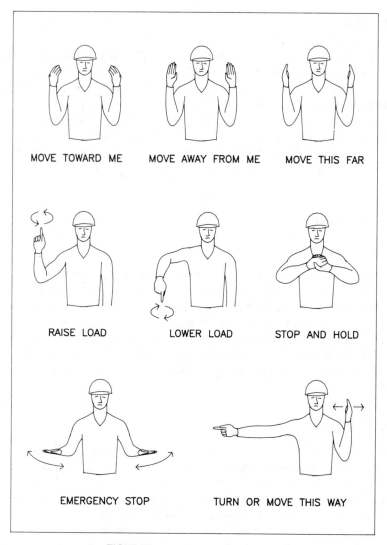

FIGURE 7.1. Common hand signals.

The "B" Word

Of course, we should not even have to discuss the subject of bribes, but in thoroughly exploring the subject of inspection, it must come up. In the role of inspector, there are many situations that occur that are conducive to the offering of bribes. It would be so easy to accept an offer of money to look the other way while a contractor installed an inferior material or did not build some item of work the way it is supposed to be built. I would like to say that this happens only in the movies but we all know that it happens in real life because so many individuals have been *caught* doing it.

In all likelihood, sometime in your career, you too will be offered money. Maybe only a small amount or some thing of small value, but it is likely that it will be enough to tempt you. The best advice I can offer is to decide what you will do in this circumstance—right now—so that you do not even have to think about it when the time comes. Accepting bribes is not only dishonest, it is illegal; and you will probably get caught. Make up your mind right now that you have the integrity to simply walk away from any offer of a bribe without further thought. The only possible exception would be that you might be cooperating with law officials in an effort to catch someone offering a bribe.

Expansion Joints

There are many applications for expansion joints in construction: building expansion joints, expansion joints in paving, drywall, plaster, and so forth. Expansion joints allow the materials to expand and shrink without wrecking the construction materials. The main point is: If there is an expansion joint in the design, expect it to work. Expect the joint to get wider and narrower as the materials expand and contract.

Do not confuse expansion joints with control joints. Control joints generally allow an initial shrinkage to take place and provide a place for a controlled crack to form. After the initial movement is complete, the control joint does not have to allow more movement. Expansion joints must take repeated movement, usually with changes in atmospheric temperature. Make sure that any expansion joint can tolerate this repeated movement.

Many places in which expansion joints are placed probably would not move if the joint were not there but because there is an expansion joint, they do move. Therefore, always look at the construction and detailing of an expansion joint as though it will move throughout the total range of movement that the design allows; because it will. Ask yourself, "Will the joint allow the full movement to take place without breaking or distorting the surrounding materials?" If the answer is "no", call it to the attention of the architect and request a revision or a clarification.

Come-Alongs

Every time I hear this term, a red flag goes up in my brain. It usually means trouble. A *come-along* is usually a cable or a chain with a hydraulic jack or a lever winch. See Figure 7.2. One end of the cable is fastened to something stationary, and the other end is fastened to something that is to be moved by pulling on the cable with the jack or winch. The come-along has legitimate uses, but I have found that it is generally used for questionable purposes. I have seen workers try to straighten a structural member, such as a steel beam

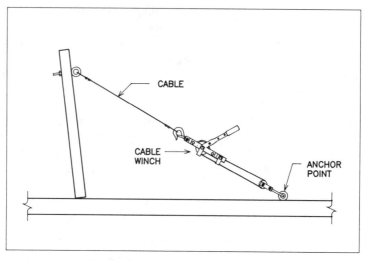

FIGURE 7.2. A typical "come-along" setup.

or open web joist, with a come-along. Obviously, this is not a legitimate usage.

During one winter a contractor called me in a panic and cried "come out here quick, we've got a wall about to fall over!" The wall was a CMU wall with face brick on the outside and a 1-in. cavity between the face brick and the CMU backup. See Figure 7.3. The wall was about 20 ft tall and 50 ft long, with control joints at each end. Just beyond each control joint was a radiused corner of the same construction. Eventually, a bond beam at the top would tie the wall to the corners, but it was not yet in place.

The outside of the wall faced north. It was a sunny day (about noon) and there was a cold wind out of the north. The wind had chilled the face brick and it contracted while the sun had warmed the CMU and it expanded. The net result was that the wall began to bow so that the upper corners became misaligned with the more rigid radiused corners. These corners were about an inch or so out of line toward the outside (north).

The contractor was convinced that the wall was about to fall over, and he already had two come-alongs attached to pull it back into alignment. I convinced him to wait until dusk and take another look at it. Sure enough, when the temperature of the two faces of the wall evened out, the wall came back into alignment. If the contractor had pulled on the wall with the come-along, it surely would have cracked and he probably would have had to tear it down and rebuild it.

"It's Not Available"

I have heard the words "it's not available" many times when a contractor wants to substitute a product for one that is specified or has been approved. Frequently, I have taken this as a challenge, spent an hour or so on the phone,

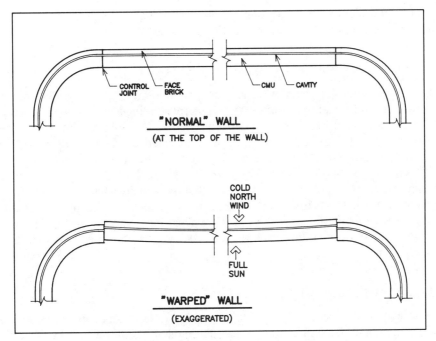

FIGURE 7.3. Tale of the "wall falling over."

and located the "unavailable," product (which was probably more expensive than the contractor had estimated). Although a specified product may not be available, this pleading is often used to gain your approval of an inferior product, so be careful.

Intimidation

Many people in the construction business know no other way to persuade others than by intimidation. This tactic is usually tried early in the project, but it can start at any time. Intimidation can take many forms. The most recognizable is a hostile threat promising bodily harm. However, it also can be in the form of a veiled threat. I have worked with two different contractors who said that they were about to go out of business anyway so if they are forced to furnish work or materials that they did not want to they would simply walk off the job. I have seen this ploy actually work! Learn to recognize a threat or an attempt at intimidation. Typically, it is unmistakable, but some are so skilled at intimidation that it may escape you.

A favorite example is one particular pier driller. If this one is asked to return to a hole to clean it out, he may throw a fit, or maybe just glare at you with that "I'd like to break your kneecaps" look. If you are confronted with this sort of intimidation, you do not have to be belligerent in return. Do not carry on a discussion with the driller. Talk to the contractor's superintendent and he will deal with the driller. Simply insist that the hole must be clean before you will allow it to be filled with concrete.

"It's Not in My Bid"

On a public project (which required open bidding) I had trouble with a subcontractor's materials submittals. He kept sending a submittal for a product that was a cut below what had been specified. I would rejected it, and he would submit it again. I finally called him and asked why he had not submitted a product that would meet the requirements of the specifications. He said, "it's not in my bid." I asked why it wasn't. He replied, "if I bid that way, I would never win a bid." Unfortunately, that is probably a true statement for a public bid, where the low bidder is almost always awarded a contract, regardless of the unsoundness of the bid. However, this is no reason to relax the requirements of the contract. This is a risk each bidder takes by submitting such a bid.

Scaling the Drawings

You will be tempted at some time or another to lay a scale on the prints to determine a dimension instead of calculating it. If the dimension is a critical one be very, very careful. Or better yet, don't. The reasons are many. Some drafters will change a dimension without redoing the drawing because it is too much trouble. Printed media are not necessarily accurate, either. If a tracing is reproduced on the typical blueprint (or blueline) machine, the print paper and the tracing go around a roller together and the difference in the radius of the paper and the tracing introduces an error. That is why overlay drafting requires flatbed printing techniques. If overlays were made on a machine with rollers, they would never register.

Noncritical dimensions, such as the location of a typical electrical outlet may be OK; but think twice before using a scale on drawings because of the high risk of error. If there is no other way, ask the architect if it is OK to scale the location.

II

SITE AND STRUCTURAL CONSTRUCTION

8

SITEWORK

LAYOUT AND SURVEYING

It is customary to have a registered surveyor place stakes marking the property lines. The surveyor may also be asked to survey and set out a marking system to locate the building and several bench marks, for convenience, and set batter boards for the building perimeter. A batter board is a horizontal board fastened to two stakes, set about 3 ft apart, near the top, at about 18 in above grade. See Figure 8.1. Marks made on the horizontal board align with the proposed line of the building. A string or wire is then stretched between the marks on two sets of batter boards to help locate foundations and grade beams. Batter boards and strings might be used for the entire perimeter of the building, and must remain until no longer needed.

A mistake in the layout at this point can have grave consequences. Many law suits have resulted from mislocated buildings. It seems that a surveyor's layout is too often taken for granted and never checked. Obviously, you should verify the location of the lines of the building with the dimensions on the drawings. You may need a helper if the dimensions are large enough.

A licensed surveyor might also be requested to lay out the roads and parking lots. If the site is complex, the surveyor may set up a grid system for locating the buildings and site features. The grid system helps in minimizing the distances that must be measured from an established location. The less the distance that must be measured, the less are the chances for error.

For grading, a surveyor must set grade stakes. These are $2'' \times 2''$ wood stakes that will have their top elevation set at the required elevation to assist the motor grader operator. These stakes usually have a coating of chalk on the top surface, usually blue (which is why they are sometimes called "blue tops") that will be scraped off by the blade on the motor grader when the

55

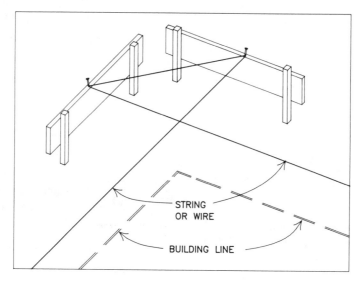

FIGURE 8.1. Batter boards.

correct grade is reached. See Figure 8.2. After the grading is complete, ask the surveyor to check critical elevations—or, better, if you can get the equipment and a helper, check them yourself.

Any existing utility lines (water pipes, sanitary or storm drain pipes, electrical conduit, telephone lines) should be located and staked. Don't be surprised if unknown lines are discovered during construction. They have probably been abandoned, but the contractor should contact the utility that is involved and verify that the line is no longer in use. I remember discovering that a contractor had drilled a pier hole through an unknown storm sewer line and filled it with concrete. However, the "abandoned" storm sewer was still in use, so he had to construct a bypass to get storm water around the filled portion of the pipe.

Existing trees or shrubs that are to remain should be clearly marked and protected during construction. The landscape architect or even the contractor may do this; otherwise mark the plants yourself. No grading should be allowed within the drip line (that is, inside the outermost edges of the upper part of the tree) of a tree that is to be saved. This applies to excavation and to fill. Either operation is detrimental to the tree's root system and will probably cause irreparable damage to such an extent that the tree will eventually die. If the grading plan calls for extensive grading within the drip line of a tree that will remain, notify the architect of this condition and request a revised plan or another strategy to save the tree.

FIGURE 8.2. A blue-top grade stake (at ground level) with a tall guard stake beside it. This particular blue-top was bright orange. Note the hay bales in the background for runoff sediment protection.

TEMPORARY DRAINAGE

Nearly every construction site will require some provisions for temporary drainage. If it is not taken into consideration, the results could cause construction delays because an area might be flooded and unavailable for construction. Some local regulations require provisions for the control of temporary drainage so that construction soil runoff won't increase the turbidity of local waters. In that case, a filtering media, such as hay bales, must be placed across the flow of the runoff. See Figure 8.2. The bales (or other media) must be staked in place if the water flow is expected to be strong enough to wash them away.

Local regulations might even require temporary (or permanent) holding basins with metered outflow. These basins help retard a local flooding condition or ensure that the runoff is not contributing an excessive amount of sedimentation to local water. Measures to control temporary drainage should be carefully detailed on the drawings and/or in the specifications. If there are no provisions, contact the architect for details.

GRADING, BACKFILLING, ENGINEERED FILLS

A site that is to receive earth fills usually must be excavated to a specific level before the filling can begin, either to remove unsuitable soils or to preserve an undisturbed layer. Whether excavation is required or not, before filling can begin the integrity of the subbase usually must be tested. This process is called *proof rolling*. The most usual unacceptable conditions are soft areas that cannot be compacted or areas that are wet and undrainable. Unacceptable conditions must be corrected, usually by deeper excavation, stabilization with soil-cement, or laying a geofabric over the unsuitable areas. The soils engineer will specify the proper measure.

Generally, the surface needs some preparation before the filling can begin. Specifications typically require the surface to be broken up with a scarifier or disks to allow a better bonding of the in situ soils with the fill material.

When the fill for a slab must have specific characteristics, such as free drainage or a low plasticity index, the fill is called an *engineered* fill. If engineered fill materials are required, they are usually found off the site, because the site soils probably do not have the requisite characteristics (which is probably the reason for needing an engineered fill in the first place). If the fill material must be imported, you should know the location of the source, and make sure that the fill material brought on the site is from the proper location. The contract will usually require a testing company to verify that the fill material meets the requirements of the specifications.

Compaction of Fills

Because soil-compacting equipment can only compact the soil to a very limited depth, all fills, regardless of the total depth or the volume, should be placed in layers, known as *lifts*. The recommended depth of the lift will be addressed in the specifications, typically 8 to 12 in. Each lift should be compacted before another lift is added.

Compaction is done in different ways, depending on the size of the fill and the materials. If the fill is small, such as backfilling a pipe trench or along a grade wall, compaction is usually done with powered hand tools. For cohesive materials a jumping-jack device that "whacks" the fill material is used;

for sand, a vibratory-type compactor is used. Larger fills require large sheep's-foot rollers (see Figure 8.3) or rubber-tired rollers that are either self-propelled or pulled by a tractor or bulldozer.

A common stipulation of a compaction specification is that the compaction be at the optimum moisture content. The soils engineer should tell the contractor if moisture needs to be added before compaction. Small fills may be wet down with a water hose, but large fills will require a water sprinkler truck.

It is wise to have the testing lab make tests before a deep fill is completed. A compaction failure in the middle of a fill could mean that the entire fill must be removed and recompacted. Of course, any fill should be tested for compaction after it is complete. If a fill is rained on before the fill is covered with a slab or paving, it usually destroys the compaction. Likewise, frost can destroy the compaction of sand fills. The point is that rain or frost may signal a need for new compaction tests.

There is always a need to stockpile something; usually stripped topsoil, to be reused later. Excavated material suitable as engineered fill could also be stockpiled. The area designated for stockpiling should be shown on the drawings. If it is not, you will be expected to designate an area. Just be sure that is out of the way of construction activities and that it will not block critical drainage.

FIGURE 8.3. A sheep's-foot roller.

Material removed from excavations that is not suitable as backfill or topsoil is called *spoil*. The specifications usually call for spoil to be removed from the site. If not, the contractor will expect an area to be designated for stockpiling or spreading it. If the documents do not address spoil or if they are not clear, check with the architect.

Blasting

Never allow blasting on a site unless it is expressly permitted by the specifications. Blasting will probably require permits from the local code authority, and should be carried out only by experts. Blasting operations should not be started without a preconstruction conference to ensure coordination on the site. During the blasting, the area should be marked or cordoned off to prevent workers from wandering into an unexpected explosion.

Grading

If an extensive amount of material must be moved during rough grading, it is usually done with a bulldozer or scrapers (also called earth movers, "pans", and "turn-a-pulls"). Scrapers are self-powered machines that have a large bucket with a blade under the belly for scooping up soil and transporting it (see Figure 8.4). They also have a mechanism for dumping the soil. Earth may also be moved with a front-end loader and dump trucks, and then spread with a bulldozer after it is dumped. These machines can achieve only an approximate finished grading.

The fine grading or finished grading must be done with a motor grader. The surveyor may have to reset the grade stakes after rough grading is complete and before the fine grading begins. Needless to say (but I shall, anyway) that finish grading should never be attempted when the ground is saturated.

Grading tolerances may or may not be established by the specifications. On many projects they become a matter of judgment. Allowable error is usually influenced by proximity to buildings or other built features of the site or to the slope of the land. In general, the closer the grading is to buildings, the more accurate it must be; and as the slope of the ground decreases, the more accurate grading must be and conversely, the greater the slope, the greater the allowable tolerance can be.

Safety

When large earth-moving equipment is moving about the site, keep a watchful eye on the traffic patterns, and if dangerous situations develop, do not hesitate to call it to the attention of the contractor. Large machinery can do a lot of damage in a collision, especially with pedestrians. All wheeled site equipment should have a loud warning device, such as a bell or a beeping horn that

FIGURE 8.4. An earth mover or scraper.

sounds when the vehicle is moving in reverse. In this situation, injuries to pedestrians are most likely.

Trenches are dangerous. Many open trenches have caved in and buried workers. Many workers have perished or been seriously injured in this way. That is why OSHA is so strict with trenches. There are many guidelines to be followed. Briefly, if the trench is dug in soil rather than rock, it is susceptible to caving. The sides of the trenches must be shored or cut to the approximate angle of repose of the material—that is, the angle the soil would assume if it were piled loosely. If the contractor proposes another method, require him or her to prove that the method has been approved by OSHA.

Water Removal

When it rains or if there is excessive ground water seeping there must be provisions to remove the standing water from excavations. It can take a long time for water accumulated in an excavation to evaporate. In fact, if the water is seeping groundwater, it will probably never evaporate. Rainwater can be removed by pumping. Some accumulation can be avoided by grading around the excavation to prevent surface runoff from going into the excavation in the first place. Watch where the discharge of any pumping is going, to preclude problems with local authorities.

If the problem of seeping groundwater is bad enough, the contractor may have to install interceptor trenches, which can be pumped out. The last resort is to install wellpoints. Wellpoints are, in essence, water wells. They are intended to remove the water from the surrounding soil, thus preventing it from seeping into the building excavation. Wellpoints have to be designed by a geologist to ensure that there are enough of them and that their capacity is sufficient to stop the seepage. Once again, watch where any pump discharge is going and make sure it meets local regulations.

Backfilling

Backfilling is the term used for filling in trenches and filling against grade beams and retaining walls. I suppose the term comes from the fact that the fill material was usually removed from the trench or excavation in the first place; and it is just being put back. In pipe trenches, the material removed is probably the best material with which to fill the trench. Verify this condition through the specifications, though, because this is not always the case.

Backfilling should not begin until the excavation is properly prepared. Pipes in trenches must be bedded—that is, surrounded with a granular fill that will not tend to move around with pressure or moisture change. Specifications usually require that grade walls or retaining walls be partially backfilled with a free-draining material, to prevent groundwater hydraulic head pressure from impinging on the structure. Check the specifications for requirements of the particular backfill location.

After the trench or excavation is ready for filling, the filling should proceed in lifts, usually of about 8 in., each one being thoroughly compacted before the next lift is added. This method should prevent the fill in the trench from subsiding in years to come. Subsidence of trench backfills typically causes problems such as standing water, cracked paving, or ruts that can damage lawn-mowing equipment.

STORM DRAINAGE

Ditches

The most basic storm water drainage feature is the drainage ditch. This is not to intimate that ditches are crude or that they are not important. In facilities where underground drainage creates a sanitation problem by providing a harborage for rodents and insects, ditches may be the only means of draining the site. It is important that ditches be properly designed in the first place, and then constructed accurately to function properly.

Ditches are usually designed marginally, because they can be a critical element in establishing the finished floor elevation of the building and, therefore, may determine the amount of fill that is necessary. Accurate grading is necessary if the ditch is to drain and not leave ponded water.

Ditches may require concrete lining or they may simply have a turf grass growing in them. If they are not paved, some attention must given to the fact that they must be regularly mowed as a part of maintenance.

Although not one of your duties, if you see the contractor locating temporary facilities that could be isolated by a drainage ditch that is too wet to cross, point it out to him or her.

Pipe

Most storm drainage systems incorporate underground piping to carry the water to the public storm drain or some other major drainage structure. The pipe may be galvanized steel or reinforced concrete. Since these pipes drain solely by gravity, the grade of the pipe must be maintained accurately. The grade is also used to determine the capacity of the pipe, and ensures that the water velocity will provide "scouring" or self-cleaning of the pipe. Similarly, low spots in a pipe cannot be tolerated because standing water provides a breeding ground for mosquitoes and other insects. Therefore, make sure that the grading conforms exactly to the drawings and is not simply a rough approximation.

The pipe must be properly bedded to achieve and maintain the proper grade. The horizontal alignment and vertical alignment (grade) should be checked before backfilling is begun. The alignment may be checked by sighting down the inside of the pipe with a transit telescope at one end of the pipe and a bright light at the other end. Some contractors use laser devices to assure alignment. If the alignment is not correct, it must be corrected before backfilling is allowed. As with all piping in trenches, the backfilling must be done properly with proper materials.

Where a branch storm drainage pipe joins a main storm line, it is sometimes permissible to chip a hole in the main pipe, seat the intersecting pipe and coat the intersection with a mortar fillet to seal the joint. The preferred method is to replace a portion of the main pipe with a special fitting that allows joining of the smaller pipe with a typical pipe joint. Check the drawings and specifications for the required methods.

In some situations, short pipes or culverts beneath a road that crosses a ditch are designed to be partially filled or silted in, but normally the grade of pipe should smoothly match the grade of the ditch. Also, at the downstream end of the pipe, a concrete apron is usually placed to help prevent erosion of the ditch just beyond the end of the culvert. Verify these conditions with the drawings.

Catch Basins and Manholes

These are the terminations and junction boxes of the gravity drainage world. Catch basins are located at the beginning of the underground drainage system. The basins are usually concrete, either cast in place or precast, with a metal grate on top. In paving, the grate is usually flat and made of heavy cast iron to withstand vehicular traffic. In lawn areas, the covers are usually "beehive" grates, which are more resistant to clogging by leaves and debris. The elevation of the rim of the grate is critical.

Manholes are used to accommodate a change in flow line between incoming and outflowing piping, as junctures between multiple pipes, and as cleanouts. Manholes may be cast-in-place concrete, precast concrete, or brick. Again, the elevation of the top of the manhole is critical

Catch basins and manholes should be cast or set in place before the piping is run, because their invert elevation sets the invert of the pipe. (The invert elevation is the elevation of the bottom inside of the pipe. The flow line is the top inside of the pipe.) Designs usually call for the bottom to be faired or filleted with grout to smooth the pathway for water flow.

For a person to get into a manhole, a ladder or ladder rungs are cast into the wall of the manhole. Manholes must also have covers, which are typically heavy cast iron so that they will not be dislodged by foot or wheel traffic. Check both against the specifications.

Headwalls

Headwalls may terminate a pipe at either end, inlet or outfall. They should be cast in place after the pipe is run. Check the section on concrete for "watch-outs." Piping may also be terminated with a flared end. In steel pipe, this is usually a prefabricated piece of galvanized steel made for the diameter of pipe. With concrete pipe, it may be a free-formed slab of mortar that is "plastered" around the end of the pipe. Check the drawings for details of each headwall or flared end. In some cases, an engineer might specify a headwall design from a local government. If this is the case, ask the engineer to secure a copy of the details for you.

Underground Drainage

Where groundwater or seeping water can accumulate against a grade wall, a basement wall, or a retaining wall, the design usually calls for subsurface drainage. There will be a free-draining fill against the wall, such as gravel, sand, or a manufactured drainage sheet (see Figure 8.5). At the bottom of the wall will be a perforated pipe, surrounded by free-draining material. The perforated pipe must slope, just like any other gravity drainage device. It must be connected to the storm drainage system or to a French drain. A French drain is a hole in the ground filled with gravel and is used in soils in which the water can percolate or leach into the surrounding soil (sort of like a reverse water well).

RAIL SIDINGS

Railroad beds are different from paving beds in that paving is intended to keep water from reaching the subgrade. A rail bed is made of a porous gravel, called *ballast,* that allows water to freely drain to the subbase. However, the

FIGURE 8.5. Top edge of a grade beam drainage sheet.

subbase must be graded to drain the water away as soon as possible. See Figure 8.6. If it is not well graded, the subbase will surely become water-logged and fail.

Rail ties serve two purposes. One is to keep the rails from sinking into the ballast. The other is to keep the rails the correct distance apart. The spacing between the ties is determined by the distance that the rails can span without excessive deflection. The ties are held in place by their own weight, by the weight of the track, and by the ballast packed between them.

The construction sequence begins with the surveyor's layout. The subbase is then prepared and graded, usually by the grading contractor. The balance of the work is typically done by a railroad contractor. The specifications will likely call for the railroad contractor to formally accept the subbase before beginning work. The ballast is added on top of the subbase. The ties are placed slightly lower than their final designed elevation. The rail is then laid and spiked to the ties. Pilot holes must be drilled for the spikes. The track is then raised by lifting on the track and tamping the ballast into place. Two operations are usually needed to get the rail level to the final elevation.

Make sure that the rails have been spiked to each tie and that the subbase

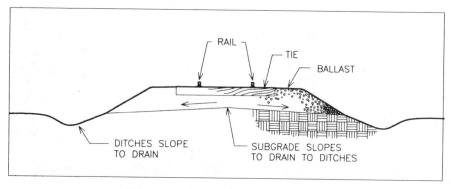

FIGURE 8.6. Section through a rail bed.

drains freely. Check the top of the rail for elevation and grade. Check the specifications for other requirements of the installation.

LANDSCAPING

Scheduling

Landscaping work should not begin before the finished grading is complete in the landscaped area. The schedule should allow plenty of time from start to finish, because landscaping will be interrupted by inclement weather at some time during construction. Ideally, landscaping should be done in the late winter so that it is ready for a full growing season when spring arrives. If this is not possible, plant materials, except grass, may be planted at any time of the year with proper precautions. Grass should not be planted in the fall or winter.

Layout

Landscaping plans are not typically dimensioned as well as a site plan. The layout must usually be transferred from the drawings to the ground by pro-portion and proximity to built features, such as buildings, paving, fences, and walks. However, the layout can still be fairly precise. You may also be able to scale the drawings to relate them to what is constructed.

You should measure the sizes of plant materials called out on the drawings, such as total height, caliper of tree trunks, or the size of the containers they were grown in. You should also measure the spacing of multiple plants, such as with mass plantings or ground covers.

Installation

Read the specifications for detailed requirements of the installation. They should tell you the makeup of the soil for planting beds, the size of holes to dig for larger plant materials, and the procedures to use for setting and backfilling. Staking of larger trees may or may not be called for. If it is, it should be detailed on the drawings. But all landscape architects do not believe in staking. The specifications may require supplemental feeding or fertilization with the installation.

The new plant materials should be protected from general construction traffic. The best method is not to guard the plants but to route traffic safely away from the planting.

See the "Mechanical" section for a discussion of landscape irrigation.

Maintenance

The landscape contractor is usually required to maintain the plant materials for a stated period. He or she may have to water from a water truck if water is not available when the installation is complete. Any plant materials that are dead before the installation has received the final inspection should be replaced. A guarantee of one or two growing seasons is typically required of a landscape contractor. Any plant materials dying during this period should also be replaced. Check the specifications for guarantees and replacement requirements. If plant materials begin to look weak or sick, inform the architect as soon as possible.

ASPHALT PAVING

Some code jurisdictions require paved fire access roads be in place before the building begins to rise above ground. This, of course, makes it necessary to construct roads early in the construction process. If this is a requirement, the paving must be protected from damage during the rest of the construction period. The best protection is to keep all traffic off the pavement. That may not be possible because of the need to get equipment across the paving or to set it up on the paving for access to the construction. Hence, contractors usually place paving *after* the heavy construction is complete. Watch carefully for and record any damage that may be caused by construction equipment.

Asphalt paving begins with a design based on intended use and the characteristics of the soil that will support the paving. Remember, the main purpose of the paving is to protect the underlying soil. Most soils that would be in the vicinity of a building project would have the capacity to support traffic if the soil could be kept dry. If the soil was impervious to water, we would not need paving. But soil is susceptible to water, so we must overlay it with an impervious material to keep it dry. That is what paving is all about. The paving must also be able to support the wheel loads, but most of this is carried by the subsurface and the base.

Thus the paving design begins with the base. Most base materials must be *proof rolled,* a process which consolidates the soil and shows up soft spots. The objective of preparing a base is to have it as uniform as possible.

In heavy, expansive clays, it may be necessary to stabilize the soil. Actually what we are talking about is stabilizing the moisture content at an optimum percentage. If the moisture content is stabile, so is the clay. Stabilization is accomplished by mixing lime, cement, or asphalt with the soils in place. The specifications will tell you what is to be used and how much to mix in. The mixing of the soil and the stabilizer must be thorough. Mixing is accomplished with a special piece of machinery pulled by a tractor. It is somewhat like a very large rototiller. The subgrade should be tested for compaction before proceeding.

Next, it may be necessary to add a compactible engineered fill or base, usually a well-graded gravel. By well graded, I mean that there are a range of sizes so that voids will be minimized. The materials that are submitted usually must be submitted to the soils engineer for approval. Of course, the material used, the thickness, and compaction must be verified against the requirements of the design. This base should be tested for the specified compaction before continuing.

Some paving designs call for a tack course (a sprayed-on liquid bitumen) to be placed directly on the base and the final surface course laid without further preparation. Other specifications call for a binder course, which is similar to a base course but has a bituminous binder mixed with the gravel. Again, a tack course is applied, and the surface course is laid.

The specifications will usually call for submittal of a design mix for the surface course. This is usually a hot-mix bituminous concrete. Some specifications merely refer to a state department of highways specification number. In this case, it is assumed that the local paving contractors are familiar with the state requirements and know what is required. In any case, check with the architect to verify that the material to be used is acceptable.

After the surface course is placed, it must be compacted by rolling with a large steel roller or a rubber-tired roller. The roller should overlap each pass by a specified amount. The surface should be rolled in two directions if at all possible.

Between courses, the surface should be checked for level with a long straightedge. Any low spots should be raked and filled with a fresh mixture, then recompacted.

Some architects and engineers like to have the paving seal-coated immediately. A seal coat is a thin layer of a liquid bituminous material that will coat the surface course and seal it. Most paving contractors and materials suppliers do not recommend seal coating until the paving has weathered for at least a year. The seal coat must have some time to set before traffic can be allowed on it. Check the specifications for requirements.

Striping is usually done before traffic is allowed on the paving. It, too, must have some time to dry before it can withstand traffic without smearing and tracking. The striping should be checked against the specifications for correct materials and against the drawings for accuracy.

9

CONCRETE

CONCRETE BASICS

Because it constitutes the main site-manufactured material on most projects, and because there are many ways to mess it up, major emphasis is given to concrete. To be effective when inspecting concrete construction, you need to understand a few fundamentals about concrete. Contrary to what some in the field seem to believe, it is easy to lower substantially the strength of concrete or the effectiveness of a concrete structure by mishandling the concrete or other components. If enough water is added, the strength can be lowered to almost nothing! If the aggregate is allowed to separate or segregate, the concrete will not be homogeneous and will not protect the reinforcing steel from corrosion.

Concrete is a complex material, and it should not be thought of simply as "mud" that cannot be mishandled. Do not allow people to talk of pouring concrete. It leaves the impression that concrete should be soupy. Concrete should be placed, not poured. It may seem like a small thing, but small things matter when you are dealing with concrete.

Concrete consists of portland cement, small aggregate (sand), large aggregate (gravel), and water. Sometimes additives are put in the mixture to alter the characteristics of the concrete in either the plastic or the cured state.

Portland cement comes in five different types. Type I is the general-purpose cement. Type II is a sulfate-resistant type to be used where soil conditions require such resistance. Type III is a high-early-strength cement, which should not be used indiscriminately because it has low sulfate resistance and produces a high heat of hydration. Type IV is a low-heat type and is to be used in large masses, such as dams. Type V is a special cement for use where especially high sulfate resistance is required. There is another type, which is not a generic, but a proprietary, shrinkage-compensating, cement.

The aggregate is a mixture of fine (sand) and large (rocks or gravel) aggregate. Aggregate is simply a filler so that less cement may be used, and rarely contributes to the strength of the concrete. When you look closely at the wet concrete flowing out of the mixing truck, you should see that all the large aggregate is completely covered with the gray water-cement paste.

The main criterion in choosing the large aggregate is the spaces it must flow through. If reinforcing steel is spaced a maximum of 1/2 in. apart, a 3/4 in. aggregate certainly will not get through. Even if the space is 3/4 in. a 3/4 in. aggregate might not get through. Wet concrete tends to bridge small openings and block passage. Potential blockages must be corrected before the concreting can begin. See Figure 9.1. When you see reinforcing congestion like that shown in the figure, examine it carefully, keeping in mind the size of the aggregate that must pass through the openings. If you think some places will not allow the aggregate to pass through easily, discuss it with the contractor. Perhaps the reinforcing can be adjusted to alleviate the restriction, or a special concrete with smaller aggregate can be used. If there is no reinforcing, there is little to limit the size of the aggregate, other than availability.

The final main ingredient is water. Water must be potable and not detrimental ("deleterious" in most specifications) to the concrete. What is critical is the ratio between water and cement. This is the single most critical element in determining the strength and durability of the hardened concrete. Let me say that it is *super critical,* and the water in the mixture should not be tampered with by anyone. Unless the batching plant is over an hour's drive from the site, all the necessary water should be added at the batching plant. None should be added at the site, by anyone. If the mixture is "too dry" it should be returned to the batching plant. To do otherwise is to jeopardize the design strength of the concrete.

Any number of additives may be included in the concrete mix. None of these should be added after the concrete leaves the batching plant. The proportions of most admixtures are too critical to leave to truck drivers or concrete finishers. Some of the admixtures used are air entraining agents, fly ash, retarders, accelerators, pozzolans, plasticizers, and super plasticizers. Most are added to improve the workability of the wet concrete, to hasten or retard the initial set, or to increase the durability of the hardened concrete.

Before any concrete is placed, the contractor should submit a design mix for each type and strength of concrete to be used. The suggested strength of a design mix can be proven either by a recent track record of testing or by making samples and testing them. The provisions of acceptance of design mixes should be detailed in the specifications. The design mix should be signed off by the engineer. If the contractor overlooks submittal of design mixes, it will delay the start of concreting.

Likewise, it is critical to make early submittal of the first reinforcing steel needed. This usually applies to footing reinforcing or to drilled pier reinforc-

FIGURE 9.1. What a mess! Look carefully at the clearances between the reinforcing before placing concrete with large, angular aggregate. In this joint, the aggregate would clog the openings and cause voids.

ing. Many a contractor has forgotten these shop drawings and has tried to coerce the site inspector to overlook the fact that the steel being placed has not been checked by the engineer.

INSPECTING THE FORMWORK

The first thing to check is the layout. If you have been following the layout from the beginning as you should have, this will be a cursory examination for missing details. The details are what generally get overlooked: for example, notches for doors, rustications, leave-outs, sleeves, dowels for tying to concrete that will be added later. Use the drawings and your tape measure. Make

FIGURE 9.2. The concrete around this base plate was not placed correctly, requiring hand chipping to correct.

FIGURE 9.3. A well-braced grade beam form.

sure the formwork will produce what the drawings call for. Remember, it is much easier to correct mistakes before they are cast in concrete. See Figure 9.2.

Check the forms for general strength. Are they secure? Shake them. Kick them. Do they move? If they do, they are not strong enough and would probably distort under the weight of wet concrete. I have seen forms completely collapse while the concrete was being placed. See Figure 9.3 for an example of a well-braced grade beam form. Will the forms leak? If they do, the cement-water paste will leak out of the mixture and result in honeycombs or weak spots. These flaws must be patched after the forms are removed, and patching concrete is always harder to do than getting the forms tight in the first place. Potential leaks must be closed. Leaking forms may require caulking. Steel pan forms have a special problem where the forms lap (see Figure 9.4). If there is a "fish mouth" or gap, the forms must be fastened together with sheet metal screws to prevent leakage.

Are the forms clean (the surface of the forms as well as the space between the forms)? Are there candy wrappers or lunch sacks lying in the formed space? Many foreign objects are unintentionally cast into concrete. I remember finding a wrecking bar neatly cast in the face of an architectural concrete

FIGURE 9.4. The gap at the edge of this metal pan form will leak concrete. It should be fastened down with sheet metal screws.

column. It was *very* obvious that the inspector had not inspected that form before the concrete was placed.

Have previously used forms been properly patched? Forms that have previously had holes drilled in them should be patched with sheet metal patches nailed over the openings. Is a form release required? A form release is a liquid (anything from old motor oil to sophisticated compounds) applied to the form to keep it from sticking to the hardened concrete. You can usually see dust sticking to the face of a form that has been coated. The formwork should be wetted with a fog spray immediately before the concrete is placed, but it should not be wetted enough to cause standing water in the bottom of the form.

INSPECTING THE REINFORCING

Has the reinforcing been properly placed according to the design? Count the bars. In the beginning, you should measure to make sure of the size of the bar. With experience, you can tell simply by their appearance. The reinforcing should be properly and securely tied at each intersection of bars to maintain its position during placing of concrete. Shake it, kick it. If it moves, it is not tied well enough and will be displaced by the placing of wet concrete. Is the steel properly supported (chairs, etc.)? See Figures 9.5 and 9.6. Check clearances between the reinforcing and the face of the forms. Make sure there is enough room to get the concrete in place without straining out the large aggregate. The specifications give the required minimum clearance. Are the laps joining continuous bars the proper dimension? Are the hidden bars in place (corner bars, dowels, etc., that may not show in a plan or section drawing)?

Reinforcing steel must be supported off the bottom of the form to allow concrete to flow under it. Some contractors may try to support reinforcing with wood blocks. Never allow this. Wood will absorb water and swell with enough force to break the concrete. Even if you believe that moisture will never reach the wood, it will eventually rot out, leaving the reinforcing steel exposed and subject to corrosion. Some specifications, however, allow reinforcing in grade beams to be supported with bricks or pieces of concrete block. The American Concrete Institute standards say that anything used to support the reinforcing steel should have a compressive strength greater than the concrete placed around it. The most appropriate support is a *chair* or *bolster*. A chair is a heavy wire device specially made for supporting reinforcing steel. See Figure 9.7. However, a chair or bolster may not have enough foot area to resist sinking into an earth form bottom, so masonry blocks may be the best support.

The steel must be clean enough that the concrete will effectively bond to it. Only when they are bonded can they act as a single structural material as they were intended. The reinforcing steel must not have dirt caked on it nor be

FIGURE 9.5. A concrete reinforcing chair (low chair).

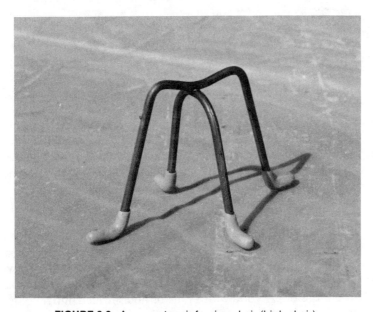

FIGURE 9.6. A concrete reinforcing chair (high chair).

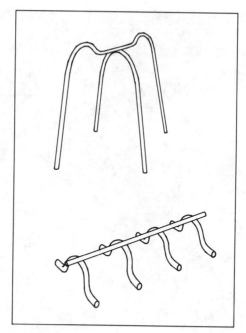

FIGURE 9.7. Concrete reinforcing chairs or bolsters.

excessively rusty. (Some say that surface rust will actually promote a better bond.) If the rust is flaky, it is too rusty.

INSPECTING IMBEDDED WORK

In nearly every mass of concrete placed, there will be imbedded stuff that adds nothing to the concrete structure, but which can compromise the structure if improperly placed. Check the locations of all imbedded items before it is time to place concrete, among which are electrical conduit, plumbing piping, sleeves and block-outs, miscellaneous imbedded anchorage devices, and possibly ducts. Ducts must be securely tied down to keep them from floating out of the wet concrete.

Anchor Bolts

Anchor bolts are always a headache because they are hard to place. The location of anchor bolts is extremely critical (see Figure 9.8). They must either be hurriedly worked into the wet concrete or placed with a template. A template is a piece of plywood with a hole or holes drilled into it conforming to the pattern of multiple anchor bolts (see Figure 9.9). The anchor bolts are

FIGURE 9.8. These anchor bolts were obviously not placed correctly.

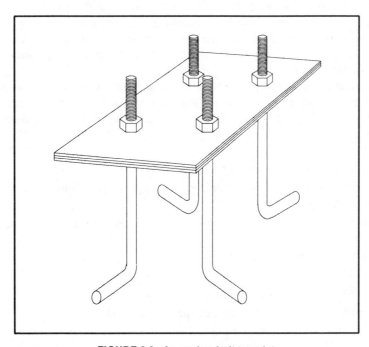

FIGURE 9.9. An anchor bolt template.

inserted in the template with a nut on top and another on the bottom to hold them in place vertically.

The template must be securely fastened to the forms or somehow located out in space for anchor bolts that are not near a form. If there is no form to fasten to, the assembly is usually tied to reinforcing steel. Make sure the fastening is secure.

If the template is large, there is a risk of having a void in the concrete under the center of the template. Concrete must be carefully placed and thoroughly vibrated to prevent voids. Occasionally even the most diligent efforts do not prevent voids. Therefore, templates should be removed soon after the concrete is placed to inspect for voids; and any voids patched with grout.

Some contractors prefer to use various devices to form a small void space around the anchor bolts so that the bolts may be bent into alignment after the concrete has set. This method is usually acceptable, but you should check with the structural engineer to make sure. The void must be grouted with a non shrinking grout after the bolt has been aligned.

CONCRETE PLACEMENT PREWORK

Before beginning a concrete placement, it is in the best interest of the project (and in your best interest) for you to ask a few questions of the person who will be in charge of the concreting. (It is not a given that there will be someone designated "in charge," but there should be). If the person who will be in charge has not covered all the bases, when crisis time arrives, you may be asked to make unnecessary compromises to make up for the superintendent's lack of planning.

As I have stated before, you should not approach this questioning in such a manner as to assume the liability for the outcome. It is done only to prevent a crisis from developing during the concreting. Here are some questions you might need to ask:

- Are there enough workers on hand?
- How is the concrete to be delivered to the forms: chuted directly into forms, buggied, pumped?
- Have circulation paths for trucks and buggies and the sequencing been worked out?
- Is all necessary equipment on hand?
  Water,
  Shovels and concrete rakes,
  Vibrator(s) (and a backup) of the proper type,
  Tremie(s) (a tremie is a portable hopper with a large pipe or snout on the bottom for placing concrete without an excessive drop),

Imbeds, anchor bolts, templates,

Surveying level (in the case of a slab),

Runways (in the case of a continuously cast slab), and

Screeds.

- If any part of the finishing is likely to be done after dark, are enough portable lights available?
- Has the testing lab been informed?
- What will the superintendent do in case of rain? A form failure? Slow delivery of concrete? Concrete trucks waiting too long (hot concrete)? Unacceptable concrete?

CONCRETE PLACEMENT

Proper placement of concrete is absolutely necessary to maintain the strength and integrity designed into it. Therefore, you should watch *all* the concrete being placed. The main goal is to make the concrete homogeneous, without voids or weaknesses. Poor placement can ruin all the careful planning and design that has gone into it. The wet concrete should be placed as nearly as possible in the area where it will remain. In other words, it is best to not have to move the concrete once it is in place in the form.

Concrete is most usually placed directly from the discharge chute on the concrete truck. If it must be transported further than the chute can reach, the most common means are the Georgia buggy, the bucket, and the tremie (see Figure 9.10). Pumping is now becoming more common as a transportation method, especially in awkward places.

The main problem encountered with faulty placement is segregation of the large aggregate from the fine aggregate and cement paste. Many common placement methods can promote segregation. Study Figures 9.11–9.13 to get a feel for things to avoid.

Before the concrete is discharged, the chute of the concrete truck should be wet down, but not enough to dilute the concrete. Make sure that this wet-down water does not go into the forms. The first bit of concrete that comes down the chute, for some reason, will be watery or have dirt clods in it. It should be dumped on the ground and not into the forms.

Concrete should not be dropped more than 3 to 5 ft when placed. Even then it should not be allowed to bounce off the form sides or off the reinforcing steel because segregation will occur. If a drop of more than 5 ft is required, or if there is a lot of reinforcing steel near the top of the form, a tremie should be used to prevent segregation.

A deep form should not be filled to the top in one lift. This is difficult to do that without creating voids; it may also overstress the formwork. The weight of wet concrete and the hydraulic head created combine to produce tremendous forces that can overcome the strongest of forms. The depth of the lifts

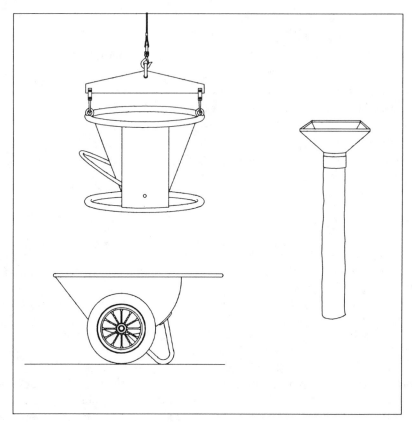

FIGURE 9.10. Concrete placing devices: (above) a crane-lifted bucket; (below) a "Georgia" buggy; (right) a tremie with an "elephant trunk."

should be stated in the specifications. It is usually in the range of 8 in. to 12 in.. Placing in lifts introduces another hazard—cold joints. If the second lift is delayed too long, the first lift begins to take an initial set. When the vibrator is used to blend the second lift into the first, the vibrator either will not penetrate the lower lift, or it will weaken it because the concrete has begun to set. What results is called a *cold joint*. There is no set rule on how much time is allowed between lifts. You must be able to feel the first lift and know that it is still plastic. If it is not, *do not* try to blend by vibration. That will weaken the concrete in the first lift. If appearance is a concern, an exposed cold joint must be patched after the forms are removed.

Inadvertent cold joints are not allowed in concrete that must be watertight because there will be a capillary path all the way through. Cold joints are sometimes planned in watertight concrete, but they always incorporate some form of a water stop. A water stop is usually a piece of flexible plastic that is placed in the center of the mass and at right angles to and across the cold joint.

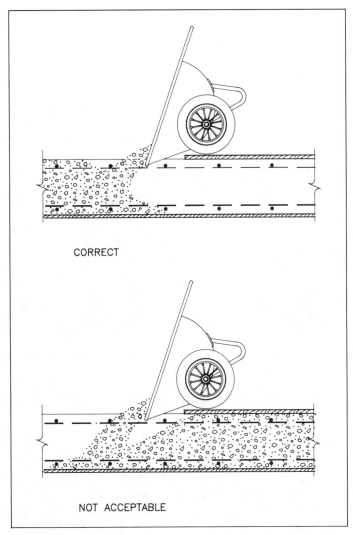

CORRECT

NOT ACCEPTABLE

FIGURE 9.11. Correct and incorrect methods for placing concrete horizontally as in a slab or a beam.

One half of the water stop is cast into the first concrete placed, and the other half is cast into the second placement. See Figure 9.14.

Failure to vibrate, or the misuse of vibrators, can cause many problems. Lazy workers discover quickly that concrete can be made to move horizontally with a vibrator much easier than with a shovel. But moving concrete with a vibrator is a sure way to promote segregation. The shovel is the proper tool for moving it. The vibrator should be used for only two reasons: to consolidate the concrete (eliminate voids and air bubbles) and to blend two

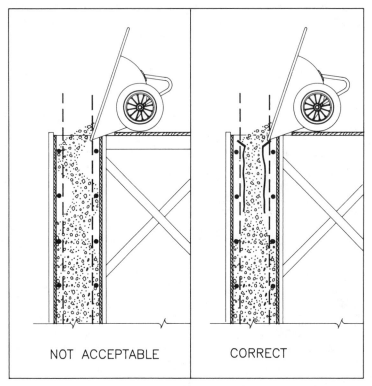

NOT ACCEPTABLE   CORRECT

FIGURE 9.12. Correct and incorrect methods for placing concrete vertically as in a wall or a column.

lifts together. The vibrator should be inserted vertically and withdrawn vertically. It should not touch the forms or the reinforcing, because segregation will occur. Because a strong vibrator has a radius of influence of about 10 in., vibrator insertions must be less than 20 in. on center to compact properly all the concrete. The vibrator should be in use all the time during concrete placement. It is difficult to overvibrate concrete, but it is easy not to vibrate it enough.

It is not unusual for a concrete foreman to look at the first concrete out of the mixing truck's chute and declare that "It is too stiff; add some water." A concrete design mix is based on a specific ratio between the elements: portland cement, sand, large aggregate, and water. Of these, the ratio between the cement and water is the most critical. This ratio should take into account all water, even that in the sand and large aggregate. It is hard enough to obtain the proper water-cement ratio with sophisticated batching equipment; trying to "eyeball" it in the field is impossible. Water should never be added to concrete after it leaves the batching plant. Only by running a slump test can one determine whether it is too stiff. If the mixture is too stiff to place, it should be returned, not watered down.

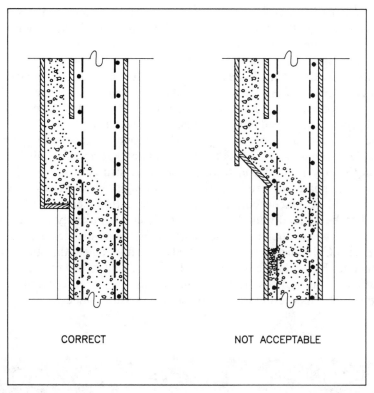

FIGURE 9.13. Correct and incorrect methods for placing concrete in a column through a side port.

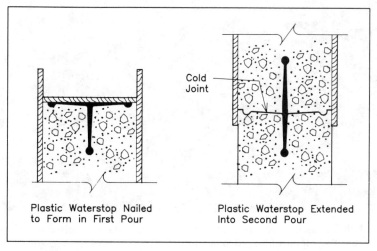

FIGURE 9.14. A plastic water stop placed in a construction joint.

The arrival of concrete trucks on the site should be monitored carefully. If the trucks are kept waiting too long before discharging the concrete, the mixture can begin to set up. If this happens, the concrete will be worthless. The average maximum time concrete can be mixed is about 90 minutes, less in very hot weather. Check the delivery ticket for the time that the truck left the batching plant. If this subject has not been covered in the specifications, reject any concrete that has been mixed over 90 minutes. There may be special provisions for reducing this time in hot weather.

Since most jobs are too large to place all the concrete at one time, joints are inevitable. Even if the job is not too large, complex forming requirements or sequencing may require construction joints. A structural design does not typically designate construction joints. They must be located in the field. Joints should be placed carefully, and the structural requirements of the element to be divided must be observed. Beams are usually divided at the third points, where the combined shear and moment stresses are least (see Figure 9.15).Columns are usually divided at the floor and at the bottom of the beam above. Floor slabs can be divided where a joint would naturally occur, typically at column lines. If you're unsure about the acceptability of the placement of construction joints, ask the structural engineer.

FIGURE 9.15. Suspended concrete after form removal. Note the shoring is founded on mud sills, and that they are wedged for a tight fit.

All construction joints must have elements that will eventually tie the structure together: continuous reinforcing, dowels, and keys. If the reinforcing is continuous, the bulkhead form must be split to allow removal after the concrete has set (see Figure 9.16).

Dowels that are intended to tie the structure together are deformed bars, not smooth ones. If the dowels are No. 3, they can usually be bent at the bulkhead and straightened after the forms are removed. More typically they are larger bars, and the bulkhead must be drilled to allow the dowels to pass through.

Keys form a joint like a tongue and groove joint in wood. The groove is usually formed in the first concrete placed, and the tongue is placed against it. This is done primarily because a groove is easier to form. It can be formed with a 2″ × 4″ nailed to the bulkhead that stops the concrete. The sides must be beveled to permit removal without spalling the sides of the groove. Manufactured steel bulkheads for slabs have the key built in and provisions for reinforcing to penetrate the bulkhead (see Figure 9.17).

If the structure is to be absolutely watertight, the construction joints will have water stops in them.

FIGURE 9.16. A bulkhead in a grade beam form. The slots that allow the reinforcing to pass through must be filled before the concrete is placed.

FIGURE 9.17. A metal bulkhead form for a slab. Note the key and the reinforcing continuing through the form.

CURING

I cannot overemphasize the importance of proper curing of concrete. Improper curing can lead to cracking, crazing, curling, and weak concrete. The cement must have time to hydrate properly in order to become strong and not be prone to excessive or uneven shrinkage. (Note: Be sure to read the section on cracks in concrete slabs.) The longer that concrete can be cured, the better. It cannot be overcured. The best curing will be affected with a wet cure. This is accomplished either by fog-spraying or by covering the concrete with wet blankets and keeping them wet. The concrete can also be wet down and covered with a vapor barrier, such as polyethylene sheets or building paper.

Because these wet methods require more labor, most contractors these days want to use a sprayed-on curing compound. I do not trust these compounds, not because they are not effective, but because the application depends on complete and effective coverage. I usually require that twice the amount recommended by the manufacturer be applied, with each coat at 90 degrees to the preceding one. Do not take this action yourself, but ensure that a curing compound is, indeed, being applied at the specified rate and that the coverage is complete. Check your specifications for the allowable project-specific curing methods.

FORM REMOVAL

Most contractors want to remove forms as early as possible, because they need them elsewhere, but sometimes they remove them too soon. Concrete relies on the formwork to support it until it is strong enough to support itself. Concrete does not reach its design strength for 28 days, but it is seldom necessary to wait that long to remove formwork. That is simply because the concrete will not yet be carrying the design load. The minimum time for form removal should be stated in the specifications. You should follow the terms to the letter and not allow early removal.

It is possible to predict the 28-day strength of concrete based on compressive strength tests at 7 days with reasonable accuracy. See Figure 9.18. If, for

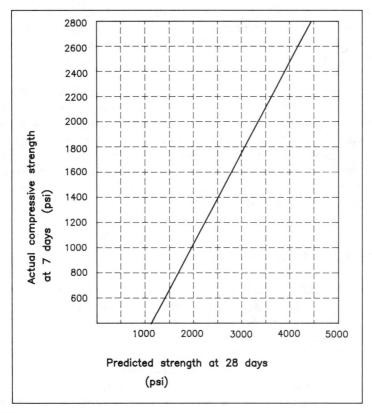

FIGURE 9.18. Predicting the strength of concrete at 28 days from the tested strength at 7 days.

instance, the 7-day tests prove the compressive strength to be 1400 psi, the predicted 28-day strength will be about 2500 psi. Of course, if the cement is high early strength or if the concrete is designed to be over 5000 psi, the chart will not apply.

Shoring for elevated structural concrete is covered later. Suffice it to say that elevated concrete must always be supported or shored even after the forms are removed. I have seen large sections of elevated concrete torn out because it was not properly shored or the shoring was removed prematurely.

WEATHER

Concrete placement should not begin if it is raining, or if there is a strong possibility of it. However, the chances of having precipitation on any given day is hard to predict. (Just ask any weatherman! And, believe me, contractors are no better at predicting rain than weathermen.) Because it is so unpredictable, the contractor should have contingency plans in case unexpected rain comes. Rain directly on fresh concrete, of course will dilute the concrete on the surface and produce an unacceptable finish. If rain does come in the middle of concreting, the form should be bulkheaded to stop the concrete and the fresh concrete covered as soon as possible.

It is easier to anticipate especially cold or hot weather. Temperature extremes create special problems for placing concrete. It used to be that when the temperature reached 40°F and below, the only thing to do was to stop placing concrete and wait until the weather warmed up. Now there are well documented techniques available that will allow for the placing of concrete throughout the winter. In the worst climates, the contractor will simply build a "cocoon" around the construction and heat it to allow construction to continue. The aggregate can even be heated, and hot water can be used to allow placement at colder temperatures.

COLD WEATHER CONCRETING

Years ago, contractors used some form of salt to keep concrete from freezing, but that is unacceptable now. Calcium chloride and sodium chloride used as anti-freezing agents are known to produce some devastating effects on reinforced concrete. They can cause such severe corrosion in reinforcing and imbedded conduit that the concrete will literally explode chunks of surface concrete outward. Check the specifications for allowable special measures and when to apply them.

Do not allow concrete to be placed on a frozen subbase. If the frozen ground is massive and cold enough, it can retard the hydration of the concrete. If the heat hydration of the concrete thaws the frozen ground, the ground will shrink enough to disturb the partially set concrete and lower the strength substantially.

Do not allow concrete to be placed if there is ice on the forms or on the reinforcing. The heat of hydration will melt the ice, but the bond between steel and concrete will be weak.

Another common technique is to use lower-slump concrete (the less water there is to freeze, the better), but check with the structural engineer first.

If the weather is cold enough, the concrete may have to be covered with insulating blankets for proper curings. See Figure 9.19.

Mixing water and aggregates may be heated before mixing to provide a measure of safety during cold-weather concreting. High-early-strength cement (Type III) may also be used to allow the concrete to reach acceptable strengths before it is exposed to cold temperatures. Normal concrete may

FIGURE 9.19. These columns have been properly protected from the cold during the curing period.

have to be protected from the cold for three days, whereas high-early-strength concrete requires only two.

The contractor may have to build a shelter to warm the ground, the forms, the reinforcing, and the newly placed concrete. The covering of the shelter need not be insulated, since it is simply a boundary between warm and cold air. The air in the shelter is not intended to be comfortable, but to keep the concrete components above freezing. If the weather is cold enough to require a shelter, the heaters must be robust. Because the products of combustion are being released into the enclosure, precautions must be taken to guard against carbon monoxide poisoning or simple oxygen depletion. Check the specifications for the temperature that will trigger cold-weather precautions (usually 40°F and falling) and for other requirements.

HOT WEATHER CONCRETING

Placed at 60°F, concrete will take an initial set in about 2-1/2 hours and will be completely firm in about 6 hours. At 100°F it may set up in as little as 45 minutes and be completely firm in 3 hours or less. Hot weather increases the need for immediate curing because the water begins to depart immediately. Therefore it is necessary to plan ahead for an efficient, expeditious system for placing and finishing of the concrete. The routine must be smooth enough that no concrete trucks are kept waiting. The concrete placed in the forms should be no more than 75 to 100°F, according to ACI. The specifications may have more specific guidelines.

Other precautionary measures can be taken, such as adding water and cement, retarders, and ice to the mixture. None of these are applicable to the field operations, and all should be reviewed by the structural engineer

Wind also affects the speed at which concrete will set up: the higher the wind, the faster the drying. This is true in all hot-weather concreting, but it is especially critical in geographic areas of low relative humidity. It can actually effect the concrete during placing, before it can be covered for curing. Therefore, it may be necessary to build shelters to protect the concrete from the wind. Check the specifications for the temperature that will trigger hot-weather precautions and for other requirements.

10

CONCRETE APPLICATIONS

PAVING

As with asphalt paving, concrete paving begins with the subbase. Since concrete will span over small irregularities in the subbase, preparation is usually not as extensive as with asphalt. However, in highly active clays, the preparation may be substantial. In any case, the subbase must be compacted and proof-rolled.

The forms should have the top surface set at the level of the top of the finished concrete surface, since most screeding devices use the top surface of the forms as a rail.

Before the concreting begins, the reinforcing and embeds should be checked. As with all concrete, the reinforcing must be located correctly in the form and secured to prevent movement during placing.

Concrete paving may be unreinforced, but dowels are usually required at joints. The dowels should be secured with devices called *dowel baskets*. Dowels are smooth rods, but they must be greased to prevent their bonding to the concrete. Some contractors prefer to use "whistles," which are light-gauge metal or plastic tubes with one end pinched closed (to resemble whistles). They also prevent dowels from bonding to the concrete (See Figure 10.1). Check the alignment of the dowels. If they are not at right angles to the joint, they will bind and stress the concrete instead of slipping as intended.During concreting, care must be exercised to prevent movement of the dowels. It is best to place concrete around the dowels with shovels until the they are covered.

The surface finish of paving is usually a broom or bag finish. The finish texture is obtained by dragging a burlap bag or a stiff broom across the

FIGURE 10.1. A dowel with a "whistle" to break the bond between dowel and concrete.

surface. This must be done after the surface sheen has disappeared and while the concrete is still plastic.

Joints should be sawed as soon as it is possible to saw without raveling. If the sawing is done too late, the cracks they are intended to prevent will have already formed and the sawing will be useless.

See the sections on cracks in concrete slabs and on caulking.

FOUNDATIONS

Foundations are typically one of three types: spread footings, drilled piers, or driven friction pilings. Less common foundations, such as dug caissons and sand-slurry drilling, will not be covered.

One of the most important aspects of spread-footing and drilled-pier foundation construction is identification of the subsurface bearing material. If the site is sandy and homogeneous, there is little to identify. A typical situation is that a particular strata beneath the surface on which the building is to be has greater bearing capacity than the surface soils. Sometimes it is only a subtle change in the soil, and sometimes it is a particular rock type or formation. The bearing material should be identified in the design, but you should rely on a geological engineer to identify that material in the field. It could be so subtle that the geotechnical person must identify it throughout the construction of the foundations. It also may be so dramatic that anyone could identify it after seeing it only once. You should also know if the foundations are to be placed on top of the strata or if they require some specific penetration into the strata, as is often the case with drilled piers.

The second most important aspect of foundation construction is measurement and payment. This is most often a variable because of the variable nature of subsurface geology. I will discuss the specifics of measurement and payment for the different foundation types, but you should make sure that it is clearly understood by all parties before the work begins. It is most difficult to negotiate payments after the fact.

Spread Footings

Some builders think that the location of spread footings is not critical. Spread footings are not intended to be loaded eccentrically. This can only be prevented in the field by accurately locating them. Of course, the tolerance is greater than for a grade beam, for instance, but they should be accurate to ± 5% of their width. Check the locations. If the top elevation is also critical to later construction, check it too.

Spread footings may be formed, or the excavation may be neat—formed by the earth. Read the requirements in the specifications for the bearing strata. A geological engineer may have to identify the bearing strata. The bottom of the footing should be on undisturbed soil unless other conditions are specifically allowed in the specifications. The bottom of the footing form should be clean and dry. The specifications will be explicit about what to do in the event that a footing is overexcavated. They will usually say that the top of the footing will remain the same and the overage filled with concrete at the contractor's expense.

There may also be stipulations about measurement and payment in the event that the depth of the bearing strata varies. In this case, it is incumbent upon you to supervise and/or verify the measurement as called for in the specifications.

Reinforcing for spread footings may be very simple, but placement deserves the same attention as in any other concrete work. Count the bars, and verify their size and locations. Look for unusual features such as hooks and multiple layers. Make sure the reinforcing is supported properly off the bottom and that the correct clearance is between the bars and between the bars and the forms.

The footing must be tied to the structure that it will support, which could be upturned reinforcing bars, vertical dowels, or anchor bolts. Bars and dowel placement are not particularly critical as long as they fall within the space allotted in the piers or grade beams. Placement of anchor bolts is extremely critical. See the section on anchor bolts. The forms must be tight and strong enough to hold the wet concrete. The bottom must be damp, but not wet.

Placing is straightforward. The concrete must not be dropped more than 2 or 3 ft, and it must be vibrated.

Depending on the design, the top elevation of the footing may or may not be critical. If there are to be short formed piers from the footing to the grade beam, the top elevation is usually not critical. If the grade beams or columns bear directly on the footing, the top elevation is critical. Determine which is the case and act accordingly. Remember, chipping out concrete to lower the top elevation is not fun and games.

Refer to the specifications for disposition of the spoil that is removed from the footing excavations.

Drilled Piers

The layout of drilled piers can be complicated. Not only must the centerline be located, but the proper type and size must be correlated with the location. Locating markers must be protected during the drilling or they will be lost, and the work must be done again.

Pier drillers are always in a hurry. They make their money by the foot of depth drilled so it is advantageous, to be fast. They tend to get edgy if delayed, and they will sometimes try to intimidate an inspector if he or she won't let them move to a new location until they better clean the bottom of the pier or worse, if the inspector makes the driller return to a previously drilled hole to clean it out. I believe some contractors use the drillers to test the mettle of a new inspector. If this seems to be the case, accept the challenge, stay cool, and come out a winner.

There are three classes of pier drilling machinery. The small tractor-mounted rigs are of limited use in most construction that you would be inspecting. The most prevalent type is the truck-mounted rig (Figure 10.2). It is usually limited as to how deep it can drill. For very large diameter or very deep piers, a crane-mounted rig with extensions for the drill stem must be employed. You have no control over the type of machinery used. Just be prepared for a drawn-out affair if the rig is too small for the job, and do not let it become an excuse for unacceptable work.

A geological engineer should be on site to identify the bearing strata. Once it has been identified, it may be clear enough that you can identify it, but do not accept this responsibility if you're not sure you can reliably identify it.

If the pier depends on any end bearing (and most do), you must examine the bottom for cleanliness. A powerful flashlight, or a large mirror and strong sunlight, is an absolute necessity. You can not expect the bottom to be surgically clean, but make sure there is no loose soil or debris left. If there is very dry, loose material on the bottom, a pail of water and a skillful driller can turn the soil into mud balls that can be picked up with the auger. If the pier is

FIGURE 10.2. A truck-mounted pier drilling rig.

not too deep, the bottom can be cleaned by hand with a long-handled shovel with a reshaped blade, called a *spoon*.

In some areas of the country, soils engineers insist that the inspector be lowered into the hole to examine the bottom for cleanliness. This practice is extremely dangerous and I do not allow it. If, however, it is permitted, the following precautions are mandatory. (1) The hole should not be smaller than 30 in. in diameter. (2) There should be two independent and substantial means of raising and lowering the inspector. (3) He or she should carry a reinforced air supply hose. The risk can also be reduced if the hole is cased from top to bottom.

Sometimes, the design calls for the pier to be belled (*under-reamed*). A bell is simply a flare on the bottom end of the pier to increase the bearing surface. Bells are typically placed in soil, but not in rock. When the bearing depth has been reached, the driller will change the auger for a barrel-shaped bit with "wings" that are extended when a plunger at the center of the barrel hits the bottom of the hole. The wings extend and cut the soil away to form the bell.

If the contract has a provision for payment of the piers by the actual amount drilled, the depth of each hole must be measured. The typical contract usually calls for measurements to be taken at the level of the bearing strata and, possibly, at the bottom of the hole. You must also know where the measurement begins at the top. It may be to the bottom of a grade beam, to the top of a grade beam, to the top of the pier, or to the top of an extension on the top of the pier. In practice, the measurement is taken to the ground level and any difference is calculated. If the pier is to be drilled into the bearing strata (called *penetration*), this dimension must be verified. Most contracts call for a minimum penetration, and if the hole is drilled too deep, the driller will probably not be paid for it. Keep your own log of pier sizes and depths, and do not rely on the contractor's log.

If the sides of the pier cave in or if excessive water seeps into the hole, the hole must be cased. If these conditions were anticipated, the design probably will call for casing to begin with. Casings may be permanent or temporary. Permanent casings are usually cardboard tubes (Sono-tubes) or corrugated metal. However, temporary casings of a fairly heavy gauge steel are more common.

The drill auger goes through the casing and the casing is advanced as the hole is drilled. If the hole is deep, casings sections must be welded together as the hole advances. The top section of casing has notches to allow the driller to turn it, to seal the casing against the bearing strata and keep out water.

As concrete is placed in the hole, the casing is withdrawn. The bottom of the casing must remain below the level of the advancing concrete to create a hydraulic head and ensure the integrity of the pier. Sometimes the casing gets stuck. In this case, it must be cut off and left in the hole.

Piers may be reinforced only in the top part, or the reinforcing may continue to the bottom. In either case, it must be prefabricated and lowered into the hole. Reinforcing consists of vertical bars tied with square ties or with a spiral. The size and number of bars should be verified. The cage, as it is called, should be fabricated longer than will be necessary. It is easy to cut off the excess, but it may not be possible to lengthen it. The cage must be lowered into the hole carefully if the pier is not cased, to prevent scuffing soil off the sides of the hole and into the bottom. A small amount of concrete can be placed in the bottom of the hole to provide protection for the steel reinforcing. It is also acceptable to tie a concrete brick on the bottom of the cage to keep it off the bottom.

Concrete should be placed in the hole as soon as possible. No pier holes should be left open over night because the soil will rebound or creep and the pier will not have the same structural integrity when placed, and because a person could fall into an open pier hole even if it is covered. Children, or even adults, could remove the covering for mischief or through curiosity. The concrete must be placed with a tremie, and the top vibrated as deeply as possible. The deeper concrete will probably be consolidated by the weight of the concrete above it.

The contract will probably call for off-site disposal of the spoil from the drilling operation.

Driven Friction Piles

Piles come in many shapes and forms: wood, steel H-shapes, steel pipes, precast and prestressed concrete, and many proprietary styles. The requirements of the specifications should be verified before driving begins.

As with all foundations, the layout must be verified. In most instances, piles will be driven in clusters and tied together with a concrete pile cap.

The bearing strata must be identified. With driven piles, what is beneath the surface cannot be seen, but the subsurface structure still has a story to tell. It tells this story through the reaction of the pile to the driving force. The typical unit of measure is blows of the driver per inch of movement of the pile. This is how the engineer knows when the pile will carry the load for which it was designed.

An experienced geological engineer should be on the site during pile driving. He or she can detect subtleties in the reaction of the pile that may indicate overdriving, rejection, or a failed pile. In the event of a failed pile, the structural engineer should be consulted for corrective action.

Piles are usually paid for by the foot. The specifications should clearly state the basis of payment. There will usually be an assumed length and anything over or under that amount will amount to an extra or a credit.

If the pile is a steel shell to be filled with concrete, the placing of the concrete should follow the same rules as for drilled piers.

Very rarely will a pile be at the correct elevation when driving is completed. The top portion must be cut off and disposed of according to the specifications (usually off site). You should know at what elevation the pile should be cut off.

For each pile driven, the following information should be recorded and kept with your project records:

1. Sizes, lengths, and locations of piles,
2. Sequence of driving,
3. Number of blows per foot for entire length of
   piles and measured set for last 10 blows (or as specified),
4. Final tip and head elevations, and
5. Driving force of each hammer blow.

GRADE BEAMS

Reread the section on formwork because all the comments apply to grade beam forming. Some techniques apply only to grade beams, one of which is neat forming. *Neat* means that one or more of the vertical faces of the grade beam is formed by the earth, not wood or steel formwork. Neat forming should be allowed only if the soil is cohesive enough to remain neat with no sloughing or caving. Make sure that the integrity of the face has not been destroyed during the placing of the reinforcing steel. Also make sure that excessive amounts of loose soil have not been left in the bottom of the form.

I defined neat as referring to only the vertical faces because it is typical for the bottom of a grade beam to be formed by the soil. There is one notable exception. Where the soil is a highly active clay, the design will call for void forms. These are waterproofed cardboard boxes placed in the bottom of a grade beam form to make a void between the bottom of the completed grade beam and the soil (see Figure 10.3). Active clay can produce unbelievable

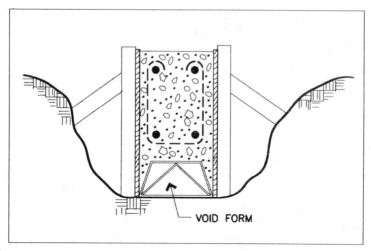

FIGURE 10.3. A trapezoidal carton void form beneath a grade beam.

forces when it is swelling from moisture change, and it can easily wreck a concrete grade beam. It can even force a grade beam off the top of piers if it is not well tied, or if it is tied, the clay can pull the pier loose.

Therefore, Be scrupulous when inspecting the placement of void forms. Obviously, they should not be crushed. Especially look around footings or piers to ensure that the soil is isolated from the bottoms of grade beams. In Figure 10.4 the void forms have been covered with a polyethylene sheet. Void forms are coated to provide some waterproofing, but they can still be ruined by a heavy rainfall. Their integrity must be checked after any exposure to water.

Another grade beam peculiarity is insulation. Sometimes, the drawings and specifications call for the inside face of the grade beam to be insulated, usually with an expanded polystyrene rigid board (Styrofoam). If the inside face of the grade beam is neat-formed, the insulation must be in place before the concrete is placed. As such, the insulation becomes a form, and it must be checked for tightness because leaks will have the same effect on the concrete.

Form ties are used to prevent the forms from spreading outward under the pressure of wet concrete. They need to be in place and properly spaced. Spreaders, usually wood, are either wedged between the inside faces of the form or nailed across the top to prevent the forms from moving inward until the concrete has been placed. If spreaders, or any wood, are left in the forms when the concrete is placed, they can swell with a force great enough to burst the concrete. Therefore, check to make sure that the spreaders can be easily removed as the concrete placing progresses.

Grade marks are marks that indicate where the top of the finished concrete should be. Sometimes the top of the form is the top grade. If the forms are too tall, the grade marks are pencil marks (not very good), nails, or strips of wood nailed at the proper height. Look to see if the grade marks are in place and easily readable.

FIGURE 10.4. Notice that the void forms do not reach to the top of the pier. That portion of the grade beam between the void form and the pier will not be isolated from the grade below.

For various reasons a grade beam must be broken by a construction joint. The contractor may not have enough forms to completely form all the grade beams at once. The construction sequence may dictate partial placement of grade beams. Construction timing may make it important to place some of the grade beams before others. What is important is that the form be blocked off to form a dead end, and you should know where this is permissible. This end form is called a *header*. The third points between footings or supports are the usual places to break it, but if there is any doubt check with the structural engineer. Headers must be split to allow the reinforcing to go through and still permit removal of the form (see Figure 9.17).

SLABS ON GRADE

Before a slab is placed, check several items. The subgrade must be tested for suitability. If the subbase is an engineered fill, it will have already been tested as a part of the filling and compaction operations.

Check the formwork and the reinforcing. If the specifications call for a vapor retarder, check it for continuity, holes, and tears (just finding them is not enough; they must also be repaired). Reinforcing bolsters are the main cause of holes. Look carefully around them. If the specifications call for the seams to be taped, make sure they are. The vapor retarder should be checked around the edges for proper termination.

If the slab is reinforced with welded wire fabric, the contractor may not want to support it off the bottom. The usual proposal is to have a worker with a hooked rod lift the fabric as the concrete is placed. The theory is that once the concrete gets beneath the fabric it will stay there. Experience (and forensic investigations after many failures) has shown that the steel does not remain off the bottom in most cases. It is probably "walked down" by the workers placing the concrete. In any case, hooking the steel is not an acceptable way to ensure that it is located off the bottom. The only acceptable way is to properly support it with chairs or bolsters.

Slabs may contain an abundance of conduit. The location of the conduit risers should have been checked before it is time to place the slab. The same applies to plumbing risers. Usually, the last things to be put in the forms before placing the concrete are sleeves and block-outs. Sometimes they are put in in a last-minute frenzy, which frequently causes errors. Be familiar with what will be sleeved and where so that checking dimensions will be easier and quicker.

If a slab is to be strip-placed (the preferred method), the forms of the strip are usually located such that the screed will reach from one form to the other. If the slab is not to be strip placed, some contractors use wooden grade stakes in the slab area to screed to. These stakes must be removed as the placing progresses. Others use mud screeds. A small pile or piles of wet concrete are placed within the area of the slab so that a screed will reach them. The top is flattened, and the height is set by using a surveyor's level. This flat plane is used like the top of the formwork or a stake to work a screed. This method will not typically yield a very accurate slab surface, but it can be acceptable if done carefully.

When workers are placing a slab, watch carefully when they screed (and later when they float) around things that protrude through the slab, such as columns, pipes, and conduit. The usual result of a lack of attention to these protrusions is a high spot at the protrusion and a low spot between protrusions (called scalloping).

Each strip should have a key form on the edge form, and sometimes dowels. This should be checked on the drawings. If the dowels are small enough in diameter, they can be bent to lie along the edge, so when the forms are removed they can be straightened to protrude into the next strip of slab. Otherwise, the form must be drilled to accept the dowels (see Figure 9.17). The form should also be split along the line of the drilled holes to make it easier to remove the form. Many contractors want to tool the edges of the strip slab, but this is usually not a good practice. If the slab is to be covered with a vinyl floor covering, the tooled joint will telegraph through the covering material. If the slab will carry wheeled vehicles, the joint should not be tooled because it will quickly begin to spall under traffic.

Construction joints are formed by placing two areas of concrete side by side at different times. They should be detailed on the drawings. *Contraction* joints are placed in monolithic concrete to create a plane of weakness, to encourage the natural shrinkage cracking to follow a predetermined line instead of occurring strictly at random. These joints are placed in a slab after the concrete is placed and finished, usually with a concrete saw. Timing of this sawing is critical. If done too soon, the edges ravel. If done too late, the slab will have already cracked and the sawed joints will be useless.

There are proprietary systems to create contraction joints in slabs. These usually consist of strips of metal or plastic placed prior to the concreting. There are also proprietary systems of metal or plastic strips that are set into the wet concrete. Concrete finishers do not like these strips because the blades of rotary finishing machines can snag them and cause a big mess. Careful placement will prevent most finishing problems.

After the slab has been cast, the specifications may call for a hardener, either a liquid, applied with a sprayer, or a dry, shake-on powder. The amount of hardener applied is critical, so there must be a way to measure the amount being applied. The manufacturer's directions should be followed, both as to amount and timing of the application.

The finish of a slab begins with screeding. Before screeding, workers may have to jitterbug the slab with a steel grating to mash the larger aggregate further from the surface. After all surface water has disappeared, the slab can be floated with a long-handled bull float. As soon as it can be walked on without leaving imprints, the slab may be steel-troweled. Some finishers try to speed up the drying of the surface moisture by sprinkling portland cement on the surface. This practice should not be allowed because it will weaken the surface. If steel troweling brings up water, the slab should be allowed to dry a while longer. The bleed water should not be troweled back into the concrete because it will produce a weak surface that will be prone to dusting.

After the slab finishing is completed, it must be cured by the method given in the specifications. The best method is the wet cure. The slab is kept damp with a fog spray of water or covered with blankets that are kept wet. The time of the cure should also be in the specifications. A more popular method is to use a curing compound, which purports to seal the concrete so that it will cure in the water in the mixture. If this method is allowed, the manufacturer's directions should be followed carefully, especially the rate of application.

A number of specialty contractors advertise their expertise in placing and finishing superflat slabs. Superflat slabs may be required on warehouse floors, where merchandise is moved by extremely tall forklift trucks. Small variations in the floor can make the vertical mast of the truck (which may have an operator at the top) sway intolerably. Tolerances for superflat slabs are stated in F-numbers. This system of measurement was developed by the Samuel Face Company, a concrete slab consultant: the higher the F-number, the flatter the slab. Not just any concrete contractor is capable of producing superflat slabs. Most of these contractors limit their activity to this special area of construction and prefer to deal directly with the owner rather than to subcontract through a general contractor.

CRACKS IN CONCRETE SLABS

Although not a problem on every project, cracks can be a major source of dispute. This section will help you evaluate the seriousness of cracks and give some criteria for acceptability. Be sure to check your specifications for acceptability criteria because they might be spelled out clearly there.

Owners are especially unhappy about cracks in concrete slabs. He or she may expect a slab that is entirely crack-free. I know two contractors that will actually buy a load of sand to spread over a newly finished slab to prevent owners from seeing hairline cracks until the slab can be covered up with a floor finish. However, even if the contractor has taken all recommended preventive measures and does a perfect job, concrete *will shrink* during the initial drying process, and as it shrinks, *it will crack*. The trick is to make it crack where you want it to—in a predetermined joint. But, I have seen many, many slabs with cracks just inches away from, and parallel to, saw-cut joints. This always means that the joints were sawed too late. The stress from shrinkage was already building up when the slab was saw cut. I have seen slabs with random cracking all over, the slab which defy rational explanation. The most usual cause of random cracking is inadequate curing. The most effective means of preventing cracks is proper curing. Unfortunately, curing is the most often overlooked or shortchanged of the measures that can be taken to prevent cracking.

Evaluating Cracks

What is an acceptable crack?—one that can be essentially ignored. What is not acceptable?—cracks that must be corrected. Several criteria must be considered:

Size of the crack (width and depth),
Location of the crack, and
Use of the slab.

Size of the Crack *Hairline* cracks appear almost to have been drawn on the surface of the concrete. If you can slip a piece of paper, or even the corner of a business card, into a crack, this is called a *small* crack. Anything larger is a *serious* crack. In this context, "serious"refers to the width of the crack, not the severity of its consequences.

The depth of a crack is immaterial in hairline and small cracks because they are ragged enough and have enough keying (interlocking of the aggregate on each side of the crack) to prevent significant differential movement (either up and down or longitudinal) of the concrete on either side of the crack. Serious cracks are a different matter, however. You can expect any serious crack to continue through the entire thickness of the slab. Then the location of the crack and final use of the slab become the determining factors.

Location of the Crack If a crack is in a predetermined joint, either a construction joint or a sawed control joint, it can be ignored for the purposes of this discussion. It probably will not be noticed any way, which is the desired result.

If a small or a serious crack is in a slab that is to be left uncovered and appearance is a factor, the concrete must be removed because any patching will be unsightly. You will notice that I did not mention hairline cracks. Hairlines are a fact of life with concrete. Chances are that you could find hairline cracking in *any* concrete slab you care to inspect. This is a case where any corrective action will probably make the slab look worse, not better; so it is best to leave it alone and go on about your business.

If a crack is in an area that is to be covered with a floor finish material, the nature of the material must be considered. Any serious crack will "telegraph" through most resilient materials and through brittle finishes (such as ceramic tile). In other words, you will still be able to see the crack in the finish materials. Ceramic tile will crack at the crack in the concrete. Resilient tile will depress or crack at the crack in the concrete. In these cases, the crack must be addressed, whether by replacing the concrete panel or by patching the crack. Carpet would not be affected by any cracking unless the crack is wide enough to insert your thumb. If the crack will be completely covered by a concrete equipment pad, a concrete locker base, or a partition, nothing need be done about the crack.

The main purpose of outside paving is to prevent water from entering the subbase; therefore, any crack larger than a hairline must be sealed. However, sealing may not be enough. If there is automobile or truck traffic on the slab, preventing differential movement becomes important because the sealant can absorb only a limited amount of such movement. Also, if differential movement is allowed, the material immediately beneath the slab at the crack will begin to "pump" and create a soft area or even a void, either of which will make the problem progressively worse until complete failure occurs.

If the slab is reinforced, differential movement is not likely. (Reinforced means a minimum of about 0.2% of the cross sectional area is steel, which is roughly equivalent to No. 3 at 18 in. o.c. each way in a 4-in. slab or No. 3 at 12 in. o.c. each way in a 6-in. slab.) If the slab is unreinforced, differential movement is highly likely, which is why dowels are used at joints in unreinforced concrete. Dowels prevent the concrete on each side of a construction joint or on each side of a crack at a saw-cut joint from moving with respect to the other, mainly up and down. Any unreinforced concrete with a serious crack should be removed and replaced. The entire panel (that is, the area between joints) should be removed.

Another consideration is underslab moisture. If underslab moisture migrates to the top of the slab, the result will be a wet slab or wet carpet or loosened tile. If underslab moisture is anticipated, there should be a vapor barrier beneath the slab, or a granular fill that will not provide a capillary path for the moisture to follow. Even with these precautions, moisture gathered beneath the slab can still find "accidental" capillary paths. If a serious crack (or even a small crack) has formed in the slab, it is highly likely that it has torn the vapor retarder, creating a path to the top of the slab. Moisture does not need pressure or a hydraulic head to travel a capillary; it is sucked right through by the capillary action itself. In these cases, every crack must be sealed to prevent the intrusion of moisture, even cracks located in joints where they are supposed to be.

Use of the Slab   Where the slab will be a wearing surface for vehicular traffic, such as fork trucks, pallet jacks, or hand trucks, any small or serious cracks (including our intentional saw-cut joints) will affect the long-term usefulness of the slab. The main concern here is spalling of the shoulders of the crack or joint. Once the shoulders begin to spall, the traffic will begin to jolt the slab on either side of the crack and lead to equipment damage, pumping of the material beneath the slab, and an eventual soft spot or void, leading to subsequent failure of the slab. Of course, it is best to replace any cracked panel. If that is not a negotiable solution, the next best course is to rout the joint with a crack chaser to a uniform width and smooth the jagged course somewhat; then caulk with a suitable semiresilient material made for this purpose. The results will not be pretty, but they will prevent further deterioration at the crack.

Corrective Measures

If cracked concrete is to be repaired or replaced, try to make sure that the cure is not worse than the problem. It is not easy to produce a good patch. The patch will probably be screeded to the existing concrete, and the shrinkage of the concrete in the patch will create a small offset at the junction of new and old concrete. This can be ground with a terrazzo grinding machine, but it will be visible if exposed and it may even show through floor coverings. Dowels should be drilled into the existing concrete and left to protrude into the new concrete to about half their length. The vapor barrier should also be restored.

Another option is removal. However, removing concrete reflects poorly on the contractor who placed it. It is not only a matter of money but a matter of pride, and could affect your relationship with the contractor for the rest of the project. Removal of concrete should be considered only as a last resort.

Cracks in Structural Concrete

Concrete will crack as it dries and cures. But when is a crack unacceptable? A partial answer is that a crack is unacceptable if moisture can reach the reinforcing and cause it to corrode. Therefore, the answer further depends on whether the crack is in concrete exposed to the weather or in concrete protected from the weather. It has been proven that if a crack is small enough, moisture will be "absorbed" or chemically combined with the cement before it reaches the reinforcing steel. In concrete not exposed to the weather, a crack that is small enough is 0.4 mm (0.016 in.) wide. In concrete exposed to weather the crack can be no larger than 0.15 mm (0.006 in.) wide. Measuring

FIGURE 10.5. Column reinforcing before installing forms and a formed column in the background.

cracks can be difficult, but a relatively simple "go/no-go" gauge can be made from wire of the appropriate size. If you have any doubt about the implications of a crack in a structural member, ask the structural engineer.

The other main consideration, of course, is appearance. This is a highly subjective call, but generally your decision to repair or not should be based on whether the crack or the repair will be more unsightly.

CONCRETE COLUMNS

Column forming presents several unique wrinkles. One is that the reinforcing steel is tied and placed before the formwork is erected. See Figure 10.5. There are exceptions. I once worked with some columns that were about 6 ft square. In that case, the formwork was built first and the reinforcing was added.

Another unique aspect of inspecting column formwork is that it *must* be plumb. Do not take it for granted that someone has plumbed it; check it yourself.

Also unique to column formwork is the depth of the concrete that can be placed. The depth is critical because of the hydraulic head that the wet concrete can place on the forms at the bottom. The designer of the formwork should determine how much concrete can be placed in a lift. Column form-

FIGURE 10.6. A closeup of column forming.

work is usually heavily reinforced near the bottom of the column (see Figure 10.6).

The depth (or height) of a column is also a factor because of the distance the concrete must fall to the bottom of a column form. Concrete must not free-fall the height of the column because segregation of the aggregate will be inevitable. Sometimes a column can be filled by using a tremie. Usually, though, auxiliary openings must be made in the side of the column form that can be opened for placing and easily closed securely enough to resist the pressure of the wet concrete. See Figure 9.13 for the proper way to place concrete through these openings.

ELEVATED CONCRETE STRUCTURES

When concrete structures are elevated, the formwork must be elevated on some sort of a vertical structure, usually many small columns of wood or steel (see Figure 10.7). The structural design of this support system is as critical as the building structure itself. It can not usually be left to intuition, but must be designed by a structural engineer. It must carry not only the weight of the wet concrete but also the weight of the people placing the concrete plus their equipment, both of which can impose lateral as well as vertical loads. The

FIGURE 10.7. Elevated concrete forming.

safety of the people must be considered as well as the structural requirements of the formwork.

One of the most important parts of elevated forming is the foundation for the first level of shoring. Shoring is usually placed on wooden boards lying on the ground, called *mud sills*. (see Figure 9.15). Make sure that these mud sills are placed on firm ground and that they have not been undermined by rainwater or water used to wash out formwork. Mud sills must not be placed on frozen ground. Shoring must be wedged tightly in place to function properly. (See Figures 9.18 and 10.8).

Placing elevated concrete needs more careful planning than does ground-level concrete. Contractors generally pump elevated concrete if it is economically feasible. But when concrete is pumped, it is important to keep the first part of the discharge from entering the forms. This part is usually a wet slurry used to lubricate the hose, and is not sound concrete.

If the concrete is not pumped, some form of vertical lift is needed to get the concrete up to the level of the forms. The most common method is directly placing the concrete with a hopper or bucket lifted by a crane. The bucket is discharged directly into the forms. If there is a large horizontal area to place, a crane may not be able to reach all parts of it. In that case, common methods are to fill the buggy at the form level from a crane-hoisted hopper, or to

FIGURE 10.8. Notice that the shore on the left is not tight against the concrete. It is virtually worthless.

discharge concrete into a buggy at ground level and lift the buggy to the form level by elevator. If there is much concrete to place, a concrete skip will be used. A skip is a hopper that is a part of a materials-lifting elevator. It can carry enough concrete to fill several buggies. Review and follow all of the guidelines for placing concrete.

After the formwork is removed, the concrete must be supported with shoring. The time requirements are stated in the specifications, and they must not be ignored or shortened. I have seen large sections of elevated concrete that had to be demolished because shoring was prematurely removed.

GANG FORMS AND SLIP FORMS

In a project where large sections of formwork may be reused, the contractor may elect to use the gang form or "flying" form technique. Multiple sections of formwork are tied together and braced to act as a unit. This form is then removed and relocated in one piece, usually with the aid of a crane (thus, the "flying" form designation). This method is usually used on multistory projects.

Another technique used on multistory construction is the slip form. This technique was developed by contractors building large concrete grain silos (see Figure 10.9). A form is constructed at ground level, and concrete is placed in the normal fashion. As the concrete near the bottom of the form takes an initial set, the form is raised (slipped) upward by a system of hydraulic jacks. These jacks work on smooth vertical bars that are roughly in the center of the form. Thus, the formwork is supported by the concrete already in place. The operation goes on more or less continuously from the bottom to the top of the structure.

Slip forming requires people who are highly experienced in the procedures and have the proper equipment to make the system work. The formwork must have multiple-level work platforms because the reinforcing steel must be placed and tied ahead of the concreting operation and any required openings must be formed. The speed of the progressive concreting must be carefully calculated so that the concrete reaches the proper strength before the form moves away from it. The average speed that the forms rise is about 12 in. per hour. The levelness of the form must be controlled to prevent the structure from bowing as it rises, and the squareness must be controlled to prevent twisting. These alignments are constantly monitored from the ground with multiple transits, theodolites, or laser instruments.

ARCHITECTURAL CONCRETE

Architectural concrete refers to concrete that will be exposed in the finished construction in a location where appearance is important. It may entail special concrete with white portland or colored cement and/or aggregates

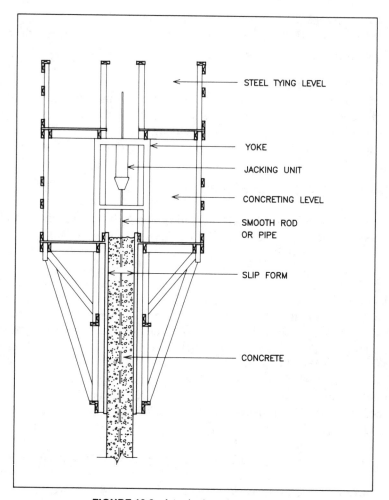

STEEL TYING LEVEL

YOKE

JACKING UNIT

CONCRETING LEVEL

SMOOTH ROD
OR PIPE

SLIP FORM

CONCRETE

FIGURE 10.9. A typical vertical slip form.

that have been selected for appearance. Arriving at special concrete formulation is not typically easy and the approved concrete mix should not be tampered with in any way at the site.

Architectural concrete also implies a special surface, either textured or exceptionally smooth. Texture may be obtained in several ways, the most common using a form liner that has the desired texture (see Figure 10.12). The main drawback to form liners is the size limitation. Any joint in the form liner will show up just like a form joint unless it is carefully treated. Joints are best accentuated with a rustication. That is subjective, though, and the design may not call for a rustication. The only alternative is careful caulking of the joint with a tough-skinning caulk. If the worker is not careful with the application, or if the caulk is soft, the joint will still show up in the finished concrete.

Architectural concrete is especially demanding because it is the classic case of "What you see is what you get." Some patching can be done, but don't let anyone tell you that the finish texturing, sandblasting, or bush hammering will erase flaws. On the contrary, they *accentuate* flaws. Patching should be done and allowed to cure before the texturing is done. The concrete mixture, formwork, placing, and vibrating are all critical with architectural concrete.

Less effective and riskier method of texturing is by using a surface retarder painted on the surface of the form. It is supposed to retard the set of the concrete at the face enough to allow removal of the form and expose the aggregate by water-blasting away some of the matrix of cement and sand. I have found that the results are somewhat unpredictable and generally uneven.

Much more so than with structural concrete, the surface of the forms is important. Soft and hard spots in wood grain will telegraph into the surface of the finished concrete. Any imperfection will show up in the finished product. Some contractors refer to architectural formwork as though the specifications called for furniture-grade work.

The details should get special attention. Most architects design architectural concrete so that the joints between individual form boards will be covered by a rustication. If the contractor ignores the design, the results will be disastrous. Do not take the placement of these details casually, because they are usually a reflection of a highly modular design theme.

Form tightness is also critical. Any leakage will create a blemish in the finished concrete, even if it cannot be detected before the texturing is done. Do not hesitate to call for caulking to ensure tight joints.

All the rules of placing must be adhered to scrupulously if there are to be no disastrous honeycombs or rock or sand pockets. Many specifications call for special high-cycle, high-energy vibrators. If so, make sure that the vibrators are the correct type. The vibrators help consolidation and drive more of the large aggregate toward the form to make the texturing more uniform. They also place much more stress on the formwork, so make sure the forms are stout.

Uniform texturing is highly critical to the success of architectural concrete. Especially with bush hammering and sand-blasting, it is difficult for any two individuals to get the same results. The areas each person works on should be carefully planned so that two different textures are not allowed to meet at obvious places, such as along a wall or a spandrel beam.

Many projects will fund an architectural concrete specialist to act as a consultant during the design phase and during the construction of architectural concrete. Most, though, do not engage one until it is apparent that the finish is not what it should be, and they are called in to fix the damage. At that point, they can do little more than minimize the effects of flaws.

CONCRETE CLEANUP, PATCHING

Cast-in-place concrete will need some attention after the forms have been removed. The amount of work required will be determined by the specifications. Fins usually appear where there are joints in the formwork. They should be removed with a hammer and smoothed with a carborundum stone. Honeycombs and voids should be filled and smoothed. If they are bad enough, some concrete may have to be removed to facilitate a sound patch.

If appearance is important, the patching material should be tested for color match before patching begins. It is best to test several mixtures at once, so that one can be chosen after the test patches have cured, rather than waiting for a sequence of tests. Patching cement is usually made with a mixture of white portland cement and normal gray portland cement, blended in different proportions for different colors or shades of patching material.

If there are large areas of honeycombing (see Figure 10.10) or exposed reinforcing steel and appearance is not a factor, patching may be best accomplished by guniting.

PRECAST CONCRETE

Precast concrete comes in two types: factory cast and site cast. Either may be architectural, structural, or a combination of both.

Site-cast concrete is usually, though not always, tilt-up. The concrete is cast in a horizontal slab and lifted (or tilted up) to a vertical position for use as building walls. Tilt-up walls are usually cast on the finished floor slab or on a "waste slab" that will be broken up and removed when the casting and lifting are complete. Panels cast on the building slab will telegraph any surface defects in the casting slab, such as construction joints or cracks (see Figure 10.11). Wall slabs may be stacked. One slab will be cast and coated with a release agent, and another slab will be cast on top of the first one. I have seen them cast in stacks up to four panels high.

Surface texture and detailing may be obtained with form liners (see Figure 10.12) or rustication strips placed in the form. Accuracy is essential when form features are placed.

Among the imbeds associated with precast concrete are welding plates and attach points to fasten the pieces of precast concrete to the structure or to each other. See Figure 10.13. Metal attaching devices must also be cast into the panel to facilitate lifting. Attaching devices for lifting are typically cast-in metal lifting loops (see Figure 10.14) or cast-in metal castings that have internal threads. The cables from the lifting crane will have attaching devices with external threads. The main problem with cast-in-place devices comes from burying them beneath the surface of the concrete so that

FIGURE 10.10. A honeycomb in concrete.

they are hard to locate. There may also be attaching points for temporary bracing to hold the panels until they can be permanently fastened to the structure.

You will find that, in most instances, once the slab has been cast it will be used in the building. The nature of tilt-up panel construction is that it is usually on the critical path, and the panels must be erected in sequence. Rejected panels can set back the schedule by an intolerable amount, so everything must be right before the panel is cast.

Alignment of precast panels is critical for a good job. The top edges must form a straight line, the joints between panels must be uniform, top to bottom, and aligned for a good caulk joint, and some provision for alignment such as shims or leveling devices is necessary. (see Figure 10.15).

Factory-cast concrete is not cast on the site. Therefore, some inspection must occur at the casting plant. Factory casting allows greater accuracy and more intricate detailing than is obtainable in the field. The factory-cast pieces should be checked thoroughly against the shop drawings. The acceptability of each piece should be determined before it leaves the plant.

Architectural precast concrete can be textured in the form or after form removal by sandblasting, bush hammering, or applying a grit-textured coating material. It may also be colored by painting or staining.

FIGURE 10.11. "Telegraphing" on a tilt-up panel cast on the building slab. Note the diamond-shaped pattern near the bottom. This was a block-out for an interior column in the casting slab.

FIGURE 10.12. Form-textured concrete.

FIGURE 10.13. Tilt-up slab forming. Note the blocked-out beam pockets and the welding plates with the studs protruding into the panel.

FIGURE 10.14. Precast panels awaiting erection. Note the lifting loops and the leveling devices.

FIGURE 10.15. A precast concrete wall panel leveling device.

PRESTRESSING CONCRETE

About the only form of prestressing that occurs on a construction site is post-tensioning. Post-tensioning is done by attaching a hydraulic pulling device to the tension strands, pulling the proper tension, and attaching a lug that prevents relaxation of the strand after the pulling device is removed (see Figure 10.16).

In some cases the retraining lugs are left in place permanently (see Figure 10.17). A recess is formed at the lug, the tendons are cut off below the

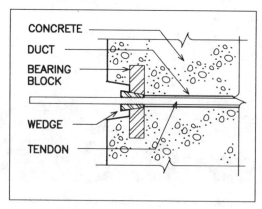

FIGURE 10.16. Posttension lug.

FIGURE 10.17. Lugs or anchor points for prestressing strands.

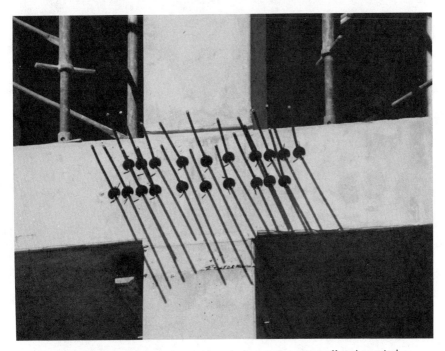

FIGURE 10.18. Prestressing tendons before they are cut off and grouted.

surface, and the recess is grouted (see Figure 10.18). In other cases the tendons are pressure-grouted after the tension has been pulled, and the lugs are removed after the grout has set up. In order to be grouted, the tendons must be in tubular ducts. Usually, the ducts and tendons are cast in the wet concrete, but sometimes only the ducts are cast in. Then the tendons are lubricated and threaded through the ducts after the concrete has set. The lubricant must be flushed out before the duct is grouted. After the grout has set, the restraints are removed. This operation is complex, and you should have the structural engineer monitor at least the start of the tensioning operation.

11

STEEL CONSTRUCTION

STRUCTURAL STEEL

When a truckload of structural steel arrives on the job site, the contractor's first task is to lay the pieces out (supported off the ground on timbers) in an orderly manner with the identifying marks visible. This procedure is called *shaking out*. Basically, a building should be built according to the drawings and specifications, not according to shop drawings. However, all the structural steel elements have been numbered on the shop drawings, and those numbers are used to identify the individual pieces of steel. There is no other way to know where each piece goes than by referring to the shop drawings.

Before erection begins, inspect the pieces. If any are bent or otherwise damaged, they must be replaced. Any that are dirty, oily, or rusty, must be cleaned before erection. Steel is extremely difficult to clean once it is in place. The cleaning is the same, but it is harder to get to without scaffolds or lifts.

Spot-check the predrilled holes. If any are out of round or oversized, probably all of them are faulty. If they are oversized, a larger-diameter bolt must be used. If the bolt will not fit, the holes must be reamed. Out-of-round holes are said to be "wallowed out". They must also be drilled out and a larger bolt used. This drilling out cannot be done by a worker with a hand drill. The holes must be square, which requires a drill press and a means to position and hold the structural member. The steel may have to be returned to the fabricator for corrections.

During installation, be certain that the pieces are installed in the correct places. There will be many pieces with the same number that are interchangeable, but pieces with different numbers are definitely not interchangeable. As the erection proceeds, temporary guys should be placed to brace the structure and to aid in plumbing and squaring the assembly. The assembled frame must be trued before the connections are made tight. Check the alignment of the structure yourself. Check for squareness in the horizontal plane and for levelness and plumbness in vertical planes.

The effects of tolerances will show up in the squaring of a steel frame. It is impossible to get all the members exactly true, but that should be the goal. When assessing the effect of a member that is not true (out of kelter), mentally build the rest of the building around the frame. Test the effect of the misalignment on the finished product. Ask yourself "can the finished materials be adjusted to overcome the misalignment of the frame?" If not, have the misalignment corrected. That may be easier said than done, though. It usually calls for a compromise to *minimize* the effect or to spread it out among several locations.

Most erectors will use erection bolts for temporary fastening during erection. These bolts are not acceptable for permanent use in the structure and should be replaced.

Metal decking is sometimes used for horizontal bracing of the structure in place of diagonal structural members and for serving as a base for the roof system. In this case, the fastening of the deck to the structure is critical. The metal deck must be fastened to the next level of structural framing (i.e., joists, purlins, or beams), the most common methods being welding or by screwing with self-drilling, self-tapping screws. The screws must be the right length to penetrate both the metal deck and the structural member, and they must be the right diameter to achieve the structural fastening necessary. The number of welds or screws and their placement (pattern) must be correct in order to achieve the structural goals. This pattern, or spacing, is not an intuitive thing; it must be calculated by the supplier or by the structural engineer. To summarize, make sure that the screws are

1. The proper diameter and length,
2. Installed with the correct spacing,
3. Going into a structural member,
4. Straight, and
5. Fully driven.

Welding is the least expensive method and is therefore preferred by most contractors. The main "watch-out" with welding is burning through the sheet metal and not getting the weld attached to the structure. Some structural engineers specify the use of welding washers. These washers reduce the incidence of nonwelds, because it will furnish the extra metal needed for the weld. However, washers will not help if the welder does not place the weld over a structural member.

Remember that the individual sheets of the metal deck must be fastened together also, including the end and side laps. Check the dimension of the lap against requirements. They may be screwed together, welded, or button punched. Check the specifications for fastening requirements.

FASTENERS, WELDING

Bolts

Three predominant methods for ensuring that bolts are tightened to their proper tension are turn-of-the-nut, torque wrenches, and snap-off lugs. Determine the appropriate method and see to it that it is applied properly. A washer must be put beneath the turned element. For example, if the nut is held and the bolt head is turned, the washer must be under the head of the bolt. For proper tension with the turn-of-the-nut method, the nut is snugged finger tight and rotated a specified number of turns—no more, no less.

Torque wrenches must be regularly calibrated and used properly to achieve an accurate tightening. The wrench is kept in motion until the proper torque value is reached. Hesitating, stopping, and restarting will result in improper final torque.

Snap-off lugs are on the nut end of the bolt. A special driver is used to turn the bolt while the nut is held motionless. When the driver has achieved the proper torque for the bolt, the lug snaps off.

All bolts should be checked to see that they have been tightened. Some of the bolts should be checked to verify that they have been *properly* tightened. The usual practice is to check one bolt on each connection. If one is found not properly tightened, all the bolts in the connection should be checked. Just one loose bolt could cause the joint to fail. However, the specifications may require that all bolts be checked by the testing company.

Not all bolts are meant to be tightened to provide friction to the connection. Bolts in a slip connection with slotted holes are a good example. Sometimes they will be detailed with double nuts so that the second nut will "jam" the first nut so that it will not loosen. This second nut is called a *jamb nut*.

At present there is a national problem with bolts that do not meet critical specifications. The problem has been investigated by Congress and is widespread. Some unscrupulous third-party brokers have been mixing untested bolts with certified bolts and selling the lot as certified. These substandard bolts have shown up in all sorts of uses, including bridge structures and airplanes. Structural bolts should be certified and have a traceable history. If you have any question about the identity, marking, or certification of structural bolts, alert the structural engineer.

Power-Actuated Fasteners

In many situations, power-actuated fasteners are the best choice, however, in two situations they are unacceptable: (1) where the fastener will be anchored in concrete and strictly in tension; or (2) where one of the parts they fasten is subject to moving loads or vibrations. Driving power-actuated fasteners into concrete presents a special installation problem. If a fastener hits a hard piece of aggregate near the end of the installation stroke, it is likely to bounce (not enough to be seen or detected) and form a poor bond with the concrete. It is

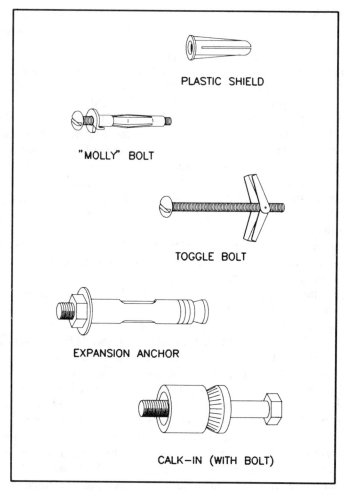

FIGURE 11.1. Common expansion anchors, roughly varying in strength from top to bottom.

susceptible to pull-out if it must secure moving loads or is put in tension. If you have any doubt about an application, consult the structural engineer.

Expansion Bolts

Expansion bolts are typically used in concrete or masonry. They come in many types and forms, from simple bolts driven with a hammer into a predrilled hole to those that drill their own hole as they are installed. The most important concern of expansion anchors is the bond (actually friction) they form with the substrate. The manufacturer publishes a theoretical pull-out value, given a type and length of anchorage. The pull-out and the size of the bolt should be checked by the structural engineer. You should only verify

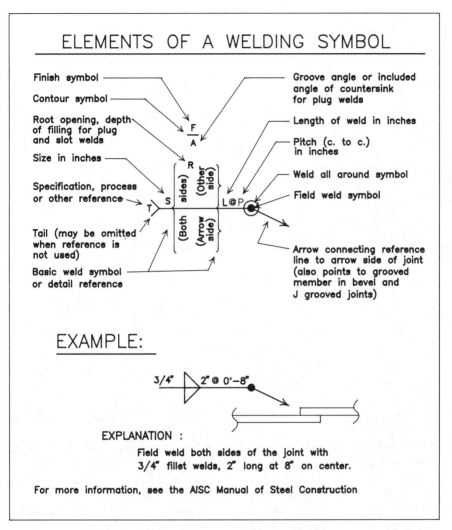

FIGURE 11.2. Standard welding symbols.

that the specified type and size is used and installed correctly. See Figure 11.1 for some common types of anchors. They are only a few of the types of expansion anchors available and are generally arranged, top to bottom, in their order of structural capacity. The upper three are usually used in hollow-wall applications.

Welding

Structural welding is not often done at the job site because it is much more expensive than shop welding or a bolted connection. However, if site welding needs to be done, read the specifications and study the drawings for welding

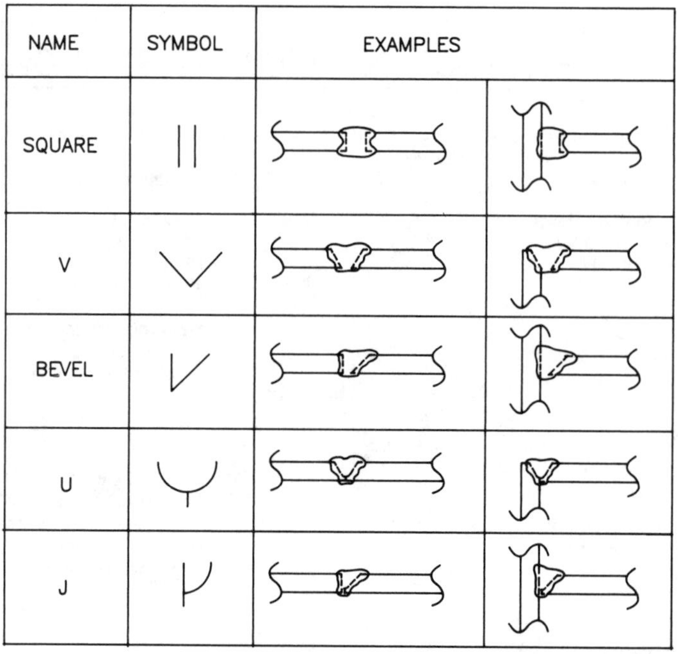

NAME	SYMBOL	EXAMPLES	
SQUARE	||		
V	\/		
BEVEL	\/		
U	\u{}		
J			

For more information, see the AISC Manual of Steel Construction.

FIGURE 11.3. How the symbols look in a weld.

details (see Figure 11.2). If the welding is critical, welders should be certified and the testing company should be involved.

Critical structural welds require preparation of the members to be welded. Cleanliness is essential. The area to be welded can not be contaminated with oil, dirt, paint, or rust. If the detail calls for a full-penetration weld, the pieces are usually beveled to assure that the weld penetrates the total depth of the member, (see Figure 11.3). Sometimes it is necessary to space the edges to be welded apart and in most of these cases, a backing plate will be required. If you have more questions about welding, the AISC *Manual of Steel Construction* is a good place to look.

Most structural welding on a site is noncritical: welding joists to beams or to joist seats in masonry or concrete, welding metal deck to joists, and such. Even these welds should be good welds and must be checked. A good weld will be neat in appearance, with splattering held to a minimum. It will not be cracked. Each bead will be continuous. The weld will be the required size. Measure the width and length of the weld for conformation.

Fastening (for supplemental framing or a hanger) to open-web steel joists should be allowed only at panel points of the lower chord, preferably close to a point where the cross bridging ties to the joist. If something must be fastened between panel points, ask the structural engineer about adding web

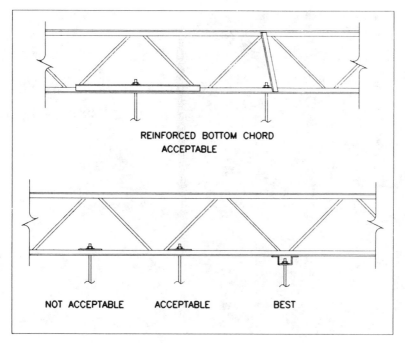

REINFORCED BOTTOM CHORD
ACCEPTABLE

NOT ACCEPTABLE   ACCEPTABLE   BEST

FIGURE 11.4. Hanging loads from open-web steel joists.

members or strengthening the bottom chord (see Figure 11.4). As usual, there are exceptions. If you have any doubts, check with the structural engineer.

Welding for piping is a different matter because the welds are critical, especially where steam is involved. Each welder must be certified. Some specifications will accept welder certification from other projects, but I prefer to have each welder weld a coupon and have it tested. Check mechanical specifications for welding and testing requirements and follow them exactly. High-pressure steam is potentially dangerous, and welding failures could be lethal.

GROUTING

Grouting structural baseplates is not merely for appearance. Grouting evenly transfers the load to the concrete so as not to point-load the concrete and cause a failure. In order to accomplish this purpose, there can be no voids in the grout. Trying to force grout under the base plate from two to four sides is a sure way to creating voids, no matter how carefully it is done. How does one insure that there are no voids? The answer is to grout from one side only, pushing a full bed of grout across the space until it comes out the other side.

FIGURE 11.5. A properly shimmed column baseplate before grouting.

Then there are no voids. It is amazing how many people in the field do not recognize this simple procedure. This method is referred to as *dry-pack*.

To provide space for grouting, a base plate is either shimmed (see Figure 11.5) or nuts are placed on the anchor bolts beneath the base plate to support it temporarily.

When flowable grout is used, the sides must be formed to retain the liquid grout until it has taken a set. The same principle applies to flowing grout: place the grout from one side only. To do otherwise would trap air pockets and voids will result.

Masonry grouting is more like concrete placing, except that the mixture must be flowable enough that vibration is not needed and the masonry is the formwork. The main thing to watch for is the possibility of voids or air pockets. If grout is placed into a dead-end pocket, it must be filled slowly to ensure that an air pocket does not form. If the masonry is very high, you might want inspection holes near the bottom, to see that the grout completely fills the voids in the masonry. The best way, though, is to grout masonry as it rises.

GENERAL CONSTRUCTION

12

CONCEALED WORK

FIREPROOFING

The only purpose of fireproofing is to protect structural members for a specified time against the heat of fire. Heat can penetrate incredibly small openings; therefore, small openings jeopardize the effectiveness of a fireproofing system and may allow the structural member to weaken before it is supposed to in a fire, thereby threatening lives. You must thoroughly inspect the integrity of the fireproofing system for each structural member. However, since not all structural members in every project receive fireproofing, nor do all members always get the same fireproofing, you must know which members are to be fireproofed and what system is used.

Fireproofing is commonly done by using sprayed-on materials (see Figure 12.1) or gypsum wallboard. There are other systems and materials, such as gypsum blocks, but they are not commonly used today. Sprayed-on materials must be inspected for coverage, thickness, and bonding, and the material must be approved. A problem with sprayed-on fireproofing can occur later in the construction sequence. Workers from different trades will scrape off the fireproofing to make way or clearance for their particular piece of construction. If this occurs, the conflict of materials must be worked out and the fireproofing restored.

Gypsum wallboard fireproofing is installed in layers. All systems require that the joints between boards be staggered from the first layer to the second (and subsequent) layers, including at corners. Some systems require the joints to be taped and bedded. Other systems require each layer to be banded. You must be thoroughly familiar with the requirements for inspecting wallboard fireproofing systems. Read the specifications and study the drawings for details. If they are not clear, ask the architect for clarification. Some

FIGURE 12.1. Sprayed-on fireproofing.

architects will simply call out "two-hour fireproofing" or will reference an industry standard. Do not assume that the installers know the standard. Secure a copy of the specific standard and judge the construction against it.

PLUMBING TESTS

A note on plumbing tests is inserted here because many pipes will be covered by general construction and they must be tested and proven leak-free while they are still accessible. For more information on the testing of pipes, consult Part IV. Generally speaking, a test consists of installing plugs in the lower end of the pipe and pressurizing it for a given period of time. Determine if a city inspection is necessary before allowing backfilling or covering with structural or finish materials.

WATERPROOFING

Waterproofing takes many different forms and must be used in various stages of the construction. The application of waterproofing is always critical, because it is nearly always covered up by subsequent construction and will be difficult, if not impossible, to repair later. For instance, in floor-slab water-proofing of an underground tunnel, the waterproofing will be on the underside of the slab. After the complete tunnel is in place, there is no way to repair the waterproofing without demolishing the tunnel and starting over again.

Waterproofing is used on tunnel floors, walls, and ceilings, on basement walls, beneath ceramic tile floors in wet areas on suspended floors, on grade beams in special situations, and beneath the first course of masonry (where it is sometimes called dampproofing). Through-wall flashing and underslab vapor barriers could also be called waterproofing. Because that waterproofing usually must resist a hydraulic head, you should think of the application as though the finished product would be on the wet side of a lake dam—any pinhole will admit water. Flashing that is not continuous, such as sill flashing for window openings, must be properly terminated. See Figure 12.2 for examples of correct and incorrect flashing terminations.

The most common waterproofing systems are asphalt-based, either hot- or cold-applied. Though rarer, coal tar is also used. In hot climates, hot-applied waterproofing probably will not work in vertical applications because it will run down the surface and puddle at the bottom. Cold-applied must then be used. Below-grade waterproofing is usually multi-course, with alternating layers of bitumen and reinforcing fabric.

Proprietary systems of sophisticated compounds that generally form a synthetic rubber when cured are also used. They are typically liquid or mastics applied with brushes or trowels. Be sure that you understand the manufacturer's requirements for installation.

Some preformed sheets (single-ply) are also used below grade. They usually consist of an elastomeric sheet with an adhesive on one face, and a removable paper facing to separate the adhesive from the next layer in the roll. It is tricky to apply because the separating paper has to be removed from the adhesive face during or before application. Wrinkles and bubbles are difficult to prevent, but they should be worked out to prevent a failure later. The size of the laps between sheets should be measured to ensure proper sealing.

With any below-grade application, it is of utmost importance to make sure the waterproofing membrane is, indeed, waterproof. The consequences are serious if leaks are discovered after the backfill is in place. Careful attention to detail is paramount. If the specifications call for a three-course application, make sure it is three courses *everywhere*. If the design calls for special techniques at joints that may move, make sure those techniques are done exactly as designed.

Another common below-grade waterproofing material is bentonite. Bentonite is a type of clay that swells dramatically when exposed to moisture and forms a relatively impervious layer to resist the intrusion of moisture. This is a simplistic explanation of a complicated chemical process that takes place, but the effect is the same. Bentonite is usually supplied as a rigid board, similar to corrugated cardboard in heavy boxes. The corrugations are filled

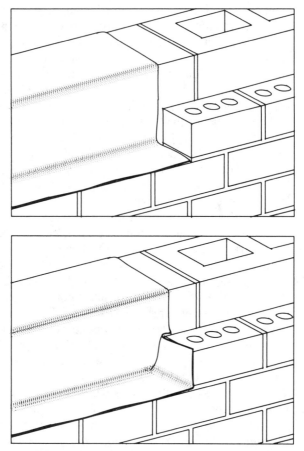

FIGURE 12.2. (top) Improper flashing termination (the moisture can simply run off the end and into the wall); (bottom) a proper flashing termination.

with bentonite, and over time the cardboard disintegrates and leaves the bentonite clay. Attention to detail is vital. Any gaps not covered by the boards must be sealed with a bentonite slurry or gel supplied for this purpose.

Most subgrade waterproofing specifications call for a protection course to keep the backfill materials from damaging the membrane during placing and compacting operations. Even with a protection course, backfilling should be done carefully, watching to make sure that the protection course itself is not damaged during backfilling.

The upper termination of basement wall or grade beam waterproofing is usually at the finished grade line. Thus, the grading is relatively critical. If the grade is not brought up high enough, the waterproofing will show, rather aesthetically undesirable. However, if the grade is too high, moisture in the soil can get behind the membrane over the top edge and negate the very reason for its being there.

13

ROOFING AND FLASHING

There have been many debates about the merits of roofing guarantees and warranties. To some, they are a necessary expense, just like insurance. To others, they are a total waste of money. What becomes clear, after years of exposure to the subject of roofing, is that the best guarantee of a good roof with a long life is to insure that the system is: (1) properly designed, (2) properly installed, and (3) properly maintained. We can only deal with one of those: the installation. However, if a manufacturer's warranty is called for, the manufacturer will probably want to inspect some of the installation and the final product before it will issue the warranty.

Especially with a built-up roof, to assure the owner that the roof is properly installed, the inspector must watch every bit of installation. Roofs are ruined by small, minor lapses in attention: inadequate bitumen between plies, foreign materials imbedded within the system, bitumen getting too hot, improper brooming, and so forth. And with single plies, every inch of every seam is critical. Only by constant attention to detail can the inspector be sure that the roof installation is a good one.

If you have other duties while roofing is progressing, one or the other must suffer. If you are in this position, you should suggest either adding a person for full-time roofing inspection or relief from your other duties to give roofing your full attention. As an owner's representative, I always insisted on full-time inspection of roofing.

If you have tough questions about roofing that your home office cannot answer, the best outside resources are the National Roofing Contractors' Association (NRCA) and the Roofing Industry Education Institute (RIEI). Other good sources are the Better Understanding of Roofing Systems Institute (BURSI), and the Midwest Roofing Contractors' Association (MRCA). You will find addresses and telephone numbers in the General References.

Roofing operations should not begin if it is raining or if there is a strong possibility of it. Because weather is so unpredictable, the contractor should have contingency plans in case of rain. If rain falls directly on unprotected insulation, the insulation will be ruined. If the membrane is not tied off, water can run under the roofing, especially on a metal deck.

If the structural deck is concrete, gypsum concrete, or insulating concrete (concrete with a perlite or vermiculite aggregate), moisture testing must be done before roofing begins to ensure that the deck is dry enough to roof over. If moisture is still coming out of the concrete, it will be trapped beneath the roofing system and ruin it.

BUILT-UP ROOFING

All roofing materials look alike. You cannot tell by looking if the proper bitumen is being used. Ply materials all look about the same. The only way to tell if the materials are as specified and approved is to look at the labels. While checking the label on the bitumen, note the equivicous temperature (EVT) (covered later). Also, make sure that the materials are being properly stored. They should be off the ground, and protected from moisture. The roof cannot be dry if the materials are wet, and only a small amount of moisture will make a wet roof.

If materials must be stored on the roof deck, they must be spread out to avoid overloading either the deck or the structure.

Materials should be hoisted over the edge of the roof, and not brought in from inside the building. This is important because many roofing materials are impossible to remove completely if accidentally spilled. For the same reason, if there are any finish materials in place, the side of the building should be covered with plastic sheets in the area of the materials hoist or bitumen pumping hose.

Before any roofing operations begin, make sure that the deck is clean and dry. If it is not dry, insist that the roofers wait for it to dry. On a metal or concrete deck, it may be acceptable to use torches to speed the drying. However, I do not allow flames of any kind on a roof; I have witnessed too many accidents associated with torches and "dragon wagons" (a contraption with ganged torches and fuel tanks on wheels). If torches are allowed, watch their use very carefully and critically, and make sure that adequate fire extinguishers are nearby.

The first layer of insulation should be mechanically fastened to prevent wind uplift and blowoff. Mechanical fastening usually means power-driven screws. The type, length, and material of the screws and, possibly, the washer should be specified. For mechanical fastening to be effective, the number and pattern of the fasteners are critical. More fasteners are usually called for around the perimeter and at the corners. Check the wording of the specifications. Fastening will be different for different wind uplift classifications. Factory Mutual has two classifications, I-60 and I-90, and each has different requirements. It may even be necessary to secure and study the RIEI publication on fastening for wind uplift.

If there is a second layer of insulation, it should be secured to the first layer with a full mopping of bitumen. The operative word is *full*—strip mopping or hit-and-miss mopping is not adequate. Joints should be staggered in both directions from the joints in the first layer. Some specifications call for the joints to be taped. The tape is usually set in hot bitumen, but check the specifications.

Many installations call for the use of tapered insulation. It may be for the entire field or only locally used for crickets. In either case, their location must be planned and carefully thought out to provide the intended slope.

If a vapor retarder is specified, it is usually installed on top of the first layer of insulation so that it is installed on top of the insulation fasteners and the fasteners will not have to penetrate the vapor retarder. The vapor retarded will probably be mopped down just as the roofing plies are, but the laps will be smaller. Check the lap dimension. The vapor retarder keeps moisture from inside the building from entering the top layer(s) of insulation, so see to it that there are no openings for moisture to travel through.

If the roofing bitumen is coal tar, the specifications will probably call for pitch dams to be installed at all roof penetrations. Pitch dams are a sort of "flashing" for the pitch, which will tend to flow at summer temperatures (see Figure 13.1). If a pitch dam is not used at a roof opening, the pitch will flow through the opening and into the interior of the building and make a real mess. A coal tar installation will also call for envelopes (folded-back plies) at all edges to keep coal tar from leaking out of the system and onto the finish materials of the wall.

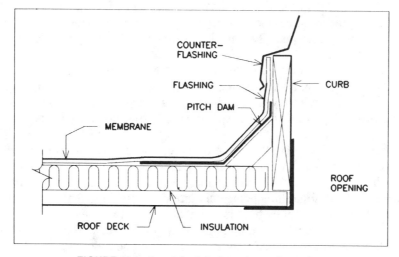

FIGURE 13.1. A metal pitch dam at a roof opening.

Shingling refers to the way in which each ply overlays the one before it. The roofing specifications will call for the plies to be shingled so that they naturally shed runoff. This is good theory, but it is not always possible nor is it always the best way to run the plies. An acceptable alternative is to run the plies parallel to the direction of runoff, but they should not be run against the flow. A possible exception to this rule is at a cricket, and it is better to continue the plies against the flow than to cut them to get the proper shingling effect over a small area.

The EVT is the temperature that must be maintained at the bucket (the last place before application to the roof) to make sure that the bitumen is hot enough to flow properly and saturate the roofing plies. The EVT is marked on the wrapper of each lug of bitumen. Check the temperature of the bitumen in the bucket several times a day during roofing operations. You should also know the maximum allowable temperature for the bitumen in the heating kettle and check it several times a day. If the bitumen is overheated, it alters the characteristics of the bitumen and will cause trouble later. If you discover overheating, notify the contractor immediately. Overheated bitumen should be discarded and the kettle charged with fresh bitumen.

You should know the proper number of plies to be applied. Markings on each ply will help, but sometimes they won't, and you must watch to verify that the minimum number of plies is furnished.

How much bitumen should be applied? The specifications will call for so many pounds per square foot or per square (100 ft²). This spec is of little use to you, however, because you have no way to determine the weight being applied until after it is done. So how can you tell if the correct amount is being applied? The correct amount is enough to guarantee a complete coating between plies and to saturate the plies and bond them. Look to see that there is complete coverage. Then a small amount of bitumen should be squished out along the edge of each ply. If the plies are organic felt, the plies should be broomed to ensure imbedment. With fiberglass plies, embedment is achieved by brooming with a specially made broom, by rolling, or by squeegeeing the plies.

End laps (where one roll of felt runs out and another is begun) should be staggered to prevent a straight-line buildup of double plies. End laps cause a plane of weakness if they are lined up, and a straight-line buildup can affect the drainage of the roof and cause ponding. The specifications will tell you the overlap dimension required for end laps.

What can go wrong at this stage of the construction? I have investigated bubbles that contained felt roll wrappers, lunch sacks, cold blobs of bitumen, and other foreign objects. The point is, what usually goes wrong is inattention, resulting in something being built into the membrane that should not be there. Or dry spots can be built in—that is, incomplete coverage of bitumen that will later cause a bubble. The plies may get skewed and cause a wrinkle or a "fish mouth" to form. The workers might not be brooming or rolling the plies down into the bitumen well enough. The roll of ply material may be defective and have wrinkles or gaps. For all these reasons, you should watch every bit of roofing as it goes down, not just watch representative work and assume the rest will be done correctly.

Any time roofing is suspended, the exposed edge of the membrane, any exposed insulation, and the roof deck near the edge of the completed roofing must be protected with temporary cutoffs. Overnight dew, rain, or any other form of moisture will penetrate unprotected edges and result in wet roofing, which must be removed before proceeding. If the plies are running at right angles to the flutes in a metal deck, temporary cutoffs are especially tedious, because each low area of the flutes must be sealed to prevent water from running down the flutes beneath the roofing system.

Make sure the surface aggregate to be applied is the proper size and type and that it is dry and clean—that is, free from trash and sand, which will hinder the embedment of the aggregate in the flood coat of bitumen. The purpose of a surface aggregate is to protect the bitumen from the effects of sunlight. If the aggregate is not well embedded, it will be blown around by wind or washed off by rain runoff and expose the bitumen to the harmful effects of the sun. If applied by hand, the flood coat should be poured, not mopped. About half the aggregate applied should be thoroughly embedded in the bitumen.

Wheeled devices are commonly used for laying plies, and for applying the flood coat and gravel in one operation. These devices are acceptable as long as they are used correctly and accomplish what the specifications have set out.

The flood coat and gravel should be applied as soon as possible after the plies are laid. If they cannot be applied immediately, the exposed plies should be glazed with a thin coating of bitumen to prevent moisture intruding into the plies. Many roofing contractors argue that glazing is not necessary with fiberglass plies because they will not absorb moisture. True, they are not as bad as organic felts, but they can still retain moisture that could get trapped by the flood coat, thus ruining the system.

FLASHING AND COUNTERFLASHING

Base flashing is made of many different materials, but it will always be somewhat like the roofing materials. The sheets are usually heavier than the roofing plies and possibly more pliable. The flashing material should completely cover the area being flashed, from the very top and extending out over the plies the required dimension (usually 2 or 3 ft). They must cover from end to end also, with special attention to corners. Do not allow a roofer to cover up gaps in the flashing (such as at corners) with roofing mastic (commonly called "pookey"). Think of the roof as a water reservoir up to the top of the flashing, and make sure the reservoir will hold water (see Figure 13.2). If the specifications call for nailing at the top, make sure it is done. Specifica-

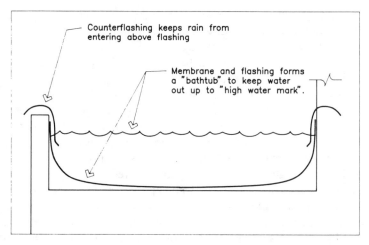

FIGURE 13.2. Flashing theory.

tions may also call for a coating to be applied to the flashing. This coating will usually be reflective (aluminum or white) to reduce the effects of ultraviolet light. Figure 13.3 is a schematic of a roof membrane–flashing–counterflashing system.

Counterflashing is usually metal: galvanized steel, factory-painted steel, copper, lead-coated copper, aluminum, or stainless steel. Different metals should not be allowed to touch. When two metals touch in the presence of an electrolyte (water is a good electrolyte), a cathodic action takes place. That is, an electric current passes between the metals, and one or both of the metals begin to corrode. This action is called *galvanic activity* (the same thing takes place inside a battery). The further apart that metals are on the chart of galvanic activity, the more corrosion is likely to take place and the more rapid it will be.

Chart of Galvanic Activity

Aluminum
Zinc
Galvanized steel
Steel
Iron
Nickel
Tin
Lead
Copper
Stainless steel
Monel

If you were to lap a piece of aluminum flashing over a sheet of stainless steel flashing on a roof, rainwater would provide an electrolyte and promote galvanic activity. One or both of the metals would quickly corrode. If dissimilar metals must touch because of some quirk of the design, they must be isolated from one another with a heavy coating of bituminous paint or even a sheet of roofing felt.

Since counterflashings are relatively light gauge metal, they are subject to a lot of linear thermal expansion and contraction. They *will* expand and contract, so keep this in mind when inspecting the methods of attachment and the joints between individual lengths of metal. These places must allow movement or the metal will tear as it shrinks or buckle as it expands. Slotted holes for fastenings and joints that allow some slippage are needed while watertightness is maintained. Many contractors will want to solder or pop-rivet joints, thinking that it will be a better job. You can be a hero by eliminating this piece of work.

As with flashing, attention to the details not covered by the drawings is essential for a watertight roof. The most commonly missed details are at terminations or intersections. If they are not shown on the drawings, use your common sense to judge the effectiveness of what the contractor provides.

As archaic as is may seem, some specifications still call for test cuts in the newly completed roof. Test cuts are 12 in. × 12 in. squares cut out of the roofing system in order to count the plies and weigh the bitumen to verify that the system is in compliance with the specifications. If the roof installation had full-time inspection, I am totally against test cuts. After all, you have gone a long way to assure that it was properly installed and a test cut will only introduce a weakened, patched scar to an otherwise perfect roof membrane. Unless there are rational, well-considered reasons for test cuts (such as

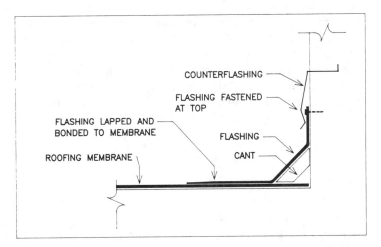

FIGURE 13.3. A schematic of a roof membrane–flashing–counterflashing system.

suspecting that the bitumen was overheated or that the bitumen is the wrong type in spite of the labeling), do not allow them.

By the way, I have seen instances of the bitumen being inadvertently mislabeled by the manufacturer. The mistake was not discovered until the roofing plies began slipping down the slope of the roof. I now require that each batch of bitumen be tested to verify the type before it is used on the roof. If this testing is not required by the specifications, check with the architect to see if it should be included.

SINGLE-PLY MEMBRANES

The body of knowledge for inspecting single-ply membranes is not as extensive as for built-up roofing. There are almost as many materials, fastening methods, and seaming systems as there are manufacturers of single plies. Your specifications may be limited and rely mainly on the specification of the particular system or the manufacturer's installation instructions. In any case, you should know what the contract requires. That could mean documents other than the architect's drawings and specifications, such as the manufacturer's instructions or specifications. You should have a copy of whatever will govern the installation, and study it thoroughly.

In almost every preformed sheet system, the most critical element is seaming. Whether solvent or heat-welded, the seam is the most vulnerable point in the system, not only the seam of the main field of roofing but also the detail seams, seams around the perimeter, and seams at roof penetrations. By the way, most of the cleaners and solvents used in single-ply seaming are pretty nasty, so read and follow the precautions on the label or on the material safety data sheet (MSDS).

Carefully note any abuse of the membrane after it has been laid. They are relatively thin and easily penetrated by sharp objects, such as nails, screws, "shoeless" ladders, scrap sheet metal, shears, knives, screwdrivers, hammer claws, and anything that might be dragged across the surface. The offenders are usually not the roofing applicators, but other workers, such as sheet metal workers and HVAC installers. Activity on the roof must be monitored after the installation is complete. If there is to be much construction traffic, it would be a good idea to require plywood walkways and laydown areas.

SHINGLES

Except for thatch, shingles are probably the oldest form of roofing, and still one of the best; the only limitation is the slope of the roof. It is the slope that makes shingles work. Shingles range from the cheapest and shortest life of roofing materials (lightweight composition shingles) to one of the most expensive with the longest life (slate). Shingles are also made of redwood and cedar, clay tile, concrete tile, and various metals.

Composition shingles on a good slope are probably the most forgiving roofing material available. But, poorly installed, they will still leak. Pay attention to the sealing-down of the tabs. Some shingles have an exposed area of bitumen that will accomplish this, but others require a hand application of bitumen to seal down the tabs.

The most important things to watch are the terminations (upper edges, lower edges, gable edges, and edges around roof penetrations) and flashing. Flashing with composition shingles may be a composition roll material or metal. The same principles apply to shingle flashing as to built-up roof flashing, but that some situations require slip flashing. Slip flashing is inserted between the shingles, shingle style, and usually turns up a vertical wall or a masonry chimney. The flashing must be inserted into the masonry and caulked or counterflashed for proper water protection.

Specialists must install clay tile or slate. Slate is brittle and must be fastened carefully to avoid breaking the shingle. Both clay and slate shingles are typically installed on a deck with a steep pitch. Working on a steeply pitched roof is dangerous. Know and understand the capabilities of the installers and watch their progress through binoculars rather than from the roof. Clay tile may be fastened with a proprietary system which, of course, requires knowledge of the system.

METAL ROOFING

There are two broad categories of metal roofing: those that are structurally self-spanning, (usually referred to as a *structural metal roof*) and those that require a structural deck for support (referred to as an *architectural metal roof*). Those that are self-spanning are usually associated with pre-engineered metal buildings, the so-called "wrinkled tin" roof. The other is the ancient art of field-fabricated standing seam, flat seam, or batten seam of copper, tern, or monel roofing. The success of either type depends partially on the slope of the roof. Field-fabricated architectural metal roofing is highly dependent on the design of the details and on the skill of the installers.

Roofing metal will expand and contract; and this movement must be accommodated. Most light-gauge metal has this accommodation built in because of the nature of the installation and the detailing. Structural metal roofing must accommodate nearly all the expansion and contraction at the ends of the long pieces. Careful attention must be given to the corrugations at the terminations also. Most configurations depend on specially formed foam rubber closure strips cut to fit the corrugations. These strips are usually installed before the metal is installed.

Flashing can be particularly hard with structural metal roofing, especially at penetrations in the field and terminal flashings at the upper end of a slope. At penetrations, make sure the water blocked by the curb can get around the curb and not run into a seam or where the corrugations stop. At top-of-slope flashings, there usually must be closures beneath the flashing to close the gap formed by the corrugations of the roofing sheet.

It is probably a good idea to test the soundness of a structural metal roof with a water hose before pronouncing it watertight. When testing, remember that rain is often wind-driven, seldom falling straight down. Water testing can produce some surprises. It will probably require a good dose of common sense to find and repair leaks revealed by testing.

HOUSEKEEPING

Good housekeeping is mandatory on a roof because

1. The work is done off the ground and safety is paramount. If a worker stumbles, he or she could fall to the ground or into hot bitumen.
2. Construction debris will eventually be walked on, and the roof is not very tolerant of this sort of abuse. Nails and screws mashed into a new membrane will cause a leak in a very short time, perhaps immediately.
3. The state of housekeeping will affect the attitudes of the workers. Although a neat roof will not guarantee a good roof, a sloppy roof will usually result in sloppy work.

14

MODULAR PLANNING, MASONRY, AND CARPENTRY

MODULAR PLANNING AND DESIGN

The modular design I am addressing here is a philosophy of design embraced by many architectural designers. It uses a modular grid (usually 4' × 4' or 5' × 5') to control and regulate the plan. The grid is usually based on the structural system, and all grid lines have the same relationship to the structural grid. All partitions are centered on a grid line, or have one face on the grid, or may be a certain distance from the grid. In any case, partitions are always located in the same relationship to the grid. Other elements may also be included, such as rustications and reveals, doors, windows, floor patterns, ceiling patterns, lighting and HVAC terminals, and even signage.

This modular design may or may not be apparent on the drawings. If the design is based on a rigid module, you should discuss with the design architect how he or she laid out the building. The architect can explain how each element is located in relation to the module or grid lines. You may be surprised how simple and yet how comprehensive the system is and how many elements are critical to the success of the modular design. If you understand the theory behind the design, it will greatly simplify your job of monitoring the layout.

MASONRY

Before inspecting masonry, you must know that the correct materials are used. Clay brick is generally classified as face brick, common brick, firebrick, or pavers. Common brick is not as strong as face brick and is usually a pink color (in some areas they are called "pinks"). Firebrick is usually larger than face brick and a light buff color. Pavers are solid, hard-fired bricks used for paving. Different sizes of bricks are available, so make sure that the brick on hand is the right size.

Concrete masonry units (CMU) can be lightweight, heavyweight, and heavy face shell types. Lightweight CMU is made with expanded shale, volcanic rock, or pumice. Heavy units are made with normal hard-rock aggregates. To provide a required fire rating, some designs will call for CMU with thicker face shells or even solid units, and they are usually made with hard-rock concrete.

Concrete masonry units are not made perfectly. Their faces might not be truly parallel and truly perpendicular. Hence, only one face of a single-wythe wall can be a planar surface. The opposite face will have irregularities, such as "tilted" faces and faces that are lower or higher than the plane of the wall. Someone (preferably the architect) must decide which face of a wall will be the "good" face. For this reason, many architects use two-wythe walls where both faces must be good.

Mortar comes in many types and classifications, and you must know that the correct mortar is used in each application. A product used in making mortar from scratch is called "masonry cement," but it is not well defined, even though you may see designations of type I and type II. Therefore, because of this dubious heritage and the black art associated with job-mixed lime-cement mortar, most specifications now call a preproportioned masonry mortar mix that requires only the addition of water. These prepared mortars are classified by type according to use, exposure, and compressive strength:

Type M	Below grade applications in contact with earth (2500 psi)
Type S	General use, good lateral force resistance (1800 psi)
Type N	General use, severe exposures (750 psi)
Type O	Interior use (350 psi)
Types PL and PM	Masonry grouts (2500 psi)

Mortar should be mixed according to the manufacturer's instructions. If unused mortar has begun to harden, it must be discarded not retempered (by adding water) and used.

The specifications may call for compressive testing of the mortar as mixed. If so, the testing company will make test cubes of mortar to be used in the compressive test.

One of the most important moments in masonry construction is the first hours of laying a wall or partition. If no one is watching when the mason begins laying masonry units, a lot of masonry could be in place before it is inspected. If the work is unacceptable, a battle ensues over whether to accept it or tear it down and start over. The mason may not understand what level of quality is expected. If modular coursing is critical (and it usually is), the mason should understand the importance of coursing. If the design calls for a clean cavity, what does that mean "fairly clean" or is a pull stick required in the cavity? If the specifications do not allow muratic acid for cleaning masonry, then mortar should be kept off the face of masonry.

The first masonry laid may serve as a sample panel, or it may actually be a sample panel that will not be incorporated into the construction. A sample should be of each type and material of masonry. It should contain any typical details, such as soldier courses or special shapes, and carefully judged and preserved. Since the quality of all subsequent masonry will be judged against this sample, it must last for the duration of the masonry work.

When masonry is laid, it must have a full bed of mortar and the head joints (vertical joints) must be full. The only exception to this is CMU where the face and back shell only must have full joints, not the part that joins the shell faces together. This exception does not apply to the first course. It must have a full bed joint through the depth of the wythe. Mortar should not be spread for more than one minute before the masonry unit is laid in it. A fast mason can accomplish this if the mortar is spread no more than 4 ft in front of laying.

When a masonry unit is laid, it must be shoved and tapped into position, with the unit always moving toward the bed and head joint. If it is moved back or lifted, even a little, it must be removed, cleaned, and relaid. Otherwise, the joint will not be full, and the masonry unit will not be bonded to the mortar. The excess mortar should squish out of the joints. After the unit is in its final position, the excess mortar should be cut off with the trowel. It may be reused on the next unit to be laid.

All masonry joints must be tooled, but special care is needed with exterior joints. The water-repelling integrity of the wall depends on it. Tooling compacts the mortar and ensures that the face of the joint is watertight. Joints must be tooled at the right time. The mortar should be thumbprint hard. If the joint is tooled too soon, it will continue to shrink and leave a hairline crack where it joins the masonry. Hairline cracks will admit water. If the joint is tooled too late, the tooling will not be effective. You must watch this step.

Masonry units must be cut with a masonry saw. The only common exception to this is for headers that do not extend beyond the first wythe. These may be broken with a masonry hammer, but the break should be neat.

Most masonry specifications will call for special shapes. Some special shapes may be as simple as a solid brick (without holes) for use where the flat face of a brick is exposed, as at corners of a soldier course or at the ends of an extended, sloping windowsill. Some special shapes may be as complicated as an scrolled cornice or trim piece. Perhaps the most common shape, other than solids, is the brick with a special angle on the end to form corners that are not a 90° angle.

Cavity wall construction calls for a clean cavity. The purpose of the cavity is to create a capillary break, so water that penetrates the outside wythe will collect in the cavity on the back face of the outside wythe, run down the cavity and out through weep holes. Boy! That sentence contains a whole mouthful of lessons.

First, the cavity must be clean, or the moisture will have a bridge to the backup wythe and defeat the purpose of the cavity. The most foolproof way to clean cavities is with pull sticks. Pull sticks are wooden sticks as wide as the cavity that are laid on the last wall reinforcing and left there until the next reinforced course is reached. At that time, the stick is lifted with pull strings or wires, lifting the loose mortar in the cavity with it. It is a real nuisance to the masons, but it will guarantee a clean cavity.

Second, there must be weep holes at the bottom of a cavity to let the moisture out. And, third, the bottom of the cavity must be flashed to direct the moisture to the weep holes and not under the backup masonry. All three elements are crucial to the performance of the wall.

Flashing built into masonry recognizes that masonry is not waterproof. Moisture will penetrate through minute cracks and be drawn into the wall by capillary action. Flashing directs this moisture to the outside instead of letting it find its way into the interior of the building. Flashing must be used beneath parapet caps, above and along spandrel beams and lintels, at windowsills, and at the bottom of all cavities. Flashing is usually shown in wall sections and details, but the method of terminating flashing is usually not shown. Refer again to Figure 12.2. You can see in the first illustration that moisture diverted by the flashing can still get into the wall around the end of the flashing. This can be prevented by building a dam at the end, as shown in the second illustration. This is a specific case, but the principle can be applied to other situations as well. Verify that the flashing material is what is specified.

When a masonry panel cannot be completed during one day's work, the termination should be stepped back (see Figure 14.1) or "toothed" (see Figure 14.2). Stepping back is preferred because the mason does not have to work new masonry units between existing units above and below, as with toothing.

Methods for fastening masonry to the structure must allow differential movement in two planes (up and down, along the length of the wall), but not the third (in and out). It must also allow the structure to move without affecting the masonry. Some acceptable anchoring techniques are shown in Figure 14.3. Anchor devices may be shown on the drawings or simply called out in the specifications.

When we speak of masonry and reinforcing, it is easy to create a misunderstanding, because there are two distinctly different types of reinforcing. Horizontal joint reinforcing, the most common, is made of heavy-gauge wire welded into a grid or truss. The second type is similar to what is used in reinforced concrete (and it serves the same purpose).

Wire reinforcing is usually called for in the specifications, but may not be shown on the drawings. Read what the specifications say about joint reinforcing because in some places it should be cut and in other places it should be continuous. Otherwise, just make sure that the wire is not lapped in such a way that the mortar joint becomes too large.

If you ask a structural engineer about masonry reinforcing, he or she will

FIGURE 14.1. This incomplete CMU partition was properly stepped when work stopped before the partition was completed.

probably not even think about wire joint reinforcing. Reinforcing to an engineer means deformed reinforcing bars. There is always a structural reason for reinforced masonry. The most common is the reinforced bond beam and the reinforced lintel. Structural considerations might require vertical reinforcing as well, which is usually detailed in the structural drawings rather than on architectural drawings. This should set off a bell in your head. There have been many projects on which the structural engineer did not understand the architectural requirements, and vice versa, and the two were never coordinated. The drawings wind up with conflicting requirements, which should be resolved before masonry construction begins.

If the wall to be reinforced is CMU, it is much harder to construct. The vertical reinforcing bars are usually placed first. That means that each block

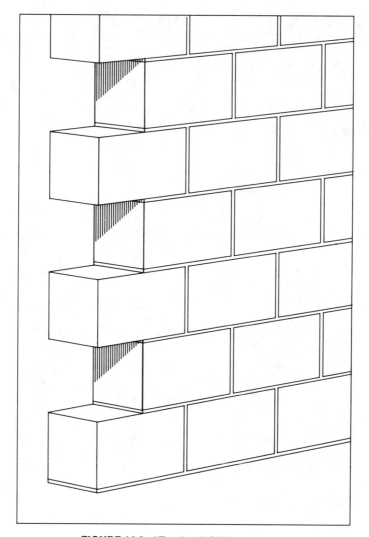

FIGURE 14.2. "Toothed" CMU masonry.

must be "threaded" onto the bars as it is laid. That makes proper laying much harder and one that bears watching for correct laying technique.

After a masonry wall is completed, it must be cleaned. How much cleaning it needs depends on how sloppy the mason was and on how important appearance is. A boiler room wall may not need much cleaning, especially if it will be painted. But a face brick wall is made of face brick because appearance is a factor. Most architects specifically forbid cleaning face brick with acid because it will burn the brick and mortar and change their color. You will have to be diligent here, because brick is hard to clean with detergent alone,

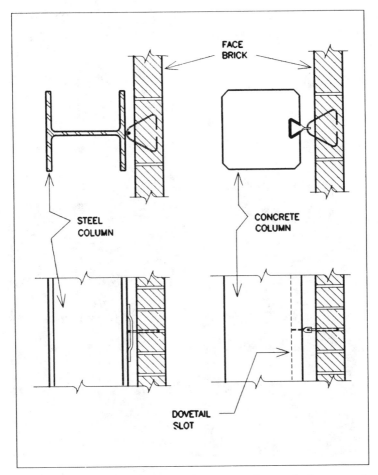

FIGURE 14.3. Typical brick anchors to columns allow vertical movement.

and the contractor will be tempted to use a weak acid (muratic acid) to reduce the labor cost. Wire brushes must not be used. They leave minute metal particles on the masonry that will oxidize and ruin its appearance.

Finished masonry in a vulnerable location, especially corners, should be protected until the construction is complete. See Figure 14.4.

CARPENTRY

Read the specifications. Know what material and what grade are required and where, and then check for visible grade markings on lumber. If there are no visible markings, assume it is the wrong material. Someone will surely volun-

FIGURE 14.4. Vulnerable finished corners should be protected.

teer to show you that it is right. Wood is usually not highly stressed, but it is good policy to require the right grade and size of lumber to be used and not to assume that almost anything will do the job. Structures can be deceiving. It is always better to be safe than to find out after a failure that you made a poor assumption.

It is especially important that lumber stored on the site be protected from the weather and off the ground. Much of the lumber used in construction is pressure-treated. It will have a characteristic pale green, blue, orange, or purple tint. All pressure-treated wood is not the same, however. Some wood is treated for water (rot) protection; other wood is treated to protect against insects. Some treatments are fire retardants. Know what treatment is required and what to look for on the site.

Architect's specifications frequently do not allow lumber to be reused— for instance, lumber used in concrete forming. If so, watch out for it. The lumber might be perfectly good, but the architect had good reasons to prohibit its reuse.

Most of the lumber on nonresidential construction is used for concrete forming. By economic necessity, it will be reused many times. This practice is acceptable as long as the lumber is not seriously structurally impaired. The nails that must be removed to enable removal of the forms must be double-headed. Otherwise, the same nails recommended for permanent construction should be used. Most building codes contain a nailing table that details the type and sizes of nails to be used in different situations. If you're unsure about the suitability of nailing, consult the table in the code.

Plywood comes in many thicknesses, types, species, grades, and sizes. The grade must be clearly marked on the full sheet. Concrete-forming specifications may actually call for a better grade of plywood than is used in the permanent construction. Plywood used structurally must be supported and nailed on all edges. Sometimes the specifications allow unsupported edges if a batten or edge clips are used. Edge clips are small, metal H-shaped devices that hold the adjacent edges in alignment. The specifications will tell you how many or what spacing to use.

One of the main things to look for on a plywood marking is the service that is intended. Plywood that can be used in moist atmospheres must have a glue that resists deterioration from moisture. It will be labeled for outside exposure, or "exterior." Some plywood is also treated with a fire retardant. It should also be well marked and verified before it is used.

Flakeboard and particleboard are not automatic substitutions for plywood. Either may possibly be used in places calling for plywood, but you should check the specifications or ask the architect to verify such substitutions.

Glue-laminated Structural Members

Glue-laminated ("glulam") members come in three general grades: industrial, utility, and architectural. The differences are mainly appearance and finishability. Erection of a glulam structure is somewhat like the erection of a steel structure, except that wood must be protected from damage by lifting cables.

The structure must be carefully squared and plumbed before decking begins. You will also need to use the shop drawings to determine which pieces go where. Glulam beams are made with a compression face (usually the top) and a tension face (usually the bottom), and there are different rules regarding splices and flaws that apply to compression areas and tension areas. They can be installed upside down! I have seen it happen. What results is a structure that is substantially weaker than designed.

All metal-connecting pieces must be well primed before the wood members are attached (unless they are galvanized). Otherwise they will quickly attract moisture into the interface between steel and wood and begin to rust. The wood members might also need to be sealed in the area of connections. Check the specifications.

If the deck is very heavy, requiring large spikes for nailing, the individual planks must be predrilled for spikes. Check to see if specifications require the end of the deck planks placed over a support or end at a random spacing. Remember that the deck is a part of the structural system, and watch the installation accordingly.

You should also determine where the conduit for lighting fixtures can be routed. Concealed conduit probably needs to be routed through voids cut into the roof insulation or into the wood deck. This requires some forethought and planning.

15

INTERIORS

DRYWALL

Drywall is the most common interior finish in use today. It used to be considered a cheap, inferior substitute for plaster and was totally unacceptable to many in the construction industry. Now it is so common that some workers take it for granted. Drywall quality can literally make or break a job, because it is close up and personal; and available for close scrutiny. The secret to good drywall is close attention to detail and a good substrate.

The most common substrate for drywall is wood or metal studs. Before wallboard is applied to the studs, check them for alignment. (Sometimes drywall framing installers take the attitude that whatever mistakes they make can be remedied with "mud" (joint compound). Look horizontally down a row of studs. If you can see misalignment or waves, they will show up in the finished product, especially in corridors, where your viewing position is parallel to the surface. Irregularities are especially apparent if there is a strong source of light, such as a window, at the end of the corridor.

If wallboard is to be applied to a masonry or concrete wall, the wall must be furred. Furring is done by fastening hat-shaped metal furring channels to the wall (see Figure 15.1). The wallboard is screwed to the furring channels as though they were metal studs.

When the wallboard installation begins, make sure that the right type and thickness are used. Check especially for the fire-rated and moisture-resistant types. Also, check the specifications for the direction of application; some specifications call for the boards to be installed horizontally, with the vertical joints staggered.

Gypsum wallboard typically comes in 4' × 8' sheets. What happens if a room has a 9-ft or 10-ft ceiling? Check the specifications for the answer.

FIGURE 15.1. A CMU wall with hat-shaped furring channels for later application of drywall.

Wallboard does come in lengths greater than 8', and the answer may be to use a longer sheet. It may also be acceptable to patch in smaller pieces to make up the required height.

See that all edges of the wallboard occur at a support. If the boards are nailed, the last stroke of the hammer should just dimple the face paper, not break it. Similarly, screw fasteners should be driven flush but should not break the face paper.

If there are any wall-mounted items to be applied later, the framing may need to be supplemented. Supplemental framing may be simply some wood blocking, or it may be a heavy structural system. Check the drawings for details.

If metal studs have wallboard on one side only, as in a chase, an acoustical separation, or an expansion joint, the back flange of the studs must be braced to resist crippling. The most common method of bracing is to fasten horizontal strips of wallboard to the backside of the studs.

If more than one layer of wallboard is hung, the joints in the second layer should not match the joints in the first layer. That means that they must be offset by at least 16 in.

Generally, a drywall partition will not continue to the overhead structure and, therefore, must be braced. Bracing is usually done with pieces of metal stud material screwed to the top runner channel and to the structure above, usually at 45° to the horizontal. This bracing should be screwed not to the underside of a metal deck but to structural members.

If the partition is to be sound-rated, there are more details to check. Specifications usually call for these partitions to be caulked at the bottom and top edges. Make sure that there is a gap large enough for the caulk, but not so large that the caulk will not bridge the gap. Most specifications do not allow electrical boxes to be placed back to back or side by side in an acoustical partition. Some even call for the boxes to be "buttered" with acoustical caulking. Buttering can be done only before the wallboard is installed.

Occasionally, someone will try to bed and tape drywall joints in one or two operations. It never works. At least three applications of bedding compound are required to make a good joint, because of the natural shrinkage from drying. The wider the bedding compound can be spread, the less apparent the joint can be made. Theoretically, a drywall should look as monolithic as a plastered wall.

Protruding joints can be hard to spot because of the different texture and color of the wallboard and bedding compound. A 3-ft-long straightedge (laid at right angles to the joint) can be helpful in pointing out unacceptable joints. If the joints are not well sanded, they will show up after the first coat of paint. The only way to remedy a bad joint after painting is to remove the paint at the bedding compound and resand it.

No "raw" edges of gypsum wallboard should be exposed. They should be finished with a casing bead, a corner bead, an expansion joint, or a similar accessory. This type of accessory usually has a flange that laps the tapered edge of the wallboard. The flange is covered with bedding compound and finished like a joint.

Expansion joints in drywall are controversial, to say the least. If a crack shows up soon after installation, someone will want to know why an expansion joint wasn't used. This is a valid question, since that is what expansion joints are for. But one cannot always guess where an expansion joint will be needed. The conservative approach says "put an expansion joint *anywhere* a crack could occur." That could require a lot of expansion joints! ASTM C 840, the specification for installation that many architects refer to, calls for expansion joints no more than 50 ft apart on ceilings (or in any ceiling area exceeding 2500 ft^2) and no more than 30 ft apart on walls.

Some architects believe drywall should be installed with no expansion joints and then install them if they are needed, after the fact. You must determine what is called for in each case. Do not try to second guess the intent of the architect if it is not clearly stated; ask.

Drywall expansion joints require that the drywall be supported on each side of the joint (see Figure 15.2). They also require expansion devices or detailing that will actually allow the expected movement. If the device or detailing does not allow free movement, the movement will occur elsewhere, probably where it is not wanted (see Figure 15.3).

FIGURE 15.2. Note the metal studs on either side of the expansion joint.

PLASTER

There are four general classifications of plaster: gypsum, cement plaster (or stucco), Imperial plaster, and synthetic thin-coat plasters. Gypsum plaster is not used much today, but it was a primary interior material up to the late 1960s. Drywall now is used where gypsum plaster was once used. Imperial plaster is a thin coating of a gypsum plaster compound that is used on a drywall substrate. The predominate plaster in use today is cement plaster. The methods and techniques are similar for gypsum and cement plaster. Synthetic thin-coat plasters are usually used as a weather covering for rigid insulation placed on the outside of the building. They are usually a part of a proprietary system of reinforcing and plastering materials. Again, verify that all the materials on the job are the ones that have been specified or approved as substitutes.

As with so many other systems, inspection of plaster construction begins with the substrate, which may be masonry, concrete, furring channels, drywall or structural studs, rigid insulation, or a steel structural member. A plaster finish cannot be true and plumb unless the substrate is. This is your first checkpoint. Make sure the substrate is true and plumb before any lathing, reinforcing, or plaster work begins. If the substrate is furring channels, make sure that the structure is well tied and rigid. If the specifications

FIGURE 15.3. Results of poor expansion joint detailing.

call for galvanized channels, make sure they are. Otherwise, they will be painted. Make sure that painted steel channels are rust-free.

If the substrate is a solid surface, such as masonry, concrete, or steel, the specifications usually call for a self-furring lath, which has "dimples" at regular intervals. These dimples are placed against the substrate and serve as a fastening point. They hold the main surface of the lath away from the substrate, to emulate furring.

All the accessories (casing beads, corner beads, expansion joints, etc.) will be fastened to the lath or to the substrate. These accessories are generically referred to as *grounds*. Technically, the term refers to the distance from the back of the lath to the face of the accessories—in other words, the thickness of the plaster. The face of the accessories will form a plane that will be the face of the finished plaster surface. The surface is "grounded" upon these faces. Hence, you must pay attention to the face surface of the accessories because that describes the surface that will result. Look for secure fastening, neatly butted or mitred corners, alignment, and proper location.

Concerning expansion joints: plaster is not a thick, strong material. It usually has a coefficient of expansion different from that of the substrate. Therefore, it must have the ability to expand and contract without cracking. Experience has shown that a plaster panel of no more than 100 sq. ft. can withstand movement without cracking. This means that expansion joints must divide the surface into panels of no more than 100 sq. ft. For an expansion joint to work, the gap must be able to open and close. If the gap is bridged by the lath, channels, or any other rigid element, the joint will not work. The opposite sides of expansion joints should be separately supported, there must be two channels (or two studs) at each expansion joint, and the lath must be cut, or expansion and contraction will be only a figment of someone's imagination.

With a stucco or gypsum system, the first coat of plaster—the scratch coat—is not critical, but it should form the basis of a good bond between the lath and the later coats of plaster. The second coat—the brown coat—should receive more attention to accuracy, because it will be the base for the finish coat. The finish coat, which is only about 1/16 to 1/8 in. thick, will impart the finished color and texture. An approved sample of the acceptable color and texture should be compared with the finished product. Discuss the desired results with the design architect. Some will expect a uniform color and texture. Others will expect plaster to look more like a natural product with some variation in color and texture. You must know what is expected in order to judge the acceptability of the finished color and texture. Remember that stucco is a portland cement product and, thus, must be cured. Fog spraying is by far the best cure.

Before any plaster is painted, it must be dry. Specifications will specify how dry plaster must be. Dryness (or wetness) of plaster is determined with a moisture meter. This device has two probes and measures the electrical resistance of the surface of the plaster between the probes (the greater the moisture, the lower the resistance).

As with other proprietary products, the specifications for synthetic thin-coat systems may be the manufacturer's specifications or installation instructions. Obtain a copy of these documents and see that they are followed.

INSULATION

Most insulation used in walls is in the form of batts or blankets, typically filled with fiberglass or rock wool. The insulation thickness greatly influences the effectiveness of the insulation. Make sure the total thickness meets the specification.

If the design calls for a vapor barrier, you must know on which side of the wall it belongs. Classically, it goes on the warm side of the wall. In most northern climes, the warm side is on the inside. But where is the warm side in an air-conditioned building in Arizona? Don't assume that you know where it goes. Determine where the *design* requires it. If a vapor barrier is to be a true barrier, the joints must be taped and careful attention paid to sealing the barrier at the top and at the bottom.

Other, more exotic, types of insulation are used for highly conditioned spaces, such as cold rooms and refrigerators. Today, this mostly consists of prefabricated panels or completely prefabricated rooms that must be installed according to the manufacturer's instructions and requirements.

Insulation in masonry construction may consist of a loose, poured granuler insulation, such as vermiculite or perlite, or rigid insulating boards of perlite, styrofoam, urethane, or polyisocyanurate. Loose insulation is usually used in the cores of concrete masonry units. Boards may be installed inside (as a substrate for the interior finish), on the outside (as the substrate for a thin synthetic plaster), or in the cavity between two wythes. Manufacturer's instructions for installation should be carefully followed.

Insulation may also be used to assist with sound separation, either in interior partitions or on top of a ceiling system. The insulation is the same as thermal insulation; the use is just different.

MISCELLANEOUS METAL FABRICATIONS

Concrete imbeds are the first miscellaneous metal fabrications to show up on the site (they better be). They must be installed in the concrete formwork or imbedded at the time the concrete is placed. Included are expansion joint anchor plates, beam and joist bearing plates, dock edge angles, grate frames, access hatch frames, attachment plates to later weld to, and so forth.

Lintels for masonry construction are the most common miscellaneous metals. They could be plates, angles, channels, or beams. Most commonly, they are angles. On outside walls, lintels usually are flashed. Watch for specified bearing area at each side of the opening.

Bollards or guard posts are installed to protect parts of the building from damage, usually by fork trucks. They are typically located to protect outside corners, wall-mounted equipment (water fountains, electrical panels, etc.), and doorways. Verify that the bollard actually protects what it is supposed to protect. I have seen bollards located at doors mounted so that a fork truck could still crash into the doorjamb or the overhead door track. It does little good like that, even though that may be where it is supposed to be located by dimension.

Most metal stairs are prefabricated (see Figure 15.4). At least there will be some measure of prefabrication. Some multirise stairs are prefabricated from bottom to top and installed as a single piece. The main thing to watch for with any stair installation is alignment with existing construction, especially the

FIGURE 15.4. Prefabricated steel pan stairs in a steel-framed building.

finished floor levels. If the treads are metal pans to be filled with concrete, they should have a temporary filling of wood if they are not concreted immediately. Empty metal-pan stairs are dangerous to walk on.

Prefabricated stair handrails can be one of the most trying pieces to fit in the entire building (see Figure 15.5). Because they are continuous, on an angle, and diving down and swooping around corners at landings many situations for dimensional and fabrication errors are possible. What usually happens is that the rails do not meet at the landing return. If the stair is an architectural feature or one that will be used frequently, it is most unwise to allow the contractor to refabricate the handrail in the field. It should go back to the shop. Sometimes, a misfabricated stair rail in an exit stairwell that is rarely used can be corrected in the field. But most attempts that I have seen look cobbled up.

Raised access floors are sometimes considered as special construction and sometimes as metal fabrications. They are becoming more common as data processing and its accompanying wiring are used in more applications. Raised access floors are available in two basic types: those with freestanding pedestals, and those in which the pedestals are tied together with beams. The beams may be made for removal without tools, or they may be bolted to the pedestals. Make sure that removable beams are not jammed in so tight that they cannot be removed. If the floor also serves as an air distribution device,

FIGURE 15.5. A complex prefabricated stair rail return.

the location of the perforated panels is important. Make sure that the contractor has provided a panel lifting device.

The most critical element of raised floors is the levelness. Check it with a surveyor's instrument in large spaces and with a long straightedge in smaller spaces. Walk over all the floor surface to check for panels that rock or pop when stepped on. The height of the pedestals is adjustable to correct these deficiencies.

Many other miscellaneous items could be mentioned. The main things to watch for in installation of miscellaneous items are proper alignment and secure fastening. Some of the miscellaneous items that may be involved are:

Ladders and ladder rungs: check spacing of rungs.

Thresholds: verify that the location conforms to the door design.

Access hatches: check for proper operation.

Grates: check for materials, spacing, and depth of bars, and proper fastening to the supporting structure.

Catwalks: Check against the design.

Entry mats: Watch for "toe stubbers."

16

WINDOWS AND DOORS

WINDOWS, CURTAIN WALL AND STOREFRONT

Nearly all curtain wall and storefront systems are made of aluminum, as are most windows. Windows are still made of steel, wood, and wood composites (vinyl overlay on wood), and some exotic systems are made entirely of glass and sealant. These exotic windows should be installed under the scrutiny of a manufacturer's representative.

Some storefront and curtain wall systems are shipped to the field knocked down, usually referred to as *stick* systems. The two main things to watch for in knocked-down systems are the alignment (square and plumb) and the jointery. If not assembled correctly and tightly, either can cause leakage and complications.

Glazing is an ambiguous term, but it is used consistently in the construction industry. Used as a noun, it typically means "glass". Used as a verb, it typically means the act of installing glass. However, some times the term signifies the materials used to install the glass, as in "glazing compound." To avoid misunderstandings, ask for a more specific term.

Glass now comes in numerous varieties. There are various combinations of tinting, reflective coatings, tempering, reinforcing, laminating, and composite insulating systems. And glass is not the only glazing material available. Acrylic plastic, polycarbonate and various laminations of glass and plastics are available. Thus, you cannot be casual about checking glass and glazing materials against the specifications.

When inspecting the installation of glass, watch for chipped pieces, scratches, and staining (which may only be seen after the system is in place and can be compared with the other glass).

Oversize pieces can sometimes be "nibbled" in the field. If the piece is to be used in a sophisticated system, though, you probably should not allow nibbling. Any piece of tempered glass that is oversize cannot be cut. It must be replaced.

Because of the proliferation of glass and plastic types, the sizes being used, and the expansion characteristics of the systems, glazing (i.e., the materials used to seal and fasten the glass in place) is now a high-tech part of a sophisticated system. The proper components must be carefully chosen and used exactly as they were intended to be. A glazing system can have many components: resilient shim blocks, gaskets, glazing tapes, metal glazing beads, and glazing compounds for structural use or for sealing. Each one has a specific job to perform in a specific way. Some spectacular failures have occurred because some component was not used or else was used incorrectly. Be sure you understand the parts of the total system and how each one must be installed.

Curtain wall, field-assembled windows, and sophisticated glazing systems are excellent candidates for mock-ups and trial runs. Installation techniques can make the difference between a smooth, successful installation and one in which problems abound and the results are unsatisfactory: the more complex the assembly, the more benefit is gained by trial runs and mock-ups. If unforeseen difficulties show up, they can be worked out before a lot of unsatisfactory work is in place.

You can disregard most of the foregoing discussion if you are inspecting wood windows, single-pane glass, and glazing compound. Glazing is simply a matter of using a good oleoresinous glazing compound and applying it neatly, making sure that the compound is pressed into place.

Glass staining is a relative newcomer to the world of construction problems. Staining could be factory-produced or caused by factors at the project site, such as rust staining, etching by the chemical action of concrete or plaster dust, and water sprinklers wetting the glass and depositing mineral residues on it. Staining is a subject for experts, but watch for it so that it may be addressed before it becomes a major problem.

The advent of single-pane reflective glass has introduced a potential problem. Even though the coating is called a "hard coat" and it must be installed on the inside, it can still be damaged by abrasive cleaners and by scraping with razor blades. This type of damage cannot be repaired in the field, so prevention is the best cure.

DOORS, FRAMES, HARDWARE

A doorframe must be plumb and square for the door to fit. But don't assume that everyone installing doorframes realizes that. Also, the hinge location must be on the correct side and properly handed (see Figure 16.1 for an explanation of hand).

Most hollow metal doorframes are constructed under the assumption that

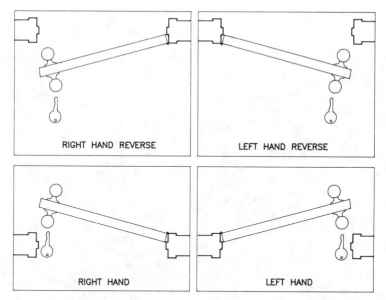

FIGURE 16.1. Standard designation of door hands.

they will be erected and the partition built to them later (see Figure 16.2), which is the best sequence. Frames may be braced in place and anchors installed as the masonry rises or as the drywall studs are installed. But what happens when the hollow metal delivery is so long that the entire project would be delayed if the contractor waited for frames before beginning partitions? Naturally, the wall construction would begin—without the frames. It is always more difficult to install frames in a completed drywall partition, but it is not impossible. (In fact, there are frames that are made specifically to install in drywall after the partition is finished. These frames are usually knocked-down frames that fasten at the corners with a "tab A in slot B" type connection and the corner joint may or may not be mitered.)

Hollow metal frames in a masonry partition can be anchored through the frame and a pipe standoff with expansion anchors (see Figure 16.3). But hollow metal frames in a masonry partition are generally filled with grout to prevent the hollow sound. The easiest way, of course, is to leave the grout out, but that may not be negotiable. In that case, the frames must be grouted *before* installation. It makes them awfully heavy and hard to install, but it is not impossible. I have seen it done several times.

If frames are dented or dinged before installation, some repair can be done with an epoxy or polyester body putty. Some contractors want to use a spackling compound, but this is not a good practice. Spackling does not adhere well to metal, and it is susceptible to deterioration from moisture.

Check the specifications for the method of joining at the corner. The joint may be a butt or a miter, and it may or may not be welded.

FIGURE 16.2. Hollow metal door frames braced in place awaiting masonry.

The specifications or drawings (usually in a door schedule) might call for hospital stops. A hospital stop is a cutoff stop to make cleaning around the frame easier (see Figure 16.4). In spite of their name, hospital stops are not used only on hospital projects but might show up on any project.

Wooden doorframes are usually prefabricated, with one face removed or loosely nailed in place. They must be set in place, plumbed, and then fastened. Look for tight joints and secure fastening.

Doors

Doors come in many shapes, sizes, materials, and configurations. They may be swinging, pivoting, sliding, folding, or overhead. They may be wood (paint grade or stain grade), hollow metal, plastic (or plastic faced), or aluminum. Specialty doors include blast-resistant doors, lead-lined doors for x-ray blocking, vault doors, refrigerator doors, and various types of jail and prison doors. During inspection, see that the right door is being installed, that it is properly installed so that it functions properly. Check the specifications for allowable tolerances.

Doors in fire-rated walls and partitions must be fire-rated and have a label attached (usually on the edge at the hinges) stating the rating. Rated doors must be installed in a similarly labeled frame. If the design calls for labeled doors and frames, look for the label and check the designation against the

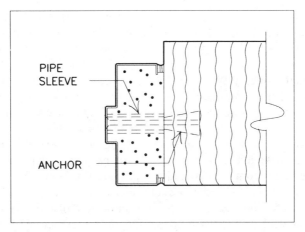

FIGURE 16.3. A pipe stand-off door frame anchor (used when the wall is in place before the frame).

design requirements. A labeled door or frame can look like just another door or frame, so you must look at the label.

Hollow metal doors must be prepared in the plant for hardware. Even though the doors and frames might be made in different places, they are prepared with templates furnished by the hardware manufacturer so that they will fit in the field. If they do not fit, some locales have people who can do a decent job of remaking the doors or frames. The job is not easy job and should not be attempted at the site.

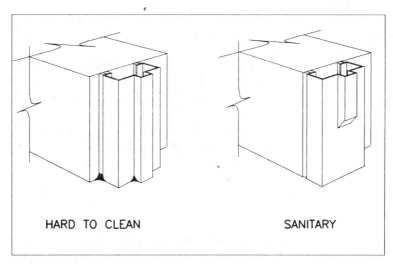

FIGURE 16.4. Door frame with hospital stop (on right).

If not prefabricated, wood doors and frames are prepared and fitted by finish carpenters at the site. Make sure that the carpenter does not trim off the bevel on the strike edge of the door. That bevel allows the door to close without hitting its back edge against the frame. It is necessary because the front and back edges pivot from the same point and, therefore, describe different arcs. The back side arch is longer than the front side arch by about 1/4 in. This 1/4 in. difference is overcome by the bevel cut on the edge. Get out a compass and prove it to yourself if you do not believe it.

Some doors have windows ("lights" in the trade) and/or louvers. Make sure they are the specified items and that the proper glazing is installed.

Overhead doors come in two major types: steel roll-up doors and upward-acting sectional doors. Overhead doors may be powered or manual, if they are small enough. The tracks for upward-acting sectional doors should slope away from the wall as they rise is so that the door rides free of friction with the wall but seals against the wall when closed. Check this seal for effectiveness.

Check both types of doors for operation. If the doors are manual, you shouldn't need excessive force to lift or close them, because their spring balances reduce the lifting force. Automatic doors should open and close without hesitation or jerky movement, and adjusted to stop clear of the opening in the up position. They should seal against the threshold. The bottom bar must have a large rubber tube along the edge containing a safety stopping device. If it encounters resistance, the door will reverse immediately. Check this feature for each door.

Horizontal sliding doors may be powered or manual (acted on by gravity). They are usually fire-rated and must have fusible links and electronic devices that close the door in case of a fire or an alarm. The closing force may be an electric operator or gravity. Some gravity-closing doors simply roll on sloped rails, and others have cables, pulleys, and suspended weights to assist the closing. Check for free movement without binding.

Rapid-rolling overhead doors have a plastic-coated fabric curtain with a metal bottom bar. It too should have an automatic reversing device built into the bottom bar.

Automatic doors can be activated in many ways. The most common is a push button actuator located on the wall beside the door. The doors can be equipped with a remote pull chord suspended from the ceiling. This type usually has a delayed automatic closing feature. Automatic doors can also be actuated by an induction loop built into the floor. This type usually has an electric eye in the opening to keep the door from closing when the opening is obstructed. Check the specifications carefully for options and required features.

Hardware

Door hinges (called *butts* in the trade) are numbered by the pair. Three hinges is a pair and a half of butts. (Trivial, but it helps if you speak the language). Butts come in many sizes and shapes, with many varied features. They can be plain or ball bearing, heavy duty, swaged or offset, self-closing, or NRP (nonrising pin for butts that must have the hinge pin on the outside). Use the hardware schedule from the supplier when checking for proper hardware. These schedules are maddeningly complex and confusing, but the only way to use one is to dive in and tough it out.

Other hinging devices do not qualify as butts. Among them are floor pivots, "Soss" hinges, and automatic operators. Pivots are concealed in the floor and require a block-out in the slab. Any special hinging devices should be carefully specified and detailed.

Latches, locksets, keys, and keying are similarly complex. Latches are fairly simple, but locksets are not. They are handed, of course, and they must have the correct level of keying and the correct function. By "correct level of keying," I mean the hierarchy designated by grand master, master, keyed alike, and so on (see Figure 16.5). Large projects can have many levels of keying in which a grand master key will open any lock on the project; a master key might open half the locks; keyed alike keys might open a dozen; and so forth. This is the heart of a security system for the project.

The available functions are an entire subject. They can have concealed or exposed button locks or lever locks, safety bolts (with a free-rolling pin that resists hacksawing), dummy knobs on one side, and many more options. The hardware schedule is essential to properly locate the latches and locksets.

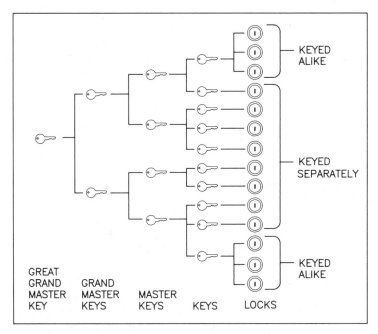

FIGURE 16.5. A hierarchical keying system.

Electric strikes or electric bolts facilitate releasing the latch from a remote location or with a card key or code keypad. The wiring must be installed with the door frame. An electric strike has conduit and wiring to the strike jamb of the frame. An electric bolt has conduit and wiring to the hinge side of the frame. An electromagnetic plate has conduit and wiring to the strike jamb. Each setup uses a remote actuator device, which might be beside the door, as with a card reader or a keypad, or in a remote location and consist of a simple button to release the door. These devices may also be connected to a computer or a recording device that is also remotely located.

These electric devices are designed to fail-safe or fail-lock if the power goes out. With a fail-safe, the bolt retracts with power outage and a fail-lock extends (or remains extended) on a power outage. Know which is required, and verify the power-out condition of the device.

Panic hardware is installed on selected doors. Some doors with panic hardware may have alarms to discourage everyday use of a door intended solely for an emergency exit. These doors may or may not have a knob on the outside.

Any door that should normally remain closed will have a closer mounted on it. Closers come in a variety of sizes and shapes. The size is designated by a number that may be unique to the manufacturer. Be sure you can identify the proper size of closer.

Door closers may be mounted on the door or the frame, on the inside or the outside, exposed or concealed within the door or the frame, or they may be built into the floor. You should know the location of each closer and how it is to be mounted. Many an architect has had a rude shock finding a closer suspended from the frame and protruding into the opening with the door open. This mounting is standard and should not be a surprise to anyone who has been careful in specifying closers and thorough in checking the hardware submittals.

Features of closers include checks that limit the angular travel of the door and the hold-open, which . . . well, you know. Coordinators are devices that apply to pairs of doors with an astragal mounted on one leaf. This device is mounted on the head of the frame at the meeting of the doors. The door with no astragal must close first, and a coordinator makes this happen. It will hold the leaf with the astragal ajar until the other one closes.

Closers must be adjusted for closing force so that they will not be too hard to open, but will not stand open in a breeze. Adjustments should be done by the hardware supplier.

Checks are like closers in that they attach to the door and the frame with a linked arm. But the only duty of a check is to limit the swing of the door. A check can also have a hold-open feature.

Exterior doors will usually have weatherstripping attached to the frame, in the form of brushes, resilient tubular seals, or brass strips. Some are adjustable, but most are not. If they are not adjustable, they must be carefully installed so that the door and weatherstripping function properly.

Closely akin to weatherstripping is sound stripping. Nearly all soundstripping is adjustable, and the adjustment should be checked. Operate doors with gaskets or compression-type sealing several times to verify that the door closes and latches as it should, and by itself if it is equipped with a closer.

The bottom may be sealed with an automatic door bottom, which is a sound seal that retracts as the door opens to reduce friction and wear. They may either be surface-mounted or built into the bottom of the door. A pin protruding from the end of the device nearest the hinges actuates the retraction and extension as it strikes the frames. The floor must be level at the door for the automatic door bottom to work properly.

Doors may also be equipped with kickplates, push plates, or pull bars. Most doors will have a bumper to protect the adjacent walls, mounted on or near the floor or on the wall at the knob location. The frame is also equipped with rubber buttons inserted into predrilled holes in the stop to cushion the door.

I have not covered the true security hardware that is used in jails and prisons because this subject is highly complex and could fill a complete book. A special consultant should be involved in selection and installation of this class of hardware.

CAULKING

Caulking materials (also correctly spelled calking) and sealants are technically different. Strictly speaking, caulking is used in a nonmoving joint, and sealants are used in moving joints.

The oldest caulking material is the common oil-based or oleoresinous type. This material retains some pliability for several years, can be installed and tooled easily, and it can be painted. Installation is easy—the more the better being the general rule, as long as it is neat. However, caulk cannot withstand much movement. Sealants must be used in moving joints, and correct installation is extremely important.

Sealants come in two basic configurations: self-leveling and thixotropic. (i.e., nonsagging). The self-leveling type is used in horizontal joints, and the thixotropic type is used in vertical or overhead joints. Sealants can also be classified as to number of parts. One-part sealants can be used straight out of the container. Higher-performance sealants are usually two-part and must be mixed before use. Most sealants in common use today are butyl, solvent-based acrylic, acrylic hybrid, polysulfide, urethane, or silicone. Verify that the sealant being used is what has been specified for the application. Most types of sealants come in a variety of colors, so be sure the right color is used.

For convenience, I will use the term *caulk* for both caulking and sealants. I have seen more faulty caulking than any other single construction element. Most caulking failures are due to neglecting the cleanliness of the joint or the depth-to-width ratio of the joint material. Both of these elements are critical.

Some substrate materials must be primed to promote adhesion of the caulking material. But if the joint is not clean, even priming will not make the caulking adhere.

Most joints to be caulked are usually much deeper than they are wide. To control the depth of the calk, workers put a backer rod in the joint. A backer rod is a round or rectangular "rope" of closed cell foam. Some construction people think that the more caulk used the better, but this wastes expensive caulking and guarantees joint failure. Caulk that is too thick has too much strength and cannot properly stretch. Therefore it cracks down the middle or separates from the side of the joint, so correct setting of the backer rod is essential, and should be closely monitored. Figure 16.6 shows how caulked

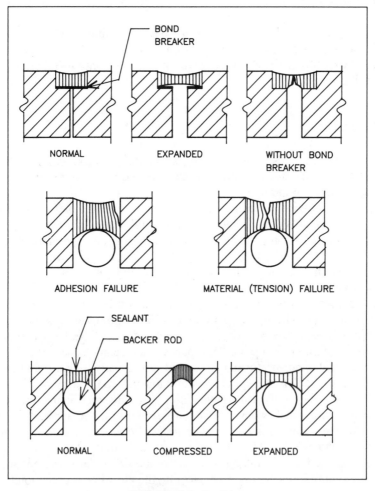

FIGURE 16.6. Caulking.

joints should behave and how they fail. A caulked joint with a bottom or shoulder should have a bond breaker on the shoulder as shown.

Another caulking situation occurs in joints in industrial floors, especially warehouse floors. Most warehouses are subjected to wheeled traffic (fork trucks, dollies, hand trucks, etc.), which are a special problem for joints. If the caulking is soft and resilient, the traffic will eventually cause spalling at the edges of joints, which creates bumps and accelerates spalling. The joints must therefore be square-shouldered and filled with a semiresilient caulking that will support the wheel loads and provide a smooth crossing of the joint. Several epoxy caulks on the market meet this need. They are not installed like sealants in a moving joint with a backer rod to control depth, but instead are installed to the full depth of the joint to be able to carry the loads to which they will be subjected.

EXTERIOR LOUVERS

Louvers are fairly simple, but they can get complicated with multiple duct connections and motorized dampers. Installing a louver is somewhat like installing a window. The head and sill must be flashed and the perimeter caulked for a weathertight installation. Louvers are usually fastened to the structure through the jambs. A substructure might be called for if the louver is large or if multiple louvers are installed in one opening. If the louver is to be connected to a duct, the details may not be clear. It would pay to be cognizant of that fact and to have thought about it beforehand.

Poorly detailed or assembled louvers can be a source of troublesome leaks that is difficult to diagnose, even where they are part of factory-assembled equipment. It pays to keep a sharp eye out for possible glitches as the installation takes place.

Louvers will probably be equipped with screens to keep out debris, rodents and birds. Insect screens are usually not appropriate because they reduce the free area of the louver too much.

Some louvers will require field painting, but this is unusual. They are more usually made of anodized aluminum, some other metal that does not require painting, or they have been factory finished.

17

FINISHES

PAINTING

Painting used to be a fairly straightforward and simple subject. This is not true today, and paints and coatings are becoming more complex every year. This is not only because of advances in chemical technology, but also because of restrictions by environmental protection legislation.

It is essential to make sure that the right painting system is being used where it is supposed to be. By system, I mean the undercoater (filler and or sealer or primer) and the top coat or coats. Some architects will specify a bewildering array of paint systems—different systems for each different substrate. The specifier was meticulous in putting this array together, and you should be no less meticulous in assuring that the correct system goes on each surface that is coated.

The first key to a good paint job is surface preparation. This can not be overemphasized. Even an whiz-bang primer can not overcome the effects of poor surface preparation. Know what is required to prepare the surface. It could be simply sanding and removing the sanding dust; or it may be sand-blasting to a near white metal. It could also consist of wiping with solvents. Do not allow a painter to apply paint to a surface that has not been properly prepared.

Do not mistake primers for fillers or sealers. Fillers are usually heavy-bodied coatings that are to used to fill the pores in concrete masonry units. Neither primers nor sealers will do the job. They will leave the surface full of pinholes. Sealers are usually intended for use on semiporous materials, such as wood. They might be used in conjunction with a primer; but they are always top-coated. Nearly any bare substrate needs a primer. In some rare instances, the finished coat material may be used as a primer. But unless this is specified, assume that there will be a primer that is different from the top-coating material. The purpose of a primer is to ensures adhesion of the painting system to the substrate.

Painting materials can contain some harmful chemicals. Each paint should have a material safety data sheet (MSDS) on the material. OSHA requires that these MSDSs be available to anyone on the site. The MSDS points out precautions that should be taken to avoid harm from the chemicals in the material. Some states and local governments have VOC limits. This is a measure of how much of the solvent will be released into the air. The MSDS or the label on the can will tell you if the product is low VOC. It is the contractor's responsibility to make sure the limits are met, but you should know about the limits and how the contractor is meeting them.

The most prevalent precaution is wearing a particular type of mask anywhere the material is being used. It makes little difference whether the paint is being applied with a brush, a roller, or by paint sprayer. The mask requirement will be very specific, and you should be properly equipped to observe the painting in progress. The most stringent requirement is for the body to be completely covered (no exposed skin) and a mask with a fresh, outside air supply. If you read the labels, you will find that most two-component epoxies and urethanes have these stringent requirements.

Remember there is usually a fire hazard associated with solvent-based paints. When painting is in progress, you should know where the fire extinguishers are. Painting materials should be properly stored.

Most specifications call for each coat of paint to be a different shade so that one can tell how many coats are on the surface. This is a good theory that works well on a sample panel (with each successive coat stopped short to reveal the under layers); but it seldom works in practice. A better practice for an inspector is to make a pencilmark in an inconspicuous place after the first color coat is in place. You should remember where you have made your marks, so that you can return and see, without a doubt, whether any paint has been applied over your marks.

If the specifications call for a minimum mil thickness, there are devices to measure both wet and dry mil thicknesses. You will probably have to call on the testing company to test the paint thickness if it is required.

Some defects you should look for are

The wrong color,

Incomplete coverage,

Streaking due to incorrectly mixed color,

Runs and sags,

Holidays or incomplete hiding,

Pinholes, and

Overspray, drips, and generally sloppy painting.

Know what is to be painted and what is not. Most architectural metals, should not be painted (aluminum, bronze, stainless steel, chrome, etc.). Galvanized steel should not be painted unless it has been factory primed. Your specifications may call for it to be painted anyway, in which case surface preparation and priming are super-critical.

The most confusing painting item is often piping. Requirements range from no painting at all to all piping completely painted. Generally it is painted only where visible. Determining the requirements for painting can sometimes be the main problem. It could be in the mechanical section, either in general requirements or in the piping section, or it could be in the architectural painting section as well. (Just hope they do not conflict!).

Be on the look-out for "hidden" painting. Some projects require the inside of ducts to be painted near the grilles or registers. A partially open ceiling might require painting of the structure, deck, conduits, and piping above the ceiling level.

The traditional skill task that separates the day laborers from the painters is the ability to cut a neat line. Watch for it. It can make or break a painting job.

Look in the specifications for a maintenance stock of paint to be left with the owner.

Wood Staining

Specifications may call for a transparent finish on wood. This refers to finishes such as clear varnishes, clear lacquer, and woods that are stained before the application of a clear finish. Most woods will darken or the grain may become more contrasty with the application of a clear finish. Generally, though, a stain is required to bring out the character of a wood or to change its character. Stains usually darken the wood, but bleaching is also considered stain. Most painters will want to have someone hand them a can of stain and say "Here, put this stain on that wood." Most properly, though, the painter should be handed a sample of the desired results and told "Here, make that wood look like this." The difference is significant.

Being a natural material wood is not uniform, as synthetic materials are. Each piece of wood is different so each piece will react differently to the application of stain. Some pieces will absorb the stain rapidly and others will resist the stain. In order to achieve the desired results, it is usually necessary to apply the stain, wipe it off, and then go back over the piece to even out the staining. It may require more stain in some areas, to leave the stain on longer before wiping, or to wipe the stain off very quickly in other areas. The point is, staining is not like painting. Application requires technique and technique requires adjustment to the methods of application to achieve the desired results.

WALL COVERING

Some vinyl wall coverings have a wide selvedge, up to 3 or 4 in. wide, On one job, it was not discovered until a lot of wall covering had been installed. It was a real mess to remove and it did not make the installers happy to have it removed. A selvedge can show a very subtle difference, but enough to be apparent after it is in place. Make sure all of it is removed as the fabric is installed.

Although it is sometimes designed that way, it is virtually impossible to terminate a wall covering at an outside corner. It *can* be done, but it will look ragged in a very short period of time (probably before the contractor leaves the job). For the covering to last, the edge must be protected usually by a piece of wood or plastic trim. Thus, it much better to terminate any wall covering at an inside corner. If the design does call for termination at an outside corner, discuss it with the architect.

After the wall covering is hung, air bubbles should be carefully worked out before the glue has set. If bubbles show up after the glue has set, it might be possible to puncture the bubble with a razor blade, inject a small amount of glue with a syringe, and roll it down, working from the outside edges of the bubble toward the puncture. Excess glue should be removed to prevent a lump where the bubble was or a stain on the fabric around the puncture.

Patterns are usually easy to match at the joints, but some can be difficult, especially in a plain, light colored, coarse-textured, raised fabric pattern such as burlap. The vertical lines are not always truly vertical or straight. If this condition exists, not much can be done about it.

RESILIENT FLOOR COVERING

Almost all concrete floor slabs need some preparation before resilient tile is laid, because the tile will telegraph imperfections through to the finished surface. Preparation usually involves filling low spots and gouges or pits with a latex-modified cement material. This material can be feather-edged and is easy to spread, but it can be a source of blemishes if carelessly applied.

Two types of resilient floor covering are used: sheet goods and tiles. The specifications should be quite definite about the materials, but sometimes the layout is left to the installer. Some specifications call for the pattern to continue through door openings without interruption. Others allow a feature strip that will be beneath the closed door. Every floor covering material has a pattern direction, however subtle, that it will show up if a mistake is made. Specifications usually will call for the pattern to all run in one direction or for an alternating checkerboard pattern. If the pattern is to run in one direction, the specifications should state the direction relative to the long dimension of the room.

The most critical element in laying floor covering is the amount of glue or mastic applied. This amount is controlled by the size and spacing of the notches in the edge of the application trowel. Mastic may be spread over a large area, but not so large that it dries before the covering is laid. If too much mastic is applied, it will eventually seep through the joints and really make a mess.

Check the specifications for a maintenance stock of tile to be left with the owner.

CARPET

There are three distinctly different methods of installing carpet: Stretched, glued down, and carpet tiles. Stretched carpet usually has a padding beneath it, which is not stretched. The holding device for the carpet is a strip of wood lath around the perimeter of the room. The lath has fine nails spaced about 4 in. apart with the pointed end up. The nails, which are angled toward the wall, grab the carpet and hold it. The angle facilitates stretching because it possible to ratchet the nail's grip on the carpet. The carpet should be stretched tight enough so that it cannot be easily removed by lifting an edge. It should be stretched evenly so as not to distort the pattern. Seams must be carefully sewn.

If the specifications call for a cushion beneath the carpet, verify the type, thickness, and method of installation.

Glued-down carpet is usually used in areas of heavy traffic or where there will be rolling-wheeled loads. The carpet is laid directly on the glued floor surface. Seams are usually made with glue, also. The predominant type of glue in use today is called *blue glue*. It allows the carpet to be removed relatively easily.

The direction of the pattern or the grain of the carpet must be watched. It may not be readily apparent, but the direction of the grain will show up if it is not the same on both sides of a seam.

Carpet tiles are gaining favor, especially in open-office applications. They can lower the installation cost, and they are generally more practical to maintain than seamless carpet. Most carpet tiles are only glued down around the perimeter of the room, whereas those in the center are laid loosely or applied with a small amount of glue. Follow the specifications for proper installation methods. As with resilient tile, the pattern or grain is important. You should know if it is supposed to be checkerboarded or run in one direction.

Carpet nearly always requires some sort of treatment at exposed edges, such as door openings or where the floor material changes to a harder surface. Usually a metal strip is nailed to the substrate and curved back to conceal and protect the raw carpet edge. A plastic or rubber strip glued to the floor may also be used. Edge protection should be called out in the specifications. Look for the correct material, shape, color, and method of fastening.

If the carpet is turned up the wall to form a base, it should have a device to finish the top edge and a cove piece to form a radius between the floor and wall. Look for these elements in the specifications.

TERRAZZO

Traditional terrazzo is properly called *venetian terrazzo*. It consists of a sand-cement setting bed and a finish material of portland cement (usually colored) and marble chips. (See the next section for very thin terrazzos with an epoxy or vinyl ester binder.) It has four basic classifications: bonded, unbonded, thin set, and full thickness. Each type calls for different installation techniques. If the specifications do not give installation details, find a copy of The Tile and Terrazzo Institute installation manual. Common to all types is the surface, comprising marble chips that are broadcast and imbedded in the cement matrix. After it has set up, the surface is wet-ground and polished. An exception to this is "rustic terrazzo" in which the surface is not ground smooth.

Also common to all types is the system of metal or plastic dividers that divides the surface into squares, rectangles, or practically any geometric shape a designer dreams up. These divider strips also provide a screed for leveling the wet surface as it is placed. Therefore, it is prudent to check closely the placement of the divider strips.

Terrazzo specifications usually call for sample panels, because the finished appearance could be altered by the color of the marble chips (which might be a mixture also) and the color of the matrix. The project might also have more than one color or style of terrazzo.

Check the finished surface for voids, rough spots, cracking, and unlevel surface. All these defects should be corrected.

SEAMLESS OR MONOLITHIC FLOORING

The designations *seamless* and *monolithic* are somewhat misleading. They usually apply to floor finish materials that are placed as grouts or liquids, and they are usually based on epoxy or vinyl ester binders. Included are grout-type toppings, thin terrazzos, and liquid-applied toppings. I say the designations are misleading because they are not truly monolithic. The materials are different from their substrate, and the substrate must usually be cured or prepared for application of the finish. In addition, seams should appear in the finish whereever seams appear in the substrate. The terms *seamless* and *monolithic* seem to be relative in that these finishes are more seamless and monolithic than ceramic tile, brick pavers, resilient tile, and traditional terrazzo.

Common to all these flooring systems is that proper surface preparation is essential. If the surface is poorly prepared, an unsatisfactory floor is guaranteed. These materials are most commonly applied to concrete substrates. Surface preparation might include detergent cleaning, acid etching, scabbling, or shot blasting. These treatments remove construction dust, surface laitance and surface contaminants and provide a profile to the surface for good mechanical bonding of the finish.

The most difficult finish to apply is the grout type. It is usually applied with a trowel. Thickness is difficult to control and impossible to judge once the material is in place. Watch during the application for methods of ensuring proper thickness and for removal of trowel marks.

Terrazzo and other liquid-applied systems are usually placed as a honey-like liquid that is squeegeed to an even application. Any aggregate that is required is then broadcast to a full even coating. After the binder has hardened, the excess aggregate is swept up and removed. Check the specifications to see if this excess aggregate is reusable. Some systems require a surface coat without an added aggregate. Terrazzo must be ground and polished after the binder has cured.

TILE

Tile includes glazed ceramic tile, unglazed mosaic tile, quarry tile, brick pavers (if set by the tilesetter's method, rather than the mason's method), and many minor varieties, such as Mexican Saltillo tile. One of three methods is used to set tile: full grout bed, thin-set grout, and mastic. To some people, the term thin-set means thin-set grout, whereas to others it means mastic set. A full-grout-bed application is most likely to be used on a floor that slopes to a drain but the substrate does not slope.

Any of the setting methods could be used on walls, but mastic is the most common.

Glazed ceramic and mosaic tiles usually come in sheets with a flexible backing. This arrange ensures proper spacing within the sheet, but you may have to closely watch for proper spacing between the sheets. Most 4.25″ × 4.25″ tile has small "knobs" on each edge to set the spacing. Mosaic tile does not have this feature, and spacing may be difficult. Many tilesetters use small plastic spacers to ensure that the joints are even.

A first-class tile installation calls for a complete set of trim pieces: inside and outside corners, bull-nose terminations, inside and outside corner junctions, and so forth. On most installations, however, the most you will see is a finished edge piece. The specifications should be clear about trim required.

Most tile installations call for some planning before setting begins. If the specifications call for matching floor and wall joints, you need to use your judgment because to match floor and wall joints everywhere is usually not possible. Consider what happens at the end of a wing wall. The thickness of the wall probably will not match the module of the tile, and some compromise should be reached beforehand. The length of a wall seldom matches the tile module, so, again, someone must decide where to take up the difference. If the area is highly visible, the design architect should decide, or at least have a strong voice in the decision. But force these decisions to be made before the tile is set, not after the job is half complete.

Intricate patterns and designs in ceramic tile are quite common now. Because the design may not be well thought out and presented on the drawings, you must take the initiative and time to study it and make sure that the resulting installation will satisfy the intent of the design.

A full wall of installed 2″ × 2″ tile clearly shows if the walls are plumb and true. Give close scrutiny to walls that will be finished with mosaic tile. Lay a straightedge and level on them. Uncased openings and outside corners should not have corner beads, because they usually cause a flare in the wall next to the corner that tile cannot overcome.

Many specifications call for colored grout. If it is not a packaged color, the mix is critical for a uniform installation. Some specifications call for "natural" grout, which means the grout is the color that results from using only gray portland cement.

When the installation is complete, look for uneven joints, damaged tiles, tiles set askew, incomplete grouting or pinholes, and overall levelness of the surface. If required by the specifications, look for the matching of floor and wall joints.

CEILINGS

Modern construction, generally uses three types of finished ceilings: plaster, gypsum wallboard, and lay-in. Plaster and drywall may be fastened directly to the structure above. Most installations call for suspended ceilings. I suspect that about 90 percent of the ceilings installed today are suspended lay-in types. That is the subject that this section deals with. Refer to the sections on plaster and drywall for those types.

Four elements determine the load-carrying capacity of a suspended, lay-in ceiling grid: the section modulus of the individual grid members, the assembly pattern of the members, the size of hanger wires, and the spacing of hanger wires.

It is not up to you to determine what capacity the grid must have; that is determined by the documents. The structural capability of the grid should be reflected by the ceiling grid shop drawing submittal. It should tell you the sections to be used and where they are used. Grid sections carry different designations. Some manufacturers simply call them "standard" or "heavy duty." Check the section modulus against the specifications.

Figure 17.1(A) shows what you usually see in a 2′ × 4′ grid pattern. What you do not see is how that grid is assembled. Three basic patterns of assembly are illustrated in B, C and D. Given the same hanger spacing, B will carry the

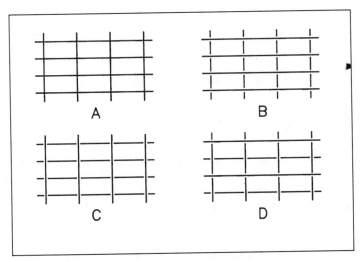

FIGURE 17.1. Ceiling grid installation options.

most load, *C* will carry less, and *D* will carry the least. Therefore, the assembly pattern may be as important to load-carrying capacity as the section modulus of the individual members. Know which pattern is called for, and verify that the grid is installed that way.

A ceiling grid is a good example of modular planning and design. It will pay off in the long run if you know what the architect had in mind when he or she laid it out. Lacking that knowledge, the installer will always begin in the center of the room with a grid member or a panel, to lay out with the largest partial panel at the wall.

An L-shaped trim piece at the wall will support the grid. You should know whether the grid is to be fastened to this trim piece or left unfastened.

If a ceiling is used in a rated fire-resistant assembly, the grid will have a distinctive appearance. Somewhere along the length of the individual members will be a weakened area in the vertical part of the tee. This area is designed such that when a member is expanded by the heat of a fire, the bottom flange will buckle sharply only in this area and the grid will remain intact so that it will not drop the panel out of the grid. The panel is what really does the protecting, so it is imperative that it remain in place to protect the structure above. Look for the weakened area of the vertical part of the grid if the ceiling is in a rated assembly. By the way, check the fire rating on the panel. Fire-rated ceiling assemblies may also require that a gypsum wallboard or ceiling panel materials box be constructed above each lighting fixture. Make sure the electricians and plumbers know this.

We usually think of lighting fixtures laying in the grid just like a ceiling panel does. Depending on the capacity of the ceiling grid and the weight of lighting fixtures, the grid may or may not be able to support them. If it cannot, the fixtures must have their own hangers. Sometimes, the grid will support heavy fixtures only if the grid is hung at each corner where a fixture will be. Be sure you understand the requirements before the ceiling and fixtures are in place.

If the fixture is smaller than the grid, such as a recessed "can" incandescent fixture, it must not be supported by a ceiling panel. The same is true for sound system speakers. The panel may support the load for the first year, but it will eventually sag and fall out of the grid.

The most common device for leveling a ceiling is the laser leveler. I don't know if these devices actually have a laser in them or just a fine beam of red light. The leveler has a rotating head with a lens that projects a "laser" red beam. It is located on a tripod or mounted on a wall and carefully leveled so that the beam of light traces the ceiling height around the perimeter of the room. The wall angle of the grid is set by the beam. As the grid is assembled, it too is leveled by the beam. Leveling should be done by adjusting the loop on the hanger wire, not by kinking the wire. A kink will eventually relax and let the ceiling sag.

As with many other finish materials, acoustical ceiling panels have a pattern direction. Pattern direction is not a factor with $2' \times 4'$ panels, but with square panels it is. Some architects want the pattern to run in the same direction, and others want it a checkerboard pattern.

As the grid is installed, make sure that there is enough clearance above the grid to maneuver the panels into place. If a wide duct is installed above the ceiling with a 1 in. clearance from the grid, it may not be possible to get the panels in. Because of the number of hangers, the panel may have to be installed through the grid opening it will lay in, and it will need more clearance than you might think.

The ceiling design may call for hold-down clips. These clips can prevent lifting of the panels due to HVAC air pressures or opening and closing of doors, or clips may also be required for a fire rating. Some architects call for panels that are beneath valves (or other devices that I will discuss later) to be left without hold-down clips and to be marked with a white thumbtack.

Some designs call for the fire sprinkler heads to be installed in a specific location within a grid, perhaps the exact center. If so, the sprinkler system installer should be made aware before he has gone too far. The installer will probably have to return to the job site to move a few heads. A head cannot be located on a grid line. It may touch it, but it may not cut through a grid piece.

All of the foregoing comments also apply to integrated ceiling systems. They are just more complex because of the integrated lighting and HVAC supply units.

Installation of a Z-spline suspension system is similar to a lay-in grid, but the tiles are usually $12'' \times 12''$. The installation of tiles on the splines must begin at one end and progress to the other end. There are provisions in concealed grid systems to incorporate access tiles. The main difference is that more attention to detail is required with a Z-spline system, because it is supposed to look like a monolithic system.

More variety is available in the panels than in the grids. Some can be look alikes, so carefully check the specifications. Panels that are routed or regressed at the perimeter (and sometimes on a pattern throughout the panel) must be hand-routed at partial, cut panels. This procedure requires craftsmanship and good judgment as to its acceptability. Check the specifications for any requirements to provide extra panels to be left with the owner.

MILLWORK AND CASEWORK

Millwork and casework apply to special items made of wood. The commonly accepted difference is that millwork is finished on the job and casework is finished in the factory or shop. Casework may imply manufactured items as opposed to custom made items, although this is not typical. Manufactured casework usually refers to factory-made items such as laboratory or kitchen cabinets. This usage gets somewhat muddled because both types of cabinets are also made in metal.

Casework, by definition, requires only the assembly of major components and installation at the job site. In some instances, the casework is not manufactured until the dimensions of the actual space can be taken and used in the manufacture. In these cases, the casework should fit precisely. However, most casework and millwork is not made to such close tolerances. Special filler pieces can be cut to fit on the job, and built-in provisions for scribing the piece or cabinet to the walls are available. A scribe is a protruding part of the cabinet that abuts the wall, usually an end piece, and may be beveled to make the trimming easier. The piece is placed close to the wall, and with a metal divider the contour of the wall is traced (or scribed) onto the protruding piece. When this edge is trimmed to the scribe mark, it will fit up to the wall perfectly.

Millwork may be delivered to the job in large pieces, broken down to many pieces or completely fabricated on the job. The specifications usually have something to say about the degree of prefabrication required.

As the pieces are installed, look at the joint lines. They should be tight and in alignment. Open all the doors. Do they fit properly? Do they latch properly? Open all the drawers. Do they slide easily? Try all the locks. Does everything fit? Is any warping evident? If the insides are supposed to be finished, check them. Are all adjustable shelves in place?

INTERIOR GRILLES AND LOUVERS

Grilles and louvers are usually covered in the mechanical sections, but because they constitute a part of the finished architecture I will address them here. As with all other hardware, what is furnished should be checked against the specifications as to size, type, fittings (such as dampers), and finish. The main thing that might be overlooked is a custom finish or field painting.

As with other finish features, fit and alignment are important. Look for gaps between the finished surface and the trim of the grille, or where the opening in the finish surface is not fully covered by the grille trim. Look for litter behind the grille. On linear grilles or other large, multisection grilles, look for alignment between the sections of grille. On floor grilles, test for rocking or any movement when it is stepped on. If they are called for in the design, make sure that return air or transfer grilles have sound-absorbing baffles or boots.

If a damper is fitted, check its operation before the balancing is done. It should move without undue force, but there should be enough resistance to keep it from moving from air pressure. After the balancing is done, with the system running, listen for rattling, whistling, or other excessive noise. Be aware that noise may be a product of the design, not necessarily the installation. Look at the direction the deflecting surfaces direct the air stream. Does it direct the air in a reasonable direction? Does the direction make sense? It could be going directly to a return air grille thereby short-circuiting the air flow.

18

ACCESSORIES AND EQUIPMENT

TOILET ACCESSORIES

Long before it is time to install recessed toilet accessories, make sure the wall is thick enough to receive the accessory. Check the shop drawing submittal for recess depths. The main item to check is the paper towel dispenser and disposal units.

After installation, count accessories, and check that each type meets the specifications. You should also inspect the following:

Check metal accessories for dents and dings.

On sanitary napkin dispensers, check for correct actuator and setup (free, coin operation, how much?).

Check mirrors for secure mounting.

Check ash trays for secure mounting.

On towel disposal units is the receptacle easily removable?

Check all locking devices.

Check toilet paper dispensers or rolls.

Test handicap rails for secure fastening and proper location.

Make sure soap dispensers are the proper type (they can be for liquid, lather, leaf, or granular soap).

Check wash fountains for good drainage of the basin and even flow of water from the spray head(s).

TOILET PARTITIONS

If toilet partitions are overhead mounted, before the ceiling is in place check for the structural channel for support of the stiles. The partitions must be the correct type and color. Check for secure fastening and alignment of the stiles to the structure and for the divider panels to the stiles and to the wall. Shake the stiles; they should not move under normal pressure. Check all for dents and dings. Check for free operation and self-closing of the doors. Test handicapped rails for secure fastening by standing on them. Check for door bumpers, clothes hangers, door latches, and package shelves. Use the specifications, the drawings, and shop drawings.

METAL LOCKERS

In the lockers, look for exterior accessories, such as sloping tops, closure trim, and finished end pieces. Check for dents, dings, and scratches in the finish. Be careful in allowing field-applied touch-up. Many lockers are finished with baked enamel and field-applied touch-up paints may not be compatible, or they may fade quicker than the factory finish.

Verify that the proper latching device is installed. Some projects call for simple gravity latches, others for integral locks, either combination- or key-operated. Open and close all doors, and operate locks if installed. Check inside the lockers for installation of shelves, hooks, and clothes rods. Check for correct numbering on the locker doors.

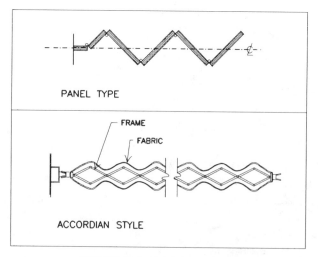

FIGURE 18.1. Folding partitions.

MOVABLE PARTITIONS

Movable partitions come in two basic varieties: accordion (or pleated) and panel type. The accordion partition is basically a metal frame covered with a heavy fabric (see Figure 18.1). The panel type is a series of rigid panels hinged at their meeting edges. Both types are suspended from an overhead track that is usually flush with the ceiling.

Another type of panel style is used in very large meeting places. The panels are not connected until they are in place, where they are locked together with a cam-locking device. These panels sometimes have movable tops or bottoms that are extended to make a more complete sound barrier.

None of these partitions has much room for error in either length or height. Accordion-type partitions can accept an opening that is too small in length, but not if it is too large. There may be some capacity for adjustment in the design of the building. If acceptable, small projections may be built out from the wall to accommodate a partition that is not long enough. Nothing can be done for a partition that is too long, except at the manufacturer's plant.

All movable partitions have one thing in common: the overhead track. These partitions can be very heavy, and all require structural support. Look for this support and the track before the ceiling is installed. Check to see that the track is level and the centerline is in the right place. Also check the distance from the floor to the track. There is not much room for error with a sound-rated partition. This would be a good "watch-out" for when placing the concrete slab. Make every effort to have the floor straight and level along the centerline of any folding partition.

For a good sound separation between spaces, a closure is needed above the track to block off the space from the ceiling to the structural deck above. This, too must be in place before the ceiling is installed.

Operate the partition to its full extension. Check for ease of movement. Check the operation of the fastening latches. Check to see that the panels or the partition can be fully nested in the open or stored position. With the partition closed check around the perimeter to see if there are any places for sound to "leak" through. A good way to do this is to turn the lights off on one side and look for light leaks from the other side.

Inspect the partition for torn fabric, dented or dinged framework, and faulty hardware. Compare the fabric and paint colors against the samples on the color board.

ELEVATORS, ESCALATORS

Elevators and escalators are specialized pieces of equipment and require specialized inspection. Both will undoubtedly require inspections by local authorities. The installation of the equipment and the check out of the operation should be a requirement of the manufacturer or installer. You should know what inspections are required and what the reporting format should be.

Most of your involvement is not with the equipment, but with the provisions of the building construction to accommodate the equipment— structural openings and clearances, the penthouse or pit, the shaft enclosure or the surrounding walls, the fit and finish of the doors, frames, and passenger cabs, and the like. The most critical of these provisions are the structural elements, for if they are not right there will be much "weeping and wailing and gnashing of teeth." Remedies usually involve chipping concrete by hand or having some of the equipment components remanufactured.

Make sure that elevator entry doorframes are fully grouted and have the correct fire-rating labels attached. Verify that the passenger cabs are correctly sized. Confirm that the finished materials are as specified and conform to the design requirements. One elevator cab will probably be outfitted to be used as a materials transporter. It should have a removable interior or studs for hanging protective pads, and a removable ceiling and a tall structural enclosure for carrying oversize materials, such as 9-ft-tall pieces of gypsum wallboard.

If the elevator is hydraulic, it will have a vertical cylinder beneath the cab that will require a vertical hole in the center of the shaft. The hole must be drilled early in the construction while the area is accessible to drilling rigs.

As a part of your checkout, call each elevator from each floor. Watch for proper operation of the annunciator lights. See that the cab floor is level with the building floor. Check the safety devices on the entry door. Place an object in the opening and see if the door reverses when the leading edge of the door touches the object.

Escalator checkout involves little more than checking for smooth operation and verifying the fit and finish of the associated trim.

MISCELLANEOUS EQUIPMENT

Electrical

If clocks are provided, check them for time setting and see that they operate. If they are slaved to a master clock, verify that they are synchronized.

If guard tour stations are required, check each location and verify that they operate properly.

Electrically operated projection screens should be let down to their full extension and then completely retracted. Check for correct operation of the limit switches. If the ceiling recess is covered by an automatic door, check for fit.

Signs

Signage includes letters mounted on walls, small sign plaques mounted on walls or on doors for identification or directions, hand-painted signs, adhesive plastic letters, changeable letter signs, plaques, and outdoor signs or mounted letters for building identification or traffic direction and control. Check size, color(s), letter style and size, placement, correct message, and security of mounting (on walls, doors, on poles).

Directories

Verify that directories and display cases are as specified and that they are properly located and securely mounted. Confirm that any accessories specified (letter kits, engraving devices, keys, etc.) have been supplied.

Food Service

An extensive food service contract may include a complete commercial kitchen, in which case a food service consultant is needed. The consultant should check out the completed installation. Minor food service equipment may be nothing more than residential kitchen equipment or a premanufactured unit kitchen. Inspection involves comparing the installation with the specifications, and checking for neatness and alignment, that all components are in working order, and checking the physical condition for scratches, dents, and dings.

In order to be ahead of the game, you must check for necessary utilities before installation or even before finish-out of the space begins. Look for sanitary sewer, water service (both hot and cold), and electrical connections. A vent hood may also be required. In a commercial kitchen, look for a fire extinguishing system in the hood.

Electric Water Coolers

Check water coolers for correct size and capacity. The manufacturer's plate located on the cooler will supply this information. Check the following:

Correct finish,
Security of mounting,
Correct fittings (bubbler, glass filler, foot operator, etc.),
Height of mounting (especially coolers installed for wheelchair users), and
Correct adjustment of the water stream.

Laboratory Equipment

Plumbing piping may be cast iron, Pyrex (glass), or Duriron. Check the specifications. The tops may be any of several materials: laminated plastic (common or chemical resistant), epoxy, or natural stone. Verify what is required. Check for correct placement and labeling of all service outlets. Verify that all services are working. Cross-check and inventory all small items. Check out the operation of doors and drawers. Check for equipment such as distilled water units, vacuum pumps, water chillers, and air compressors.

Make sure the sash on fume hoods operates smoothly, and check the operation of the fan. If emergency shower and eyewash stations are installed, find a water bucket and test the operation.

Miscellaneous Devices

Miscellaneous devices include mailboxes, mail chutes, and laundry chutes. Accommodations for vertical chutes and built-in mailboxes must be accounted for long before their installation. Check devices against the specifications and for neat, secure installation with no snags along the length of chutes.

Dock Equipment

An early watch-out is for pit-mounted dock levelers. These pits must be built into the structure, starting with the grade beam. Most will have angles on the edges of the pit and some may even have metal liners. If they have electrically powered hydraulic systems, they will also need electrical conduit.

A full complement of dock door equipment may include dock levelers, trailer levelers, trailer restraints and associated controls and signal lights, grade beam bumper pads, protective bollards, door pads or shelters (sometimes called seals), and a bracket-mounted light and fan. Check each item against the specifications. Look for proper mounting and alignment, and for physical damage. Make sure they work. Operate the dock levelers. Hydraulic operation should be smooth and accurate. A spring-operated leveler should be easy to release: it should spring up to its full height and be easy to "walk down." The lip should extend fully. If there is an interlocked system consisting of a retaining hook and signal lights, test for proper operation.

Flagpoles

One of the most important parts of a flagpole installation is electrical grounding (flagpoles make very effective and attractive lightning rods). Check the lanyards for easy operation. Verify that all the hardware called for is installed (snap hooks, etc.). Check for plumbness. Confirm that the correct taper has been supplied. A straight taper is just that; an entasis taper has a slight "bulge." (You all learned about entasis on classical Greek and Roman columns in school, didn't you?) Check for physical damage.

Trash Compactors

Trash compactors typically require electric power, water for washdown, and an equipment-mounting pad. Check the equipment against the specifications and run the equipment to verify proper operation. Equipment for trash or garbage storage and removal is often supplied by the provider of the removal service. In this case, the type and size of equipment may not be known at the time of design. This typically provokes a mad scramble to provide the necessary electrical power, sanitary drains, wash stations, mounting pad, and the like. Try to plan ahead and make sure the necessary services are available with the least disruption or demolition.

19

FURNITURE

When inspecting furniture, the first task is to take inventory. If there is a lot of furniture, this task is not easy; it is dull and repetitive, but it must be done. Good organization can make it easier, though. You might identify and locate identical office or workstation layouts and check all those at the same time. Plan ahead to make the job go faster, and more accurately. It is best to have a pictorial catalog to verify the configuration of each piece. Count the pieces (chairs, etc.), and make sure each piece is in its proper location. Check upholstery fabrics for color, pattern, and type (weave, etc.). Look for dents, dings, and scratches on metal pieces.

For open-office panels and workstations verify the layout and makeup of each workstation. Check the panels for configuration: Are they supposed to be acoustical, magnetic, plain fabric, trim, tackable? Check electrical outlets, telephone outlets, computer hookups, and task lighting.

Look at the castors on office chairs. Large ones are for use on carpet, small ones work only on hard surfaces. Office chairs may be any combination of swivel, tilt, or adjustable height.

Open all drawers and doors. Try all locks, and check for correct level of keying. Make sure dividers and accessories are inside drawers and cabinets.

Check all miscellaneous items of furnishings, such as artwork, lamps, rugs, planters, and sand urns. Wastebaskets, ashtrays, and various desk accessories may also be in the furnishings contract.

IV

MECHANICAL AND ELECTRICAL

20

PLUMBING

GENERAL CONSIDERATIONS

I am not going to attempt to make a mechanical or electrical expert out of you with this manual. (I couldn't do that anyway, because I am not an expert in these subjects, either.) But there are plenty of things to watch out for in mechanical and electrical installations that do not require expertise in those disciplines. For starters, all the pieces and parts must be accounted for and they must all be as specified. All HVAC and electrical terminal devices are visible and part of the architectural environment of the building, so they must meet the same standards of acceptability that apply to everything else that can be seen.

They must be square with the lines of the building.

They must be neat and secure.

They must work as they were intended to work.

The "hidden" parts of the systems must be securely mounted, and all the connections must be complete and tight.

These things are all essentially nontechnical and require only common sense to inspect. I will try to give you enough information to be able to decide when you should call on the engineers for answering questions, working out solutions to problem situations, or to perform some of the inspection.

COORDINATION WITH OTHER TRADES

Coordination between trades must become a way of life when dealing with mechanical and electrical systems. Many opportunities exist for interference and conflicting requirements, especially above ceilings (see Figure 20.1).

FIGURE 20.1. Good example of a crowded ceiling space. Lighting, ducts, and pipes all compete for space.

Examine these situations on the drawings so that you can forestall potential conflicts. After they occur it often becomes a battle over who will move his or her work to accommodate the other. Many times, it is not simply a matter of deciding who has the greatest will power, but a matter of actually having to engineer a solution. This is best left to the design engineers, not to negotiations between contractors and subcontractors.

Some prime areas to examine for interferences are located at

Interior roof drain leaders: They are usually large-diameter pipe, they must slope from the drain to the downcomer, and they must be insulated.

Soil lines in multistory construction: They must slope.

The ductwork that occurs near the air handling unit, where the ducts are the largest and hardest to relocate.

Ducts and pipes are usually not shown on the same drawings and therefore have a propensity for conflict. Many times I have seen ductwork designed to fill the space between the structure and the top of the ceiling, totally oblivious to the fact that a recessed lighting fixture must be installed directly beneath

FIGURE 20.2. This photo points out a lack of coordination. Notice the disconnected fire sprinkler line with the hanger rod dangling down.

the duct. Lighting patterns are typically rigid, highly visible, and difficult to rearrange.

Another prime place to watch for interference is where pipes designed by different disciplines cross; for instance, roof drain pipes and sanitary sewer pipes. Both depend on slope for drainage, and it may not be easy to alter the slope of either pipe. Roof drain lines and fire water main runs are another good example. Both tend to be large pipe and difficult to relocate. Interference between ducts and fire water mains is also frequent (see Figure 20.2). In the typical construction sequence, the fire sprinkler system piping is installed first, plumbing piping, major conduit, and ductwork are installed next, then small conduit, and finally the ceiling and lighting. Installers seem willing to deal with work that has already been installed, but they could have problems watching out for things that will be installed later.

Also watch for conflicts on the site. They typically occur between storm drainage lines and sanitary sewers because both must slope and they are usually relatively large diameter pipe. Watch for conflicts between other underground utilities such as water supply, electrical service, fire protection lines, and natural gas lines. Note that water supply lines should always pass above sanitary sewers when they must cross.

LANDSCAPE IRRIGATION

The layout of an irrigation system is probably only second in importance to the type of heads installed. The layout is designed to cover completely all the plant materials. Any gaps in the coverage of the irrigation system, especially in lawn areas, will show up as dried up plants. Brown plants do not usually add to the appearance of a landscape design. Irrigation layouts are not usually dimensioned, so you need another way to locate heads. The most accurate way is by reference to existing features, such as walkways, paving, fences, retaining walls, or the building.

If sprinkler heads have to be placed along a long run of curbing or sidewalk, they should be spaced as much like the drawings as possible. Look for clues such as X number of heads, spaced equally, the first head at the intersection of curb and walk, last head at the corner of the property line, and so forth.

Layout also includes the type of head used in a particular location. The basic head types are sprinkler, spray, mist, and bubbler. Mist and bubbler heads are usually located in beds so that they can be raised well above the grade. Sprinkler heads are set low so that a mower can pass over them without damage. Sprinkler heads can be pop-up or plug-in types. They can spray water all around the head, or they can spray a revolving-stream. The revolving-stream type covers more area than the spray type. Finally, the arc that is sprinkled can be a complete circle, a half-circle, or any division of a circle. Check each location, and make sure the correct head has been installed and that it has been properly adjusted. Plug-in heads of the large impact-operated type may be located in remote locations.

Piping is usually plastic with solvent welded connections. Connections should be tested for leaks before the system is backfilled. Check the control system on the drawings and make sure that the installation conforms to the design. It is wise to run the system through a complete cycle before you leave the site. Check for coverage of the heads and for timing and sequencing of the control system. Also check for backflow prevention because it is required by code.

Backfilling of irrigation piping is just as important as any other backfilling on the project. Improper compaction will result in shallow trenches where the fill has settled after a watering season. But turf will probably be established by then, so refilling the trench will result in torn up turf.

PLUMBING FIXTURES

Inspecting plumbing fixtures involves verifying that they are the exact make, model, and color specified and that the proper hardware is installed. Never allow any fixture, especially a china one, that is chipped or cracked to be installed.

Wall-mounted water closets (WCs) and some lavatories require a device called a chair, which is a support device imbedded in the chase wall. For a WC, it usually combines the support framework and the plumbing to which the WC is attached (see Figure 20.3). When the wall is completed, only the pipe opening and four threaded studs will be seen. The WC is bolted to the studs. A preformed caulk ring is placed between the pipe opening and the WC china for a seal. A chair for a lavatory usually has a metal plate at the height of the lavatory (see Figure 20.4) or two arms sticking out of the wall, which support the lavatory.

Two easily overlooked devices are hammer chambers and vacuum breakers. Hammer chambers prevent the classic pipe "hammer" that occurs when the water valve is suddenly closed. Hammer is more than a disturbing noise; it destroys piping and its supports. Hammer chambers are installed at the top of the supply riser, just before the faucet (or valve for a WC or urinal). It has a resilient top chamber that absorbs the shock and prevents the hammer. Early hammer chambers were simply an extension of the riser that was capped. Air trapped in the dead-end pipe cushioned the hammer. This type, however, has a tendency to fill with water and cease functioning. Hammer chambers are installed behind the wall, so you must look for them before the wall is completed.

FIGURE 20.3. Water closet chair carriers.

FIGURE 20.4. Lavatory support chairs.

Vacuum breakers are usually installed on any faucet that is threaded for a hose. They will not allow the hose to back-siphon standing water. Look for them on mop sinks and basins, laboratory sinks, and outdoor faucets. They could be a separate device or combined with the faucet and are identified by a dome "hat."

Watch for the location of cleanouts. If not planned in advance they can wind up in the worst places, such as on the walls of executive conference rooms or the president's office. You would not want a floor mounted cleanout in the middle of the main entry, now would you?

PIPING

You can learn a lot about workers' attitudes by noticing how neatly or how haphazardly the piping is installed. It should all run parallel or perpendicular to the building lines and generally be as high as possible. Make sure the routing allows enough room if the pipe is to be insulated. Make sure that piping does not block access to other pieces of equipment. It will be a lot easier to watch what is going on in the first place than it is to persuade a pipe fitter to move a pipe.

Watch for the placement of unions. Unions are generally not necessary for installation of a system, but they can sure be important when it comes time to maintain the system. Look for them downstream of valves and near any piece of equipment. Try to visualize how you would remove a piece of equipment. If you had to remove a long pipe with threaded connections on both ends, you need a union.

Materials

Verify that all piping is the proper material and size. It may be copper, black steel, galvanized steel, cast iron, ductile iron, a composite of metal with a plastic lining, plastic (be careful, there are several, very different, types), stainless steel or glass. Each type is suitable for use in a limited number of applications. Even with so many types to choose from, there may be some of each variety on a project.

You also have to check the strength of the pipe in some cases; for instance black iron (steel) pipe will be clearly marked with the schedule type. If you have doubt about the type of pipe to be used, check the specifications. If they don't help, ask the mechanical engineer.

Support

Pipes that are not buried must usually be supported off the building structure. Especially look out for vertical runs. It is easy to forget that they, too, must be supported. Supports are sometimes not adequately detailed on the drawings, so use your judgment. Most pipes can be hung simply by using good, common sense, experience and intuition. Remember that, when filled with liquid, large pipes become a much greater load—too great to be judged by intuition. Any pipe larger than 1 in. should be hung with care. First check the specifications, then consult the mechanical engineer.

Supports can be brackets off a wall or a column, or brackets, hangers, or trapezes hung from the structure. No piping should be unsecured laterally. Pipes (or conduit either for that matter) must not simply lay on their support. They should at least be restrained from movement at right angles to their length. Especially tempting, but not acceptable, is laying pipes on top of a suspended ceiling or on the bottom chord of bar joists. Ceilings are usually designed only to carry their own weight and, perhaps the lighting, but not piping and conduit. The bottom chords of bar joists are designed to resist tension, not bending loads. Any load should hang only from panel points of bar joists. Pipes themselves should not be used as structural support (see Figure 20.5).

Generally, loads may be hung from any point on wide-flange steel beams or concrete beams. Hangers are fastened to steel beams with beam clamps: holes are not to be drilled in the steel. Read the section on fasteners for a discussion of anchoring to concrete.

All-thread rods are all right in most applications, but some engineers (and

FIGURE 20.5. A saddle used to hang a load and avoid the pipe.

some applications) prohibit its use. Most engineers will not permit perforated steel banding material to be used for hangers either.

Pipes carrying hot liquids or steam must have provisions for expansion and contraction. This class of piping should have been subjected to a stress analysis and properly detailed for stress relief on the drawings. Steam lines will have expansion loops (see Figure 20.6).

Joints

Many joints must be made in piping, and joints are the weak link in the chain. Pipe never leaks, but the joints do. Since piping is usually hidden when the building is complete, it must be tested before it is concealed. The specifications will tell you the type of test that should be applied, the duration of the test (in some cases), and what constitutes acceptable results.

Joints may be threaded, soldered, compression devices, welded, solvent welded, patented no-hub joints, or simple bell-and-spigot. Threaded, soldered, and No-Hub are the most common in building construction. As pipe

FIGURE 20.6. Expansion loops in steam lines.

fitters are making threaded joints watch cutting and threading operations to see that the workers are beveling the inside surface, removing burrs, and cleaning debris out of the pipe before joining.

The highly labor-intensive bell-and-spigot joints in sanitary sewer systems have largely been replaced by various no-hub (see Figure 20.7) and O-ring systems. Check the specifications or submittals for acceptability of systems.

Most plumbing specifications do not allow Teflon tape to be used on threaded pipe joints in place of pipe dope. The reason is that it is easy to apply too much tape and the excess tends to get into the piping and eventually lodge in a valve or some other sensitive plumbing apparatus. Check your specifications.

Pipe Insulation

Several types of insulation for different applications could be found on the project. Verify that all piping designed to be insulated is covered with the right insulation system. If a vapor barrier is called for, go over the installation carefully, looking for inadvertent breaks in the barrier. Bends are especially subject to breaks.

Do not allow such antics as cutting insulation around existing construction (see Figure 20.8). Verify that pipes have been tested before insulation begins.

FIGURE 20.7. "No-hub" plumbing joints.

Natural Gas Piping

Gas piping, especially natural gas piping, deserves special caution. Always assume that a gas pipe will leak. Consider what will happen when that occurs. If the pipe is beneath a concrete slab with a grade beam all around it, the slab will become a reservoir for the escaping gas. Sooner or later, a spark will ignite the gas, causing a tremendous explosion. Many lives have been lost in this very manner.

Lines that run beneath concrete, whether it be a building slab or paving, should be sleeved with another pipe that is vented to the open air at both ends. This arrangement protects the line and allows escaping gas to be diluted by the surrounding air. Use the same logic on any concealed gas pipe. If the design has overlooked a concealed gas pipe situation, alert the architect.

FIGURE 20.8. The pipe insulation was cut back to clear the stud. This is definitely not a good practice.

Valves

There are many different types of valves and each type has particular applications. For instance, globe valves are used in applications where the purpose of the valve is to throttle the flow of the liquid. It will allow partially open operation to adjust the flow as required. The angle valve is identical in purpose and operation to the globe valve, but the flow is usually somewhat smoother. Gate valves are used where positive closure is required. It is intended to be either on or off and not used for partial flows. Check valves allow liquid to flow in one direction but not in the opposite direction. Figures 20.9 and 20.10 show these valve types. Differences in individual makes and sizes may exist, but by knowing what goes on inside you can probably recognize the type by its appearance. These valves are threaded in smaller sizes and flanged in larger sizes.

Butterfly valves (see Figures 20.11 and 20.12) are sometimes substituted for gate valves. They are generally less expensive and more adaptable to motorized actuators. When closed, they do not make as good a seal as a gate valve, nor when open are they as open as a gate valve. Make sure that butterfly valves are acceptable before allowing their use. Butterfly valves are usually clamped in place between flanges or with special compression fittings.

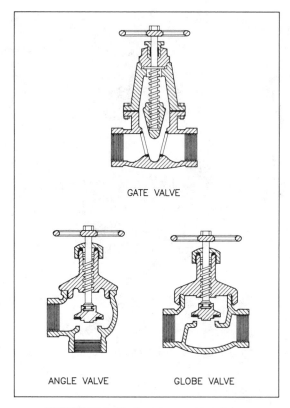

GATE VALVE

ANGLE VALVE   GLOBE VALVE

FIGURE 20.9. The most common valves.

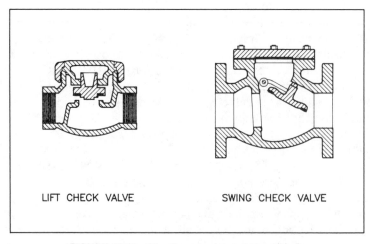

LIFT CHECK VALVE   SWING CHECK VALVE

FIGURE 20.10. Check valves (prevent backflow).

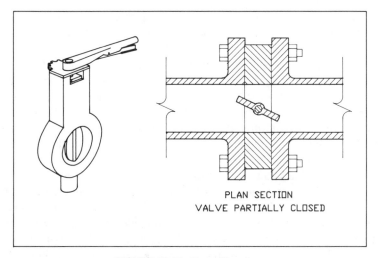

PLAN SECTION
VALVE PARTIALLY CLOSED

FIGURE 20.11. Butterfly valve.

FIGURE 20.12. Butterfly valves.

Ball valves are most often found in smaller piping and are usually welded or soldered in place. There are applications for large ball valves, but they are not common in building construction (see Figure 20.13).

The specifications usually, but not always, give a type number to each type of valve used in the design. Sometimes, only the applications for which the valve type is to be used is specified. The size of some valves is critical, and the system may not function with the wrong size valve installed. I have included illustrations of the common valves used in building construction. If there is any doubt to the proper type or size of valve to use, call the mechanical engineer.

Codes require backflow prevention to prevent contamination of a city water supply. How can a building's water system contaminate a city water supply? Suppose a hose is attached to an open faucet, and the open end of the hose is lying in a mud puddle. If a fire breaks out nearby and the fire department opens the fire hydrants, the demand puts a suction on the hose in the mud puddle. There is nothing to prevent the dirty water from being drawn into the city water supply. For this reason some codes require vacuum breakers on hose bibs, which is one form of backflow prevention.

Most codes require some type of backflow preventer between the city water supply and the building system. It can be as simple as a double check valve or as complicated as a reduced-pressure backflow preventer. Be able to identify the type used and know what is specified. Check valves are common backflow preventers. Figure 20.10 shows two common check valves.

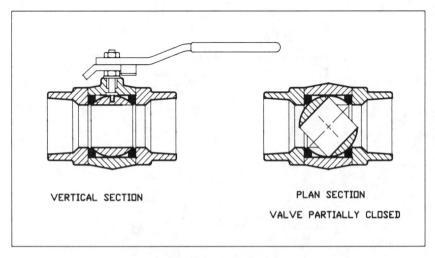

VERTICAL SECTION

PLAN SECTION

VALVE PARTIALLY CLOSED

FIGURE 20.13. Ball valve.

Thrust Blocks

When water (or any fluid) abruptly starts or stops flowing, it tries to transfer its kinetic energy to the pipeline carrying it. If this were allowed to happen, the pipe would flex at any change in the direction of the pipe. Repeated flexing would induce fatigue and eventual rupture of the pipe or fitting. Thrust blocks are masses of concrete placed at strategic points on a buried pipeline, such as at bends, to prevent this stressing of the pipeline.

Thrust blocks are usually detailed generically on the drawings and are not called for at specific locations. Therefore, it is a matter of judgment as to where the generic details should apply. Try to visualize what will happen if the pipe is allowed to move along its long axis. That should tell you where to resist this thrust with a thrust block. If in doubt, contact the engineer.

Special Systems

Laboratory, electronics, and medical buildings, will have special systems, including various gases (especially oxygen), vacuum, chilled water, deionized (DI) water and compressed air. Almost all of these systems have special requirements. Study the specifications carefully.

Sanitizing

All pipes except sanitary sewer lines and closed-loop lines (steam, heating and cooling water, etc.) must be sanitized before they can be used. The specifications will advise you on methods.

21

HVAC AND MECHANICAL

HVAC DUCTWORK

Study the design as shown on the drawings. Try to understand how it works and why the ducting is routed the way it is. Look for possible interferences. Look for in-duct devices, such as dampers, reheat coils, smoke detectors, temperature sensors, sound attenuators (more about these later), and the like. Look for terminal devices such as mixing boxes, variable air volume (VAV) boxes, flex duct, integrated ceiling devices, linear grille boots, grilles, and registers. The better you understand the system, the easier it will be for you to inspect.

Hangers, Supports

Nearly all ducts must be hung from the structure. The sizes and shapes of some ducts will present challenges, which are not addressed on the drawings or in the specifications. It is most desirable to have all hangers vertical, but that is not always possible. Angled hangers are acceptable, but the laws of physics cannot be repealed to allow an unusual solution to hanging a duct. In other words, an isolated angled hanger is not permitted; at least two are needed to balance out the horizontal thrust. This can be deceiving because the rigidity of a duct may make a single angled hanger appear to work. But it is placing the stress on the ductwork. Eventually, it will deflect, twist, or sag, and probably open a joint, allowing air to leak out.

A duct should not be used as a structural support for a hanger. However, this happens frequently, because avoiding it makes the situation more complicated (see Figure 21.1). But those complications are necessary. Never allow a duct to be used as a structural support for a hanger.

FIGURE 21.1. A saddle used to hang a load and avoid the duct.

Check your specifications for allowable hanging devices. Watch especially for devices or equipment associated with the ductwork that may be heavier than ductwork, such as in-line fans, mixing boxes, and VAV boxes (see Figure 21.2). Hanging of this type of equipment should be detailed on the drawings or on shop drawings. They should *not* be supported by the ductwork.

Access

A duct system of any complexity cannot be installed and forgotten. There will be dampers to adjust, motors and fans to maintain, drive belts to replace, and control devices to maintain. All these activities require that the devices be accessible. In this day and age of the lay-in ceiling, we tend to forget about access, because a lay-in system virtually assures unlimited access. But what about ducts that are so close to the ceiling that the lay-in panels can not be removed? What about gypsum board ceilings in toilets? What about a device that is mounted 40 feet above the floor and the floor is covered with manufacturing equipment?

Obviously, these situations should be handled and solved during design. Don't be too quick to point fingers, though, because two-dimensional drawings do not always reveal three-dimensional problems. You have a unique

FIGURE 21.2. A variable air volume (VAV) box before installation of the ductwork. Note the steam-heated reheat coils.

opportunity to ambush problems like this because you can watch the workers installing the device and see how accessible it really is. If there are access problems, consult the architect.

Insulation

Ducts must usually be insulated, either on the inside or on the outside. Design reasons exist for each method, and it should be clearly shown on the drawings. However, you will have to study the specifications to determine the materials and methods to be used to insulate ducts. Check the insulation for completeness, sealing of joints, and terminations.

Vibration Isolation and Sound Attenuators

As applied to ductwork, vibration isolation is usually used to isolate the ductwork from a noisy, vibrating fan. It is typically in the form of a flexible bellows. Watch for complete sealing of joints and freedom of movement. The source of the vibration and the duct downstream of the bellows should not have a common support structure. Sound attenuators are also intended to block noise from a loud, boisterous fan from traveling down the duct system and into rooms that are supposed to be quiet. They are usually inserted in the duct as close as possible to the source of the noise.

Grilles and Registers

By most definitions a grille is a static fixture, and a register has either adjustable outlet vanes or a volume damper or both. Check that the proper fixture has been used in the proper place. Check for security of fastening and for leakage of air around the trim. Check registers for freedom of movement of the vanes and the correct aiming or adjustment of the vanes. Volume dampers should be set during the balancing of the HVAC system. Naturally, check for visible dents and dings and scratches.

Turning Vanes

Turning vanes are inserted in ducts to help the airstream turn corners. They are usually used in corners where space limitations prevent a large-radius turn in the duct. The specifications call out places where turning vanes are required, and some will be shown on the drawings. Look inside the ducts before they are closed off to verify that the required turning vanes are in place.

Splitter Dampers

Splitter dampers are used to help the balancing process (see Figure 21.3). The important things to check are that splitter dampers have been installed where they are called for by the design and that the control is accessible.

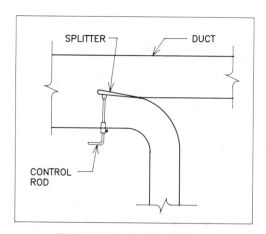

FIGURE 21.3. A splitter damper.

Fire Dampers

When a duct passes through a fire wall, fire dampers are required. In the event of a fire, the flames will quickly melt the thin metal of ductwork. Where the duct passes through a fire wall (or used to pass through a fire wall), the wall will be left with an opening that cancels the effectiveness of the fire separation provided by the fire wall. Therefore, a damper must be installed in the duct at the fire wall, which will close when a fusible link melts and remain in place if the duct melts away, thereby protecting the opening in the fire wall. Therefore, look for fire dampers where any duct passes through a fire wall (see Figure 21.4).

Obstructions

Sometimes a duct installer encounters an unexpected conflict between pipes or beams, and there is no way to route the duct around the obstruction. It may be possible to pass the obstruction through the duct if the obstructing member is small enough (see Figure 21.5). As shown in the upper illustration, the duct may need to be widened to allow enough area for efficient airflow. Always check with the mechanical engineer to verify the feasibility of the solution.

FIGURE 21.4. A square fire damper for a round duct at a fire separation wall.

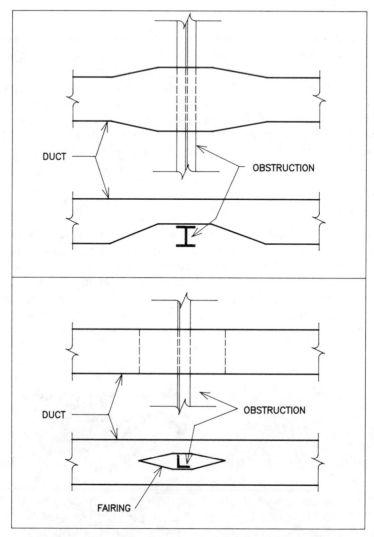

FIGURE 21.5. Possible ways of resolving duct obstructions.

Balancing

An HVAC system is designed to provide a specific amount of air through each supply grille or register. The system must be balanced to provide the designed airflow, which is the purpose for all the balancing dampers. Each one must be adjusted to balance the system and ensure proper airflow. Verification of correct airflow and balancing of the system are best left to experts. You simply need to know that the system must be balanced. Therefore, the technicians doing the work must be able to reach the damper controls. Make sure that all controls can be located and accessed (see Figures 21.6 and 21.7). Specifications usually call for a report on the balancing.

Special Watch-outs

I have been involved in several projects where the area above the ceiling is used as a return air plenum; some of the partitions continued above the ceiling and are sealed to the structure above (for a sound separation), and the mechanical engineers were not aware of the barriers. Consequently, there was no provision for return air to get through the partition and back to the main air handling unit. This situation not only required a hole in the partition (of the correct size), but the opening also required baffles to prevent sound transmission through the hole.

In some situations, the architect will call for the inside of a duct to be painted flat black just inside of registers and grilles to prevent the duct from showing through the grille. Be alert for this and see that the painting is done before grilles are installed.

FIGURE 21.6. Note the balancing damper control near the white sticker.

FIGURE 21.7. Volume damper in a round duct take-off.

MECHANICAL EQUIPMENT

Boilers

Check the ASME inspection plate against the specification. Follow the piping diagram on the drawings and verify the correct hookup. Check pipe sizes, and look for valves and gauges where shown on the drawings. Look at the stack and make sure the proper clearances from building structure have been maintained. Check the height of the stack above the roof. The mechanical engineer or manufacturer's representative should be involved in the checkout and start-up of the boiler.

Direct-fired Heaters

If the heater is gas-fired, verify that the flue is installed. Check the following:

Cap or draft device on top of the flue,
Hanging or mounting,
Correct piping, either natural gas or steam and condensate return,

Power to the fan and proper turning direction of the fan, and
Controls (switch or thermostat).

Chillers

Check the following:

Vibration isolators, and make sure that the hold-down bolts have been
loosened.

Pipe routing and required valves and gauges.

Continuity of insulation.

Belt Drives

Most mechanical equipment transmits power from the motor to the driven
shaft by belt drives. They may be as simple as single V-belts and pulleys or as
complex as multiple belts and sheaves or synchronous drives that are cogged
or toothed. The belts must be matched to the sheaves. Multiple-belt drives
should be fitted with matched sets of belts.

Alignment of the drive sheave and the driven sheave is essential for
efficient operation and long life of the belts and the equipment. The sheaves
must be aligned in the vertical and horizontal planes and must be parallel.
Belts must never be sprung or levered onto the sheaves. The sheaves should
be moved until the belt or belts can be installed without force.

Proper tension is also important. The proper tensioning method is to adjust
the center distance between the shafts until the belts appear taut. Run the
equipment under full load for a few minutes and retension the belts. If the
belts squeal or slip, apply more tension. Properly tensioned belts will deflect
under thumb pressure, and there will be a slight bulge on the slack side when
running under load. If you have any doubt about proper tension, consult the
belt manufacturer. They always have more precise tensioning recommendations that depend on the specific belt make and model and the pressure
required to deflect the belt a standard distance.

Compressors

Verify the piping arrangement and the installation of all the ancillary pieces of
equipment (dryer, filters, coolers, etc.) Involve the mechanical engineer in
the checkout of the system.

Built-up HVAC Units

Check for accessibility to the interior of the enclosure. Verify the structure
and air-tightness of the enclosure. Check for proper condensate drainage.
Involve the mechanical engineer in the checkout of the system.

Packaged HVAC Units

Check the following:

Proper drainage of condensate,
Clean filters,
Belts for proper type, alignment, and tension,
Rotation of blower wheel,
Proper flashing for roof-mounted units,
Weathertightness of housing,
Coils for cleanliness,
Thermostat operation, and
Free operation of dampers.

Split HVAC Units

Make sure that any exposed refrigerant line is insulated. Check

Weathertightness of refrigerant and return lines where they enter the building,
Thermostat operation,
Evaporators for proper condensate drainage,
Clean filters, and clean coils, and
Condenser coils for cleanliness.

Cooling Towers

Check belts for proper type, alignment, and tension. Check the blower for proper rotation. Check watertightness of return basin.

Air Handlers

Check for free rotation of the blower wheel. Check for bearing sideplay. Make sure that the blower wheel turns in the right direction. Check belts for proper type, alignment, and tension. Check filters for cleanliness.

Exhausters

Check blower for proper rotation and secure mounting. Check roof flashing. Check for free operation of backdraft damper.

Vibration Isolation

Rotating equipment such as blowers, pumps, compressors, and fans often produce vibration that can be transmitted to the building structure and cause unacceptable vibration or noise where there should be none. Vibration isolation devices can totally or partially eliminate the noise. Isolation devices may be as simple as resilient pads between the equipment and the floor (see Figure 21.8). Even resilient pads may be somewhat complicated devices that are "tuned" to dampen certain frequencies of vibration.

Next to pads, the most common form of isolation is spring isolators. In the typical installation, they are mounted outboard of the equipment frame so that they do not raise the total height of the equipment substantially. This

FIGURE 21.8. Note the resilient block vibration isolation on this pump pad.

type isolator may also be tuned for a specific range of frequencies. Spring isolators may also be used on hanging equipment by inserting an isolator on each hanger support.

When equipment imparts low frequencies (which are harder to counteract), the specifications may require an inertial pad. This is a concrete pad, usually placed in a steel frame immediately below the piece of equipment, that is suspended, with the equipment on the spring isolators. The inertial pad gives the equipment more mass, which makes it harder for built-in vibration to shake the assembly.

Check all isolation devices against the requirements in the specifications.

Controls

Temperature control may be electric or pneumatic. Either type incorporates thermostats to sense the temperature of the air and to set the desired temperature. Verify that all required thermostats are installed and working. We are all familiar with wall-mounted thermostats, but some installations call for thermostats to be located in the return airstream inside the return air duct, usually just behind the grille.

Look for required pressure-sensing devices in ductwork and in plenums. They will usually be located near the fan or near a grille or register. Pressure-sensing devices usually control the operators on dampers, which in turn control the pressure that builds up in the duct or plenum.

Look for required smoke detectors in ductwork.

Central electronic energy management systems can be incredibly complex. They should always be checked out by the mechanical engineer or by a representative of the system manufacturer. Just try to ensure that all the sensing and control devices are in place and connected before the system is checked out.

FIRE PROTECTION

Site

If the project is large enough for several separate systems and, therefore, multiple fire protection risers, there may be a requirement for a loop around the building. Each riser should have a post-indicator valve (PIV) between the fire loop and the riser. The PIV is a red device about 2 or 3 ft tall with a built-in sign showing whether the valve is on or off. These valves must be located away from the building (the distance is set by code) so that one can be manipulated safely out of the reach of a falling building wall.

A fire-loop design may call for different materials for piping placed under a roadway, near a fire hydrant, near a PIV, or at other special locations. It is especially important to verify that all required thrust blocks have been placed on the site piping because they must bear the thrust of large surges.

Building

The building portion of a sprinkler system consists of the risers and the main piping. If the building has more than one sprinkler system, one riser is needed for each system. The code may require that the riser be accessible from outside the building as well as inside. Risers are usually complicated piping assemblies that must be verified visually by reference to the drawings (see Figure 21.9). They must usually be painted red.

Planning the Distribution Piping

The distribution piping for sprinkler systems may be designed by the sprinkler subcontractor, who may not be aware of the water piping, conduits, cable trays, and ducts that have to share the space with sprinkler piping, and

FIGURE 21.9. A fire sprinkler riser. Note the double-check backflow preventer.

sprinkler piping is usually installed first. You should know where potential conflicts are likely to occur and be ready to alert the contractor.

When the sprinkler subcontractor is installing the system, there will probably be no way to determine accurately where the final location of each head will be if the space is a finished space with a ceiling. In most projects the drops (the vertical pipe that begins at the horizontal pipe and terminates with a sprinkler head) will be installed from tees in the main line and left unfinished until the ceiling grid is installed. At that time, the subcontractor will return and adjust the drops as necessary to properly locate the heads.

Heads

Make sure that the heads are the proper type and have the correct melting point. Make sure that they are properly located to produce an effective spray. Sidewall types may require a diverter above the head. Make sure the heads are *not* painted. Check the location horizontally and vertically. Some designs may call for the heads to be recessed in the ceiling with a pop-off cover that is flush with the ceiling.

22

ELECTRICAL

LIGHTING FIXTURES

Study the drawings for the types of fixtures, and correlate the fixture types with the schedule of fixtures or with the information in the specifications on fixture types. Study the shop drawings or lighting submittal. Become familiar with the locations of each type of fixture. Look at the mounting; it may be surface-mounted, recessed, pendent, hanging, or lay-in (in a lay-in ceiling system or an integrated ceiling system in which the lighting is combined with the ceiling system and the HVAC). Check to make sure each installed fixture is the correct type.

Check the mounting, especially for lay-in and hanging fixtures. Lay-in fixtures may need to be independently hung if the ceiling grid is not made to support the fixture. The grid might need hanging wires at each corner of the opening where a lighting fixture is placed. Check the load carrying capacity of the grid system, and make sure that it has not been exceeded. Lay-in ceiling panels should not be used to support any lighting fixture.

Hanging fixtures should be detailed on the drawings. They cannot be hung from just anything handy. If they are not detailed and the hanging does not make sense, discuss it with the electrical engineer and the structural engineer.

Check the switching to see that it conforms to the design, especially switching that uses contactors. Contactors are heavy-duty secondary switches that can handle a greater electrical load than an ordinary light switch can. The light switch activates the contactor, which in turn activates the lighting fixtures. Make sure all the switches are in a logical place and accessible. I have found lighting switches located behind open office partitions where they were hard to see and impossible to work. Check out lighting controls such as dimmers.

231

Turn off all the lights and see if the right fixtures remain on for night lighting. Also, have the contractor trip the proper breaker or breakers to see that the emergency lighting comes on. Check each emergency fixture in the building to verify that it works. At the same time check all exit lights. They too should be lit when the power is off.

Operate any high-bay lamp-changing devices. Most will lower the fixture to floor level for easy lamp changing. If the design calls for a lamp-changing pole device, verify that it has been supplied.

Don't forget to check the outdoor lighting. Check out automatic devices that turn on the outside lighting with either a timer or a photocell. Outdoor light poles may also have fixture-lowering devices. Operate each one to verify that it operates. Verify the aiming of lighting that is intended to wash the building in light.

Check out any passive controls such as infrared sensors, and sound or movement detectors that automatically turn lights on and off. Check timed energy-saving systems that turn off all lights at a predetermined time. Some systems are equipped with override buttons that will turn banks of lights back on after the automatic device has turned them off. These buttons are usually timed, and the lights will go off again after a specified time. Check them for the required time delay.

Special lighting, such as theatrical stage lighting, athletic field lighting, and gymnasium lighting must be aimed. Specifications usually call for a lighting level survey and a report on this sort of lighting. Changeable theatrical lighting that is attached to flying battens and operated from busses should be checked to see that it works. Theatrical controls should be verified, but this is usually handled by the installer or a special consultant. These controls are quite complex in a sophisticated installation.

Verify that every lamp in the building is operating. Finally, read what the specifications have to say about lamp replacement. Some specifiers require that all lamps used during construction will be changed before the project is handed over to the owner.

WIRING, CONDUIT

Specifications usually state that conduit will be run level and true to line or truly vertically, running at right angles or parallel to the lines of the building. Of course, this is not necessary for the wiring nor for the electricity to flow. But neatness and attention to detail is a clue to the attitude of the electricians. If they are meticulous about conduit runs, they are more likely to be meticulous about making connections, which are critical. Electrical connections are the most likely place for the electrical system to give trouble in the future, and it will be terribly time-consuming to check each and every connection. But if the conduit runs demonstrate sloppy workmanship, it might be a good idea to inspect all connections thoroughly.

It is perfectly legitimate to use lubricating compounds to assist in pulling wires through the conduit. Make sure that the lubricant is approved.

Do not allow an electrical worker to lay conduit on a suspended ceiling grid for support. These grids are usually designed to carry only ceiling loads. Sometimes they will not even carry lighting fixtures. Similarly, conduit any larger than 1 in. should not be laid on the bottom chord of bar joists without checking with the structural engineer.

Be aware that doors that are remotely operated, either by an electric strike, electric bolt, or electromagnetic plate, must have conduit and wiring to the doorframe. An electric strike will have conduit and wiring to the strike jamb of the frame. An electric bolt must have conduit and wiring to the hinge side of the frame. An electromagnetic plate has conduit and wiring to the strike jamb. Each door has a remote actuator device, which may be beside the door, as with a card reader or a keypad. It may be in a remote location and consist of a simple button to release the door. These devices may also be connected to a computer or a recording device that is also remotely located. These devices also require a source of power.

Site Wiring

Buried conduit is usually encased in "red concrete." This is just what it seems to be—concrete with red dye. Its purpose is to warn diggers to stop when they hit red concrete. Check the specifications for requirements for buried conduit.

Telephone lines may be run in a duct bank, which is a vitrified clay tile block with square cells running the length of each piece. When laid end to end, they form a raceway of square cells. The joints must be sealed to prevent water intrusion. The bank may be encased in concrete for the same purpose. A duct bank may also be multiple conduits encased in concrete

In some installations direct burial of cable is acceptable. Check the specifications for what is allowed. The cable can be buried in a trench and backfilled. It is more common, however, for it to be laid with a device that cuts through the soil and inserts the cable as it goes, leaving no trench behind.

ELECTRICAL DEVICES

All connections should be made in outlet boxes or junction boxes ("j-boxes"). Most j-boxes have knockout plugs for connection of conduit. Any unused open plug openings should be covered. All j-box covers should be in place at completion.

Convenience outlets should be securely mounted, true to the lines of the building. It is not a good practice to allow back-to-back outlet boxes, one serving each side of the wall. It *must* not be allowed in a sound-rated wall.

Check for required pull cords in empty conduit for wiring to be pulled later.

They might be for telephone lines, computer cables, or simply for additional electric power.

Check the operation of switches, especially ganged switches, three- or four-way switches, and switches with remote contactors. Check the operation of variable lighting controls. Also check them on a low light setting for excessive heat.

It is good practice to coordinate the location of switches and thermostats so that the wall does not appear cluttered.

Do not allow lighting fixtures or speakers to be mounted in the middle of a lay-in ceiling panel without supplemental support. They may do fine for a year or so, but eventually the panel will sag and even fall out of the grid.

ELECTRICAL SWITCHGEAR, PANELS

Check the labeling of panels and circuits. Look for neat routing of wiring. Verify that all connections have been made. Make sure there are no tripped circuit breakers. The electrical engineer should be called on for a complete checkout of complicated switchgear.

EMERGENCY GENERATORS

Emergency power is usually provided by generators driven by an internal combustion engine. If the load is significant, the engine will be diesel. Emergency power should be set to start up after a power outage for a stipulated time. Check the engine to make sure that it runs properly, that the generator produces an output, and that the switchgear actually switches the load to the generator. If the generator is located inside the building, make sure that the cooling system has adequate airflow and that the exhaust is vented to the outside.

SECURITY SYSTEMS

Security systems usually include more than simple electrical equipment. The discussion of total, sophisticated security systems is beyond the scope of this manual. In this context security systems mean the burglar alarm and fire alarm system.

These systems have two main parts: detection devices and alarms. Detection for fire alarms may be provided by smoke detectors or by manual pullboxes. A fire alarm may also be triggered by a positive flow of water in the fire sprinkler system. The alarm may be a simple "paddle" alarm that is mechanically operated by the flowing water in the fire riser. Verify the proper operation of all detection devices.

Detection for security may be by infrared sensors, motion detectors, or breaks in a continuous wiring circuit. Infrared sensors and motion detectors sound an alarm when a preset detection parameter is exceeded. Continuous circuits are characterized by metallic tape around the perimeter of the glass in windows and doors and by contact plates on doors and operable windows. When the circuit is broken, an alarm sounds. Continuous circuits require testing for continuity before the system is activated.

Make sure that the alarm system works properly with exit devices. They may release the latches of exit doors that are electrically operated, and may release the hold-open devices of doors that should automatically close with an alarm.

A central control or enunciator panel may be required. An enunciator panel will energize lights to show where an alarm has been activated. Check it for proper operation.

The security system may include alarms on certain doors or windows that are locally activated. They are typically integrated with panic hardware and will sound when the door or window is opened.

A closed-circuit television (CCTV) system may also be included. This requires a station from which the remote cameras are monitored. A monitor may be dedicated to one camera or scan among several cameras. Cameras may be fixed or pan types, which scan the area by oscillating back and forth slowly. They may even have the ability to zoom with a telephoto lens. Make sure that each camera actually covers its designated area and that there are no unforeseen obstructions or unacceptable glare that prevents a clear view.

PUBLIC ADDRESS OR SOUND SYSTEMS

You may find two completely different classes of sound systems: one that is rudimentary and intended for voice transmission only (commonly called public address or PA), or one that is high fidelity for the high-quality amplification and transmission of voice and music. The first type is usually for room-to-room communication and only requires that all parts are accounted for, that the amplifier works, and that all speakers are installed, hooked up, and functioning. Any other requirements will be stated in the specifications.

The second type is usually installed in an auditorium or other public space and may require the services of an audio specialist. The speakers must usually be aimed and tuned to ensure even coverage of sound (by broadcasting white noise and the system must be tuned for accurate frequency response. This requires sophisticated electronic equipment and knowledge of how to use it.

Sound Masking Systems

To improve acoustical performance and privacy in open-office systems, sound-masking systems are often used. These systems are noisemakers that raise the ambient noise level, not enough to be annoying, but enough to increase privacy. The noise devices are usually small speakers located above the ceiling system that emit a hiss somewhat like an HVAC sound. Some devices may be exposed and mounted on the open office system panels. Locations and adjustment of the individual devices are important. Adjustment may be at each device or at a central control unit. Check the specifications for requirements for locations and adjustment.

PHONE SYSTEMS

You will find that the phone company always requires at least one 4′ × 8′ fire-retardant plywood panel to be mounted in any building with more than two or three phones. Access to this panel should not be obstructed by other equipment. Most contracts call for pull chords in empty conduit for later pulling of the phone cables. Some fire codes require that phone wiring routed above suspended ceilings be in conduit or be a wire type with a special outer insulation (usually Teflon).

Large and elaborate telephone systems may require provisions somewhat like a computer room—that is, raised flooring and in-room air conditioners. These systems usually need an uninterruptable power system (UPS) also. They consist of banks of wet-cell batteries, which are continuously trickle-charged, and a power conditioner that removes instantaneous power fluctuations and provides switching for power interruptions. These are very special systems that must be well-documented in the specifications.

V

FINAL INSPECTION AND PROJECT CLOSEOUT

23

COMPLETION

A GENERIC INSPECTION

If an inspection subject is not covered in this manual, do not despair. There are some common elements that apply to nearly every inspection. Some of these elements apply to the subjects that are covered, even though they might not be specifically mentioned. I say nearly because there are always some subjects that are so oddball that generalities may not apply, but these are definitely the exception and they are rare.

First study the drawings and read the specifications. In the drawings, check the dimensions; look for critical or unusual placement. See how each element relates to other elements of construction or to finishes. See how the element fits into the sequence of construction. Determine where errors might show up. Determine what effect errors might have on other elements of construction.

In the specifications, look for installation instructions and tolerances. Determine how quality is defined. Is is clearly stated and objective? If not, do the specifications call for a sample or a mock-up? There must be some way to determine the acceptability of the installed work. If this is not adequately addressed in the specifications, ask the architect or engineer to tell you what is critical. Since it is not a part of the contract at this point, you should talk with the contractor's superintendent and negotiate the acceptability criteria. The contractor is just as interested in this as you are, because he or she does not want you to make a subjective judgment and delay the project.

Check the approved shop drawings for changes from the drawings or specifications. Determine how the elements are shipped. Are they knocked down, partially assembled, or fully assembled? How do they go together in the field?

Armed with this information, you can now proceed to make a checklist or a list similar to the memory joggers included in this manual. Now you can inspect with confidence, even though the subject is not covered in the manual.

SITE: FINAL INSPECTION

It is possible to have two different final inspections. Take, for instance, a project in which the contractor does not purchase and install furniture and movable equipment. It will be necessary to have final inspection of the building construction after it is complete and before the equipment and furniture installation begins. If the furniture installer scuffs the walls or breaks out a window pane, the contractor will not want to pay for it. Conversely, the installer will not want to pay for a broken glass pane if it was broken before work started. An inspection must be conducted to ascertain the condition of the building before the equipment or furniture installation begins, for the benefit of the contractor and the installer.

A final inspection is also held for the owner. This inspection should be only a walk-through and should not be held until after all the discrepancies from the actual final inspection have been corrected.

The purpose of a final inspection is to allow the owner to occupy the building and to facilitate final payment to the contractor. The building may be in various states of completion. Of course, the more finished it is, the better. The contractor is still responsible for completing the punch list, but he should not be expected to perform maintenance on the building by repairing damage to it caused by the owner when moving in and using the facility.

The owner's representative should accompany you on the final inspection, and his or her comments should be added to the punch list. There may be a tendency on the part of this representative to request work that is not a part of the contract, to expand the scope, or to ask for better quality than is required. He or she may also want to add items that are actually design-related. You should add all these items to the punch list, and the architect, the owner, and the contractor will be responsible for resolving disputes.

Site Inspection

Walk around the site. Look for discrepancies such as large rocks or dirt clods, settling backfill where pipes have been run, ponding water, and incomplete work, such as unpainted ferrous metal, missing irrigation heads, missing signs, and so forth.

BUILDING: FINAL INSPECTION

Walk around the outside of the building and look for missing caulking, "B-holes" in masonry, unclean surfaces, and so on.

Carry a floor plan to note where discrepancies occur (room number, door number, window number, etc.). Carry a notepad or a recorder to note all the items.

Look at finishes for cleanliness, fit, trim, and so forth. Look at painting for good straight lines, overspray, drips, evenness, and such.

When you see a small flaw, do not "pat it down", "kick it up." But use discretion. If a small flaw can be repaired by touch-up, gluing, and patting down, don't try to destroy it.

Open and close all doors, check closer action, latch operation, key operation, and free swing with no dragging. Look at the bottom edge of the door for finish, check for weatherstripping and sound stripping. Check electric strikes and card-key operators.

Operate all operable windows.

Operate all folding partitions.

Turn on and off all switches for lights, fans, projection screens, and so forth. Are all light bulbs in place and burning? Are the lenses clean?

On millwork open and close all doors and drawers.

Flush all water closets and urinals: turn on each water faucet.

Look for damage to finish materials.

Check supply of required maintenance materials stocks to be furnished to the owner.

Electrical Check lighting fixtures for complete lamping and working lamps.

Check lighting fixture lenses for cleanliness.

Check all lighting switches and dimmers for correct operation.

Are all electrical panels labeled?

Circuit breakers identified? Spare wire ends taped or covered?

Mechanical Make sure all filters and strainers are in place and clean.

Any dripping pipes should be routed to drains.

FURNISHINGS: FINAL INSPECTION

Count all pieces. Check for colors and finishes of wood metal and fabric. Check for correct location of individual pieces. Make sure the configuration of each workstation is correct.

Check open-office panels for configuration: are they supposed to be acoustical, magnetic, plain fabric, trim. Check electrical outlets and switches in open-office partitions.

Open all drawers and doors.

Work all locks; check for correct level of keying.

Look for dents and dings.

Check for accessories such as sand urns, coat racks, waste receptacles, planters and vases, rugs or mats, wall hangings, and artwork.

Check all signs and graphics for correctness and completeness.

PROJECT CLOSEOUT

In most cases, the specifications will be crystal clear about closeout procedures. Most call for submittal of project records documents, operation and maintenance data, and warranties. Delivery of spare parts and maintenance materials may be included as part of the closeout procedures. Some contracts call for a final cleaning and equipment adjusting as a closeout procedure. Some contracts also call for a written certification by the contractor that the work has been reviewed and is ready for the final inspection by the architect, and submission of the final application for payment as "triggers" for the final inspection and closeout procedures.

Included in the project documents submittal should be the marked-up copy of the contract drawings and specifications that reflect as-built conditions, addenda, change orders, approved shop drawings, product data, and samples.

Spare parts and maintenance materials should be accompanied by a written inventory.

Project closeout also includes removal of temporary facilities, such as the construction office, storage buildings, temporary power and water, construction roads and parking, sample panels and mock-ups, and construction signs. It may also include cleaning and repair of permanent facilities used during construction.

Verify each of these requirements with the specifications and check for other requirements of the closeout procedure.

INSPECTION MEMORY JOGGERS

These supplemental "memory joggers" are intended to be used in the field or in the office before leaving for the field. The most benefit will be gained by reading the book cover to cover and then using the memory joggers to refresh your memory for specific tasks.

Layout and Surveying

1. Read the Specifications.
2. Study the drawings.
3. Has a surveyor been used? Is he or she registered?
4. Have bench marks been set? Are they marked and guarded?
5. Have property lines been located?
6. Are facilities properly located?
7. Are batterboards set and properly located?
8. Are geometrics (layout of roads and walks) complete?
9. Have existing utilities been located and marked?
10. Have trees that are to remain been marked?

Records and Daily Log

1. Daily log:
   a. The weather,
   b. Work taking place,
   c. If significant, work not taking place,
   d. Estimate of the work force (by major subcontractors),
   e. Major equipment on site, and
   f. Visitors to the site.
2. Records:
   a. All correspondence,
      Directives to the contractor,

Answers to questions and interpretations of the drawings and specifications,

Written communication with your office;
b. Log of telephone conversations,
c. Schedules and schedule changes,
d. Drawings and specifications,
e. The agreement,
f. Revisions and change orders, and
g. Shop drawings and submittals,

Grading, Backfilling Engineered Fills

1. Read the specifications.
2. Study the drawings and details.
3. During grading:
   a. Study the contours.
   b. Do spot checks to verify proper grades.
   c. Verify any critical grades.
4. During backfilling:
   a. Are excavations ready for backfills?
      Is the area clean?
      Has piping, etc., been inspected?
   b. Is proper material being used?
   c. Is backfill being placed in lifts? Have the lifts? been properly compacted?
5. For engineered fills:
   a. Has the subgrade been accepted?
   b. Has a geological engineer identified and qualified fill material?
   c. Do you know that fills are coming from the right source?
   d. Are fills being placed in proper lifts?
   e. Has the subgrade surface been loosened to accept fills?
   f. Are lifts being compacted and tested?
6. For temporary drainage:
   a. Is temporary drainage required? Has it been established?
   b. Is runoff control required? Has it been established?
7. Is stockpiling of topsoil required? Has the stockpile area been identified?
8. Is spoil being properly disposed?
9. Is soil stabilization required? Check the specifications.

10. During blasting:
    a. Have the required permits been secured?
    b. Is the blasting being conducted with expert supervision?
    c. Are safety rules being carefully followed?
11. During grading:
    a. Are grade stakes set?
    b. Does earth-moving equipment have the required warning devices for moving in reverse?
    c. Spot-check finished grades.
12. When dewatering, check pump discharge runoff control.

Storm Drainage

1. Read the specifications.
2. Study the drawings and details.
3. Inspect materials for compliance with the specifications.
4. Check that catch basins and manholes:
    a. Are properly located,
    b. Have correct rim elevation, and
    c. Have flow line at the correct elevation.
5. Are headwalls properly located? Is flow line at proper elevation?
6. For pipe check for:
    a. Proper materials and types,
    b. Trenches shored or properly sloped,
    c. Correct bedding, and
    d. Correct grade and slope.

Concrete

1. Read the specifications.
2. Look at the reinforcing steel shop drawings.
3. Study the architect's or engineer's drawings.
4. Inspect the formwork.
    a. Are the forms in good shape?
    b. Have the surfaces been cleaned and properly patched?
    c. Have forms been coated with a form release?
    d. Are the joints tight? Are they properly located?
    e. Are the dimensions right? Check for formwork features: chambers, joint rustications, keys, etc.
    f. Are grade marks in place?

g. Check bracing, shoring, and ties. Are spreaders in place, and can they be easily removed?

h. Check the forms for cleanliness. Is there trash in the bottom? Have they been properly wetted? Is there any standing water?

i. Check sleeves and leave-outs, embedments, conduit, and j-boxes.

j. Check void forms. Are they watertight? Are any crushed? Are any of them soggy or likely to crush under the weight of wet concrete

k. Check vapor barrier for completeness, tears, holes, etc.

5. Inspect the reinforcing steel.

a. Before steel is placed, check for cleanliness (dirt, rust), proper manufacture (foreign?), cracks, etc.

b. Check placement. Measure for clearances. Check for reinforcing not shown on the drawings. Are corner bars in place? Are laps the correct length? Are bolsters and/or chairs in place?

c. Check the steel for proper sizes in proper places. Count the bars. Do they conform to the design?

d. Is the reinforcing properly tied? Is it properly supported? Shake it and see if it will move when the concrete is placed.

6. Before concrete is placed, make sure that:

a. There are enough people to do the job.

b. All necessary equipment is on hand:

> Water,
> Shovels,
> Vibrator (and a backup),
> Imbeds,
> Surveying level (in the case of a slab),
> Runways (in the case of a slab), and
> Screeds

c. The survey instrument (level) is in place to set grades.

d. The testing company has been alerted.

e. Circulation paths and sequencing have been worked out.

f. You know if concrete is to be chuted directly into forms, or buggied, or pumped.

g. The "super" knows what to do in case of

> Rain,
> A form failure,
> Slow delivery of concrete,
> Concrete trucks waiting too long (hot concrete), or
> Unacceptable concrete

7. Watch concrete placement—*all of it!*
   a. Check delivery tickets.
   b. Monitor truck time in waiting.
   c. Allow no water to be added to the mix at the site, unless you are located more than an hour from the batch plant.
   d. Is the concrete being placed in lifts?
   e. Is concrete being properly vibrated? Are the workers moving the concrete with the vibrator or properly with shovels or rakes?
   f. If the concrete is being dropped more than 3 ft, is a tremie being used?
   g. Have bulkheads been placed? Are the bulkheads split for reinforcing? Are they keyed?
   h. Check for surface leave-outs and elevation changes.
   i. Have grade stakes or grade marks been properly set?
   j. Are the workers properly controlling the finished grade of the concrete?
8. When testing samples:
   a. Read the specifications.
   b. Cylinders: pass bucket or wheelbarrow completely through stream of discharging concrete. Do not collect samples with test cylinders. Place concrete in correct lifts into cylinders, rod properly, do not store beside construction road
   c. Slump tests: Pass bucket or wheelbarrow completely through stream of discharging concrete. Place concrete in correct lifts into form, and rod properly.
9. Ensure proper finishing and curing.
10. Check timing and execution of saw cutting.
    a. Are the lines to be saw-cut clearly marked?
    b. Is the saw operator following the lines accurately?
    c. Is the concrete raveling at the saw blade?
11. For form removal and shoring removal timing:
    a. Check the specifications or with the structural engineer for timing.
    b. Are the workers using any removal techniques that damage the concrete?
12. Have all form tie holes been patched?

Concrete Paving

1. Read the specifications.
2. Study the drawings and details.

3. Inspect materials.
4. Review concrete inspection memory joggers.
5. Check layout and geometrics.
6. Check jointing and bulkheading.
    a. Proper joint locations
    b. Proper details (keys, dowels)
7. Check reinforcing.
8. Check elevations.
9. Check for proper curing.
10. Check saw cutting.

Asphalt Paving

1. Read the specifications.
2. Study the drawings and details.
3. Inspect materials.
4. Verify subgrade as to:
    a. Grading,
    b. Stabilization, and
    c. Compaction.
5. Are the layers the proper thickness and number?
6. Is the paving being properly compacted?
7. Check for low spots ("birdbaths").
8. Verify requirements for seal coating.
9. Check striping dimensions.

Foundation

1. Read the specifications.
2. Study the drawings and details.
3. Inspect materials.

Spread Footings

1. Check the layout and locations of footings.
2. Check the size and type of footing at each location.
3. Has the geological engineer identified the bearing strata?
4. Is the bottom clean?
5. Keep records for measurement and payment.
6. Inspect reinforcing.
7. Are dowels and/or anchor bolt locations correct?
8. Check top elevation.

9. Check for proper placement of concrete.
10. Check for proper curing of concrete.

Drilled Piers

1. Check the layout and locations of piers.
2. Check the size and type of pier at each location.
3. Is the driller properly lined up on the pier location?
4. Is the drilling tower vertical?
5. Are the workers keeping the spoil out of the hole?
6. Has the contractor made provisions to remove the spoil?
7. Has the geological engineer identified the bearing strata?
8. Measure the depth of the hole (usually at the top of the bearing strata and again at the bottom of the completed hole to determine that the pier will penetrate the strata the required amount).
9. Is the bottom clean?
10. Is there any caving, or any water in the bottom?
11. Has required underream been done?
12. Check measurements for
    a. Bottom elevation,
    b. Top of bearing strata, and
    c. Bottom of hole.
13. For cased piers:
    a. Is the casing sealing out water?
    b. Is a head of concrete being maintained as the casing is removed?
14. When setting the reinforcing:
    a. Is the reinforcing cage the correct length?
    b. Are the steel members the right size?
    c. Is the reinforcing cage being lowered without caving in the sides of the hole?
15. Is a tremie being used to place the concrete?
16. Is the top portion being vibrated?
17. Is any forming above grade proper?
18. Check top of pier elevation.
19. Check location and type of dowels or anchor bolts.

Driven Friction Piles

1. Check pile layout and driving sequence.
2. Is geological engineer monitoring driving?
3. Has bearing depth been identified?

4. Monitor driving, overdriving, and rejection.
5. Record measurement for payment.
6. Check for proper reinforcing and setting.
7. Check for proper placing of concrete.
8. Is the top elevation correct?
9. Check for proper disposing of cutoffs.
10. For pile caps, check:
    a. Physical dimensions and forming,
    b. Reinforcing, and
    c. Proper concrete placing and curing.
11. On the project documents record:
    a. Sizes, lengths, and locations of piles,
    b. Sequence of driving,
    c. Number of blows per foot for entire length of piles and measured set for last (number specified) blows,
    d. Drilling hole diameters,
    e. Final tip and head elevations, and
    f. Driving force of each hammer blow.

Grade Beam

1. Read the specifications.
2. Study the drawings and details.
3. Inspect materials.
4. Review concrete inspection memory joggers.
5. Check that required void forms are in place and in good condition.
6. Check required insulation.
7. Check "neat" forming for sloughing or caving.
8. Check that grade marks have been set and are clear.
9. Check headers or bulkheads for:
    a. Proper location, and
    b. Proper details (key, dowels, split forms, waterstops).
10. Check that spreaders are adequate and easily removable.
11. Check that snap ties are in place, correctly spaced and the proper type.

Concrete Slab

1. Read the specifications.
2. Study the drawings and details.
3. Inspect materials.
4. Review the inspecting concrete memory joggers.

5. Check electrical and plumbing placements.
6. Check for imbeds:
   a. Block-outs,
   b. Sleeves, and
   c. Anchor bolts.
7. Check vapor retarder.
8. Review placing sequence.
9. Review placement and details of construction joints.
10. Check preparations for hardener and/or curing compound application.
11. Review and observe placing.
12. Observe finishing.
13. Check for proper saw cutting.
14. Check for proper curing.

Concrete Column

1. Read the specifications.
2. Study the drawings and details.
3. Inspect materials.
4. Review the inspecting concrete memory joggers.
5. Check plumbing of forms.
6. Verify proper placing techniques.

Elevated Concrete

1. Read the specifications.
2. Study the drawings and details.
3. Inspect materials.
4. Review the inspecting concrete memory joggers.
5. Check the formwork for strength and safety.
6. Check shoring for mud sills on a sound bearing.
7. Verify proper placing techniques.
8. Check reshoring after form removal.

Architectural Concrete

1. Read the specifications.
2. Study the drawings and details.
3. Inspect materials.
4. Review the inspecting concrete memory joggers.
5. Check joint and rustication details.
6. Check modular detail dimensions.

7. Review patching techniques.
8. During sandblasting, bush hammering, rubbing, etc.:
   a. Does the work match the sample panel?
   b. If more than one person is doing texturing, have starting and finishing places been determined?
   c. Have all repairs been completed before start of texturing?

Concrete Cleanup

1. Read the specifications.
2. Study the drawings and details.
3. Inspect materials.
4. Check that fins are knocked off.
5. During patching, check for:
   a. Spalling,
   b. Honeycombs, and
   c. Sand streaks.
6. Check that stains have been treated.

Precast Concrete

1. Read the specifications.
2. Study the drawings and details.
3. Inspect materials.
4. Check imbeds for:
   a. Connection welding plates, and
   b. Lifting connection inserts.
5. Check reinforcing.
6. Verify measurements.
7. During erection:
   a. Verify attachments.
   b. Check plumb and trueness.
8. Check joints for uniformity.
9. Check texturing.

Prestressed Concrete

1. Read the specifications.
2. Study the drawings and details.
3. Inspect materials.
4. Verify the strength of concrete before tensioning.
5. Check tensioning of tendons.

6. Verify security of restraining wedges.
7. Check cleanliness of ducts before grouting.
8. Verify complete grouting.
9. Verify strength of grout before releasing tension.

Structural Steel

1. Read the specifications.
2. Study the drawings and details.
3. Inspect materials.
4. Review erection sequence.
5. Verify that proper pieces are in proper places.
6. Check leveling and truing.
7. Check bolts for:
   a. Proper type and number, and
   b. Tensioning.
8. Check welding for
   a. Location and size, and
   b. Certified welders.

Grouting

1. Read the specifications.
2. Study the drawings and details.
3. Inspect materials.
4. Spot-check baseplates and verify proper techniques to prevent formation of voids.
5. For masonry:
   a. Check reinforcing.
   b. Verify proper technique to prevent formation of voids.

Fastener

1. Read the specifications.
2. Study the drawings and details.
3. Inspect materials.
4. For bolts:
   a. Check for oversize or out-of-round holes.
   b. Verify proper type and size of bolts.
   c. Check tensioning technique.
   d. Check tension.

5. For welding:
   a. Verify that welders are certified.
   b. Check type and size of weld.
6. For expansion anchors:
   a. Verify proper type and size.
   b. Check tightness of installed fastener.
7. For anchor bolts:
   a. Check for voids, if installed with templates.
   b. Verify proper location.
   c. Check for proper length and size.
8. For grouted anchors:
   a. Check for proper type and size.
   b. Check location.
   c. Verify proper grouting technique.

Fireproofing

1. Read the specifications.
2. Study the drawings and details.
3. Inspect materials.
4. Verify proper type for location.
5. For sprayed fireproofing, check density, coverage, and thickness.
6. For gypsum wallboard:
   a. Verify proper materials.
   b. Verify proper system for location.
   c. Check number of layers.
   d. Check for staggered joints.
   e. Check for fastening details, strapping, bed, and tape.
7. Check later for integrity of coverage (see if any has been removed to make clearance for later materials).

Plumbing

1. Read the specifications.
2. Study the drawings and details.
3. Inspect materials.
4. Verify required tests.
5. Verify code official check.
6. Check required paperwork.

Waterproofing

1. Read the specifications.
2. Study the drawings and details.
3. Inspect materials.
4. Verify proper type in proper location.
5. Check basement walls; tunnel floors, walls, and ceilings; grade beams beneath the first course of masonry (dampproofing), Through-wall flashing and underslab vapor barriers.
6. Are there any openings or pinholes?
7. For multicourse, are the right number of courses there? Everywhere? Is there reinforcing fabric?
8. In prefabricated sheets:
   a. Are wrinkles and bubbles worked out?
   b. Is the size of the laps between sheets correct?
9. Does betonite have complete coverage?
10. Is the protection course in place?
11. Is the upper termination of basement wall or grade beam waterproofing at the finished grade line?

Roofing

1. Read the specifications; memorize the drawings.
2. Check labels on materials: bitumen, plies, insulation, base flashing material, screw fasteners.
3. Check roofer's equipment: kettle, pig, brooms, lifts, buckets.
4. Check fastener criteria; wind uplift category; pattern of fasteners.
5. Check EVT.
6. Are materials being stored off the ground? Are they being kept dry?
7. Are any materials stored on the roof? Are they properly spread out?
8. Are materials being hoisted over the edge of the roof? Is building protection in place?
9. Is the deck clean and dry?
10. Are fire extinguishers nearby?
11. When installing insulation:
    a. Check that first layer of insulation is mechanically fastened.
    b. Check that screws are the correct type, length, and material. Is a washer called for?
    c. Is uplift classification I-60 or I-90?
    d. Check that number and pattern of fasteners are correct.

e. Verify complete mopping for second layer, staggered joints, and no piece smaller than 12″ × 12″.

f. Check insulation tapers, crickets, etc.

12. Is vapor retarder used?
13. If the roofing bitumen is coal tar, have pitch dams been installed?
14. Check kettle temperature and EVT at bucket.
15. Check number of plies at start.
16. Are plies running in proper direction?
17. Check for adequate bitumen between plies.
18. Check lap dimension.
19. Secure water cutoffs at end of day.
20. Verify that roof is glazed at end of day, flood coated, and graveled within three days.
21. For the surface aggregate:

    a. Is gravel dry and free from trash and sand?

    b. Is it the aggregate the proper size and type?

22. Set roof drains with hot application, not after roofing has cooled.
23. Allow no open flames on roof ("dragon wagons," torches).
24. Inspect flashing and counterflashing for:

    a. Extending over the plies the required dimension (usually 2 or 3 ft),

    b. Cover from end to end and at corners,

    c. Nailing at the top,

    d. Coating to be applied to the flashing,

    e. Dissimilar metals coated with a bituminous paint to separate them,

    f. Allowance for linear expansion and contraction,

    g. Solder or pop-riveted joints, and

    h. Watertight terminations or intersections.

    i. Do not allow a roofer to cover up uncovered areas with roofing mastic.

Chart of Galvanic Activity

Aluminum
Zinc
Galvanized steel
Steel
Iron
Nickel
Tin

Lead

Copper

Stainless steel

Monel

25. For single-ply membranes:
    a. Do you have manufacturer's instructions or specifications or whatever will govern the installation?
    b. Check each seam in the field.
    c. Check each seam in flashings.
    d. Is protection provided for later workers?
26. For shingles:
    a. Are proper materials used?
    b. Do they have proper lap?
    c. Check terminations and flashing.
    d. For composition shingles check the proper sealing down of the individual shingles.
27. For metal roofing:
    a. Are there provisions for expansion and contraction?
    b. Are terminations watertight?
    c. Are foam rubber or metal closure strips in place?
    d. During flashing, at penetrations make sure the water blocked by the curb can get around the curb and will not run into a seam or where the corrugations stop.
    e. For top-of-slope flashings, the closures beneath the flashing are to close the gap formed by the corrugations of the roofing sheet.
28. Are nails and screws picked up, openings protected, and rubbish removed?

Masonry

1. Read the specifications.
2. Study the drawings and details.
3. Inspect materials.
    a. Are materials what is specified? Are masonry units the right size, color, and texture? Are they clean? Are they wet? Is mortar as specified?
    b. Are certifications available?
    c. Check concrete masonry units, brick, face brick, mortar, accessories, (ties, reinforcing, lintels,), grout, flashing materials,
4. Approve sample panel(s).

5. Inspect substrates for:
   a. Proper size and location, lines and levels, and
   b. Cleanliness.
6. At the start of masonry work, inspect:
   a. Proper layout and horizontal coursing, and
   b. Laying procedures:
      (1) Full head and bed joints,
      (2) Not moving masonry units,
      (3) Units shoved and tapped into position,
      (4) Mortar spread no more than 4 ft in front of laying,
      (5) Conformance to sample panel,
      (6) Mortar being kept off face of masonry, and
      (7) Properly tooled joints; proper timing.
7. For the cavity wall:
   a. Is the cavity kept clean? Is the pull stick in the cavity?
   b. Are flashing and weep holes in place at bottom of the cavity?
   c. Are ties and reinforcing the proper type and correctly located?
8. Is the top of the wall being protected at night? Have incomplete walls been stepped or toothed?
9. Is the mortar type correct?

Type M	Below-grade applications in contact with earth (2500 psi)
Type S	General use, good lateral force resistance (1800 psi)
Type N	General use, severe exposures (750 psi)
Type O	Interior use (350 psi)

   Types PL and PM are masonry grouts (2500 psi)
10. Is mortar mixed according to the manufacturer's instructions?
11. Is there any retempered mortar? Is spent mortar discarded?
12. Has the "good" face of the CMU been designated?
13. Masonry units must be cut with a masonry saw.
14. Are flashing terminations watertight?
15. Do masonry anchors to structure allow vertical and horizontal movement?
16. Is horizontal joint reinforcing cut and continuous at proper places? Are joints lapped?
17. Inspect structural reinforcing for:
    a. Proper size and location, and
    b. Conflicts between joint reinforcing and structural reinforcing or architectural details?

18. Is masonry cleaned without acid and with brushes (no wire)?

Carpentry

1. Read the specifications.
2. Study the drawings and details.
3. Inspect materials.
   a. Are grade markings on lumber checked?
   b. Is pressure treated lumber the proper type?
   c. Is any previously used lumber being reused?
4. Are the proper size and number of nails used?

Drywall

1. Read the specifications.
2. Study the drawings and details.
3. Inspect materials.
4. Check studs for alignment.
5. Verify that right type and thickness of wallboard is being used. Is it fire-rated and moisture-resistant?
6. Verify direction of application.
7. Verify that face paper is not broken with nails or screws.
8. Verify that all edges of the wallboard occur at a support.
9. Check for supplemental framing.
10. If wallboard is on one side only, is the back flange of the studs braced?
11. If there is more than one layer of wallboard, are joints in the second layer offset by at least 16 in.?
12. Is there overhead bracing to structure?
13. In sound-rated partitions:
    a. Are the edges caulked?
    b. Are electrical boxes back to back or side-by-side?
    c. Are boxes to be "buttered" with acoustical caulking.
14. Check bed and tape joints with 3-ft-long straightedge.
15. Check that "raw" edges of gypsum are finished with:
    a. Casing bead,
    b. Corner bead, or
    c. Expansion joint.
16. Verify that expansion joints are ASTM specification C 840 and that:
    a. Joints in ceilings are no more than 50 ft on center, and no area exceeds 2500 sq. ft. without a joint. Joints installed wherever furring or joist direction changes.

    b. Joints are no more than 30 ft on center on walls; full height openings count as expansion joints.

Plaster

1. Read the specifications.
2. Study the drawings and details.
3. Inspect materials.
4. Is the substrate acceptable?
    a. Is it true and plumb?
    b. Are furring channels well tied and rigid? If the specifications call for galvanized channels, make sure they are. Otherwise, they will be painted. Make sure that painted steel channels are rust-free.
5. Accessories–look for secure fastening, neatly butted or mitered corners, alignment, and proper location.
6. Expansion joints: There must be two channels (or two studs) at each expansion joint, and the lath must be cut.
7. Is there an approved sample of the finish on the site?
8. Verify curing method.

Insulation

1. Read the specifications.
2. Study the drawings and details.
3. Inspect materials.
4. Are the proper type and thickness being used in the proper place?
5. Is the vapor barrier on the right face?
6. If there is a vapor barrier, check taping and sealing.

Miscellaneous Metal Fabrications

1. Read the specifications.
2. Study the drawings and details.
3. Inspect materials.
4. Check:
    a. Concrete imbeds,
    b. Stairs and handrails,
    c. Thresholds–verify that the location conforms to the door design,
    d. Access hatches for proper operation,
    e. Grates–materials, spacing, and depth of the bars, proper fastening to the supporting structure,
    f. Ladders and spacing of imbedded rungs,

g. Lintels for required bearing on each side of the opening,

h. Bollards to verify that it protects what it is supposed to protect,

i. Catwalks against the design, and

j. Entry mats for "toe stubbers."

5. Is fastening secure?

6. Is the imbed installed true to the lines of the building?

7. For raised access floors:

a. Verify type, either freestanding pedestals or beam-braced, lift-out, or bolted (check for ease of removal).

b. Check levelness.

c. Check location of perforated panels where the floor also serves as an air distribution device.

d. Make sure that the contractor has provided a panel-lifting device.

Windows

1. Read the specifications.

2. Study the drawings and details.

3. Inspect materials.

4. Verify anchoring details.

5. Verify flashing details.

6. Check glazing requirements.

Doors, Frames, and Hardware

1. Read the specifications.

2. Study the drawings and details.

3. Inspect materials.

4. Is the door frame plumb and square?

5. Are hollow metal frames filled with grout?

6. Are frames dented or dinged?

7. Check the specifications for the method of joining at the corner. The joint may be a butt or a miter, and it may or may not be welded.

8. Is the proper door installed? Is it properly installed? Does it function properly? Are the tolerances within allowances?

9. Are doors in fire-rated walls and partitions fire-rated? Is the label attached (usually on the edge at the hinges) stating the rating? Are the frames labeled?

10. Are the correct number and style of hinges installed? Does the schedule call for a nonrising pin?

11. Check latches, locksets, keys, and keying for correct location and function.

12. Check for electric strikes or electric bolts.
13. Check panic hardware.
14. Check closer for proper size, mounting, and adjustment. Also check for "hold-open" feature, checks, and coordinators.
15. Check for weatherstripping or sound stripping. With sound stripping check for automatic door bottom.
16. Check for kickplates, push plates, or pull bars, bumpers, or stops.
17. Have rubber buttons been inserted into the frames?

Caulking

1. Read the specifications.
2. Study the drawings and details.
3. Inspect materials.
4. Has the joint been properly cleaned?
5. Is priming required?
6. If a backer rod is called for, has it been installed to the proper depth?
7. If a bond breaker is called for, has it been properly installed?
8. Is the proper material being installed? Is it the right color?
9. Check for painting over of moving joints.

Louvers

1. Read the specifications.
2. Study the drawings and details.
3. Inspect materials and verify that the configuration agrees with submittals and proper finish is applied.
4. Check necessary subframing.
5. Verify anchoring details.
6. Check flashing details.
7. Verify attachment to ductwork.

Painting

1. Read the specifications.
2. Study the drawings and details.
3. Inspect materials.
4. Are the Material Safety Data Sheets (MSDS) on the site and available?
5. Does the paint meet the VOC limits?
6. Are fire extinguishers in handy locations?
7. Are masks necessary?

8. Is the correct painting system being used? Is paint applied in the proper location?
9. Has the surface been properly prepared?
10. Is the correct filler or sealer being used. If a filler is being applied, is it covering and properly filling?.
11. Use hidden pencil marks to help determine if specified number of coats have been applied.
12. If critical, check minimum mil thickness, wet and dry mil thicknesses.
13. Look for

> Wrong color,
>
> Incomplete coverage,
>
> Streaking due to improper mixing,
>
> Runs and sags,
>
> Holidays or incomplete hiding,
>
> Pinholes, and
>
> Overspray, drips, and sloppy painting.

14. Is wood staining even and does it match samples?
15. Check the specifications for painting of piping.
16. Watch out for "hidden" painting:
    a. Inside ducts near the grilles or registers, and
    b. Partially open ceiling where the structure, deck, conduits, and piping need painting.
17. Watch painters cut a line.
18. Verify maintenance stock of paint to be left with the owner.
19. Verify that painting materials are being stored.

Wall Covering

1. Read the specifications.
2. Study the drawings and details.
3. Inspect materials.
4. Is the selvedge removed completely?
5. Watch for pattern match.
6. Verify removal of bubbles and excess glue.
7. Verify outside corner treatment.

Floor Coverings

1. Read the specifications.
2. Study the drawings and details.
3. Inspect materials.

4. Verify the starting point, pattern direction, and need for "feature strip" beneath the closed door.

5. Verify that the proper trowel is used to spread the mastic.

6. Verify maintenance stock of tile to be left with the owner.

Carpet

1. Read the specifications.
2. Study the drawings and details.
3. Inspect materials.
4. Verify layout and pattern direction.
5. Check glue and gluing.
6. When carpet is stretched, check the pad, stretching, and seaming.
7. Check terminations.

Tile

1. Read the specifications.
2. Study the drawings and details.
3. Inspect materials.
4. Check layout for details of matching joints from floor to wall, and patterns.
5. Check substrate.
6. Watch the start of tile setting and check for even joints and proper installation.
7. Make sure grouting properly fills joints and does not leave pinholes.
8. Verify requirements for trim pieces.
9. Verify need for expansion joints in large expanses of tile.
10. Watch for unacceptable surface produced by drywall corner beads.

Ceilings

1. Read the specifications.
2. Study the drawings and details.
3. Inspect materials.
4. Verify the size and spacing of hanger wires.
5. Verify the assembly pattern of the grid members.
6. For a rated fire-resistant assembly:
   a. Check rating of grid members and panels.
   b. Check for requirement to build boxes over lighting fixtures.
7. Allow no conduit to be laid on grid.
8. Check for independent hanging of lighting fixtures.

9. Check for lighting fixtures or speakers supported by a ceiling panel.
10. Check that leveling is done by adjusting the loop on the hanger wire, not by kinking the wire.
11. Check direction of pattern with square panels.
12. Verify clearance above the grid to maneuver the panels into place.
13. Verify hold-down clips.
14. Verify location of fire sprinkler heads.
15. Verify maintenance stock of panels to be left with the owner.

Millwork

1. Read the specifications.
2. Study the drawings and details.
3. Inspect materials.
4. Is the installation true to building lines and being scribed to walls?
5. Open all the doors.
    a. Do they fit properly?
    b. Do they latch properly?
6. Open all the drawers. Do they slide easily?
7. Does everything fit? Is there any warpage?
8. Try all the locks.

Toilet Accessories

1. Read the specifications.
2. Study the drawings and details.
3. Inspect materials.
4. Check metal accessories for dents and dings.
5. On sanitary napkin dispensers, check for correct actuator and set-up (free, coin operation, how much?).
6. Check mirrors for secure mounting.
7. Check ash trays for secure mounting.
8. On towel disposal units, is the receptacle easily removable?
9. Check all locking devices.
10. Count accessories.
11. Check toilet paper dispensers or rolls.
12. Test handicap rails for secure fastening and proper location.
13. Make sure soap dispensers are the proper type (liquid, lather, leaf, or granular soap).
14. Check wash fountains for good drainage of the basin and even flow of water from the spray head(s).

Toilet Partitions

1. Are the partitions the correct type and color?
2. Check for secure fastening and alignment of the stiles to the structure, and of the divider panels to the stiles and to the wall. Shake the stiles. They should not move under normal pressure.
3. Check all for dents and dings.
4. Check for free operation and self-closing of the doors.
5. Test handicapped rails for secure fastening by standing on them.
6. Check for accessories: door bumpers, clothes hangers, door latches, and package shelves.

Metal Lockers

1. Look for exterior accessories such as sloping tops, closure trim, and finished end pieces.
2. Check for dents, dings, and scratches in the finish.
3. Verify that the proper latching device is installed.
4. Open and close all doors, and operate locks if installed.
5. Check inside the lockers for accessory hardware: shelves, hooks, and clothes rods.
6. Check for correct numbering on the locker doors.

Elevators, Escalators

1. Verify required "official" inspections.
2. Check the structural openings and clearances, the penthouse or pit, the shaft enclosure, or the surrounding walls.
3. Check the fit and finish of the doors, frames, and passenger cabs, etc.
4. Verify that entry doorframes have the correct fire-rating labels attached and that they are fully grouted.
5. Verify that the passenger cabs are the proper size.
6. Verify that the finished materials are as specified.
7. Check designated freight elevator for removable interior, or studs for hanging protective pads, and removable ceiling.
8. Call each elevator from each floor. Watch for proper operation of the annunciator lights. See that the cab floor is level with the building floor.
9. Check the safety devices on the entry door.

Miscellaneous Equipment

1. Check clocks for time setting and operation. If they are slaved to a master clock, verify synchronization.

2. If guard tour stations are required, check each location and verify that they operate properly.
3. Check signs for:
   a. Size,
   b. Color(s),
   c. Letter style and size,
   d. Placement,
   e. Correct message, and
   f. Security of mounting (on walls, doors, on poles).
4. Verify that directories and display cases are as specified, properly located, and securely mounted and that specified accessories (letter kits, engraving devices, keys, etc.) have been supplied.
5. For food service equipment:
   a. Check against the specification for correctness.
   b. Check the installation for neatness and alignment.
   c. Verify that all components are in working order.
   d. Check for scratches, dents, and dings.
   e. In a commercial kitchen, look for a fire extinguishing system in the hood.
6. For electric water coolers:
   a. Check for correct size and capacity.
   b. Check for correct finish.
   c. Check for security of the mounting.
   d. Check for correct fittings: bubbler, glass filler, foot operator, etc.
   e. Check height of mounting, especially those installed for wheelchair users.
   f. Check for correct adjustment of the water stream.
7. For laboratory equipment:
   a. Check for smooth operation of the sash on fume hoods.
   b. Check fan operation.
   c. Find a water bucket and check out the operation of the emergency shower and eyewash stations.
   d. Check piping against the specifications.
   e. Verify that the correct top material has been supplied.
   f. Check for correct labeling of all service outlets.
   g. Cross-check and inventory all small items.
   h. Check the operation of doors and drawers.
   i. Check for equipment such as distilled water units, vacuum pumps, water chillers, and air compressors.

8. Check mail and laundry chutes against the specifications and for neat, secure installation with no "snags" along the length.
9. For dock equipment:
   a. Check dock levelers, trailer levelers, trailer restraints and associated controls and signal lights, grade beam bumper pads, protective bollards, door pads or shelters (sometimes called seals), and a bracket-mounted light and fan.
   b. Check each against the specifications.
   c. Check for proper mounting and alignment.
   d. Check the operation.
   e. Check for physical damage.
   f. Operate the dock levelers. Hydraulic operation should be smooth and accurate. A spring-operated leveler should be easy to release (it should spring up to its full height) and "walk down." The lip should extend fully.
10. Check flagpoles for:
    a. Correct taper,
    b. Proper grounding,
    c. Easy operation of lanyards,
    d. Installation of all hardware called for: snap hooks, etc., and
    e. Physical damage.

Movable Partitions

1. Read the specifications.
2. Study the drawings and details.
3. Inspect materials. Look for tears in fabric, scratches on wood or metal parts, dents or dings in metal parts.
4. Check for proper fit.
5. Check for ease of movement.
6. Check for latching.
7. Check sound-rated partitions for leaks (look for light leaks).
8. Does the folded partition fit into the enclosure? Will the enclosure door close?

Furniture

1. Read the specifications.
2. Study the drawings and details.
3. Take inventory.
   a. Use a pictorial catalog.

b. Count pieces, chairs, etc.

c. Check upholstery fabrics for color, pattern, and type (weave, etc.).

4. Make sure each piece is in its proper location.
5. Look for dents, dings, and scratches on metal pieces.
6. For open office panels and work stations:
   a. Verify layout and makeup of each work station.
   b. Check the panels for configuration: are they supposed to be acoustical, magnetic, plain fabric, tackable?
   c. Check electrical outlets, telephone outlets, and computer hookups.
   d. Check task lighting.
7. Check the type of casters on office chairs.
8. Check office chairs for swivel, tilt, or adjustable height.
9. Open all drawers and doors.
   a. Work all locks; check for correct level of keying.
   b. Check the panels for configuration: are they supposed to be acoustical, magnetic, plain fabric, tackable?
10. Check all miscellaneous items: Artwork, lamps, rugs, planters, and sand urns. Wastebaskets, ashtrays, and various desk accessories may also be in the furnishings contract.

Landscape Irrigation

1. Read the specifications.
2. Study the drawings and details.
3. Inspect materials.
4. Check layout of system and location of heads.
5. Check for leaks.
6. Verify backfilling materials and operations.
7. Check timing and sequencing of control system.
8. Verify that heads cover the area adequately with water.

Coordination of Mechanical Systems

1. Read the specifications.
2. Study the drawings and details.
3. Inspect materials.
4. Check interior roof drains for interferences with:
   a. Plumbing drain lines,
   b. Fire sprinkler lines, and
   c. Ductwork.

5. Check plumbing drain lines for interference with:
   a. Interior roof drains,
   b. Fire sprinkler lines, and
   c. Ductwork.
6. Check large ductwork near air handling units for interference with:
   a. Plumbing lines,
   b. Fire sprinkler lines, and
   c. Lighting fixtures.

Plumbing

1. Read the specifications.
2. Study the drawings and details.
3. Inspect materials and verify their suitability and size for the application.
4. Check routing (square and true to lines of building).
5. Check for necessary unions.
6. Check for accessibility after finishes are in place.
7. Verify support and provisions for expansion.
   a. Are beam clamps used (no drilling into beams)?
   b. Are items hung from panel points of joists or with bottom chord reinforced?
   c. Verify requirements as to all-thread or perforated strap hangers.
   d. Verify support of vertical runs.
8. Check cutting and threading for:
   a. Beveling of inside surface, and
   b. Removal of debris from inside of pipe.
9. Check joints for leakage, pipe dope, or teflon tape.
10. Verify testing before backfilling, covering with finish materials, or insulation.
11. Check insulation for:
    a. Complete coverage and covering requirements.
    b. Verify type and thickness.
12. Check valves for type, size, and accessibility.
13. Check backflow prevention for location, type, and proper direction of flow.
14. Check all buried piping for required thrust blocks.
15. Verify sanitizing.

Plumbing Fixtures

1. Read the specifications.
2. Study the drawings and details.
3. Inspect materials and verify proper style and color for location.
4. Check fixtures for chips or cracks, proper hardware, and secure mounting and alignment.
5. Check specifications for requirements for caulking to wall.
6. Check for required accessories, such as hammer chambers and vacuum breakers.

HVAC and Ductwork

1. Read the specifications.
2. Study the drawings and details.
3. Inspect materials.
4. Verify sizes and routing.
5. Check hanging.
   a. Verify that duct span is not exceeded.
   b. Check angled hangers for pairing.
6. Check in-duct devices, including:
   a. Volume dampers and fire dampers,
   b. Fire dampers,
   c. Splitter dampers,
   d. Reheat coils,
   e. Smoke detectors,
   f. Temperature and pressure sensors,
   g. Turning vanes, and
   h. Sound attenuation devices.
7. Check insulation for complete coverage and type and thickness.
8. Check access to control devices and their covering requirements.
9. Check terminal devices, including:
   a. Grilles and registers:
      (1) Correct type and size,
      (2) Adjustment of dampers and vanes,
      (3) Security of fastening,
      (4) Appearance, and
      (5) Proper finish.
   b. Mixing boxes, and
   c. VAV boxes.

10. Check for air leakage.
11. Check for sound attenuation devices, such as:
    a. In-duct,
    b. On hangers, and
    c. Flexible couplings.
12. Verify balancing.

Mechanical Equipment

1. Read the specifications.
2. Study the drawings and details.
3. Inspect materials.
4. For boilers check piping, valves, and ASME inspection plate.
5. On direct-fired unit heaters, check:
    a. Venting,
    b. Piping,
    c. Controls, and
    d. Aiming.
6. For chillers check
    a. Piping and valves, and
    b. Vibration isolation.
7. Check belt drives for:
    a. Proper type belts,
    b. Alignment of pulleys or sheaves,
    c. Correct tension, and
    d. Sets are matched in multiple-belt installations.
8. For compressors check:
    a. Accessories (dryer, filters, coolers), and
    b. Piping and valves.
9. For air handler units check:
    a. Soundness of housing (structural; air and water tightness),
    b. Belts and pulleys or sheaves (see above), and
    c. Vibration isolation.
10. Check HVAC units for:
    a. Soundness of housing (structural; air and water tightness),
    b. Condensate drainage (water tightness, connected to proper drain line),
    c. Piping and valves,
    d. Proper flashing (when roof-mounted),
    e. Cleanliness of coils,

f. Clean filters,

g. Belts and pulleys or sheaves (see above), and

h. Vibration isolation.

11. Verify that HVAC controls are installed, including:

a. Thermostats,

b. Pressure-sensing devices,

c. Smoke detectors, and

d. Damper actuators.

Fire Protection

1. Read the specifications.
2. Study the drawings and details.
3. Inspect materials.
4. For the site, check:

a. Size and layout,

b. PIVs for location, and

c. Required thrust blocks.

5. For the building check:

a. Layout,

b. Location and type of heads,

c. Temperature rating of heads,

d. Heads unpainted,

e. Location and accessibility of sectional valves, and

f. Splash protection at test outlet.

Lighting

1. Read the specifications.
2. Study the drawings and details.
3. Inspect materials.
4. Verify that the proper fixtures are installed according to plan.

a. Verify finish of fixture.

b. Verify lamping.

5. Check mounting.
6. Check switching for correct operation, including:

a. Contactors,

b. Single-pole, three-way, switches,

c. Dimmers, and

d. Passive sensors.

7. Check night lighting.

8. Check emergency lighting.
9. Operate high-bay fixture-lowering devices.
10. On outdoor lighting:
    a. Verify actuation (timer or light sensing devices),
    b. Check aiming, and
    c. Operate fixture-lowering devices.
11. Verify that all lamps are in place and operating.
12. Verify requirements for replacing lamps.

Electrical Devices

1. Read the specifications.
2. Study the drawings and details.
3. Inspect materials.
4. Check conduit for true and square routing.
5. Check for pull cords in empty conduit.
6. Check security and hanging of conduit.
7. Check for wiring to electrically operated doors.

Final Inspection

1. Read the specifications.
2. Study the drawings and details.
3. Walk around the site. Look for discrepancies, such as:
   a. Large rocks or dirt clods,
   b. Settling backfill where pipes have been run,
   c. Ponding water, and
   d. Incomplete work, such as unpainted ferrous metal, missing irrigation heads, missing signs, etc.
4. Walk around the outside of the building. Look for missing caulking, "B-holes" in masonry, unclean surfaces, etc.
5. Carry a floor plan to note where discrepancies occur (room number, door number, window number, etc.). Carry a note pad or a recorder to note all items.
6. Look at finishes for cleanliness, fit, trim, etc. Look at painting for good straight lines, overspray, drips, evenness, etc.
7. Open and close all doors.
   a. Check closer action.
   b. Check for free swing with no dragging.
   c. Check latch and key operation.
   d. Look at bottom edge of door for finish.

e. Check for weatherstripping and sound stripping.

f. Check electric strikes, card-key operators.

8. Operate all operable windows.
9. Operate all folding partitions.
10. Turn all switches on and off for lights, fans, projection screens, etc.
    a. Are all light bulbs in place and burning?
    b. Are the lenses clean?
11. Open and close all doors and drawers.
12. Flush all water closets and urinals; turn on each water faucet.
13. Look for damage to finish materials.
14. Check supply of required maintenance materials stocks to be furnished to the owner.

Electrical

1. Check lighting fixtures for complete lamping and correct operation.
2. Check lighting fixture lenses for cleanliness.
3. Check all lighting switches and dimmers for correct operation.
4. For electrical panels check that:
   a. All are panels labeled.
   b. Circuit breakers are identified.
   c. Spare wire ends are taped or covered.

Mechanical

1. Make sure all filters and strainers are in place and clean.
2. Any dripping pipes should be routed to drains.

Furnishings Final Inspection

1. Count pieces, chairs, etc.
   a. Check for colors and finishes of wood metal and fabric.
   b. Check for correct location of individual pieces.
   c. Make sure the configuration of each work station is correct.
2. Check open office panels for correct configuration.
   a. Are they supposed to be acoustical, magnetic, plain fabric?
   b. Check electrical outlets and switches in open office partitions.
3. Open all drawers, doors.
4. Work all locks; check for correct level of keying.
5. Look for dents and dings.

6. Check for accessories, such as sand urns, coatracks, waste receptacles, planters and vases, rugs or mats, wall hangings, and artwork.
7. Check all signs and graphics for correctness and completeness.

Project Closeout

1. Check the specifications for procedures.
2. Submit project records documents, operation and maintenance data, and warranties.
3. Check for final cleaning and equipment adjusting.
4. Spare parts and maintenance materials and written inventory should be submitted.
5. Verify removal of temporary facilities:
   a. Construction office and storage buildings,
   b. Temporary power and water,
   c. Construction roads and parking,
   d. Sample panels and mock-ups, and
   e. Construction signs.
6. Permanent facilities used during construction must be cleaned and repaired.

GENERAL REFERENCES

ORGANIZATIONS

Air-Conditioning and Refrigeration Institute
1591 Wilson Boulevard
Arlington, VA 22209

American Association of State Highway and Transportation Officials (AASHTO)
444 North Capital Street, N.W.
Washington, DC 20001

American Concrete Institute (ACI)
P.O. Box 19150
Detroit, MI 48219

American Institute of Architects (AIA)
1735 New York Avenue, N.W.
Washington, DC 20006

American Institute of Steel Construction (AISC)
400 North Michigan Avenue, 8th fl
Chicago, IL 60611

American Institute of Timber Construction (AITC)
333 W. Hampden Avenue
Englewood, CO 80110

American Iron and Steel Institute (AISI)
1000 16th Street, N.W.
Washington, DC 20036

American National Standards Institute (ANSI)
1430 Broadway
New York, NY 10018

American Plywood Association (APA)
Box 11700
Tacoma, WA 98411

American Society of Heating, Refrigeration and Air Conditioning Engineers
(ASHRE)
1791 Tullie Circle, N.E.
Atlanta, GA 30329

American Society of Mechanical Engineers (ASME)
345 East 47th Street
New York, NY 10017

American Society for Testing Materials (ASTM)
1916 Race Street
Philadelphia, PA 19103

American Welding Society (AWS)
550 LeJeune Road, N.W.
Miami, FL 33135

Architectural Woodwork Institute (AWI)
2310 South Walter Reed Drive
Arlington, VA 22206

Asphalt Institute (AI)
Asphalt Institute Building
College Park, MD 20740

Better Understanding of Roofing Systems Institute (BURSI)
P.O. Box 5108
Denver, CO 80217

Building Officials & Code Administrators International (BOCA)
4051 W. Flossmoor Road
Country Club Hills, IL 60478-5795

Concrete Reinforcing Steel Institute (CRSI)
933 Plum Grove Road
Schaumburg, IL 60195

Construction Specifications Institute (CSI)
601 Madison Street
Alexandria, VA 22314-1791

Council of American Building Officials (CABO)
5203 Leesburg Pike, Suite 708
Falls Church, VA 22041

Door and Hardware Institute (DHI)
7711 Old Springhouse Road
McLean, VA 22102

Factory Mutual (FM)
1151 Boston-Providence Turnpike
P.O. Box 688
Norwood, MA 02062

Institute of Electrical and Electronics Engineers (IEEE)
345 East 47th Street
New York, NY 10017

International Conference of Building Officials (ICBO)
5360 S. Workman Mill Road
Whittier, CA 90601

Military Specification (MIL)
Naval Publications and Forms Center
5801 Tabor Avenue
Philadelphia, PA 19120

National Association of Architectural Metal Manufacturers (NAAMM)
221 North LaSalle Street
Chicago, IL 60601

National Fire Protection Association (NFPA)
Battery March Park
Quincy, MA 02269

National Ready Mixed Concrete Association
900 Spring Street
Silver Spring, MD 20910

National Roofing Contractors' Association (NRCA)
One O'Hare Center, 6250 River Road.
Rosemont, IL 60018

Roofing Industry Education Institute (RIEI)
14 Inverness Drive East
Building H, Suite 110
Englewood, CO 80112

Portland Cement Association (PCA)
542 Old Orchard Road
Skokie, IL 60077-1083

Prestressed Concrete Institute (PCI)
201 North Wells Street
Chicago, IL 60606

Steel Structures Painting Council (SSPC)
4400 Fifth Avenue
Pittsburgh, PA 15213

Southern Building Code Congress International (SBCCI)
900 Montclair Road
Birmingham, AL 35213

Steel Deck Institute (SDI)
P.O. Box 9506
Canton, OH 44711

Steel Door Institute (SDI)
712 Lakewood Center North
14600 Detroit Avenue
Cleveland, OH 44107

Steel Joist Institute (SJI)
1205 48th Avenue North, Suite A
Myrtle Beach, SC 29577

Sheet Metal and Air Conditioning Contractors' National Association (SMACNA)
8224 Old Courthouse Road
Vienna, VA 22180

Tile Council of America, Inc. (TCA)
Box 326
Princeton, NJ 08540

Underwriters' Laboratories, Inc. (UL)
333 Pfingston Road
Northbrook, IL 60062

PUBLICATIONS

ICBO: Field Inspection Manual (for code inspectors)

ASTM C94: Standard Specification for Ready Mixed Concrete

ACI 117: Tolerances for Concrete Construction

ACI 302: Recommended Practice for Concrete Floor and Slab Construction

ACI 305: Hot-Weather Concreting

ACI 306: Cold-Weather Concreting

ACI 308: Standard Practice for Curing Concrete

ACI SP-15: Field Reference Manual U.S. Army Technical Manual TM 5-742, "Concrete and Masonry"

Concrete Construction & Estimating, PCA

IS214.02T: Removing Stains and Cleaning Concrete Surfaces, PCA

INDEX

281